Calvin's Bible Commentaries: Habakkuk, Zephaniah, and Haggai

By

John Calvin

Translated by

John King

First published in 1847

Published by Left of Brain Books

Copyright © 2023 Left of Brain Books

ISBN 978-1-397-66888-2

First Edition

All rights reserved. No part of this publication may be reproduced, distributed, or transmitted in any form or by any means, including photocopying, recording, or other electronic or mechanical methods, without the prior written permission of the publisher, except in the case of brief quotations permitted by copyright law. Left of Brain Books is a division of Left Of Brain Onboarding Pty Ltd.

PUBLISHER'S PREFACE

About the Book

"The father of modern reformed theology, Calvin was born in 1509, and after Martin Luther was a premiere leader in the Protestant movement. Quoting Charles Spurgeon: "It would not be possible for me too earnestly to press upon you the importance of reading the expositions of that prince among men, John Calvin..." Quoting Arminius: "I affirm that he excels beyond comparison in the interpretation of Scripture, and that his commentaries ought to be more highly valued than all that is handed down to us by the Library of the Fathers; so that I acknowledge him to have possessed above most others, or rather above all other men, what may be called an eminent gift of prophecy"."

(Quote from Spurgeon's "Commenting and Commentaries", 1876)

About the Author

John Calvin (1509 - 1564)

"John Calvin was born "John Cauvin" on July 10, 1509 at Noyon in France. His father, Gerard Cauvin was a church leader holding ecclesiastical offices for the lordship of Noyon. Calvin's mother was Jeanne le Franc, the daughter of an innkeeper at Cambrai, who afterwards came to reside at Noyon. Gerard Cauvin was esteemed as a man of considerable wisdom and prudence, and his wife was said to be that rare combination of both a godly and attractive lady. She bore him five sons, of whom John was the second. John Calvin lived to the age of 55, dying on May 27, 1564.

John Calvin's father destined him from the start for an ecclesiastical career, and paid for his education in the household of the noble family of Hangest de Montmor. In May 1521 he was appointed to a chaplaincy in the cathedral of Noyon. The plague having visited Noyon, the young Hangests were sent to Paris in August 1523, and Calvin accompanied them. He lived with his uncle and attended as an out-student the College de la Marche. From the College de la Marche he moved to the College de Montaigu, where the atmosphere was more ecclesiastical and where he had for instructor a Spaniard who is described as a man of learning and to whom Calvin was indebted for some sound training in dialectics and the scholastic philosophy. John Calvin speedily outstripped all his competitors in grammatical studies, and by his skill and acumen as a student of philosophy, and debate. Although not yet ordained, Calvin preached several sermons to the people."

(Quote from greatsite.com)

CONTENTS

PUBLISHER'S PREFACE
TRANSLATOR'S PREFACE 1
COMMENTARY ON HABAKKUK 5
   CALVIN'S PREFACE TO HABAKKUK 6
      CHAPTER 1 7
      CHAPTER 2 39
      CHAPTER 3 100
COMMENTARY ON ZEPHANIAH 136
   CALVIN'S PREFACE TO ZEPHANIAH 137
      CHAPTER 1 138
      CHAPTER 2 174
      CHAPTER 3 199
COMMENTARY ON HAGGAI 241
   CALVIN'S PREFACE TO HAGGAI 242
      CHAPTER 1 244
      CHAPTER 2 269
SCRIPTURE TRANSLATIONS 304
   HABBAKUK 305
   ZEPHANIAH 310
   HAGGAI 316
   ENDNOTES 320

TRANSLATOR'S PREFACE

THE present Volume, though it contains the Works of These Prophets, is yet considerably smaller in size than the preceding Volumes; but the last will more than compensate for this deficiency.

The two first Prophets, Habakkuk and Zephaniah, lived before the Captivity; and the other, Haggai began his prophetic office about sixteen years after the return of the great body of the people from Babylon by the permission given them by King Cyrus.

It is commonly thought that Habbakuk prophesied after Zephaniah, though placed before him in our Bibles. The reign of Jehoiakin is assigned as his age, about 608 years before Christ, while Zephaniah performed his office in the reign of Josiah, about 30 years earlier. Like the other prophets he is mainly engaged in reproving the extreme wickedness of the people, on account of which he denounces on them the judgments of God, while he gives occasional intimations of a better state of things, and affords some glimpses of the blessings of the gospel.

In the first Chapter he begins with a complaint as to the oppression which he witnessed, foretells the dreadful invasion of the Chaldeans, describes the severity which would be exercised by them, and appeals to God on the subject. In the second he waits for an answer, receives it, and predicts the downfal of the Chaldeans, and refers to blessings in reserve for God's people. The third contains what is called the "Prayer of Habakkuk," an ode of a singular character, in which he briefly describes, for the encouragement of the faithful, the past interpositions of God on behalf of his people, and concludes with expressing a full and joyful confidence in God, notwithstanding' the evils which were coming on the nation.

"The style of Habakkuk," Says Bishop Lowth, "is poetical, especially in his Ode, which may justly be deemed one of the most complete of its kind." [1] And in describing the character of this ode he says — "The Prophet indeed embellishes the whole of this poem with a magnificence equal to its commencement, selecting from so great an abundance of wonderful events the grandest, and setting them forth in the most splendid dress, by images and figures, and the most elevated diction; the high sublimity of which he augments and enhances by the elegance of a remarkable conclusion: so that hardly any thing of this kind would be more beautiful or more perfect than this poem, were it not for one or two spots of obscurity which are to be found in it, occasioned, as it seems, by its ancientness." [2]

Zephaniah was in part contemporary with Jeremiah, that is, during the former portion of the reign of Josiah. He foretells the Fall Of Nineveh, (Zep 2:13,) and mentions "the remnant of Baal," (Zep 1:4,) two things which prove that he prophesied during the former half of that king's reign; for Nineveh was destroyed about the sixteenth year of his reign, and it was after that time that the worship of Baal was demolished by that king.

The sins of The Jews and their approaching judgments occupy the first Chapter. The second contains an exhortation to Repentance, encouraged by a promise of protection during the evils that God would bring on neighboring nations. In the third the Prophet particularizes the sins of Jerusalem, announces its punishment, and then refers to the future blessings which God would freely confer on His Church.

The style of Zephaniah has been represented as being in some parts prosaic; and Lowth says that "he seems to possess nothing remarkable or superior in the arrangement of his matter or in the elegance of his diction." [3] But it is Henderson's opinion that "many of the censures that have been passed on his language are either without foundation or much exaggerated." He appears to be as poetic in his ideas as most of the Prophets, and in the manner in which he arranges them, though he deals not much in parallelisms, which constitute a prominent feature in Hebrew poetry.

The matters handled by the Prophet are said by Marckius to be "most worthy of God, whether we regard His serious reproofs or His severe threatenings, or His kind warnings, or His gracious promises, which especially appertain to the dispensation of the New Testament. In all these particulars he not only agrees with the other prophets, but also adopts their expressions." [4] He then gives the following examples: —

Zephaniah 1:6 compared with Jer 15:6

Zephaniah 1:15 compared with Joel 2:1, 2

Zephaniah 1:18 compared with Eze 7:19, and Jer 4:27

Zeph. 2:8, 9 compared with Jer 48:2, and Eze 25:1

Zeph. 3:3, 4 compared with Ezek. 22:26, 27, 28, etc.

It does not appear at what time Haggai returned from exile, though probably at the first return of the Jews under Zerubbabel, before Christ 536. But he did not commence his prophetic office till about sixteen years after; and he delivered what his Book contains in the space of three months. His messages, which are five, [5] are very short; and hence some have concluded that they are but summaries of what he had delivered.

Much of this Book is historical, interspersed with what is conveyed in a poetic style. The Prophet, in the first Chapter, remonstrates with the people, who were very attentive to their own private concerns, but neglected to build the Lord's Temple; he refers to the judgments with which they had been visited on this account, encourages them to undertake the work, and promises them the favor of God; and then he tells us of his success. In the second Chapter he removes an apparent ground of discouragement, the temple then in building being not so splendid as the former, and promises an additional glory to it, evidently referring to the Gospel times. He then warns them against relaxing in their work and thinking it enough merely to offer sacrifices, assures them of God's blessing, and concludes with a special promise to Zerubbabel.

What Lowth says of this Prophet's style, that "it is altogether prosaic," is not strictly true; for there are some parts highly poetical. See Hag 1:6, and from 8 to 11 inclusive. "The style of Haggai," observes Henderson, "is not distinguished by any peculiar excellence; yet he is not destitute of pathos and vehemence, when reproving his countrymen for their negligence, exhorting them to the performance of duty."

Though in some instances our Commentator may not give the precise import of a passage, yet he never advances but what is consistent with Divine Truth, and always useful and practical, and often what betokens a profound acquaintance with the operations of the human mind under the various trials and temptations which we meet with in this life; so that the observations made are ever interesting and instructive. Calvin never deduces from a passage what is in itself erroneous or unsound, though in all cases he may not deduce what the text may legitimately warrant. There is, therefore, nothing dangerous in what he advances, though it. may not be included in the passage explained. But for the most part his application of doctrine is what may be fully justified, and is often very striking, and calculated to instruct and edify.

Some may think that our Author does not always give that full range of meaning to the promises and predictions which he explains. A reason for this may probably be found in the fact, that most of the Commentators who had preceded him had indulged in very great extravagancies on the subject; and a reaction generally drives men to an opposite extreme. But it is very seldom that Calvin can be justly charged with a fault of this kind; for, entertaining the profoundest veneration for the Word of God, he strictly followed what he conceived the words imported, and what he apprehended to be the general drift of a passage. Possibly, in the estimation of those who possess a very vivid imagination, he may be thought to have kept too closely to what the text and the context require; but in explaining the Divine Oracles, nothing is more to be avoided than to let loose the imagination, and nothing is more necessary than to possess a sound judgment, and to exercise it in the fear of God, and with prayer for His guidance and direction.

J.O.
THRUSSINGTON
October 1848.

COMMENTARY ON HABAKKUK

CALVIN'S PREFACE TO HABAKKUK

NOW follows The Prophet Habakkuk; [6] but the time in which he discharged his office of a Teacher is not quite certain. The Hebrews, according to their usual manner, unhesitatingly assert that he prophesied under the king Manasseh; but this conjecture is not well founded. We are however led to think that this prophecy was announced when the contumacy of the people had become irreclaimable. It is indeed probable, from the complaint which we shall have presently to notice, that the people had previously given many proofs of irremediable wickedness. To me it appears evident that the Prophet was sent, when others had in vain endeavored to correct the wickedness of the people. But as he denounces an approaching judgement on the Chaldeans, he seems to have prophesied either under Manasseh or under the other kings before the time of Zedechiah; but we cannot fix the exact time. [7]

The substance of the Book may be thus stated: — In the First chapter he complains of the rebellious obstinacy of the people, and deplores the corruptions which then prevailed; he then appears as the herald of God, and warns the Jews of their approaching ruin; he afterwards applies consolation, as God would punish the Chaldeans when their pride became intolerable. In the second chapter he exhorts the godly to patience by his own example, and speaks at large of the near ruin of Babylon; and in the third chapter, as we shall see, he turns to supplication and prayer.

We shall now come to the words.

CHAPTER 1

Lecture One Hundred and Sixth

Habakkuk 1:1

1. The burden which Habakkuk the prophet did see.

1. Onus quod vidit Chabakuk Propheta.

The greater part of interpreters refer this burden to the Chaldeans and the monarchy of Babylon; but of this view I do not approve, and a good reason compels me to dissent from their opinion: for as the Prophet addresses the Jews, and without any addition calls his prophecy a burden, there is no doubt but that he refers to them. Besides, their view seems wholly inconsistent, because the Prophet dreads the future devastation of the land, and complains to God for allowing His chosen and elect people to be so cruelly treated. What others think is more correct — that this burden belonged to the Jews.

What the Prophet understood by the word משא, mesha, has been elsewhere stated. Habakkuk then reproves here his own nation, and shows that they had in vain disdainfully resisted all God's prophets, for they would at length find that their threatening would be accomplished. The burden, then, which the Prophet Habakkuk saw, was this — That God, after having exercised long forbearance towards the Jews, would at length be the punisher of their many sins. It now follows —

Hab. 1:2, 3

2. O LORD, how long shall I cry, and thou wilt not hear! even cry out unto thee of violence, and thou wilt not save!

2. Quousque, Jehova, clamabo, et non exaudies? Vociferabor ad te ob violentiam, et non servabis?

3. Why dost thou shew me iniquity, and cause me to behold grievance? for spoiling and violence are before me: and there are that raise up strife and contention.

3. Quare ostendis mihi iniquitatem, et moestiam aspicere facis? Et direptio et violentia in conspectu meo? et est qui litem et contentionem excitet.

As I have already reminded you, interpreters think that the Prophet speaks here of future things, as though he had in his view the calamity which he afterwards mentions; but this is too strained a meaning; I therefore doubt not but that the Prophet expostulates here with God for so patiently indulging a reprobate people. For though the Prophets felt a real concern for the safety of the people, there is yet no doubt but that they burned with zeal for the glory of God; and when they saw that they had to contend with refractory men, they were then inflamed with a holy displeasure, and undertook the cause of God; and they implored His aid to bring a remedy when the state of things had become desperate. I therefore consider that the Prophet here solicits God to visit these many sins in which the people had hardened themselves. And hence we conclude that he had previously exercised his office of a teacher; for it would have been otherwise improper for him to begin his work with such a complaint and expostulation. He had then by experience found that the people were extremely perverse. When he saw that there was no hope of amendment, and that the state of things was becoming daily worse, burning with zeal for God, he gave full vent to his feelings. Before, then, he threatens the people with the future vengeance of God, he withdraws himself, as it were, from intercourse with men, and in private addresses God himself.

We must bear this first in mind, that the Prophet relates here the secret colloquy he had with God: but it ought not to be ascribed to an unfeeling disposition, that in these words he wished to hasten God's vengeance against his own kindred; for it behaved the Prophet not only to be solicitous for the salvation of the people, but also to feel a concern for the glory of God, yea, to burn with a holy zeal. As, then, he had in vain labored for a length of time, I doubt not but that, being as it were far removed from the presence of all witnesses, he here asks God, how long he purposed thus to bear with the wickedness of the people. We now apprehend the design of the Prophet and the import of his words.

But he says first, How long, Jehovah, shall I cry, and thou hearest not? How long shall I cry to thee for violence, that is, on account of violence, and thou savest not? We hence learn, that the Prophet had often prayed God to correct the people for their wickedness, or to contrive some means to prevent so much licentiousness in sinning. It is indeed probable that the Prophet had prayed as long as there was any hope; but when he saw that things were past recovery, he then prayed more earnestly that God would undertake the office of a judge, and chastise the people. For though the Prophet really condoled with those who perished, and was touched, as I have said, with a serious concern for their public safety, he yet preferred the glory of God: when, therefore, he saw that boldness in sin increased through impunity, and that the Jews in a manlier mocked God when they found that they could sin without being punished, he could not endure such unbridled wantonness. Besides, the Prophet may have spoken thus, not only as expressing his own feeling, but what he felt in common with all the godly; as though he had undertaken here a public duty, and utters a complaint common to all the faithful: for it is probable that all the godly, in so disordered a state of things, mourned alike. How long, then, shall I cry? How long, he says, shall I cry on account of violence? that is, When all things are in disorder, when there is now no regard for equity and justice, but men abandon themselves, as it were with loose reins, unto all kinds of wickedness, how long, Lord, wilt thou take no notice? But in these words the Prophet not only egresses his own feelings, but makes this kind of preface, that the Jews might better understand that the time of vengeance was come; for they were become not only altogether intolerable to God, but also to his servants. God indeed had suspended his judgement, though he had been often solicited to execute it by his Prophet. It hence appears, that their wickedness had made such advances that it would be no wonder if they were now severely chastised by the Lord; for they had by their sins not only provoked him against them, but also all the godly and the faithful.

He afterwards adds, How long wilt thou show me iniquity, and make me to see trouble? Here the Prophet briefly relates the cause of his indignation, — that he could not, without great grief, yea, without anguish of mind, behold such evils prevailing among God's chosen people; for they who apply this to the Chaldeans, do so strainedly, and without any necessity, and they have not observed the reason which I have stated — that the Prophet does not here teach the Jews, but prepares them for a coming judgement, as they could not but see that they were justly condemned, since they were proved guilty by the cry and complaints made by all the godly.

Now this passage teaches us, that all who really serve and love God, ought, according to the Prophet's example, to burn with holy indignation whenever they see wickedness reigning without restraint among men, and especially in the Church of God. There is indeed nothing which ought to cause us more grief than to see men raging with profane contempt for God, and no regard had for his law and for divine truth, and all order trodden under foot. When therefore such a confusion appears to us, we must feel roused, if we have in us any spark of religion. If it be objected, that the Prophet exceeded moderation, the obvious answer is this, — that though he freely pours forth his feelings, there was nothing wrong in this before God, at least nothing wrong is imputed to him: for wherefore do we pray, but that each of us may unburden his cares, his griefs, and anxieties, by pouring them into the bosom of God? Since, then, God allows us to deal so familiarly with him, nothing wrong ought to be ascribed to our prayers when we thus freely pour forth our feelings, provided the bridle of obedience keeps us always within due limits, as was the case with the Prophet; for it is certain that he was retained under the influence of real kindness. Jeremiah did indeed pray with unrestrained fervor (Jer 15:10): but his case was different from that of our Prophet; for he proceeds not here to an excess, as Jeremiah did when he cursed the day of his birth, and when he expostulated with God for being made a man of contention. But our Prophet undertakes here the defense of justice; for he could not endure the law of God to be made a sport, and men to allow themselves every liberty in sinning.

We now, then, see that the Prophet can be justly excused, though he expostulates here with God, for God does not condemn this freedom in our prayers; but, on the contrary, the end of praying is, that every one of us pour forth, as it is said in the Psalms, his heart before God. As, then, we communicate our cares and sorrows to God, it is no wonder that the Prophet, according to the manner of men, says, Why dost thou show me iniquity, and make me to see trouble? Trouble is to be taken here in an active sense, and the verb מיבת, tabith, has a transitive meaning. [8] Some render it, Why dost thou look on trouble? as though the Prophet indignantly bore the connivance of God. But the context necessarily requires that this verb should be taken in a transitive sense. "Why dost thou show me iniquity?" and then, "and makest me to look on violence?" He says afterwards, in the third place, in my sight is violence. But I have said, that the word trouble is to be taken actively; for the prophet means not that he was worn out with weariness, but that wicked men were troublesome to the good and the innocent, as it is usually the case when a freedom in sinning prevails.

And why, he says, are violence and plunder in my sight? and there is he who excites, etc.? The verb אשנ, nusha means not here to undertake, as some render it; but, on the contrary, to raise. Others render it, "Who supports," but this is frigid. Therefore the translation which I have stated is the most suitable — And why is there one who excites strife and contention?

But the Prophet here accuses them only of sins against the second table of the law: he speaks not of the superstitions of people, and of the corrupted worship of God; but he briefly says, that they had no regard for what was just and right: for the stronger any one was, the more he distressed the helpless and the innocent. It was then for this reason that he mentioned iniquity, trouble, plunder, violence, contention, strife. In short, the Prophet here deplores, that there was now no equity and no brotherly kindness among the people, but that robberies, rapines, and tyrannical violence prevailed everywhere. It follows —

Habakkuk 1:4

4. Therefore the law is slacked, and judgement doth never go forth: for the wicked doth compass about the righteous; therefore wrong judgement proceedeth.

4. Propterea dissolvitur (vel, debilitatur) lex, et non egredietur perpetuo judicium (vel, non egreditur:) quia impius circumdat justum, propterea impius circumdat justum, propterea egredietur judicium perversum.

The Prophet confirms here what I have already said, and brings an excuse for his zeal; he proves that he was not without reason led to so great a warmth; for he saw that the law of God was trodden as it were under foot; he saw men so hardened in every kind of sin, that all religion and the fear of God had nearly been extinguished. Hence I have already said, that the Prophet was not here impelled by a carnal passion, as it often happens to us, when we defend ourselves from wrongs done to us; for when any one of us is injured, he immediately becomes incensed, while, at the same time, we suffer God's law to be a sport, His whole truth to be despised, and everything that is just to be violated. We are only tender on what concerns us individually, and in the meantime we easily forgive when God is wronged, and His truth despised. But the Prophet shows here that he was not made indignant through a private feeling, but because he could not bear the profanation of God's worship and the violation of His holy law.

He therefore says, that the law was dissolved or weakened, as though he said that God's law had no longer any authority or regard. Let us hence learn to rouse up ourselves, for we are very frigid, when the ungodly openly despise and even mock God. As, then, we are too unconcerned in this respect, let us learn, by the Prophet's example, to stimulate ourselves. For even Paul also shows, in an indirect way, that there is just reason for indignation — 'Be ye angry,' he says, 'and sin not,' (Eph 4:26); that is, every one ought to regard his own sins, so as to become an enemy to himself; and he ought also to feel indignant whenever he sees God offended.

This rule the Prophet now follows, Weakened, he says, is the law [9] We know that when a sinful custom prevails, there is but little authority in what is taught: nor are human laws only despised when men's audacity breaks through all restraints, but even the very law of God is esteemed as nothing; for they think that everything erroneously done, by the consent of all, is lawful. We now then see that the Prophet felt great anguish of mind, like holy Lot (Ge 19:1-38.), when he saw every regard for God almost extinct in the land, and especially among the chosen people, whom God had above all others consecrated to himself.

He then adds, judgement goes not forth perpetually. Absurdly do many regard this as having been said in the person of foolish men, who think that there is no such thing as divine providence, when things in the world are in a disordered state: but the Prophet simply says, that all justice was suppressed. We have nearly the very same complaint in Isa 59:4. He then says, that judgement did not go forth perpetually, because the ungodly thought that no account was to be given by them. When, therefore, any one dared to say a word against them, they immediately boiled with rage, and like wild beasts fiercely attacked him. All then were silent, and nearly made dumb, when the ungodly thus prevailed and gathered boldness from the daily practice of licentiousness. Hence, 'Go forth perpetually does not judgement;' that is, "O Lord, things are now past hope, and there appears to be no end to our evils, except thou comest soon and applies a remedy beyond what our flesh can conceive." For the wicked, he says, surround the righteous; that is, when there was any one who continued to retain some regard for religion and justice, immediately the wicked rose up against him on every side and surrounded him before and behind; so it happened, that no one dared to oppose the torrent, though frauds, rapines, outrages, cruelty, and even murders everywhere prevailed; if any righteous men still remained, they dared not come forth into the public, for the wicked beset them on all sides.

He afterwards adds, Therefore perverted judgement goes forth. The Prophet now rises higher, that even the rulers themselves increased the rage for evils, and as it were supplied fuel to their wickedness, as they confounded all distinction between right and wrong: for the Prophet speaks not here of private wrongs which any one might have done, but he speaks of the very rulers, as though he said, "There might have been one remedy, the judges might have checked so great an audacity; but they themselves stretch out their hands to the wicked and help them." Hence the tribunals, which ought to have been sacred, were become as it were dens of thieves. The word משפט, meshiphith is taken properly in a good sense: Is not judgement then a desirable thing? Yes, but the Prophet says, that it was perverted. It was then by way of concession that judgement is mentioned; for he afterwards adds a word to it, by which he shows that the administration of the laws was evil and injurious: for when any one oppressed had recourse to the assistance of the laws, he was plundered. In short, the Prophet means, that all things in private and in public were corrupt among the people. It now follows —

Habakkuk 1:5

5. Behold ye among the heathen, and regard, and wonder marvellously: for I will work a work in your days, which ye will not believe, though it be told you

5. Videte in gentibus, et aspicite, et admiramini, admiramini; quia opus operans in diebus vestris, non credetis, quum narratum fuerit.

The Prophet turns his discourse to the Jews, after having related the private colloquy, in which he expostulated with God for having so patiently borne with the obstinate wickedness of the nation. Being now as it were furnished with God's command, (as the case really was,) he performs the office of a herald, and proclaims an approaching destruction. He indeed adopts a preface, which ought to have awakened drowsy and careless minds. He says — look, see, be astonished, be astonished; these repetitions do not a little increase the alarm; he twice bids them to see, and he twice exhorts them to be astonished, or to wonder. He then briefly proclaims the judgement of God, which he afterwards more fully describes. We now, then, perceive the object of the Prophet, and the manner in which he proceeds with his subject.

And he bids those among the nations to behold, as though he had said, that they were unworthy to be taught in the school of God; he therefore appointed other masters for them, even the Chaldeans, as we shall presently see. He might have said — look to God; but as the Prophet had so long spent his labor in vail and without profit while teaching them, he sets over them the Chaldeans as teachers. Behold, he says, ye teachers among the Gentiles. There is here indeed an implied contrast, as thought he said — "God has hitherto often recalled you to himself, and has offered himself to you, but ye have refused to look to him; now then, as he is wearied with exercising patience so long, he appoints for you other teachers; learn now from the Gentiles what ye leave hitherto refused to learn from the holy mouth of Cod himself".

The Greek translators no doubt read בגוריט, for their version is — "Behold, ye despisers." [10] But in Hebrew there is no ambiguity as to the word.

He afterwards adds — And wonder ye, wonder [11] By these words the prophets express how dreadful God's judgement would be, which would astonish the Jews themselves. Had they not been extremely refractory they might have quietly received instruction, for God would have addressed them by his prophets, as though they had been his own children. They might thus, with composed minds, have listened to God speaking to them; but the time was now come when they were to be filled with astonishment. We hence see that the Prophet meant this in a few words — that there would be a new mode of teaching, which would overwhelm the unwilling with astonishment, because they would not endure to be ruled in a gentle manner, when the Lord required nothing from them but to render themselves teachable.

After having said that God's judgement would be dreadful, he adds that it was nigh at hand — a work, he says, will he work in your days, etc. They had already been often warned of that vengeance, but as they had for a long time disregarded it, they did ever remain sunk in their own self-delusions, like men who are wont to protract time and hunt on every side for some excuse for indulging themselves. So then when the people became hardened against all threatening, they thought that God would ever bear with them; hence the Prophet expressly declares, that the execution of that which they regarded as a fable was near at hand — He will work, he says, this work in your days

He then subjoins — ye will not believe when it shall be told you; that is, God will execute such a punishment as will be incredible and exceed all belief. The Prophet no doubt alludes to the want of faith in the people, and indirectly reproves them, as though he said — "Ye have hitherto denied faith to God's word, but ye shall at length find that he has told the truth; and this ye shall find to your astonishment; for as his word has been counted by you incredible, so also incredible shall be his judgement." In short, the Prophet intimates this — that though the Prophets had been derided by the Jews, and despised as inventors of fables, yet nothing had been said by them which would not be fully accomplished. This reward then was to be paid to all the unbelieving; for God would in the most dreadful manner avenge their impiety, so that they should themselves be astonished and become an astonishment to others. We now perceive what the Prophet meant by saying that the Jews would not believe the work of God when told them, that is, the vengeance which he will presently describe.

This passage is quoted by Paul, and is applied to the punishment then awaiting the Jews; for Paul, after having offered Christ to them, and seeing that many of them regarded the preaching of Gospel with scorn, added these words — "see," he said, "and be astonished, for God will work a work in your days which ye shall not believe." Paul at the same time made a suitable application of the Prophet's words; for as God had once threatened his people by his Prophet Habakkuk, so he was still like himself; and since had so severely vindicated the contempt of his law as to his ancient people, he could not surely bear with the impiety of that people whom he found to have acted so malignantly and so ungratefully, yea so wantonly and perversely, as to reject his grace; for this was the last remedy for the Jews. No wonder then that Paul set before them this vengeance, when the

Jews of his time persisted through their unbelief to reject Christ. Now follows the explanation -

Habakkuk 1:6

6. For, lo, I raise up the Chaldeans, that bitter and hasty nation, which shall march through the breadth of the land, to possess the dwellingplaces that are not theirs.

6. Quia ecce ego excito Chaldaeos, gentem asperam, et praecipitem, quae incedet per latitudines terrae, ad possidendum tabernacula non sua.

This verse is added by the Prophet as an explanation; for it was not enough to speak generally of God's work, without reminding them that their destruction by the Chaldeans was nigh at hand. He does not indeed in this verse explain what would be the character of that judgement which he had mentioned in the last verse Hab 1:5; but he will do this in what follows. Now the Prophets differ from Moses in this respect, for they show, as it were by the finger, what he threatened generally, and they declare the special judgements of God; as it is indeed evident from the demonstrative adverb, "Behold." How necessary this was, we may gather from the perverseness of that people; for how distinctly soever the Prophets showed to them God's judgements, so that they saw them with their eyes, yet so great was their insensibility, that they despised denunciations so apparent. What, then, would have been done, if the Prophets had only said in general, 'God will not spare you!' This, then, is the reason why the Prophet, having spoken of God's terrible vengeance, now declares in express terms, that the Chaldeans were already armed by Him to execute His judgement. The rest we leave for tomorrow.

PRAYER

Grant, Almighty God, that as our sins cry continually to heaven, each of us may turn to repentance, and by condemning ourselves of our own accord may anticipate thy judgement, and thus stir up ourselves to repentance, that being received into favor, we may find thee, whom we have provoked to take vengeance, to be indeed our Father: and may we be so preserved by thee in this world, that having at length put off all our vices, we may attain to that perfection of purity, to which thou invites us; and thus lead us more and more to thyself by thy Spirit, and separate us from the corruptions of this world, that we may glorify thee before men, and be at last made partakers of that celestial glory which has been purchased for us by the blood of thy only begotten Son. Amen.

LECTURE ONE HUNDRED AND SEVENTH

In the lecture of yesterday the Prophet began to show from whom the Jews were to expect the vengeance of God, even from the Chaldeans, who would come, not by their own instinct, but by the hidden impulse of God. God indeed testifies that he should be the author of this war, and that the Chaldeans would fight, as it were, under his auspices. I am he, he says, who excites, etc. Then by calling the Chaldeans a bitter and hasty nation, he intended seriously to terrify the Jews, who had heedlessly despised all threatenings. [12] It was not indeed a subject of praise to the Chaldeans, that they were bitter and impetuous: but the Lord could turn these vices to a good purpose, inasmuch as he elicits light from darkness. When, therefore, we read that the Chaldeans were bitter, and also hasty, God thus intimates that he can employ the vices of men in executing his judgements, and yet contract hence no spot nor blemish; for we cannot possibly pollute him with our filth, as he scatters it far away by the brightness of his justice and equity.

He afterwards adds, They shall march through the latitudes [13] of the earth, to possess habitations not their own. He means that there would be no obstacles in the way of the Chaldeans, but that they would spread themselves over the whole earth, and occupy regions far remote. For they who fear, dare not thus disperse themselves, but, on the contrary, they advance cautiously with a collected army; but those, who have already obtained victory, march on to lay waste the land. This is what the Prophet says the Chaldeans would do.

The meaning is — that they would not come to carry on an uncertain warfare, but that they would enjoy a victory; for they would by an impetuous course fill the land, so as to occupy tents or habitations not their own. It was indeed a matter of blame in the Chaldeans, that they thus made inroads on their own neighbors: but, as I have said, God intended only to fill the Jews with terror, because he found that all threatenings were despised. He therefore meant to show how terrible the Chaldeans would be, and he confirms the same in the next verse.

Habakkuk 1:7

7. They are terrible and dreadful: their judgement and their dignity shall proceed of themselves.

7. Terribilis et metuenda ipsa, ab ipsa judicium ejus (pro jure ponitur hoc nomen,) et exultatio (vel, dignitas) ejus egredietur.

By saying that the Chaldeans would be terrible and dreadful, he praises not their virtues; but, as I have already reminded you, he shows that they would be prepared to do his service by executing his vengeance: and he so regulated his judgement, that he used their cruelty for a good purpose. Thus we see that the worst of men are in God's hand, as Satan is, who is their head; and yet that God is not implicated in their wickedness, as some insane men maintain; for they say — That if God governs the world by his providence, he becomes thus the author of sin, and men's sins are to be ascribed to him. But Scripture teaches us far otherwise, — that the wicked are led here and there by the hidden power of God, and that yet the fault is in them, when they do anything in a deceitful and cruel manner, and that God ever remains just, whatever use he may make of instruments, yea, the very worst.

But when the Prophet adds, that its judgement would be from the nation itself, he means that the Chaldeans would act according to their own will. When any one indeed obeys laws, and willingly submits to them, he will freely allow either judges or umpires in case of a dispute; but he who will have all things done according to his own purpose repudiates all judges. The Prophet therefore means, that the Chaldeans would be their own judges, so that the Jews or others would complain in vain for any wrongs done to them. "They shall be," he says, "their own judges, and shall execute judgement, for they will not accept any arbitrators." The word judgement, taken in a good sense, is put here for law (jus); as though he said, "Whatever the Chaldeans will claim for themselves, theirs shall it be; for no one will dare to interfere, and they will not submit to the will of others; but their power shall be for law, and their sword for a tribunal." We now understand the Prophet's meaning; and we must ever bear in mind what I have already said, — That God had no participation in these vices; but it was necessary that the stubbornness of an irreclaimable people should be thus corrected, or at least broken down. The Lord in the meantime could use such instruments in such a way as to preserve some moderation in his judgements. It follows —

Habakkuk 1:8

8. Their horses also are swifter than the leopards, and are more fierce than the evening wolves: and their horsemen shall spread themselves, and their horsemen shall come from far; they shall fly as the eagle that hasteth to eat.

8. Et velociores pardis equi ejus, et acutiores lupis vespertinis: et multiplicati sunt equites ejus, et equites ejus e longinquo venient; volabunt quasi aquila festinans ad comedendum (vel, ad cibum.)

The design of these figurative expressions is the same. The Prophet had spoken of the cruelty of those enemies whom the Jews despised: he now adds, that they would be so active as to surpass in velocity both leopards and eagles, or to be at least equal to them. He then says first, that their horses would be swifter then leopards. The Jews might have eluded his threatenings, or at least have cherished their insensibility by a vain confidence, as we see how this vice prevails in the world; for they might have thought thus within themselves, "The Chaldeans are far away, and the danger of which the Prophet speaks cannot be so near at hand." Hence he declares that their horses would be swifter than leopards.

He then adds, that they would be fiercer than the evening wolves. The wolf is a rapacious animal; and when he ranges about all the day in vain seeking what he may devour, then in the evening hunger kindles his rage. There is, therefore, nothing more dreadful than hungry wolves. But, as I have said, except they find some prey about the evening, they become the more furious. We shall meet with the same simile in Zep 3:1. We now see the drift of the Prophet's words.

He adds that their horsemen would be numerous [14] He now sets forth their power, lest the Jews should have recourse to vain hopes, because they might obtain some help either from the Egyptians or other neighbors. The Prophet shows that all such hopes would be wholly vain; for had they gathered auxiliaries from all quarters, still the Chaldeans would exceed them in power and number.

He afterwards says, that their horsemen would come from a distance. Though they should have a long journey, yet weariness would not hinder and delay them in coming from a remote part. The toil of travelling would not weaken them, until they reached Judea. How so? Because it will fly, he says, (he speaks throughout of the nation itself,) as an eagle hastening to devour. This metaphor is also most suitable to the present purpose; for it signifies, that wherever the Chaldeans saw a prey, they would instantly come, as an eagle to any carcass it may observe. Let the distance be what it may, as soon as it sees a prey, it takes a precipitate flight, and is soon present to devour; for the rapidity of eagles, as it is well known, is astonishing.

We now see that what we learn from the Prophet's words is substantially this, — that God's judgement ought to have been feared, because he purposed to employ the Chaldeans as his servants, whose cruel disposition and inhumanity would be dreadful: he also shows that the Chaldeans would be far superior in power and number; and in third place he makes it known, that they would possess an astonishing rapidity, and that though length of journey might be deemed a hindrance, they would yet be like eagles, which come like an arrow from heaven to earth, whenever a prey is observed by them. And eagles are not only rapid in their flight, but they possess also sharpness of sight; for we know that the eyes of eagles are remarkably keen and strong: and it is said that they cast away their young, if they find that they cannot look steadily at the sun; for they regard them as spurious. The Prophet then intimates that the Chaldeans would from a distance observe their prey: as the eagles, who are endued with incredible quickness of sight, see from mid air every carcass lying on the ground; so also would the Chaldeans quickly discover a prey, and come upon it in an instant. Let us proceed.

Habakkuk 1:9

9. They shall come all for violence: their faces shall sup up as the east wind, and they shall gather the captivity as the sand.

9. Tota (semper de ipsa gente loquitur, hoc est. totus ipse populus) ad praedam venict; occursus vultus ipsorum (jam in plurali numera loquitar) ventus orientalis, et colliget quasi arenam captivitatem.

By saying that they would come to the prey, he means that they would have no trouble or labor, for they would be victorious before they had any contest, or had any war with their enemies. The meaning then is, that the Chaldeans would not come to spend much time in warfare, as when there is a strong power to resist; but that they would only come for the booty, for the Jews would be frightened, and instantly submit themselves. And by these words the Prophet intimates, that there would be neither strength nor courage in a people so refractory: for God thus debilitates the hearts of those who fiercely resist his word. Whenever, then, men become strong against God, he so melts their hearts, that they cannot resist their fellow-mortals; and thus he mocks their confidence, or rather their madness. Lest then the Jews should still harbor any hope from the chance of war, the Prophet says that the Chaldeans would only come for the prey, for all would become subject to them.

He afterwards adds, that the meeting of their faces would be like the oriental wind. The word המג, gime, means what is opposite; and its derivative signifies meeting or opposition (occursus.) We indeed know that the east wind was very injurious to the land of Judea, that it dried up vegetation, yea, that it consumed as it were the whole produce of the earth. The violence of that wind was also very great. Hence whenever the Prophets wished to express a violent impetuosity, they added this comparison of the east wind. It was therefore the same as though the Prophet had said that the Jews would now in vain flatter themselves; for as soon as they perceived the blowing of the east wind, they would flee away, knowing that they would be wholly unable to stand against it. [15]

Hence follows what is added by the Prophets, He shall gather the captivity like the sand; that is, the king of Babylon shall without any trouble subdue all the people, and collect captives innumerable as the sand; for by the sand of the sea is meant an immense number of men. In short, the Prophet shows that the Jews were already conquered; because their striving and their contest had been with God, whom they had so often and so obstinately provoked; and also, because God had chosen for himself such servants as excelled in quickness, and power, and cruelty. This is the sum of the whole. He afterwards adds —

Habakkuk 1:10

10. And they shall scoff at the kings, and the princes shall be a scorn unto them: they shall deride every strong hold; for they shall heap dust, and take it.

10. Et ipse reges ridebit, et principes subsannatio ei; ipse omnem munitionem subsannabit; congregabit pulverem et capiet eam.

The Prophet concludes the subject which he has been hitherto pursuing. He says that the Chaldeans would not come to engage in a doubtful war, but only to triumph over conquered nations. We indeed know that the Jews, though not excelling either in number or in riches, were yet so proud, that they looked down, as it were, with contempt on other nations, and we also know, that they vainly trusted in vain helps; for as they were in confederacy with the Egyptians, they thought themselves to be beyond the reach of danger. Hence the Prophet says, that kings and princes would be only a sport to the Chaldeans, and their fortresses would be only a derision to them. How so? For they will gather dust, he says; that is, will make a mound of the dust of the earth, and will thus penetrate into all fortified cities.

In short the Prophet intended to cut off every hope from the Jews, that they might humble themselves before God; or he intended to take away every excuse if they repented not, as it indeed happened; for we know that they did not repent notwithstanding these warnings, until vengeance at length fully overtook them. He then adds —

Habakkuk 1:11

11. Then shall his mind change, and he shall pass over, and offend, imputing this his power unto his god.

11. Tunc mutabit spiritum, et transgredietur, et impie aget: haec virtus ejus deo ipsius.

The Prophet now begins to give some comfort to the faithful, lest they should succumb under so grievous evils. He has hitherto directed his discourse to that irreclaimable people, but he now turns to the remnant; for there were always among them some of the faithful, though few, whom God never neglected; yea, for their sake often he sent his prophets; for though the multitude derived no benefit, yet the faithful understood that

God did not threaten in vain, and were thus retained in his fear. This was the reason why the prophets were wont, after having spoken generally, to come down to the faithful, and as it were to comfort them apart and privately. And this difference ought to be noticed, as we have said elsewhere; for when the prophets denounce God's wrath, the discourse then is directed indiscriminately to the whole body of the people; but when they add promises, it is then as though they called the faithful to a private conference, and spake in their ear what had been committed to them by the Lord. The truth might have been useful to all, had they returned to a right mind; but as almost the whole people had hardened themselves in their vices, and as Satan had rendered stupid the minds and hearts of nearly all, it behaved the Prophet to have a special regard to the chosen of God. We now then apprehend his design.

And he says — now he will change his spirit. He bids the faithful to entertain hope, because the Chaldeans, after having poured forth all their fury, will be punished by the Lord for their arrogance, for it will be intolerable. This may indeed seem frigid to ungodly men; for what wonder is it that the Chaldeans, after having obtained so many victories, should grow haughty and exult in their success, as is commonly the case? But as this is a fixed principle with us, that men's pride becomes intolerable to God when they extremely exult and preserve no moderation — this is a very powerful argument — that is, that whosoever thus raises his horns shall suddenly be laid prostrate by the Lord. And Scripture also ever sets this before us, that God beats down supercilious pride, and does this that we may know that destruction is nigh all the ungodly, when they thus grow violently mad, and know not that they are mortals. It was then for this reason that the Prophet mentions what he says here; it was that the faithful might hope for some end to the violence of their enemies, for God would check their pride when they should transgress. But he says — then He will change his spirit; not that there was before any humility in the Chaldeans, but that success inebriated them, yea, and deprived them of all reason. And it is a common thing that a person who has fortune as it were in his hand, forgets himself, and thinks himself no longer a mortal. Great kings do indeed confess that they are men; but we see how madness lays hold on them; for, as I have said, being deluded by prosperity, they deem themselves to be nothing less than gods.

The Prophet refers here to the king of Babylon and all his people. He will change, he says, his spirit; that is, success will take away from him whatever reason and moderation he had. Now since the proud betray themselves and their disposition when fortune smiles on them, let us learn to form our judgement of men according to this experiment. If we would judge rightly of any man we must see how he bears good and bad fortune; for it may be that he who has borne adversity with a patient, calm and resigned mind, will disappoint us in prosperity, and will so elate himself as to be wholly another man. The Prophet then does not without reason speak of a change of spirit; for though the Chaldeans were before proud, they were not so extremely haughty as when their pride passed all bounds, after their many victories. He will change then his spirit; not that the Chaldeans were another kind of people, but that the Lord thus discovered their madness which was before hid.

He then adds — *he will pass over*. The Prophet intended to express that when the Lord suffered the Chaldeans to rule far and wide, a way was thus opened for his judgements, which is far different from the judgement of the flesh. For the more power men acquire the more boldness they assume; and it seemed to tend to the establishing of their power that they knew how to use their success. But the Lord, as I have said, was secretly preparing a way to destroy them, when they thus became proud and passed all bounds; hence the Prophet does not simply condemn the haughtiness and pride of the Chaldeans, but shows that a way is already open, as it were, for God's judgement, that he might destroy them, inasmuch as they would render themselves intolerable.

He afterwards adds — *and shall act impiously*. The verb משׁא, *ashem* I refer to the end of the verse — where he ascribes his power to his own god. And the Prophet adds this explanation, in order that the Jews might know what kind of sin would be the sin of the king of Babylon. He then charges him with sacrilege, because he would think that he had become the conqueror of Judea through the kindness of his idol, so that he would make nothing of the power and glory of the true God. Since then the Babylonian would transfer God's glory to his own idol, his own ruin would be thus made ripe; for the Lord would undertake his own cause, and execute vengeance on such a sacrilege; for he speaks here no doubt of the Babylonian, and according to his view, when he says —

This his strength is that of his god; but were any inclined to explain this of the true God, as some do, he would make a harsh and a forced construction; for the Babylonians did not worship the true God, but were devoted, as it is well known, to their own superstitions. The Prophet then no doubt makes known here to the faithful the pride with which the Babylonians would become elated, and thus provoke God's wrath against themselves; and also the sacrilegious boasting in which they would indulge, ascribing the victories given them to their own idols, which could not be done without daring reproach to the true God. [16] It now follows —

Habakkuk 1:12

12. Art thou not from everlasting, O LORD my God, mine Holy One? we shall not die. O LORD, thou hast ordained them for judgement; and, O mighty God, thou hast established them for correction.

12. Annon tu ab initio, (vel, jampridem,) Jehova, Deus meus? sanctus meus, non moriemur; Jehova, ad judicium posiusti eum; et fortis, ad castigationem fundasti eum.

The Prophet now exulting, according to what all the faithful feel, shows the effect of what he has just mentioned; for as ungodly men wantonly rise up against God, and, while Satan renders them insane, throw out swelling words of vanity, as though they could by speaking confound earth and heaven; so also the faithful derive a holy confidence from God's word, and set themselves against them, and overcome their ferocity by the magnanimity and firmness of their own minds, so that they can intrepidly boast that they are happy and blessed even in the greatest miseries.

This then is what the prophet means when he adds — Art not thou our God? The question is much more emphatical than if he had simply declared that the true God was worshipped in Judea, and would therefore be the protector of that nation; for when the Prophet puts a question, he means, according to what is commonly understood in Hebrew, that the thing admits of no doubt. "What! art not thou our God?" We hence see that there is a contrast between the wicked and impious boastings in which the profane indulge, and the holy confidence which the faithful have, who exult in their God. But that the discourse is addressed to God rather than to the ungodly is not done without reason, for it would have been useless to contend with the wicked. This is indeed sometimes necessary, for when the reprobate openly reproach God we cannot restrain ourselves; nor is it right that we refrain from testifying that we regard all their slanders as of no account; but we cannot so courageously oppose their audacity as when we have the matter first settled between us and God, and be able to say with the Prophets — "Thou art our God." Whosoever then would boldly contend with the ungodly must first have to do with God, and confirm and ratify as it were that compact which God has proposed to us, even that we are his people, and that he in his turn will be always our God. As then God thus covenants with us, our faith must be really made firm, and then let us go forth and contend against all the ungodly. This is the order which the Prophet observes here, and what is to be observed by us — Art not thou our God?

He also adds — long since, מדקם, mekodam, by which word the Prophet invites the attention of the faithful to the covenant which God had made, not yesterday nor the day before that, with his people, but many ages before, even 400 years before he redeemed their fathers from Egypt. Since then the favor of God to the Jews had been confirmed for so long a time, it is not without reason that the Prophet says here — Thou art our God from the beginning; that is, "the religion which we embrace has been delivered to us by thy hands, and we know that thou art its author; for our faith recumbs not on the opinion of men, but is sustained by thy word. Since, then, we have found so often and in so many ways, and for so many years, that thou art our God, there is now no room for doubt." [17]

He then subjoins — we shall not die. What the Jews say of this place, that it had been corrected by the scribes, seems not to me probable; for the reason they give is very frivolous. They suppose that it was written lo tamut, Thou diest not, and that the letter nun had been introduced, "we shall not die," because the expression offended those scribes, as though the Prophet compared God to men, and ascribed to him a precarious immortality; but they would have been very foolish critics. I therefore think that the word was written by the Prophet as we now read it, Thou art our God, we shall not die. Some explain this as a prayer — "let us not die;" and the future is often taken in this sense in Hebrew; but this exposition is not suitable to the present passage; for the Prophet, as I have already said, rises up here as a conqueror, and disperses as mists all those foolish boastings of which he had been speaking, as though he said — "we shall not die, for we are under the protection of God."

I have already explained why he turns his discourse to God: but this is yet the conclusion of the argument, — that as God had adopted that people, and received them into favor, and testified that he would be their defender, the Prophet confidently draws this inference, — that this people cannot perish, for they are preserved by God. No power of the world, nor any of its defences, can indeed afford us this security; for whatever forces may all mortals bring either to protect or help us, they shall all perish together with us. Hence, the protection of God alone is that which can deliver us from the danger of death. We now perceive why the Prophet joins together these two things, "Thou art our God," and "We shall not die;" nor can indeed the one be separated from the other; for when we are under the protection of God, we must necessarily continue safe and safe for ever; not that we shall be free from evils, but that the Lord will deliver us from thousand deaths, and ever preserve our life in safety. When only he affords us a taste of eternal salvation, some spark of life will ever continue in our hearts, until he shows to us, when at length redeemed, as I have already said, from thousand deaths, the perfection of that blessed life, which is now promised to us, but as yet is looked for, and therefore hid under the custody of hope.

PRAYER

Grant, Almighty God, that since thou settest around us so many terrors, we may know that we ought to be roused, and to resist the sloth and tardiness of our flesh, so that thou mayest fortify us by a different confidence: and may we so recumb on thine aid, that we may boldly triumph over our enemies, and never doubt, but that thou wilt at length give us the victory over all the assaults of Satan and of the wicked; and may we also so look to thee, that our faith may wholly rest on that eternal and immutable covenant, which has been confirmed for us by the blood of thy only Son, until we shall at length be united to him who is our head, after having passed through all the miseries of the present life, and having been gathered into that eternal inheritance, which thy Son has purchased for us by his own blood. Amen.

LECTURE ONE HUNDRED AND EIGHTH

We began yesterday to explain the words of the Prophet, by which he encouraged himself and the faithful, and obtained support under circumstances bordering on despair; for he turned to God, when he saw the wicked, not only elated with prosperity, but also pouring forth blasphemies against the living God. The Prophet then says, that those who are under God's protection shall not perish. Of this he felt assured within himself. The declaration, as I have said, is much more striking, as the Prophet turns all his thoughts towards God, than if he had publicly and loudly declared what he testified, as it were, in a private conference.

But it was not without reason that he said, "Thou, my God, my holy one;" as though he had said, "I trust in thee, inasmuch as I am one of thy chosen people." He does not indeed speak here in his own private name, but includes with himself the whole Church; for this privilege belonged to all the children of Abraham, as they had been set apart by the gratuitous adoption of God, and were a royal priesthood. This is the reason why the Prophet says, Thou, my God, my holy one. For the Jews were wont thus to call God, because they had been chosen from the rest of the world. And their holiness was, that God had deigned to take them as his people, having rejected others, while yet there was by nature no difference between them. [18]

There is, moreover, much weight in the words which follow, Jehovah! for judgement has thou set him. This temptation ever occurs to us, whenever we strive to put our trust in God — What does this mean? for God now forsakes us, and exposes us to the caprice of the wicked they are allowed to do what they please, and God interferes not. How, then, can we cherish hope under these perplexities?" The Prophet now sets up a shield against this temptations — "Thou," he says, "hast appointed him for judgement." For he ascribes it to God's providence, that the Assyrians had with so much wantonness wasted the land, or would waste it when they came; for he speaks of things yet future — "Thou," he says, "hast appointed him for judgement."

This is a truth much needed: for Satan darkens, as with clouds, the favor of God, when any adversity happens to us, and when God himself thus proves our faith. But adversities are as it were clouds, excluding us from seeing God's fervor, as the light of the sun appears not to us when the sky is darkened. If, indeed, the mass of evils be so great and so thick, that our minds are overwhelmed, they are not clouds, but the thick darkness of night. In that case our faith cannot stand firm, except the providence of God comes to our view, so that we may know, in the midst of such confusion, why he permits so much liberty to the wicked, and also how their attempts may turn out, and what may be the issue. Except then we be fully persuaded, that God by his secret providence regulates all these confusions, Satan will a hundred times a day, yea every moment, shake that confidence which ought to repose in God. We now see how opportunely the Prophet adds this clause. He had said, "Art not thou our God? we shall not die." He now subjoins this by way of anticipation, "The Assyrians indeed do lay waste thy land as with an unbridled wantonness, they plunder thy people, and with impunity slay the innocent; but, O Lord, this is not done but by thy permission: Thou overrules all these confused proceedings, nor is all this done by thee without a cause. Thou, Jehovah, hast for judgement appointed him. — Judgement is to be taken for chastisement.

But the Prophet repeats the same thing, and, being strong, thou hast for correction established him. Some render צור, tsur strong, in the accusative case, and give a twofold explanation. One party apply the term to the Jews, who were to be subdued by hard means, since they were so refractory; and hence they think that the Jews are called strong, because they were like stones. Others give this meaning, Thou hast made him strong to correct; that is, Thou hast given him strength, by which he will chastise us. But as this is one of God's titles, I doubt not but that the two clauses correspond. He now, then, gives this name to God. Having given him his name as an eternal God, Thou, Jehovah, etc.; he now calls him strong. He puts צור, tsur to correspond with Jehovah; and then to correct, to correspond with judgement. We hence see how well the whole context agrees, and how the words answer, the one to the other. Then it is, Thou, strong one, hast established him to correct. But why does the Prophet call him strong? though this title, as I have said, is commonly ascribed to God, yet the Prophet, I have no doubt, had regard to the circumstances at the time. It is indeed difficult to retain this truth, — that the world is ruled by the secret counsel of God, when things are turned upside down: for the profane then glamour against God, and charge him with listlessness; and others cry out, that all things are thus changed fortuitously and at random; and hence they call fortune blind. It is then difficult, as I have said, to retain a fast hold on this truth. The Prophet, therefore, in order to support his own weakness, sets before himself this title of God, Thou, the strong God, or the rock, etc.; for צור, tsur means properly a rock, but it is to be taken here for God of strength. Why? "Behold, we indeed see revolutions, which not only make our faith to totter, but also dissipate as it were all our thoughts: but how much soever the world revolve in confusion, yet God is a rock; His purpose fails not, nor wavers; but remains ever firm." We now then see why the Prophet calls God strong. [19]

Thou the strong one, he says, hast established him. He expresses more by the word established, than in the first clause: for he prepared himself with firmness against continued evils, in case God (as it might be easily conjectured) would not give immediate relief to his people, but add calamities to calamities. Should God then join evils to evils, the Prophet prepares himself for perseverance; "Thou," he says, "the strong one hast established him;" that is, "Though the Assyrian should not only like a whirlwind or a violent tempest rush upon us, but also continue to oppress us, as though he were a pestilence attached to the land, or some fixed mountain, yet thou, Lord, hast established him." For what purpose? to correct. But the Prophet could not have said this, had he not known that God justly chastised his people. Not only for his own sake did he say this; but he intended also, by his own example, to lead the faithful to make the same holy and pious confession.

The two clauses of this sentence then are these, that though the Assyrian would rage with unbridled wantonness, like a cruel wild beast, he would yet be restrained by the hidden power of God, to whom it peculiarly belongs to overrule by his secret providence the confusions of this world. This is one thing. The Prophet also ascribes justice to God's power, and thus confesses his own guilt and that of the people; for the Lord would justly use so severe a scourge, because the people needed such a correction. Let us now go on —

Habakkuk 1:13

13. Thou art of purer eyes than to behold evil, and canst not look on iniquity: wherefore lookest thou upon them that deal treacherously, and holdest thy tongue when the wicked devoureth the man that is more righteous than he?

13. Mundus es oculis, ne videas malum, et aspicere ad molestiam non potes (non poteris, adverbum;) quare aspicis transgressores? dissimulas quum impius devorat justiorem se?

The Prophet here expostulates with God, not as at the beginning of the chapter; for he does not here, with a holy and calm mind, undertake the defense of God's glory, but complains of injuries, as men do when oppressed, who go to the judge and implore his protection. This complaint, then, is to be distinguished from the former one; for at the beginning of the chapter the Prophet did not plead his own cause or that of the people; but zeal for God's glory roused him, so that he in a manner asked God to take vengeance on so great an obstinacy in wickedness; but he now comes down and expresses the feelings of men; for he speaks of the thoughts and sorrows of those who had suffered injuries under the tyranny of their enemies.

And he says, O God, thou art pure in eyes, thou lookest not on evil. Some render the verb רוהט, theur in the imperative mood, clear the eyes; but they are mistaken; for the verse contains two parts, the one contrary to the other. The Prophet reasons from the nature of God, and then he states what is of an opposite character. Thou, God, he says, art pure in eyes; hence thou canst not look on evil; it is not consistent with thy nature to pass by the vices of men, for every iniquity is hateful to thee. Thus the Prophet sets before himself the nature of God. Then he adds, that experience is opposed to this; for the wicked, he says, exult; and while they miserably oppress the innocent, no one affords any help. How is this, except that God sleeps in heaven, and neglects the affairs of men? We now then understand the Prophet's meaning in this verse. [20]

By saying that God is pure in eyes, he assumes what ought to be deemed certain and indubitable by all men of piety. But as God's justice does not always appear, the Prophet has a struggle; and he shows that he in a manner vacillated, for he did not see in the state of things before him what yet his piety dictated to him, that is, that God was just and upright. It is indeed true, that the second part of the verse borders on blasphemy: for though the Prophet ever thought honourably and reverently of God, yet he murmurs here, and indirectly charges God with too much tardiness, as he connived at things, while he saw the just shamefully oppressed by the wicked. But we must notice the order which the Prophet keeps. For by saying that God is pure in eyes, he no doubt restrains himself. As there was danger lest this temptation should carry him too far, he meets it in time, and includes himself, in a manner, within this boundary — that we ought to retain a full conviction of God's justice. The same order is observed by Jeremiah when he says, 'I know, Lord, that thou art just, but how is it that the ungodly do thus pervert all equity? and thou either takest no notice, or dost not apply any remedy. I would therefore freely contend with thee.' The Prophet does not immediately break out into such an expression as this, "O Lord, I will contend with thee in judgement:" but before he mentions his complaint, knowing that his feelings were strongly excited, he makes a kind of preface, and in a manner restrains himself, that he might check that extreme ardor which might have otherwise carried him beyond due bounds; "Thou art just, O Lord," he says. In a similar manner does our prophet speak here, Thou art pure in eyes, so as not to behold evil; and thou canst not look on trouble

Since, he says, thou canst not look on trouble, we find that he confirms himself in that truth — that the justice of God cannot be separated from his very nature: and by saying, לכות אל, la tucal, "thou canst not," it is the same as though he had said, "Thou, O Lord, art just, because thou art God; and God, because thou art just." For these two things cannot be separated, as both the eternity, and the very being of God, cannot stand without his justice. We hence see how strenuously the Prophet struggled against his own impetuosity, so that he might not too much indulge himself in the complaint, which immediately follows.

For he then asks, according to the common judgement of the flesh, Why dost thou look on, when the ungodly devours one more just than himself? The Prophet here does not divest God of his power, but speaks in doubt, and contends not so much with God as with himself. A profane man would have said, "There is no God, there is no providence," or, "He cares not for the world, he takes his pleasure in heaven." But the Prophet says, "Thou seest, Lord." Hence he ascribes to God what peculiarly belongs to him — that he does not neglect the world which he has created. At the same time he here inclines two ways, and alternates; Why does thou look on, when the ungodly devours one more just than himself? He says not that the world revolves by chance, nor that God takes his delight and ease in heaven, as the Epicureans hold; but he confesses that the world is seen by God, and that he exercises care over the affairs of men: notwithstanding, as he could not see his way clear in a state of things so confused, he argues the point rather with himself than with God. We now see the import of this sentence. The Prophet, however, proceeds —

Hab. 1:14, 15

14. And makest men as the fishes of the sea, as the creeping things, that have no ruler over them?

14. Facis hominem quasi pisces maris, quasi reptile, quod caret duce (ad verbum, non est dux in illo.)

15. They take up all of them with the angle, they catch them in their net, and gather them in their drag: therefore they rejoice and are glad.

15. Totum hamo suo attrahet, colliget in sagenam suam, et congregabit in rete suum; propterea gaudebit et exultabit (hoc est, gaudet et exultat.)

He goes on, as it has been said, in his complaint; and by a comparison he shows that the judgement would be such as though God turned away from men, so as not to check the violence of the wicked, nor oppose his hand to their wantonness, in order to restrain them. Since, then, every one would oppress another as he exceeded him in power, and would with increased insolence rise up against the miserable and the poor, the Prophet compares man to the fish of the sea, — "What can this mean?" he says. "For men have been created after God's image: why then does not some justice appear among them? When one devours another, and even one man oppresses almost the whole world, what can be the meaning of this? God seems to sport with human affairs. For if he regards men as his children, why does he not defend them by his power? But we see one man (for he speaks of the Assyrian king) so enraged and so cruel, as though the rest of the world were like fish or reptiles." Thou makes men, he says, like reptiles or fishes; and then he adds, He draws up the whole by his hook, he collects them into his drag, he gathers then into his net, he exults [21]

We now see what the Prophet means — that God would, as it were, close his eyes, while the Assyrians wantonly laid waste the whole world: and when this tyranny should reach the holy land, what else could the faithful think but that they were forsaken by God? And there is nothing, as I have already said, more monstrous, than that iniquitous tyranny should thus prevail among men; for they have all, from the least to the greatest, been created after God's image. God then ought to exercise peculiar care in preserving mankind; his paternal love and solicitude ought in this respect to appear evident: but when men are thus destroyed with impunity, and one oppresses almost all the rest, there seems indeed to be no divine providence. For how will it be that he will care for either birds, or oxen, or asses, or trees, or plants, when he will thus forsake men, and bring no aid in so confused a state? We now understand the drift of what the Prophet says.

But yet he does not, as I have already said, take away from God his power, nor does he here rail against fortune, as many cavillers do. Thou makest men, he says: he ascribes to God what cannot be taken from him, — that he governs the world. But as to God's justice, he hesitates, and appeals to God. Though the Prophet seems here to rush headlong like insane men; yet if we consider all things, we shall see that he strenuously contended with his temptations, and even in these words some sparks at least of faith will shine forth, which are sufficient to show to us the great firmness of the Prophet. For this especially is worthy of being noticed, — that the Prophet turns himself to God. The Epicureans, when they glamour against God, for the most part, seek the ear of the multitude; and so they speak evil of God and withdraw themselves at a distance from him; for they do not think that he exercises any care over the world. But the Prophet continually addresses God. He knew then that God was the governor of all things. He also desires to be extricated from thoughts so thorny and perplexing; and from whom does he seek relief? From God himself. When the profane wantonly deride God, they indulge themselves, and seek nothing else but to become hardened in their own impious conjectures: but the Prophet comes to God himself, "How does this happen, O Lord?" As though he had said,

"Thou sees how I am distracted, and also held fast bound — distracted by many absurd thoughts, so that I am almost confounded, and held fast bound by great perplexities, from which I cannot extricate myself. Do thou, O Lord, unfold to me these knots, and concentrate my scattered thoughts, that I may understand what is true, and what I am to believe; and especially remove from me this doubt, lest it should shake my faith; O Lord, grant that I may at length know and fully understand how thou art just, and overrules, consistently with perfect equity, those things which seem to be so confused."

It also happens sometimes that the ungodly, as it were, openly revile God, a satanic rage having taken possession on them. But the case was far different with the Prophet; for finding himself overwhelmed and his mind not able to sustain him under so heavy trials, he sought relief, and as we have said, applied to God himself.

By saying, He therefore rejoices and exults, he increases the indignity; for though the Lord may for a time permit the wicked to oppress the innocent, yet when he finds them glorying in their vices and triumphing, so great a wantonness ought the more to kindle his vengeance. That the Lord then should still withhold himself, seems indeed very strange. But the Prophet proceeds —

Habakkuk 1:16

16. Therefore they sacrifice unto their net, and burn incense unto their drag; because by them their portion is fat, and their meat plenteous.

16. Propterea sacrificabit sagenae suae, et suffitum offeret reti suo, quia in illis pinguis portio ejus, et cibus ejus lautus.

The Prophet confirms the closing sentence of the last verse; for he explains what that joy was of which he had spoken, even the joy by which the wicked, as it were, designedly provoke God against themselves. It is indeed an abominable thing when the ungodly take delight in their vices; but it is still more atrocious when they deride God himself. Such, then, is the account now added by the Prophet, as though he had said, "Not only do the ungodly felicitate themselves while thou sparest them, or for a time bearest with them; but they now rise up against thee and deride all thy majesty, and openly blaspheme against heaven itself; for they sacrifice to their own net, and offer incense to their drag." By this metaphor the Prophet intimates, that the wicked do not only become hardened when they succeed in their vices, but that they also ascribe to themselves the praise of justice; for they consider that to be rightly done which has been attended with success. They thus dethrone God, and put themselves in his place. We now then see the Prophet's meaning.

But this passage discovers to us the secret impiety of all those who do not serve God sincerely and with an honest mind. There is indeed imprinted on the hearts of men a certain conviction respecting the existence of a God; for none are so barbarous as not to have some sense of religion: and thus all are rendered inexcusable, as they carry in their hearts a law which is sufficient to make them a thousand times guilty. But at the same time the ungodly, and those who are not illuminated by faith, bury this knowledge, for they are enveloped in themselves: and when some recollection of God creeps in, they are at first impressed, and ascribe some honor to him; but this is evanescent, for they soon suppress it as much as they can; yea they even strive to extinguish (though they cannot) this knowledge and whatever light they have from heaven. This is what the Prophet now graphically sets forth in the person of the Assyrian king. He had before said,

"This power is that of his God." He had complained that the Assyrians would give to their idols what was peculiar to God alone, and thus deprive him of his right: but he says now, that they would sacrifice to their own drag, and offer incense to their net. This is a very different thing: for how could they sacrifice to their idols, if they ascribed to their drag whatever victories they had gained? Now, by the words drag and net, the Prophet means their efforts, strength, forces, power, counsels, and policies as they call them, and whatever else there be which profane men arrogate to themselves. But what is it to sacrifice to their own net? The Assyrian did this, because he thought that he surpassed all others in craftiness, because he thought himself so courageous as not to hesitate to make war with all nations, regarding himself well prepared with forces and justified in his proceedings; and because he became successful and omitted nothing calculated to ensure victory. Thus the Assyrian, as I have said, regarded as nothing his idols; for he put himself in the place of all the gods. But if it be asked whence came his success, we must answer, that the Assyrian ought to have ascribed it all to the one true God: but he thought that he prospered through his own velour. If we refer to counsel, it is certain that God is he who governs the counsels and minds of men; but the Assyrian thought that he gained everything by his own skill. If, again, we speak of strength, whence was it? and of courage, whence was it, but from God? but the Assyrian appropriated all these things to himself. What regard, then, had he for God? We see how he now takes away all honor even from his own idols, and attributes everything to himself.

But this sin, as I have already said, belongs to all the ungodly; for where God's Spirit does not reign, there is no humility, and men ever swell with inward pride, until God thoroughly cleanse them. It is then necessary that God should empty us by his special grace, that we may not be filled with this satanic pride, which is innate, and which cannot by any means be shaken off by us, until the Lord regenerates us by his Spirit. And this may be seen es specially in all the kings of this world. They indeed confess that kings rule through God's grace; and then when they gain any victory, supplications are made, vows are paid. But were any one to say to those conquerors, "God had mercy on you," the answer would be, "What! was then my preparation nothing? did I not provide many things beforehand? did I not attain the friendship of many? did I not form confederacies? did I not foresee such and such disadvantages? did I not opportunely provide a remedy?" In a word, they sacrifice apparently to God, but afterwards they have a regard mainly to their drag and their net, and make nothing of God.

Well would it be were these things not so evident. But since the Spirit of God sets before us a lively image of the fact, let us learn what true humility is, and that we then only have this, when we think that we are nothing, and can do nothing, and that it is God alone who not only supports and continues us in life, but also governs us by his Spirit, and that it is he who sustains our hearts, gives courage, and then blesses us, so as to render prosperous what we may undertake. Let us hence learn that God cannot be really glorified, except when men wholly empty themselves.

He then adds, because in (or by) them is his fat portion and his rich meat. Though some render הארב, berae, choice meat, and others, fat meat, I yet prefer the meaning of rich. [22] His meat then will be rich. The Prophet intimates here that men are so blinded by prosperity that they sacrifice to themselves, and hence the more deserving of reproof is their ingratitude; for the more liberally God deals with us the more reason, no doubt, there is why we ought to glorify him. But when men, well supplied and fully satisfied, thus swell with pride and sacrifice to themselves, is not their impiety in this manner more completely discovered? But the Prophet not only proves that the Assyrians abused God's bounty, but he shows in their person what is the disposition of the whole world. For when men accumulate great wealth, and pile up a great heap from the property of others, they become more and more blinded. We hence see that we ought justly to fear the evil of prosperity, lest our fatness should so increase that we can see nothing; for the eyes are dimmed by excessive fatness. Let this then be ever remembered by us. The Prophet then concludes his discourse: but as one verse of the first chapter only remains, I shall briefly notice it.

Habakkuk 1:17

17. Shall they therefore empty their net, and not spare continually to slay the nations?

17. An propterea extendet [23] sagenam suam, et assiduus erit ad occidendas gentes, ut non parcat (alii vertuat, annon negative; atqui debuisset esse [הלא על-כו])?

This is an affirmative question, "Shall they therefore;" which, however, requires a negative answer. Then all interpreters are mistaken; for they think that the Prophet here complains, that he presently extends his net after having made a capture, but he rather means, "Is he ever to extend his net?" that is, "How long, O Lord, wilt thou permit the Assyrians to proceed to new plunders, so as to be like the hunter, who after having taken a boar or a stag, is more eager, and immediately renews his hunting; or like the fisherman, who having filled his little ship, with more avidity pursues his vocation? Wilt thou, Lord, he says, suffer the Assyrians to become more assiduous in their work of destruction?" And he shows how unworthy they were of God's forbearance, for they slew the nations. "I speak not here," he says, "either of fish or of any other animal, nor do I speak of this or that man, but I speak of many nations. As these slaughters are thus carried on through the whole world, how long, Lord, shall they be unpunished? for they will never cease." We now see the purport of the Prophet's complaint; but we shall find in the next lecture how he recovers himself.

PRAYER

Grant, Almighty God, that as it cannot be but that, owing to the infirmity of our flesh, we must be shaken and tossed here and there by the many turbulent commotions of this world, — O grant, that our faith may be sustained by this support — that thou art the governor of the world, and that men were not only once created by thee, but are also preserved by thy hand, and that thou art also a just judge, so that we may duly restrain ourselves; and though we must often have to bear many insults, let us yet never fail, until our faith shall become victorious over all trials, and until we, having passed through continued succession of contests, shall at length reach that celestial rest, which Christ thy Son has obtained for us. Amen.

CHAPTER 2

Lecture One Hundred and Ninth

Habakkuk 2:1

1. I will stand upon my watch, and set me upon the tower, and will watch to see what he will say unto me, and what I shall answer when I am reproved.

1. Super speculam meam stabo, et statuam me super arcem, et speculabor ad videndum quid loquatur mecum, et quid respondeam ad increpationem meam.

We have seen in the first chapter Hab 1:2-3 that the Prophet said in the name of all the faithful. It was indeed a hard struggle, when all things were in a perplexed state and no outlet appeared. The faithful might have thought that all things happened by chance, that there was no divine providence; and even the Prophet uttered complaints of this kind. He now begins to recover himself from his perplexities; and he ever speaks in the person of the godly, or of the whole Church. For what is done by some interpreters, who confine what is said to the prophetic office, I do not approve; and it may be easy from the contempt to learn, that the Prophet does not speak according to his private feeling, but that he represents the feelings of all the godly. So then we ought to collect this verse with the complaints, which we have before noticed; for the Prophet, finding himself sinking, and as it were overwhelmed in the deepest abyss, raises himself up above the judgement and reason of men, and comes nearer to God, that he might see from on high the things which take place on earth, and not judge according to the understanding of his own flesh, but by the light of the Holy Spirit. For the tower of which he speaks is patience arising from hope. If indeed we would struggle perseveringly to the last, and at length obtain the victory over all trials and conflicts, we must rise above the world.

Some understand by tower and citadel the Word of God: and this may in some measure be allowed, though not in every respect suitable. If we more fully weigh the reason for the metaphor, we shall be at no loss to know that the tower is the recess of the mind, where we withdraw ourselves from the world; for we find how disposed we are all to entertain distrust. When, therefore, we follow our own inclination, various temptations immediately lay hold on us; nor can we even for a moment exercise hope in God: and many things are also suggested to us, which take away and deprive us of all confidence: we become also involved in variety of thoughts, for when Satan finds men wandering in their imaginations and blending many things together, he so entangles them that they cannot by any means come nigh to God. If then we would cherish faith in our hearts, we must rise above all these difficulties and hindrances. And the Prophet by tower means this, that he extricated himself from the thoughts of the flesh; for there would have been no end nor termination to his doubts, had he tried to form a judgement according to his own understanding; I will stand, he says, on my tower, [24] I and I will set myself on the citadel. In short, the sentence carries this meaning — that the Prophet renounced the judgement of men, and broke through all those snares by which Satan entangles us and prevents us to rise above the earth.

He then adds, I will watch to see what he may say to me, that is, I will be there vigilant; for by watching he means vigilance and waiting, as though he had said, "Though no hope should soon appear, I shall not despond; nor shall I forsake my station; but I shall remain constantly in that tower, to which I wish now to ascend: I will watch then to see what he may say to me." The reference is evidently to God; for the opinion of those is not probable, who apply this "saying" to the ministers of Satan. For the Prophet says first, 'I will see what he may say to me,' and then he adds, 'and what I shall answer.' They who explain the words 'what he may say,' as referring to the wicked who might oppose him for the purpose of shaking his faith, overlook the words of the Prophet, for he speaks here in the singular number; and as there is no name expressed, the Prophet no doubt meant God. But were the words capable of admitting this explanation, yet the very drift of the argument shows, that the passage has the meaning which I have attached to it. For how could the faithful answer the calumnies by which their faith was assailed, when the profane opprobriously mocked and derided them — how could they satisfactorily disprove such blasphemies, did they not first attend to what God might say to them? For we cannot confute the devil and his ministers, except we be instructed by the word of God. We hence see that the Prophet observes the best order in what he states, when he says in the first place, 'I will see what God may say to me;' and in the second place, 'I shall then be taught to answer to my chiding;' [25] that is, "If the wicked deride my faith, I shall be able boldly to confute them; for the Lord will suggest to me such things as may enable me to give a full answer." We now perceive the simple and real meaning of this verse. It remains for us to accommodate the doctrine to our own use.

It must be first observed, that there is no remedy, when such trials as those mentioned by the Prophet in the first chapter Hab 1:4-17 meet us, except we learn to raise up our minds above the world. For if we contend with Satan, according to our own view of things, he will a hundred times overwhelm us, and we can never be able to resist him. Let us therefore know, that here is shown to us the right way of fighting with him, when our minds are agitated with unbelief, when doubts respecting God's providence creep in, when things are so confused in this world as to involve us in darkness, so that no light appears: we must bid adieu to our own reason; for all our thoughts are nothing worth, when we seek, according to our own reason, to form a judgement. Until then the faithful ascend to their tower and stand in their citadel, of which the Prophet here speaks, their temptations will drive them here and there, and sink them as it were in a bottomless gulf. But that we may more fully understand the meaning, we must know, that there is here an implied contrast between the tower and the citadel, which the Prophet mentions, and a station on earth. As long then as we judge according to our own perceptions, we walk on the earth; and while we do so, many clouds arise, and Satan scatters ashes in our eyes, and wholly darkens our judgement, and thus it happens, that we lie down altogether confounded. It is hence wholly necessary, as we have before said, that we should tread our reason under foot, and come nigh to God himself.

We have said, that the tower is the recess of the mind; but how can we ascend to it? even by following the word of the Lord. For we creep on the earth; nay, we find that our flesh ever draws us downward: except then the truth from above becomes to us as it were wings, or a ladder, or a vehicle, we cannot rise up one foot; but, on the contrary, we shall seek refuges on the earth rather than ascend into heaven. But let the word of God become our ladder, or our vehicle, or our wings, and, however difficult the ascent may be, we shall yet be able to fly upward, provided God's word be allowed to have its own authority. We hence see how unsuitable is the view of those interpreters, who think that the tower and the citadel is the word of God; for it is by God's word, as I have already said, that we are raised up to this citadel, that is, to the safeguard of hope; where we may remain safe and secure while looking down from this eminence on those things which disturb us and darken all our senses as long as we lie on the earth. This is one thing.

Then the repetition is not without its use; for the Prophet says, On my tower will I stand, on the citadel will I set myself. He does not repeat in other words the same thing, because it is obscure; but in order to remind the faithful, that though they are inclined to sloth, they must yet strive to extricate themselves. And we soon find how slothful we become, except each of us stirs up himself. For when any perplexity takes hold on our minds, we soon succumb to despair. This, then, is the reason why the Prophet, after having spoken of the tower, again mentions the citadel.

But when he says, I will watch to see, he refers to perseverance; for it is not enough to open our eyes once, and by one look to observe what happens to us; but it is necessary to continue our attention. This constant attention is, then, what the Prophet means by watching; for we are not so clear-sighted as immediately to comprehend what is useful to be known. And then, though we may once see what is necessary, yet a new temptation can obliterate that view. It thus happens, that all our observations become evanescent, except we continue to watch, that is, except we persevere in our attention, so that we may ever return to God, whenever the devil raises new storms, and whenever he darkens the heavens with clouds to prevent us to see God. We hence see how emphatical is what the Prophet says here, I will watch to see. The Prophet evidently compares the faithful to watchmen, who, though they hear nothing, yet do not sleep; and if they hear any noise once or twice, they do not immediately sound an alarm, but wait and attend. As, then, they who keep watch ought to remain quiet, that they may not disturb others, and that they may duly perform their office; so it behaves the faithful to be also tranquil and quiet, and wait patiently for God during times of perplexity and confusion.

Let us now inquire what is the purpose of this watching: I will watch to see, he says, what he may say to me. There seems to be an impropriety in the expression; for we do not properly see what is said. But the Prophet connects together here two metaphors. To speak strictly correct, he ought to have said, "I will continue attentive to hear what he may say;" but he says, I will watch to see what he may say. The metaphor is found correctly used in Ps 85:8,

"I will hear what God may say; for he will speak peace to his people."

There also it is a metaphor, for the Prophet speaks not of natural hearing: "I will hear what God may speak," what does that hearing mean? It means this, "I will quietly wait until God shows his favor, which is now hid; for he will speak peace to his people;" that is, the Lord will never forget his own Church. But the Prophet, as I have said, joins together here two metaphors; for to speak, or to say, means no other thing than that God testifies to our hearts, that though the reason for his purpose does not immediately appear to us, yet all things are wisely ruled, and that nothing is better than to submit to his will. But when he says, "I will see, and I will watch what he may say," the metaphor seems incongruous, and yet there appears a reason for it; for the Prophet intended to remind us, that we ought to employ all our senses for this end, — to be wholly attentive to God's word. For though one may be resolved to hear God, we yet find that many temptations immediately distract us. It is not then enough to become teachable, and to apply our ears to hear his voice, except also our eyes be connected with them, so that we may be altogether attentive.

We hence see the object of the Prophet; for he meant to express the greatest attention, as though he had said, that the faithful would ever wander in their thoughts, except they carefully concentrated both their eyes and their ears, and all their senses, on God, and continually restrained themselves, lest vagrant speculations or imaginations should lead them astray. And further, the Prophet teaches us, that we ought to have such reverence for God's word as to deem it sufficient for us to hear his voice. Let this, then, be our understanding, to obey God speaking to us, and reverently to embrace his word, so that he may deliver us from all troubles, and also keep our minds in peace and tranquillity.

God's speaking, then, is opposed to all the obstreperous clamours of Satan, which he never ceases to sound in our ears. For as soon as any temptation takes place, Satan suggests many things to us, and those of various kinds: — "What will you do? what advice will you take? see whether God is propitious to you from whom you expect help. How can you dare to trust that God will assist you? How can he extricate you? What will be the issue?" As Satan then disturbs us in various ways, the Prophet shows that the word of God alone is sufficient for us all, then, who indulge themselves in their own counsels, deserve to be forsaken by God, and to be left by him to be driven up and down, and here and there, by Satan; for the only unfailing security for the faithful is to acquiesce in God's word.

But this appears still more clear from what is expressed at the close of the verse, when the Prophet adds, and what I may answer to the reproof given me; for he shows that he would be furnished with the best weapons to sustain and repel all assaults, provided he patiently attended to God speaking to him, and fully embraced his word: "Then," he says, "I shall have what I may answer to all reproofs, when the Lord shall speak to me". By "reproofs," he means not only the blasphemies by which the wicked shake his faith, but also all those turbulent feelings by which Satan secretly labors to subvert his faith. For not only the ungodly deride us and mock at our simplicity, as though we presumptuously and foolishly trusted in God, and were thus over-credulous; but we also reprove ourselves inwardly, and disturb ourselves by various internal contentions; for whatever comes to our mind that is in opposition to God's word, is properly a chiding or a reproof, as it is the same thing as if one accused himself, as though he had not found God to be faithful. We now, then see that the word "reproof" extends farther than to those outward blasphemies by which the unbelieving are wont to assail the children of God; for, as we have already said, though no one attempted to try our faith, yet every one is a tempter to himself; for the devil never ceases to agitate our minds. When, therefore, the Prophet says, what I may answer to reproof, he means, that he would be sufficiently fortified against all the assaults of Satan, both secret and external, when he heard what God might say to him.

We may also gather from the whole verse, that we can form no judgement of God's providence, except by the light of celestial truth. It is hence no wonder that many fall away under trials, yea, almost the whole world; for few there are who ascend into the citadel of which the Prophet speaks, and who are willing to hear God speaking to them. Hence, presumption and arrogance blind the minds of men, so that they either speak evil of God who addresses them, or accuse fortune, or maintain that there is nothing certain: thus they murmur within themselves, and arrogate to themselves more than they ought, and never submit to God's word. Let us proceed, -

Hab. 2:2, 3

2. And the LORD answered me, and said, Write the vision, and make it plain upon tables, that he may run that readeth it.

2. Et respondit mihi Jehova et dixit, Scribe visionem, et explana super tabulas, ut currat legens in ea:

3. For the vision is yet for an appointed time, but at the end it shall speak, and not lie: though it tarry, wait for it; because it will surely come, it will not tarry.

3. Quia adhuc visio ad tempus statutum, et loquetur ad finem, et non mentietur; si moram fecerit, expecta eam; quia veniendo veniet, et non tardabit.

The Prophet now shows by his own example that there is no fear but that God will give help in time, provided we bring our minds to a state of spiritual tranquillity, and constantly look up to him: for the event which the Prophet relates, proves that there is no danger that God will frustrate their hope and patience, who lift up their minds to heaven, and continue steadily in that attitude. Answer me, he says, did Jehovah, and said. There is no doubt but that the Prophet accommodates here his own example to the common instruction of the whole Church. Hence, by testifying that an answer was given him by God, he intimates that we ought to entertain a cheerful hope, that the Lord, when he finds us stationed in our watch-tower, will in due season convey to us the consolation which he sees we need.

But he afterwards comes to the discharge of his prophetic office; for he was bid to write the vision on tables, and to write it in large letters, that it might be read, and that any one, passing by quickly, might be able by one glance to see what was written: and by this second part he shows still more clearly that he treated of a common truth, which belonged to the whole body of the Church; for it was not for his own sake that he was bid to write, but for the edification of all.

Write, then, the vision, and make it plain; for ראב, bar properly means, to declare plainly. [26] Unfold it then, he says, on tables, that he may run who reads it; that is, that the writing may not cause the readers to stop. Write it in large characters, that any one, in running by, may see what is written. Then he adds, for the vision shall be for an appointed time

This is a remarkable passage; for we are taught here that we are not to deal with God in too limited a manner, but room must be given for hope; for the Lord does not immediately execute what he declares by his mouth; but his purpose is to prove our patience, and the obedience of our faith. Hence he says, the vision, is for a time, and a fixed time: for דעומ, muod means a time which has been determined by agreement. But as it is God who fore appoints the time, the constituted time, of which the Prophet speaks, depends on his will and power. The vision, then, shall be for a time. He reproves here that immoderate ardor which takes hold on us, when we are anxious that God should immediately accomplish what he promises. The Prophet then shows that God so speaks as to be at liberty to defer the execution of his promise until it seems good to him.

At the end, he says, it will speak [27] In a word, the Prophet intimates, that honor is to be given to God's word, that we ought to be fully persuaded that God speaks what is true, and be so satisfied with his promises as though what is promised were really possessed by us. At the end, then, it will speak and it will not lie [28] Here the Prophet means, that fulfillment would take place, so that experience would at length prove, that God had not spoken in vain, nor for the sake of deceiving; but yet that there was need of patience; for, as it has been said, God intends not to indulge our fervid and importunate desires by an immediate fulfillment, but his design is to hold us in suspense. And this is the true sacrifice of praise, when we restrain ourselves, and remain firm in the persuasion that God cannot deceive nor lie, though he may seem for a time to trifle with us. It will not, then, lie

He afterwards adds, If it will delay, wait for it. He again expresses still more clearly the true character of faith, that it does not break forth immediately into complaints, when God connives at things, when he suffers us to be oppressed by the wicked, when he does not immediately succor us; in a word, when he does not without delay fulfill what he has promised in his word. If, then, it delays, wait for it. He again repeats the same thing, coming it will come; that is, however it may be, God, who is not only true, but truth itself, will accomplish his own promises. The fulfillment, then, of the promise will take place in due time.

But we must notice the contrariety, If it will delay, it will come, it will not delay. The two clauses seem to be contrary the one to the other. But delay, mentioned first, has a reference to our haste. It is a common proverb,

"Even quickness is delay to desire." We indeed make such haste in all our desires, that the Lord, when he delays one moment, seems to be too slow. Thus it may come easily to our mind to expostulate with him on the ground of slowness. God, then, is said on this account to delay in his promises; and his promises also as to their accomplishment may be said to be delayed. But if we have regard to the counsel of God, there is never any delay; for he knows all the points of time, and in slowness itself he always hastens, however this may be not comprehended by the flesh. We now, then, apprehend what the Prophet means. [29]

He is now bidden to write the vision, and to explain it on tables. Many confine this to the coming of Christ; but I rather think that the Prophet ascribes the name of vision to the doctrine or admonition, which he immediately subjoins. It is indeed true, that the faithful under the law could not have cherished hope in God without having their eyes and their minds directed to Christ: but it is one thing to take a passage in a restricted sense as applying to Christ himself, and another thing to set forth those promises which refer to the preservation of the Church. As far then as the promises of God in Christ are yea and amen, no vision could have been given to the Fathers, which could have raised their minds, and supported them in the hope of salvation, without Christ having been brought before them. But the Prophet here intimates generally, that a command was given to him to supply the hearts of the godly with this support, that they were, as we shall hereafter more clearly see, to wait for God. The vision, then, is nothing else than an admonition, which will be found in the next and the following verses.

He uses two words, to write and to explain; which some pervert rather than rightly distinguish: for as the Prophets were wont to write, and also to set forth the summaries or the heads of their discourses, they think that it was a command to Habakkuk to write, that he might leave on record to posterity what he had said; and then to publish what he taught as an edict, that it might be seen by the people passing by, not only for a day or for a few days. But I do not think that the Prophet speaks with so much refinement: I therefore consider that to write and to explain on tables mean the same thing. And what is added, that he may run who reads it, is to be understood as I have already explained it; for God intended to set forth this declaration as memorable and worthy of special notice. It was not usual with the Prophets to write in long and large characters; but the Prophet mentions here something peculiar, because the declaration was worthy of being especially observed. What is similar to this is said in Isa 8:1, 'Write on at table with a man's pen.' By a man's pen is to be understood common writing, such as is comprehended by the rudest and the most ignorant. To the same purpose is what God bids here his servant Habakkuk to do. Write, he says how? Not as Prophecies are wont to be written, for the Prophets set before the people the heads of their discourses; but write, he says, so that he who runs may read, and that though he may be inattentive, he may yet see what is written; for the table itself will plainly show what it contains.

We now see that the Prophet commends, by a peculiar eulogy, what he immediately subjoins. Hence this passage ought to awaken all our powers, as God himself testifies that he announces what is worthy of being remembered: for he speaks not of a common truth; but his purpose was to reveal something great and unusually excellent; as he bids it, as I have already said, to be written in large characters, so that those who run might read it.

And by saying that the vision is yet for a time, he shows, as I have briefly explained, what great reverence is due to heavenly truth. For to wish God to conform to our rule is extremely preposterous and unreasonable: and there is no place for faith, if we expect God to fulfill immediately what he promises. It is hence the trial of faith to acquiesce in God's word, when its accomplishment does in no way appear. As then the Prophet teaches us, that the vision is yet for a time, he reminds us that we have no faith, except we are satisfied with God's word alone, and suspend our desires until the seasonable time comes, that which God himself has appointed. The vision, then, yet shall be. But we are inclined to reduce, as it were, to nothing the power of God, except he accomplishes what he has said: "Yet, yet," says the Prophet, "the vision shall be;" that is, "Though God does not stretch forth his hand, still let what he has spoken be sufficient for you: let then the vision itself be enough for you; let it be deemed worthy of credit, so that the word of God may on its own account be believed; and let it not be tried according to the common rule; for men charge God with falsehood, except he immediately yields to their desires. Let then the vision itself be counted sufficiently solid and firm, until the suitable time shall come." And the word מועד, muod, ought to be noticed; for the Prophet does not speak simply of time, but, as I have already said, he points out a certain and a preordained time. When men make an agreement, they on both sides fix the day: but it would be the highest presumption in us to require that God should appoint the day according to our will. It belongs, then, to him to appoint the times, and so to govern all things, that we may approve of whatever he does.

He afterwards says, And it will speak at the end, and it will not lie. The same is the import of the expression, it will speak at the end; that is, men are very perverse, if they wish God to close his mouth, and if they wish to deny faith to his word, except he instantly fulfill what he speaks. It will then speak; that is, let this liberty of speaking be allowed to God. And there is always an implied contrast between the voice of God and its accomplishment; for we are to acquiesce in God's word, though he may conceal his hand: though he may afford no proof of his power, yet the Prophet commands this honor to be given to his word. The vision, then, will speak at the end

He now expresses more clearly what he had before said of the preordained time; and thus he meets the objections which Satan is wont to suggest to us: "How long will that time be delayed? Thou indeed namest it as the preordained time; but when will that day come?" "The Lord," he says, "will speak at the end;" that is, "Though the Lord protracts time, and though day after day we seem to live on vain promises, yet let God speak, that is, let him have this honor from you, and be ye persuaded that he is true, that he cannot disappoint you; and in the meantime wait for his power; wait, so that ye may yet remain quiet, resting on his word, and let all your thoughts be confined within this stronghold — that it is enough that God has spoken. The rest we shall defer until to-morrow.

PRAYER

Grant, Almighty God, that as thou sees us laboring under so much weakness, yea, with our minds so blinded that our faith falters at the smallest perplexities, and almost fails altogether, — O grant that by the power of thy Spirit we may be raised up above this world, and learn more and more to renounce our own counsels, and so to come to thee, that we may stand fixed in our watch tower, ever hoping, through thy power, for whatever thou hast promised to us, though thou shouldst not immediately make it manifest to us that thou hast faithfully spoken; and may we thus give full proof of our faith and patience, and proceed in the course of our warfare, until at length we ascend, above all watch towers, into that blessed rest, where we shall no more watch with an attentive mind, but see, face to face, in thine image, whatever can be wished, and whatever is needful for our perfect happiness, through Christ our Lord. Amen.

LECTURE ONE HUNDRED AND TENTH

The Prophet taught us yesterday, that we ought to allow God his right of speaking to us, and of sustaining us by his own word, until the ripe time shall come, when he shall really fulfill what he has promised. Then an exhortation follows, added at the close of the verse — that we are to exercise patience; and the Apostle also, referring to this passage in Heb 10:38, makes a similar application. He indeed quotes what we shall find in the next verse, 'The just by his faith shall live;' but he had in view the whole context; and at the same time he reminds us of the Prophet's object here in exalting the authority of God's word. The exhortation, then, is briefly this — that though God may keep us in suspense, we yet ought not to cast away hope, for he knows when it is expedient for us that he should stretch forth his hand. And as there are two clauses, as I said yesterday, which seem at first sight to be inconsistent the one with the other, the Prophet very fitly joins them together, and considers them to be in perfect harmony; for though God may appear to delay, yet he is not slower than what is necessary and expedient. Let us then be fully persuaded that there is in God prudence and wisdom enough to assist us as soon as it may be needful. The Prophet now reminds us that it is no wonder if God seems to us to delay, for we are too hasty in our desires. Let therefore this fervor be restrained, so that we may subject our feelings to the providence and purpose of God. Let us now proceed —

Habakkuk 2:4

4. Behold, his soul which is lifted up is not upright in him: but the just shall live by his faith.

4. Ecce exaltatio, (vel, qui se munit, ut alii vertunt,) non recta est anima ejus in ipso: justus autem in fide sua vivet.

This verse stands connected with the last, for the Prophet means to show that nothing is better than to rely on God's word, how much soever may various temptations assault our souls. We hence see that nothing new is said here, hut that the former doctrine is confirmed — that our salvation is rendered safe and certain through God's promise alone, and that therefore we ought not to seek any other haven, where we might securely sustain all the onsets of Satan and of the world. But he sets the two clauses the one opposed to the other: every man who would fortify himself would ever be subject to various changes, and never attain a quiet mind; then comes the other clause — that man cannot otherwise obtain rest than by faith.

But the former part is variously explained. Some interpreters think the word הלפע, ophle, to be a noun, and render it elevation, which is not unsuitable; and indeed I hesitate not to regard this as its real meaning, for the Hebrews call a citadel לפוע, ouphel, rightly deriving it from לפע, ophle, to ascend. What some others maintain, that it signifies to strengthen, is not well founded. Some again give this explanation — that the unbelieving seek a stronghold for themselves, that they may fortify themselves; and this makes but little difference as to the thing itself. But interpreters vary, and differ as to the meaning of the sentence; for some substitute the predicate for the subject, and the subject for the predicate, and elicit this meaning from the Prophet's words — "Every one whose mind is not at ease seeks a fortress, where he may safely rest and strengthens himself;" and others give this view — "He who is proud, or who thinks himself well fortified, shall ever be of an unquiet mind." And this latter meaning is what I approve, only that I retain the import of the word הלפע, ophle, as though it was said — "where there is an elation of mind there is no tranquillity."

Let us see first what their view is who give the other explanation. They say that the unbelieving, being obstinate and perverted in their minds, ever seek where they may be in safety, for they are full of suspicions, and having no regard to God they resort to the world for those remedies, by which they may escape evils and dangers. This is their view. But the Prophet, as I have already said, does here, on the contrary, denounce punishment on the unbelieving, as though he had said — "This reward, which they have deserved, shall be repaid to them — that they shall always torment themselves." The contrast will thus be more obvious; and when we say that God punishes the unbelieving, when he suffers them to be driven here and there, and also harasses their minds with various tormenting thoughts, a more fruitful doctrine is elicited. When therefore the Prophet says that there is no calmness of mind possessed by those who deem themselves well fortified, he intimates that they are their own executioners, for they seek for themselves many troubles, many sorrows, many anxieties, and contrive and mingle together many designs and purposes; now they think of one thing, then they turn to another; for the Hebrews say that the soul is made right when we acquiesce in a thing and continue in a tranquil state of mind; but when confused thoughts distract us, then they say that our soul is not right in us. We now perceive the real meaning of the Prophet.

Behold, he says: by this demonstrative particle he intimates that what he teaches us may be clearly seen if we attend to daily events. The meaning then is, that a proof of this fact exists evidently in the common life of men — that he who fortifies himself, and is also elated with self confidence, never finds a tranquil haven, for some new suspicion or fear ever disturbs his mind. Hence it comes that the soul entangles itself in various cares and anxieties. This is the reward, as I have said, which is allotted by God's just judgement to the unbelieving; for God, as he testifies by Isaiah, offers to us rest; and they who reject this invaluable benefit, freely offered to them by God, deserve that they should not only be tormented in one way, but be also harassed by endless agitations, and that they should also vex and torment themselves. It is indeed true that he who is fortified may also acquiesce in God's word; but the word הלפע, ophle, refers to the state of the mind. Whosoever, then, swells with vain confidence, when he finds that he has many auxiliaries according to the flesh, shall ever be agitated, and will at length find that there is nowhere rest, except the mind recumbs on God's grace alone. We now understand the import of this clause. ³⁰

It follows, but the just shall live by his faith. The Prophet, I have no doubt, does here place faith in opposition to all those defences by which men so blind themselves as to neglect God, and to seek no aid from him. As men therefore rely on what the earth affords, depending on their fallacious supports, the Prophet here ascribes life to faith. But faith, as it is well known, and as we shall presently show more at large, depends on God alone. That we may then live by faith, the Prophet intimates that we must willingly give up all those defences which are wont to disappoint us. He then who finds that he is deprived of all protections, will live by his faith, provided he seeks in God alone what he wants, and leaving the world, fixes his mind on heaven.

As תגומא, amunat, is in Hebrew truth, so some regard it as meaning integrity; as though the Prophet had said, that the just man has more safety in his faithfulness and pure conscience, than there is to the children of this world in all those munitions in which they glory. But in this case they frigidly extenuate the Prophet's declaration; for they understand not what that righteousness of faith is from which our salvation proceeds. It is indeed certain that the Prophet understands by the word תגומא, amunat, that faith which strips us of all arrogance, and leads us naked and needy to God, that we may seek salvation from him alone, which would otherwise be far removed from us.

Now many confine the first part to Nebuchadnezzar, but this is not suitable. The Prophet indeed speaks to the end of the chapter of Babylon and its ruin; but here he makes a distinction between the children of God, who cast all their cares on him, and the unbelieving, who cannot go forth beyond the world, where they seek to be made secure, and gather hence their defences in which they confide. And this is especially worthy of being observed, for it helps us much to understand the meaning of the Prophet; if this part — "Behold the proud, his soul is not right in him," be applied to Nebuchadnezzar, the other part will lose much of its import; but if we consider that the Prophet, as it were, in these two tablets, shows what it is to glory in our own powers or in earthly aids, then what it is to repose on God alone will appear much more clear, and this truth will with more force penetrate into our minds; for we know how much such comparisons illustrate a subject which would be otherwise obscure or less evident. For if the Prophet had only declared that our faith is the cause of life and salvation, it might indeed be understood; but as we are disposed to entertain worldly hopes, the former truth would not have been sufficient to correct this evil, and to free our minds from all vain confidence. But when he affirms that all the unbelieving are deceived, while they fortify or elate themselves, be cause God will ever confound them, and that though no one disturbs them outwardly, they will yet be their own tormentors, as they have nothing that is right, nothing that is certain; when therefore all this is said to us, it is as though God drew us forcibly to himself, while seeing us deluded by the allurements of Satan, and seeing us too inclined to be taken with deceptions, which would at length lead us to destruction.

We now, then, perceive why Habakkuk has put these two things in opposition the one to the other — that the defences of this world are not only evanescent, but also bring always with them many tormenting fears — and then, that the just lives by his faith. And hence also is found a confirmation of what I have already touched upon, that faith is not to be taken here for man's integrity, but for that faith which sets man before God emptied of all good things, so that he seeks what he needs from his gratuitous goodness: for all the unbelieving try to fortify themselves; and thus they strengthen themselves, thinking that anything in which they trust is sufficient for them. But what does the just do? He brings nothing before God except faith: then he brings nothing of his own, because faith borrows, as it were, through favor, what is not in man's possession. He, then, who lives by faith, has no life in himself; but because he wants it, he flies for it to God alone. The Prophet also puts the verb in the future tense, in order to show the perpetuity of this life: for the unbelieving glory in a shadowy life; but the Lord will at last discover their folly, and they themselves shall really know that they have been deceived. But as God never disappoints the hope of his people, the Prophet promises here a perpetual life to the faithful.

Let us now come to Paul, who has applied the Prophet's testimony for the purpose of teaching us that salvation is not by works, but by the mercy of God alone, and therefore by faith. Paul seems to have misapplied the Prophet's words, and to have used them beyond what they import; for the Prophet speaks here of the state of the present life, and he has not previously spoken of the celestial life, but exhorted, as we have seen, the faithful to patience, and at the same time testified that God would be their deliverer; and now he adds, the just shall live by faith, though he may be destitute of all help, and though he may be exposed to all the assaults of fortune, and of the wicked, and of the devil. What has this to do, some one may say, with the eternal salvation of the soul? It seems, then, that Paul has with too much refinement introduced this testimony into his discussion respecting gratuitous justification by faith. But this principle ought ever to be remembered — that whatever benefits the Lord confers on the faithful in this life, are intended to confirm them in the hope of the eternal inheritance; for however liberally God may deal with us, our condition would yet be indeed miserable, were our hope confined to this earthly life. As God then would raise up our minds to the hopes of eternal salvation whenever he aids us in this world, and declares himself to be our Father; hence, when the Prophet says that the faithful shall live, he certainly does not confine this life to so narrow limits, that God will only defend us for a day or two, or for a few years; but he proceeds much farther, and says, that we shall be made really and truly happy; for though this whole world may perish or be exposed to various changes, yet the faithful shall continue in permanent and real safety. Hence, when Habakkuk promises life in future to the faithful, he no doubt overleaps the boundaries of this world, and sets before the faithful a better life than that which they have here, which is accompanied with many sorrows, and proves itself by its shortness to be unworthy of being much desired.

We now perceive that Paul wisely and suitably accommodates to his subject the Prophet's words — that the just lives by faith; for there is no salvation for the soul except through God's mercy.

Quoting this place in Ro 1:17, he says that the righteousness of God is in the gospel revealed from faith to faith, and then adds,

"As it is written, The just shall live by faith."

Paul very rightly connects these things together that righteousness is made known in the Gospel — and that it comes to us by faith only; for he there contends that men cannot obtain righteousness by the law, or by the works of the law; it follows that it is revealed in the Gospel alone: how does he prove this? By the testimony of the Prophet Habakkuk —

"If by faith the just lives, then he is just by faith; if he is just by faith, then he is not so by the works of the law."

And Paul assumes this principle, to which I have before referred — that men are emptied of all works, when they produce their faith before God: for as long as man possesses anything of his own, he does not please God by faith alone, but also by his own worthiness.

If then faith alone obtains grace, the law must necessarily be relinquished, as the apostle also explains more clearly in the third chapter of the Epistle to the Galatians Ga 3:11:

'That righteousness,' he says, 'is not by the works of the law, is evident; for it is written, The just shall live by faith, and the law is not of faith.'

Paul assumes that these, even faith and law, are contrary, the one to the other; contrary as to the work of justifying. The law indeed agrees with the gospel; nay, it contains in itself the gospel. And Paul has solved this question in the first chapter of the Epistle to the Romans, Ro 1:1-32 by saying, that the law cannot assist us to attain righteousness, but that it is offered to us in the gospel, and that it receives a testimony from the law and the Prophets. Though then there is a complete concord between the law and the gospel, as God, who is not inconsistent with himself, is the author of both; yet as to justification, the law accords not with the gospel, any more than light with darkness: for the law promises life to those who serve God; and the promise is conditional, dependent on the merits of works. The gospel also does indeed promise righteousness under condition; but it has no respect to the merits of works. What then? It is only this, that they who are condemned and lost are to embrace the favor offered to them in Christ.

We now then see how, by the testimony of our Prophet, Paul rightly confirms his own doctrine, that eternal salvation is to be attained by faith only; for we are destitute of all merits by works, and are constrained to stand naked and needy before God; and then the Lord justifies us freely.

But that this may be more evident, let us first consider why men must come altogether naked before God; for were there any worthiness in them, the Lord would by no means deprive them of such an honor. Why then does the Lord justify us freely, except that he may thereby appear just? He has indeed no need of this glory, as though he could not himself be glorified except by doing wrong to men. But we obtain righteousness by faith alone for this reason, because God finds nothing in us which he can approve, or what may avail to obtain righteousness. Since it is so, we then see that to be true which the Holy Spirit everywhere declares respecting the character of men. Men indeed glory in a foolish conceit as to their own righteousness: but all philosophic virtues, as they call them, which men think they possess through free-will, are mere fumes; nay, they are the delusions of the devil, by which he bewitches the minds of men, so that they come not to God, but, on the contrary, precipitate themselves into the lowest deep, where they seek to exalt themselves beyond measure. However this may be, let us be fully convinced, that in man there is not even a particle either of rectitude or of righteousness; and that whatever men may try to do of themselves, is an abomination before God. This is one thing.

Now after God has stretched forth his hand to his elect, it is still necessary that they should confess their own want and nakedness, as to justification; for though they have been regenerated by the Spirit of God, yet in many things they are deficient, and thus in innumerable ways they become exposed to eternal death in the sight of God; so that they have in themselves no righteousness. The Papists differ from us in the first place, imagining as they do, that there are certain preparations necessary; for that false notion about free-will cannot be eradicated from their hearts. As then they will have man to be endued with free- will, they always connect with it some power, as though they could obtain grace by their own doings. They indeed confess that man of himself can do nothing, except by the helping grace of God; but in the meantime they blend, as I have said, their own fictitious preparations. Others confess, that until God anticipates us by his grace, there is no power whatever in free-will; but afterwards they suppose that free-will concurs with God's grace, as it would be by itself inefficient, except received by our consent. Thus they always reserve for men some worthiness; but a greater difference exists as to the second subject: for after we have been regenerated through God's grace, the Papists imagine that we are justified by the merits of works. They confess, that until God anticipates us by his grace, we are condemned and cannot attain salvation except through the assisting grace of God; but as soon as God works in us, we are then, they say, able to attain righteousness by our own works.

But we object and say, that the faithful, after having been regenerated by the Spirit of God, do not fulfill the law: they allow this to be true, but say that they might if they would, for that God has commanded nothing which is above what men are capable of doing. And this also is a most pernicious error. They are at the same time forced to confess, that experience itself teaches us that no man is wholly free from sin: then some guilt always remains. But they say, that if we kept half the law, we could obtain righteousness by that half. Hence, if one by adultery offended God and thus becomes exposed to eternal death, and yet abstains from theft, he is just, they say, because he is no thief. He is an adulterer, it is true; but he is yet just in part, because he keeps a part of the law; and they call this partial righteousness. But God has not promised salvation to men, except they fully and really fulfill whatever he has commanded in his law. For it is not said, "He that fulfill a part of the law shall live;" but he who shall do these things shall live in them. Moses does not point out two or three commandments, but includes the whole law (Le 18:5.) There is also a declaration made by James,

'He who has forbidden to commit adultery, has also forbidden to steal: whosoever then transgresses the law in one particular, is a transgressor of the whole law' (Jas. 2:8, 11):

he is then excluded from any hope of righteousness. We hence see that the papists are most grossly mistaken, who imagine, that men, when they keep the law only in part, are just.

Were there indeed any one found who strictly kept God's law, he could not be counted just, except by virtue of a promise. And here also the Papists stumble, and are at the same time inconsistent with themselves; for they confess that merits do not obtain righteousness for men by their own intrinsic worth, but only by the covenant of the law. But as soon as they have said this, they immediately forget themselves, and say what is contrary, like men carried away by passion. Were then the Papists to join together these two things — that there is no righteousness except by covenant, and that there is a partial righteousness they would see that they are inconsistent: for where is this partial righteousness? If we are not righteous except according to the covenant of the law, then we are not righteous except through a full and perfect observance of the law. This is certain.

They go astray still more grievously as to the remission of sins; for as it is well known, they obtrude their own satisfactions, and thus seek to expiate the sins of men by their own merits, as though the sacrifice of Christ was not sufficient for that purpose. Hence it is that they will not allow that we are gratuitously justified by faith; for they cannot be brought to acknowledge a free remission of sins; and except the remission of sins be gratuitous, we must confess that righteousness is not by faith alone, but also by merits. But the whole Scripture proves that expiation is nowhere else to be sought, except through the sacrifice of Christ alone. This error, then, of the Papists is extremely gross and false. They further err in pleading for the merits of works; for they boast of their own inventions, the works of supererogation, or as they call them, satisfactions. And these meritorious works, under the Papacy, are gross errors and worthless superstitions, and yet they toil in them and lacerate themselves, nay, they almost wear out themselves. If they mutter many short prayers, if they run to altars and to various churches, if they buy masses, in a word, if they accumulate all these fictitious acts of worship, they think that they merit righteousness before God. Thus they forget their own saying, that righteousness is by covenant; for if it be by covenant, it is certain that God does not promise it to fictitious works, which men of themselves invent and contrive. It then follows, that what men bring to God, devised by themselves, cannot do anything towards the attainment of righteousness.

There is also another error which must be noticed, for in good works they perceive not those blemishes which justly displease God, so that our works might be deservedly condemned were they strictly examined and tried. The Papists rightly say, that we are not justified by the intrinsic worthiness of works, but afterwards they do not consider how imperfect our works are, for no work proceeds from mortal man which can fully answer to what God's covenant requires. How so? For no work proceeds from the perfect love of God, and where the perfect love of God does not exist, there is corruption there. It hence follows, that all our works are polluted before God; for they flow not except from the impure fountain of the heart. Were any to object and say, that the hearts of men are cleansed by the regeneration of the Spirit, we allow this; but at the same time much filth always remains in our hearts, and it ought to be sufficient for us to know that nothing is pure and genuine before God except where the perfect love of him exists.

As, then, the Papists are blind to all these things, it is no wonder that they with so much hostility contend with us about righteousness, and can by no means allow that the righteousness of faith is gratuitous, for from the beginning this figment about free- will has been resorted to — "if men of themselves come to God, then they are not freely justified." They, then, as I have said, imagine a partial righteousness, they suppose the deficiency to be made up by satisfactions, they have also, as they say, their devotions, that is, their own contrived modes of worship. Thus it comes, that they ever persuade themselves that the righteousness of man, at least in part, is made up by himself or by works. They indeed allow that we are justified by faith, but when it is added, by faith alone, then they begin to be furious; but they consider not that righteousness, if obtained by faith, cannot be by works, for Paul, as I have shown above, reasons from the contrary, when he says, that righteousness, if it be by the works of the law, is not by faith, for faith, as it has been said, strips man of everything, that he may seek of God what he needs. But the Papists, though they think that man has not enough for himself, do not yet acknowledge that he is so needy and miserable, that righteousness must be sought in God alone. But yet sufficiently clear is the doctrine of Paul, and if Paul had never spoken, reason itself is sufficient to convince us that men cannot be justified by faith until they cast away every confidence in their own works, for if righteousness be of faith, then it is of grace alone, and if by grace alone, then it cannot be by works. It is wholly puerile in the Papists to think, that it is partly by grace and partly by the merits of works; for as salvation cannot be divided, so righteousness cannot be divided, by which we attain salvation itself. As, then, faith acquires for us favor before God, and by this favor we are counted just, so all works must necessarily fall to the ground, when righteousness is ascribed to faith.

PRAYER

Grant, Almighty God, that as the corruption of our flesh ever leads us to pride and vain confidence, we may be illuminated by thy word, so as to understand how great and how grievous is our poverty, and be thus taught wholly to deny ourselves, and so to present ourselves naked before thee, that we may not hope for righteousness or for salvation from any other source than from thy mercy alone, nor seek any rest but only in Christ; and may we cleave to thee by the sacred and inviolable bond of faith, that we may boldly despise all those empty boastings by which the ungodly exult over us, and that we may also so cast ourselves down in true humility, that thereby we may be carried upward above all heavens, and become partakers of that eternal life which thine only begotten Son has purchased for us by his own blood. Amen.

LECTURE ONE HUNDRED AND ELEVENTH

We yesterday compared this passage of Habakkuk with the interpretation of Paul, who draws this inference, that we are justified by faith without the works of the law, because the Prophet teaches us that we are to live by faith, for the way of life and of righteousness is the same, inasmuch as life is not to be otherwise sought by us than through the paternal favor of God. This then is our life — to be united to God; but this union with God cannot be hoped for by us while he imputes sins to us; for as he is just and cannot deny himself, iniquity must be ever hated by him. Then as long as he regards us as sinners, he must necessarily hold us as hateful to him. Where the hatred of God is, there is death and ruin. It then follows, that we can have no hope of life until we be reconciled to God, and there is no other way by which God can restore us to favor, but by regarding and counting us as just. It hence follows, that Paul reasons correctly, when he leads us from life to righteousness; for they are two things which are connected and inseparable.

Hence the error of the Papists comes to light, who think that to be justified is nothing else but to be renewed in righteousness, in order that we may lead a pious and a holy life. Hence their righteousness is a quality. But Paul's view is very different, for he connects our justification and salvation together, inasmuch as God cannot be propitious to us without being reconciled to us. And how is this done even by not imputing to us our sins. Hence they speak correctly and truly express what the Holy Spirit everywhere teaches us, who call it imputative righteousness, for they thus show that it is not a quality, but, on the contrary, a relative righteousness, and therefore we said yesterday that he who lives by faith derives life from another, and that every one who is just by faith, is just through what is not in himself, even through the gratuitous mercy of God.

We now then see how suitably Paul joins righteousness with life, and adduces the Prophet's testimony to prove gratuitous justification, who affirms that we are to live by faith. But it is no wonder that the Papists go in so many ways astray in this instance, for they even differ with us in the meaning of the word faith. Hence it is that they so obstinately deny that we are justified by faith alone. They are forced, as we have said yesterday, to admit the righteousness of faith; but the exclusive particle they cannot endure; for they imagine that it is a moulded faith that justifies, and this moulded or formed faith is piety, or the fear of God. And by calling faith unformed they seem to think that we can embrace the promises of God without the fruit of regeneration, which is very absurd, as though faith were not the peculiar gift of the Spirit, and a pledge of our adoption. But these are principles of which the Papists are wholly ignorant; for they are given up to a reprobate mind, so that they stumble at the very first elements of religion.

But it is sufficient for us, in order to understand this passage, to know that we live by faith; for our life is a shadow or a passing cloud; and hence our only remedy is to seek life from God alone. And how does God communicate this life to us? even by gratuitous promises which we embrace by faith; hence salvation is by faith. Now, salvation cannot be ascribed to faith and to works too; for faith refers the praise for life and salvation to God alone, and works show that something is due to man. Faith, then, as to justification, entirely excludes all works, so that they come to no account before God; and hence I have said that salvation is by faith; for we are accepted of God by gratuitous remission of sins. The union of God with us is true and real salvation; but no one can be united to God without righteousness, and there is found in us no righteousness; hence God himself freely imputes it to us; and as we are justified freely, so our salvation is said to be gratuitous.

I will not now repeat what may be said of justification by faith; for it is better to proceed with the Prophet's subject, only it may be necessary to add two things to what has been said. The Prophet testified to the men of his age that salvation is by faith; it then follows that they had regard to Christ; for without relying on a mediator they could not have trusted in God. For as our righteousness is said to be the remission of sins, so a sacrifice must necessarily intervene, by which God is pacified, so as not to impute our sins. They had indeed their sacrifices according to the law; but these were to direct their minds to Christ; for they were by no means acceptable to God, except through that Mediator on whom our faith at this day is founded. There is also another thing: the Prophet, by distinctly expressing that the just live by faith, clearly shows, that through the whole course of this life we cannot be deemed just in any other way than by a gratuitous imputation. He does not say that the children of Adam, born in a state exposed to eternal death, do recover life by faith; but that the just, who are now endued with the true fear of God, live by faith; and thus refuted is the romance about initial justification. Let us now then proceed -

Habakkuk 2:5

5. Yea also, because he transgresseth by wine, he is a proud man, neither keepeth at home, who enlargeth his desire as hell, and is as death, and cannot be satisfied, but gathereth unto him all nations, and heapeth unto him all people.

5. Quanto magis (vel, etiam certe) vino transgrediens vir superbus, et non habitabit, quid dilatat quasi sepulchrum animam suam, et est similis morti, (ipse quasi mors, ad verbum,) et non satiabitur (non satiatur, significat actum continuum,) et colliget ad se omnes gentes, et coacervabit ad se omnes populos.

The Prophet has taught us that a tranquil state of mind cannot be otherwise had than by recumbing on the grace of God alone; and that they who elate themselves, and fly in the air, and feed on the wind, procure for themselves many sorrows and inquietudes. But he now comes to the king of Babylon, and also to his kingdom; for in my judgement he speaks not only of the king, but includes also that tyrannical empire with its people, and represents them as a great company of robbers. He then says in short, that though the Babylonians, like drunken men, hurried here and there without any control, yet God's vengeance, by which they were to be brought to nothing, was nigh at hand. What ever therefore the Prophet subjoins to the end of the chapter tends to confirm his doctrine, which we have already explained — that the just shall live by faith. We cannot indeed be fully convinced of this except we hold firmly this principle — that God cares for us, and that the whole world is governed by his providence; so that it cannot be but that he will at length check the wicked, and punish their sins, and deliver the innocent who call upon him. Unless this be our conviction, there can be no benefit derived from our faith; we might indeed be a hundred times deceived; for experience teaches us that the hopes of men, as long as they are fixed on the earth, are vain and delusive, as they are only mere imaginations. Except then God governs the world there is no salvation to the faithful; for God in that case would delude them with vain promises, and they would flatter themselves with an empty prospect, or hope for that which is not. Hence the Prophet shows how it is that the just shall live by faith; and that is because the Lord will defend all who call upon him, and that inasmuch as he is the just Judge of all the world, he will finally execute judgement on all the wicked, though for a time they act wantonly, and think that they shall escape punishment, because God does not execute upon them immediate vengeance. We now perceive the design of the Prophet.

As to the words, these two particles, אף כי, aph ki, when joined together, amplify the meaning; and some render them — "how much more;" others take them as a simple affirmative, and render them "truly." I approve of a middle course, and render them "yea, truly;" (Etiam certe;) and they are so taken as I think, in Ge 3:1, Satan thus asked the woman — yea, truly! Est-ce pour vrai? for the question is that of one doubting, and yet it refers to what is certain, — "How comes it that God should interdict the eating of the fruit? yea, is it so truly? can it be so? So it is in this place, yea, truly, says the Prophet. That it is an amplification may be gathered from the context. He had said before that they who elevate themselves, or seem to themselves to be well fortified, are fearful in their minds, and driven backwards and forwards. He now advances another step — that when men are borne along by unrestrained wantonness, and promise themselves all things, as though there was no God, they surpass even the drunken, being hurried on by blind cupidity. When therefore men thus abandon themselves, can they escape the judgement of God? Far less bearable is such a madness than that simple arrogance of which he had spoken in the last verse. Thus then are the two verses connected together, — "Yea, truly, he who in his pride is like a drunken man, and restrains not himself, and who is even like to wild beasts or to the grave, devouring whatever meets them — he surely will not at length be endured by God." Vengeance, then, is nigh to all the proud, who are cruelly furious, passing all bounds and without any fear.

But interpreters differ as to the import of the words which follow. Some render בוגד, bugad, to deceive, and it means so in some places; and they render the clause thus — "Wine deceives a proud man, and he will not dwell." This is indeed true, but the meaning is strained; I therefore prefer to follow the commonly received interpretation — that the proud man transgresses as it were through wine. At the same time I do not agree with others as to the expression "transgressing as through wine." Some give this version — "Man addicted to wine or to drunkenness transgresses;" and then they add — "a proud man will not inhabit;" but they pervert the sentence, and mangle the words of the Prophet; for his words are — By wine transgressing the proud man: he does not say that a man addicted to wine transgresses; but he compares the proud to drunken men, who, forgetting all reason and shame, abandon themselves unto all that is disgraceful; for the drunken distinguishes nothing, and becomes like a brute animal, so that he shuns nothing that is base and unbecoming. This is the reason why the Prophet compares proud men to the drunken, who transgress through wine, that is, who observe no moderation, but indulge themselves in excesses. We now then understand the real meaning of the Prophet, which many have not perceived. [31]

As to the word inhabiting I take it in a metaphorical sense, as signifying to rest or to continue in the same place. The drunken are borne along by a certain excitement; so they do not restrain themselves, for they have no power over their feet or their hands: but as wine excites them, so they ramble here and there like insane persons. As then such an unruly temper lays hold on and bewilders drunken men, so the Prophet very aptly says that the proud man never rests.

And the reason follows, (provided the meaning be approved,) because he enlarges as the grave his soul he is like to death. This is then the insatiableness which he had mentioned — that the proud cannot be satisfied, and therefore include heaven and earth and sea within the compass of their desires. Since then they thus run here and there, it is no wonder that the Prophet says that they do not rest. He enlarges then as the grave his soul; and then he adds — he heaps together, or congregates, or collects to himself all nations, and accumulates to himself all people; that is, the proud man keeps within no moderate limits; for though he were able to make one heap of all nations, he would yet think that not enough, like Alexander, who wept because he had not then enjoyed the empire of the whole world; and had he enjoyed it his tears would not have been dried; for he had heard that, according to the opinion of Democritus, there were many worlds. What did he mean? even this "Were I to obtain the empire of the world, I should still be poor; for if there are more worlds I should still wish to devour them all." These proud men surpass every kind of drunkenness.

We now apprehend the meaning of the words; and though they contain a general truth, yet the Prophet no doubt applies them to the king of Babylon and to all the Chaldeans; for as it has been said, he includes the whole nation. He shows then here, that the Chaldeans were much worse and less excusable than those who with great fierceness elated themselves, for their rage carried them farther, as they wished to swallow up the whole world. But in order to express this more fully, he says that they were like drunken men; and he no doubt indirectly derides here the counsels of princes, who think themselves to be very wise, when either by deceit they oppress their neighbors, or by artful means seize for themselves on the lands of others, or by some contrivance, or even by force of arms, take possession of them. As princes take wonderful delight in their iniquities, so the Prophet says that they are like drunken men who transgress by wine, that is, who are completely overcome by excessive drinking; and at the same time he shows the cause of this drunkenness by mentioning the words ריהי רבג, "proud man." As then they are proud, so all their crafts are like the freaks of drunkenness, that is, furious, as when a man is deprived of reason by wine. Having thus spoken of the Babylonians he immediately adds —

Habakkuk 2:6

6. Shall not all these take up a parable against him, and a taunting proverb against him, and say, Woe to him that increaseth that which is not his! how long? and to him that ladeth himself with thick clay!

6. Annon ipsi omnes super eum parabolam (vel apophthegma) tollent? et dicterium aenigmaticum (vel aenigmatum; alii [מליצה] vertunt interpretationem; sed dicemus de vocibus) ei (vel super eum,) et dicet, Vae qui mutiplicat non sua (vel ex non suis, qui sese locupletat ex alieno); quousque? et qui accumulat (vel aggravat) super se densum lutum.

Now at length the Prophet denounces punishment on the Babylonian king and the Chaldeans; for the Lord would render them a sport to all. But some think that a punishment is also expressed in the preceding verse, such as awaits violent robbers, who devour the whole world. But I, on the contrary, think that the Prophet spoke before of proud cruelty, and simply showed what a destructive evil it is, being an insatiable cupidity; and now, as I have stated, he comes to its punishment; and he says first, that all the people who had been collected as it were into a heap, would take up a parable or a taunt, in order to scoff at the king of Babylon. When therefore the Chaldeans should possess the empire of almost the whole world, and subject to their power all their neighboring nations, all these would at length take up against them parables and taunts; and what would be said everywhere would be this — Woe to him who increases and enriches himself by things not his own. How long? that is, Is this to be perpetual? All then who thus increase themselves heap on themselves thick clay, by which they shall at last be overthrown.

With regard to the words, לשמ, meshil is a short saying or a pithy sentence, and worthy to be remembered, as we have noticed elsewhere. Some render it parable. As to the word הצילמ, melitse, it probably signifies a scoff or a taunt, by which any one is reproved; for it comes from פול, luts, which means to laugh at one or to deride him. It is indeed true, that the Hebrews call a rhetorician or an interpreter פילמ, melits; and hence some render הצילמ, melitse, interpretation; but it is not suitable to this passage; for the Prophet speaks here of taunts that would be cast against the king of Babylon. For as he had as with an open mouth swallowed up all, so also all would eagerly prick him with their goads, and disdainfully deride him. The word he afterwards adds תודיח, chidut, is to be read, I have no doubt, in the genitive case. [32] I therefore do not approve of adding a copulative, as many do, and read thus — "a taunt and an enigma." This word comes from the verb דוח, chud, which is to speak enigmatically; hence תודיח, chidut, are enigmas, or metaphors, or obscure sentences; and we know that when we wish to touch a man to the quick, there is more sharpness when we use an obscure word, which contains a metaphor or ambiguity, or something of this kind. It is not therefore without reason that the Prophet calls taunts, enigmas, תודיח, chidut, that is, obscure words, which bite or prick men sharply, as it were with goads. Hence in all scoffs a figurative language ought to be used; and except the expression be ambiguous or alliterative, or, in short, contain such metaphors as it is not necessary to recite here, there would be in it no beauty, no aptness. When therefore men wish to form biting taunts, they obscure what might be plainly said by some indirect metaphor; and this is the reason why the Prophet speaks here of a taunt that is enigmatical, for it is on that account more severe.

And he shall say. There is a change of number in this verb, but it does not obscure the sense. [33] The particle יוה may be rendered "woe"; or it may be an exclamation, as when one is attracted by some particular sight, caca or sus; and so it is taken often by the Hebrews, and the context seems to favor this meaning, for "woe" would be frigid. When the Prophets pronounce a curse on the wicked, it is no doubt a dreadful threat; but what is found here is a taunt, by which the whole world would deride those haughty tyrants who thought that they ought to have been worshipped as gods. He! they say, where is he who multiplies himself by what belongs to another? and then, How long is this to be? even such accumulate on themselves thick clay; that is, they sink themselves in deep caverns, and heap on themselves mountains, by which they become overwhelmed. We now understand the meaning of the Prophet's words.

What seems here to be the singing of triumph before the victory is no matter of wonder; for our faith, as it is well known, depends not on the judgement of the flesh, nor regards what is openly evident; but it is a vision of hidden things, as it is called in Heb 11:1, and the substance of things not seen. As then the firmness of faith is the same, though what it apprehends is remote, and as faith ceases not to see things hidden, — for through the mirror of God's word it ascends above heaven and earth, and penetrates into the spiritual kingdom of God, — as faith, then, possesses a view so distant, it is not to be wondered that the Prophet here boldly triumphs over the Babylonians, and now prescribes a derisive song for all nations, that the proud, who had previously with so much cruelty exalted themselves, might be scoffed at and derided.

But were any to ask, whether it be right to assail even the wicked with scoffs and railleries, the question is unsuitable here; for the Prophet does not here refer to what is lawful for the faithful to do, but speaks only of what is commonly done by men: and we know that it is almost natural to men, that when those whom they had feared and dared not to blame as long as they were in power, are overthrown, they break forth against them not only with many complaints and accusations, but also with wanton rudeness. As, then, it usually happens, that all triumph over fallen tyrants, and throw forth their taunts, and all seek in this way to bite, the Prophet describes this regular course of things. It is not, however, to be doubted, but that he composed this song according to the nature of the case, when he says, that they were men who multiplied their own by what belonged to others; that is, that they gathered the wealth of others. It is indeed true, that many things are commonly spread abroad, for which there is no reason nor justice; but as some principles of equity and justice remain in the hearts of men, the consent of all nations is as it were the voice of nature, or the testimony of that equity which is engraven on the hearts of men, and which they can never obliterate. Such is the reason for this saying; for Habakkuk, by introducing the people as the speakers, propounded, as it were, the common law of nature, in which all agree; and that is, — that whosoever enriches himself by another's wealth, shall at length fall, and that when one accumulates great riches, these will become like a heap to cover and overwhelm him. And if any one of us will consult his own mind, he will find that this is engraven on his very nature.

How, then, does it happen, that many should yet labor to get for themselves the wealth of others, and strive for nothing else through their whole life, but to spoil others that they may enrich themselves? It hence appears that men's minds are deprived of reason by sottishness, whenever they thus addict themselves to unjust gain, or when they give themselves loose reins to commit frauds, robberies, and plunders. And thus we perceive that the Prophet had not without reason represented all the proud and the cruel as drunken.

Then follow the words, עד-מתי, od-mati, how long? This also is the dictate of nature; that is, that an end will some time be to unjust plunders, though God may not immediately check plunderers and wicked men, who proceed and effect their purposes by force and slaughters, and frauds and evildoings. In the mean time the Prophet also intimates, that tyrants and their cruelty cannot be endured without great weariness and sorrow; for indignity on account of evil deeds kindles within the breasts of all, so that they become wearied when they see that wicked men are not soon restrained. Hence almost the whole world sound forth these words, How long, how long? When any one disturbs the whole world by his ambition and avarice, or everywhere commits plunders, or oppresses miserable nations, — when he distresses the innocent, all cry out, How long? And this cry, proceeding as it does from the feeling of nature and the dictate of justice, is at length heard by the Lord. For how comes it that all, being touched with weariness, cry out, How long? except that they know that this confusion of order and justice is not to be endured? And this feeling, is it not implanted in us by the Lord? It is then the same as though God heard himself, when he hears the cries and greenings of those who cannot bear injustice.

But let us in the meantime see that no one of us should have to say the same thing to himself, which he brings forward against others. For when any avaricious man proceeds through right or wrong, as they say, when an ambitious man, by unfair means, advances himself, we instantly cry, How long? and when any tyrant violently oppresses helpless men, we always say, How long? Though every one says this as to others, yet no one as to himself. Let us therefore take heed that, when we reprove injustice in others, we come without delay to ourselves, and be impartial judges. Self love so blinds us, that we seek to absolve ourselves from that fault which we freely condemn in others. In general things men are always more correct in their judgement, that is, in matters in which they themselves are not concerned; but as soon as they come to themselves, they become blind, and all rectitude vanishes, and all judgement is gone. Let us then know, that this song is set forth here by the Prophet, drawn, as it were, from the common feeling of nature, in order that every one of us may put a restraint on himself when he discharges the office of a judge in condemning others, and that he may also condemn himself, and restrain his desires, when he finds them advancing beyond just bounds.

We must also observe what he subjoins, — that the avaricious accumulate on themselves thick clay. This at first may appear incredible; but the subject itself plainly shows what the Prophet teaches here, provided our minds are not so blinded as not to see plain things. Hardly indeed an avaricious man can be found who is not a burden to himself, and to whom his wealth is not a source of trouble. Every one who has accumulated much, when he comes to old age, is afraid to use what he has got, being ever solicitous lest he should lose any thing; and then, as he thinks nothing is sufficient, the more he possesses the more grasping he becomes, and frugality is the name given to that sordid, and, so to speak, that servile restraint within which the rich confine themselves. In short, when any one forms a judgement of all the avaricious of this world, and is himself free from all avarice, having a free and unblessed mind, he will easily apprehend what the Prophet says here, — that all the wealth of this world is nothing else but a heap of clay, as when any one puts himself of his own accord under a great heap which he had collected together.

Some refer this to the walls of Babylon, which were built of baked bricks, as it is well known; but this is too farfetched. Others think that the Prophet speaks of the last end of us all; for they who possess the greatest riches, being at last thrown into the grave, are covered with earth: but this also is not suitable here, any more than when they apply it to Nebuchadnezzar, that is, to that sottishness by which he had inebriated himself almost through his whole life; or when others apply it to Belshazzar, his grandson, because when he drank from the sacred vessels of the temple, he uttered slanders and blasphemies against God. These explanations are by no means suitable; for the Prophet does not here speak of the person of the king alone, but, as it has been solid, he, on the contrary, summons to judgement the whole nation, which had given itself up to plunders and frauds and other evil deeds.

Then a general truth is to be drawn from this expression that all the avaricious, the more they heap together, the more they lade themselves, and, as it were, bury themselves under a great load. Whence is this? Because riches, acquired by frauds and plunders, are nothing else than a heavy and cumbrous lump of earth: for God returns on the heads of those who thus seek to enrich themselves, whatever they have plundered from others. Had they been contented with some moderate portion, they might have lived cheerfully and happily, as we see to be the case with all the godly; who though they possess but little, are yet cheerful, for they live in hope, and know that their supplies are in God's hand, and expect everything from his blessing. Hence, then, their cheerfulness, because they have no anxious fears. But they who inebriate themselves with riches, find that they carry a useless burden, under which they lie down, as it were, sunk and buried.

PRAYER

Grant, Almighty God, that as thou deignest so far to condescend as to sustain the care of this life, and to supply us with whatever is needful for our pilgrimage — O grant that we may learn to rely on thee, and so to trust to thy blessing, as to abstain not only from all plunder and other evil deeds, but also from every unlawful coveting; and to continue in thy fear, and so to learn also to bear our poverty on the earth, that being content with those spiritual riches which thou offerest to us in thy gospel, and of which thou makes us now partakers, we may ever cheerfully aspire after that fullness of all blessings which we shall enjoin when at length we shall reach the celestial kingdom, and be perfectly united to thee, through Christ our Lord. Amen.

LECTURE ONE HUNDRED AND TWELFTH

Habakkuk 2:7

7. Shall they not rise up suddenly that shall bite thee, and awake that shall vex thee, and thou shalt be for booties unto them?

7. Annon repente consurgent qui te mordeant, et evigilabunt qui te exagitent, et eris in conculcationes ipsis?

The Prophet proceeds with the subject which we have already begun to explain; for he introduces here the common taunts against the king of Babylon and the whole tyrannical empire, by which many nations had been cruelly oppressed. He therefore says that enemies, who should bite him, [34] would suddenly and unexpectedly rise up. Some expound this of worms, but not rightly: for God not only inflicted punishment on the king when dead, but he intended also that there should be on earth an evident and a memorable proof of his vengeance on the Babylonians, by which it might be made known to all that their cruelty could not be suffered to go unpunished.

The words, Shall not they rise suddenly, are emphatical, both as to the question and as to the word, עתפ, peto, suddenly. We indeed know that interrogations are more common in Hebrew than in Greek and Latin, and that they are stronger and more forcible. Our Prophet then speaks of what was indubitable. He adds, suddenly; for the Babylonians, relying on their own power, did not think that any evil was nigh them; and if any one dared to rise up against them, this could not have been so sudden, but they could have in time resisted and driven far away every danger. They indeed ruled far and wide; and we know that the wicked often sleep when they find themselves fortified on all sides. But the Prophet declares here that evil was nigh them, which would suddenly overwhelm them. It now follows —

Habakkuk 2:8

8. Because thou hast spoiled many nations, all the remnant of the people shall spoil thee; because of men's blood, and for the violence of the land, of the city, and of all that dwell therein.

8. Quia tu spoliasti gentes multas, spoliabunt te omnes reliquiae populorum propter sanguines hominis et violentiam terrae, urbis et omnium habitantium in ea.

The Prophet here expresses more clearly why the Babylonians were to be so severely dealt with by God. He shows that it would be a just reward that they should be plundered in their turn, who had previously given themselves up to plunder, violence, and cruelty. Since, then, they had exercised so much inhumanity towards all people, the Prophet intimates here that God could not be deemed as treating them cruelly, by inflicting on them so severe a punishment: he also confirms the former truth, and recalls the attention of the faithful to the judgement of God, as a main principle to be remembered; for when things in the world are in a state of confusion, we despond, and all hope vanishes, except this comes to our mind — that as God is the judge of the world it cannot be otherwise but that at length all the wicked must appear before his tribunal, and give there an account of all their deeds; and Scripture, also, is wont to set God before us as a judge, whenever the purpose is to allay our troubles. The Prophet now does the same thing: for he says, that robbers should soon come upon the Babylonians, who would plunder them; for God, the judge of the world, would not at last suffer so many plunders to be unpunished.

But it was everywhere known that the Babylonians had, beyond all bounds and moderation, given themselves up to plunder, so that they spared no nations. Hence he says, because thou hast plundered many nations; and on this he enlarges; because the Babylonians had not only done wrongs to a few men, or to one people, but had marched through many countries. As, then, they had taken to themselves so much liberty in doing evil, the Prophet draws this conclusion — that they could not escape the hand of God, but that they were at length to find by experience that there was a God in heaven, who would repay them for their wrongs.

He says also, Spoil thee shall the remnant of all people. This admits of two expositions; it may mean, that the people, who had been plundered by the Chaldeans, would take revenge on them: and he calls them a remnant, because they were not entire; but yet he intimates that they would be sufficient to take vengeance on the Babylonians. This view may be admitted, and yet we may suppose, that the Prophet takes in other nations, who had never been plundered; as though he had said — "Thou hast indeed spoiled many nations; but there are other nations in the world whom thy cruelty could not have reached. All the people then who remain in the world shall strive to outdo one another in attacking thee; and canst thou be strong enough to resist so great a power?" Either of these views may be admitted; that is, that in the wasted and plundered countries there would be still a remnant who would take vengeance, — or that the world contained other people who would willingly undertake this cause and execute vengeance on the Babylonians; for God would by his secret influence fulfill by their means his purpose of punishing them.

He then adds, on account of man's blood; that is, because thou hast shed innocent blood, and because thou hast committed many plunders; for thou hast not only injured a few men, but thy daringness and cruelty have also extended to many nations. He indeed mentions the earth, and also the city. Some confine these words to the land of Judea and to Jerusalem, but not rightly; for the Prophet speaks here generally; and to the land, he joins cities and their inhabitants. [35]

But this verse contains a truth which applies to all times. Let us then learn, during the licentious success of tyrants, to raise up our minds to heaven's tribunal, and to nourish our patience with this confidence, that the Lord, who is the judge of the world, will recompense these cruel and bloody robbers, and that the more licentious they are, the heavier judgement is nigh them; for the Lord will awaken and raise up as many to execute vengeance as there are men in the world, who by shedding blood will inflict punishment, though they may not intend to fulfill his purpose. God can indeed (as it has been often observed) execute his judgements in a wonderful and sudden manner. Let us hence also learn to restrain our evil desires; for none shall go unpunished who will allow themselves to injure their brethren; though they may seem to be unpunished for a time, yet God, who is ever the same, will at length return on their heads whatever they have devised against others, as we shall presently see again. He now adds —

Habakkuk 2:9

9. Woe to him that coveteth an evil covetousness to his house, that he may set his nest on high, that he may be delivered from the power of evil!

9. Vae concupiscenti concupiscentiam malam domui suae, ut ponat in excelso nidum suum, quo se eripiat e manu (id est, e potestate) infortunii (mali, ad verbum.)

Habakkuk proceeds in exciting the king of Babylon by taunts; which were not scurrilous jests, but contained serious threatening; for, as it has been already said, the Prophet here introduces indeed the common people, but in that multitude we are to recognize the innumerable heralds of God's vengeance: and hence he says, Woe to him who coveteth, etc.; or we may say, He! for it is a particle of exclamation, as it has been said: He! thou, he says, who covetest an evil covetousness to thy house, and settest on high thy nest: but what shall happen? The next verse declares the punishment.

The clause, Woe to him who covets an evil covetousness to his house, may be read by itself, — that this cupidity shall be injurious to his house; as though he had said, "Thou indeed wouldest provide for thy house by accumulating great riches; but thy house shall find this to be evil and ruinous. So the word רע, roe, evil, might be referred to the house; but the verse is best connected by reading the whole together; that is, that the Babylonians not only provided for themselves, while they with avidity plundered and collected much wealth from all quarters; but that they wished also to make provisions for their sons and grandsons: and we also see, that avarice has this object in view; for they who are anxiously bent on the accumulation of riches do not only regard what is needful for themselves to pass through life, but also wish to leave their heirs rich. Since then the avaricious are desirous of enriching for ever their houses, the prophet, deriding this madness, says, Woe to him who covets an evil covetousness to his house; that is, who wishes not only to abound and be satiated himself, but also to supply his posterity with abundance.

He adds another vice, which is almost ever connected with the former — that he may set, he says, his nest on high; for the avaricious have a regard to this — to fortify themselves; for as an evil conscience is always fearful, many dangers come across their minds — "This may happen to me," and then, "My wealth will procure for me the hatred and envy of many. If then some danger be at hand, I shall be able to redeem my life many times;" and he also adds, "Were I satisfied with a moderate portion, many would become my rivals; but when my treasures surpass what is common, then I shall be as it were beyond the reach of men; and when others envy one another, I shall escape." So the avaricious think within themselves when they are ardently bent on accumulating riches, and form for themselves a great heap like a nest; for they think that they are raised above the world, and are exempt from the common lot of men, when surrounded by their riches.

We now then see what the Prophet means: Woe, he says, to him who wickedly and intemperately covets. And why does he so do? To enrich his posterity. And then he adds, to him who covets that he may set his nest on high; that is, that he may by wealth fortify himself, that he may be able to drive away every danger, and be thus exempt from every evil and trouble. And he adds, that he may deliver himself from the power of evil; he expresses now more clearly what I have said — that the rich are inebriated with false confidence, when they surpass all others; for they think not themselves to be mortals, but imagine that they have another life, as though they had a world of their own, free from all dangers. But while the avaricious thus elevate themselves by a proud confidence, the Prophet derides their madness. He then subjoins their punishment —

Habakkuk 2:10

10. Thou hast consulted shame to thy house by cutting off many people, and hast sinned against thy soul.

10. Consultasti in ignominiam domui tuae (vel, conflasti tuo consilio probrum et dedecus domui tuae) exidendo populos multos; et peccasti in animam tuam.

The Prophet again confirms the truth, that those who count themselves happy, imagining that they are like God, busy themselves in vain; for God will turn to shame whatever they think to be their glory, derived from their riches. The avaricious indeed wish, as it appears from the last verse, to prepare splendor for their posterity, and they think to render illustrious their race by their wealth; for this is deemed to be nobility, that the richer any one is the more he excels, as he thinks, in dignity, and the more is he to be esteemed by all. Since, then, this is the object of almost all the avaricious, the Prophet here reminds them, that they are greatly deceived; for the Lord will not only frustrate their hopes, but will also convert their glory into shame. Hence he says, that they consult shame to their family.

He includes in the word consult, all the industry, diligence, skill, care, and labor displayed by the avaricious. We indeed see how very sagacious they are; for if they smell any gain at a distance, they draw it to themselves, night and day they form new designs, that they may circumvent this person and plunder that person, and accumulate into their heap whatever money they can find, and also that they may join fields to fields, built great palaces, and secure great revenues. This is the reason why the Prophet says, that they consult shame. What is the object of all their designs? for they are, as we have said, very sharp and keen-sighted, they are also industrious, and torment themselves day and night with continual labor; for what purpose are all these things? even for this, that their posterity may be eminent, that their nobility may be in the mouth of all, and spread far and wide. But the Prophet shows that they labor in vail; for God will turn to shame whatever they in their great wisdom contrived for the honor of their families. The more provident then the avaricious are, the more foolish they are, for they consult nothing but disgrace to their posterity.

He adds, though thou cuttest off many people. This seems to have been expressed for the sake of anticipating an objection; for it might have seemed incredible that the Babylonians should form designs disgraceful to their posterity, when their fame was so eminent, and Babylon itself was like an idol, and the king was everywhere regarded with great reverence and also fear. Since then the Babylonians had made such advances, who could have thought it possible that what the Prophet declares here should take place? But, as I have already said, he meets these objections, and says, "Though the Babylonians shall conquer many enemies, and overthrow strong people, yet this will be of no advantage to them; nay, even that will turn out to their disgrace which they think will be to their glory."

To the same purpose is what he adds, thou hast sinned against thy soul. Some give this version, "Thou hast sinned licentiously" or immoderately; others, "Thy soul has sinned," but these pervert the Prophet's meaning; for what he intended was nothing else but the evils which the avaricious and the cruel bring on themselves, and which will return on their own heads. When therefore the Babylonians contrived ruin for the whole world, the Prophet predicts that an end, very different from what they thought, would be to them: thou hast sinned, he says, against thine own soul; [36] that is, the evil which thou didst prepare to bring on others, shall be made by God to fall on thine own head.

And this kind of declaration ought to be carefully noticed; that is, that the ungodly, while they trouble all, and harass all, while they torment one, plunder another, oppress another, do always sin against their own souls; that is, they do not cause so such loss and sorrow to others as to themselves: for the Lord will make the evil they intend for others to return on themselves. He does not speak here of guilt, but of punishment, when he says, "Thou hast sinned against thy soul;" that is, thou shalt receive the reward due to all thy sins. We now then see what the Prophet means. It now follows —

Habakkuk 2:11-13

11. For the stone shall cry out of the wall, and the beam out of the timber shall answer it.

11. Quia lapis ex muro clamabit, et lignum ex tabulato (ad verbum est, ex ligno,) respondebit ei.

12. Woe to him that buildeth a town with blood, and stablisheth a city by iniquity!

12. Vae aedificanti urbem in sanguinibus, et paranti civitatem in iniquitate.

13. Behold, is it not of the LORD of hosts that the people shall labour in the very fire, and the people shall weary themselves for very vanity?

13. Annon ecce a Jehova exercituum? ideo laborabunt populi in igne et gentes in vanitate (hoc est, frustra fatigabuntur.)

There is here introduced by the Prophet a new personification. He had before prepared a common song, which would be in the mouth of all. He now ascribes speech to stones and wood, of which buildings are formed. The stone, he says, shall cry from the wall, and the wood from the chamber; that is, there is no part of the building that will not cry out that it was built by plunder, by cruelty, and, in a word, by evil deeds. The Prophet not only ascribes speech to wood and stone, but he makes them also respond one to the other as in a chorus, as in lyrics there are voices which take up the song in turns. The stone, he says, shall cry from the wall, and the wood shall respond to it from the chamber; [37] as though he said, "There will be a striking harmony in every part of the building; for the wall will begin and will utter its song, 'Behold I have been built by blood and by iniquity;' and the wood will utter the same, and will cry, 'Woe;' but all in due order; there will be no confused noise, but as music has distinct sounds, so also the stones will respond to the wood and the wood to the stones, so that there may be, as they say, corresponding voices."

The stone, then, from the wall shall cry, and the wood shall answer — what will it answer? — Woe to him who builds a city by blood, and who adorns his city by iniquity. By blood and by iniquity he understands the same thing; for though the avaricious do not kill innocent men, they yet suck their blood, and what else is this but to kill them by degrees, by a slow tormenting process? For it is easier at once to undergo death than to pine away in want, as it happens to helpless men when spoiled and deprived of all their property. Wherever there is wanton plundering, there is murder committed in the sight of God; for as it has been said, he who spares not the helpless, but drinks up their blood, doubtless sins no less than if he were to kill them.

But if this personification seems to any one strange, he must consider how incredible seemed to be what the Prophet here teaches, and how difficult it was to produce a conviction on the subject. We indeed confess that God is the judge of the world; nay, there is no one who does not anticipate his judgement by condemning avarice and cruelty; the very name of avarice is infamous and hated by all: the same may be said of cruelty. But yet when we see the avaricious in splendor and in esteem, we are astounded, and no one is able to foresee by faith what the Prophet here declares. Since, then our dullness is so great, or rather our sottishness, it is no wonder that the Prophet should here set before us the stones and the wood, as though he said, "When all prophecies and all warnings become frigid, and God himself obtains no credit, while openly declaring what he will do, and when his servants consume their labor in vain by warning and crying, let now the stones come forth, and be teachers to you who will not give ear to the voice of God himself, and let the wood also cry out in its turn." This, then, is the reason why the Prophet introduces here mute things as the speakers, even to awaken our insensibility.

Then he adds, Shall it not be, behold, from Jehovah of hosts? [38] Some give a wrong version, "Is not this," as though הנה, ene, were put here instead of a pronoun demonstrative; but they extenuate and obscure the beauty of the expression; nay, they pervert the meaning of the Prophet: for when he says, הנה, ene, behold, he refers not to what he had said, nor specifies any particular thing, and yet he shows, as it were by the finger, the judgement of God, which he bids us to expect; as though he said, "Shall not God at length have his turn, when the avaricious and the cruel have obtained their triumphs in the world, and darkened the minds and thoughts of all, as though no account were to be given by them before the tribunal of God? Shall not God sometime show that it is his time to interpose?" When, therefore, he says, Shall it not be, behold, from Jehovah? it is an indefinite mode of speaking; he does not say, This or that shall be from the God of hosts; but, Shall it not be, behold, from Jehovah of hosts? that is, God seems now indeed to rest, and on this account men indulge themselves with greater boldness; but he will not always remain still, Shall not God then come forth, who seems now to be unconcerned? Something there will at length be from the God of hosts. And the demonstrative particle confirms the same thing: Behold, he says, as though he would show to the faithful as in a picture the tribunal of God, which cannot be seen by us now but by faith. He says, Behold, will not there be something from the God of hosts? that is, Will not God at length stretch forth his hand, to show that he is not unconcerned, but that he cares for the affairs of men? In a word, by this mode of speaking is pointed out to us the change, which we are to hole for, inasmuch as it cannot be soon realised.

Hence he concludes, The people, then, labor in the fire, and the people weary themselves in vain. To labor in the fire means the same thing as to take in hand an unprofitable work, the fruit of which is immediately consumed. Some say that people labor in the fire, because Babylon had been built by a great number of men, and at length perished by fire; but this explanation seems far-fetched. I take a simpler view — that people labor in the fire, like him who performs a work, and a fire is put under it and consumes it; or like him, who with great labor polishes his own work, and a fire is prepared, which destroys it while in the hands of the artifices. For it is certain that the Prophet repeats the same thing in another form, when he says, קיר-ידב, bedi-rik, with vanity, or for vanity. We now then apprehend his object.

We may here collect a useful doctrine — that not only the fruit of labor shall be lost by all who seek by wicked means to enrich themselves, but also that were the whole world favorable and subservient to them, the whole would yet be useless; as it happened to the king of Babylon, though he had many people ready to obey him. But the Prophet derides all those great preparation; for God had fire at hand to consume whatever they had so eagerly contrived who wished to spend all their labor to please one man. He at length adds —

Habakkuk 2:14

14. For the earth shall be filled with the knowledge of the glory of the Lord, as the waters cover the sea.

14. Quia replebitur terra cognitione gloriae Jehovae, sicuti aquae operiunt mare.

The Prophet briefly teaches us here, that so remarkable would be God's judgement on the Babylonians that his name would thereby be celebrated through the whole world. But there is in this verse an implied contrast; for God appeared not in his own glory when the Jews were led away into exile; the temple being demolished and the whole city destroyed; and also when the whole easterly regions was exposed to rapine and plunder. When therefore the Babylonians were, after the Assyrians, swallowing up all their neighbors, the glory of God did not then shine, nor was it conspicuous in the world. The Jews themselves had become mute; for their miseries had, as it were, stupefied them; their mouths were at least closed, so that they could not from the heart bless God, while he was so severely afflicting them. And then, in that manifold confusion of all things, the profane thought that all things here take place fortuitously, and that there is no divine providence. God then was at that time hid: hence the Prophet says, Filled shall be the earth with the knowledge of God; that is, God will again become known, when by stretching forth his hand he will execute vengeance on the Babylonians; then will the Jews, as well as other nations, acknowledge that the world is governed by God's providence, as it had been once created by him.

We now understand the Prophet's meaning, and why he says, that the earth would be filled with the knowledge of God's glory; for the glory of God previously disappeared from the world, with regard to the perceptions of men; but it shone forth again, when God himself had erected his tribunal by overthrowing Babylon, and thereby proved that there is no power among men which he cannot control. We have the same sentence in Isa 11:9. [39] The Prophet there speaks indeed of the kingdom of Christ; for when Christ was openly made known to the world, the knowledge of God's glory at the same time filled the earth; for God then appeared in his own living image. But yet our Prophet uses a proper language, when he says that the earth shall then be filled with the knowledge of God's glory, when he should execute vengeance on the Babylonians. Hence incorrectly have some applied this to the preaching of the gospel, as though Habakkuk made a transition from the ruin of Babylon to the general judgement: this is a strained exposition. It is indeed a well-known mode of speaking, and often occurs in the Psalms, that the power, grace, and truth of God are made known through the world, when he delivers his people and restrains the ungodly. The same mode the Prophet now adopts; and he compares this fullness of knowledge to the waters of the sea, because the sea, as we know, is so deep, that there is no measuring of its waters. So Habakkuk intimates, that the glory of God would be so much known that it would not only fill the world, but in a manner overflow it: as the waters of the sea by their vast quantity cover the deep, so the glory of God would fill heaven and earth, so as to have no limits. If, at the same time, there be a wish to extend this sentence to the coming of Christ, I do not object: for we know that the grace of redemption flowed in a perpetual stream until Christ appeared in the world. But the Prophet, I have no doubt, sets forth here the greatness of God's power in the destruction of Babylon. [40]

PRAYER

Grant, Almighty God, that as we are so inclined to do wrong, that every one is naturally disposed to consider his own private advantage — O grant that we may confine ourselves by that restraint which thou layest on us by thy Prophets, so that we may not allow our coveting to break forth so as to commit wrong or iniquity, but confine ourselves within the limits of what is just, and abstain from what belongs to others: may we also so learn to console ourselves in all our distresses, that though we may be justly oppressed by the wicked, we may yet rely on thy providence and righteous judgement, and patiently wait until thou deliverest us, and makes it manifest that whatever the wicked devise for our ruin, so cleaves to themselves as to return and recoil at length on their own heads; and may we so fight under the banner of the Cross, as to possess our souls in patience, until we at length shall attain that blessed life which is laid up in heaven for us, through our Lord Jesus Christ. Amen.

LECTURE ONE HUNDRED AND THIRTEENTH

Hab. 2:15, 16

15. Woe unto him that giveth his neighbour drink, that puttest thy bottle to him, and makest him drunken also, that thou mayest look on their nakedness!

15. Vae qui potat socium suum (vel, amicum;) conjungis (conjungens) calorem tuum (vel, utrem tuum; alii vertunt, adhibes venenum tuum, vel, iram tuam; alii intendens iram;) atque etiam inebrias, ut aspicias super nuditates eorum (id est, verenda.)

16. Thou art filled with shame for glory: drink thou also, and let thy foreskin be uncovered: the cup of the Lord's right hand shall be turned unto thee, and shameful spewing shall be on thy glory.

16. Saturatus es ignominia ex gloria (vel, pro gloria;) bibe etiam tu et discooperire (vel, sopiares;) fundetur super te calix dexterae Jehovae, et vomitus ignominiae super gloriam tuam.

This passage, in which the Prophet condemns the king of Babylon for his usual practice of rendering drunk his friends, is frigidly interpreted by most expounders. It has been already often said how bold the Jews are in contriving what is fabulous; when nothing certain occurs to them, they divine this or that without any discrimination or shame. Hence they say, that Nebuchadnezzar was given to excess, and led all whom he could into a participation of the same vice. They also think that his associates were captive kings, as though he bid them for the sake of sport to be brought to his table, and by drinking to their health, forced them to intoxication, that he might laugh at them when they made themselves base and ridiculous. But all this is groundless; for there is no history that relates any such thing. It is, however, easy to see that another matter is here treated of by the Prophet; for he does not speak of the king only, but he refers to the whole empire. I therefore doubt not but that this whole discourse, in which the Babylonian king is condemned for making drunk his associates or friends, is metaphorical or allegorical. But before I proceed further on the subject, I shall say something as to the words; for the meaning of the Prophet will thereby be made more evident.

Woe, he says, to him who gives his friend drink; then he adds, רתמח חפסמ, mesephech chemetak, "who joinest and bottle." המח, cheme, is taken in Hebrew for a bottle; and we know, and it is sufficiently evident from Scripture, that the Jews used bottles of skin, as there are casks and larger vessels with us. Since, then, they put their wine into bottles, these were often taken for their cups, as it is in our language, when one says, Des flacons, des bouteilles. Hence some give this explanation — that the king of Babylon brought forth his flagons, that he might force to intoxication, by excessive drinking, those who could not and dared not to resist his will. But others render המח, cheme, wrath, with a preposition understood: and in order that nothing may be understood, some render the participle, חפסמ, "displaying," that is, "his fury." But as המח, cheme, means to be hot, we may, therefore, properly give this version, "Uniting thy heat;" that is, "It is not enough for thee to inebriate others, except thou implicates them with thyself." We now perceive the meaning of this phrase. He adds, And thou also dost inebriate. We may hence learn that the Prophet had no other thing in view, but to show that the king of Babylon sought for himself many associates in his intemperance or excess: at the same time he takes, as I have said, excess in a metaphorical sense. I shall presently explain more fully what all this means; but now we only expound the words. And thou, he says, dost also inebriate: the particle אף, as it is well known, is laid down for the sake of amplifying. After having said, Thou unitest thy heat; that is, thou exhales thine intemperance, so that others also contract the same heat with thyself, he immediately adds, Thou inebriatest them. It follows, that their nakedness may be made open; that is, that they may disclose themselves with shame. The following verse I shall defer until we shall see more clearly what the Prophet had in view. [41]

As I have already said the Prophet charges the Babylonian king with having implicated neighboring kings in his own evil desires, and with having in a manner inebriated them. He indeed compares the insatiable avarice of that king to intemperance; for as it is the object of drunken men not to drink what may suffice them, but to glut themselves with wine, so also when avarice is dominant in the hearts of men, they are seized with a certain kind of fury, like a person who has an immoderate love for wine. This is the reason for the metaphor; for the Babylonian king, when he thirsted for the blood of men, and also for wealth and kingdoms, led into the same kind of madness many other kings; for he could not have succeeded except he had allured the favor of many others, and deceived them with vain expectations. As a person who gives himself up to drinking wishes to leave associates, so Habakkuk lays the same thing to the charge of the king of Babylon; for being himself addicted to insatiable avarice, he procured associates to be as it were his guests, and quaffed wine to them, that is, elicited their cupidity, that they might join him in his wars; for each hoped for a part of the spoil after victory. Since, then, he had thus blinded many kings, they are said to have been inebriated by him. We indeed know that such allurements infatuate the minds and hearts of men; for there is no intoxication that stultifies men more than that eager appetite by which they devour both lands and seas.

We now then apprehend what the Prophet meant — that the Babylonian king not only burnt with his own avarice, but kindled also, as it were, a flame in others, like drunken men who excite one another. As then he had thus inflamed all the neighboring kings to rush headlong without any consideration and without any shame, like a person suffocated and overcome by excessive drinking; so the Prophet designates this inflaming as quaffing wine to them.

And this metaphor ought to be carefully observed; for we see at this day as in a mirror what the Prophet teaches here. For all the great princes, when they devise any plans of their own, send their ambassadors here and there, and seek to involve with themselves other cities and princes; and as no one is willing to endanger himself without reason, they set forth many fallacious allurements. And when any city fears a neighboring prince, it will seek to fortify itself by a new protection; so a treaty, when offered, becomes like a snare to it. And then when any inferior prince wishes to enlarge his borders, or to revenge himself, he willingly puts on arms, nay, anxiously, that he may be able, by the help of a greater, to effect his purpose, which he could not otherwise accomplish. Thus we see that dukes and counts, as they are called, and free cities, are daily inebriated. They who are chief kings, abounding in wine, that is, full of many vain promises, give to drink, as it were with full flagons, bidding wine to be brought forth on a well furnished table — "I will make thine enemy to give way to thee, and thou shalt compel him according to thy wish, and when I shall obtain the victory a part of the spoil shall be allotted to thee; I desire nothing but the glory. With regard to you, the free cities, see, ye tremble continually;

now if you lie under my shadow, it will be the best security for you." Such quaffing is to be found at this day almost throughout the whole of Europe.

Then the Prophet does not without reason commemorate this vice in the king of Babylon — that he made those associates drunk whom he had bound to himself by perfidious treaties; for as it has been said, there is no intoxication so dangerous as this madness; that is, when any one promises this or that to himself, and imagines what does not exist. Hence he not only says, that the Babylonian king gave drink to his friends, but also that he joined his bottles; as though he had said that he was very liberal, nay, prodigal, while seeking associates in his intemperance; for if one condition did not suffice, another was added — "Behold, my king is prepared; but if he is not enough another will be joined with him." They thus then join together their heat. If we take המה, cheme, for a bottle, then to join together their bottles would mean, that they accumulated promises until they inebriated those whom they sought to deceive. But if the other interpretation be more approved, which I am disposed to follow, then the meaning would be — They join together their own heat, that is, they implicate others with themselves; as they burn themselves with insatiable cupidity, so they spread this ardor far and wide, so that the desires of many become united.

He afterwards adds — that thou mayest see their nakedness. It was not indeed an object to the king of Babylon to disclose the reproach of all those whom he had induced to take part in his wars; but we know that great kings are wont to neglect their friends, to whom at first they promise every thing. When a king wishes to entice to himself a free city or an inferior prince, he will say — "See, I seek nothing but to be thy friend". We indeed see how shamefully they perjure themselves; nor is it enough for them to utter these perjuries in their courts; but not many years pass away before our great kings make public their abominable perjuries; and it appears immediately afterwards that they thus seek, without any shame, to mock both God and all mankind. After testifying that they seek nothing except to defend by their protection what is right and just, and to resist the tyranny and pride of others, they immediately draw back when anything adverse afterwards happens, and the city, which had hoped everything from so liberal a king, is afterwards forced to submit and to agree with its enemies, and to manage matters anyhow; thus its nakedness is disclosed. In the same manner also are inferior princes deprived of their power. And to whom is this to be imputed but to the principal author? For when any one, for the sake of ambition or avarice, leads others to inconvenience or to damage, he may justly and correctly be said to disclose their nakedness. We now apprehend the Prophet's real meaning, which interpreters have not understood. I come now to the next verse —

He says that he is satiated with shame instead of glory. Some give this rendering — "Thou art satiated with shame more than glory;" but this does not suit the passage; for the Prophet does not mean that the Babylonian king was satiated with his own reproach, but rather with that of others. Secondly, the particle מ, mem, is not put here in a comparative sense, but the clause is on the contrary to be understood thus — "By thy glory, or, on account of thy glory, thou art satiated with shame". It must also in the third place be observed, that punishment is not what the Prophet describes in these words; for it immediately follows — שתה גם התה, shite gam ate, "drink thou also." He comes now to punishment. By saying, then, that the king of Babylon was satiated with shame on account of glory, it is the same as though he had said, that while he was intent on increasing his own glory he brought all others to shame. It is indeed the common game of great kings, as it has been said, to enlarge their own power at the expense and loss of others. They would, indeed, if they could, render their friends safe; but when any one loses ground in their favor they neglect him. We see how at this day great kings, raising great armies, shed innocent blood. When a slaughter is made in war they express their grief, but it is only on account of their own glory or advantage. They will in words profess that they sympathise with the miserable men who faithfully spent their life for them, but they have for them no real concern. As, then, great kings draw human blood, and care nothing when many perish for their sake, the Prophet justly says, That the king of Babylon was satiated with shame on account of glory; that is, that while he was seeking his own glory he was satiated with the reproaches of many; for many perished on his account, many had been robbed of their power, or were afterwards to be robbed — for the Prophet refers not here to what had taken place, but he speaks of things future; and the past tense of verbs was intended to express certainty; and we know that this was a common mode of speaking with the Prophets. [42]

He now adds — drink thou also. We hence see that the king of Babylon was secure as long as he remained untouched, though his alliance and friendship had proved ruinous to many. As long then as his kingdom flourished, the king of Babylon cared but little for the losses of others. Hence the Prophet says — "Thou shalt also drink; thou thinkest that others only shall be punished, as though thou were not exposed to God's judgement; but thou shalt come in thy turn and drink;" — in what way? He speaks here allegorically of the vengeance which was nigh the king of Babylon — "Thou, also," he says, "shalt drink and become a reproach," or, shalt be uncovered.

The word לרע, orel, means in Hebrew the foreskin; and the foreskinned, or uncircumcised, was the name given to the profane and the base, or the contaminated; and hence many give this rendering — "Thou also shalt become ignominious;" but others express more clearly the Prophet's meaning by this version — "Thou shalt be uncovered." Yet their opinion is not amiss who think that there is here a change of letters, that לרעה, eorel, is put for לערה, erol; and לער, rol, means to be cast asleep; and it well suits a drunken man to say that he is stupefied. But as the Prophet had spoken of nakedness, I retain the word as it is; and thus the two clauses will correspond — Then thou shalt drink and be uncovered

Then follows the explanation — Poured forth [43] into thee shall be the cup of Jehovah's right hand; that is, "the Lord shall in his time be thy cup-bearer; as thou hast inebriated many nations, and under the pretense of friendship hast defrauded those who, being bound to thee by treaties, have been ruined; so the Lord will now recompense thee with the reward which thou hast deserved: As thou hast been a cup-bearer to others, so the Lord will now become thy cup-bearer, and will inebriate thee, but after another manner." We indeed know what the Scripture everywhere means by the cup of God's hand — even vengeance of every kind. God strikes some with giddiness and precipitates them, when deprived of all humanity, into a state of madness; others he infatuates by insensibility; some he deprives of all understanding, so that they perceive nothing aright; against others he rouses up enemies, who treat them with cruelty. Hence the Lord is said to extend his cup to the wicked whenever he takes vengeance on them.

Therefore he adds — the reproach of spewing shall be on thy glory. The word וקיקלון, kikolun, is a compound. [44] We have already seen that קלון, kolun, is shame; and now he speaks of shameful spewing. And this may be referred to the king of Babylon — that he himself would shamefully spew out what he had before intemperately swallowed down; or it might be fitly applied to his enemies — that they would spew in the face of the king of Babylon.

The end of which Habakkuk speaks, awaits all tyrants, who disturb the world by their cupidity. Ambition does indeed so infatuate them, that they neither spare human blood, nor hesitate to endanger their nearest and most friendly associates. Since then an insatiable thirst for glory thus inflames them, the Prophet justly allots to them this reward — that they shall receive filthy and shameful spewing instead of that glory, in seeking which they observed no limits. Let us now proceed -

Habakkuk 2:17

17. For the violence of Lebanon shall cover thee, and the spoil of beasts, which made them afraid, because of men's blood, and for the violence of the land, of the city, and of all that dwell therein.

17. Quia violentia Libani operiet te et praedatio animalium, quae terruit ea (vel, quae contrivit,) propter sanguines hominis et violentiam terrae, urbis et omnium habitantium in ea.

We may hence easily learn, that the Prophet has not been speaking of drunkenness, but that his discourse, as we have explained, was metaphorical; for here follows a reason, why he had denounced such a punishment on the king of Babylon, and that was, because he had exercised violence, not only against all nations indiscriminately, but also against the chosen people of God. He had before only set forth in general the cruelty with which the king of Babylon had destroyed many nations; but he now speaks distinctly of the Jews, in order to show that God would in a peculiar manner be the avenger of that cruelty which the Chaldeans had employed towards the Jews, because the Lord had taken that people under his own protection. Since then the king of Babylon had assailed the children of God, who had been adopted by him, and whose defender he was, he denounces upon him here a special punishment. We thus see that this discourse is properly addressed to the Jews; for he intended to bring them some consolation in their extreme evils, so that they might strengthen their patience; for they were thereby made to see that the wrongs done to them were come to a reckoning before God.

By Libanus then we are to understand either Judea or the temple; for Libanus, as it is well known, was not far from the temple; and it is elsewhere found in the same sense. But if any extends this to the land of Judea, the meaning will be the same; there will be but little or no difference as to the subject that is handled. Because the violence then of Libanus shall overwhelm thee

Then come the words, the pillaging of beasts. Interpreters think that the Chaldeans and Assyrians are here called תומהב, bemutt, beasts, as they had been savage and cruel, like wild beasts, in laying waste Judea; but I rather understand by the beasts of Libanus those which inhabited that forest. The Prophet exaggerates the cruelty of the king of Babylon by this consideration, that he had been an enemy to brute beasts; and I consider the pronoun relative רשא, asher, which, to be understood before the verb ותיחי, ichiten, which may be taken to mean, to tear, or to frighten, Some give this rendering, "The plundering of beasts shall tear them;" as though he had said, "The Babylonians are indeed like savage beasts, but they shall be torn by their own plundering:" but another sense will be more suitable that the plundering of beasts, which terrified them, shall overwhelm thee; for the same verb, יסב, icas, shall cover or overwhelm the king of Babylon, is to be repeated here. He adds at last the clause, which was explained yesterday. We now perceive the meaning of the Prophet to be — that the king of Babylon would be justly plundered, because he had destroyed the holy land and iniquitously attacked God's chosen people, and had also carried on his depredations through almost the whole of the Easter world.
[45] It now follows —

Habakkuk 2:18

18. What profiteth the graven image that the maker thereof hath graven it; the molten image, and a teacher of lies, that the maker of his work trusteth therein, to make dumb idols?

18. Quid prodest sculptile? quia sculpsit illud fictor ejus conflatile et doctorem mendacii; quia confidit fictor figmento suo, ut faciat idola muta.

The Prophet now advances farther, and shows that whatever he had predicted of the future ruin of Babylon and of its monarchy, proceeded from the true God, from the God of Israel: for it would not have been sufficient to hold, that some deity existed in heaven, who ruled human affairs, so that it could not be, but that tyrants would have to suffer punishment for their cruelty. We indeed know that such sayings as these were everywhere common among heathen nations — that justice sits with Jupiter — that there is a Nemesis — that there is Divine vengeance. Since then such a conviction had ever been imprinted on the hearts of men, it would have been a frigid and almost an empty doctrine, had not the Prophet introduced the God of Israel. This is the reason why he now derides all idols, and claims for God the government of the whole world, and clearly shows that he speaks of the Jews, because they worshipped no imaginary gods, as the heathen nations, but plainly understood him to be the creator of heaven and earth, who revealed himself to Abraham, who gave his law by the hand of Moses. We now perceive the Prophet's design.

As then the king of Babylon did himself worship his own gods, the Prophet dissipates that vain confidence, by which he might be deceived and deceive others. Hence he says, What avails the graven image? He speaks here contemptuously of images formed by men's hands. And he adds a reason, because the maker has graven it, he says. Interpreters give a sense that is very jejune, as though the Prophet had said, "What avails a graven image, when it is graven or melted by its artifices?" But the Prophet shows here the reason why the worship of idols is useless, and that is, because these gods are made of dead materials. And then he says, "What deity can the artifices produce?" We hence see that a reason is given in these words, and therefore we may more clearly render them thus — "What avails the graven image, when the framer has graven it?" that is, since the graven image has its origin from the hand and skill of man, what can it avail? He then adds, he has formed a molten image; that is, though the artifices has given form to the metal, or to the wood, or to the stone, yet he could not have changed its nature. He has indeed given it a certain external appearance; but were any one to ask what it is, the answer would surely be, "It is a graven image." Since then its nature is not changed by the work of man, it evidently appears, how stupid and mad must all those be who put their trust in graven images. [46]

He then adds, and a teacher of falsehood. He added this clause, because men previously entertain false notions, and dare not to form a judgement on the matter itself. For, how comes it that a piece of wood or a stone is called a god? Had any one asked the sages at Rome or at Athens, or in other cities, who thought all other nations barbarous, What is that? on seeing a Jupiter made of silver; or of wood, or of stone, the answer would have been, "It is Jupiter, it is God." But how could this be? It is a stone, a piece of wood, or of silver. They would yet have asserted that it was God. Whence came this madness? Even from this, because men were bewitched, so that seeing they saw not; they wilfully closed their eyes, and resolved to be blind, being unwilling to understand. This is the reason why the Prophet, by way of anticipation, says, the artificer has formed — what has he formed? a graven image and a teacher of falsehood. The material remains the same, but a false notion prevails, for men think idols to be gods. How come they to think so? It is no doubt the teaching of falsehood, a mere illusion. He then confirms the same thing; the fashioner, or the artificer, he says, trusts in his own work, or in what he has formed. How is this? Must they not be void of sense and reason who trust in lifeless things? "The workman," as Isaiah says, "will take his instruments, will form an idol, and then he will bow the knee, and call it his god; yet it is the work of his own hands." What! art not thou thyself a god? thou knowest thine own frailty, and yet thou createst new gods! Even in this manner does the Prophet confirm what he had previously said, that men are extremely stupid, nay, that they are seized with monstrous sottishness, when they ascribe a kind of deity to wood, or to a stone, or to metal. How so? because they are, he says, false imaginations.

And he adds, that he may make dumb idols. He again repeats what he had said, — that the nature of the material is not changed by men's workmanship, when they form to themselves gods either from wood or from stone. How so? because they cannot speak. To the same purpose is what immediately follows; the next verse must therefore be added. We shall afterwards say something more on the general subject.

Habakkuk 2:19

19. Woe unto him that saith to the wood, Awake; to the dumb stone, Arise, it shall teach! Behold, it is laid over with gold and silver, and there is no breath at all in the midst of it.

19. Vae qui dicit ligno, Expergiscere; excitare, lapidi muto (mortuo,) ipse docebit: Ecce, ipse (vel ipsum lipsum, si vefaremus ad lignum; ipse ergo) opertus est auro et argento; et nullus spiritus in medio ejus.

He pursues, as I have said, the same subject, and sharply inveighs against the sottishness of men, that they call on wood and stone, as though there were some hidden power in them. They say to the wood, Awake; for they implored help from their idols. Shall it teach? Some render it thus as a question; but I take it in a simpler form, "It will teach;" that is, "It is a wonder that ye are so wilfully foolish; for were God to send to you no

Prophet, were there no one to instruct you, yet the wood and the stone would be sufficient teachers to you: ask your idols, that is, ascertain rightly what is in them. Doubtless, the god that is made of wood or of stone, sufficiently declares by his silence that he is no god. For there is no motion in wood and stone. Where there is no vigor and no life, is it not right to feel assured, that there is no deity? There are, indeed, many creatures endued with feeling and motion; but the God who gives power, and motion, and feeling to the whole world, and to all its parts, does he not surpass in these respects all his creatures? Since, then, wood and stone are silent, they are teachers sufficient for you, provided ye be apt scholars."

We hence see how the Prophet in this way amplifies the insensibility of men; for they did not perceive what was quite manifest. The design of what follows is the same. Behold, it is covered over with gold and silver; that is, it is made splendid: for idolaters think that their gods are better when adorned with gold and silver; but yet there is no breath in the midst of them. "Look," he says, "within; look within, and ye shall see that they are dead." [47] The rest we shall dilate on to-morrow.

PRAYER

Grant, Almighty God, that as there is in us so little of right judgement, and as our minds are blind even at mid-day, — O grant, that thy Spirit may always shine in us, and that being attentive to the light of thy word, we may also keep to the right way through the whole course of our pilgrimage, and subject to thee both ourselves and every action of our life, so that we may not be led by any allurements into the same ruin with the ungodly, who would deceive and entrap us, and who lie in wait on every side; but that being ruled by the counsel of thy Spirit, we may beware of all their intrigues: and may we, especially as to our spiritual life, be so given up to thee alone, as ever to keep ourselves far away from the defilements of all people, and so remain in the pure worship of thy majesty, that the ungodly may never draw us away into the same delusions with themselves, by which Satan so mightily deceives them; but may we follow Him as our leader whom thou wouldst have to be our ruler, even Christ thy Son, until he at length gathers us all into that celestial kingdom which he has purchased for us by his own blood. Amen.

LECTURE ONE HUNDRED AND FOURTEENTH

We said yesterday, that the Prophet speaks now of idols, that he might deprive the king of Babylon of his vain confidence: for though heathens claim everything to themselves and to their own powers, yet their superstition in some measure dementates them. Hence the Prophet shows, that that tyrant in vain trusted in his idols, since they were things of nought. But the reasons by which he refutes idolatry ought to be noticed: he says, that the artifices, who formed gods, were not able to change the nature of the material, for the wood remained wood, and stone continued to be stone, and that the workmen and artifices in forming it did nothing more than make a molten image. The material then remained still the same. As to the image itself, the Prophet says, that it was mere falsehood and deception; yea, that gods made of wood or of silver, or of any other material, were instructors and teachers of falsehood, for they allured simple souls: and Satan spread his snares before men, when he set before their eyes these visible figures, and persuaded them that they contained something divine. Then this reasoning of the Prophet ought to be carefully observed; for he reminds us, that fictitious gods are made of lifeless and perishable materials, and that images are only the juggleries of Satan.

That saying of Gregory is common among the Papists, that images are the books of the ignorant; for such was his answer to Serenus, bishop of Marseilles, who turned out images from all the churches (Lib. 9, Epist. 9.) He said that he approved of his object, in wishing to correct the superstition which prevailed among the people, but that he had done what was not right in wholly taking away images, the books of the ignorant. But let us consider whether more faith is due to Gregory, a man imbued with many errors, (as that age was very corrupt), or to the Prophet Habakkuk, and also to Jeremiah, who announces nearly the same sentiment. Though, then, there is some speciousness in idols, yet the Prophet here reminds us that they are nothing but the impostures of Satan; for they teach falsehood. The reason also that is given is deserving of notice — that the workmen put their hope in what they themselves have formed. And it is indeed a thing most preposterous, that a mortal man should form his own god, and then imagine that something divine is enclosed in the very form, for deity is not in the material. The material is disregarded when unformed; but not so when it attains a beautiful shape. While the tree grows, while it produces flowers and fruit, it is deemed, as it really is, a dead thing; but when a piece of it is formed in the figure of a man, it is believed to be a god! But it is extremely absurd to suppose that the hand of the artifices gives deity to a dead material; for the wood is dead, and nothing is perceived but the shape given to it by man. Since, then, the artifices trusts in what he has formed, it is what seems beyond anything strange. It is hence quite evident, that men are wholly demented by the devil, when they worship their own workmanship.

But now, in order to press the matter more fully on idolaters, the Prophet upbraids them for calling on the wood and on the stone to awake. It is certain, that when idolaters bow the knee before what they have themselves formed, they still imagine that there are celestial gods; but when before a figure of wood or stone they call upon God, it is the same thing as though they expected help from the wood and stone; for the question is not here what idolaters imagine, but the thing itself is to be regarded; and this is what the Prophet most fully and plainly condemns. Since, then, the superstitious are wont to address their prayers to wood and stone, he says, that they make to themselves gods, to whom they sacrifice. And the Prophet rightly refers in express terms to this kind of service; for the chief sacrifice which God bids to be offered to him, and demands from us, is to call on him; for we thus testify that life and all things belonging to salvation are found alone in him. Since, then, the majesty of God appears especially from having this testimony borne to him, that he is the fountain of life and of all blessings, every one who prostrates himself before a stone or wood, and implores the aid of a visible god, transfers, no doubt, the glory of the eternal God to a dead piece of wood or to a stone. If, then, we wish to be free from every superstition, let us remember this truth, that then only we have the only true God, when we direct our prayers and supplications to him alone, or, in a word, when we call on him alone. When we have recourse to dead idols, God is deprived of his own right. We may call him God a hundred times, but we give him an empty title, and one of no value, except we pray to him alone.

The Prophet, in the last place, derides the madness of men, by saying that the very idols teach: for, as it was said yesterday, the clause is not to be read as a question, as some do; but in order more sharply to reprove the stupidity of men, the Prophet says, "Doubtless the very figures themselves, except ye are wholly senseless, will teach you." He had before said, it is true, that they were the teachers of falsehood and vanity; but he speaks now of another kind of teaching, that if men wisely attended to the thing itself, they might soon learn from a mere view of their gods, that they were most palpably the deceits of Satan; for if any one looked on the idols with a clear eye, he would see that they were a dead material, and would see that great wrong is done to God by transforming him into a likeness of what is dead.

We now understand the Prophet's meaning, when he says, That idols themselves are sufficient, and more than sufficient teachers, when men are teachable, and lend an attentive ear. He means not, as it was said yesterday, that idols teach fallaciously to the destruction of men, while something divine is ascribed to them; but he says that they teach, if any one of a sane mind, and free from error, comes to view the idol, and forms a judgement of the thing itself. But superstition occupies the minds of men; and hence it is that all become the scholars of Satan, and no one applies his mind to understand the doctrine he mentions here. In short, idols teach naturally, and they teach through the artifice and delusion of Satan. They teach naturally; for by their silence they show that they are not gods, inasmuch as there is no strength in them. They teach, also, by the artifice of the devil; for they are made to claim a kind of divinity, and thus dazzle the minds of men, who are already corrupted by their own delusions. To the first teaching, of which the Prophet now speaks, none apply their minds; for almost all renounce nature wholly: this only lays hold on them — that idols are gods; for they make an image of the heavenly and eternal God, from whom we are at a great distance, and who does not otherwise descend to us, except through visible representations!

The same truth the Prophet confirms when he says, that though these gods are covered over with gold and silver, there is no breath in them, or in the midst of them. In short, he means that they are mere masks; for no divinity can be without life. As then idols are dead things, it follows that they are the most palpable impostures of Satan, by which he fascinates the minds of men, when they thus devote themselves to dead things.

Moreover, whatever is here said against idols, most certainly applies to the superstitions of popery. They deny that they give divine honors to their idols; but let us consider what the Prophet says. They indeed sacrifice to gold and silver, and then bend their knees before their images, and do not think that God is near them, except in these figures. Let them show, then, that the Prophet reasons here foolishly, or let them be held guilty according to the declaration, as it were, of the Holy Spirit, when they thus present their prayers before idols. It now follows —

Habakkuk 2:20

20. But the Lord is in his holy temple: let all the earth keep silence before him.

20. Jehova autem in templo sanctitatis suae (id est, in templo sancto suo:) sileat a facie ejus omnis terra.

After having taught us that the Babylonians were deceived in expecting any help from their idols, and were deluded by Satan, Habakkuk now recalls the attention of the faithful to the only true God; for it would not have been enough to take away from the Babylonians the false confidence which they had in their idols, except the Israelites, on the other hand, trusting in the grace of the true God, were fully persuaded that God was on their side, as he had taken them under his protection.

And we ought carefully to observe this order; for we see that many boldly deride all the superstitions which prevail in the world, and at the same time daringly and with cyclopic fury despise the true God. How many are at this day either Epicureans or Lucianians, who prate jestingly and scoffingly against the superstitions of the papacy, but in the meantime they are not influenced by any fear of God? If, however, we are to choose one of two evils, superstition is more tolerable than that gross impiety which obliterates every thought of a God. It is indeed true, that the more the superstitious toil in their delusions, the more they provoke God's wrath against them; for they transfer his glory to dead things; but yet they retain this principle — that honor and worship are due to God: but the profane, in whom there is no religion whatever, not only change God from what he is, but also strive as far as they can to reduce him to nothing. Hence I have said, that the order which the Prophet observes here ought to be maintained. For, after having overturned the false illusions of the devil, by which he deludes the superstitious, by setting before them a mere shadow in the place of the true God, he now sets up the true worship of the only true God. Then the Prophet has hitherto been endeavoring to subvert superstitions, but he now builds up: for except God, when idols are pulled down, ascends his own tribunal, and shines there as supreme according to his right, it would be better, at least it would be more tolerable, as I have said, that superstitions should be left entire.

He now says that God is in his own temple or palace: this word is often taken for heaven, but is applied to the sanctuary. Many consider that the reference is made to heaven; as though the Prophet had said, that the true God, who is the artificer and creator of heaven and earth, is not to be seen in a visible form, nor covered over with gold and silver, nor represented by wood or stone; but that he rules in heaven, and fills heaven with his infinite glory and this view is by no means unsuitable. But as he here specially addresses the Jews, it seems to me more probable that he speaks of the temple, where God then designed to be worshipped, and sacrifices to be offered to him for it would not have been sufficient to set God, the creator of heaven and earth, in opposition to the superstitions of all the nations; but it was also necessary to introduce the contrast between the God of Israel and all those gods who then had obtained a name and reputation in the world, as they had been formed by the will of men. The God of Israel was indeed the creator of heaven and earth; but he had made himself known by his law, he had revealed himself to men, so that his majesty was not hidden; for when we speak of God, we are lost except he comes to us, and in a manner exhibits himself to us; for the capacity of our understanding is not so great that it can penetrate above all heavens. Hence the majesty of God is in itself incomprehensible to us; but he makes himself known by his works and by his word. Now as the Israelites worshipped, and surely knew that they worshipped the only true God, the Prophet here rightly confirms them in the hope they derived from the teaching of the law — that God was their Father, inasmuch as he had adopted them. If any prefer to take the word for heaven, I do not object; and that meaning, as I have said, is not unsuitable. But as the Prophet seems to me to have a special vies to his own people, to whom he was appointed a teacher; it is more probable that the word, temple or palace, is here to be understood of the sanctuary.

If any raises the objection that there is then no difference between the God of Israel and the gods of the Gentiles, for he also dwells in an earthly habitation, the answer is obviously this — that though God is said to dwell between the cherubim, he has not been represented by an image, as though he had anything like to wood or stone, or possessed any likeness to human bodies. All these delusions were banished from the Temple; for he commanded his worshipers to look up to heaven. There was an intervening veil, that the people might understand that they could not otherwise come to God than through that celestial model, the and types of which they saw in the altar of incense, in the altar on which they sacrificed, in the table of the shewbread, in short, in all other services of the Temple. And there is another difference to be noticed; for though there was there the golden altar, though there was there the ark of the covenant, and the altar on which the victims were immolated, yet inscribed on all these typical representations was the word of God, by which alone true religion was to be distinguished from all false inventions. For whatever specious appearance of reason may therefore be in fictitious modes of worship, men have no authority to render them lawful; but so much reverence is due to the only true word of God, that it ought to overrule all other reasons. And besides, this word, as I have hinted already, did not retain the Jews in these delusions, but elevated their minds to heaven. We now then see that there was a wide difference between the Temple which was at Jerusalem, and the temples which the superstitious had then built for themselves throughout the world; for God ruled over the Jews, so that they could not have been deluded. And at this day, where the word of God shines among us, we can follow it with safety. And, further, God did spiritually draw to himself his own servants, though he employed, on account of their ignorance, certain outward elements. Hence the Prophet justly says, that God was in his palace or his Temple; for the Israelites knew of a certainty that they did not worship a fictitious God, since in his law he had revealed himself to them, and had chosen the sanctuary, where he intended to be worshipped in a typical, and yet in a spiritual manner.

He then adds, Let all the earth be silent before him. Habakkuk, no doubt, commends the power of God, that the Israelites might proceed with alacrity in their religious course, knowing it to be a sufficient security to be under the protection of the only true God, and that they might not seek after the superstitions of the nations, nor be carried here and there, as it often happens, by vain desires. Keep silence, then, he says, let all the earth. He shows that though the Israelites might be far inferior to the Babylonians and other nations, and be far unequal to them in strength, military art, forces, and, in short, in all things of this kind, yet they would be always safe under the guardianship of God; for the Lord was able to control whatever power there might be in the world.

We now see what the Prophet had in view: for he does not here simply exhort all people to worship God, but shows, that thought men may grow mad against him, he yet can easily by his hand subjugate them; for after all the tumults made by kings and their people, the Lord can, by one breath of his mouth, dissipate all their attempts, however furious they may be. This, then, is the silence of which the Prophet now speaks. But there is another kind of silence, and that is, when we willingly submit to God; for silence in this respect is nothing else but submission: and we submit to God, when we bring not our own inventions and imaginations, but suffer ourselves to be taught by his word. We also submit to him, when we murmur not against his power or his judgements, when we humble ourselves under his powerful hand, and do not fiercely resist him, as those do who indulge their own lusts. This is indeed, as I have said, a voluntary submission: but the Prophet here shows that there is power in God to lay prostrate the whole world, and to tread it under his feet, whenever it may please him; so that the faithful have nothing to fear, for they know that their salvation is secured; for though the whole world were leagued against them, it yet cannot resist God. Now follows a prayer: —

CHAPTER 3

Habakkuk 3:1

1. A prayer of Habakkuk the prophet upon Shigionoth.

1. Precatio Chabakuk Prophetae super ignorantiis (vel, super canticis, aut instrumentis musicis.)

There is no doubt but that the Prophet dictated this form of prayer for his people, before they were led into exile, that they might always exercise themselves in the study of religion. We indeed know that God cannot be rightly and from the heart worshipped but in faith. Hence, in order to confine the dispersed Israelites within due limits, so that they might not fall away from true religion, the Prophet here sets before them the materials of faith, and stimulates them to prayer: and we know, that our faith cannot be supported in a better way than by the exercise of prayer.

Let us then bear in mind, that the way of fostering true religion, prescribed here to the miserable Israelites while dispersed in their exile, was to look up to God daily, that they might strengthen their faith; for they could not have otherwise continued in their obedience to God. They would, indeed, have wholly fallen away into the superstitions of the Gentiles, had not the memory of the covenant, which the Lord had made with them, remained firm in their hearts: and we shall presently see that the Prophet lays much stress upon this circumstance.

He calls it his own prayer, [48] not because he used it himself privately, or composed it for himself, but that the prayer might have some authority among the people; for they knew that a form of prayer dictated for them by the mouth of a Prophet, was the same as though the Spirit itself was to show them how they were to pray to God. The name, then, of Habakkuk is added to it, not because he used it himself, but that the people might be more encouraged to pray, when they knew that the Holy Spirit, through the Prophet, had become their guide and teacher.

There is some difficulty connected with the word תוניגש, sheginut. The verb שגג, shegag, or הגש, shege, means, to act inconsiderately; and from הגש, shege, is derived ויגשן, shegiun. Many render it, ignorance; some, delight. Some think it to be the beginning of a song; others suppose it to be a common melody; and others, a musical instrument. Thus interpreters differ. In the seventh Psalm David, no doubt, calls either a song or some musical instrument by the word ויגשן, shegiun. Yet some think that David bears testimony there to his own innocency; and that, as he was not conscious of having done wrong, his own innocency is alone signified by the title: but this is a strained view. The word is taken in this place, almost by common consent, for ignorances: and we know that the Hebrews denominate by ignorances all errors or falls which are not grievous, and such things as happen through inadvertence; and by this word they do not extenuate their faults, but acknowledge themselves to be inconsiderate when they offend. Then ויגשן, shegiun, is no excusable ignorance, which men lay hold on as a pretext; but an error of folly and presumptions, when men are not sufficiently attentive to the word of God. But perhaps the word תוניגש, sheginut, being here in the plural number, ought to be taken for musical instruments. Yet as I would not willingly depart from a received opinion, and as there is no necessity in this case to constrain us to depart from it, let us follows what had been already said, — that the Prophet dictates here for his people a form of prayer for ignorances, that is, that they could not otherwise hope for God's forgiveness than by seeking his favor. [49] And how can we be reconciled to God, except by his not imputing to us our sins?

But the Prophet, by asking for the pardons of ignorances, does not omit more grievous sins; but intimates that though their conscience does not reprove men, they are yet not on that account innocent and without guilt; for they often inconsiderately fall, and their faults are not to be excused for inadvertence. It is, then, the same thing as though the Prophet reminded his own people, that there was no remedy for them in adversity but by fleeing to God, and fleeing as suppliants, in order to solicit his forgiveness; and that they were not only to acknowledge their more grievous sins, but also to confess that they were in many respects guilty; for they might have fallen through error a thousand times, as we are inconsiderate almost through the whole course of our life. We now, then, perceive what this word means, and why the Prophet spoke rather of ignorances than of other sins. But I shall not proceed farther now, as there is some other business.

PRAYER

Grant, Almighty God, that as thou hast deigned to make thyself known to us by thy word, and as thou elevates us to thyself in a way suitable to the ignorance of our minds, — O grant, that we may not continue fixed in our stupidity, but that we may put off all superstitions, and also renounce all the thoughts of our flesh, and seek thee in the right way; and may we suffer ourselves to be so ruled by thy word, that we may purely and from the heart call upon thee, and so rely on thine infinite power, that we may not fear to despise the whole world, and every adversity on the earth, until, having finished our warfare, we shall at length be gathered into that blessed rest, which thine only-begotten Son has procured for us by his own blood — Amen.

LECTURE ONE HUNDRED AND FIFTEENTH

Habakkuk 3:2

2. O Lord, I have heard thy speech, and was afraid: O Lord, revive thy work in the midst of the years, in the midst of the years make known; in wrath remember mercy.

2. Jehova, audivi vocem tuam (auditum tuum, ad verbum, [שמעד]; [50]) Jehova, opus tuum in medio annorum vivifica illud (sed relativum pronomen abundat;) in medio annorum notum fac; in ira misericordiae recorderis.

The Prophet says here, in the name of the whole people, that he was terrified by the voice of God, for so I understand the word, though in many places it means report, as some also explain it in this place. But as the preaching of the Gospel is called in Isa 53:1, העמש, shemoe, report, it seems to me more suitable to the present passage to render it the voice of God; for the general sentiment, that the faithful were terrified at the report of God, would be frigid. It ought rather to be applied to the Prophecies which have been already explained: and doubtless Habakkuk did not intend here to speak only in general of God's power; but, as we have seen in the last lecture, he humbly confesses the sins of the people, and then prays for forgiveness. It is then not to be doubted but that he says here, that he was terrified by the voice of God, that is, when he heard him threatening punishment so grievous. He then adds, Revive thy work in the middle of the years, and make it known. At last, by way of anticipation, he subjoins, that God would remember his mercy, though justly offended by the sins of the people.

But by saying, that he feared the voice of God, he makes a confession, or gives an evidence of repentance; for we cannot from the heart seek pardon, unless we be first made humble. When a sinner is not displeased with himself, and confesses not his guilt, he is not deserving of mercy. We then see why the Prophet speaks here of fear; and that is, that he might thus obtain for himself and for others the favor of God; for as soon as a sinner willingly condemns himself, and does not do this formally, but seriously from the heart, he is already reconciled to God; for God bids us in this way to anticipate his judgement. This is one thing. But if it be asked, for what purpose the Prophet heard God's voice; the obvious answer is, — that as it is not the private prayer of one person, but of the whole Church, he prescribes here to the faithful the way by which they were to obtain favor from God, and turn him to mercy; and that is, by dreading his threatening and by acknowledging that whatever God threatened by his Prophets was near at hand.

Then follows the second clause, Jehovah! in the middle of the years revive thy work. By the work of God he means the condition of his people or of the Church. For though God is the creator of heaven and earth, he would yet have his own Church to be acknowledged to be, as it were, his peculiar workmanship, and a special monument of his power, wisdom, justice, and goodness. Hence, by way of eminence, he calls here the condition of the elect people the work of God; for the seed of Abraham was not only a part of the human race, but was the holy and peculiar possession of God. Since, then, the Israelites were set apart by the Lord, they are rightly called his work; as we read in another place,

"The work of thine hands thou wilt not despise," Ps 138:8.

And God often says, "This is my planting," "This is the work of my hands," when he speaks of his Church.

By the middle of the years, he means the middle course, as it were, of the people's life. For from the time when God chose the race of Abraham to the coming of Christ, was the whole course, as it were, of their life, when we compare the people to a man; for the fullness of their age was at the coming of Christ. If, then, that people had been destroyed, it would have been the same as though death were to snatch away a person in the flower of his age. Hence the Prophet prays God not to take away the life of his people in the middle of their course; for Christ having not come, the people had not attained maturity, nor arrived at manhood. In the middle, then, of the years thy work revive; that is, "Though we seem destined to death, yet restore us." Make it known, he says, in the middle of the years; that is, "Show it to be in reality thy work." [51]

We now apprehend the real meaning of the Prophet. After having confessed that the Israelites justly trembled at Cod's voice, as they saw themselves deservedly given up to perdition, he then appeals to the mercy of God, and prays God to revive his own work. He brings forward here nothing but the favor of adoption: thus he confesses that there was no reason why God should forgive his people, except that he had been pleased freely to adopt them, and to choose them as his peculiar people; for on this account it is that God is wont to show his favor towards us even to the last. as, then, this people had been once chosen by God, the Prophet records this adoptions, and prays God to continue and fulfill to the end what he had begun. With regard to the half course of life, the comparison ought to be observed; for we see that the race of Abraham was not chosen for a short time, but until Christ the Redeemer was manifested. Now we have this in common with the ancient people, that God adopts us, that he may at length bring us into the inheritance of eternal life. Until, then, the work of our salvation is completed, we are, as it were, running our course. We may therefore adopt this form of prayer, which is prescribed for us by the Holy Spirit, — that God would not forsake his ohm work; in the middle of our course.

What he now subjoins — in wrath remember mercy, is intended to anticipate an objection; for this thought might have occurred to the faithful — "there is no ground for us to hope pardon from God, whom we have so grievously provoked, nor is there any reason for us to rely any more on the covenant which we have so perfidiously violated." The Prophet meets this objection, and he flees to the gracious favor of God, however much he perceived that the people would have to suffer the just punishment of their sins, such as they deserved. He then confesses that God was justly angry with his people, and yet that the hope of salvation was not on that account closed up, for the Lord had promised to be propitious. Since God then is not inexorable towards his people — nay, while he chastises them he ceases not to be a father; hence the Prophet connects here the mercy of God with his wrath.

We have elsewhere said that the word wrath is not to be taken according to its strict sense, when the faithful or the elect are spoken of; for God does not chastise them because he hates them; nay, on the contrary, he thereby manifests the care he has for their salvations. Hence the scourges by which God chastises his children are testimonies of his love. But the Scripture represents the judgement with which God visits his people as wrath, not towards their persons but towards their sins. Though then God shows love to his chosen, yet he testifies when he punishes their sins that iniquity is hated by him. When God then comes forth as it were as a judge, and shows that sins displease him, he is said to be angry with the faithful; and there is also in this a reference to the perceptions of men; for we cannot, when God chastises us, do otherwise than feel the accusations of our own conscience. Hence then is this hatred; for when our conscience condemns us we must necessarily acknowledge God to be angry with us, that is with respect to us. When therefore we provoke God's wrath by our sins we feel him to be angry with us; but yet the Prophet collects together things which seem wholly contrary — even that God would remember mercy in wrath; that is, that he would show himself displeased with them in such a way as to afford to the faithful at the same time some taste of his favor and mercy by finding him to be propitious to them.

We now then perceive how the Prophet had joined the last clause to the foregoing. Whenever, then, the judgement of the flesh would lead us to despair, let us ever set up against it this truth — that God is in such a way angry that he never forgets his mercy — that is, in his dealings with his elect. It follows —

Habakkuk 3:3

3. God came from Teman, and the Holy One from mount Paran. Selah. His glory covered the heavens, and the earth was full of his praise.

3. Deus de Theman veniet, et Sanctus e monte Paran. Selach. [52] Operuit coelos decor (vel, gloria) ejus; laude ejus plena est terra.

This verse interpreters explain in two ways. Some construe the verb in the future tense in the past time — "God went forth from Teman, and the holy one from mount Paran"; for a verb in the past tense follows. But others consider it to be in the optative mood — "May God come, or go forth, from Teman, and the holy one from mount Paran;" as though the Prophet prayed God to come as the defender of his people from mount Sinai, where the law was promulgated and the covenant ratified, which God had formerly made with Abraham and his posterity. I rather subscribe to their opinion who think that the manifestation of God, by which he had testified that he was the guardian of that people, is repeated by the Prophet. As, then, God had so made known his glory on mount Sinai, that it was evident that that nation was under his protection, so the Prophet, with the view of strengthening himself and others, records what was well known among the whole people — that is, that the law was given on mount Sinai, which was a testimony of singular favor; for God then by a new pledge testified, that the covenant formerly made with Abraham was firm and inviolable. The reason why Habakkuk does not mention mount Sinai, but Teman and Paran, seems to some to be this — because these mountains were nearer the Holy Land, though this view, I fear, will appear too refined; I therefore take this simple view — that instead of mentioning mount Sinai, he paraphrastically designates it by mount Paran and the desert of Teman. Some suppose these to be two mountains; but I know not whether Teman ought to be understood only as a mountain; it seems on the contrary to have been some large tract of country. It was a common thing among the Jews to add this name when they spoke of the south, as many nations were wont to give to winds the names of some neighboring places; so when the Jews wished to designate a wind from Africa, they called it Teman. "It is a Teman wind;" and so when they spoke of the south, they said Teman.

However this may be, it is certain that the desert of Teman was nigh to Sinai, and also that mount Paran was connected with that desert. As then they were places towards the south, and nigh to mount Sinai, where the law had been proclaimed, the Prophet records here, in order to strengthen the faith of the whole people, that God had not in vain gone forth once from Teman, and there appeared in his celestial power; for God then openly showed, that he took under his guardianship the children of Abraham, and that the covenant which he had formerly made with him was not vain or of no effect. Since, then, God had testified this in so remarkable and wonderful a manner, the Prophet brings forward here that history which tended especially to confirm the faith of the godly — God went forth once from Teman, and the holy one from mount Paran.

For it was not God's will that the memory of that manifestation should be obliterated; but he had once appeared with glory so magnificent, that the people might feel assured that they would ever be safe, for they were protected by God's hand, and that full of power, as the fathers had once known by manifest and visible evidences; and hence the Prophet represents God's going forth from mount Paran as a continued act, as though he rendered himself visible chiefly from that place. Nor is this representation new; for we see, in many other places, a living picture, as it were, set before the eyes of the faithful, in order to strengthen them in their adversity, and to make them assured that they shall be safe through God's presence. The Lord, indeed, did not daily fulminate from heaven, nor were there such visible indications of his presence as on mount Sinai; but it behaved the people to feel assured that he was the same God who had given to their fathers such clear evidence of his power, and that he is also at this time, and to the end of the world, endued with the same power, though it be not rendered visible.

We now then apprehend the design of the Prophet: God then came from Teman, and the holy one from mount Paran. We must also observe, that the minds of the godly were recalled to the spectacle on mount Sinai, when they were drawn away into exile, or when they were in the power of their enemies. They might indeed have then supposed, that they were wholly forsaken. Obliterated then must have been the memory of that history, had not this remedy been introduced. It is, therefore, the same as though the Prophet had said — "Though God now hides his power, and gives no evidence of his favor, yet think not that he formerly appeared in vain to your fathers as one clothed with so great a power, when the law was proclaimed on mount Sinai. It follows —

Habakkuk 3:4

4. And his brightness was as the light; he had horns coming out of his hand: and there was the hiding of his power.

4. Et splendor quasi lux fuit; cornua e manu ejus ei, et ibi absconsio fortitudinis ejus.

He confirms the declaration which I have explained that God, when he intended his presence to be made known to his people, gave evidences of his wonderful power, capable of awakening the minds of all. He then says, that the brightness was like light. By the word רוא, aur, is doubtless meant the light, which diffuses itself through the whole world, and proceeds from the sun. Then he says, that the brightness which appeared on mount Sinai was equal to the light of the sun, capable of filling the whole world. He adds, that horns were to him from the hand. Some render it, splendor; but ןרק, coren, properly means a horn, and םינרק, corenium, is here in the dual number: it is therefore more probable, that the Prophet ascribes horns to God, carried in both hands; and it more corresponds with what immediately follows, that "there was the hiding of his strength," or that "there was his power hidden." They who render the word, splendours, think that what had been said is repeated, that is, that the brightness was like light; but they are mistaken, for we may collect from the verse that two different things are expressed by the Prophet: he first speaks of the visible form of God; and then he adds his power, designating it metaphorically by horns, which is common in Scripture. Indeed this mode of speaking occurs often. He then says, that God came armed with power, when he gave the law to his people; for he bore horns in his hands, where his strength was hid. [53]

As to the word hiding, some indeed give this refined view, that God then put forth his strength, which was before hidden. But this is a very strained explanation. To me it seems evident, that the Prophet in the first place says, that God's glory was conspicuous, capable of irradiating the whole world like the light of the sun; and he then adds, that this splendor was connected with power, for God carried horns in both his hands, where his strength was laid: and he says, that it was hid, because God did not intend to make known his power indiscriminately throughout the world, but peculiarly to his own people; as it is also said in Ps 31:20, that

"the greatness of his goodness is laid up for the faithful alone,
who fear and reverence him."

As then it is said, that the goodness of God is laid up for the faithful, for they enjoy it as children and members of the household; so also the power of God is said to be laid up, because he testifies that he is armed with power to defend his Church, that he may render safe the children of Abraham, whom he has taken under his protection. It afterwards follows —

Habakkuk 3:5

5. Before him went the pestilence, and burning coals went forth at his feet.

5. Coram facie ejus ambulavit pestis, et egredietur carbo ignitus (vel, ustio) ad pedes ejus.

The Prophet repeats here, that God came armed to defend his people, when he went forth from Teman; for he connects with it here the deliverance of the people. He does not indeed speak only of the promulgation of the law, but encourages all the godly to confidence; for God, who had once redeemed their fathers from Egypt, remained ever like himself, and was endued with the same power.

And he says, that before God's face walked the pestilence; this is to be referred to the Egyptians; and that ignited coal proceeded from his feet. Some render רשף, reshoph, exile; but its etymology requires it to be rendered burning or ignited coal, and there is no necessity to give it another meaning. [54]

The import of the whole is — that Cod had put to flight all the enemies of his people; for we know that the Egyptians were smitten with various plagues, and that the army of Pharaoh was drowned in the Red Sea. Hence, the Prophet says, that God had so appeared from Teman, that the pestilence went before him, and then the ignited coal; in short, that the pestilence and ignited coal were God's officers, which were ready to perform his commands: as when a king or a judge, having attendants, commands them to put this man in prison, and to punish another in a different way; so the Prophet, giving us a representation of God, says, that all kinds of evils were ready to obey his orders, and to destroy his and their enemies. He does not then intend here to terrify the faithful in mentioning the pestilence and the ignited coal; but, on the contrary, to set before their eyes evidences of God's power, by which he could deliver them from the hand of their enemies, as he had formerly delivered their fathers from Egypt. By God's feet, he then means his going forth or his presence; for I do not approve of what some have said, that ignited coals followed, when pestilence had preceded; for both clauses are given in the same way. It follows —

Habakkuk 3:6

6. He stood, and measured the earth: he beheld, and drove asunder the nations; and the everlasting mountains were scattered, the perpetual hills did bow: his ways are everlasting.

6. Stetit et mensus est terram; aspexit et dissolvit gentes; et afflicti sunt montes aeterni; incurvati sunt colles seculi; itinera seculi ei.

He says that God possessed every power to subdue the earth to himself, and that he could at his will destroy it, yea, dissolve mountains as veil as nations. Some of the Jews understood this of the ark, which stood at that time in Gilead. They then suppose that the Prophet meant this in short — that when God chose a place for the ark of the covenant in Gilgal, that he determined then what he would do, and that he then in his secret counsel divided the land, so that each should have his portion by lot. This, it is true, was accomplished shortly after, for Joshua, as we know, divided it by lot between the tribes. But what the Jews affirm of the ark seems to me strained and frigid. Habakkuk, on the contrary, means by the word stand, that God was openly conspicuous, like him who assumes an erect posture, so that he is seen at a distance. In this sense we are to take the expression that God stood.

The measuring, of the earth is not to be confined to Judea, but is to be extended to the whole world. God, he says, has measured the earth. To measure the earth is what properly belongs to a sovereign king; and it is done that he may assign to each his portion. Except God, then, had a sovereign right over the earth and the whole world, Habakkuk would not have ascribed to him this office; and this we learn from the verse itself, for he immediately subjoins, that the nations, as it were, melted away, that the mountains were destroyed, that the hills were bowed down

We hence see that by earth we are not to understand Judea only, but the whole world; as though he had said, that when God appeared on mount Sinai, he made it fully evident that the earth was under his power and authority, so that he could determine whatever he pleased, and prescribe limits to all nations. For he does not speak of God here as having, like a surveyor, a measuring line; but he says, that he measured the earth as one capable even then of changing the boundaries of the whole world; nay, he intimates that it was he himself who had at first created the earth and assigned it to men. It is indeed true that the nations did not then melt away, nor were the mountains demolished, nor the hills bowed down; but the Prophet simply means, that God's power then appeared, which was capable of shaking the whole world.

But he calls these the mountains of eternity and the hills ages, which had been from the beginning fixed on their own foundations. For if an earthquake happens on a plain, it seems less wonderful; and then if any of those mountains cleave, which are not so firmly fixed, it may be on account of some hollow places; for when the winds fill the caverns, they are forced to burst, and they cleave the mountains and the earth. But the Prophet relates an unusual thing, and wholly different from the ordinary course of nature — that the mountains of eternity, which had been from the beginning, and had remained without any change, were thus demolished and bowed down. In short, the Prophet intended by all means to raise up to confidence the minds of the godly, so that they should become fully persuaded that God's power to deliver them would be the same as that which their fathers had formerly experienced; for there is no other support under adverse, and especially under despairing circumstances, than that the faithful should know that they are still under the protection of that God who has adopted them. This is the reason why the Prophet amplifies, in so striking a manner, on the subject of God's power.

And hence also he subjoins, that the ways of ages are those of God. Some render the clause, "the ways of the world." The word עולם, oulam, however, means properly an age, or perpetual time. The Prophet, I have no doubt, means by ways of ages, the wonderful means which God is wont to adopt for the defense of his Church; for we are ever wont to reduce God's wonder to our own understanding, while it is his purpose to perfect, in a manner that is wonderful, the work of our salvation. Hence the Prophet bids the faithful here to raise upwards their thoughts, and to conceive something greater of God's power than what they can naturally comprehend. If we take the ways of eternity, in this sense, then they are to be understood as in opposition to those means which are known and usual. They are his daily ways, when the sun rises and sets, when the spring succeeds the winter, when the earth produces fruit; though even these are so many miracles, yet they are his common ways. But God has ways of eternity that is he has means unknown to us by which he can deliver us from death, whenever it may please him.

But yet, if any prefer taking the ways of eternity as signifying the continued power of God, which has ever appeared from the beginning, the sense would be appropriate and not less useful: for it especially avails to confirm our faith, when we consider that God's power has ever been the same from the creation of heaven and earth, that it has never been lessened or undergone any change. Since, then, God has successively manifested his power through all ages, we ought hence to learn that we have no reason to despair, though he may for a time conceal his hand; for he is not on that account deprived of his right. He ever retains the sovereignty of the world. We ought, then, to be attentive to the ways of ages, that is, to the demonstration of that power, which was manifested in the creation of the world, and still continues to be manifested. [55] It follows —

Habakkuk 3:7

7. I saw the tents of Cushan in affliction: and the curtains of the land of Midian did tremble.

7. Pro iniquitate (vel, pro nihilo, alii vertunt) vidi tentoria Chusan (vel, Aethiopiae;) contremiscent cortinae (vel, pelles) terrae Madian.

The Prophet relates here, no doubt, whatever might bring comfort to the miserable Jews, as they thought themselves rejected and in a manner alienated from God. Hence the Prophet mentions here other deliverances, which were clear evidences of God's constant favor towards his chosen people. He had hitherto spoken of their redemption, and he will presently return to the same subject: but he introduces here other histories; as though he had said, that it was not only at one time that God had testified how much he loved the race of Abraham, and how inviolable was the covenant he had made; but that he had given the same testimonies at various times: for as he had also defended his people against other enemies, the conclusion was obvious, that God's hand was thus made manifest, that the children of Abraham might know that they were not deceived, when they were adopted by him.

Hence Habakkuk mentions the tents of Chushan as another evidence of God's power in preserving his people, and the curtains of Midian; for we know how wonderful was the work, when the Jews were delivered by the hand of Gideon; and the same was the case with respect to the king of Chosen.

We now, then, understand the design of the Prophet: for as he knew that the time was near when the Jews might succumb to despair in their great adversities, he reminds them of the evidences of God's favor and power, which had been given to their fathers, that they might entertain firm hope in time to come, and be fully persuaded that God would be their deliverer, as he had been formerly to their fathers.

Prayer

Grant, Almighty God, that as we have a continual contest with powerful enemies, we may know that we are defended by thine hand, and that even thou art fighting for us when we are at rest; so that we may boldly contend under thy protection, and never be wearied, nor yield to Satan and the wicked, or to any temptations; but firmly proceed in the course of our warfare: and however much thou mayest often humble us, so as to make us to tremble under thine awful judgement, may we yet never cease to entertain firm hope, since thou hast once promised to be to us an eternal Father in thine eternal and only-begotten Son, but being confirmed by the invincible constancy of faith, may we so submit ourselves to thee, as to bear all our afflictions patiently, till thou gatherest us at length into that blessed rest, which has been procured for us by the blood of thine own Son. Amen.

LECTURE ONE HUNDRED AND SIXTEENTH

We said yesterday that the Prophet spoke of the king of Chusan and of the Midianites, in order to strengthen the minds of the godly, and to set before their eyes the continued aid of God, so that they might venture to feel assured that he would not act otherwise towards the Church to the end of the world, then what he had done from the beginning. The meaning, then, is sufficiently evident. We must now consider the words.

Some understand by the word, אוֹן, aun, nothing, or vanity; as though the Prophet had said, that the tells of Cushan had been reduced to nothing: but another sense is more probable; I have seen the tents of Cushan on account of his iniquity; [56] that is, the reward which God had repaid, for the iniquity of the king of Cushan had been made manifest. The Prophet says that he had seen it, because it was evident and known to all. We now perceive what is meant that God had been a just judge against the army of Cushan; for as they had unjustly assailed the Israelites, so a just reward was rendered to them. The account of this we have in Judges 3. Chusan, the king of Mesopotamia, had well-nigh destroyed the Israelites, when the Lord put him to flight with all his forces. Some render the words, "The tents of Ethiopia," as though it was written thus; but this is strained, and contrary to the rules of grammar; and besides, the following clause confirms what I have said; for the Prophet mentions the slaughter with which God destroyed the Midianites, who had also nearly overwhelmed the miserable people. He says that their curtains trembled, or their dwellings: for God, without the hand or sword of men, drove them into such madness, that they slew one another, as the sacred history testifies. See Judg. 6:1, Judg. 7:1. It now follows —

Habakkuk 3:8

8. Was the Lord displeased against the rivers? was thine anger against the rivers? was thy wrath against the sea, that thou didst ride upon thine horses and thy chariots of salvation?

8. An contra fluvios iratus es, Jehova? an contra fluvios indignatio tua? an contra mare furor tuus (vel, ira tua)? quia equitasti super equos tuos; quadridge tuae salus.

The Prophet here applies the histories to which he has already referred, for the purpose of strengthening the hope of the faithful; so that they might know these to be so many proofs and pledges of God's favor towards them, and that they might thus cheerfully look for his aid, and not succumb to temptation in their adversities. When he asks, was God angry with the rivers and the sea, he no doubt intended in this way to awaken the thoughts of the faithful, that they might consider the design of God in the works which he had already mentioned; for it would have been unreasonable that God should show his wrath against rivers and the sea; why should he be angry with lifeless elements? The Prophet then shows that God had another end in view when he dried the sea, when he stopped the course of Jordan, and when he gave other evidences of his power. Doubtless God did not regard the sea and the rivers; for that would have been unreasonable. It then follows that these changes were testimonies of God's favor towards his Church: and hence the Prophet subjoins, that God rode on his horses, and that his chariots were for salvation to his people. [57] We now perceive the Prophet's meaning, which interpreters have not understood, or at least have not explained.

We now, then, see why the Prophet puts these questions: and a question has much more force when it refers to what is in no way doubtful. What! can God be angry with rivers? Who can imagine God to be so unreasonable as to disturb the sea and to change the nature of things, when a certain order has been established by his own command? Why should he dry the sea, except he had something in view, even the deliverance of his Church? except he intended to save his people from extreme danger, by stretching forth his hand to the Israelites, when they thought themselves utterly lost? He therefore denies, that when God dried the Red Sea, and when he stopped the flowing of Jordan, he had put forth his power against the sea or against the river, as though he was angry with them. The design of God, says the Prophet, was quite another; for God rode on his horses, that is, he intended to show that all the elements were under his command, and that for the salvation of his people. That God, then, might be the redeemer of his Church, he constrained Jordan to turn back its course, he constrained the Red Sea to make a passage for his miserable captives, who would have otherwise been exposed to the slaughter of their enemies. There was indeed no hope of saving Israel, without a passage being suddenly opened to them through the Red Sea.

Hence all these miracles were designed to show that God had become the redeemer of his Church, and had put forth his power for the salvation of those whom he had taken under his protection: and it is easy from this fact to conclude, that the same help ought to be expected from God by posterity; for God was not induced by some sudden impulse to change the nature of things, but exhibited a proof of his favor: and his grace is perpetual, and flows in an even course, though not according to the apprehension of men; for it suffers some interruptions, because God exercises the faithful under the cross; yet his goodness never ceases. It hence follows that the faithful are to entertain hope; for God, when he pleases, and when he sees it expedient, will really show the same power which was formerly exhibited to the fathers. It now follows —

Habakkuk 3:9

9. Thy bow was made quite naked, according to the oaths of the tribes, even thy word. Selah. Thou didst cleave the earth with rivers.

9. Nudando nudatus fuit (vel, manifestatione manifestus fuit) arcus tuus; juramenta Tribuum, sermo: Selach: fluviis scindes terram.

The Prophet explains the same thing more clearly in this verse — that the power of God was formerly manifested for no other reason but that the children of Abraham might be taught to expect from him a continued deliverance: for he says that the bow of God was made bare. By the bow, he means also the sword and other weapons; as though he had said, that God was then armed, as we have found declared before. God therefore was then furnished with weapons, and marched to the battle, having undertaken the cause of his chosen people, that he might defend them against the wicked. Since it was so, we hence see that these miracles were not to avail only for one period, but were intended perpetually to encourage the faithful to look ever for the aid of God, even in the midst of death; for he can find escapes, though they may not appear to us.

We now see the import of the text; but he emphatically adds, The oaths of the tribes; for hereby he more fully confirms that God had not then assisted the children of Abraham, so as to discard them afterwards; but that he had really proved how true he was in his promises; for by the oaths of (or to) the tribes he means the covenant that God had made not only with Abraham, but also with his posterity for ever. He puts oaths in the plural number, because God had not only once promised to be a God to Abraham and to his seed, but had often repeated the same promise, in order that faith might be rendered more certain, inasmuch as we have need of more than one thing to confirm us. For we see how our infirmity always vacillates, unless God supplies us with many props. As, then, God had often confirmed his servant Abraham, the Prophet speaks here of his oaths: but then as to the substance, the oath of God is the same; which was, that he had taken the race of Abraham under his protection, and promised that they should be to him a peculiar people, and, especially, that he had united the people under one head; for except Christ had been introduced, that covenant of God would not have been ratified nor valid. As, then, God had once included every thing when he said to Abraham, "I am God Almighty, and I shall be a God to you and to your children;" it is certain that nothing was added when God afterwards confirmed the faith of Abraham: but yet the Prophet does not without reason use the plural number; it was done, that the faithful might recomb with less fear on God's promise, seeing, that it had been so often and by so many words confirmed.

He calls them too the oaths to the tribes: for though God had spoken to Abraham and afterwards to Moses, yet the promise was deposited in the hands of Abraham, and of the patriarchs, and afterwards in those of Moses, that the people might understated that it belonged equally to them; for it would have been no great matter to promise what we read of to a few men only. But Abraham was as it were the depository; and it was a certain solemn stipulation made with his whole race. We hence see why the Prophet here mentions the tribes rather than Abraham, or the patriarchs or Moses. He had indeed a special regard to those of his own time, in order to confirm them, that they might not doubt but that God would extend to them also the same power. How so? Because God had formerly wrought in a wonderful manner for the deliverance of his people. Why? That he might prove himself to be true and faithful. In what respect? Because he had said, that he would be the protector of his people; and he did not adopt a few men only, but the whole race of Abraham. Since it was so, why should not his posterity hope for that which they knew was promised to their fathers? for the truth of God can never fail. Though many ages had passed away, the faith of his people ought to have remained certain, for God intended to show himself to be the same as he had been formerly known by their fathers.

He afterwards adds רמא, amer, which means a word or speech; but it is to be taken here for a fixed and an irrevocable word. The word, רמא, amer, he says; that is, as they say, the word and the deed: for when we say, that words are given, we often understand that those who liberally promise are false men, and that we are only trifled with and disappointed when we place confidence in them. But the term, word, is sometimes taken in a good sense. "This is the word," we often say, when we intend to remove every doubt. We now then perceive what the Prophet meant by adding רמא amer, the word. "O Lord, thou hast not given mere words to and people; but what has proceeded from thy mouth has been found to be true and valid. Such, therefore, is and faithfulness in thy promises, that we ought not to entertains the least doubt as to the event. As soon as thou givest to us any hope, we ought to feel assured of its accomplishment, as though it were not a word but the exhibition of the thing itself." In short, by this term the Prophet commends the faithfulness of God, lest we should harbour doubts as to his promises. [58]

He then says, that by rivers had been cleft the earth. He refers, I doubt not, to the history we read in Nu 14; for the Lord, when the people were nearly dead through thirst, drew forth water from the rock, and caused a river to flow wherever the people journeyed. As then he had cleft the earth to make a perpetual course for the stream, and thus supplied the people in dry places with abundance of water, the Prophet says here, that the earth had been cleft by rivers or streams. It was indeed but one river; but he amplifies, and justly so, that remarkable work of God. He afterwards adds —

Habakkuk 3:10

10. The mountains saw thee, and they trembled: the overflowing of the water passed by: the deep uttered his voice, and lifted up his hands on high.

10. Viderunt me, timuerunt montes; inundatio (vel, gurges) aquarum transivit; dedit abyssus vocen suam; in altum manus suas sustulit (vel, altitudo, [רום]; potest tam in casu nominandi legi quam in accusative.)

Habakkuk proceeds with the history of the people's redemption. We have said what his object was, even this that the people, though in an extreme state of calamity, might yet entertain hope of God's favor; for he became not a Redeemer to the race of Abraham for one time, but that he might continue the same favor to them to the end.

He says that mountains had seen and grieved. Some explain this allegorically of kings, and say, that they grieved when envy preyed on them: but this view is too strained. The Prophet, I have no doubt, means simply, that the mountains obeyed God, so as to open a way for his people. At the same time, the verb לול, chul, signifies not only to grieve, but also to bring forth, and then to fall and to abide in the same place. We might then with no less propriety read thus — see thee did the mountains, and were still, or fell down; that is, they were subservient to thy command, and did not intercept the way of thy people. I think the real meaning of the Prophet to be, that God had formerly imprinted on all the elements evident marks of his paternal favor, so that the posterity of Abraham might ever confide in him as their deliverer in all their distresses: and even the context requires this meaning; for he subjoins -

The stream or the inundation of waters, etc.: and this second part cannot be explained allegorically. We then see, that the import of the words is — That God removed all obstacles, so that neither mountains, nor waters, nor sea, nor rivers, intercepted the passage of the people. He says now, that the inundation of waters had passed away. This applies both to Jordan and to the Red Sea; for God separated the Red Sea, so that the waters stood apart, contrary to the laws of nature, and the same thing happened to Jordan; for the flowing of the water was stayed, and a way was opened, so that the people passed over dryshod into the land of Canaan. Thus took place what is said by the Prophet, the stream of waters passed away. We indeed know that such is the abundance of waters in the sea and in the rivers, that they cannot be dried up: when therefore waters disappear, it is what is beyond the course of nature. The Prophet, therefore, records this miracle, that the faithful might know, that though the whole world were resisting, their salvation would still be certain; for the Lord can surmount whatever impediments there may be.

He then ascribes life to waters; for he says, that the abyss gave its voice, and also, that the deep lifted up its hands; or that the abyss with uplifted hands was ready to obey God. It is a striking personification; for though the abyss is void of intelligence, and it cannot speak, yet the Prophet says, that the abyss with its voice and uplifted hands testified its obedience, when God would have his people to pass through to the promised land. When anxious to testify our obedience, we do this both with our voice and in our gesture. When any one is willing to do what is commanded, he says, "Here I am," or "I promise to do this." As, then, servants respond to others, so the Prophet says, that a voice was uttered by the abyss. The abyss indeed uttered no voice; but the event itself surpassed all voices. Now when a whole people meet together, they raise their hands; for their consent cannot be understood except by the outstretching of the hands, and hence came the word hand-extending, χειροτονια. This similitude the Prophet now takes, and says, that the abyss raised up its hands; that is, shows its consent by this gesture. As when men declare by this sign that they will do what they are bidden; so also the abyss lifted up its hands. If we read, The deep raised up its hands, the sense will be the same. [59] Let us proceed -

Habakkuk 3:11

11. The sun and moon stood still in their habitation: at the light of thine arrows they went, and at the shining of thy glittering spear.

11. Sol, luna stetit in habitaculo, ad lucem sagittarum tuarum ambulabunt, ad splendorum fulguris hastae tuae.

Here the Prophet refers to another history; for we know that when Joshua fought, and when the day was not long enough to slay the enemies, the day was prolonged according to his prayer, (Jos 10:12.) He seems indeed to have authoritatively commanded the sun to stay its course: but there is no doubt, but that having been answered as to his prayer, when he expressed this, he commanded the sun, as he did, through the secret impulse of the Holy Spirit: and we know that the sun would not have stopped in its course, except the moon also was stayed. There must indeed have been the same action as to these two luminaries.

Hence Habakkuk says, that the sun and moon stood still in their habitation; that is, that the sun then rested as it were in its dwelling. When it was hastening in its course, it then stood still for the benefit of God's people. The sun then and the moon stood, — How? At the light of thy arrows shall they walk. Some refer this to the pillar of fire, as though the Prophet had said, that the Israelites walked by that light, by which God guided them: but I doubt not but that this is said of the sun. The whole sentence is thus connected — that the sun and moon walked, not as from the beginning, but at the light of God's arrows; that is, when instead of God's command, which the sun had received from the beginning as its direction, the sun had God's arrows, which guided it, retarded its course, or restrained the velocity which it had before. There is then an implied contrast between the progress of the sun which it had by nature to that day, and that new direction, when the sun was retained, that it might give place to the arrows of God, and to the sword and the spear; for by the arrows and the spear he means nothing else but the weapons of the elect people; for we know, that when that people fought under the protection of God, they were armed as it were from above. As then it is said of Gideon, "The sword of God and of Gideon;" so also in this place the Prophet calls whatever armor the people of Israel had, the arrows of God and his spear; for that people could not move — no, not a finger's breadth — without the command of God. The sun then was wont before to regard the ordinary command, of which we read in Genesis; but it was then directed for another purpose: for it had regard to the arrows of God flying on the earth as lightning; and it had regard to the arrows, as though it stood astonished and dared not to advance. Why? because it behoved it to submit to God while he was carrying on war. ⁶⁰ We now then perceive how much kindness is included in these words.

What, therefore, we have already referred to, ought to be borne in mind — that in this place there is no frigid narrative, but such things are brought before the faithful as avail to confirm their hope, that they may feel assured, that the power of God is sufficient for the purpose of delivering them; for it was for this end that he formerly wrought so many miracles. It follows —

Habakkuk 3:12

12. Thou didst march through the land in indignation, thou didst thresh the heathen in anger.

12. In ira calcasti terram (vel, ambulasti super terram; [צעד] enim significat ambulare;) in ira (est tamen aliud nomen, ergo vertamus uno loco, indignationem, vel, furorem, — in furore) triturasti gentes (vel, triturabis.)

The Prophet relates here the entrance of the people into the land of Canaan, that the faithful might know that their fathers would not have obtained so many victories had not God put forth the power and strength of his hand. Hence he says, that God himself had trampled on the land in anger. For how could the Israelites have dared to attack so many nations, who had lately come forth from so miserable a bondage? They had indeed been in the desert for forty years; but they were always trembling and fearful, and we also know that they were weak and feeble. How then was it, that they overcame most powerful kings? that they made war with nations accustomed to war? Doubtless God himself trod down the land in his wrath, and also threshed the nations: as it is said in Ps 44:5,

"It was not by their own sword that they got the land of Canaan; neither their own power, nor their own hand saved them; but the Lord showed favor to them, and became their Deliverer."

Justly then does the Prophet ascribe this to God, that he himself walked over the land; for otherwise the Israelites would never have dared to move a foot. Doubtless, they could never have been settled in that land, had not God gone before them. Hence when God did tread on the land in his anger, then it became a quiet habitation to the children of Abraham; warlike nations were then easily and without much trouble conquered by the Israelites, though they were previously very weak.

We now see, that the Prophet sets forth here before the eyes of the people their entrance into the land, that they might know that God did not in vain put to flight so many nations at one time; but that the land of Canaan might be the perpetual inheritance of his chosen people.

The Prophet changes often the tenses of the verbs, inconsistently with the common usage of the Hebrew language; but it must be observed, that he so refers to those histories, as though God were continually carrying on his operations; and as though his presence was to be looked for in adversities, the same as what he had granted formerly to the fathers. Hence the change of tenses does not obscure the sense, but, on the contrary, shows to us the design of the Prophet, and helps us to understand the meaning. It follows at length -

Habakkuk 3:13

13. Thou wentest forth for the salvation of thy people, even for salvation with thine anointed; thou woundedst the head out of the house of the wicked, by discovering the foundation unto the neck. Selah.

13. Egressus es in salutem populi tui, in salutem cum Christo tuo; transfodisti caput e domo impii, nudando fundamentum usque ad collum. Selah.

The Prophet applies again to the present state of the people what he had before recorded — that God went forth with his Christ for the salvation of his people. Some consider that there is understood a particle of comparison, and repeat the verb twice, "As thou didst then go forth for the deliverance of thy people, so now wilt thou go forth for the deliverance of thy people with thy Christ." But this repetition is strained. I therefore take the words of the Prophet simply as they are — that God went forth for the deliverance of his people. But when God's people are spoken of, their gratuitous adoption must ever be remembered. How was it that the children of Abraham became the peculiar people of God? Did this proceed from any worthiness? Did it come to them naturally? None of these things can be alleged. Though then they differed in nothing from other nations, yet God was pleased to choose them to be a people to himself. By the title, the people of God, is therefore intimated their adoption. Now this adoption was not temporary or momentary, but was to continue to the end. Hence it was easy for the faithful to draw this conclusion — that they were to hope from God the same help as what he had formerly granted to the fathers.

Thou wentest forth, he says, for the salvation, for the salvation of thy people. He repeats the word salvation, and not without reason; for he wished to call attention to this point, as when he had said before — that God had not in vain manifested, by so many miracles, his power, as though he were angry with the sea and with rivers, but had respect to the preservation of his people. Since then the salvation of the Church has ever been the design of God in working miracles, why should the faithful be now cast down, when for a time they were oppressed by adversities? for God ever remains the same: and why should they despond, especially since that ancient deliverance, and also those many deliverances, of which he had hitherto spoken, are so many evidences of his everlasting covenant. These indeed ought to be connected with the word of God; that is, with that promise, according to which he had received the children of Abraham into favor for the purpose of protecting them to the end. "For salvation, for salvation," says the Prophet, and that of his elect people.

He adds, with thy Christ. This clause still more confirms what Habakkuk had in view — that God had been from the beginning the deliverer of his people in the person of the Mediator. When God, therefore, delivered his people from the hand of Pharaoh, when he made a way for them to pass through the Red Sea, when he redeemed them by doing wonders, when he subdued before them the most powerful nations, when he changed the laws of nature in their behalf — all these things he did through the Mediator. For God could never have been propitious either to Abraham himself or to his posterity, had it not been for the intervention of a Mediator. Since then it has ever been the office of the Mediator to preserve in safety the Church of God, the Prophet takes it now for granted, that Christ was now manifested in much clearer light than formerly; for David was his lively image, as well as his successors. God then gave a living representation of his Christ when he erected a kingdom in the person of David; and he promised that this kingdom should endure as long as the sun and moon should shine in the heavens. Since, then, there were in the time of Habakkuk clearer prophecies than in past times respecting the eternity of this kingdom, ought not the people to have taken courage, and to have known of a certainty that God would be their Deliverer, when Christ should come? We now then apprehend the meaning of the Prophet. [61] But I cannot now go farther; I shall defer the subject until tomorrow.

Prayer

Grant, Almighty God, that as thou hast so often and in such various ways testified formerly how much care and solicitude thou hast for the salvation of those who rely and call on thee, — O grant, that we at this day may experience the same: and though thy face is justly hid from us, may we yet never hesitate to flee to thee, since thou hast made a covenant through thy Son, which is founded in thine infinite mercy. Grant then, that we, being humbled in true penitence, may so surrender ourselves to thy Son, that we may be led to thee, and find thee to be no less a Father to us than to the faithful of old, as thou everywhere testifies to us in thy word, until at length being freed from all troubles and dangers, we come to that blessed rest which thy Son has purchased for us by his own blood. Amen.

LECTURE ONE HUNDRED AND SEVENTEENTH

We explained yesterday why the Prophet says that God went forth for the salvation of the elect people with his Christ. His purpose was to confirm still more the faithful in the hope of their deliverance; for God is not only the same, and never changes his purpose, but the same Mediator also performs his office, through whom the people were formerly preserved. We must also notice this difference, to which I referred yesterday; for as God had then more clearly manifested Christ, with more cheerfulness it behaved the faithful to go on, as they had so remarkable a pledge of God's favor, inasmuch as God had promised that the kingdom of God would be for ever.

He adds, that wounded was the head from the house of the wicked; that is, that there was no power which had not been laid prostrate by God for the sake of his people; and we know that all the great kings were formerly destroyed, in order that favor might be shown to God's people. The other comparison seems different, and yet its object is the same — that God had made bare the foundation to the neck; that is, that he had destroyed from the roots his enemies; for by foundation he means, in a metaphorical sense, whatever stability there was in these enemies, and that this was torn up and overthrown to the very neck, that is, to the very summit; for the body of men, we know, is covered from the neck to the feet. And he says that their houses, that is their families, were made bare to the neck, for the Lord had destroyed them all from the bottom to the top. We now understand what the Prophet meant.

As to the word סלה, selah, I have hitherto said nothing; but I shall now briefly refer to what the Hebrew interpreters think. Some explain it by לעולם, laoulam, "for ever;" and by עד ועד, od uod, "yet and yet;" as though, when this word is inserted, the Holy Spirit pronounced what is to be for ever. Others render it by אמן, amen, as though God testified that what is said is true and indubitable. But as it never occurs except in this song and in the Psalms, and does not always comport with what they say, that is, that it denotes certainty or perpetuity, I prefer embracing the opinion of those who think that it refers to singing, and not to things. And what they add is also probable, if we regard its etymology, for the word means to raise or to elevate; and it was therefore put down to remind the singers to raise their voice. But as it is a thing of no great importance, it is enough shortly to state what others think. Let us now go on —

Habakkuk 3:14

14. Thou didst strike through with his staves the head of his villages: they came out as a whirlwind to scatter me: their rejoicing was as to devour the poor secretly.

14. Perforasti baculis ejus caput villarum ejus; prosilierunt instar turbinis ad dispellendum me; exultatio eorum sicut ad vorandum pauperem in abscondito.

At the beginning of this verse the Prophet pursues the same subject — that God had wounded all the enemies of his people; and he says that the head of villages or towns had been wounded, though some think that פרזים, perezim, mean rather the inhabitants of towns; for the Hebrews call fortified towns or villages פרזות, perezut, and the word is commonly found in the feminine gender; but as it is here a masculine noun, it is thought that it means the inhabitants. At the same time this does not much affect the subject; for the Prophet simply means, that not only things had been overthrown by God's hand, but also all the provinces under their authority; as though he had said that God's vengeance, when his purpose was to defend his people, advanced through all the villages and through every region, so that not a corner was safe. [62] But we must also notice what follows — with his rods. The Prophet means that the wicked had been smitten by their own sword. Though the word rods is put here, it is yet to be taken for all kinds of instruments or weapons; it is the same as though it was said that they had been wounded by their own hands. [63]

We now perceive the import of this clause — that God not only put forth his strength when he purposed to crush the enemies of his people, but that he had also smitten them with infatuation and madness, so that they destroyed themselves by their own hands. And this was done, as in the case of the Midianites, who, either by turning their swords against one another, fell by mutual wounds, or by slaying themselves, perished by their own hands. (Jud 7:2.) We indeed often read of the wicked that they ensnared themselves, fell into the pit which they had made, and, in short, perished through their own artifices; and the Prophet says here that the enemies of the Church had fallen, through God's singular kindness, though no one rose up against them; for they had transfixed or wounded themselves by their own staff. Some read — "Thou hast cursed his sceptres and the head of his villages;" but the interpretation which I have given is much more appropriate.

He adds, that they came like a whirlwind. It is indeed a verb in the future tense; but the sentence must be thus rendered — "When they rushed as a whirlwind to cast me down, when their exultation was to devour the poor in their hiding-places." It is indeed only a single verb, but it comes from רעס, sor, which means a whirlwind, and we cannot render it otherwise than by a paraphrase. They rushed, he says, like a whirlwind. The Prophet here enlarges on the subject of God's power, for he had checked the enemies of his people when they rushed on with so much impetuosity. Had their advance been slow God might have frustrated their attempts without a miracle, but as their own madness rendered them precipitate, and made them to be like a whirlwind, God's power was more clearly known in restraining such violence. We now understand the import of what is here said; for the Prophet's special object is not to complain of the violent and impetuous rage of enemies, but to exalt the power of God in checking the violent assaults of those enemies whom he saw raging against his people.

He subjoins, their exultation was to devour the poor. He intimates that there was nothing in the world capable of resisting the wicked, had not God brought miraculous help from heaven; for when they came to devour the poor, they came not to wage war, but to devour the prey like wild beasts. Then he says, to devour the poor in secret. He means, that the people of God had no strength to resist, except help beyond all hope came from heaven. [64]

The import of the whole is — that when the miserable Israelites were without any protection, and exposed to the rage and cruelty of their enemies, they had been miraculously helped; for the Lord destroyed their enemies by their own swords; and that when they came, as it were to enjoy a victory, to take the prey, they were laid prostrate by the hand of God: hence his power shone forth more brightly. It follows —

Habakkuk 3:15

15. Thou didst walk through the sea with thine horses, through the heap of great waters.

15. Viam fecisti in mari equis tuis per acervum aquarum magnarum.

Some read, "Thou hast trodden thy horses in the sea;" but it is a solecism, that is quite evident. Others, "Thou hast trodden in the sea by thy horses." But what need is there of seeking such strained explanations, since the verb דרך, darek, means to go or to march? The Prophet's meaning is by no means doubtful — that God would make a way for himself in the sea, and on his own horses. How? even when great waters were gathered into a mass. The Prophet again refers to the history of the passage through the Red Sea; for it was a work of God, as it has been said, worthy of being remembered above all other works: it is therefore no wonder that the Prophet dwells so much in setting forth this great miracle. Thou then didst make a way for thy horses — where? in the sea; which was contrary to nature. And then he adds, The heap of waters: for the waters had been gathered together, and a firm and thick mass appeared, which was not according to nature; for we know that water is a fluid, and that hardly a drop of water can stand without flowing. [65] How then was it that he stopped the course of Jordan, and that the Red Sea was divided? These were evidences of God's incomprehensible power, and rightly ought these to have added courage to the faithful, knowing, as they ought to have done, that nothing could have opposed their salvation, which God was not able easily to remove, whenever it pleased him. It follows —

Habakkuk 3:16

16. When I heard, my belly trembled; my lips quivered at the voice: rottenness entered into my bones, and I trembled in myself, that I might rest in the day of trouble: when he cometh up unto the people, he will invade them with his troops.

16. Audivit, et contremuit (vel, tumultuatus est) venter meus; ad vocem trepidarunt labia mea; ingressa est putredo in ossa mea; et apud me tumultuatus sum (ad verbum, tumultuabitur; sed diximus heri de temporibus verborum,) ad ascendedum ad populum, excidet eum (vel, colliget se.)

Those interpreters are mistaken in my view, who connect the verb, "I have heard," with the last verse, as though the Prophet had said, that he had conceived dread from those evidences of God's power: for the Prophet had no occasion to fear in regarding God as armed with unexpected power for the salvation of his people; there was no reason for such a thing. Hence these things do not agree together. But he returns again to that dread which he had entertained on account of God's voice in those terrific threatening which we before referred to. We must always bear in mind the Prophet's design — that his object was to humble the faithful, that they might suppliantly acknowledge to God their sins and solicit his forgiveness. His purpose also was to animate them with strong hope, that they might nevertheless look for deliverance. He had already said at the beginning, "Lord, I have heard thy voice; I feared." He now repeats the same thing: for if he had spoken only of that terrific voice, the faithful might have been overwhelmed with despair; he therefore wished opportunely to prevent this evil, by interposing what might have comforted them. For this reason he recited these histories, by which God had proved that he was armed with invincible power to save his Church. Having done this, he applies his general doctrine to present circumstances, and says, "I have heard." What had he heard? even those judgements with which God had determined to visit the contumacy of his people. Since, then, God had threatened his people with a horrible destruction, the Prophet says now, that he had heard and trembled, so that he had been confounded. He speaks in the singular number; but this was done, as we have said, because he represented the whole people, as was the case before (which escaped my notice) when he said, his enemies came like whirlwind to cast him down; for certainly he did not then speak of himself but of the ancient people. As, then, the Prophet here undertakes the cause of the whole Church, he speaks as though he were the collective body of the people: and so he says that he had heard; but the faithful speak here as with one mouth, that they had heard, and that their inside trembled

Some read, "I was dismayed, or I feared, and my inside trembled at his voice." He takes לוק, kul, voice, not for report, but, as it has been said, for threatening. The faithful, then, declare here, that they dreaded the voice of God, before he had executed his judgements, or before he inflicted the punishment which he had threatened. He says, quiver did my lips. The verb ללצ, tsalel, means sometimes to tingle, and so some render it here, "Tingle did my lips;" but this is not suitable, and more tolerable is the rendering of others, "Palpitate did my lips." The Hebrews say that what is meant is that motion in the lips which fear or trembling produces. I therefore render the words, "quiver did my lips;" as when one says in our language, Mes levres ont barbate; that is, when the whole body shakes with trembling, not only a noise is made by the clashing of the teeth, but an agitation is also observed in the lips.

Enter, he says, did rottenness into my bones and within myself I made a noise, (it is the verb זגר, regaz, again,) or I trembled. No doubt the Prophet describes here the dread, which could not have been otherwise than produced by the dreadful vengeance of God. It hence follows that he does not treat here of those miracles which were, on the contrary, calculated to afford an occasion of rejoicing both to the Prophet and to the whole of the chosen people; but that the vengeance of God, such as had been predicted, is described here.

He now adds, That I may rest in the day of affliction [66] There seems to be here an inconsistency — that the Prophet was affected with grief even to rottenness, that he trembled throughout his members with dread, and now that all this availed to produce rest. But we must inquire how rest is to be obtained through these trepidations, and dreads, and tremblings. We indeed know that the more hardened the wicked become against God, the more grievous ruin they ever procure for themselves. But there is no way of obtaining rest, except for a time we tremble within ourselves, that is, except God's judgement awakens us, yea, and reduces us almost to nothing. Whosoever therefore securely slumbers, will be confounded in the day of affliction; but he who in time anticipates the wrath of God, and is touched with fear, as soon as he hears that God the judge is at hand, provides for himself the most secure rest in the day of affliction. We now then see, that the right way of seeking rest is set forth here by the Prophet, when he says, that he had been confounded, and that rottenness had entered into his bones that he could have no comfort, except he pined away as one half-dead: and the design of the Prophet, as I have already said, was to exhort the faithful to repentance. But we cannot truly and from the heart repent, until our sins become displeasing to us: and the hatred of sin proceeds from the fear of God, and that sorrow which Paul regards as the mother of repentance. (2Co 7:10.)

This exhortation is also very necessary for us in the present day. We see how inclined we are by nature to indifference; and when God brings before us our sins, and then sets before us his wrath, we are not moved; and when we entertain any fear, it soon vanishes. Let us, then, know that no rest can be to us in the day of distress, except we tremble within ourselves, except dread lays hold on all our faculties, and except all our soul becomes almost rotten. And hence it is said in Ps 4:4, "Tremble, and ye shall not sin." And Paul also shows that the true and profitable way of being angry is, when one is angry with his sins (Eph 4:26,) and when we tremble within ourselves. In the same manner does the Prophet describe the beginnings of repentance, when he says, that the faithful trembled in their bowels, and were so shaken within, that even their lips quivered, and, in short, (and this is the sum of the whole,) that all their senses felt consternation and fear.

He says, When he shall ascend: he speaks, no doubt, of the Chaldeans; When therefore the enemy shall ascend against the people, that he may cut them off: for הדג or דוג, gade or gud, means to cut off, and it means also to gather, and so some render it, "that he may gather them:" but the other meaning is better, "when the enemy shall ascend, that he may cut them off." If one would have the word God to be understood, I do not object: for the Prophet does not otherwise speak of the Chaldeans than as the ministers and executioners of God's wrath.

In short, he intimates, that they who had been moved and really terrified by God's vengeance, would be in a quiet state when God executed his judgements. How so? because they would calmly submit to the rod, and look for a happy deliverance from their evils; for their minds would be seasonably prepared for patience, and then the Lord would also console them, as it is said in Ps 51:17, that he despises not contrite hearts. When, therefore, the faithful are in a suitable time humbled, and when they thus anticipate the judgement of God, they then find a rest prepared for them in his bosom. It follows —

Hab. 3:17, 18

17. Although the fig tree shall not blossom, neither shall fruit be in the vines; the labour of the olive shall fail, and the fields shall yield no meat; the flock shall be cut off from the fold, and there shall be no herd in the stalls:

17. Quia ficus non florebit, et nullus erit fructus in veneis; fraudabit opus olivae, et agri non producent cibum (ad verbum, non faciet cibum; est mutatio numeri, sed esset asperior illa translatio; Agri igitur non producent cibum: porro hac voce comprehendi triticum, legumina, et quae ad victum pertinent, satis liquet;) excissum est ab ovili pecus, et nullus bos in stabulis:

18. Yet I will rejoice in the Lord, I will joy in the God of my salvation.

18. Ego autem in Jehova exultabo, laetabor in Deo salutis meae.

The Prophet declares now at large what that rest would be of which he had spoken; it would be even this — that he would not cease to rejoice in God, even in the greatest afflictions. He indeed foresees how grievous the impending punishment would be, and he warns also and arouses the faithful, that they might perceive the approaching judgement of God. He says, Flourish shall not the fig, and no fruit shall be on the vines; fail shall the olive. First, the fig shall not flourish; then, the fields shall produce nothing; and lastly, the cattle and the sheep shall fail. Though the figs produce fruit without flowering, it is not yet an improper use of פרח, perech, which means strictly to bud. [67] He means that the desolation of the land was nigh at hand, and that the people would be reduced to extreme poverty. But it was an instance of rare virtue, to be able to rejoice in the Lord, when occasions of sorrow met him on every side.

The Prophet then teaches us what advantage it is to the faithful seasonably to submit to God, and to entertain serious fear when he threatens them, and when he summons them to judgement; and he shows that though they might perish a hundred times, they would yet not perish, for the Lord would ever supply them with occasions of joy, and would also cherish this joy within, so as to enable them to rise above all their adversities. Though, then, the land was threatened with famine, and though no food would be supplied to them, they would yet be able always to rejoice in the God of their salvation; for they would know him to be their Father, though for a time he severely chastised them. This is a delineation of that rest of which he made mention before.

The import of the whole is — "Though neither the figs, nor the vines, nor the olives, produce any fruit, and though the field be barren, though no food be given, yet I will rejoice in my God;" that is, our joy shall not depend on outward prosperity; for though the Lord may afflict us in an extreme degree, there will yet be always some consolation to sustain our minds, that they may not succumb under evils so grievous; for we are fully persuaded, that our salvation is in God's hand, and that he is its faithful guardian. We shall, therefore, rest quietly, though heaven and earth were rolled together, and all places were full of confusion; yea, though God fulminated from heaven, we shall yet be in a tranquil state of mind, looking for his gratuitous salvation.

We now perceive more clearly, that the sorrow produced by the sense of our guilt is recommended to us on account of its advantage; for nothing is worse than to provoke God's wrath to destroy us; and nothing is better than to anticipate it, so that the Lord himself may comfort us. We shall not always escape, for he may apparently treat us with severity; but though we may not be exempt from punishment, yet while he intends to humble us, he will give us reasons to rejoice: and then in his own time he will mitigate his severity, and by the effects will show himself propitious to us. Nevertheless, during the time when want or famine, or any other affliction, is to be borne, he will render us joyful with this one consolation, for, relying on his promises, we shall look for him as the God of our salvation. Hence, on one side Habakkuk sets the desolation of the land; and on the other, the inward joy which the faithful never fail to possess, for they are upheld by the perpetual favor of God. And thus he warns, as I have said, the children of God, that they might be prepared to bear want and famine, and calmly to submit to God's chastisements; for had he not exhorted them as he did, they might have failed a hundred times.

We may hence gather a most useful doctrine, — That whenever signs of God's wrath meet us in outward things, this remedy remains to us — to consider what God is to us inwardly; for the inward joy, which faith brings to us, can overcome all fears, terrors, sorrows and anxieties.

But we must notice what follows, In the God of my salvation: for sorrow would soon absorb all our thoughts, except God were present as our preserver. But how does he appear as such to the faithful? even when they estimate not his love by external things, but strengthen themselves by embracing the promise of his mercy, and never doubt but that he will be propitious to them; for it is impossible but that he will remember mercy even while he is angry. It follows —

Habakkuk 3:19

19. The Lord God is my strength, and he will make my feet like hinds' feet, and he will make me to walk upon mine high places. To the chief singer on my stringed instruments.

19. Jehova Dominus fotitudo mea, et ponet pedes meos quasi cervarum, et super excelsa mea ambulare me faciet. Prefecto in Neginothai (vel, in pulsationibus meis, vel, musicis instrumentis.)

He confirms the same truth, — that he sought no strength but in God alone. But there is an implied contrast between God and those supports on which men usually lean. There is indeed no one, who is not of a cheerful mind, when he possesses all necessary things, when no danger, no fear is impending: we are then courageous when all things smile on us. But the Prophet, by calling God his strength, sets him in opposition to all other supports; for he wishes to encourage the faithful to persevere in their hope, however grievously God might afflict them. His meaning then is, — that even when evils impetuously rage against us, when we vacillate and are ready to fall every moment, God ought then to be our strength; for the aid which he has promised for our support is all-sufficient. We hence see that the Prophet entertained firm hope, and by his example animated the faithful, provided they had God propitious, however might all other things fail them.

He will make, he says, my feet like those of hinds. I am inclined to refer this to their return to their own country, though some give this explanation, — "God will give the swiftest feet to his servants, so that they may pass over all obstacles to destroy their enemies;" but as they might think in their exile that their return was closed up against them, the Prophet introduces this most apt similitude, that God would give his people feet like those of hinds, so that they could climb the precipices of mountains, and dread no difficulties: He will then, he says, give me the feet of hinds, and make me to tread on my high places. Some think that this was said with regard to Judea, which is, as it is well known, mountainous; but I take the expression more simply in this way, — that God would make his faithful people to advance boldly and without fear along high places: for they who fear hide themselves and dare not to raise up the head, nor proceed openly along public roads; but the Prophet says, God will make me to tread on any high places

He at last adds, To the leader on my beatings. The first word some are wont to render conqueror. This inscription, To the leader, חצנמל, lamenat-sech, frequently occurs in the Psalms. To the conqueror, is the version of some; but it means, I have no doubt, the leader of the singers. Interpreters think that God is signified here by this title, for he presides over all the songs of the godly: and it may not inaptly be applied to him as the leader of the singers, as though the Prophet had said, — "God will be a strength to me; though I am weak in myself, I shall yet be strong in him; and he will enable me to surmount all obstacles, and I shall proceed boldly, who am now like one half-dead; and he will thus become the occasion of my song, and be the leader of the singers engaged in celebrating his praises, when he shall deliver from death his people in so wonderful a manner." We hence see that the connection is not unsuitable, when he says, that there would be strength for him in God; and particularly as giving of thanks belonged to the leader or the chief singer, in order that God's aid might be celebrated, not only privately but at the accustomed sacrifices, as was usually the case under the law. Those who explain it as denoting the beginning of a song, are extremely frigid and jejune in what they advance; I shall therefore pass it by.

He adds, on my beatings. This word, תוניגנ, neginoth, I have already explained in my work on the Psalms. Some think that it signifies a melody, others render it beatings (pulsationes) or notes (modos;) and others consider that musical instruments are meant. [68] I affirm nothing in a doubtful matter: and it is enough to bear in mind what we have said, — that the Prophet promises here to God a continual thanksgiving, when the faithful were redeemed, for not only each one would acknowledge that they had been saved by God's hand, but all would assemble together in the Temple, and there testify their gratitude, and not only with their voices confess God as their Deliverer, but also with instruments of music, as we know it to have been the usual custom under the Law.

PRAYER

Grant, Almighty God, that as we cease not daily to provoke thy wrath against us, and as the hardness and obstinacy of our flesh is so great, that it is necessary for us to be in various ways afflicted, — O grant, that we may patiently bear thy chastisements, and under a deep feeling of sorrow flee to thy mercy; and may we in the meantime persevere in the hope of that mercy, which thou hast promised, and which has been once exhibited towards us in Christ, so that we may not depend on the earthly blessings of this perishable life, but relying on thy word may proceed in the course of our calling, until we shall at length be gathered into that blessed rest, which is laid up for us in heaven, through Christ one Lord. Amen.

COMMENTARY ON ZEPHANIAH

CALVIN'S PREFACE TO ZEPHANIAH

ZEPHANIAH is placed the last of the Minor Prophets who performed their office before the Babylonian Captivity; and the inscription shows that he exercised his office of teaching at the same time with Jeremiah, about thirty years before the city was destroyed, the Temple pulled down, and the people led into exile. Jeremiah, it is true, followed his vocation even after the death of Josiah, while Zephaniah prophesied only during his reign.

The substance of his Book is this: He first denounces utter destruction on a people who were so perverse, that there was no hope of their repentance; — he then moderates his threatening, by denouncing God's judgments on their enemies, the Assyrians, as well as others, who had treated with cruelty the Church of God; for it was no small consolation, when the Jews heard that they were so regarded by God, that he would undertake their cause and avenge their wrongs. He afterwards repeats again his reproofs, and shortly mentions the sins which then prevailed among the elect people of God; and, at the same time, he turns his discourse to the faithful, and exhorts them to patience, setting before them the hope of favor, provided they ever looked to the Lord; and provided they relied on the gratuitous covenant which he made with Abraham, and doubted not but that he would be a Father to them, and also looked, with a tranquil mind, for that redemption which had been promised to them. This is the sum of the whole Book.

CHAPTER 1

LECTURE ONE HUNDRED AND EIGHTEENTH

ZEPHANIAH 1:1

1. The word of the LORD which came unto Zephaniah the son of Cushi, the son of Gedaliah, the son of Amariah, the son of Hizkiah, in the days of Josiah the son of Amon, king of Judah.

1. Sermo Jehovae, qui fuit ad Zephaniam, filium Chusi, filii Gedoliae, filii Amariae, filii Chizkiae, in diebus Josiae, filii Amon, regis Jehudah.

Zephaniah first mentions the time in which he prophesied; it was under the king Josiah. The reason why he puts down the name of his father Amon does not appear to me. The Prophet would not, as a mark of honor, have made public a descent that was disgraceful and infamous. Amon was the son of Manasseh, an impious and wicked king; and he was nothing better than his father. We hence see that his name is recorded, not for the sake of honor, but rather of reproach; and it may have been that the Prophet meant to intimate, what was then well known to all, that the people had become so obdurate in their superstitions, that it was no easy matter to restore them to a sound mind. But we cannot bring forward anything but conjecture; I therefore leave the matter without pretending to decide it.

With regard to the pedigree of the Prophet, I have mentioned elsewhere what the Jews affirm — that when the Prophets put down the names of their fathers, they themselves had descended from Prophets. But Zephaniah mentions not only his father and grandfather, but also his great-grandfather and his great-great-grandfather; and it is hardly credible that they were all Prophets, and there is not a word respecting them in Scripture. I do not think, as I have said elsewhere, that such a rule is well-founded; but the Jews in this case, according to their manner, deal in trifles; for in things unknown they hesitate not to assert what comes to their minds, though it may not have the least appearance of truth. It is possible that the father, grandfather, the great-grandfather, and the great-great-grandfather of the Prophet, were persons who excelled in piety; but this also is uncertain. What is especially worthy of being noticed is — that he begins by saying that he brought nothing of his own, but faithfully, and, as it were, by the hand, delivered what he had received from God.

With regard, then, to his pedigree, it is a matter of no great moment; but it is of great importance to know that God was the author of his doctrine, and that Zephaniah was his faithful minister, who introduced not his own devices, but was only the announcer of celestial truth. Let us now proceed to the contents -

Zeph. 1:2, 3

2. I will utterly consume all things from off the land, saith the Lord

2. Perdendo perdam (vel, colligendo colligam) omnia ex superficie terrae, dicit Jehova.

3. I will consume man and beast; I will consume the fowls of the heaven, and the fishes of the sea, and the stumblingblocks with the wicked; and I will cut off man from off the land, saith the Lord.

3. Perdam (vel, colligam) hominem et bestiam; perdam autem avem coelorum, et pisces maris; et offendicula erunt impiis; et excidam hominem e superficie terrae, dicit Jehova.

It might seem at the first view that the Prophet dealt too severely in thus fulminating against his own nation; for he ought to have begun with doctrine, as this appears to be the just order of things. But the Prophet denounces ruin, and shows at the same time why God was so grievously displeased with the people. We must however remember, that the Prophet, living at the same period with Jeremiah, had regard to the stubbornness of the people, who had been already with more than sufficient evidence proved to have been guilty. Hence he darts forth as of a sudden and denounces the wickedness of the people, which had been already exposed; so there was to be no more contention on the subject, for their iniquity had become quite ripe. And no doubt it was ever the object of the Prophets to unite their endeavors so as to assist one another: and this united effort ought ever to be among all the servants of God, that no one may do anything apart, but with joined efforts they may promote the same object, and at the same time strive mutually to confirm the common truth. This is what our Prophet is now doing.

He knew that God would have used various means to restore them, had not the corruption of the people become now past recovery. Having observed that all others had spent their labor in vain, he directly attacks the wicked men who had, as it were designedly, cast aside every fear of God, and shook off every shame. Since, then, it was openly evident that with determined rebellion they resisted God, it was no wonder that the Prophet began with so much severity.

But here a difficulty meets us. He said in the first verse, that he thus spoke under Josiah; but we know that the land was then cleansed from its superstitions. For we learn, that when that pious king attained manhood, he labored most strenuously to restore the pure worship of God; and when all places were full of wicked superstitions, he not only constrained the tribe of Judah to adopt the true worship of God, but he also stimulated his neighbors who had remained and were dispersed through the land of Israel. Since, then, the pious king had strenuously and courageously promoted the interest of true religion, it seems a wonder that God was still so much displeased. But we must remember, that though Josiah sincerely worshipped God, yet the people were not really changed; for it has often happened, that God roused the chief men and leaders, while few, or hardly any, followed them, but only yielded a feigned obedience. This was no doubt the case in the time of Josiah; the hearts of the people were alienated from God and true religion, so that they chose rather to rot in their filth than to return to the true worship of God. And that this was the case soon appeared by the event; for Josiah did not reign long after he had cleansed the land from its defilements, and Jehoahaz succeeded him; and then the people immediately relapsed into their idolatry; and though for three months only his successor reigned, yet true religion was in that short time abolished. It is hence an obvious conclusion, that the people had ever been wedded to impiety, and that its roots were hidden in their hearts; though they apparently pretended to worship God, and, in order to please the king, embraced the worship divinely prescribed in their law; yet the event proved that it was a mere act of dissimulation, yea, of perfidy. Then after Jehoahaz followed Jehoiakim, and no better was their condition down to the time of Zedekiah; in short, no remedy could be found for their unhealable wound.

It hence plainly appears, that though Josiah made use of all means to revive the true and unadulterated worship of God in Judea, he did not yet gain his object. And we hence clearly learn how hard were the trials he sustained, seeing that he effected nothing, though at great hazard he attempted to restore the worship of God. When he found that he labored in vain, he no doubt had to contend with great difficulties; and this we know by our own experience. When hope of success shines on us, we easily overcome all troubles, however arduous our work may be; but when we see that we strive in vain, we become dejected: and when we see that our labor succeeds only for a few years, our spirit grows faint. Josiah surmounted these two difficulties; for the perverseness of the people was sufficiently evident, and he was also reminded by two Prophets, Jeremiah and Zephaniah, that the people would still cherish their impious perverseness. When, therefore, he plainly saw that his labor was almost in vain, he might have fainted in the middle of his course, or, as they say, at the starting-place. And since the benefit was so small during his reign, what could he have hoped after his death?

This example ought at this day to be carefully observed: for though God now appears to the world in full light, yet very few there are who submit themselves to his word; and of this small number fewer still there are who sincerely and without any dissimulation embrace sound doctrine. We indeed see how great is their inconstancy and indifference. For they who pretend great zeal for a time very soon vanish and fall away. Since then the perversity of the world is so great, sufficient to deject the minds of God's servants a hundred times, let us learn to look to Josiah, who in his own time left undone nothing, which might serve to establish the true worship of God; and when he saw that he effected but little and next to nothing, he still persevered, and with firm and invincible greatness of mind proceeded in his course.

We may also derive hence an admonition no less useful not to regard ours as the golden age, because some portion of men profess the pure worship of God: for many, by no means wicked men, think, that almost all mortals are like angels, as soon as they testify in words their approbation of the gospel: and the sacred name of Reformation is at this day profaned, when any one who shows as it were by a nod only that he is not wholly an enemy to the gospel, is immediately lauded as a person of extraordinary piety. Though then many show some regard for religion, let us yet know that among so large a number there are many hypocrites, and that there is much chaff mixed with the wheat: and that our senses may not deceive us, we may see here, as in a mirror, how difficult it is to restore the world to the obedience of God, and utterly to root up all corruptions, though idols may be taken away and superstitions be abolished. No doubt Josiah had regard to everything calculated to cleanse the Church, and had recourse to the advice of Jeremiah and also of Zephaniah; we yet see that he did not attain the object he wished, for God now became more grievously displeased with his people than under Manasseh, or under Amon. These wicked kings had attempted to extinguish all true religion; they had cruelly raged against all God's servants, so that Jerusalem became almost drenched with innocent blood: and yet God seems here to have manifested greater displeasure under Josiah than during the previous cruelty and so many impieties. But as I have already said, there is no reason why we should despond, though the world by its ingratitude may close up the way against us; and however much may Satan also by this artifice strive to discourage us, let us still perseveringly go on according to the duties of our calling.

But it may be now asked, why God denounces his vengeance on the beasts of the field, the birds of heaven, and the fishes of the sea; for how much soever the Jews may have provoked him by their sins, innocent animals ought to have been spared. If a son is not to be punished for the fault of his father, Eze 18:4, but that the soul that has sinned is to die, why did God turn his wrath against fishes and other animals? This seems to have been a hasty and unreasonable infliction. But let this rule be first borne in mind — that it is preposterous in us to estimate God's doings according to our judgment, as froward and proud men do in our day; for they are disposed to judge of God's works with such presumption, that whatever they do not approve, they think it right wholly to condemn. But it behaves us to judge modestly and soberly, and to confess that God's judgments are a deep abyss: and when a reason for them does not appear, we ought reverently and with due humility to hook for the day of their full revelation. This is one thing. Then it is meet at the same time to remember, that as animals were created for man's use, they must undergo a lot in common with him: for God made subservient to man both the birds of heaven, and the fishes of the sea, and all other animals. It is then no matter of wonder, that the condemnation of him, who enjoys a sovereignty over the whole earth, should reach to animals. And we know that the world was not made subject to corruption willingly — that is, naturally; but because the contagion from Adam's fall diffused itself through heaven and earth. Hence the sun and the moon, and all the stars, and also all the animals, the earth itself, and the whole world, bear marks of God's wrath, not because they have provoked it through their own fault, but because the whole world is involved in man's curse. The reason then is, because all things were created for the sake of man. Hence there is no ground to conclude, that God acts with too much severity when he executes his vengeance on innocent animals, for he can justly involve in the same ruin with man whatever he has created for his use.

But the reason also is sufficiently plain, why the Prophet speaks here of the beasts of the earth, the fishes of the sea, and the birds of heaven: for we find that men grow torpid, or rather stupid in their own indifference, except they are forcibly roused. It was, therefore, necessary for the Prophet, when he saw the people so hardened in their wickedness, and that he had to do with men past recovery, to set clearly before them these judgments of God, as though he had said — "Ye lie down securely, and indulge yourselves, when God is coming forth prepared for vengeance: but his wrath shall not only proceed against you, but will also lay hold on the harmless animals; for ye shall see a horrible judgment executed on your oxen and asses, on the birds and the fishes. What will become of you when God's wrath shall be thus kindled against the unhappy creatures who have committed no sins? Shall ye indeed escape unpunished?" We now understand why the Prophet does not speak here of men only, but collects with them the beasts of the earth, the fishes of the sea, and the birds of the air.

He says first, By removing I will remove all things from the face of the land; he afterwards enumerates particulars: but immediately after he clearly shows, that God would not act rashly and inconsiderately while executing his vengeance, for his sole purpose was to punish the wicked, There shall be, he says, stumblingblocks to the ungodly; [69] it is the same as though he said — "When I cite to God's tribunal both the fishes of the sea and the birds of heaven, think not that God's controversy is with these creatures which are void of reason, but they are to sustain a part of God's vengeance, which ye have through your sins deserved." The Prophet then does here briefly show, that what he had before threatened brute creatures with, would come upon them on men's account; for God's design was to execute vengeance on the wicked; and as he saw that they were extremely torpid, he tried to awaken them by manifest tokens, so that they might see God the avenger as it were in a striking picture. And at the same time he also adds, I will remove man from the face of the land. He does not speak now of fishes or of other animals, but refers to men only. Hence appears more clearly what I have said — that the Prophet was under the necessity of speaking as he did, owing to the insensibility of the people. He now adds —

Zephaniah 1:4

4. I will also stretch out mine hand upon Judah, and upon all the inhabitants of Jerusalem; and I will cut off the remnant of Baal from this place, and the name of the Chemarims with the priests;

4. Et extendam manum meam super Jehudah, et super omnes incolas Jerusalem; et excidam ex loco hoc reliquias Baal, et nomen cultorum cum sacerdotibus.

The Prophet explains still more clearly why he directed his discourse in the last verse against the beasts of the earth and the birds of heaven, even for this end — that the Jews might understand that God was angry with them. I will stretch forth, he says, my hand on Judah and on Jerusalem. God, then, by executing his vengeance on animals, intended to exhibit to the Jews, as in a picture, the dreadfulness of his wrath, which yet they despised and regarded as nothing. The stretching forth of God's hand I have elsewhere explained; and it means even this — that he stretches forth his hand when he acts in an unusual manner, and employs means beyond what is common. We indeed know that God has no hands, and we also know that he performs all things by his command alone: but as everything seen in the world is called the work of his hands, so he is said to stretch forth his hand when he mentions a work that is remarkable and worthy of being remembered. In a like manner, when I intend to do some slight work, I only move my hand; but when I have some difficult work to do, I prepare myself more carefully, and also stretch forth my arms. This metaphor, then, is intended only for this purpose, to render men more attentive to God's works, when he is set forth as stretching forth his hand.

But he says, on Judah and on the inhabitants of Jerusalem. The kingdom of Israel had now been abolished, and the ten tribes had been led into exile; and a few only of the lowest and the poorest remained. The Jews thought themselves safe for ever, because they had escaped that calamity. This is the reason why the Prophet declares that God's judgment was impending not only over the kingdom of Judah, but also over the holy city, which thought itself exempt from all such evil, because there were the sacrifices performed, and there was the royal city, and, in short, because God had testified that his habitation was to be there for ever. Since, then, by this vain confidence the inhabitants of Jerusalem deceived themselves and others, Zephaniah specifically addresses them. And as he had before spoken of the wicked, he intended here, no doubt, sharply to reprove the Jews, as though he said by way of anticipation, There is no reason for you to enquire who are the wicked; for ye yourselves are they, even ye who are the holy people of God and God's chosen inheritance, ye who are the race of Abraham, who flatter yourselves so much on account of your excellency; ye are the wicked, who have not hitherto ceased to provoke the vengeance of God. And at the same time he shows, as it were by the finger, some of their sins, though he mentions others afterwards: but he speaks now of their superstitions.

I will cut off, he says, the remnants of Baal and the name of Chamerim. The severity of the Prophet may seem here again to be excessive, for being so incensed against superstitions which had been abolished by the great zeal and singular diligence of the king; but, as we have already intimated, he regarded not so much the king as the people. For though they dared not openly to adulterate God's worship, they yet cherished those corruptions at home to which they had before been accustomed, as we see to be done at this day. For when it is not allowed to worship idols, many mutter their prayers in secret and invoke their idols: and, in short, they are restrained only by the fear of men from manifesting their own impiety; and in the meantime, they retain before God the same abominations. So it was in the time of Josiah; the people were wedded to their corruptions, and this we may easily conclude from the words of Zephaniah: for the remnants of Baal were not seen in the temple, nor in the streets, nor in their chapels, nor in the high places; but their hidden impiety is here discovered by the Spirit of God; and no doubt their sin was the more heinous and less excusable, because the people refused to follow their pious leader. It was indeed the most abominable ingratitude; for when they saw that the right worship was restored to them, they preferred to remain fixed in their own filth, rather than to return to God, even when they had liberty to do so, and also when that pious king extended his hand to them.

As to the word כמרים, camerim, it designated either the worshipers of Baal or some such men as our monks at this day: and they are supposed by some to have been thus called, because they were clothed in black vestments; while others think that they derived this name from their fervor, because they were madly devoted to their superstitions, or because they had marks on their foreheads, or because they imposed, as is commonly the case, on the simple by the ardor of their zeal. The name is also found in 2Ki 23:1 in the account given of Josiah: for it is said there, that the כמרים, camerim, were taken away, together with other abominations of superstition. But as Zephaniah connects priests with them, it is probable that they were a kind of people like the monks, who did not themselves offer sacrifices, but were a sort of attendants, who undertook vows and offered prayers in the name of the whole people. For what some think, that they were thus called because they burnt incense, appears not to me probable; for then they must have been priests. They were then inferior to the sacrificers, and occupying a station between them and the people, like the monks and hermits of this day, who deceive foolish men by their sanctity. Such, then, were the Camerim. [70]

But as Josiah could not attain his object, so as immediately to cleanse the land from these pollutions, we need not wonder that at this day we are not able immediately to remove superstitions from the world: but let us in the meantime ever proceed in our course. Let those endued with authority, who bear the sword, that is, all magistrates, perform their office with greater diligence, inasmuch as they see how difficult and protracted is the contest with the ministers of idolatry. Let also the ministers of the gospel earnestly cry against idolatry, and all ungodly ceremonies, and not desist. Though they may not effect as much as they wish, yet let them follow the example of Josiah. If God should in the meantime thunder from heaven, let them not be discouraged, but, on the contrary, know that their labor is approved by him, and never doubt of their own safety; for though all were destroyed, their godly efforts would not be in vain, nor fail of a reward before God. Thus, then, ought all God's servants to animate themselves, each in his particular sphere and vocation, whenever they have to contend with superstitions, and with such corruptions as vitiate and adulterate the pure worship of God.

PRAYER

Grant, Almighty God, that as we are so prone to corruptions, and so easily turn from the right course after having commenced it, and so easily degenerate from the truth once known, — O grant, that, being strengthened by thy Spirit, we may persevere to the end in the right way which thou showest to us in thy word, and that we may also labor to restore the many who abandon themselves to various errors; and though we may effect nothing, let us not yet be led away after them, but remain firm in the obedience of faith, until having at length finished all these contests, we shall be gathered into that blessed rest which is prepared for us in heaven, through Christ our Lord. Amen.

LECTURE ONE HUNDRED AND NINETEENTH

ZEPHANIAH 1:5

5. And them that worship the host of heaven upon the housetops; and them that worship and that swear by the LORD, and that swear by Malcham;

5. Et super eos qui adorant super tecta militiam coelorum, et eos qui adorant et jurant per Jehovam, et jurant per regem suum.

Zephaniah pursues the subject contained in the verse I explained yesterday. For as the majority of the people still adhered to their superstitions, though the pure worship of the law had been restored by Josiah, the Prophet threatens here, that God would punish such ingratitude. As then he had spoken in the last verse of the worshipers of Baal and their sacrifices, so now he proceeds farther — that the Lord would execute vengeance on the whole people, who prayed to the host of heaven, or bowed themselves down before the host of heaven. It is well known that those stars are thus called in Scripture to which the gentiles ascribed, on account of their superior lustre, some sort of divinity. Hence it was, that they worshipped the sun as God, called the moon the queen of heaven, and also paid adoration to the stars. The people, then, did not only sin in worshipping Baal, but were also addicted to many superstitions, as we see to be the case whenever men degenerate from the genuine doctrine of true religion; they then seek out various inventions on all sides, so that they observe no limits and keep within no boundaries.

But he says, that they worshipped the stars on their roofs. It is probable that they chose this higher place, as interpreters remind us, because they thought that they were more seen by the stars the nearer they were to them. For as men are gross in their ideas they never think God propitious to them except he exhibits some proof or sign of a bodily presence; in short, they always seek God according to their own earthly notions. Since, then, the Jews thought that there were so many Gods as there are stars in heaven, it is no wonder that they ascended to the roofs of their houses, that they might be, as it were, in the sight of their gods, and thus not lose their labor; for the superstitious never think that their devotion is observed by God, unless they have before their eyes, as we have just said, some sign of his presence.

We now then see how this verse stands connected with the last. God declares that he would punish all idolaters; but as the Jews worshipped Baal, the Prophet first condemned that strange religion; and now he adds other devices, to which the Jews perversely devoted themselves; for they worshipped also all the stars, ascribing to them some sort of divinity. Then he mentions all those who worshipped and swore by their own king, and swore by Jehovah

By these last words the Prophet intimates, that the Jews had not so repudiated the law of God but that they boasted that they still worshipped the God who had adopted them, and by whom they had been redeemed, who had commanded the temple to be built for him, and an altar on mount Sion. They then did not openly reject the worship of the true God, but formed such a mixture for themselves, that they joined to the true God their own idols, as we see to be the state of things at this day under the Papacy. It seems a sufficient excuse to foolish men that they retain the name of God; and they confidently boast that the true God is worshipped by them; and yet we see that they mix together with this worship many of the delusions of Satan; for under the Papacy there is no end to their inventions. When any devise some peculiar mode of worship, it is then connected with the rest; and thus they form such a mixture, that from one God, divided into many parts, they bring forth a vast troop of deities. As then at this day the Papists worship God and idols too, so Zephaniah had to condemn the same wickedness among the Jews.

We here learn that God's name was not then wholly obliterated, as though the world had openly fallen away from God; for though they worshipped Jupiter, Mercury, Apollo, and other fictitious gods, they yet professed to worship the only true and eternal God, the Creator of heaven and earth. What then was it that the Prophet condemned that they were not content with what the law simply and plainly prescribed, but that they devised for themselves various and strange modes of worship; for when men take to themselves such a liberty as this, they no longer worship the true God, how much soever they may pretend to do so, inasmuch as God repudiates all spurious modes of worship, as he testifies especially in Ezekiel 20 — Go ye, he says, worship your idols. He shows that all kinds of worship are abominable to him whenever men depart in any measure from his pure word. For we must hold this as the main principle — that obedience is more valued by God than all sacrifices. Whenever men run after their own inventions they depart from the true God; for they refuse to render to him what he principally requires, even obedience.

But our Prophet speaks according to the common notions of men; for they pretended to be the true worshipers of God, while they still adhered to their own inventions. They did not, indeed, properly speaking, worship the true God; but as they thought, and openly professed to do this, Zephaniah, making this concession, says — God will not suffer his own worship to be thus profaned: ye seek to blend it with that of your idols; this he will not endure. Ye worship the true God, and ye worship your idols; but he would have himself to be worshipped alone; and this he deserves. But the partition which ye make is nothing else than the mangling of true worship; and God will not have himself to be thus in part worshipped. We now understand what the Prophet means here; for the Jews covered their abominations with the pretext that their purpose was to worship the God of Abraham: the Prophet does not simply deny this to be done by them, but declares that this worship was useless and disapproved by God; nay, he proceeds farther, and says that this worship, made up of various inventions, was an abominable corruption which God would punish; for he can by no means bear that there should be such an alliance — that idols should be substituted in his place, and that a part of his glory should be transferred to the inventions of men. This is the true meaning.

We hence learn how greatly deceived the Papists are, who think it enough, provided they depart not wholly from the worship of the only true God; for God allows and approves of no worship except when we attend to his voice, and turn not aside either to the left hand or to the right, but acquiesce only in what he has prescribed.

It is nothing strange that he connects swearing with worship, for it is a kind of divine worship. Hence the Scripture, stating a part for the whole, often mentions swearing in this sense, as including the service due to God. But the Prophet pronounces here generally a curse on all the superstitious, who worshipped fictitious gods; and then he adds one kind of worship, and that is swearing. I shall not here speak at large, nor is it — necessary, on the subject of swearing. We know that the use of an oath is lawful when God is appealed to as a witness and a judge, on important occasions; for God's name may be interposed when a matter requires proof, and when it is important; but God's name is not to be introduced thoughtlessly. Hence two things are especially required in an oath — that all who swear by his name should present themselves with reverence before his tribunal, and acknowledge him to be the avenger if they take his name falsely or inconsiderately This is one thing. Then the matter itself, on account of which we swear, must be considered; for if men allow themselves to swear by God's name respecting things which are trifling and frivolous, it is a shameful profanation, and by no means to be borne. For it is a singular favor on the part of God, that he allows us to take his name when there is any controversy among us, and when a confirmation is necessary. As then we thus receive through kindness the name of God, it is surely a great favor; for how great is the sanctity of that name, though it serves even earthly concerns? God then does so far accommodate himself to us, that it is lawful for us to swear by his name. Hence a greater seriousness ought to be observed by us in oaths, so that no one should dare to interpose an oath except when necessity requires; and we should also especially take heed lest God be called a witness to what is false. For how great a sacrilege it is to cover a falsehood with his name, who is the eternal and immutable truth! They then who swear falsely by his name change God, as far as they can, into what he is not. We now sufficiently understand how swearing is a kind of divine worship, because his honor is thereby given to God; for his majesty is, as it were, brought before us, and as it is his peculiar office to know and to discover hidden things, and also to maintain the truth, this his own work is ascribed to him. Now when any one swears by a mortal, or by the sun, or by the moon, or by creatures, he deprives God in part of his own honor.

We hence see that in superstitious oaths there was a clear proof of idolatry. This is the reason why the Prophet here condemns those who did swear by Jehovah and by Malkom; that is, who joined their idols with the true and eternal God when they swore. For it is a clear precept of God's law, 'By the name of thy God shalt thou swear.' De 6:13. And when the Prophets speak of the renovation of the Church, they use this form — 'Ye shall swear by the name of God;' 'To me shall bend every knee;' 'Every tongue shall swear to me.' What does all this mean? The whole world shall acknowledge me as the true God; and as every knee shall bow to me, so every one will submit himself to my judgment. We may hence doubtlessly conclude, that God is deprived of his right, whenever we swear by the sun, or by the moon, or by the dead, or by any creatures.

This evil has been common in all ages; and it prevails still at this day under the Papacy. They swear by the Virgin, by angels, and by the dead. They do not think that they thus take away anything from the sovereignty of the only true God; but we see what he declares respecting them. The Papists therefore foolishly excuse themselves, when they swear by their saints: for they cannot elude the charge of sacrilege, which the Holy Spirit has stamped with perpetual infamy, since he has said, that all those are abominable in the sight of God who swear by any other name than his own: and the reason is evident, for the sun, moon, and stars, and also dead or living men, are honored with the name of God, when they are set up as judges. For they who swear by the sun, do the same as though they said — The sun is my witness and judge; that is, The sun is my God. They who swear by the name of a king, or as profane men swore formerly, By the genius of their king, ascribe to a mortal what is peculiar to the true God alone. But when any one swears by heaven or the temple, and does not think that there is any divinity in the heavens or in the temple, it is the same as though he swore by God himself, as it appears from Mt 23:20-22; and Christ, when he forbade us to swear by heaven or by the earth, did not condemn such modes of swearing as inconsistent with his word, but as only useless and vain. At the same time he showed that God's name is profaned by such expressions: 'They who swear by heaven, swear also by him who inhabits heaven; they who swear by the temple, swear also by him who is worshipped in the temple, and to whom sacrifices are offered.' When one swears by his head or by his life, it is a protestation, as though he said — As my life is dear to me. But they who swear by the saints, either living or dead, ascribe to mortals what is due to God. They who swear by the sun, place a dead created thing on the throne of God himself.

As to the term מכלם, melkom, it may be properly rendered, their king; for מלך, melak, as it is well known, means a king; but it is here put in construction, מכלם, melkom, their king; they swear by their own, king [71] The Prophet, I doubt not, alludes to the word מולך, Molok, which is derived from the verb, to reign: for though that word was commonly used by all as a proper name, it is yet certain that that false god was so called, as though he was a king: and the Prophet increases the indignity by saying — They swear by Malkom. He might have simply said, They swear by Moloch; but he says, They swear by Malkom; that is, They forget that I am their king, and transfer my sovereignty to a dead and empty image. God then does here, by an implied contrast, exaggerate the sin of the Jews, as they sought another king for themselves, when they knew that under his protection they always enjoyed a sure and real safety. Let us now proceed —

Zephaniah 1:6

6. And them that are turned back from the LORD; and those that have not sought the LORD, nor enquired for him.

6. Et qui retro aguntur, ne sequantur Jehovam, (ad verbum est, de-post Jehovam.) et qui non quaerunt Jehovam, neque investigant eum.

The Prophet seems here to include, as it were, in one bundle, the proud despisers of God, as well as those idolaters of whom he had spoken. It may yet be, that he describes the same persons in different words, and that he means that they were addicted to their own superstitions, because they were unwilling to serve God sincerely and from the heart, and even shunned everything that might lead their attention to true religion. And this view I mostly approve; for what some imagine, that their gross contempt of God is here pointed out, is not sufficiently supported. I therefore rather think that the idolaters are here reproved, that they might not suppose that they could by subterfuges wash away their guilt; for they were wont to cover themselves with the shield of ignorance, when they were overcome, and their impiety was fully proved: I did not think so; but, on the contrary, my purpose was to worship God. Since, then, the superstitious are wont to hide themselves under the covering of ignorance, the Prophet here defines the idolatry of the people, and briefly shows that it was connected with obstinacy and wickedness.

They did not seek Jehovah; but, on the contrary, they turned willfully away from him, and sought, as it were designedly, to extinguish true religion. Nor was it to be wondered at, that so grievous and severe a sentence was pronounced on them; for they had been taught by the law how God was to be served. How was it, then, that errors so gross had crept in? Doubtless, God had kindled the light of celestial truth, which clearly showed the way of true religion; but as men ever seek to perform some frivolous trifles, the Israelites and the Jews, when they felt ashamed openly and manifestly to reject the true God, labored at the same time to add many ceremonies, that their impiety might be thus concealed. This is the reason why the Prophet says that they turned back; that is, that they could not be excused on the ground of ignorance, but that they were perfidious and apostates, who had preferred their own idols to the true God; though they knew that he could not be rightly worshipped, but according to the rule prescribed in the law, they yet neglected this, and heaped together many superstitions.

And, doubtless, we shall find that the fountain of all false worship is this — that men are unwilling truly and from the heart to serve God; and, at the same time, they wish to retain some appearance of religion. For there is nothing omitted in the law that is needful for the perfect worship of God: but as God requires in the law a spiritual worship, hence it is that men seek hiding-places, and devise for themselves many ceremonies, that they may turn back from God, and yet pretend that they come to him. While they sedulously labor in their own ceremonies, it is indeed true that the worship of God and religion are continually on their lips: but, as I have said, it is all hypocrisy and deception; for they accumulate ceremonies, that there might be something intervening between God and them. It is not, therefore, without reason that the Prophet here accuses the Jews that they turned back from Jehovah, and that they sought him not. How so? For there was no need of a long, or of a difficult, or of a perplexed enquiry; for the Lord had freely offered himself to them. How, then, was it that they were blind in the midst of light, except that they knowingly and willfully followed their own inventions? [72]

The same is the case at this day with the Papists: for though they may glamour a hundred times that they seek to worship God, it is quite evident that they willfully go astray; inasmuch as they so delight themselves with their own inventions, that they do not purely and from the heart devote and consecrate themselves to God.

We now, then, see that this verse was added, as an explanation, by the Prophet, that he might deprive the Jews of their false plea of ignorance, and show that they sinned willfully; for they would have been sufficiently taught by the law, had they not adopted their own inventions, which dazzled their eyes and all their senses. It follows —

Zephaniah 1:7-9

7. Hold thy peace at the presence of the Lord God: for the day of the Lord is at hand: for the Lord hath prepared a sacrifice, he hath bid his guests.

7. Tace a facie Domini Jehovae, quia propinquus dies Jehova, quia paravit Jehova sacrificium, (vel, ordinavit, [הכין],) sanctificavit invitatos suos.

8. And it shall come to pass in the day of the Lord's sacrifice, that I will punish the princes, and the king's children, and all such as are clothed with strange apparel.

8. Et erit, in die sacrificii Jehovae tunc visitabo super Principes, et super filios Regis, et super omnes qui induti sunt vestitu extraneo.

9. In the same day also will I punish all those that leap on the threshold, which fill their masters' houses with violence and deceit.

9. Et visitabo super omnem qui tripudiat super limen in die illo, qui replent domum dominorum suorum violentia et fraude.

The Prophet confirms here what he has previously taught, when he bids all to be silent before God; for this mode of speaking is the same as though he had said, that he did not terrify the Jews in vain, but seriously set before them God's judgment, which they would find by experience to be even more than terrible. He also records some of their sins, that the Jews might know that he did not threaten them for nothing, but that there were just causes why God declared that he would punish them. This is the substance of the whole.

Let us first see what the Prophet means by the word, silence. Something has been said of this on the second chapter of Habakkuk. We said then that by silence is meant submission; and to make the thing more clear, we said that we were to notice the contrast between the silence to which men calmly submit, and the contumacy, which is ever clamorous: for when men seek to be wise of themselves, and acquiesce not in God's word, it is then said, that they are not silent, for they refuse to give a hearing to his word; and when men give loose reins to their own will, they observe no bounds. Until God then obtains authority in the world, all places are full of clamor, and the whole life of men is in a state of confusion, for they run to and fro in their wanderings; and there is no restraint where God is not heard. It is for the same reason that the Prophet now demands silence: but the expression is accommodated to the subject which he handles. To be silent at the presence of God, it is true, is to submit to God's authority; but the connection is to be considered; for Zephaniah saw then that God's judgment was despised and regarded as nothing; and he intimates here that God had so spoken, that the execution was nigh at hand. Hence he says, Be silent, [73] that is, Know ye, that I have not spoken merely for the purpose of terrifying you; but as God is prepared to execute vengeance, of this he now reminds you, that if there be any hope of repentance, ye may in time seek to return into favor with him; if not, that ye may be without excuse.

We now then understand why the Prophet bids them to be silent before the Lord Jehovah: and the context is a confirmation of the same view; for the reason is added, Because the day of Jehovah is nigh. For profane men ever promise to themselves some respite, and think that they gain much by delay: the Prophet, on the contrary, does now expose to scorn this self-security, and says, that the day of Jehovah was nigh at hand. It is then the same thing as though he had said, that his judgment ought to have been quickly anticipated, and even with fear and trembling.

He afterwards employs a metaphor to set forth what he taught, — that God had prepared a sacrifice, yea, that he had already appointed and set apart his guests. By the word, sacrifice, the Prophet reminded them, that the punishment of which he had spoken would be just, and that the glory of God would thereby shine forth. We indeed know how ready the world is to make complaints; when it is pressed by God's hand, it expostulates on account of too much rigor; and many in an open manner give utterance to their blasphemies. As then they own not God's justice in his punishment, the Prophet calls it a sacrifice; and sacrifices, we know, are evidences of divine worship, and he who offers a sacrifice to God, owns him to be just. So also by this kind of speaking Zephaniah intimates that God would not act a cruel part in cutting off the city Jerusalem and its inhabitants; for this would be a sacrifice, according to the language often employed by the Prophets, and especially by Isaiah, who says of Bozrah, 'A sacrifice is prepared in Bozrah,' Isa 34:6;) and who says also of Jerusalem itself, 'Oh! Ariel! Ariel!' Isa 29:1, where Jerusalem itself is represented as the altar; as though he had said, In all the streets, in the open places, there shall be altars to me; for I will collect together great masses of men, whom I shall slay as a sacrifice to me. For all who were not willing to render worship to God, and who did not freely offer themselves as spiritual victims to him, were to be drawn to the slaughter, and were at the same time called sacrifices. So the executions on the gallows, when the wicked suffer, may be said to be sacrifices to God: for the Lord arms the magistrate with the sword to restrain wickedness, that the wicked may not have such liberty as to banish all equity from the world. The cities also, which, being forcibly taken, are subject to a slaughter, and the fields, where armies are slain, become altars, for God makes the rebellious a sacrifice, because they refuse willingly to offer themselves.

So also in this place the Prophet says, Jehovah has prepared for himself a sacrifice, — Where? At Jerusalem, through the whole city, as it has appeared from the quotation from Isaiah; for as they had not rightly sacrificed to God on Mount Sion, but vitiated his whole worship, God himself declares, that he would become a priest, that he might slay, as he thought right, those beasts, who had obstinately refused his yoke: And he has prepared his guests. But I cannot finish today.

PRAYER

Grant, Almighty God, that as we continue in so many ways to provoke against us thy wrath, we may patiently bear the punishment, by which thou wouldest correct our faults, and also anticipate thy judgment: and since thou art pleased to recall us in due time to thyself, let us not turn deaf ears to thy counsels, but so obey and submit ourselves to thee, that we may become partakers of that mercy, which thou offerest to us, provided we seek to be reconciled to thee, and so proceed in thy service, that under the government of Christ thy Son, whom thou hast appointed to be our supreme and only king, we may so strive to be wholly devoted to thee that thou mayest be glorified through our whole life, until we become at length partakers of that celestial glory, which has been procured for us by the blood of thy only-begotten Son. Amen

LECTURE ONE HUNDRED AND TWENTIETH

We stated yesterday why God compares the slaughter of the wicked to a sacrifice, — because in punishing the ungodly, he shows himself to be the judge of the world: and this slaying is a sacrifice of sweet odour, because it makes known this glory. And he immediately adds, that he had prepared his guests. The word he uses is שדק, kodash, which means to sanctify, but is often to be taken in a different sense. It may be explained as meaning, that God had prepared his guests: but as there is an express mention made of sacrifice, Zephaniah, I have no doubt, continues the same metaphor. The meaning then is, that the Chaldeans, who were ministers of God's vengeance, were already not only chosen for the purpose of executing it, but were divinely consecrated for that end: and this unwelcome saying was uttered by the Prophet, that he might more sharply touch the feelings of his own nation. The Jews ought indeed to have acknowledged God's judgment even when executed by heathens; but this they would not have done, had they not understood, that these were, in exercising their cruelty, as it were, the priests of God; for the royal priesthood at Jerusalem had been profaned. We now then see why the Prophet says, that those were sanctified by the Lord who had been invited to feed on the flesh of the chosen people, as they were wont to eat of the remainder of their sacrifices on festal days. [74] Let us now proceed.

I yesterday repeated this verse, And it shall be, on the day of the sacrifice of Jehovah, that I will then visit the princes, and the sons of the king, and those who are clothed with strange apparel. The Prophet shows, that he not only threatened the common people, but also the chief leaders, so that he spared not even the king's sons. He attacks then here the principal men among the people; for they were justly led to punishment in the first place, as they had been to others the cause of their errors. We indeed know, that they who excel in dignity give a much greater offense when they abuse their power in promoting what is sinful. Hence it was, that God seemed often to have sent his Prophets to them only. For though the low and the humble in the community were not exempt from punishment, yet it was but reasonable that God should more severely punish their leaders. Hence the Prophet now says, that God would visit the princes and the king's sons [75] He did not indeed intend here to flatter obscure men, as though God meant to overlook them: but as the king and his counselors had more grievously sinned, the more angry was God with them. We also know, that kings and others, who exercise power, are not easily moved, for the splendor of their fortune blinds them; and they think that they are in a manner exempt from laws, because they occupy a higher station. We now then see why the Prophet speaks especially of the princes and the king's sons.

He also adds, And those who wear foreign apparel [76] Some refer this to the worshipers of Baal, or his priests; but the context does not allow us to apply it to any but to courtiers, whose great delight was in apparel: for what Christ says is proved by the experience of all ages to be too true, — that they who wear soft clothing are in king's courts. Mt 11:8. And it is probable, that courtiers, through a foolish affectation, often changed their clothes; as it is the case with men who seek to appear great, they devise daily some new way for spending money; and though they may be more splendidly clothed than needful, yet they think it almost too sordid to wear the same apparel for a whole month; and that their prodigality may be more evident, they change also the forms of their dress. This affectation prevails far too much at this day in the world. But even then in the age of the Prophet, as it appears, the courtiers and those who had power among the people, often changed their dress, that they might the more display their pomp and attract the admiration of the simple and poor people. And it was not simple ambition, but it brought with it a contempt for others; for the rich in this way upbraided the poor, that they themselves were alone worthy of this superfluity and opulence. It was not enough for them, that they were clothed for their own comfort, and also that ornament and splendor were added; but they would have willingly made bare all others: and as it was a shame to do this, they yet showed, as far as they could, by their superfluous abundance, that they were alone worthy of such display. It was then no wonder that the Lord threatened them with so much severity.

As this vice in course of time had greatly increased, this passage of the Prophet deserves particular notice. And the more luxurious men become and the more they indulge in such varieties, and thus manifest their pride, the more carefully we ought to learn to restrain the desires of our flesh, that they may not leap over the bounds of moderation; and let those who abound in wealth be contented with what is modest and becoming; and let them especially abstain from that absurd affectation, which the Prophet evidently condemns here. It may however have been, that the Jews then sought new and unusual fashions as to their clothes from remote countries, like the French at this day, who delight in the Turkish habit; for they have too much intercourse with Turkey. So also at that time a foolish desire had possessed the hearts of the people, so as to wish to ingratiate themselves with the Chaldeans, and to make friends of them by a likeness in dress. And we may learn this from a passage in Ezekiel, where he compares them to harlots or to foolish lovers Eze 23:2, etc.:) for as lovers paint harlots on walls, and whoremongers and adulterers do the same; so Ezekiel accuses the Jews, that they were so inflamed with a mad desire of making a covenant with the Chaldean nation, that they had their images painted in their chambers. They also no doubt imitated their dress, in order to show that they regarded it a great happiness, if they became their friends and confederates.

Now follows what I repeated also yesterday, I will visit every one who danceth on the threshold. Some explain this of the worshipers of Baal, but improperly; for as I have already said, the context will not allow us to understand this except of the servants of princes, who cruelly harassed the people and deprived helpless men of their property, who were not able to resist them. The Prophet then, after having spoken of the chief governors of the kingdom and of the king's sons, now comes to their servants, who, like hunting dogs, were ready to seize everywhere on the prey. They who understand this to be said of the sacrifices of Baal, adduce a passage from sacred history, — that since the image of Dagon had been found on the threshold of the temple, they dared not to tread on the threshold, but leaped over it: but this is too far-fetched. Others also bring expositions of a different kind; but the Prophet, I have no doubt, refers here to the liberty they took in plundering, when he says, that they danced on the threshold, as persons triumphing; for he afterwards adds, that they filled, by rapine and fraud, the houses of the princes. To leap or dance then on the threshold is no other thing than to take possession of the houses of other people, and insolently to triumph over them, as it is usually done by conquerors. For he who takes possession of what belongs to another, does not quietly rest there as in his own habitation, but boasts and exults. So also here, the Prophet paints to the life that wantonness, which the servants of princes showed, when they entered into the houses of others. He therefore says, that they danced, and said, This is my house; and who will dare to say a word to the contrary? Since then the servants of princes took so much liberty, the Prophet here denounces on them the vengeance of God. [77]

He then adds, that they filled their masters' houses by rapine and fraud. By rapine and fraud he means the prey gathered, partly by armed force, and partly by deceit and craft; for courtiers have their nets by which they lay in wait for helpless men. But if they cannot obtain by fraud what they hope for, they leave recourse to armed force. However this may be, they enrich themselves, sometimes by plundering, and sometimes by fraud. Hence the Prophet mentions both here. It follows —

Zephaniah 1:10

10. And it shall come to pass in that day, saith the LORD, that there shall be the noise of a cry from the fish gate, and an howling from the second, and a great crashing from the hills.

10. Et erit in die illa, dicit Iehova, vox clamoris a porta piscium, et ululatus a secundda (ad verbum; sed multi intelligunt scholam,) et contritio magna a collibus.

He confirms here the same truth, and amplifies and illustrates it by a striking description; for we know how much a lively representation avails to touch the feelings, when the event itself is not only narrated, but placed as it were before our eyes. So the Prophet is not content with plain words, but presents a scene, that the future destruction of Jerusalem might appear in a clearer light. But as I have elsewhere explained this mode of speaking, I shall not dwell on the subject now.

He says, that there would be the voice of crying from the gate of the fishes. He names here three places in Jerusalem, and afterwards he adds a fourth. But as we do not understand the situation of the city, sufficient for us is this probable conjecture, — that he refers to parts opposite to one another; as though he had said, that no corner of the city would be in a quiet state, when the Lord roused up war. Let us then suppose it to be triangular, and let the gate of the fishes be one side, and let the second gate or the school be on the other; and let the part nigh the hills form the third side. What some say, that the hills mean palaces, I do not approve of; nor is it consistent with the context: but we ought to bear in mind what I have already stated, that the Prophet here denounces ruin on every part of the city, so that the Jews would in vain seek refuges for themselves; for by running here and there, they would find all places full of crying and howling. There shall be then the voice of crying from the gate of the fishes. Why the Prophet calls it the gate of the fishes we cannot for certainty say, except that it is a probable conjecture, that either some fish-pond was near it, or that the fish-market was nigh.

As to the word הנשמ, meshene, the majority of interpreters think that it means the place where the priests explained the law and devoted themselves to the study of it; and they adduce a passage from 2Ki 22:14, where it seems, as there is mention made of priests, the word is taken in this sense. But as gates are spoken of here, and as the Hebrews often call whatever is second in order by this word, as the second part in buildings and also in towns and in other places, is thus called, we may take it here in this sense, that is, as meaning that gate which was next to the first in general esteem. But as the subject has little to do with the main point, I dismiss it. [78]

He says in the last place, that there would be a great breach in the hills. He refers, I have no doubt, to that part of the city which was contiguous to the mountains. However this may be, it was the Prophet's object to include here the whole city, that he might shake off from the Jews all vain confidence, and show that there would be no escape, when the Lord stretched forth his hand to punish their sins. It now follows —

Zephaniah 1:11

11. Howl, ye inhabitants of Maktesh, for all the merchant people are cut down; all they that bear silver are cut off.

11. Ululate habitatores loci concavi; quia exterminatus est populos mercatorum, excisi sunt omnes onusti pecunia.

The Prophet addresses the merchants here who inhabited the middle part of the city, and hence thought themselves farther off from all danger and trouble. As then they were concealed as it were in their hiding-places, they thought that no danger was nigh them; and thus security blinded them the more. After having spoken of the king's palace and of the princes and their servants, Zephaniah now turns his discourse to the merchants.

And he calls them the inhabitants of the hollow place, שתכמ, mecatesh. The verb שתכ, catash, means to be hollow; hence the Hebrews call a hollow place שתכמ, mecatesh. So Solomon calls a mortar by this name, because it is hollow: [79] and we learn also from other parts of scripture that the word means sometimes either a cavern or some low place. But we know that merchants have for the most part their streets on level ground, and it is for their advantage, as they have goods to carry. It may then have been, that at Jerusalem there was a large company of merchants in that part of the city, which was in its situation low. But they who regard it as a proper name, bring nothing either of reason or probability to confirm their opinion: and it is also evident from the context that merchants are here addressed, for cut off, he says, is the mercantile people. The word ענן,

canon, means a merchant. Some think that the Jews are here, as often elsewhere, called Canaan, because they were become degenerate, and more like the Canaanites than the holy fathers, from whom they descended. [80] But the Prophet speaks here no doubt of merchants, for an explanation immediately follows, all who are laden with money. And he says that merchants were laden with money, because they would not transact business without making payments and counting money, and also, because merchants for the most part engrossed by their gainful arts a great portion of the wealth of the world.

We now then understand what the Prophet means: He threatens howling to the merchants, who were concealed in their hidden places, for they occupied that part of the city, as I have already said, which was below the hills; and he then makes use of the word כנען, canon, a trafficker; and lastly he speaks of their wealth, as it is probable that they became rich through frauds and most dishonest means, and shows that their money would be useless to them, for they would find in it no defense, when the Lord extended his hand to punish them. It now follows —

Zephaniah 1:12

12. And it shall come to pass at that time, that I will search Jerusalem with candles, and punish the men that are settled on their lees: that say in their heart, The LORD will not do good, neither will he do evil.

12. Et erit in tempore illo, serutabor Ierusalem in lucernis, et visitabo super homines, qui congelati sunt in faecibus suis, et dicunt in cordibus suis, Neque benefaciet Iehova, neque malefaciet.

The Prophet addresses here generally the despisers of God, who were become hardened in their wickedness. But before he openly names them, he says that the visitation would be such, that God would search every corner, so that no place would remain unexplored. For to visit with candles, or to search with candles, is so to examine all hidden places or coverts, that nothing may escape. When one intends to plunder a city, he first enters into the houses, and takes away whatever he finds; but when he thinks that there are some hidden treasures, he descends into the secret cells; and then if there be no light there, he lights a candle, and carefully looks here and there, that he may not overlook anything. By this comparison then God intimates, that Jerusalem would be so plundered, that nothing whatever would remain. Hence he says, I will search it with candles. We indeed know that nothing is hid from God; but it is evident, that he is constrained to borrow comparisons from the common practice of men, because he could not otherwise express what is necessary for us to know. The world indeed deal with God as men do with one another; for they think that he can be deceived by their craftiness. He therefore laughs to scorn this folly, and says, that he would have candles to search out whatever was concealed.

Now, as impiety had possessed the minds of almost all the people, he says, I will visit the men, who on their lees are congealed. This may indeed be only understood of the rich, who flattered themselves in their prosperity, and feared nothing, and were thus congealed on their lees: but Zephaniah shows in the words which follow, that he had in view something more atrocious, that is, that they said that neither good nor evil proceeded from God. At the same time, these two things may be suitably joined together — that he reproves here their self-security, produced by wealth — and that he also accuses the careless Jews of that gross contempt of God which is afterwards mentioned. And I am disposed to take this view, that is, that the Jews, inebriated with prosperity, became hardened, as men contract hardness often by labor — and that they so collected lees through too much quietness and abundance of things, that they became wholly stupid, and could be touched by no truth made known to them. Hence in the first place the Prophet says, that God would visit with punishment a carelessness so extreme, when men not only slumbered in their prosperity, but also became congealed in their own stupidity, so as to be almost void of sense and understanding. When one addresses a dead mass, he can effect nothing: and so the Prophet compares careless men to a dead and congealed mass; for stupidity had so bound up all their senses, that they could not be either allured by the goodness of God, or terrified by his threatenings. Congealing then is nothing else but that hardness or contumacy, which is contracted by self-indulgences, and particularly when the minds of men become almost stupefied. [81] And by lees he means sinful indulgences, which so infatuate all the senses of men, that no light nor sincerity remains.

He then mentions what they said in their hearts. He expresses here what that carelessness which he condemned brings with it — even that wicked men fearlessly mock God. What it is to speak in the heart, is evident from many parts of Scripture; it means to determine anything within: for though the ungodly do not openly proclaim what they determine in their minds, they yet reason within themselves, and settle this point — that either there is no God, or that he rests idly in heaven. 'Said has the ungodly in his heart, No God is.' Why in the heart? Because shame or fear prevents men from openly avowing their impiety; yet they cherish such thoughts in the heart and assent to them. Now here is described by the Prophet the height of impiety, when he says, that men drunk with pleasures robbed God of his office as a judge, saying, that he does neither good nor evil. And it is probable that there were then many at Jerusalem and throughout Judea who thus insolently despised God as a judge. But Zephaniah especially speaks of the chief men; for such above all others deride God, as the giants did, and look down as from on high on his judgments. There is indeed much insensibility among the common people; but there is more madness in the pride of great men, who, trusting in their power, think themselves exempt from the authority of God.

But what I have just said must be borne in mind, that an unhealable impiety is described by the Prophet, when he accuses the Jews, that they did not think God to be the author either of good or of evil; because God is thus deprived of his dignity; for except he is owned as the judge of the world, what becomes of his dignity? The majesty, or the authority, or the glory of God does not consist in some imaginary brightness, but in those works which so necessarily belong to him, that they cannot be separated from his very essence. It is what peculiarly belongs to God, to govern the world, and to exercise care over mankind, and also to make a difference between good and evil, to help the miserable, to punish all wickedness, to check injustice and violence. When any one takes away these things from God, he leaves him an idol only. Since, then, the glory of God consists in his justice, wisdom, judgment, power, and other attributes, all who deny God to be the governor of the world entirely extinguish, as much as they can, his glory. Even so do heathen writers accuse Epicures; for as he dared not to deny the existence of some god, like Diagoras and some others, he confessed that there are some gods, but shut them up in heaven, that they might enjoy there their leisure and delights. But this is to imagine a god, who is not a god. It is then no wonder that the Prophet condemns with so much sharpness the stupidity of the Jews, as they thought that neither good nor evil proceeded from God. But there was also a greater reason why God should be so indignant at such senselessness: for whence was it that men entertained such an opinion or such a delirious thought, as to deny that God did either good or evil, except that they attempted to drive God far away from them, that they might not be subject to his judgment.

They therefore who seek to extinguish the distinction between right and wrong in their consciences, invent for themselves the delirious notion, that God concerns not himself with human affairs, that he is contented with his own celestial felicity, and descends not to us, and that adversity as well as prosperity happens to men by chance.

We hence see how men seek willfully and designedly to indulge the notion, that neither good nor evil comes from God: they do this, that they may stupefy their own consciences, and thus precipitate themselves with greater liberty into sin, as though they were free to do anything with impunity, and as though there was no judge to whom an account is to be rendered.

And hence I have said, that it is the very summit of impiety when men strengthen themselves in this error, that God rests in heaven, and that whatever miseries they endure in this world happen through fortunes and that whatever good things they have are to be ascribed either to their own industry or to chance. And so the Prophet briefly shows in this passage that the Jews were past recovery, that no one might feel surprised, that God should punish with so much severity a people who had been his friends, and whom he had adopted in preference to the whole world: for he had set apart the race of Abraham, as it is well known, as his chosen and holy people. God's vengeance on the children of Abraham might have appeared cruel or extremely rigid, had it not been expressly declared that they had advanced so far in impiety as to seek to exclude God from the government of the world, and to deprive him of his own peculiar office, even that of punishing sin, of defending his own people, of delivering them from all evils, of relieving all their miseries. Since, then, they thus shut up God in heaven, and gave the governing power on earth to fortune, it was an intolerable stupidity, nay, wholly diabolical. It was therefore no wonder that God was so severely indignant, and stretched forth his hand to punish their sin, as their disease had become now incurable.

PRAYER

Grant, Almighty God, that as almost the whole world breaks out into such excesses, that there is no moderation, no reason, — O grant, that we may learn not only to confine ourselves within those limits which thou dost approve and command, but also to delight and glory in the smallness of our portion, inasmuch as the wealth, and honors, and pleasures of the world so fascinate the hearts and minds of all, that they elevate themselves into heaven, and carry on war, as it were, avowedly with thee. Grant also to us, that in our limited portion we may be in such a way humbled under thy powerful hand, as never to doubt but that thou wilt be our deliverer even in our greatest miseries; and that ascribing to thee the power over life and death, we may feel fully assured, that whatever afflictions happen to us, proceed from thy just judgment, so that we may be led to repentance, and daily exercise ourselves in it, until we shall at length come to that blessed rest which is laid up for us in heaven, through Christ our Lord. Amen.

LECTURE ONE HUNDRED AND TWENTY-FIRST

Zephaniah 1:13

13. Therefore their goods shall become a booty, and their houses a desolation: they shall also build houses, but not inhabit them; and they shall plant vineyards, but not drink the wine thereof.

13. Et erit substantia eorum in direptionem, et domus eorum in vastitatem; et aedificabunt domos, neque habitabunt; et plantabunt vineas, neque bibent vinum earum.

Zephaniah pursues the same subject — that God, after long forbearance, would punish his rebellious and obstinate people. Hence he says, that they were now delivered, even by God himself, into the hands of their enemies. They indeed knew that many were inimical to them; but they did not consider God's judgment, as God himself elsewhere complains — that they did not regard the hand of him who smote them. Isa 9:13. Our Prophet, therefore, declares now that they were given up to destruction, and that their enemies would find no trouble nor difficulty in invading the land, since all places would be open to plunder. And he recites what is found in Le 26:20; for the Prophets were interpreters of the law, and the only difference between Moses and them is, that they apply his general truth to their own time. The Prophet now pursues this course, as though he had said, that God had not in vain or to no purpose threatened this evil in his law; for the Jews would find by experience that this would really be the case, and that it had been truly said, that the fruit of the land, their habitations, and other comforts of life, would be transferred to others. It now follows —

Zephaniah 1:14

14. The great day of the Lord is near, it is near, and hasteth greatly, even the voice of the day of the Lord: the mighty man shall cry there bitterly.

14. Propinquus dies Jehovae magnus, propinquus et festinans valde; vox diei Jehovae amara (ut alii vertunt,) vociferabitur illic fortis (vel, amarum, aut, amare illic vociferabitur fortis; alii secus ditinguunt, Vox diei Jehovae amara vociferabitur, aut, amare; postea, illic fortis.)

The Prophet in this verse expresses more clearly what I have already stated — That God would be the author of all the evils which would happen to the Jews; for as they grew more insensible in their sins, they more and more provoked God's wrath against themselves. It is therefore no common wisdom to consider God's hand when he strikes or chastens us. This is the reason why the Prophet now calls the attention of the Jews to God, that they might not fix their minds, as it is commonly done, on men only. At the same time, he tries to shake off their torpor by declaring that the day would be terrible, and that it was also now near at hand. We indeed know that hypocrites trifle with God, except they feel the weight of his wrath, and that they protract time, and promise themselves so long a respite, that they never awake to repentance. Hence the Prophet in the first place shows, that whatever evils then impended over the Jews were not only from men, but especially from God. This is one thing; and then, in order thoroughly to touch stupid hearts, he says, that the day would be terrible; and lastly, that they might not deceive themselves by vain flatteries, he declares that the day was at hand. These three things must be noticed in order that we understand the Prophet's object.

But he says at the beginning of the verse, that the great day of Jehovah was nigh. In these words he includes the three things to which I have already referred. By calling it the day of Jehovah, he means, that whatever evils the Jews suffered, ought to have been ascribed to his judgment; and by calling it the great day, his object was to strike terror; as well as by saying, in the third place, that it was nigh. We hence see that three things are included in these words. But the Prophet more fully explains what might, on account of the brevity of his words, have seemed not quite clear.

Near, he says, is the day, and quickly hastens. Men, we know, are wont to extend time, that they may cherish their sins; for though they cannot divest themselves of every feeling as to religion, or shake it off, they yet imagine for themselves a long distance between them and God; and by such an imagination they find ease for themselves. Hence the Prophet declares the day to be nigh; and as it was hardly credible that the destruction of which he spake was near, he adds, that the day was quickly hastening; as though he had said, that they ought not to judge by the present state of things what God would do, for in a moment his wrath would pass through from east to west like lightning. Men need long preparation when they determine to execute their vengeance; but God has no need of much preparation, for his own power is sufficient for him when he resolves to destroy the wicked. We now, then, see why it was added by the Prophet, that the day would quickly hasten.

He now repeats that the day of Jehovah and his voice would cry out bitterly. I have stated three renderings as given by interpreters. Some read thus — The day of Jehovah shall be bitter; there the strong shall cry aloud. This meaning is admissible, and a useful instruction may from it be elicited; as though the Prophet had said, that no courage could bring help to men, or be an aid to them, against God's vengeance. Others give this rendering, that the day would bitterly cry out, for there would be the strong, that is, the strength of enemies would break down whatever courage the Jews might have. But this second meaning seems forced; and I am disposed to adopt the third — that the voice of the day of Jehovah would bitterly cry out. And he means the voice of those who would have really to know God as a judge, whom they had previously despised; for God would then put forth his power, which had been an object of contempt, until the Jews had by experience felt it. [82]

As to the Prophet's design, there is no ambiguity: for he seeks here to rouse the Jews from their insensibility, who had so hardened themselves against all threatening, that the Prophets were not able to convince them. Since, then, they had thus hardened themselves against every instruction and all warnings, the Prophet here says, that the voice of God's day would be different: for God's voice had sounded through the mouth of the Prophets, but it availed not with the deaf. An awful change is here announced; for the Jews shall then cry aloud, as the roaring of the divine voice shall then terrify them, when God shall really show that he is the avenger of wickedness — When therefore he shall ascend his tribunal, then ye shall cry. His messengers now cry to you in vain, for ye close up your ears; ye shall cry in your turn, but it will be in vain.

But if one prefers to take it as one sentence, The voice of the day of Jehovah, there strong, shall bitterly cry out, the meaning will be the same as to the main point. I would not, therefore, contend about words, provided we bear in mind what I have already said — that Zephaniah sets here the cry of the distressed people in opposition to the voices of the Prophets, which they had despised, yea, and for the most part, as it appears from other places, treated with ridicule. However this may have been, he indirectly condemns their false confidence, when he speaks of the strong; as though he had said, that they were strong only for their own ruin, while they opposed God and his servants; for this strength falls at length, nay, it breaks itself by its own weight, when God rises to judgment. It follows —

Zeph. 1:15, 16

15. That day is a day of wrath, a day of trouble and distress, a day of wasteness and desolation, a day of darkness and gloominess, a day of clouds and thick darkness,

15. Dies excandescentiae, dies ille, dies angustiae et afflictionis, dies tumultus, et vastationis, dies tumultus et vastationis, dies tenebrarum et caliginis, dies nubis et nebulae;

16. A day of the trumpet and alarm against the fenced cities, and against the high towers.

16. Dies tubae et clangoris super urbes munitas, et super arces excelsas.

The Prophet shows here how foolish they were who extenuated God's vengeance, as hypocrites and all wicked men are wont to do. Hence he accuses the Jews of madness, that they thought that the way of reconciliation would be easy to them, when they had by their perverseness provoked God to come against them as an armed enemy. For though the ungodly do not promise to themselves anything of God's favor, yet they entertain vain imaginations, as though he might with no trouble be pacified: they do not think that he will be propitious to them, and yet in the meantime they deride his vengeance. Against this kind of senselessness the Prophet now inveighs. We have stated in other places, that these kinds of figurative expressions were intended solely for this end — to constrain men to entertain some fear, for they willfully deluded themselves: for the Prophets had to do, partly with open despisers of God, and partly with his masked worshipers, whose holiness was hypocrisy.

This, then, was the reason why he said, that that day would be a day of wrath, and also a day of distress and of affliction, [83] of tumult and desolation, [84] of darkness and of thick darkness, of clouds and of mist. In short, he intended to remove from the Jews that confidence with which they flattered themselves, yea, the confidence which they derived from their contempt of God: for the flesh is secure, while it has coverts, where it may withdraw itself from the presence of God. True confidence cannot exceed moderation, that is, the confidence that is founded on God's word, for thus men come nigh to God: but the flesh wishes for no other rest but in the forgetfulness of God. And we have already seen in the Prophet Amos, (Am 5:18,) why the day of Jehovah is painted as being so dreadful; he had, as I have said, to contend with hypocrites, who made an improper use of God's name, and at the same time slumbered in gross insensibility. Hence Amos said, It will be a day, not of light, but of darkness; not of joy, but of sorrow. Why then do ye anxiously expect the day of the Lord? For the Jews, glorying in being the chosen people of God, and trusting only in their false title of adoption, thought that everything was lawful for them, as though God had renounced his own authority. And thus hypocrites ever flatter themselves, as though they held God bound to them. Our Prophet does not, as Amos, distinctly express these sentiments, yet the meaning of the words is the same, and that is, that when God ascends his tribunal, there is no hope for pardon. He at the same time cuts off from them all their vain confidences; for though God excludes all escapes, yet hypocrites look here and there, before and behind, to the right hand and to the left.

The Prophet therefore intimates, that there would be everywhere darkness and thick darkness, clouds and mists, affliction and distress, — Why? because it would be the day of wrath; for God, after having borne patiently a long time with the Jews, and seen that they perversely abused his patience, would at length put forth his power. And that they might not set up their own strongholds against God, he says, that war was proclaimed against the fortified cities and high citadels. We hence see that he deprives the Jews of all help, in order that they might understand that they were to perish, except they repented, and thus return into favor with God. It shall then be a day of the trumpet and of shouting, [85] — How? on all fortified cities. For the Jews, as it is usually done, compared the strength of their enemies with their own. It was not their purpose to go forth beyond their own borders: and they thought that they would be able to resist, and be sufficiently fortified, if any foreign enemy invaded them. The Prophet laughs to scorn this notion, for God had declared war against their fortified cities. It follows —

Zephaniah 1:17

17. And I will bring distress upon men, that they shall walk like blind men, because they have sinned against the LORD: and their blood shall be poured out as dust, and their flesh as the dung.

17. Et coarctabo hominem (vel, homines,) et ambulabunt tanquam caeci, quia contra Iehovam impie egerunt; et fundetur sanguis quasi pulvis; et caro eorum erit tanquam stercora.

He confirms what I have already stated — that though other enemies, the Assyrians or Chaldeans, attacked the Jews, yet God would be the principal leader of the war. God then claims here for himself what the Jews transferred to their earthly enemies: and the Prophet has already often called it the day of Jehovah; for God would then make known his power, which had been a sport to them. He therefore declares in this place, that he would reduce man to distress, so that the whole nation would walk like the blind — that, being void of counsel, they would stumble and fall, and not be able to proceed in their course: for they are said to go astray like the blind, who see no end to their evils, who find no means to escape ruin, but are held as it were fast bound. And we must ever bear in mind what I have already said — that the Jews were inflated with such pride, that they heedlessly despised all the Prophets. Since then they were thus wise in themselves, God denounces blindness on them.

He subjoins the reason, Because they had acted impiously towards Jehovah [86] By these words he confirms what I have already explained — that the intermediate causes are not to be considered, though the Chaldeans took vengeance on the Jews; for there is a higher principle, and another cause of this evil, even the contempt of God and of his celestial truth; for they had acted impiously towards God. And by these words the Prophet reminds the Jews, that no alleviation was to be expected, as they had not only men hostile to them, but God himself, whom they had extremely provoked.

Hence he adds, Poured forth shall be your blood as dust [87] They whom God delivered up to extreme reproach were deserving of this, because he had been despised by them. Their flesh, [88] he says, shall be as dung. Now, we know how much the Jews boasted of their preeminence; and God had certainly given them occasion to boast, had they made a right and legitimate use of his benefits; but as they had despised him, they deserved in their turn to be exposed to every ignominy and reproach. Hence the Prophet here lays prostrate all their false boastings by which they were inflated; for they wished to be honorable, while God was despised by them. At last he adds —

Zephaniah 1:18

18. Neither their silver nor their gold shall be able to deliver them in the day of the Lord's wrath; but the whole land shall be devoured by the fire of his jealousy: for he shall make even a speedy riddance of all them that dwell in the land.

18. Etiam argentum eorum, etiam aurum eorum, nihil proficiet ad liberandos ipsos in die excandescentiae Jehovae, et in igne indignationis ejus evorabitur omnis terra; quia consumptionem et quidem definitam (vel, horribilem, vel, celerem) facet cum omnibus incolis terrae.

He repeats what he has already said — that the helps which the Jews hoped would be in readiness to prevent God's vengeance would be vain. For though men dare not openly to resist God, yet they hope by some winding courses to find out some way by which they may avert his judgment. As then the Jews, trusting in their wealth, and in their fortified cities, became insolent towards God, the Prophet here declares, that neither gold nor silver should be a help to them. Let them, he says, accumulate wealth; though by the mass of their gold and silver they form high mountains for themselves, yet they shall not be able to turn aside the hand of God, nor be able to deliver themselves, — and why? He repeats again the same thing, that it would be the day of wrath. We indeed know, that the most savage enemies are sometimes pacified by money, for avarice mitigates their cruelty; but the Prophet declares here, that as God would be the ruler in that war, there would be no redemption, and therefore money would be useless: for God could by no means receive them into favor, except they repented and truly humbled themselves before him.

He therefore adds, that the land would be devoured by the fire of God's jealousy, or indignation. He compares God's wrath to fire; for no agreement can be made when fire rages, but the more materials there are the more will there be to increase the fire. So then the Prophet excludes the Jews from any hope of deliverance, except they reconciled themselves to God by true and sincere repentance; for a consummation, he says, he will make as to all the inhabitants of the land, and one indeed very quick or speedy. [89] In short, he means, that as the Jews had hardened themselves against every instruction, they would find God's vengeance to be such as would wholly consume them, as they would not anticipate it, but on the contrary enhance it by their pride and stupidity, and even deride it. Now follows —

CHAPTER 2

Zeph. 2:1, 2

1. Gather yourselves together, yea, gather together, O nation not desired;

1. Colligite vos, et colligite gens non amabilis;

2. Before the decree bring forth, before the day pass as the chaff, before the fierce anger of the Lord come upon you, before the day of the Lord's anger come upon you.

2. Antequam pariat decretum, sicut stipula transibit die, antequam veniat super eos furor irae Iehovae, antequam veniat super eos dies irae Iehovae.

The Prophet, after having spoken of God's wrath, and shown how terrible it would be, and also how near, now exhorts the Jews to repentance, and thus mitigates the severity of his former doctrine, provided their minds were teachable. We hence learn that God fulminates in his word against men, that he may withhold his hand from them. The more severe, then, God is, when he chastises us and makes known our sins, and sets before us his wrath, the more clearly he testifies how precious and dear to him is our salvation; for when he sees us rushing headlong, as it were, into ruin, he calls us back by threatening and chastisements. Whenever, then, God condemns us by his word, let us know that he will be propitious to us, if, touched with true repentance, we flee to his mercy; for to effect this is the design of all his reproofs and threatening.

There follows then a seasonable exhortation, after the Prophet had spoken of the dreadfulness of God's vengeance. Gather yourselves, he says, gather, ye nation not worthy of being loved. Others read — Search among yourselves, search; and interpreters differ as to the root of the verb; some derive it from קשש, koshesh, and others from קוש, kush; while some deduce the verb from the noun קש kosh, which signifies chaff or stubble. But however this may be, I consider the real meaning of the Prophet to be — Gather yourselves, gather; for this is what grammatical construction requires. I do not see why they who read search yourselves, depart from the commonly received meaning, except they think that the verb gather does not suit the context; but it suits it exceedingly well. Others with more refinement read thus — Gather the chaff, gather the chaff, as though the Prophet ridiculed the empty confidence of the people. But as I have already said, he no doubt shows here the remedy, by which they might have anticipated God's judgment, with which he had threatened them. He indeed compares them to stubble, as we find in the next verse, but he shows that still time is given them to repent, so that they might gather themselves, and not be dissipated; as though he said — The day of your scattering is at hand; ye shall then vanish away like chaff, for ye shall not be able to stand at the breath of the Lord's wrath. But now while God withholds himself, and does not put forth his hand to destroy you, gather yourselves, that ye may not be like the chaff. There are then two parts in this passage; the first is, that if the Jews abused, as usual, the forbearance of God, they would become like the chaff, for God's wrath would in a moment scatter them; but the Prophet in the meantime reminds them that a seasonable time for repentance was still given them; for if they willingly gathered themselves, God would spare them. Before then the day of Jehovah's wrath shall come; gather, he says, yourselves [90]

But the way of gathering is, when men do not vanish away in their foolish confidences, or when they do not indulge their own lusts; for whenever men give loose reins to wicked licentiousness, and thus go astray in gratifying their corrupt lusts, or when they seek here and there vain confidences, they expose themselves to a scattering. Hence the Prophet exhorts them to examine themselves, to gather themselves, and as it were to draw themselves together, that they might not be like the chaff. Hence he says, — gather yourselves, yea, gather, ye nation not loved

Some take the participle נכסף, necasaph, in an active sense, as though the Prophet had said that the Jews were void of every feeling, and had become wholly hardened in their stupidity. But I know not whether this can be grammatically allowed. I therefore follow what has been more approved. The nation is called not worthy of love, because it did not deserve mercy; and God thus amplifies and renders illustrious his own grace, because he was still solicitous about the salvation of those who had willfully destroyed themselves, and rejected his favor. Though then the Jews had by their depravity so alienated themselves from God, that there was no reason why he should save them, he yet still continued to call them back to himself. It is therefore a remarkable proof of the unfailing grace of God, when he shows love to a nation wholly worthy of being hated, and is concerned for its safety. [91]

He then adds, Before the decree brings forth. Here the Prophet asserts his own authority, and that of God's other servants: for the Jews thought that all threatening would come to nothing, as it is the case with most men at this day who deride every true doctrine, as though it were nothing but an empty sound. Hence the Prophet ascribes birth to his doctrine. It is indeed true, that the word decree has a wider meaning; but the Prophet does not speak here of the hidden counsel of God. He therefore calls that a decree, which God had already declared by his servants: and the meaning is, that it is not beating the air when God denounces his vengeance on sinners by his Prophets, but that it is a fixed and unchangeable decree, which shall at length be effected. But the similitude of birth is most apposite; for as the embryo lies hid in the womb, and then emerges in due time into light; so God's vengeance, though hid for a time, will yet in due season be accomplished, when God sees that men's wickedness is past a remedy. We now understand why the Prophet says, that the time was near when the decree should bring forth.

Then he says, Pass away shall the chaff in a day. Some read, Before the day comes, when the stubble (or chaff) shall pass away. But I take מוֹץ, ium, in another sense, as meaning that the Jews shall quickly pass away as the chaff; the like expression we have also met in Hosea. He says then that the Jews would perish in a day, in a short time, and as it were in a moment; though they thought that they would not be for a long time conquered. Pass away, he says, shall they like chaff [92]

Then he adds, Before it comes, the fury of Jehovah's wrath; the day of Jehovah's wrath, gather ye yourselves. He says first, before it comes upon you, the fury of wrath, and then, the day of wrath. He repeats the same thing; but some of the words are changed, for instead of the fury of wrath, he puts in the second clause, the day of wrath; as though he had said, that they were greatly deceived if they thought that they could escape, because the Lord deferred his vengeance. How so? For the day, which was nigh, though not yet arrived, would at length come. As when one trusting in the darkness of the night, and thinking himself safe from the danger of being taken, is mistaken, for suddenly the sun rises and discovers his hiding-place; so the Prophet intimates, that though God was now still, it would yet be no advantage to the Jews: for he knew the suitable time. Though then he restrained for a time his wrath, he yet poured it forth suddenly, when the day came and the iniquity of men had become ripe.

PRAYER

Grant, Almighty God, that as we continue in various ways to provoke thy wrath, we may at length be awakened by the blasting of that trumpet which sounds in our ears, when thou proclaimest that thou wilt be the judge of the world, and testifies also the same so plainly in the gospel, so that we may, with our minds raised up to thee, learn to renounce all the depraved lusts of the world, and that having shaken off our torpidity, we may so hasten to repent, that we may anticipate thy judgment, and so find that we are reconciled to thee, as to enjoy thy goodness, and ever to retain the taste of it, in order that we may be enabled to renounce all the allurements and pleasures of this world, until we shall at length come to that blessed rest, where we shall be filled with that unspeakable joy, which thou hast promised to us, and which we hope for in Christ our Lord. Amen.

LECTURE ONE HUNDRED AND TWENTY-SECOND

Zephaniah 2:3

3. Seek ye the Lord, all ye meek of the earth, which have wrought his judgment; seek righteousness, seek meekness: it may be ye shall be hid in the day of the Lord's anger.

3. Quaerite Jehovam omnes mansueti terrae, qui judicium ejus fecerunt (pro fecistis;) quaerite justitiam, quaerite mansuetudinem, si forte abscondamini in die irae Jehovae.

Here the Prophet turns his discourse to a small number, for he saw that he could produce no effect on the promiscuous multitude. For had his doctrine been addressed in common to the whole people, there were very few who would have attended. We would therefore have been discouraged had he not believed that some seed remained among the people, and that the office of teaching and exhorting had not been in vain committed to him by God. But he shows at the same time that the greater part were wholly given up to destruction. We now see why the Prophet especially addresses the meek of the land; for few undertook the yoke, though they had been already broken down by many calamities. And it hence appears that the fruit of correction was not found equal in all, for God had chastised the good and the bad, the whole people, from the least to the greatest; they had all been laid prostrate by many evils, yet the same ferocity remained, as God complains in Isaiah, that he labored in vain in punishing that refractory nation. Isa 1:5

But we are here taught that though ministers of the word may think that they spend their labor to no purpose, while they sing to the deaf, as the proverb is, they ought not yet to depart from the course of their vocation; for there will ever be some who will really show, after a long time, that they had been divinely and wonderfully saved, so as not to perish with others. But what the Prophet had especially in view was to show, that the faithful ought not to regard what the multitude may do, or how they live; but that when God invites them to repentance, and gives them a hope of pardon, they ought without delay to come to him, that they might not perish with the rest. And it deserves to be noticed, that when God raises his voice, some harden others, and thus men lead one another into ruin. Thus it happens that all teaching becomes unsuccessful. Hence the Prophet applies a remedy, by showing how preposterous it is when some follow others; for in this way they increase the ranks of the rebellious; but that if there be any who are meek, they ought to be teachable, when God stretches forth his hand and shows that he will be propitious, provided they return to the right way.

He calls them meek who had profited under the scourges of God; for the Hebrews consider םיונע, onuim, to be the afflicted, deriving the word from הנע, one, to afflict, or to be humble. But as men for the most part are not subdued except by scourges, they call, by a metaphor, םיונע, onuim, the meek, such as have been subdued: for men grow wanton in their pleasures, and abundance commonly produces insolence; but by adversity they learn to become meek. Hence our Prophet calls those the meek of the land who were submissive to God, after having been chastised by him. For we know, that though God may smite the wicked, they yet continue to have a stiff and iron neck and a brazen front: but the faithful are tamed, as Jeremiah confesses as to himself; for he says that he was like an untamed heifer before he was chastised by God's scourges. So the Prophet directs his discourse to the few who had felt the afflicting hand of God, and had been thus humbled. [93]

He bids them to seek Jehovah, and yet he says that they had wrought his judgment. These two clauses seem inconsistent with each other; for if they had been previously alienated from God, justly might the Prophet bid them to return to the right way; but as they had devoted themselves to religion, and formed their life according to the rule of uprightness, the Prophet seems to have exhorted them without reason to seek God. But the passage is worthy of special notice; for we hence learn that even the best are roused by God's scourges to seek true religion with greater ardor than they had before done. Though then it be our object to serve God and to follow his word, yet when calamities arise and God appears as a judge, we ought to be stimulated to greater care and diligence; for it never is the case that any one of us fully performs his duty. Let us then remember, that we are roused by God whenever adversity impends over us, and when God himself shows by manifest signs that he is displeased. This is the reason why the Prophet bids the pious doers of righteousness to seek God, however much they were before devoted to what was just and upright.

There was also another reason: we know how grievously faith is tried, when the good and wicked are indiscriminately and without any difference chastised by God's hand; for the godly are then tempted to think that it avails them nothing that they have labored sincerely to serve God; they think that this has all been in vain and to no purpose, for they are brought into the same miseries with others. As then this temptation is enough to shake even the strongest, the Prophet here exhorts the faithful to persevere, as though he had said, that in the first confusion no difference would be found between the good and the wicked as to their circumstances, for God would afflict both alike, but that the end would be different; and that there was therefore no reason for them to despond or to think it of no advantage to seek God: for he would at length really show that he approved of their integrity; as though he had said, God will not remunerate you at the first moment; but your patience will at length find that he is a just judge, who has regard for his people, and delivers them in their extremity.

To do the judgment of God in this place is to form the life according to the righteousness of the law. The word משפט, meshepheth, has various meanings in Scripture. Sometimes, and indeed often, it designates the punishment which God allots to the wicked: but it frequently means equity or the rule of right living. Hence to do judgment is to observe what is righteous and just, to abstain from what is wrong and injurious. But the

Prophet calls it the judgment of God, because it is what he prescribes in his word and what he approves. For we know that men blend various things, by which they would prove themselves to be just and righteous: but they deceive themselves, except they form their life especially according to what God requires. We now perceive what the Prophet means; and he afterwards defines what it is to seek God; for the latter part of the verse is added as an explanation, that the faithful might understand how God is to be sought.

For hypocrites, as soon as God invites them, accumulate many rites, and weary themselves much in things of no value. In short, they think that they have sufficiently sought God when they have performed a number of ceremonies. But by over-acting they trifle as it were with God, and thus deceive themselves. Thus we see repentance profaned. They under the Papacy prattle enough about repentance, but when they are asked to define it, they begin with contrition; and yet no displeasure at sin is mentioned by them, nor any real love of righteousness, but they talk about attrition and contrition, and then immediately they leap to confession; and this is the principal part of repentance: they afterwards come to satisfactions. Thus repentance among the Papists is nothing else but a some kind of mistaken solicitude, by which they labor to pacify God, as though they came nigh him: nay, the satisfactions of the Papacy are nothing else but obstructions between God and men.

This evil has been common in all ages. The Prophet, therefore, does not without reason define what the true and rightful way of seeking God is, and that is, when righteousness is sought, when humility is sought. By righteousness he understands the same thing as by judgment; as though he had said, Advance in a righteous and holy course of life, for God will not forget your obedience, provided your hearts grow not faint, and ye persevere to the end. We hence see that God complains, not only when we obtrude external pomps and devices I know not what, as though he might like a child be amused by us; but also when we do not sincerely devote our life to his service. And he adds humility to righteousness; for it is difficult even for the very best of men not to murmur against God when he severely chastises them. We indeed find how much their own delicacy embitters the minds of men when God appears somewhat severe with them. Hence the Prophet, in order to check all clamors, exhorts the faithful here to cultivate humility, so that they might patiently bear the rigor by which God would try them, and might suffer themselves to be ruled by his hand. Peter had the same thing in view when he said, Humble yourselves under the mighty hand of God. (1Pe 5:6.) We now then see why the Prophet requires from the faithful not only righteousness but also humility; it was, that they might with composed minds wait for the deliverance which God had promised. They were not in the interval to murmur, nor to give vent to their own perverse feelings, however severely God might treat them.

We may hence gather a profitable instruction: The Prophet does not address here men who were depraved and had wholly neglected what was just and right, but he directs his discourse to the best, the most upright, the most holy: and yet he shows that they had no other remedy, but humbly and patiently to bear the chastisement of God. It then follows that no perfection can be found among men, such as can meet the judgment of God. For were any to object and say, that they devoted themselves to righteousness, there is yet a just reason why they should humble themselves; for we are all guilty before God, and no one can clear himself, inasmuch as when any one examines his own conscience, he finds that he is not free from sin. However conscious then we may be of acting uprightly, and God himself may be a judge to us, and the Holy Spirit the witness of our true and real integrity; yet when the Lord summons us before his tribunal, let us all, from the least to the greatest, learn to confess ourselves guilty and exposed to judgment.

He afterwards adds, If it may be (or, it may be) ye shall be concealed [94] in the day of Jehovah's anger. The Prophet speaks not doubtingly, as though the faithful were uncertain as to God's favor: but he had another thing in view, — that though no hope remained as to the perceptions of men, yet the faithful would not lose their labor, if they sought God; for in their worst circumstances they would find him propitious to them and their safety secured by his kindness. Hence we see, that the Prophet in these words points out the disastrous character of the event, but no deficiency in the love of God. Though the Lord is ready to pardon, nay, of his own self anticipates his people, and kindly invites them to himself; it is yet necessary for them to consider how wonderful is his power in preserving his elect, when all things seem desperate. It may then be, he says, when the Jews understood that all things were in a state of extreme despair: and the Prophet said this, partly that the reprobate and the perverse might know that they were to perish, and partly that the faithful might appreciate the more the favor of God, when they saw themselves delivered from death by a miracle, and found that it would be a kind of resurrection, when God became their deliverer. Hence the Prophet, in order to commend to God's children his salvation, which he offers them, and to render more illustrious God's favor, makes use of the particle ילוא, auli, it may be. In the meantime he fulminates, as I have already said, against the reprobate, that they might understand that it was all over with them. It follows —

Zeph. 2:4, 5

4. For Gaza shall be forsaken, and Ashkelon a desolation: they shall drive out Ashdod at the noon day, and Ekron shall be rooted up.

4. Quia Aza derelicta erit, et Aksalon in vastiationem; Asdod in meridie expellent, et Ekron dissipabitur.

5. Woe unto the inhabitants of the sea coast, the nation of the Cherethites! the word of the LORD is against you; O Canaan, the land of the Philistines, I will even destroy thee, that there shall be no inhabitant.

5. Heus habitatores funiculi maris (vel, regionis) gens Cretim; sermo Iehovae contra vos Canaan, terra Philistim; et exterminabo te, ne sit habitator.

The Prophet begins here to console the elect; for when God's vengeance had passed away, which would only be for a time against them, the heathens and foreigners would find God in their turn to be their judge to punish them for the wrongs done to his people; though some think that God's judgment on the Jews is here described, while yet the Prophet expressly mentions their neighbors: but the former view seems to me more suitable, — that the Prophet reminds the faithful of & future change of things, for God would not perpetually afflict his chosen people, but would transfer his vengeance to other nations. The meaning then is — that God, who has hitherto threatened the Jews, would nevertheless be propitious to them, not indeed to all the people, for a great part was doomed to destruction, but to the remnant, whom the Lord had chosen as a seed to himself, that there might be some church remaining. For we know, that God had always so moderated the punishment he inflicted on his people, as not to render void his covenant, nor abolish the memory of Abraham's race: for this reason he was to come forth as their Redeemer.

Since then the Prophet speaks here against Gaza, and Ashkelon, and Ashdod, and Akron, and the Philistine, and the Cretians and others, he intended no doubt to add courage to the faithful, that they might not despair of God's mercy, though they might find themselves very grievously oppressed; for he could at length put an end to his wrath, after having purged his Church of its dregs. And this admonition the faithful also need, that they may not envy the wicked and the despisers of God, as though their condition were better or more desirable. For when the Lord spares the wicked and chastens us, we are tempted to think that nothing is better than to shake off every yoke. Lest then this temptation should have assailed the faithful, the Prophet reminded them in time, that there was no reason why the heathens should flatter or congratulate themselves, when God did not immediately punish them; for their portion was prepared for them.

He mentions Gaza first, a name which often occurs in scripture. The Hebrews called it Aza; but as ע, oin, is the first letter, the Greeks have rendered it Gaza, and heathen authors have thought it to be a Persia word, and it means in that language a treasure. But this is a vain notion, for it is no doubt a Hebrew word. He then adds Ashkelon, a city nigh to Gaza. In the third place he mentions Ashdod, which the Greeks have translated Azotus, and the Latins have followed the Greeks. He names Ekron in the last place. All these cities were near to the Jews, and were not far from one another towards the Moabites and the Idumeans. [95]

He then adds, Ho! (or, woe to, הוי) the inhabitants of the line of the sea. The region of the sea he calls Galilee; and he joins the Kerethites and the Philistine. Some think that he alludes to the troops, who carried on war under David; for he had chosen his garrison soldiers from that nation, that is, from the people of Galilee, and had called them Kerethites and Philistine. But I know not whether the Prophet spoke so refinedly. I rather think, that he refers here to those heathen nations, which had been hostile to the Jews, though vicinity ought to have been a bond of kindness. Hence he includes them all in the name of Canaan: for I do not take it here, as some do, as signifying merchants; for the Prophet evidently means, that however called, they were all Canaanites, who had been long ago doomed to destruction. Since then those regions had been enemies to the Jews, the Prophet intimates that God would become the defender of his chosen people.

The word of Jehovah is against you. God, who has hitherto threatened his own people, summons you to judgment. Think not that you will escape unpunished for having vexed his Church. For though God designed to prove the patience of his people, yet neither the Moabites, nor the rest, were excusable when they cruelly oppressed the Jews; yea, when they purposed through them to fight with God himself, the creator of heaven and earth. He afterwards adds, There shall be no inhabitant, for God would destroy them all. We now see that the Prophet had no other design but to alleviate the bitter grief of the faithful by this consolation, — that their miseries would be only for a time, and that God would ere long punish their enemies. It follows —

Zeph. 2:6, 7

6. And the sea coast shall be dwellings and cottages for shepherds, and folds for flocks.

6. Et erit funiculus maris (id est, regio; sed metaphorice Hebraei vocant regionem, funiculum, propter distributionem) habitaculum caulis pastorum et septa ovium.

7. And the coast shall be for the remnant of the house of Judah; they shall feed thereupon: in the houses of Ashkelon shall they lie down in the evening: for the LORD their God shall visit them, and turn away their captivity.

7. Et erit regio reliquiis domus Jehudah, apud eos pascentur, in domibus Ascalon vesperi accubabunt; quia visitabit Jehova Deus ipsorum ipsos, et reducet captivitatem eorum.

The Prophet confirms what he has before said respecting the future vengeance of God, which was now nigh at hand to the Moabites and other neighboring nations, who had been continually harassing the miserable Jews. Hence, he says, that that whole region would become the habitation of sheep. It is a well known event, that when any country is without inhabitants shepherds occupy it; for there is no sowing nor reaping there, but grass alone grows. Where, therefore, there is no cultivation, where no number of men are found, there shepherds find a place for their flocks, there they build sheep cots. It is, therefore, the same as though the

Prophet had said, that the country would be desolate, as we find it expressed in the next verse. [96]

He immediately adds, but for a different reason, that the coast of the sea would be a habitation to the house of Judah. And there is here a striking divergence from the flocks of shepherds to the tribe of Judah, which was as it were, the chosen flock of God. The Prophet then, after having said that the region would be waste and desolate, immediately adds, that it would be for the benefit of the chosen people; for the Lord would grant there to the Jews a safe and secure rest. But the Prophet confines this to the remnant; for the greater part, as we have already seen, were become so irreclaimable, that the gate of mercy was completely closed against them. The Prophet, at the same time, by mentioning a remnant, shows that there would always be some seed from which God would raise up a new Church; and he also encourages the faithful to entertain hope, so that their own small number might not terrify them; for when they considered themselves and found themselves surpassed by a vast multitude, they might have thought that they were of no account. Lest then they should be disheartened the Prophet says that this remnant would be the object of God's care; for when he would visit the whole coast of the sea and other regions, he would provide there for the Jews a safe habitation and refuge.

That line then, he says, shall be for the residue of the house of Judah; feed shall they in Ashkelon, and there shall they lie down in the evening; that is, they shall find in their exile some resting-place; for we know that the Jews were not all removed to distant lands; and they who may have been hid in neighboring places were afterwards more easily gathered, when a liberty to return was permitted them. This is what the Prophet means now, when he says, that there would be a refuge in the night to the Jews among the Moabites and other neighboring nations.

A reason follows, which confirms what I have stated, for Jehovah their God, he says, will visit them. We hence see that the Prophet mitigates here the sorrow of exile and of that most grievous calamity which was nigh the Jews, by promising to them a new visitation of God; as though he had said, Though the Lord seems now to rage against you, and seems to forget his own covenant, yet he will again remember his mercy, when the suitable time shall come. And he adds, he will restore their captivity; and he added this, that he might show that his favor would prove victorious against all hindrances. The Jews might indeed have raised this objection, Why does not the Lord help us immediately; but he, on the contrary, allows our enemies to remove us into exile? The Prophet here calls upon them to exercise patience; and yet be promises, that after having been driven into exile, they should again return to their country; for the Lord would not suffer that exile to be perpetual. It now follows —

Zephaniah 2:8

8. I have heard the reproach of Moab, and the revilings of the children of Ammon, whereby they have reproached my people, and magnified themselves against their border.

8. Audivi opprobrium Moab, et contumelias filiorum Ammon, quibus exprobrarunt populo meo, et se extulerunt contra terminum ipsorum.

The Prophet confirms what I have just said of God's vengeance against foreign enemies. Though all the neighboring nations had been eager in their hostility to the Jews, yet we know that more hatred, yea and more fury, had been exhibited by these two nations than by any other, that is, by the Moabites and the Ammonites, notwithstanding their connection with them by blood, for they derived their origin from Lot, who was Abraham's nephew. Though, then, that connection ought to have turned the Moabites and the Ammonites to mercy, we yet know they always infested the Jews with greater fury than others, and as it were with savage cruelty. This is the reason why the Prophet speaks now especially of them. Some indeed take this sentence as spoken by the faithful; but the context requires it to be ascribed to God, and no doubt he reminds them that he looked down from on high on the proud vauntings of Moab which he scattered in the air, as though he had declared that it was not hidden or unknown to him how cruelly the Moabites and Ammonites raged against the Jews, how proud and inhuman they had been. And this was a very seasonable consolation. For the Jews might have been swallowed up with despair, had not this promise been made to them. They saw the Moabites and the Ammonites burning with fury, when yet they had not been injured or provoked. They also saw that they made gain and derived advantage from the calamities of a miserable people. What could the faithful think? These wicked men not only harassed them with impunity, but their cruelty and perfidy towards them was gainful. Where was God now? If he regarded his own Church, would he not have interposed? Lest then a temptation of this kind should upset the faithful, the Prophet introduces God here as the speaker, —

I have heard, he says, the reproach of Moab; I have heard the revilings of Amman: "Nothing escapes me; though I do not immediately show that these things are regarded by me, yet I know and observe how shamefully the Moabites and the Ammonites have persecuted you: they at length shall find that I am the guardian of your safety, and that you are under my protection." We now apprehend the Prophet's design. Nearly the same words are used by Isaiah, Isa 16:1, and also by Jeremiah Jer 48:1, they both pursue the subject much farther, while our Prophet only touches on it briefly, for we see that what he says is comprised in very few words. But by saying that the reproach of Moab and the revilings of the children of Amman had come into remembrance before God, what he had in view was — that the Jews might be assured and fully persuaded that they were not rejected and forsaken, though for a time they were reproachfully treated by the wicked. The Prophet indeed takes the words reproach and revilings, in an active sense. [97]

He then adds, By which they have upbraided any people. God intimates here that he does not depart from his elect when the wicked spit, as it were, in their faces. There is indeed nothing which so much wounds the feelings of ingenuous minds as reproach; there is not so much bitterness in hundred deaths as in one reproach, especially when the wicked licentiously triumph, and do this with the applauding consent of the whole world; for then all difference between good and evil is confounded, and good conscience is as it were buried. But the Prophet shows here, that the people of God suffer no loss when they are thus unworthily harassed by the wicked and exposed to their reproach.

He at last subjoins that they had enlarged over their border. Some consider mouth to be understood — they have enlarged the mouth against their border; and the word, it is true, without any addition, is often taken in this sense; but in this place the construction is fuller, for the words על-גבולם, ol-gebulam, over their border, follow the verb. The Prophet means that God's wrath had been provoked by the petulance of both nations, for they wished to break. up, as it were, the borders, which had been fixed by God. The land of Canaan, we know, had been given to the Jews by an hereditary right; — When the Most High, says Moses, divided the nations, he set a line for Jacob. De 32:8. It is indeed true that the possessions of the nations were allotted to them by the hidden counsel of God; but there was a special reason as to his chosen people; for the Lord had made Abraham the true possessor of that land, even for ever. Ge 17:8. Now the Moabites were confined, as it were, to a certain place; the Lord had assigned to them their own inheritance. When, therefore, they sought to go beyond and to invade the land of the Jews, God's wrath must have been kindled against them; for they thus fought, not against mortals, but against God himself; for by removing the borders fixed by him, they attempted to subvert his eternal decree. We now then understand why the Prophet says that the children of Moab and of Ammon had enlarged over the border of those who had been placed in the land of Canaan by God's hand; for they not only sought to eject their neighbors, but wished and tried to take away from God's hand that inheritance which the Lord had given to Abraham, and given, as I have said, in perpetuity. [98]

PRAYER

Grant, Almighty God, that as thou hast been pleased to consecrate us a peculiar people to thyself, we may be mindful of such an invaluable favor, and devote ourselves woody to thee, and so labor to cultivate true sincerity as to bear the marks of thy people and of thy holy Church: and as we are so polluted by so many of the defilements of our own flesh and of this world, grant that thy Holy Spirit may cleanse us more and more every day, until thou bringest us at length to that perfection to which thou invites us by the voice of thy gospel, that we may also enjoy that blessed glory which has been provided for us by the blood of thy only begotten Son. Amen.

LECTURE ONE HUNDRED AND TWENTY-THIRD

Zeph. 2:9, 10

9. Therefore as I live, saith the LORD of hosts, the God of Israel, Surely Moab shall be as Sodom, and the children of Ammon as Gomorrah, even the breeding of nettles, and saltpits, and a perpetual desolation: the residue of my people shall spoil them, and the remnant of my people shall possess them.

9. Propterea vivo ego, dicit Jehova exercituum, Deus Israel, quod Moab sicuti Sodoma erit, et filii Ammon sicuti Gomorrha, productio urticae et fodina salis, et vastitas in perpetuum: reliquiae populi mei diripient eos, et residuum gentis meae possidebit eos.

10. This shall they have for their pride, because they have reproached and magnified themselves against the people of the Lord of hosts.

10. Hoc illis pro superbis sua, quia exprobrarunt et insultarunt super populum Jehovae exercituum.

In order to cheer the miserable Jews by some consolation, God said, in what we considered yesterday, that the wantonness of Moab was known to him; he now adds, that he would visit with punishment the reproaches which had been mentioned. For it would have availed them but little that their wrongs had been observed by God, if no punishment had been prepared. Hence the Prophet reminds them that God is no idle spectator, who only observes what takes place in the world; but that there is a reward laid up for al the ungodly. And these verses are to be taken in connection, that the faithful may know that their wrongs are not unknown to God, and also that he will be their defender. But that the Jews might have a more sure confidence that God would be their deliverer, he interposes an oath. God at the same time shows that he is really touched with when he sees his people so cruelly and immoderately harassed, when the ungodly seem to think that an unbridled license is permitted them. God therefore shows here, that not only the salvation of his people is an object of his care, but that he undertakes their cause as though his anger was kindled; not that passions belong to him but such a form of speaking is adopted in order to express what the faithful could never otherwise conceive an idea of, that is, to express the unspeakable love of God towards them, and his care for them.

He then says that he lives, as though he had sworn by his own life. As we have elsewhere seen that he swears by his life, so he speaks now. Live do I, that is, As I am God, so will I avenge these wrongs by which my people are now oppressed. And for the same reason he calls himself Jehovah of hosts, and the God of Israel. In the first clause he exalts his own power, that the Jews might know that he was endued with power; and then he mentions his goodness, because he had adopted them as his people. The meaning then is that God swears by his own life; and that the Jews might not think that this was done in vain, his power is brought before them, and then his favor is added.

Moab, he says, shall be like Sodom, and the sons of Ammon like Gomorrah, even for the production of the nettle and for a mire of salt; [99] that is, their lands should be reduced to a waste, or should become wholly barren, so that nothing was to grow there but nettles, as the case is with desert places. As to the expression, the mine (fodina) or quarry of salt, it often occurs in scripture: a salt-pit denotes sterility in Hebrew. And the Prophet adds, that this would not be for a short time only; It shall be (he says) a perpetual desolation. He also adds, that this would be for the advantage of the Church; for the residue of my people shall plunder them, and the remainder of my nation shall possess them. He ever speaks of the residue; for as it was said yesterday, it was necessary for that people to be cleansed from their dregs, so that a small portion only would remain; and we know that not many of them returned from exile.

The import of the whole is, that though God determined to diminish his Church, so that a few only survived, yet these few would be the heirs of the whole land, and possess the kingdom, when God had taken vengeance on all their enemies.

It hence follows, according to the Prophet, that this shall be to them for their pride. We see that the Prophet's object is, to take away whatever bitterness the Jews might feel when insolently slandered by their enemies. As then there was danger of desponding, since nothing, as it was said yesterday, is more grievous to be borne than reproach, God does here expressly declare, that the proud triumph of their neighbors over the Jews would be their own ruin; for, as Solomon says, 'Pride goes before destruction.' Pr 16:18. And he again confirms what he had already referred to — that the Jews would not be wronged with impunity, for God had taken them under his guardianship, and was their protector: Because they have reproached, he says, and triumphed over the people of Jehovah of hosts. He might have said, over my people, as in the last verse; but there is something implied in these words, as though the Prophet had said, that they carried on war not with mortals but with God himself, whose majesty was insulted, when the Jews were so unjustly oppressed. It follows —

Zephaniah 2:11

11. The Lord will be terrible unto them: for he will famish all the gods of the earth; and men shall worship him, every one from his place, even all the isles of the heathen.

11. Terribilis Iehova super eos, quia consumpsit omnes deos terrae: et adorabit eum quisque ex loco suo, omnes insulae gentium.

He proceeds with the same subject, — that God would show his power in aiding his people. But he calls him a terrible God, who had for a time patiently endured the wantonness of his enemies, and thus became despised by them: for the ungodly, we know, never submit to God unless they are constrained by his hand; and then they are not bent so as willingly to submit to his authority; but when forced they are silent. [100] This is what the Prophet means in these words; as though he had said, that the wicked now mock God, as they disregard his power, but that they shall find how terrible an avenger of his people he is, so that they would have to dread him. And then he compares the superstitions of the nations with true religion; as though he had said, that this would be to the Jews as a reward for their piety, inasmuch as they worshipped the only true God, and that all idols would be of no avail against the help of God. And this was a necessary admonition; for the ungodly seemed to triumph for a time, not only over a conquered people, but over God himself, and thus gloried in their superstitious and vain inventions. The Prophet, therefore, confirms their desponding minds; for God, he says, will at length consume all the gods of the nations

The verb הזר, reze, means strictly to make lean or to famish, but is to be taken here metaphorically, as signifying to consume. God then will famish all the inventions of the nations: and he alludes to that famine which idols had occasioned through the whole world; as though he had said, that God's glory would shortly appear, which would exterminate whatever glory the false gods had obtained among them, so that it would melt away like fatness.

He at last adds, that the remotest nations would become suppliants to God; for by saying, adore him shall each from his place, [101] he doubtless means, that however far off the countries might be, the distance would be no hindrance to God's name being celebrated, when his power became known to remote lands. And, for the same reason, he mentions the islands of the nations, that is, countries beyond the sea: for the Hebrews, as it has been elsewhere observed, call those countries islands which are far distant, and divided by the sea. [102] In short, the Prophet shows, that the redemption of the people would be so wonderful, that the fame of it would reach the farthest bounds of the earth, and constrain foreign nations to give glory to the true God, and that it would dissipate all the mists of superstition, so that idols would be exposed to scorn and contempt. It follows —

Zephaniah 2:12

12. Ye Ethiopians also, ye shall be slain by my sword.

12. Etiam vos Ethiopes, interfecti gladio meo ipsi (alii vertunt, cum ipsis.)

The Prophet extends farther the threatened vengeance, and says, that God would also render to the Ethiopians the reward which they deserved; for they had also harassed the chosen people. But if God punished that nation, how could Ammon and Moab hope to escape? For how could God spare so great a cruelty, since he would visit with punishment the remotest nations? For the hatred of the Moabites and of the Ammonites, as we have said, was less excusable, because they were related to the children of Abraham. They ought, on this account, to have mitigated their fierceness: besides, vicinity ought to have rendered them more humane. But as they exceeded other nations in cruelty, a heavier punishment awaited them. Now this comparison was intended for this end — that the Jews might know that God would be inexorable towards the Moabites, by whom they had been so unjustly harassed, since even the Ethiopians would be punished, who yet were more excusable on account of their distance.

As to the words, some regard the demonstrative pronoun המה, eme, they, as referring to the Babylonians, and others, to the Moabites. I prefer to understand it of the Moabites, if we read, like them, or with them, as these interpreters consider it: for they regard the particle תא, at, with, or כ, caph, like, to be understood, Ye Ethiopians shall be slain by my sword like them, or with them. It would in this case doubtless apply to the Moabites. But it seems to me that the sentence is irregular, even ye Ethiopians, and then, they shall be slain by any sword. The Prophet begins the verse in the second person, summoning the Ethiopians to appear before God's tribunal; he afterwards adds in the third person, they shall be slain by my sword. [103]

God calls whatever evils were impending over the Ethiopians his sword; for though they were destroyed by the Chaldeans yet it was done under the guidance of God himself. The Chaldeans made war under his authority, as the Assyrians did, who had been previously employed by him to execute his vengeance. It follows —

Zephaniah 2:13

13. And he will stretch out his hand against the north, and destroy Assyria; and will make Nineveh a desolation, and dry like a wilderness.

13. Et extendet manum suam ad Aquilomen, et perdet Assyriam, et ponet Ninevem in vastitatiem, desolationem instar deserti.

The Prophet proceeds here to the Assyrians, whom we know to have been special enemies to the Church of God. For the Moabites and the Ammonites were fans only, as we have elsewhere seen, as they could not do much harm by their own strength. Hence they stirred up the Assyrians, they stirred up the Ethiopians and remote nations. The meaning, then, is, that no one of all the enemies of the Church would be left unpunished by God, as every one would receive a reward for his cruelty. He speaks now of God in the third person; but in the last verse God himself said, that the Ethiopians would be slain by his sword. The Prophet adds here, He will extend his hand to the north; that is, God will not complete his judgments on the Ethiopians; but he will go farther, even to Nineveh and to all the Assyrians.

Nineveh, we know, was the metropolis of the empire, before the Assyrians were conquered by the Babylonians. Thus Babylon then recovered the sovereignty which it had lost; and Nineveh, though not wholly demolished, was yet deprived of its ruling power, and gradually lost its name and its wealth, until it was reduced into a waste; for the building of Ctesiphon, as we have elsewhere seen, proved its ruin. But the Prophet, no doubt, proceeds here to administer comfort to the Jews, lest they should despair, while the Lord did not interfere. And the extension of the hand means as though he said, that his own time is known to the Lord, and that he would put forth his power when needful. Assyria was north as to Judea: hence he says, to the north will the Lord extend his hand, and will destroy Assyria; he will make Nineveh a desolation, that it may be like the desert. It follows —

Zephaniah 2:14

14. And flocks shall lie down in the midst of her, all the beasts of the nations: both the cormorant and the bittern shall lodge in the upper lintels of it; their voice shall sing in the windows; desolation shall be in the thresholds: for he shall uncover the cedar work.

14. Et cubabunt in medio ejus greges, omnes bestiae gentium: etiam onocrotalus, etiam noctua (alii vertunt, pro onocrotalo, ibin, alii, cuculum; alii, pro noctua, ericium) in postibus ejus pernoctabunt; vox cantabit in fenestra, in poste vastitatis (alii vertunt, corvum; sed nomen vastitatis, quod postulat ratio grammaticae, retinendum nobis est,) quia nudavit cedrum (vel, contignationem.)

The Prophet describes here the state of the city and the desolation of the country. He says, that the habitations of flocks would be in the midst of the city Nineveh. The city, we know, was populous; but while men were so many, there was no place for flocks, especially in the middle of a city so celebrated. Hence no common change is here described by the Prophet, when he says, that flocks would lie down in the middle of Nineveh; and he adds, all wild beasts. For beasts, which seek seclusion and shun the sight of men, are wont to come forth, when they find a country desolate and deserted; and they range then at large, as it is the case after a slaughter in war; and when any region is emptied of its inhabitants, the wolves, the lions, and other wild beasts, roam here and there at full liberty. So the Prophet says, that wild beasts would come from other parts and remote places, and find a place where Nineveh once stood. [104] He adds that the bitterns, or the storks or the cuckoos, and similar wild birds would be there. [105] As to their various kinds, I make no laborious research; for it is enough to know the Prophet's design: besides, the Jews themselves, who boldly affirm that either the bittern or the stork is meant, yet adduce nothing that is certain. What, in short, this description means, is — that the place, which before a vast multitude of men inhabited, would become so forsaken, that wild beasts and nocturnal birds would be its only inhabitants.

But we must bear in mind what I have stated, that all these things were set before the Jews, that they might patiently bear their miseries, understanding that God would become their defender. For this is the only support that remains for us under very grievous evils, as Paul reminds us in the first chapter of the Second Epistle to the Thessalonians; for he says, that the time will come when the Lord shall give to us relief and refreshment, and that he will visit our adversaries with punishment 2Th 1:1.

The Prophet mentions especially Nineveh, that the Jews might know that there is nothing so great and splendid in the world which God does not esteem of less consequence than the salvation of his Church, as it is said in Isaiah, I will give Egypt as thy ransom. So God threatens the wealthiest city, that he might show how much he loved his chosen people. And the Jews could not have attributed this to their own worthiness; but the cause of so great a love depended on their gratuitous adoption. It afterwards follows —

Zephaniah 2:15

15. This is the rejoicing city that dwelt carelessly, that said in her heart, I am, and there is none beside me: how is she become a desolation, a place for beasts to lie down in! every one that passeth by her shall hiss, and wag his hand.

15. Haec urbs exultabunda, quae sedebat confidenter, quae dicebat in corde suo, Ego et non praeter me amplius: quomodo facta est in vastationem, cubile animalibus? Quisquis transierit (vel, omnis viator) super eam subilabit, agitabit manum suam.

He seems to have added this by way of anticipation, lest the magnificent splendor of the city Nineveh should frighten the Jews, as though it were exempt from all danger. The Prophet therefore reminds them here, that though Nineveh was thus proud of its wealth, it could not yet escape the hand of God; nay, he shows that the greatness, on account of which Nineveh extolled itself, would be the cause of its ruin; for it would cast itself down by its own pride: as a wall, when it swells, will not long stand; so also men, when they inwardly swell, and vent their own boastings, burst; and though no one pushes them down, they fall of themselves. Such a destruction the Prophet denounces on the Ninevites and the Assyrians.

This, he says, is the exulting city, which sat in confidence. Isaiah reprobates in nearly the same words the pride of Babylon: but what Isaiah said of Babylon our Prophet justly transfers here to Nineveh. But he no doubt had respect to the Jews, and exhibits Nineveh in its state of ruin, lest the power of that city should dazzle their eyes; for we are seized with wonder, when anything grand and splendid presents itself to us. Here then Zephaniah makes a representation of Nineveh and sets it before the Jews: Behold, he says, ye see this city full of exultation; ye also see that it rests as in a state of safety; for it is conscious of no fear; it regards itself exempt from the common lot of men, as though it was built in the clouds. This city, he says, is above all others celebrated; but let not frail and evanescent splendor terrify you; for God will doubtless in his own time overthrow it and reduce it to nothing.

Let us also in the meantime observe what I have lately referred to, — that the cause of the ruin of Nineveh is described, which was, that it had promised to itself a perpetuity in the world. But let us remember, that in this city is presented to us an example, which belongs in common to all nations, — that God cannot endure the presumption of men, when inflated by their own greatness and power, they do not think themselves to be men, nor humble themselves in a way suitable to the condition of men, but forget themselves, as though they could exalt themselves above the heavens.

But it is necessary to examine the words: Nineveh said in her heart, I, and besides me no other. By these words the Prophet means, that Nineveh was so blinded by its splendor that it now defied every change of fortune. Had Babylon spoken thus, it would have been no wonder, for it had taken from Nineveh its sovereignty. But we see that the same pride infatuates people as well as superior kings; for each thinks himself to be great alone, and when he compares himself with others, he looks on them as far below him, as though they were placed beneath his feet. Thus then the Prophet shows in few words what was the cause of the ruin of Nineveh: it thought that its condition on the earth was fixed and perpetual. If then we desire to be protected by God's hand, let us bear in mind what our condition is, and daily, yea, hourly prepare ourselves for a change, except God be pleased to sustain us. Our stability is to depend only on the aid of God, and from consciousness of our infirmity, to tremble in ourselves, lest a forgetfulness of our state should creep in.

He afterwards adds, How has it become a desolation? The Prophet accommodates his words to the capacities of men: for the ruin of Nineveh might have appeared incredible. Hence the Prophet by a question rouses the minds of the faithful, that they might not doubt the truth of what God declared, for he would work in an extraordinary manner. This how then intimates, that the Jews ought not to be incredulous, while thinking that Nineveh was on all sides fortified, so as to prevent the occurrence of anything disastrous: for God would, in a wonderful manner and beyond what is usual, overthrow it. How, then, has it become a desolation, a resting-place for beasts?

He then subjoins, Every one who passes by will hiss and shake his hand. The Prophet seems to point out the future reproach of Nineveh, and to confirm also by a different mode of speaking what he had before said, that its ruin would be wonderful; for the shaking of the hand and hissing are marks of reproach: Behold Nineveh, which so much flattered itself! we now see only its sad ruins. The Prophet, I have no doubt, means here by hissing and the shaking of the hind, that Nineveh would become an ignominious spectacle to all people: and the same mode of speaking often occurs in the Prophets. All shall hiss at thee; that is, I will make thee a reproach and a disgrace. Then the Prophet, as I have already said, still declares the same truths that the ruin of Nineveh would be like a miracle; for all those who pass by would be amazed; as though he had said, Behold, they will hiss — What is this? and then they will shake the hand — What can be firm in this world? We see the principal seat of empire demolished, and differing nothing from a desert. We now perceive the meaning of the Prophet.

As this doctrine is also necessary for us at this day, we must notice the circumstances to which we have referred. If, then, our enemies triumph now, and their haughtiness is intolerable, let us know, that the sooner the vengeance of God will overtake them; if they are become insensible in their prosperity, and secure, and despise all dangers, they thus provoke God's wrath, and especially if to their pride and hardness they add cruelty, so as basely to persecute the Church of God, to spoil, to plunder, and to slay his people, as we see them doing. Since then our enemies are so wanton, we may see as in a mirror their near destruction, such as is foretold by the Prophet: for he spoke not only of his own age, but designed to teach us, by the prophetic spirit, how dear to God is the safety of his Church; and the future lot of the ungodly till the end of the world will no doubt be such as Nineveh is described here to have been that though they swell with pride for a time, and promise themselves every success against the innocent, God will yet put a stop to their insolence and check their cruelty, when the proper time shall come. I shall not today begin the third chapter, for it contains a new subject.

PRAYER

Grant, Almighty God, that as thou triest us in the warfare of the cross, and arouses most powerful enemies, whose barbarity might justly terrify and dishearten us, were we not depending on thine aid, — O grant, that we may call to mind how wonderfully thou didst in former times deliver thy chosen people, and how seasonably thou didst bring them help, when they were oppressed and entirely overwhelmed, so that we may learn at this day to flee to thy protection, and not doubt, but that when thou becomest propitious to us, there is in thee sufficient power to preserve us, and to lay prostrate our enemies, how much soever they may now exult and think to triumph above the heavens, so that they may at length know by experience that they are earthly and frail creatures, whose life and condition is like the mist which soon vanishes: and may we learn to aspire after that blessed eternity, which is laid up for us in heaven by Christ our Lord. Amen.

CHAPTER 3

LECTURE ONE HUNDRED AND TWENTY-FOURTH

Zeph. 3:1, 2

1. Woe to her that is filthy and polluted, to the oppressing city!

1. Vae pollutae et inquinatae, urbi direptrici (vel, fraudatrici.)

2. She obeyed not the voice; she received not correction; she trusted not in the LORD; she drew not near to her God.

2. Non audivit ad vocem; non suscepit disciplinam (vel, correctionem;) in Iehova non est confisa; ad Deum suum non appropinquarit.

The Prophet speaks here again against Jerusalem; for first, the Jews ought ever to have been severely reproved, as they were given to many sins; and secondly, because there was always there some seed which needed consolation: and this has been the way pursued, as we have hitherto seen, by all the Prophets. But we must also bear in mind, that the books now extant were made up of prophetic addresses, that we might understand what was the sum of the doctrine delivered.

The Prophet here makes this charge against the Jews, that they were polluted and become filthy. And he addresses Jerusalem, where the sanctuary was; and it might therefore seem to have been superior to other cities; for God had not in vain chosen that as the place for his worship. But the Prophet shows how empty and fallacious was any boasting of this kind; for the city which God had consecrated for himself had polluted itself with many sins. The Prophet seems to allude to the ancient rites of the law, which, though many, had been prescribed, we know, by God, that the people might observe a holy course of life: for the ceremonies could not of themselves wash away their filth; but the people were instructed by these external things to worship God in a holy and pure manner. As then they often washed themselves with water, and as they carefully observed other rites of outward sanctity, the Prophet derides their hypocrisy, for they did not regard the real design of the ceremonies. Hence he says, that they were polluted, though in appearance they might be deemed the most pure; for they were defiled as to their whole life. [106]

He adds that the city was הנויה, eiune; some render it the city of dove, or, a dove; for the word has this meaning: and they take it metaphorically for a foolish and thoughtless city, as we find it to be so understood in Ho 7:11; where Ephraim was said to be a dove, because the people were void of reason and knowledge, and of their own accord exposed themselves to traps and snares. Some then consider this place to have this meaning, — that Jerusalem, which ought to have been wise, was yet wholly fatuitous and foolish. But it may be easily gathered from the context, that the Prophet means another thing, even this, — that Jerusalem was given to plunder and fraud; for the verb הני, ine, signifies to defraud and to take by force what belongs to another; and it means also to circumvent as well as to plunder. He therefore means no doubt, that Jerusalem was a city full of every kind of iniquity, as he had before called it a polluted city; and then he adds an explanation.

The Prophet in the first verse seems to have in view the two tables of the law. God, we know, requires in the law that his people should be holy; and then he teaches the way of living justly and innocently. Hence when the Prophet called Jerusalem a polluted city, he meant briefly to show that the whole worship of God was there corrupted, and that no regard for true religion flourished there; for the Jews thought that they had performed all their duty to God, when they washed away their filth by water. Such was the extremely foolish notion which they entertained: but we know and they ought to have known that the worship of God is spiritual. He afterwards adds, that the city was rapacious, under which term he includes every kind of injustice.

It follows, She heard not the voice, she received not correction. The Prophet now explains and defines what the pollution was of which he had spoken: for true religion begins with teachableness; when we submit to God and to his word, it is really to enter on the work of worshipping him aright. But when heavenly truth is despised, though men may toil much in outward rites, yet their impiety discovers itself by their contumacy, inasmuch as they suffer not themselves to be ruled by God's authority. Hence the Prophet shows, that whatever the Jews thought of their purity at

Jerusalem, it was nothing but filth and pollution. He says, that they were unteachable, because they did not hear the Prophets sent to them by God.

This ought to be carefully noticed; for without this beginning many torment themselves in the work of serving God, and do nothing, because obedience is better than sacrifice. If, then, we wish our efforts to be approved by God, we must begin with faith; for except the word of God obtains credit with us, whatever we may offer to him are mere human inventions. It is, in the second place, added, that they did not receive correction; and this was no superfluous addition. For when God sees that we are not submissive, and that we do not willingly come to him when he calls us, he strengthens his instruction by chastisements. He allures us at first to himself, he employs kind and gentle invitations; but when he sees us delaying, or even going back, he begins to treat us more roughly and more severely: for teaching without the goads of reproof would have no effect. But when God teaches and reproves in vain, it then appears that our disposition is wicked and perverse. So the Prophet intended here to show the wickedness of his people as extreme, by saying, that they heard not the voice nor received correction; as though he had said, that the wickedness of his people was unhealable, for they not only rejected the doctrine of salvation, when offered, but also obstinately rejected all warnings, and would not bear any correction.

But we must bear in mind, that the Prophet had to do with that holy people whom God had chosen as his peculiar treasure. There is therefore no reason why those who profess the name of Christians at this day should exempt themselves from this condemnation; for our condition is not better than the condition of that people. Jerusalem was in an especial manner, as we have already said, the sanctuary, as it were, of God: and yet we see how severely the Prophet reproves Jerusalem and all its inhabitants. We have no cause to flatter ourselves, except we willingly submit to God, and suffer ourselves to be ruled by his word, and except we also patiently bear correction, when his teaching takes no suitable effect, and when there is need of sharp goads to stimulate us.

He afterwards adds, that it did not trust in the Lord, nor draw nigh to its God. The Prophet discovers here more clearly the spring of impiety — that Jerusalem placed not the hope of salvation in God alone; for from hence flowed all the mass of evils which prevailed; because if we inquire how it is that men burn with avarice, why they are insatiable, and why they wantonly defraud and plunder one another, we shall find the cause to be this — that they trust not in God. Rightly then does the Prophet mention this here, among other pollutions at Jerusalem, as the chief — that it did not put its trust in God. The same also is the cause and origin of all superstitions; for if men felt assured that God alone is enough for them, they would not follow here and there their own inventions. We hence see that unbelief is not only the mother of all the evil deeds by which men willfully wrong and injure one another, but that it is also the cause of all superstitions.

He says, in the last place, that it did not draw nigh to God. The Prophet no doubt charges the Jews that they willfully departed from God when he was nigh them; yea, that they wholly alienated themselves from him, while he was ready to cherish them, as it were, in his own bosom. This is indeed a sin common to all who seek not God; but Jerusalem sinned far more grievously, because she would not draw nigh to God, by whom she saw that she was sought. For why was the law given, why was adoption vouchsafed, and in short, why had they the various ordinances of religion, except that they might join themselves to God? 'And now Israel,' said Moses, 'what does the Lord thy God require of thee, except to cleave to him?' God thus intended his law to be, as it were, a sacred bond of union between him and the Jews. Now when they wandered here and there, that they might not be united to him, it was a diabolical madness. Hence the Prophet here does not only accuse the Jews of not seeking God, but of withdrawing themselves from him; and thus they were ungovernable. The Lord sought to tame them; but they were like wild beasts. It now follows —

Zephaniah 3:3

3. Her princes within her are roaring lions; her judges are evening wolves; they gnaw not the bones till the morrow.

3. Principes ejus in medio ejus, leones rugientes; judices ejus lupi vespertini, non lacerant ad mane (alii non differunt, nempe ossa comminuere; sed [גרם], proprie significat, conterere vel, frangere ergo de ossibus loquitur Propheta, quod scilicet non expectarent usque ad mane, ut ipsa contererent dentibus; sed prae fame, vel potius rabie praedam statim lacerarent; imo etiam contererent ossa dentibus.)

The Prophet now explains what we have stated respecting plunder and fraud. He confirms that he had not without reason called Jerusalem הניה, eiune, a rapacious city, or one given to plunder; for the princes were like lions and the judges like wolves. And when he speaks of judges, he does not spare the common people; but he shows that all orders were then corrupt: for though no justice or equity is regarded by the people, there will yet remain some shame among the judges, so as to retain the people at least within some limits, that an extreme licentiousness may not prevail: but when robbery is practiced in the court of justice, what can be said of such a city? We hence see that the Prophet in these words describes an extreme confusion: The princes of Jerusalem, he says, are lions. And we have elsewhere similar declarations; for the Prophets, when it was their object to condemn all from the least to the greatest, did yet direct their discourse especially to the judges.

And this is worthy of being noticed, for there was then no Church of God, except at Jerusalem. Yet the Prophet says, that the judges, and prophets, and priests, were all apostates. What comfort could the faithful have had? But we hence see that the fear of God had not wholly failed in his elect, and that they firmly and with an invincible heart contended against all offenses and trials of this kind. Let us also learn to fortify ourselves at this day with the same courage, so that we may not faint, however much impiety may everywhere prevail, and all religion may seem extinct among men.

But we may also hence learn, how foolishly the Papists pride themselves in their vain titles, as though they thought that God was bound as it were to them, because they have bishops and pastors. But the Prophet shows, that even those who performed the ordinary office of executing the laws could yet be the wicked and perfidious despisers of God. He also shows, that neither prophets nor priests ought to be spared; for when God sets them over his Church, he gives them no power to tyrannize, so that they might dare to do anything with impunity, and not be reproved. For though the priesthood under the law was sacred, we yet see that it was subject to correction. So let no one at this day claim for himself a privilege, as though he was exempt from all instruction and reproof, while occupying a high station among the people of God.

He distinguishes between princes and judges; and the reason is, because the kingdom was as yet standing. So the courtiers, who were in favor and authority with the king, drew a part of the spoil to themselves, and the judges devoured another part. Though Scripture often makes no difference between these two names, yet I doubt not but he means by שרים, sherim, princes, the chiefs who were courtiers; and he calls them שפטים, shephtim, judges, who administered justice. And he says that the judges were evening wolves, that is, hungry, for wolves become furious in the evening when they have been roaming about all day and have found nothing. As their want sharpens the savageness of wolves, so the Prophet says that the judges were hungry like evening wolves, whose hunger renders them furious. And for the same purpose he adds, that they broke not the bones in the morning; that is, they waited not till the dawn to break the bones; [107] for when they devoured the flesh they also employed their teeth in breaking the bones, because their voracity was so great. We now apprehend the Prophet's meaning. It afterwards follows —

Zephaniah 3:4

4. Her prophets are light and treacherous persons: her priests have polluted the sanctuary, they have done violence to the law.

4. Prophetae ejus leves (vel, futiles,) viri transgressionum; sacerdotes ejus polluerunt sanctum (vel, sanctuarium,) sustulerunt legem.

The Prophet again reverts to the pollution and filth of which he has spoken in the first verse. He shows that he had not without reason cried against the polluted city; for though the Jews used their washings, they could not yet make themselves clean in this manner before God, as the whole of religion was corrupted by them.

He says that the Prophets were light. He alone speaks here, and he condemns the many. We hence see that there is no reason why the ungodly should allege their great number, when God by his word accuses them, as the Papists do at this day, who deny it to be right in one or two, or few men, to speak against their impiety, however bad the state of things may be; there must be the consent of the whole world, as though the Prophet was not alone, and had not to contend with a great many. It is indeed true that he taught at the same time with the Prophet Jeremiah, as we have elsewhere seen; but yet hardly two or three did then discharge faithfully their office of teaching; and from this and other places we learn that the false Prophets, relying on their number, were on that account bolder. But Zephaniah did not for this reason cease to cry against them. However much then the false Prophets raged against him, and terrified him by the show of their number, he still exercised his liberty in condemning them. So at this day, though the whole world should unite in promoting impiety, there is yet no reason why the few should be disheartened when observing the worship of God perverted; but they ought on the contrary to encourage themselves by this example, and strenuously to resist thousands of men if necessary; for no union formed by men can possibly lessen the authority of God.

It now follows that they were men of transgressions. What we render light, others render empty; (vacuous;) but the word פחזים, puchezim, means strictly men of nought, and also the rash, and those who are void of judgment as well as of all moderation. In short, it is the same as though the Prophet had said that they were stupid and blind; and he says afterwards that they were fraudulent, than which there is nothing more inconsistent with the Prophetic office. But Zephaniah shows that the whole order was then so degenerated among the people, that the thickest darkness prevailed among those very leaders whose office it was to bring forth the light of celestial truth. And he makes a concession by calling them Prophets. The same we do at this day when we speak of Popish bishops. It is indeed certain that they are unworthy of so honorable a title; for they are blinder than moles, so that they are far from being overseers. We also know, that they are like brute beasts; for they are immersed in their lusts: in short, they are unworthy to be called men. But we concede to them this title, in order that their turpitude may be more apparent. The Prophet did the same, when he said, that the Jews did not draw nigh to their God; he conceded to them what they boasted; for they ever wished to be regarded as the holy and peculiar people of God: but their ingratitude did hence become more evident, because they went back and turned to another object, when God was ready to embrace them, as though they designedly meant to show that they had nothing to do with him. It is then the same manner of speaking, that Zephaniah adopts here, when he says, that the Prophets were light and men of transgressions. [108]

He then adds, The priests have polluted the holy place. The tribe of Levi, we know, had been chosen by God; and those who descended from him, were to be ministers and teachers to others: and for this reason the Lord in the law ordered the Levites to be dispersed through the whole country. He might indeed have given them as to the rest, a fixed habitation; but his will was, that they should be dispersed among the whole population, that no part of the land should be without good and faithful ministers. The Prophet now charges them, that they had polluted the holy place. By the word שדק, kodash the Prophet means whatsoever is holy; at the same time he speaks of the sanctuary. Moreover, since the sanctuary was as it were the dwelling-place of God, when the Prophets speak of divine worship and religion, they include the whole under the word, Temple, as in this place. He says then that the sanctuary was polluted by the priests, and then that they took away or subverted the law. [109]

We here see how boldly the Prophet charges the priests. There is then no reason why they who are divinely appointed over the Church should claim for themselves the liberty of doing what they please; for the priests might have boasted of this privilege, that without dispute everything was lawful for them. But we see that God not only calls them to order by his Prophets, but even blames them more than others, because they were less excusable. Now the Papists boast, that the clergy, even the very dregs collected from the filthiest filth, cannot err; which is extremely absurd; for they are not better than the successors of Aaron. But we see what the Prophet objects now to them, — that they subverted the law: he not only condemns their life, but says also, that they were perfidious towards God; for they strangely corrupted the whole truth of religion. The Papists confess, that they indeed can sin, but that the sin dwells only in their moral conduct. They yet seek to exempt themselves from all the danger of going astray. Though the Levitical priests were indeed chosen by the very voice of God, we yet see that they were apostates. But God confirms the godly, that they might not abandon themselves to impiety, though they saw their very leaders going astray, and rushing headlong into ruin. For it behaved the faithful to fortify themselves with constancy, when the priests not only by their bad conduct withdrew the people from every fear of God, but also perverted every sound doctrine; it behaved, I say, the faithful to remain then invincible. Though then at this day those who hold the highest dignity in the Church neglect God and even despise every celestial truth, and thus rush headlong into ruin, and though they attempt to turn God's truth into falsehood, yet let our faith continue firm; for John has not without reason declared, that it ought to be victorious against the whole world. 1Jo 5:4. It follows —

Zephaniah 3:5

5. The just Lord is in the midst thereof; he will not do iniquity: every morning doth he bring his judgment to light, he faileth not; but the unjust knoweth no shame.

5. Iehova justus in medio ejus, non faciet iniquitatem: mane, mane judicium suum proferet in lucem, non deficiet: neque tamen congnoscet iniquus pudorem.

Here the Prophet throws back against hypocrites what they were wont to pretend, when they sought wickedly to reject every instruction and all warnings; for they said, that God dwelt in the midst of them, like the Papists at the present day, who raise up this as their shield against us, — that the Church is the pillar of the truth. Hence they think that all their wicked deeds are defended by this covering. So the Jews at that time had this boast ever on their lips, — We are notwithstanding the holy people of God, and he dwells in the midst of us, for he is worshipped in the Temple, which has been built, not according to men's will, but by his command; for that voice proceeded not from earth, but came from heaven, 'This is my rest for ever, here will I dwell.' Ps 132:14. Since then the Jews were inflated with this presumption, the Prophet concedes what they claimed, that God dwelt among them; but it was for a far different purpose, which was, that they might understand, that his hand was nigh to punish their sins. This is one thing.

Jehovah is in the midst of them; Granted, he says; I allow that he dwells in this city; for he has commanded a temple to be built for him on Mount Sion, he has ordered a holy altar for himself; but why does God dwell among you, and has preferred this habitation to all others? Surely, he says, he will not do iniquity. Consider now what the nature of God is; for when he purposed to dwell among you, he certainly did not deny himself, nor did he cease to be what he is. There is therefore no reason for you to imagine, as though God intended, for the sake of those to whom he bound himself, to throw aside his own justice, or intended to pollute himself by the defilements of men. He warns the Jews, that they absurdly blended these things together. God then who dwells in the midst of you, will not do iniquity; that is, He will not approve of your evil deeds; and though he may for a time connive at them, he will not yet bear with them continually. Do not therefore foolishly flatter yourselves, as though God were the approver of your wickedness.

Some apply this to the people, — that they ought not to have done iniquity; but this is a strained exposition, and altogether foreign to the context. Most other interpreters give this meaning, that God is just and will do no iniquity, for he had sufficient reasons for executing his vengeance on a people so wicked. They hence think, that the Prophet anticipates the Jews, lest they murmured, as though the Lord was cruel or too rigid. He will not do iniquity, that is, Though the Lord may inflict on you a most grievous punishment, yet he cannot be arraigned by you as unjust; and ye in vain contend with him, for he will ever be found to be a righteous judge. But this also is a very frigid explanation. Let us bear in mind what I have already said, — that the Prophet here, by way of irony, concedes to the Jews, that God dwelt among them, but afterwards brings against them what they thought was a protection to them, — God dwells in the midst of you; I allow it, he says; but is not he a just God? Do not then dream that he is one like yourselves, that he approves of your evil deeds. God will not do iniquity; ye cannot prevail with him to renounce himself, or to change his own nature. Why then does God dwell in the midst of you? In the morning, in the morning, he says, his judgment will he bring forth to light; the Lord will daily bring forth his judgment. How this is to be understood, we shall explain tomorrow.

PRAYER

Grant, Almighty God, that inasmuch as thou hast deigned to favor us with an honor so invaluable, as to adopt us for a holy people to thee, and to separate us from the world, — O grant, that we may not close our eyes against the light of thy truth, by which thou showest to us the way of salvation; but may we with true docility follow where thou callest us, and never cast away the fear of thy majesty, nor mock thee with frivolous ceremonies, but strive sincerely to devote ourselves wholly to thee, and to cleanse ourselves from all defilements, not only of the flesh, but also of the spirit, that by thus seeking true holiness, we may aspire after and diligently labor for that heavenly perfection, from which we are as yet far distant; and may we in the meantime, relying on the favor of thy only-begotten Son, lean on thy mercy; and while depending on it, may we ever grow up more and more into that true and perfect union, reserved for us in heaven, when we shall be made partakers of thy glory, through Christ our Lord. Amen.

LECTURE ONE HUNDRED AND TWENTY-FIFTH

We began yesterday to explain the passage, where the Prophet says, that God dwelt at Jerusalem, but that he was notwithstanding just, and could not possibly associate with the ungodly and the wicked, because he changes not his nature to suit the humor of men.

It now follows, In the morning, in the morning, his judgment will he bring forth to light: by which words he means, either that God would be the avenger of wickedness, which seems to escape, as it were, his eyes, while he delays his punishment, or that he is ready to restore his people, whenever they are attentive to instruction. If the former view be approved, the sense will be this, — that hypocrites foolishly flatter themselves, when God spares them; for he will suddenly ascend his tribunal that he may visit them with punishment. Some however choose to apply this to the judgments executed on the Gentiles, of which the Jews had not once nor twice been reminded, but often, that they might in time repent. But there is no doubt but that the Prophet refers here to a judgment belonging to the Jews.

Let us now see whether this judgment is pronounced or inflicted. It would not ill suit the passage to understand it of the vengeance which God was hastening to execute, for the Jews were worthy of what had been severely threatened, because they falsely professed his name; and while they absurdly boasted that he dwelt among them, they withdrew themselves very far from him. It is however no less suitable to refer this to teaching, so that the Prophet thus enhanced the sin of the people, because they had hardened themselves after so many and so constant warnings, which continually sounded in their ears, as God elsewhere complains, that though he rose early, and indeed daily, this solicitude had been without its fruit. The verb in the future tense will thus signify a continued act, for God ceased not to exhort to repentance those wretched beings who had ears which were deaf. And this view strikingly corresponds with what immediately follows, that he fails not; for such a perseverance was a proof of unwearied mercy, when God continued to send Prophets one after the other.

He now adds, The wicked knows no shame. He means what he has just referred to — that the people had become so hardened in their wickedness that they could not be reformed, either by instruction or by threats, or by the scourges of God.

If we refer judgment to teaching, which I approve, the meaning will be — that though God, by making known daily his law, kindled as it were a lamp, which discovered all evils, yet the ungodly were not ashamed. But if we understand it, as they say, of actual judgment, the meaning will be in substance the same — that the ungodly repented not, though the hand of God openly appeared; and though he rose to judgment, yet he says, they knew not what it was to feel ashamed. As to the main subject there is no ambiguity; for the Prophet means only that the people were past recovery; for though God proved himself a judge by manifest evidences, and even by his own law, they yet felt no shame, but went on in their wicked courses. The word judgment, in the singular number, seems to have been put here in the sense of a rule, by which men live religiously and justly, and a rule which ought to make men ashamed. [110] It now follows —

Zeph. 3:6, 7

6. I have cut off the nations: their towers are desolate; I made their streets waste, that none passeth by: their cities are destroyed, so that there is no man, that there is none inhabitant.

6. Excidi gentes; vastate sunt arces earum; perdidi vicos earum, ut nemo transeat; vastatae sunt urbes earum, ut non sit vir, no sit qui habitet.

7. I said, Surely thou wilt fear me, thou wilt receive instruction; so their dwelling should not be cut off, howsoever I punished them: but they rose early, and corrupted all their doings.

7. Dixi, certe timebis me, suscipies disciplinam; et non excidetur habitatio ejus, quicquid visitavi super eam: certe properarunt, corruperunt omnia studia sua.

Here the Prophet shows in another way that there was no hope for a people, who could not have been instructed by the calamities of others, to seek to return to God's favor. For God here complains that he had in vain punished neighboring nations, and made them examples, in order to recall the Jews to himself. Had they been of a sane mind they might have been led, by their quiet state, while God spared them, to consider what they had deserved — If this is done in the green tree, what at length will be done in the dry? They might then have thought within themselves, that a most grievous calamity was at hand, except they anticipated God's wrath, which had grown ripe against them; and God also testified that he intended by such examples to stay the judgment which he might have already justly executed on them. As they then even hastened it, it is evident that their wickedness was past remedy. This is the sum of the whole.

He says first, I have cut off nations; by which words he shows that he warned the Jews to repent, not only by one example, but by many examples; for not one instance only of God's wrath had appeared, but God had on all sides manifested himself to be a judge, in inflicting punishment on one nation after another. Since then they had been so often warned, we may hence learn that they were wholly blinded by their wickedness.

He now enhances the atrocity of the punishment inflicted, and says, that citadels had been demolished and streets cut off, that no one passed through; and then, that cities had been reduced to solitude, so that there was no inhabitant. For when punishment is of an ordinary kind, it is wont, for the most part, to be disregarded; but when God showed, by so remarkable proofs, that he was displeased with the nations, that is, with the ignorant, who in comparison with the Jews were innocent, how could such an instance as this be disregarded by the Jews, whom God thus recalled to himself, except that they were of a disposition wholly desperate and irreclaimable? We now then see why the Prophet enlarges on the punishments which, having been inflicted on the nations, ought to have been considered by the Jews. [111]

He now subjoins the object which God had in view, I said, Surely thou wilt fear me. Here God assumes the character of man, as he does often elsewhere: for he does not wait for what is future, as though he was doubtful; but all things, as we know, are before his eyes. Hence God was not deceived, as though something had happened beyond his expectation; but as I have already said, he undertakes here the character of man; for he could not otherwise have sufficiently expressed how inexcusable the Jews were who had despised all his warnings. For what was God's design when he punished the heathens, one nation after another, except that the Jews might be awakened by the evils of others, and not provoke his wrath against themselves? Paul makes use of the same argument.

'On account of these things,' he says,
'the wrath of God comes upon all the unbelieving.'

Ro 1:17.

Inasmuch as men for the most part deceive themselves by self-flatteries and cherish with extreme indulgence their own wickedness, Paul says, that the wrath of God comes on the unbelieving: and it is a singular proof of God's love, that he does not immediately assail us, but sets before us the examples of others. As when any one lays hold of his servant in the presence of his son, and punishes him severely, the son must be moved by the sight, except he be wholly an abandoned character: however, in such a case the father's love manifests itself; for he withholds his hand from his son and inflicts punishment on the servant, and this for the benefit of his son, that he may learn wisdom by what another suffers. God declares in this place that he had done the same; but he complains that it had been without benefit, for the Jews had frustrated his purpose.

It may be here asked, whether men so frustrate God that he looks for something different from what happens. I have already said, that God speaks after the manner of men, and in a language not strictly correct: and hence we ought not here to enter or penetrate into the secret purpose of God, but to be satisfied with this reason, — that if we profit nothing when God warns us either by his word or by his scourges, we are then equally guilty, as though he was deceived by us: and hence also the madness of those is reproved, who are unwilling to ascribe anything to God but what is conveyed in these common forms of speech: God says, that he wills the salvation of all, 1Ti 2:4;) hence there is no election, which makes a distinction between one man and another; but the Lord leaves the whole human race to their free-will, so that every one may provide for himself as he pleases; otherwise the will of God must be twofold. So unlearned men vainly talk; and such not only show their ignorance in religion, but are also wholly destitute of common sense. For what is more absurd than to conclude, that there is a twofold will in God, because he speaks otherwise with us than is consistent with his incomprehensible majesty? God's will then is one and simple, but manifold as to the perceptions of men; for we cannot comprehend his hidden purpose, which angels adore with reverence and humility. Hence the Lord accommodates himself to the measure of our capacities, as this passage teaches us with sufficient clearness. For if we receive what the fanatics imagine, then God is like man, who hopes well, and finds afterwards that he has been deceived: but what can be more alien to his glory? We hence see how these insane men not only obscure the glory of God, but also labor, as far as they can, to reduce his whole essence to nothing. But this mode of speaking ought to be sufficiently familiar to us, — that God justly complains that he has been deceived by us, when we do not repent, inasmuch as he invites us to himself, and even stimulates us, I said, Surely thou wilt fear me

This word said, ought not then to be referred to the hidden counsel of God, but to the subject itself, and that is, that it was time to repent. Who would not have hoped but that you would have returned to the right way? When the next house was on fire, how was it possible for you to sleep, except ye were extremely stupid? And when so many examples were presented before your eyes without any advantage, it is evident that there is no more any hope of repentance. Thou, then, wilt fear me; that is, God might have hoped for some amendment, though he had not yet touched you even with his smallest finger; for ye beheld, while in a tranquil state, how severely he punished the contempt of his justice as to the heathens. He uses a similar language in Isa 5:4,

'My vine, what have I done to thee? or what could I have done to thee more than what I have done? I expected thee to bring forth fruit; but, behold, thou hast brought forth wild grapes.'

God in that passage expostulates with the Jews as though they had by their perfidiousness deceived him. But we know, that whatever happens was known to him before the creation of the world: but, as I have already said, the fact itself is to be regarded by us, and not the hidden judgment of God.

He afterwards adds, Thou wilt receive correction; that is, thou wilt be hereafter more tractable: for monstrous is our stupidity, when we fear not God's vengeance; when yet it evidently appears that we are warned, as I have already said, to repent, by all the examples of judgments which are daily presented to us. But if we proceed in our wickedness, what else is it but to kick against the goad, as the old proverb is? In short, we here see described an extreme wickedness and obstinacy, which admitted of no remedy.

Hence the Prophet adds again, And cut off should not be her habitation, howsoever I might have visited her; that is, though the Jews had already provoked me, so that the punishment they have deserved was nigh; yet I was ready to withdraw my hand and to forgive them, if they repented: not that God ever turns aside from his purpose, for there is no shadow of turning in him; but he sets before them the fact as it was; for the subject here, as I have said, is not respecting the secret purpose of God, but we ought to confine ourselves to the means which he employs in promoting our salvation. God had already threatened the Jews for many years; he had as yet deferred to execute what he had threatened. In the meantime his wrath had been manifested through the whole neighborhood; the heathen nations had suffered the severest judgments. God here declares, that he had been so lenient to his people as to give time to repent; and he complains that he had delayed in vain, for they had gone on in their wickedness, and had mocked, as it were, his patience. When, therefore, he says, Cut off should not be her habitation, howsoever I might have visited her, or have visited her, he pursues still the same mode of speaking, that is, that he was prepared to forgive the Jews, though he had before destined them to destruction; not that he, as to himself, would retract that sentence; but that he was still reconcilable, if the Jews had been touched by any feeling of repentance. [112]

He at last adds, Surely, (some render it, but,) surely they have hastened. The verb מכשׁ, shecam, means properly to rise early, but is to be taken metaphorically in the sense of hastening; as though he had said, They run headlong to corrupt their ways. God had said that he had been indulgent to them for this end — that he might lead them by degrees to repentance: now he complains, that they on the contrary had run another way, when they saw that he suspended his judgments, as though it was their designed object to accelerate his wrath. Thus they hastened to corrupt their ways. The meaning, then, is that this people were not only irreclaimable in their obstinacy, but that they were also sottish and presumptuous, as though they wished to hasten the judgment, which the Lord was ready for a time to defer. It now follows —

Zephaniah 3:8

8. Therefore wait ye upon me, saith the Lord, until the day that I rise up to the prey: for my determination is to gather the nations, that I may assemble the kingdoms, to pour upon them mine indignation, even all my fierce anger: for all the earth shall be devoured with the fire of my jealousy.

8. Propterea expectate me, dicit Jehova, usque ad diem quo surgam ad praedam; quia judicium meum (hoc est, decretum est mihi,) ut colligam gentes, ut congregem regna; ut effundam super ipsa (regna, vel, super

ipsas gentes) indignationem meam, totum furorem irae meae; quia igne zeli (vel, indignationis meae) vorabitur tota terra.

God here declares that the last end was near, since he had found by experience that he effected nothing by long forbearance, and since he had even found the Jews becoming worse, because he had so mercifully treated them. Some think that the address is made to the faithful, that they might prepare themselves to bear the cross; but this view is foreign to the subject of the Prophet: and though this view has gained the consent of almost all, I yet doubt not but that the Prophet, as I have now stated, breaks out into a complaint, and says, that God would not now deal in words with a people so irreclaimable.

Look for me, he says; that is, I am now present fully prepared: I have hitherto endeavored to turn you, but your hearts have become hardened in depravity. But inasmuch as I have lost all my labor in teaching, warning, and exhorting you, even when I presented to you examples on every side among heathen nations, which ought to have stimulated you to repentance, and inasmuch as I have effected nothing, it is now all over with you — Look for me: I shall no more contend with you, nor is there any ground for you to hope that I shall any more send Prophets to you.

Look then for me, until I shall rise — for what purpose? to the prey. Some render the word דעל, laod, forever; but the Prophet means, that God was so offended with the contumacy oú the people, that he would now plunder, spoil and devour, and forget his kindness, which had been hitherto a sport to them — I shall come as a wild beast; as lions rage, lacerate, tear, and devour, so also will I now do with you; for I have hitherto too kindly and paternally spared you. We hence see that these things are not to be referred to the hope and patience of the godly; but that God on the contrary does here denounce final destruction on the wicked, as though he had said — I bid you adieu; begone, and mind your own concerns; for I will no longer contend with you; but I shall shortly come, and ye shall find me very differentfrom what I have been to you hitherto. We now see that God, as it were, repudiates the Jews, and threatens that he would come to them with a drawn sword; and at the same time he compares himself to a savage and cruel wild beast.

He afterwards adds — For my judgment is; that is, I have decreed to gather all nations. We have elsewhere spoken of this verb אסף, asaph; it is the same in Hebrew as the French trousser. It is then my purpose to gather, that is, to heap together into one mass all nations, to assemble the kingdoms, so that no corner of the earth may escape my hand. But he speaks of all nations and kingdoms, that the Jews might understand that his judgment could no longer be deferred; for if a comparison be made between them and the heathen nations, judgment, as it is written, is wont to begin with the house of God, 1Pe 4:17; and further, they were less excusable than the unbelieving, who went astray, which is nothing strange, in darkness, for they were without the light of truth. God then threatens nations and kingdoms, that the Jews might know that a most dreadful punishment was impending over their heads, for they had surpassed all others in wickedness and evil deeds. [113] He afterwards adds —

Zephaniah 3:9

9. For then will I turn to the people a pure language, that they may all call upon the name of the LORD, to serve him with one consent.

9. Certe tunc convertam ad populos labium purum, ut invocent omnes nomen Jehovae, ut serviant ei humero uno.

The Prophet now mitigates the asperity of his doctrine, which might have greatly terrified the godly; nay, it might have wholly disheartened them, had no consolation been applied. God then moderates here what he had previously threatened; for if the Prophet had only said this — My purpose is to gather all the nations, and thus the whole earth shall be devoured by the fire of indignation, what could the faithful have concluded but that they were to perish with the rest of the world? It was therefore necessary to add something to inspire hope, such as we find here.

We must at the same time bear in mind what I have reminded you of elsewhere — that the Prophet directs his discourse one while to the faithful only, who were then few in number, and that at another time he addresses the multitude indiscriminately; and so when our Prophet threatens, he regards the whole body of the people; but when he proclaims the favor of God, it is the same as though he turned his eyes towards the faithful only, and gathered them into a place by themselves. As for instance, when a few among a people are really wise, and the whole multitude unite in hastening their own ruin, he who has an address to make will make a distinction between the vast multitude and the few; he will severely reprove those who are thus foolish, and live for their own misery; and he will afterwards shape his discourse so as to suit those with whom he has not so much fault to find. Thus also the Lord changes his discourse; for at one time he addresses the ungodly, and at another he turns to the elect, who were but a remnant. So the Prophet has hitherto spoken by reproofs and threatening, for he addressed the whole body of the people; but now he collects, as I have said, the remnant as it were by themselves, and sets before them the hope of pardon and of salvation.

Hence he says, But then [114] (for I take כי, ki, as an adversative) will I turn to the people a pure lip. God intimates that he would propagate his grace wider, after having cleansed the earth; for he will be worshipped not only in Judea, but by foreign nations, and even by the remotest. For it might have been objected, Will God then extinguish his name in the world? For what will be the state of things when Judea is overthrown and other nations destroyed, except that God's name will be exposed to reproach! It will nowhere be invoked, and all will outvie one another in blasphemies against him. The Prophet meets this objection, and says, that God has in his own hand the means by which he will vindicate his own glory; for he will not only defend his Church in Judea, but will also gather into it nations far and wide, so that his name shall be everywhere celebrated.

But he speaks first of a pure lip, I will turn, he says, to the nations a pure lip. By this word he means, that the invocation of God's name is his peculiar work; for men do not pray through the suggestion of the flesh, but when God draws them. It is indeed true, that God has ever been invoked by all nations; but it was not the right way of praying, when they heedlessly cast their petitions into the air: and we also know, that the true God was not invoked by the nations; for there was no nation then in the world which had not formed for itself some idol. As then the earth was full of innumerable idols, God was not invoked except in Judea only. Besides, though the unbelieving had an intention to pray to God, yet they could not have prayed rightly, for prayer flows from faith. God then does not without reason promise, that he would turn pure lips to the nations; that is, that he would cause the nations to call on his name with pure lips. We hence then learn what I have stated — that God cannot be rightly invoked by us, until he draws us to himself; for we have profane and impure lips. In short, the beginning of prayer is from that hidden cleansing of the Spirit of which the Prophet now speaks.

But if it be God's singular gift, to turn a pure lip to the nations, it follows that faith is conferred on us by him, for both are connected together. As God then purifies the hearts of men by faith, so also he purifies their lips that his name may be rightly invoked, which would otherwise be profaned by the unbelieving. Whenever they pretend to call on God's name, it is certain that it is not done without profanation.

As to the word all, it is to be referred to nations, not to each individual; for it has not been that every one has called on God; but there have been some of all nations, as Paul also says in the first chapter of the first Epistle to the Corinthians 1Co 1:1: for in addressing the faithful, he adds, 'With all who call on the name of the Lord in every place' — that is, not only in Judea; and elsewhere he says,

'I would that men would stretch forth hands to heaven in every place.' (1Ti 2:8.)

He afterwards adds, That they may serve him with one shoulder; that is, that they may unitedly submit to God in order to do him service; for to serve him with the shoulder is to unite together, so as to help one another. The metaphor seems to have been derived from those who carry a burden; for except each assists, one will be overpowered, and then the burden will fall to the ground. We are said then to serve God with one shoulder when we strive by mutual consent to assist one another. And this ought to be carefully noticed, that we may know that our striving cannot be approved by God, except we have thus the same end in view, and seek also to add courage to others, and mutually to help one another. Unless then the faithful thus render mutual assistance, the Lord cannot approve of their service. [115]

We now see how foolishly they talk who so much extol free-will and whatever is connected with it: for the Lord demands faith as well as other duties of religion; and he requires also from all, love and the keeping of the whole law. But he testifies here that his name cannot be invoked, as the lips of all are polluted, until he has consecrated them, cleansing by his Spirit what was before polluted: and he shows also that men will not undertake the yoke, unless he joins them together, so as to render them willing. I must not proceed farther.

PRAYER

Grant, Almighty God, that since it is the principal part of our happiness, that in our pilgrimage through this world there is open to us a familiar access to thee by faith, — O grant, that we may be able to come with a pure heart to thy presence: and when our lips are polluted, O purify us by thy Spirit, so that we may not only pray to thee with the mouth, but also prove that we do this sincerely, without any dissimulation, and that we earnestly seek to spend our whole life in glorifying thy name, until being at length gathered into thy celestial kingdom, we may be truly and really united to thee, and be made partakers of that glory, which has been procured for us by the blood of thy only-begotten Son. Amen.

LECTURE ONE HUNDRED AND TWENTY-SIXTH

Zephaniah 3:10

10. From beyond the rivers of Ethiopia my suppliants, even the daughter of my dispersed, shall bring mine offering.

10. Trans fluvios Ethiopiae supplicantes mihi (vel, supplices mei;) filia dispersorum meorum offerent munus meum (hoc est, mihi; nam [י] affixum accipitur loco pronominis [אלי
].)

Interpreters agree not as to the meaning of this verse; for some of the Hebrews connect this with the former, as though the Prophet was still speaking of the calling of the Gentiles. But others, with whom I agree, apply this to the dispersed Jews, so that the Prophet here gives hope of that restoration, of which he had before spoken. They who understand this of the Gentiles, think that Atharai and Phorisai are proper names. But in the first place, we cannot find that any nations were so called; and then, if we receive what they say, these were not separate nations, but portions of the Ethiopians; for the Prophet does not state the fact by itself, that Atharai and Phorisai would be the worshipers of God; but after having spoken of Ethiopia, he adds these words: hence we conclude, that the Prophet means this, — that they would return into Judea from the farthest region of the Ethiopians to offer sacrifices to God. And as he mentions the daughter of the dispersion, we must understand this of the Jews, for it cannot be applied to the Ethiopians. And this promise fits in well with the former verse: for the Prophet spoke, according to what we observed yesterday, of the future calling of the Gentiles; and now he adds, the Jews would come with the Gentiles, that they might unite together, agreeing in the same faith, in the true and pure worship of the only true God. He had said, that the kingdom would be enlarged, for the Church was to be gathered from all nations: he now adds, that the elect people would be restored, after having been driven away into exile.

Hence he says, Beyond the rivers of Ethiopia shall be my suppliants: for עתר, otar, means to supplicate; but it means also sometimes to be pacified, or to be propitious; and therefore some take עתרים, otarim, in a passive sense, they who shall be reconciled to God; as though he had said, God will at length be propitious to the miserable exiles, though they have been cast away beyond the rivers of Ethiopia: they shall yet again be God's people, for he will be reconciled to them. As David calls Him the God of his mercy, because he had found him merciful and gracious, (Ps 59:17,) so also in this place they think that the Jews are said to be the עתרי, the reconciled of Jehovah, because he would be reconciled to them. But this exposition is too forced: I therefore retain that which I have stated, — that some suppliants would come to God from the utmost parts of Ethiopia, not the Ethiopians themselves, but the Jews who had been driven there.

To the same purpose is what is added, The daughter of my dispersed; for פוץ, puts, means to scatter or to disperse. [116] Hence by the daughter of the dispersed he means the gathered assembly of the miserable exiles, who for a time were considered as having lost their name, so as not to be counted as the people of Israel. These then shall again offer to me a gift, that is, they are to be restored to their country, that they may there worship me after their usual manner. Now though this prophecy extends to the time of the Gospel, it is yet no wonder, that the Prophet describes the worship of God such as it had been, accompanied with the ceremonies of the Law. We now then perceive what Zephaniah means in this verse, — that not only the Gentiles would come into the Church of God, but that the Jews also would return to their country, that they might together make one body. It follows, —

Zephaniah 3:11

11. In that day shalt thou not be ashamed for all thy doings, wherein thou hast transgressed against me: for then I will take away out of the midst of thee them that rejoice in thy pride, and thou shalt no more be haughty because of my holy mountain.

11. In die illo non erubesces ob omnia facta tua, quibus praevaricata es contra me; quia tunc auferam e medio tui qui exultant superbia tua; et non adijicies ad superbiendum posthac (hoc est, non adjicies superbire) in monte sanctitatis meae.

Here the Prophet teaches us, that the Church would be different, when God removed the dross and gathered to himself a pure and chosen people: and the Prophet stated this, that the faithful might not think it hard that God so diminished his Church that hardly the tenth part remained; for it was a sad and a bitter thing, that of a vast multitude a very few only remained. It could not then be, but that the ruin of their brethren greatly affected the Jews, though they knew them to be reprobate. We indeed see how Paul felt a sympathy, when he saw that his own nation were alienated from God. Ro 9:1. So it was necessary that some consolation should be given to the faithful, that they might patiently bear the diminution of the Church, which had been previously predicted. Hence the Prophet, that he might moderate their grief, says, that this would be for their good; for in this manner the reproaches were to be removed, by which the Jewish name had been polluted, and rendered abominable.

Thou shalt not be ashamed, he says, for the sins by which I have been offended. Why? For thou shalt be cleansed; for it is God's purpose to reserve a few, by whom he will be purely worshipped. Some think that he does not speak here of the remission of sins, but on the contrary, of a pure and holy life, which follows regeneration; as though he had said, "There will be no reason any more for thee to be ashamed of thy life; for when I shall chasten you, ye will then fear me, and your correction will be conducive to a newness of life: since then your life will not be the same as formerly, and since my glory shall shine forth among you, there will be no cause why ye should be ashamed." But this is a strained view, and cannot be accommodated to the words of the Prophet; for he says, Thou shalt no more be ashamed of the sins by which thou hast transgressed against me. We hence see that this cannot be otherwise applied than to the remission of sins. But the last clause has led interpreters astray, for the Prophet adds, For I will take away from the midst of thee those who exult: but the Prophet's design, as I have stated, was different from what they have supposed; for he shows that there was no reason for the Jews to lament and deplore the diminution of the Church because the best compensation was offered to them, which was, that by this small number God would be purely served.

For when the body of the people was complete, it was, we know, a mass of iniquity. How then could Israel glory in its vast number, since they were all like the giants carrying on war against God? When now God collects a few only, these few would at length acknowledge that they had been preserved in a wonderful manner, in order that religion and the true worship of God should not be extinguished in the earth.

We now perceive the Prophet's design; but I will endeavor to render this clearer by a comparison: Suppose that in a city licentiousness of life so prevails that the people may seem to be irreclaimable; when it happens that the city itself falls away from its power and pristine state, or is in some other way reformed, not without loss, and is thus led to improve its morals, this would be a compensation to the good, and would give courage to the godly and ease their grief, so that they would patiently submit, though the city had not the same abundance, nor the same wealth and enjoyments. How so? because they who remained would form a body of people free from reproach and disgrace. When disease is removed from the human body, the body itself is necessarily weakened; and it is sometimes necessary to amputate a member, that the whole body may be preserved. In this case there is a grievous diminution, but as there is no other way of preserving the body, the remedy ought to be patiently sustained. In a similar manner does the Prophet now speak of the city Jerusalem: Thou shalt not be ashamed of the sins by which thou hast transgressed against me. How so? Because they were to be separated from the profane and gross despisers of God; for as long as the good and the evil were mixed together, it was a reproach common to all. Jerusalem was then a den of robbers; it was, as it were, a hell on earth; and all were alike exposed to the same infamy, for the pure part could not be distinguished, as a mass of evil prevailed everywhere. The Prophet now says, Thou shalt not be ashamed of thy former infamy. Why? "Because God will separate the chaff from the wheat, and will gather the wheat; ye shall be, as it were, in the storehouse of God; the chosen seed shall alone remain; there will be such purity, that the glory of the Lord shall shine forth among you: ye shall not therefore be ashamed of the disgraceful deeds by which ye are now contaminated."

We now apprehend the meaning of the words. But it may seem strange that the Prophet should say, that sins should be covered by oblivion, which the Jews ought indeed to have thought of often and almost at all times, according to what Ezekiel says,

'Thou wilt then remember thy ways, and be ashamed,' (Eze 16:61)

that is, when God shall be pacified. Ezekiel says, that the fruit of repentance would be, that the faithful, covered with shame, would condemn themselves. Why so? Because the reprobate proceed in their wicked courses, as it were, with closed eyes, and as it has been previously said, they know no shame: though God charges them with their sins, they yet despise and reject every warning with a shameless front; yea, they kick against the goads. Since it is so, justly does Ezekiel say, that shame would be the fruit of true repentance, according to what Paul also says in the sixth chapter to the Romans Ro 6:1, "Of which ye are now ashamed." He intimates, that when they were sunk in their unbelief, they were so given to shameful deeds, that they perceived not their abomination. They began therefore to be ashamed, when they became illuminated. The Prophet seems now to cut off this fruit from repentance: but what he says ought to be otherwise understood, that is, that the Church would be then free from reproach; for the reprobate would be separated, all the filth would be taken away, when God gathered only the remnant for himself; for in this manner, as it has been said, the wheat would be separated from the chaff. Thou shalt not then be ashamed in that day of evil deeds; for I will take away from the midst of thee those who exult. He shows how necessary the diminution would be; for all must have perished, had not God cut off the putrid members. How severe soever then and full of pain the remedy would be, it ought yet to be deemed tolerable; for the Church, that is the body, could not otherwise be preserved.

But it may be again objected — That the Church is cleansed from all spots, inasmuch as the reprobate are taken away; for he says, Thou shalt not be ashamed of the evil deeds by which thou hast sinned, literally, against me, that is, by which thou hast transgressed against me. God here addresses, it may be said, the faithful themselves: He then does not speak of the evil deeds of those whom the Lord had rejected. But the answer is easy: When he says, that the Church had sinned, he refers to that mixture, by which no distinction is made between the wheat and the chaff. We may say that a city is impious and wicked, when the majority so much exceeds in number the good, that they do not appear. When therefore among ten thousand men there are only thirty or even a smaller number who are anxious for a better state of things, the whole number will be generally counted wicked on account of the larger portion, for the others are hid, and, as it were, covered over and buried. Justly then and correctly does Zephaniah declare, that the Jews had transgressed against God; for in that mixed multitude the elect could not have been distinguished from the reprobate. But he now promises that there would be a distinction, when God took away the proud, who exulted in vain boasting. For he says, I will take away from the midst of thee those who exult in thy pride

Some render the word in the abstract, the exultations of thy pride: but the term עליזי, found here, is never in construction rendered exultations. It is therefore no doubt to be understood of men. He then names the pride of the people; and yet he addresses the elect, who were afterwards to be gathered. What does this mean? even what we have already stated, that before the Church was cleansed from her pollution and filth, there was a common exultation and insolence against God; for these words were everywhere heard —

"We are God's holy people,
we are a chosen race,
we are a royal priesthood,
we are a holy inheritance."
Ex 19:6.

Since, then, these boastings were in the mouth of them all, the Prophet says, that it was the pride of the whole people. I will then take away, he says, from the midst of thee those who exult in thy pride [117]

He afterwards adds, Thou shalt no more add to take pride in my holy mountain. Here the Prophet points out the main spring of the evil, because the Jews had hardened themselves in a perverse self-confidence, as they thought that all things were lawful for them, inasmuch as they were God's chosen people. Jeremiah also in a similar manner represents their boasting as false, when they pretended to be the temple of God. Jer 7:4. So our Prophet condemns this pride, because they concealed their sins under the shadow of the temple, and thought it a sufficient defense, that God dwelt on Mount Sion. To show, then, that the people were unhealable, without being cleansed from this pride, the Prophet says, I will take away those who exult — How did they exult? in thy pride: and what was this pride? that they inhabited the holy mount of God, besides which there was no other sanctuary of God on earth. As then they imagined that God was thus bound to them, they insolently despised all admonitions, as though they were exempt from every law and restraint. Thou shalt not then add to take pride in my holy mountain

We now then see how careful we ought to be, lest the favors of God, which ought by their brightness to guide us to heaven, should darken our minds. But as we are extremely prone to arrogance and pride, we ought carefully to seek to conduct ourselves in a meek and humble manner, when favored with God's singular benefits; for when we begin falsely to glory in God's name, and to put on an empty mask to cover our sins, it is all over with us; inasmuch as to our wickedness, to our contempt of God, and to other evil lusts and passions, there is added perverseness, for we persevere in our course, as it were, with an iron and inflexible neck. Thus, indeed, it happens to all hypocrites, who elate themselves through false pretenses as to their connection with God. It follows —

Zeph. 3:12, 13

12. I will also leave in the midst of thee an afflicted and poor people, and they shall trust in the name of the Lord.

12. Et residuum faciam in medio tui populum afflictum et pauperem; et sperabunt in nomine Iehovae.

13. The remnant of Israel shall not do iniquity, nor speak lies; neither shall a deceitful tongue be found in their mouth: for they shall feed and lie down, and none shall make them afraid.

13. Residuum Israel non perpetrabunt iniquitatem (hoc est, reliquae; ad verbum est, residuum; sed quia nomen est collectivum, ideo mutatur numerus,) et non loquentur mendacium, et non invenietur in ore ipsorum lingua dolosa (vel, lingua fraudis;) quoniam ipsi pascentur et accubabunt; et nemo erit exterrens.

Here the Prophet pursues the same subject — that God would provide for the safety of his Church, by cutting off the majority of the people, and by reserving a few; for his purpose was to gather for himself a pure and holy Church, as the city had previously been full of all uncleanness. It ought, then, to have been a compensation to ease their grief, when the godly saw that God would be propitious to them, though he had treated them with great severity. And we must bear in mind what I have before stated — that the Church could not have been preserved without correcting and subduing that arrogance, which arose from a false profession as to God. Zephaniah takes it now as granted, that pride could not be torn away from their hearts, except they were wholly cast down, and thus made contrite. He then teaches us, that as long as they remained whole, they were ever proud, and that hence it was necessary to apply a violent remedy, that they might learn meekness and humility; which he intimates when he says, that the residue of the people would be humble and afflicted; for if they had become willingly teachable, there would have been no need of so severe a correction. In short, though the faithful lament that God should thus almost annihilate his Church, yet in order that they might not murmur, he shows that this was a necessary remedy. How so? because they would have always conducted themselves arrogantly against God, had they not been afflicted. It was, therefore, needful for them to be in a manner broken, because they could not be bent. I will, then, he says, make the residue an afflicted and a poor people

The word, יני, oni, means humble; but as he adds the word לד, dal, he no doubt shows that the Jews could not be corrected without being stripped of all the materials of their glorying. [118] They were, indeed, extremely wedded to their boastings; yea, they were become hardened in their contempt of God. He therefore says, that this fruit would at last follow, that they would trust in the Lord, that is, when he had laid them prostrate.

This verse contains a most useful instruction: for first we are taught that the Church is subdued by the cross, that she may know her pride, which is so innate and so fixed in the hearts of men, that it cannot be removed, except the Lord, so to speak, roots it out by force. There is then no wonder that the faithful are so much humbled be the Lord, and that the lot of the Church is so contemptible; for if they had more vigor, they would soon, as is often the case, break out into an insolent spirit. That the Lord, then, may keep his elect under restraint, he subdues and tames them by poverty. In short, he exercises them under the cross. This is one thing.

We must also notice the latter clause, when he says, They shall trust in the Lord, that is, those who have been reduced to poverty and want. We hence see for what purpose God deprives us of all earthly trust, and takes away from us every ground of glorying; it is, that we may rely only on his favor. This dependence ought not, indeed, to be extorted from us, for what can be more desirable than to trust in God? But while men arrogate to themselves more than what is right, and thus put themselves in the place of God, they cannot really and sincerely trust in him. They indeed imagine that they trust in God, when they ascribe to him a part of their salvation; but except this be done wholly, no trust can be placed in God. It is hence necessary that they who ascribe to themselves even the smallest thing, should be reduced to nothing: and this is what the Prophet means. Let us further know, that men do not profit under God's scourges, except they wholly deny themselves, and forget their own power, which they falsely imagine, and recomb on him alone.

But the Prophet speaks of the elect alone; for we see that many are severely afflicted, and are not softened, nor do they put off their former hardihood. But the Lord so chastises his people, that by the spirit of meekness he corrects in them all pride and haughtiness. But by saying, They shall trust in the name of Jehovah, he sets this trust in contrast with the pride which he had previously condemned. They indeed wished to appear to trust in the name of God, when they boasted of Mount Sion, and haughtily brought forward the adoption by which they had been separated from heathen nations; but it was a false boasting, which had no trust in it. To trust, then, in the name of Jehovah is nothing else than sincerely to embrace the favor which he offers in his word, and not to make vain pretenses, but to call on him with a pure heart and with a deep feeling of penitence.

For the same purpose he adds, The residue of Israel shall no more work iniquity nor speak falsehood; nor shall there be found a deceitful tongue in their mouth. The Prophet continues the same subject — that the Church is not to be less esteemed when it consists only of a few men; for in the vast number there was great filth, which not only polluted the earth by its ill savor, but infected heaven itself. Since then Jerusalem was full of iniquities, as long as the people remained entire, the Prophet adduces this comfort, that there was no reason for sorrow, if from a vast number as the sand of the sea, and from a great multitude like the stars, God would only collect a small band; for by this means the Church would be cleansed. And it was of great importance that the filth should be cleansed from God's sanctuary; for what could have been more disgraceful than that the holy place should be made the lodging of swine, and that the place which God designed to be consecrated to himself, should be profaned? As then Jerusalem was the sanctuary of God, ought not true religion to have flourished there? But when it became polluted with every kind of filth, the Prophet shows that it ought not to have seemed grievous that the Lord should take away that vast multitude which falsely boasted that they professed his name. They shall not then work iniquity

Under one kind of expression he includes the whole of a righteous life, when he says, They shall not speak falsely, nor will there be found a deceitful tongue. It is indeed sufficient for the practice of piety or integrity of life to keep the tongue free from frauds and falsehood; but as it cannot be that any one will abstain from all frauds and falsehood, except he purely and from the heart fears God, the Prophet, by including the whole under one thing, expresses under the word tongue what embraces complete holiness of life.

It may be now asked, whether this has ever been fulfilled. It is indeed certain, that though few returned to their own country, there were yet many hypocrites among that small number; for as soon as the people reached their own land, every one, as we find, was so bent on his own advantages, that they polluted themselves with heathen connections, that they neglected the building of the temple, and deprived the priests of their tenths, that they became cold in the worship of God. With these things they were charged by Haggai, Zechariah, and Malachi. Since these things were so, what means this promise, that there would be no iniquity when God had cleansed his Church? The Prophet speaks comparatively; for the Lord would so cleanse away the spots from his people that their holiness would then appear more pure. Though then many hypocrites were still mixed with the good and real children of God, it was yet true that iniquity was not so prevalent, that frauds and falsehood were not so rampant among the people as they were before.

He afterwards adds, For they shall feed and lie down, and there will be none to terrify them. He mentions another benefit from God — that he will protect his people from all wrongs when they had repented. We must ever bear in mind what I have stated — that the Prophet intended here to heal the sorrow of the godly, which might have otherwise wholly dejected their minds. That he might then in some measure alleviate the grief of God's children, he brings forward this argument — "Though few shall remain, it is yet well that the Lord will cleanse away the filth of the holy city, that it may be justly deemed to be God's habitation, which was before the den of thieves. It is not then a loss to you, that few will dwell in the holy land, for God will be a faithful guardian of your safety. What need then is there of a large multitude, except to render you safe from enemies and from wild beasts? What does it signify, if God receives you under his protection, under the condition that ye shall be secure, though not able to resist your enemies? Though one cannot defend another, yet if God be your protector, and ye be made to live in peace under the defense which he promises, there is no reason why ye should say, that you have suffered a great loss, when your great number was made small. It is then enough for you to live under God's guardianship; for though the whole world were united against you, and ye had no strength nor defense yourselves, yet the Lord can preserve you; there will be no one to terrify you

And this argument is taken from the law; for it is mentioned among other blessings, that God would render safe the life of his people; which is an invaluable blessing, and without which the life of men, we know, must be miserable; for nothing is more distressing than constant fear, and nothing is more conducive to happiness than a quiet life: and hence to live in quietness and free from all fear, is what the Lord promises as a chief blessing to his people.

PRAYER

Grant, Almighty God, that since the depravity of our nature is so great, that we cannot bear prosperity without some wantonness of the flesh immediately raging in us, and without becoming even arrogant against thee, — O grant, that we may profit under the trials of the cross; and when thou have blest us, may we with lowly hearts, renouncing our perverseness, submit ourselves to thee, and not only bear thy yoke submissively, but proceed in this obedience all our life, and so contend against all temptations as never to glory in ourselves, and feel also convinced, that all true and real glory is laid up for us in thee, until we shall enjoy it in thy celestial kingdom, through Christ our Lord. Amen.

LECTURE ONE HUNDRED AND TWENTY-SEVENTH

Zeph. 3:14, 15

14. Sing, O daughter of Zion; shout, O Israel; be glad and rejoice with all the heart, O daughter of Jerusalem.

14. Exulta filia Sion (vel, jubila; exulta Israel; gaude et exulta toto corde filia Ierjusalem.

15. The Lord hath taken away thy judgments, he hath cast out thine enemy: the king of Israel, even the Lord, is in the midst of thee: thou shalt not see evil any more.

15. Abstulit Iehova judicia tua, purgando avertit inimicos tuos; rex Israel Iehova in medio tui; non videbis malum amplius.

The Prophet confirms what he has been teaching, and encourages the faithful to rejoice, as though he saw with his eyes what he had previously promised. For thus the Prophets, while encouraging the faithful to entertain hope, stimulate them to testify their gratitude, as though God's favor was already enjoyed. It is certain, that this instruction was set before the Jews for this purpose, — that in their exile and extreme distress they might yet prepare themselves to give thanks to God, as though they were already, as they say, in possession of what they had prayed for. But we must remember the design of our Prophet, and the common mode of proceeding which all the Prophets followed; for the faithful are exhorted to praise God the same as if they had already enjoyed his blessings, which yet were remote, and seemed concealed from their view.

We now then perceive what the Prophet meant in encouraging the Jews to praise God: he indeed congratulates them as though they were already enjoying that happiness, which was yet far distant: but as it is a congratulation only, we must also bear in mind, that God deals so bountifully with his Church as to stimulate the faithful to gratitude; for we pollute all his benefits, except we return for them, as it has been stated elsewhere, the sacrifice of praise: and as a confirmation of this is the repetition found here, which would have otherwise appeared superfluous. "Exult, daughter of Sion, shout, be glad; rejoice with all thine heart, daughter of Jerusalem."
[119]

But the Prophet was not thus earnest without reason; for he saw how difficult it was to console the afflicted, especially when God manifested no evidence of hope according to the perception of the flesh; but his purpose was by this heap of words to fortify them, that they might with more alacrity struggle with so many hard and severe trials.

He then adds, that God had taken away the judgments of Zion. By judgments, he means those punishments which would have been inflicted if it had been the Lord's purpose to deal according to strict justice with the Jews, as when any one says in our language, J'ai brule tous tes proces. He intimates then that God would no more make an enquiry as to the sins of his people. The word משפט, meshiphath, we know, has various meanings in Hebrew; but in this place, as I have said, it means what we call in French, Toutes procedures. In short, God declares that the sins of his people are buried, so that he in a manner cuts off his character as a judge, and remits his own right, so that he will no more contend with the Jews, or summon them, as they say, to trial. Jehovah then will take away thy judgments [120]

Then follows an explanation, By clearing he has turned aside all enemies; [121] for we know that war is one of God's judgments. As then God had punished the Jews by the Assyrians, by the Egyptians, by the Chaldeans, and by other heathen nations, he says now, that all enemies would be turned away. It hence follows, that neither the Assyrians nor the Chaldeans had assailed them merely through their own inclination, but that they were, according to what has been elsewhere stated, the swords, as it were, of God.

It afterwards follows, The king of Israel is Jehovah in the midst of thee. Here the Prophet briefly shows, that the sum of real and true happiness is then possessed, when God declares, that he undertakes the care of his people. God is said to be in the midst of us, when he testifies that we live under his guardianship and protection. Properly speaking, he never forsakes his own; but these forms of speech, we know, are to be referred to the perception of the flesh. When the Lord is said to be afar off, or to dwell in the midst of us, it is to be understood with reference to our ideas: for we think God to be then absent when he gives liberty to our enemies, and we seem to be exposed as a prey to them; but God is said to dwell in the midst of us when he protects us by his power, and turns aside all assaults. Thus, then, our Prophet now says, that God will be in the midst of his Church; for he would really and effectually prove that he is the guardian of his elect people. He had been indeed for a time absent, when his people were deprived of all help, according to what Moses expresses when he says, that the people had denuded themselves, because they had renounced God, by whose hand they had been safely protected, and were also to be protected to the end. Ex 32:25

He lastly adds, Thou shalt not see evil. Some read, "Thou shalt not fear evil," by inserting ו, iod; but the meaning is the same: for the verb, to see, in Hebrew is, we know, often to be taken in the sense of finding or experiencing. Thou shalt then see no evil; that is, God will cause thee to live in quietness, free from every disturbance. If the other reading, Thou shalt not fear evil, be preferred, then the reference is to the blessing promised in the law; for nothing is more desirable than peace and tranquillity. Since then this is the chief of temporal blessings, the Prophet does not without reason say, that the Church would be exempt from all fear and anxiety, when God should dwell in the midst of it, according to what he says in Ps 46:1. It now follows —

Zeph. 3:16, 17

16. In that day it shall be said to Jerusalem, Fear thou not: and to Zion, Let not thine hands be slack.

16. In die illa dicitur Jerosolymae, Ne timeas; Sion, ne pigrescant (vel, solvantur, name [רפה] significat lentum esse, vel, remissum, vel, dissolutum; ne ergo pigrescant) manus tuae.

17. The LORD thy God in the midst of thee is mighty; he will save, he will rejoice over thee with joy; he will rest in his love, he will joy over thee with singing.

17. Iehova Deus tuus in medio tui fortis servabit; exultabit (vel, gaudebit) super te in laetitia; quiescet (silebit ad verbum, vel, quietus erit) in amore suo; exultabit super te cum jubilatione.

The Prophet proceeds still to confirm the same truth, but employs a different mode of speaking. It shall, he says, be then said everywhere to Zion, Fear not, let not thine hands be let down, etc. For these words may no less suitably be applied to the common report or applause of all men, then to the prophetic declaration; so that the expression, It shall be said, may be the common congratulation, which all would vie to offer. The import of the whole is, that Jerusalem would be so tranquil that either the Prophets, or all with common consent would say, "Thou enjoyest thy rest: for God really shows that he cares for thee; there is therefore no cause for thee hereafter to fear." For there is expressed here a real change: since the Jews had been before in daily fear, the Prophet intimates, that they would be so safe from every danger, as to be partakers of the long-wished-for rest, with the approbation even of the whole world. Hence, it shall be said — by whom? either by the Prophets, or by common report: it makes no great difference, whether there would be teachers to announce their state joyful and prosperous, or whether all men would, by common consent, applaud God's favor, when he had removed from his people all wars, troubles, and fears, so as to make them live in quietness.

It shall then be said to Jerusalem, fear not; Sion! let not thine hands be relaxed. By saying Fear not, and let not thine hands be relaxed, he intimates, that all vigor is so relaxed by fear, that no member can perform its function. But by taking a part for the whole, he understands by the word hands, every other part of the body; for by the hands men perform their works. Hence in Scripture the hands often signify the works of men. The meaning then is — that God's Church would then be in such a state of quietness as to be able to discharge all its duties and transact its concerns peaceably and orderly. And it is what we also know by experience, that when fear prevails in our hearts we are as it were lifeless, so that we cannot raise even a finger to do anything: but when hope animates us, there is a vigor in the whole body, so that alacrity appears everywhere. The Prophet, no doubt, means here, that God thus succors his elect, not that they may indulge in pleasures, as is too often the case, but that they may, on the contrary, strenuously devote themselves to the performance of their duties. We ought therefore to notice the connection between a tranquil state and diligent hands; for, as I have said, God does not free us from all trouble and fear, that we may grow torpid in our pleasures, but that we may, on the contrary, be more attentive to our duty. Sion, then! let thine hands be no more torpid — Why?

Jehovah, he says, in the midst of thee strong, will save. He repeats what he had said, but more fully expresses what might have appeared obscure on account of its brevity. He therefore shows here more at large the benefit of God's presence — that God will not dwell idly in his Church, but will be accompanied with his power. For what end? To save. We hence see that the word רובג, gebur, ascribed to God, is very emphatical; as though he had said, that God would not be idle while residing in the midst of his Church, but would become its evident strength. And it is worthy of notice, that God exhibits not himself as strong that he may terrify his elect, but only that he may become their preserver.

He afterwards adds, He will rejoice over thee with gladness. This must be referred to the gratuitous love of God, by which he embraces and cherishes his Church, as a husband his wife whom he most tenderly loves. Such feelings, we know, belong not to God; but this mode of speaking, which often occurs in Scripture, is thus to be understood by us; for as God cannot otherwise show his favor towards us and the greatness of his love, he compares himself to a husband, and us to a wife. He means in short — that God is most highly pleased when he can show himself kind to his Church.

He confirms and shows again the same thing more clearly, He will be at rest (or silent) in his love. The proper meaning of שרח, charesh, is to be silent, but it means here to be at rest. The import is, that God will be satisfied, as we say in French, Il prendra tout son contentement; as though he had said that God wished nothing more than sweetly and quietly to cherish his Church. As I have already said, this feeling is indeed ascribed to God with no strict correctness; for we know that he can instantly accomplish whatever it pleases him: but he assumes the character of men; for except he thus speaks familiarly with us, he cannot fully show how much he loves us. God then shall be at rest in his love; that is, "It will be his great delight, it will be the chief pleasure of thy God when he cherishes thee: as when one cherishes a wife most dear to him, so God will then rest in his love." He then says, He will exult over thee with joy [122]

These hyperbolic terms seem indeed to set forth something inconsistent, for what can be more alien to God's glory than to exult like man when influenced by joy arising from love? It seems then that the very nature of God repudiates these modes of speaking, and the Prophet appears as though he had removed God from his celestial throne to the earth. A heathen poet says, —

**Not well do agree, nor dwell on the same throne, Majesty and love.
(Ovid. Met. Lib. 2: 816-7.)**

God indeed represents himself here as a husband, who burns with the greatest love towards his wife; and this does not seem, as we have said, to be suitable to his glory; but whatever tends to this end — to convince us of God's ineffable love towards us, so that we may rest in it, and being weaned as it were from the world, may seek this one thing only, that he may confer on us his favor — whatever tends to this, doubtless illustrates the glory of God, and derogates nothing from his nature. We at the same time see that God, as it were, humbles himself; for if it be asked whether these things are suitable to the nature of God, we must say, that nothing is more alien to it. It may then appear by no means congruous, that God should be described by us as a husband who burns with love to his wife: but we hence more fully learn, as I have already said, how great is God's favor towards us, who thus humbles himself for our sake, and in a manner transforms himself, while he puts on the character of another. Let every one of us come home also to himself, and acknowledge how deep is the root of unbelief; for God cannot provide for our good and correct this evil, to which we are all subject, without departing as it were from himself, that he might come nigher to us.

And whenever we meet with this mode of speaking, we ought especially to remember, that it is not without reason that God labors so much to persuade us of his love, because we are not only prone by nature to unbelief, but exposed to the deceits of Satan, and are also inconstant and easily drawn away from his word: hence it is that he assumes the character of man. We must, at the same time, observe what I have before stated — that whatever is calculated to set forth the love of God, does not derogate from his glory; for his chief glory is that vast and ineffable goodness by which he has once embraced us, and which he will show us to the end.

What the Prophet says of that day is to be extended to the whole kingdom of Christ. He indeed speaks of the deliverance of the people; but we must ever bear in mind what I have already stated — that it is not one year, or a few years, which are intended, when the Prophets speak of future redemption; for the time which is now mentioned began when the people were restored from the Babylonian captivity, and continues its course to the final advent of Christ. And hence also we learn that these hyperbolic expressions are not extravagant, when the Prophets say, Thou shalt not afterwards fear, nor see evil: for if we regard the dispersion of that people, doubtless no trial, however heavy, can happen to us, which is not moderate, when we compare our lot with the state of the ancient people; for the land of Canaan was then the only pledge of God's favor and love. When, therefore, the Jews were ejected from their inheritance, it was, as we have said elsewhere, a sort of repudiation; it was the same as if a father were to eject from his house a son, and to repudiate him. Christ was not as yet manifested to the world. The miserable Jews had an evidence, in figures and shadows, of that future favor which was afterwards manifested by the gospel. Since, then, God gave them so small an evidence of his love, how could it be otherwise but that they must have fainted, when driven far away from their land? Though the Church is now scattered and torn, and seems little short of being ruined, yet God is ever present with us in his only-begotten Son: we have also the gate of the celestial kingdom fully opened. There is, therefore, administered to us at all times more abundant reasons for joy than formerly to the ancient people, especially when they seemed to have been rejected by God. This is the reason why the Prophet says, that the Church would be lessened by calamities, when God again gathered it. But that redemption of the people of Israel ought at this day to be borne in mind by us; for it was a memorable work of God, by which he intended to afford a perpetual testimony that he is the deliverer of all those who hope in him. It follows —

Zephaniah 3:18

18. I will gather them that are sorrowful for the solemn assembly, who are of thee, to whom the reproach of it was a burden.

18. Afflictos a tempore (vel, pro tempore, vel, ad tempus, ut alii vertunt) congregabo qui ex te erunt: onus (vertunt quidam, sed active accipere Propheta potius, qui sistinuerunt ergo) super eam opprobrium.

He proceeds here with the same subject, but in different words; for except some consolation had been introduced, what the Prophet has hitherto said would have been frigid; for he had promised them joy, he had exhorted the chosen of God to offer praise and thanksgiving; but they were at the same time in a most miserable state. It was hence necessary to add this declaration respecting the exiles being gathered.

But he says at the time. Some read, in respect to time; but this is obscure and strained. Others render it, at the time; but it means strictly from the time; though מ, mem, may sometimes be rendered as a particle of comparison. Interpreters do not seem to me rightly to understand the Prophet's meaning: for I do not doubt but that he points out here the fixed time of deliverance, as though he had said, I will again gather thine afflicted, and those who have endured thy reproach. When? at the time, ממועד, memuod; that is, at the determined or fixed time: for מועד, muod, is not taken in Hebrew for time simply, but for a predetermined time, as we say in French, Un terme prefix I will then gather thine afflicted, but not soon. Our Prophet then holds the faithful here somewhat in suspense, that they might continue in their watch tower, and patiently wait for God's help; for we know how great is our haste, and how we run headlong when we hope for anything; but this celerity, according to the old proverb, is often delay to us. Since, then, men are always carried away by a certain heat, or by too much impetuosity, to lay hold on what may happen, the Prophet here lays a restraint, and intimates that God has his own seasons to fulfill what he has promised, that he will not do so soon, nor according to the will of men, but when the suitable time shall come. And this time is that which he has appointed, not what we desire.

He then adds, Who have sustained reproach for her. In this second clause the Prophet no doubt repeats the same thing; but at the same time he points out, not without reason, their condition — that the Jews suffered reproach and contumely at the time of their exile, and that on account of being the Church; that is, because they professed to worship their own God; for on account of his name the Jews were hated by all nations, inasmuch as their religion was different from the superstitions of all heathens. It could not hence be, but that the unbelieving should vex them with many reproaches, when they were carried away into exile, and scattered in all directions. [123]

He had said before, I will gather the afflicted; but he now adds, I will gather those who have sustained reproach. I have stated that some read, A burden upon her is reproach; but no sense can be elicited from such words. The Prophet does here no doubt obviate a temptation which awaited God's children, who would have to experience in exile what was most grievous to be borne; for they were to be exposed to the taunts and ridicule of all nations. Hence he seasonably heals their grief by saying, that though for a time they would be laughed at by the ungodly, they would yet return to their own country; for the Lord had resolved to gather them. But we must ever remember what I have said — that God would do this in his own time, when he thought it seasonable. It follows —

Zephaniah 3:19

19. Behold, at that time I will undo all that afflict thee: and I will save her that halteth, and gather her that was driven out; and I will get them praise and fame in every land where they have been put to shame.

19. Ecce ego conficiens omnes oppressores tuos (qui te humiliant, ad verbum) in tempore illo; et servabo claudicantem, et reducam expulsam ad faciendum eos in laudem et nomen in terra opprobrii ipsorum.

He confirms here what I have referred to in the last verse that God would overcome all obstacles, when his purpose was to restore his people. On this the Prophet, as we have said, dwells, that the Jews might in their exile sustain themselves with the hope of deliverance. As, then, they could not instantly conceive what was so incredible according to the perceptions of the flesh, he testifies that there is sufficient power in God to subdue all enemies.

At that time, he says, he repeats what had been stated before — that his people must wait as long as God pleases to exercise them under the cross; for if their option had been given to the Jews, they would have willingly continued at their ease; and we know how men are wont to exempt themselves from every trouble, fear, and sorrow. As therefore men naturally desire rest and immunity from all evil, the Prophet here exhorts the faithful to patience, and shows, that it cannot be that God will become their deliverer, except they submit to his chastisement; at that time then. It is ever to be observed, that the Prophet condemns that extreme haste which usually takes hold of men when God chastises them. However slowly then and gradually God proceeds in the work of delivering his own, the Prophet shows here, that there was no reason for them to despair, or to be broken down in their spirits. [124]

He then subjoins, that he would save the halting, and restore the driven away. By these words he means, that though the Church would be maimed and torn, there would yet be nothing that could hinder God to restore her: for by the halting and the driven away he understands none other than one so stripped of power as wholly to fail in himself. He therefore compares the Church of God to a person, who, with relaxed limbs, is nearly dead. Hence, when we are useless as to any work, what else is our life but a languor like to death? But the Prophet declares here, that the seasonable time would come when God would relieve his own people: though they were to become prostrate and fallen, though they were to be scattered here and there, like a torn body of man, an arm here and a leg there, every limb separated; yet he declares that nothing could possibly prevent God to gather his Church and restore it to its full vigor and strength. In short, he means that the restoration of the Church would be a kind of resurrection;

for the Lord would humble his people until they became almost lifeless, so as not to be able to breathe: but he would at length gather them, and so gather them that they would not only breathe but be replenished with such new vigor as though they had received no loss. I cannot finish the whole today.

PRAYER

Grant, Almighty God, that as we are at this day so scattered on account of our sins, and even they who seem to be collected in thy name and under thy authority, are yet so torn by mutual discords, that the safety of thy Church hangs as it were on a thread, while in the meantime thine enemies seem with savage cruelty to destroy all those who are thine, and to obliterate thy gospel, — O grant, that we may live in quietness and resignation, hoping in thy promises, so that we may not doubt, but that thou in due time will become our deliverer: and may we so patiently bear to be afflicted and cast down by thee, that we may ever raise up our groans to heaven so as to be heard through the name of thy Son, until being at length freed from every contest, we shall enjoy that blessed rest which is laid up for us in heaven, and which thine only begotten Son has procured for us. Amen.

LECTURE ONE HUNDRED AND TWENTY-EIGHTH

We stopped yesterday at the latter clause of the last verse but one of the Prophet Zephaniah, where God promises that the Jews, who had been before not only obscure, but also exposed to all kinds of reproaches, would again become illustrious; for to give them for a name and for a praise, is no other thing than to render them celebrated, that they might be, as they say, in the mouth of every one.

And he says, in the land of their shame, or reproach; for they had been a mockery everywhere; as the unbelieving thought that they deluded themselves with a vain hope, because they boasted that God, under whose protection they lived, would be their perpetual guardian, though they were driven away into exile. Hence an occasion for taunt and ridicule was given. But a change for the better is here promised; for all in Assyria and Chaldea would have to see that this was a people chosen by God; so that there would be a remarkable testimony among all nations, that all who trust in

God are by no means disappointed, for they find that he is faithful in his promises. The last verse follows —

Zephaniah 3:20

20. At that time will I bring you again, even in the time that I gather you: for I will make you a name and a praise among all people of the earth, when I turn back your captivity before your eyes, saith the LORD.

20. In tempore illo reducam vos, in tempore illo colligam vos; quia ponam vos in nomen et laudem per cunctos populos terrae, (vel, inter cunctos populos terrae,) quam reducam captivitates vestras in oculis vestris, dicit Jehova.

He repeats the same things, with some change in the words; and not without reason, because no one of then thought that the Jews, who were cast as it were into the grave, would ever come forth again, and especially, that they would be raised unto such dignity and unto so elevated an honor. As then this was not probable, that Prophet confirms his prediction — I will restore you, says God, I will gather you, even because I have given you a name; that is, it is my resolved and fixed purpose to render you celebrated: but here again are laid down the words we have already noticed.

He afterwards adds — When I shall restore your captivities. The plural number is to be noticed; and not rightly nor prudently is what has been done by many interpreters, who have rendered the word in the singular number; for the Prophet mentions captivities designedly, as the Jews had not only been driven into exile, but had also been scattered through various countries, so that they were not one captive people, but many troops of captives. Hence his purpose was to obviate a doubt; for it would not have been enough that one captivity should be restored, except all who had been dispersed were collected into one body by the wonderful power of God. And hence he adds before your eyes, that the Jews might be convinced that they should be eye-witnesses of this miracle, which yet they could hardly conceive, without raising up their thoughts above the world.

COMMENTARY ON HAGGAI

CALVIN'S PREFACE TO HAGGAI

AFTER the return of the people, they were favored, we know, especially with three Prophets, who roused their fainting hearts, and finished all predictions, until at length the Redeemer came in his appointed time. During the time of The Babylonian Exile the office of teaching was discharged among the captives by Ezekiel, and also by Daniel; and there were others less celebrated; for we find that some of the Psalms were then composed, either by the Levites, or by some other teachers. But these two, Ezekiel and Daniel, were above all others eminent. Then Ezra and Nehemiah followed them, the authority of whom was great among the people; but we do not read that they were endued with the Prophetic gift.

It then appears certain that three only were divinely inspired to proclaim the future condition of the people.

Daniel had before them foretold whatever was to happen till the coming of Christ, and his Book is a remarkable mirror of God's Providence; for he paints, as on a tablet, three things which were to be fulfilled after his death, and of which no man could have formed any conjecture. He has given even the number of years from the return of the people to the building of the Temple, and also to the death of Christ. But we must come to the other witnesses, who confirmed the predictions of Daniel. The Lord raised up three witnesses — Haggai, Zechariah, and Malachi. [125]

The first [126] condemned the sloth of the people; for, being intent on their own advantages, they all neglected the building of the Temple; and he shows that they were deservedly suffering punishment for their ingratitude; for they despised God their Deliverer, or at least honored him less than they ought to have done, and deprived him of the worship due to him. He then encouraged them to hope for a complete restoration, and showed that there was no reason for them to be disheartened by difficulties, and that though they were surrounded by enemies, and had to bear many evils, and were terrified by threatening edicts, they ought yet to have entertained hope; for the Lord would perform the work which he had begun — to restore their ancient dignity to his people, and Christ also would at length come to secure the perfect happiness and glory of the Church.

This is the sum of the whole. I now come to the words.

CHAPTER 1

Haggai 1:1

1. In the second year of Darius the king, in the sixth month, in the first day of the month, came the word of the LORD by Haggai the prophet unto Zerubbabel the son of Shealtiel, governor of Judah, and to Joshua the son of Josedech, the high priest, saying,

1. Anno secundo Darii regis, mense sexto, die primo mensis, datus fuit sermo Jehovae in manum Chaggai Prophetae ad Zerubbabel, filium Sealtiel, ducem Jehudah, et ad Jehosuah, filium Jehosadak, sacerdotem magnum, dicendo—

The Prophet mentions here the year, the month, and the day in which he began to rouse up the people from their sloth and idleness, by the command of God; for every one studied his own domestic interest, and had no concern for building the Temple.

This happened, he says, in the second year of Darius the king. Interpreters differ as to this time; for they do not agree as to the day or year in which the Babylonian captivity began. Some date the beginning of the seventy years at the ruin which happened under Jeconiah, before the erasing of the city, and the destruction of the Temple. It is, however, probable, that a considerable time had passed before Haggai began his office as a Prophet; for Babylon was taken twenty years, or little more, before the death of king Cyrus; his son Cambyses, who reigned eight years, succeeded him. The third king was Darius, the son of Hystaspes, whom the Jews will have to be the son of Ahasuerus by Esther; but no credit is due to their fancies; for they hazard any bold notion in matters unknown, and assert anything that may come to their brains or to their mouths; and thus they deal in fables, and for the most part without any semblance of truth. It may be sufficient for us to understand, that this Darius was the son of Hystaspes, who succeeded Cambyses, (for I omit the seven months of the Magi; for as they crept in by deceit, so shortly after they were destroyed;) and it is probable that Cambyses, who was the first-born son of Cyrus, had no male heir. Hence it was that his brother being slain by the consent of the nobles, the kingdom came to Darius. He, then, as we may learn from histories, was the third king of the Persians. Daniel says, in the fifth chapter Da 5:1, that the city of Babylon had been taken by Cyrus, but that Darius the Mede reigned there.

But between writers there is some disagreement on this point; though all say that Cyrus was king, yet Xenophon says, that Cyaxares was ever the first, so that Cyrus sustained only the character, as it were, of a regent. But Xenophon, as all who have any judgement, and are versed in history, well know, did not write a history, but fabled most boldly according to his own fancy; for he invents the tale that Cyrus was brought up by his maternal grandfather, Astyages. But it is evident enough that Astyages had been conquered in war by Cyrus. [127] He says also that Cyrus married a wife a considerable time after the taking of Babylon, and that she was presented to him by his uncle Cyaxares, but that he dared not to marry her until he returned to Persia, and his father Cambyses approved of the marriage. Here Xenophon fables, and gives range to his own invention, for it was not his purpose to write a history. He is a very fine writer, it is true; but the unlearned are much mistaken who think that he has collected all the histories of the world. Xenophon is a highly approved philosopher, but not an approved historian; for it was his designed object fictitiously to relate as real facts what seemed to him most suitable. He fables that Cyrus died in his bed, and dictated a long will, and spoke as a philosopher in his retirement; but Cyrus, we know, died in the Scythian war, and was slain by the queen, Tomyris, who revenged the death of her son; and this is well known even by children. Xenophon, however, as he wished to paint the image of a perfect prince, says that Cyrus died in his bed. We cannot then collect from the Cyropaeda, which Xenophon has written, anything that is true. But if we compare the historians together, we shall find the following things asserted almost unanimously: — That Cambyses was the son of Cyrus; that when he suspected his younger brother he gave orders to put him to death; that both died without any male issue; and that on discovering the fraud of the Magi, [128] the son of Hystaspes became the third king of the Persian. Daniel calls Darius, who reigned in Babylon, the Mede; but he is Cyaxares. This I readily admit; for he reigned by sufferance, as Cyrus willingly declined the honor. And Cyrus, though a grandson of Astyages, by his daughter Mandane, was yet born of a father not ennobled; for Astyages, having dreamt that all Asia would be covered by what proceeded from his daughter, was easily induced to marry her to a stranger. When, therefore, he gave her to Cambyses, his design was to drive her to a far country, so that no one born of her should come to so great an empire: this was the advice of the Magi. Cyrus then acquired a name and reputation, no doubt, only by his own efforts; nor did he venture at first to take the name of a king, but suffered his uncle, and at the same time his father-in-law, to reign with him; and yet he was his colleague only for two years; for Cyasares lived no longer than the taking of Babylon.

I come then now to our Prophet: he says, In the second year of Darius it was commanded to me by the Lord to reprove the sloth of the people. We may readily conclude that more than twenty years had elapsed since the people began to return to their own country. [129] Some say thirty or forty years, and others go beyond that number; but this is not probable. Some say that the Jews returned to their country in the fifty-eighth year of their captivity; but this is not true, and may be easily disproved by the words of Daniel as well as by the history of Ezra. Daniel says in the ninth chapter Da 9:1 that he was reminded by God of the return of the people when the time prescribed by Jeremiah was drawing nigh. And as this happened not in the first year of Darius, the son of Hystaspes, but about the end of the reign of Belshasar before Babylon was taken, it follows that the time of the exile was then fulfilled. We have also this at the beginning of the history, 'When seventy years were accomplished, God roused the spirit of Cyrus the king.' We hence see that Cyrus had not allowed the free return of the people but at the time predicted by Jeremiah, and according to what Isaiah had previously taught, that Cyrus, before he was born, had been chosen for this work: and then God began openly to show how truly he had spoken before the people were driven into exile. But if we grant that the people returned in the fifty-eighth year, the truth of prophecy will not appear. They therefore speak very thoughtlessly who say that the Jews returned to their country before the seventieth year; for thus they subvert, as I hare said, every notion of God's favor.

Since then seventy years had elapsed when Babylon was taken, and Cyrus by a public edict permitted the Jews to return to their country, God at that time stretched forth his hand in behalf of the miserable exiles; but troubles did afterwards arise to them from their neighbors. Some under the guise of friendship wished to join them, in order to obliterate the name of Israel; and that they might make a sort of amalgamation of many nations. Then others openly carried on war with them; and when Cyrus was with his army in Scythia, his prefects became hostile to the Jews, and thus a delay was effected. Then followed Cambyses, a most cruel enemy to the Church of

God. Hence the building of the Temple could not be proceeded with until the time of this Darius, the son of Hystaspes. But as Darius, the son of Hystaspes, favored the Jews, or at least was pacified towards them, he restrained the neighboring nations from causing any more delay as to the building of the Temple. He ordered his prefects to protect the people of Israel, so that they might live quietly in their country and finish the Temple, which had only been begun. And we may hence conclude that the Temple was built in forty-six years, according to what is said in the second chapter of John [130] (Joh 2:1); for the foundations were laid immediately on the return of the people, but the work was either neglected or hindered by enemies.

But as liberty to build the Temple was given to the Jews, we may gather from what our Prophet says, that they were guilty of ingratitude towards God; for private benefit was by every one almost exclusively regarded, and there was hardly any concern for the worship of God. Hence the Prophet now reproves this indifference, allied as it was with ungodliness: for what could be more base than to enjoy the country and the inheritance which God had formerly promised to Abraham, and yet to make no account of God, nor of that special favor which he wished to confer — that of dwelling among them? An habitation on mount Sion had been chosen, we know, by God, that thence might come forth the Redeemer of the world. As then this business was neglected, and each one built his own house, justly does the Prophet here reprove them with vehemence in the name and by the command of God. Thus much as to the time. And he says in the second year of Darius, for a year had now elapsed since liberty to build the Temple had been allowed them; but the Jews were negligent, because they were too much devoted to their own private advantages.

And he says, that the word was given by his hand to Zerubbabel, the son of Shealtiel, and to Joshua, the son of Josedech. We shall hereafter see that this communication had a regard without distinction to the whole community; and, if a probable conjecture be entertained, neither Zerubbabel nor Joshua were at fault, because the Temple ass neglected; nay, we may with certainty conclude from what Zechariah says, that Zerubbabel was a wise prince, and that Joshua faithfully discharged his office as a priest. Since then both spent their labor for God, how was it that the Prophet addressed them? and since the whole blame belonged to the people, why did he not speak to them? why did he not assemble the whole multitude? The Lord, no doubt, intended to connect Zerubbabel and Joshua with his servant as associates, that they three might go forth to the people, and deliver with one mouth what God had committed to his servant Haggai. This then is the reason why the Prophet says, that he was sent to Zerubbabel and Joshua.

Let us at the same time learn, that princes and those to whom God has committed the care of governing his Church, never so faithfully perform their office, nor discharge their duties so courageously and strenuously, but that they stand in need of being roused, and, as it were, stimulated by many goads. I have already said, that in other places Zerubbabel and Joshua are commended; yet the Lord reproved them and severely expostulated with them, because they neglected the building of the Temple. This was done, that they might confirm by their authority what the Prophet was about to say: but he also intimates, that they were not wholly free from blame, while the people were thus negligent in pursuing the work of building the Temple.

Zerubbabel is called the son of Shealtiel: some think that son is put here for grandson, and that his father's name was passed over. But this seems not probable. They quote from the Chronicles a passage in which his father's name is said to be Pedaiah: but we know that it was often the case among that people, that a person had two names. I therefore regard Zerubbabel to have been the son of Shealtiel. He is said to have been the governor [131] of Judah; for it was necessary that some governing power should continue in that tribe, though the royal authority was taken away, and all sovereignty and supreme power extinguished. It was yet God's purpose that some vestiges of power should remain, according to what had been predicted by the patriarch Jacob,

'Taken away shall not be the scepter from Judah, nor a leader from his thigh, until he shall come;' etc. (Ge 49:10.)

The royal scepter was indeed taken away, and the crown was removed, according to what Ezekiel had said, 'Take away the crown, subvert, subvert, subvert it,' (Ezek. 21:26, 27;) for the interruption of the government had been sufficiently long. Yet the Lord in the meantime preserved some remnants, that the Jews might know that that promise was not wholly forgotten. This then is the reason why the son of Shealtiel is said to be the governor of Judah. It now follows —

Haggai 1:2-4

2. Thus speaketh the Lord of hosts, saying, This people say, The time is not come, the time that the Lord's house should be built.

2. Sic dicit Iehova exercituum, dicendo, Populus isti dicunt (hoc est, dicit,) Non venit tempus domui Iehovae ad aedificandum.

3. Then came the word of the Lord by Haggai the prophet, saying,

3. Et datus fui sermo Iehovae in manu Chaggai Prophetae, dicendo,

4. Is it time for you, O ye, to dwell in your ceiled houses, and this house lie waste?

4. An tempus vobis, ut habitatis vos in domibus vestris tabulatis, et domus haec deserta?

They who think that seventy years had not passed until the reign of Darius, may from this passage be easily disproved: for if the seventy years were not accomplished, an excuse would have been ready at hand, — that they had deferred the work of building the Temple; but it was certain, that the time had then elapsed, and that it was owing to their indifference that the Temple was not erected, for all the materials were appropriated to private uses. While then they were thus taking care of themselves and consulting their own interest, the building of the Temple was neglected. That the Temple was not built till the reign of Darius, this happened, as we have said, from another cause, because the prefects of king Cyrus gave much annoyance to the Jews, and Cambyses was most hostile to them. But when liberty was restored to them, and Darius had so kindly permitted them to build the Temple, they had no excuse for delay.

It is however probable that they had then many disputes as to the time; for it may have been, that they seizing on any pretext to cover their sloth, made this objection, — that many difficulties had occurred, because they had been too precipitate, and that they had thus been punished for their haste, because they had rashly undertaken the building of the Temple: and we may also suppose that they took another view of the time as having not yet come, for easily might this objection occur to them, — "It is indeed true that the worship of God is deservedly to be preferred to all other things;

but the Lord grants us this indulgence, so that we are allowed to build our own houses; and in the meantime we attend to the sacrifices. Have not our fathers lived many ages without a Temple? God was then satisfied with a sanctuary: there is now an altar erected, and there sacrifices are offered. The Lord then will forgive us if we defer the building of the Temple to a suitable time. But in the meantime every one may build his own house, so that afterwards the Temple may at leisure be built more sumptuously." However this may have been, we find that true which I have often stated, — that the Jews were so taken up with their own domestic concerns, with their own ease, and with their own pleasures, that they made very little account of God's worship. This is the reason why the Prophet was so greatly displeased with them.

He declares what they said, This people say, The time is not yet come to build the house of Jehovah [132] He repeats here what the Jews were wont to allege in order to disguise their sloth, after having delayed a long time, and when they could not, except through consummate effrontery, adduce anything in their own defense. We however see, that they hesitated not to promise pardon to themselves. Thus also do men indulge themselves in their sins, as though they could make an agreement with God and pacify him with some frivolous things. We see that this was the case then. But we may also see here, as in a mirror, how great is the ingratitude of men. The kindness of God had been especially worthy of being remembered, the glory of which ought to have been borne in mind to the end of time: they had been restored from exile in a manner beyond what they had ever expected. What ought they to have done, but to have devoted themselves entirely to the service of their deliverer? But they built, no, not even a tent for God, and sacrificed in the open air; and thus they wilfully trifled with God. But at the same time they dwelt at ease in houses elegantly fitted up.

And how is the case at this day? We see that through a remarkable miracle of God the gospel has shone forth in our time, and we have emerged, as it were, from the abodes below. Who does now rear up, of his own free-will, an altar to God? On the contrary, all regard what is advantageous only to themselves; and while they are occupied with their own concerns, the worship of God is cast aside; there is no care, no zeal, no concern for it; nay, what is worse, many make gain of the gospel, as though it were a lucrative business. No wonder then, if the people have so basely disregarded their deliverance, and have almost obliterated the memory of it. No less shameful is the example witnessed at this day among us.

But we may hence also see how kindly God has provided for his Church; for his purpose was that this reproof should continue extant, that he might at this day stimulate us, and excite our fear as well as our shame. For we also thus grow frigid in promoting the worship of God, whenever we are led to seek only our own advantages. We may also add, that as God's temple is spiritual, our fault is the more atrocious when we become thus slothful; since God does not bid us to collect either wood, or stones, or cement, but to build a celestial temple, in which he may be truly worshipped. When therefore we become thus indifferent, as that people were thus severely reproved, doubtless our sloth is much more detestable. We now see that the Prophet not only spoke to men of his age, but was also destined, through God's wonderful purpose, to be a preacher to us, so that his doctrine sounds at this day in our ears, and reproves our torpor and ungrateful indifference: for the building of the spiritual temple is deferred, whenever we become devoted to ourselves, and regard only what is advantageous to us individually. We shall go on with what follows tomorrow.

PRAYER

Grant, Almighty God, that as we must carry on a warfare in this world, and as it is thy will to try us with many contests, — O grant, that we may never faint, however extreme may be the trials which we shall have to endure: and as thou hast favored us with so great an honor as to make us the framers and builders of thy spiritual temple, may every one of us present and consecrate himself wholly to thee: and, inasmuch as each of us has received some peculiar gift, may we strive to employ it in building this temple, so that thou mayest be worshipped among us perpetually; and especially, may each of us offer himself wholly as a spiritual sacrifice to thee, until we shall at length be renewed in thine image, and be received into a full participation of that glory, which has been attained for us by the blood of thy only-begotten Son. Amen.

LECTURE ONE HUNDRED AND TWENTY-NINTH

When the Prophet asks, whether the time had come for the Jews to dwell in splendid and well furnished houses, and whether the time had not come to build the Temple, he intimates, that they were trifling in a very gross manner with God; for there was exactly the same reason for building the

Temple as for building the city. How came they to be restored to their country, but that God performed what he had testified by the mouth of Jeremiah? Hence their return depended on the redemption promised to them: it was therefore easy for them to conclude, that the time for building the Temple had already come; for the one could not, and ought not to have been separated from the other, as it has been stated. He therefore upbraids them with ingratitude, for they sought to enjoy the kindness of God, and at the same time disregarded the memorial of it.

And very emphatical are the words, when he says, Is it time for you to dwell in houses? [133] For there is implied a comparison between God, whose Temple they set no value on, and themselves, who sought not only commodious, but sumptuous dwellings. Hence the Prophet inquires, whether it was consistent that mortal men, who differ not from worms, should possess magnificent houses, and that God should be without his Temple. And to the same purpose is what he adds, when he says, that their houses were boarded; for ספונים, saphunim, means in Hebrew what we express by Cambrisees [134] Since then they were not satisfied with what was commodious, without splendor and luxury being added, it was extremely shameful for them to rob God at the same time of his Temple, where he was to be worshipped. It now follows —

Hag. 1:5, 6

5. Now therefore thus saith the LORD of hosts; Consider your ways.

5. Et nunc sic dicit Iehova exercituum, Adjicite cor vestrum ad vias vestras;

6. Ye have sown much, and bring in little; ye eat, but ye have not enough; ye drink, but ye are not filled with drink; ye clothe you, but there is none warm; and he that earneth wages earneth wages to put it into a bag with holes.

6. Seminastis multum, et intulistis parum; comedere, et non ad satietatem; bibere, et non ad ebrietatem; vestire, et non ad calorem cuique; et qui colligit mercedem, colligit mercedem in sacculum perforatum.

Here the Prophet deals with the refractory people according to what their character required; for as to those who are teachable and obedient, a word is enough for them; but they who are perversely addicted to their sins must be more sharply urged, as the Prophet does here; for he brings before the Jews the punishments by which they had been already visited. It is commonly said, that experience is the teacher of fools; and the Prophet has this in view in these words, apply your hearts to your ways; [135] that is, "If the authority of God or a regard for him is of no importance among you, at least consider how God deals with you. How comes it that ye are famished, that both heaven and earth deny food to you? Besides, though ye consume much food, it yet does not satisfy you. In a word, how is it that all things fade away and vanish in your hands? How is this? Ye cannot otherwise account for it, but that God is displeased with you. If then ye will not of your own accord obey God's word, let these judgements at least induce you to repent." It was to apply the heart to their ways, when they acknowledged that they were thus famished, not by chance, but that the curse of God urged them, or was suspended over their heads. He therefore bids them to receive instruction from the events themselves, or from what they were experiencing; and by these words the Prophet more sharply teaches them; as though he had said, that they profited nothing by instruction and warning, and that it remained as the last thing, that they were to be drawn by force while the Lord was chastising them.

He says that they had sown much, and that small was the produce. They who render the clause in the future tense, wrest the meaning of the Prophet: for why did he say, apply your heart to your ways, if he only denounced a future punishment? But, as I have already stated, he intimates, that they very thoughtlessly champed the bridle, for they perceived not that all their evils were inflicted by God's hand, nor did they regard his judgement as righteous. Hence he says, that they had sowed much, and that the harvest had been small; and then, that they ate and were not satisfied; that they drank and had not their thirst quenched; that they clothed themselves and were not warmed. How much soever they applied those things which seemed necessary for the support of life, they yet availed them nothing. And God, we know, does punish men in these two ways either by withdrawing his blessings, by rendering the earth and and the heavens dry; or by making the abundant produce unsatisfying and even useless. It often happens that men gather what is sufficient for support, and yet they are always hungry. It is a kind of curse, which appears very evident when God takes away their nourishing power from bread and wine, so that they supply no support to man. When therefore fruit, and whatever the earth produces for the necessities of man, give no support, God proves, as it were by an outstretched arm, that he is an avenger. But the other curse is more frequent; that is, when God smites the earth with drought, so that it produces nothing. But our Prophet refers to both these kinds of evils. Behold, he says, Ye have sown much and ye gather little; and then he says, Though ye are supplied with the produce of wine and corn, yet with eating and drinking ye cannot satisfy yourselves; nay, your very clothes do not make you warm. They might have had a sure hope of the greatest abundance, had they not broken off the stream of God's favor by their sins. Were they not then extremely blind this experience must have awakened them, according to what is said in the first chapter of Joe 1:1

He says at the end of the verse, He who gains wages, gains then for a perforated bag. By these words he reminds them, that the vengeance of God could not only be seen in the sterility of the earth, and in the very hunger of men, who by eating were not satisfied; but also in their work, for they wearied themselves much without any profit, as even the money cast into the bag disappeared. Hence he says, even your work is in vain. It was indeed a most manifest proof of God's wrath, when their money, though laid up, yet vanished away. [136]

We now see what the Prophet means: As his doctrine appeared frigid to the Jews and his warnings were despised, he treats them according to the perverseness of their disposition. Hence he shows, that though they disregarded God and his Prophets, they were yet sufficiently taught by his judgements, and that still they remained indifferent. He therefore goads them, as though they were asses, that they might at length acknowledge that God was justly displeased with them, and that his wrath was conspicuous in the sterility of the land, as well as in everything connected with their life; for whether they did eat or abstained from food, they were hungry; and when they diligently labored and gathered wages, their wages vanished, as though they had cast them into a perforated bag. It follows —

Hag. 1:7, 8

7. Thus saith the Lord of hosts; Consider your ways.

7. Sic dicit Iehova exercituum, Ponite cor vestrum super vias vestras;

8. Go up to the mountain, and bring wood, and build the house; and I will take pleasure in it, and I will be glorified, saith the Lord.

8. Ascendite in montem et afferte lignum, et aedificate domum (vel, hance domum;) et propitius ero in ea (vel, mihi placebit in ea;) et glorificabor, dicit Iehova.

The Prophet now adds, that since the Jews were thus taught by their evils, nothing else remained for them but to prepare themselves without delay for the work of building the Temple; for they were not to defer the time, inasmuch as they were made to know, that God had come forth with an armed hand to vindicate his own right: for the sterility of which he had spoken, and also the famine and other signs of a curse, were like a drawn sword in the hand of God; by which it was evident, that he intended to punish the negligence of the people. As God then had been robbed of his right, he not only exhorted the people by his Prophets, but also executed his vengeance on this contempt.

This is the reason why the Prophet now says, Apply your heart, and then adds, Go up to the mountain, bring wood, etc. And this passage strikingly sets forth why God punished their sins, in order that they might not only perceive that they had sinned, but that they might also seek to amend that which displeased God. We may also, in the second place, learn from what is said, how we are to proceed rightly in the course of true repentance. The beginning is, that our sins should become displeasing to us; but if any of us proceed no farther, it will be only an evanescent feeling: it is therefore necessary to advance to the second step; an amendment for the better ought to follow. The Prophet expresses both here: He says first, Lay your heart on your ways; that is, "Consider whence comes this famine to you, and then how it is that by laboring much ye gain nothing, except that God is angry with you." Now this was what wisdom required. But he again repeats the same thing, Lay your heart on your ways, that is, "Not only that sin may be hated by you, but also that this sloth, which has hitherto offended God and provoked his wrath, may be changed into strenuous activity." Hence he says, Go up to the mountain, and bring wood, and let the house be built

If any one is at a loss to know why the Prophet insists so much on building the Temple, the ready answer is this that it was God's design to exercise in this way his ancient people in the duties of religion. Though then the Temple itself was of no great importance before God, yet the end was to be regarded; for the people were preserved by the visible Temple in the hope of the future Christ; and then it behaved them always to bear in mind the heavenly pattern, that they might worship God spiritually under the external symbols. It was not then without reason that God was offended with their neglect of the temple; for it hence clearly appeared, that there was no care nor zeal for religion among the Jews. It often was the case that they were more sedulous than necessary in external worship, and God scorned their assiduity, when not connected with a right inward feeling; but the gross contempt of God in disregarding even the external building, is what is reprehended here by the Prophet.

He afterwards adds, And I will be propitious in it, or, I will take pleasure in it. Some read, It will please me; and they depart not from the real meaning of the verb: for הצר, retse — is to be acceptable. But more correct, in my view, is the opinion of those who think that the Prophet alludes to the promise of God; for he had said, that he would on this condition dwell among the Jews, that he might hear their prayers, and be propitious to them. As, then, the Jews came to the Temple to expiate their sins, that they might return to God's favor, it is not without reason that God here declares that he would be propitious in that house.

'If any one sin,' said Solomon, 'and entering this house, shall humbly pray, do thou also hear from thy heavenly habitation.' (1Ki 8:30.)

We further know that the covering of the ark was called the propitiatory, because God there received the suppliant into favor. This meaning, then, seems the most suitable — that the Prophet says, that if the Temple was built, God would be there propitious. But it was a proof of extreme impiety to think that they could prosper while God was adverse to them: for whence could they hope for happiness, except from the only fountain of all blessings, that is, when God favored them and was propitious to them? And how could his favor be sought, except they came to his sanctuary, and thence raise up their minds by faith to heaven? When, therefore, there was no care for the Temple, it was easy to conclude that God himself was neglected, and regarded almost with scorn. We then see how emphatically this was added, I will be propitious there, that is, in the Temple; as though he had said, "Your infirmity ought to have reminded you that you have need of this help, even of worshipping me in the sanctuary. But as I gave you, as it were, a visible mirror of my presence among you, when I ordered a Temple to be built for me on mount Sion, when ye despise the Temple, is it not the same as though I was rejected by you?"

He then adds, And I shall be glorified, saith Jehovah. He seems to express the reason why he should be propitious; for he would then see that his glory was regarded by the Jews. At the same time, this reason may be taken by itself, and this is what I prefer. [137] The Prophet then employs two goads to awaken the Jews: When the Temple was built, God would bless them; for they would have him pacified, and whenever they found him displeased, they might come as suppliants to seek pardon; this was one reason why it behaved them strenuously to undertake the building of the Temple. The second reason was, that God would be glorified. Now, what could have been more inconsistent than to disregard God their deliverer, and so late a deliverer too? But how God was glorified by the Temple I have already briefly explained; not that it added anything to God; but such ordinances of religion were then necessary, as the Jews were as yet like children. It now follows —

Haggai 1:9

9. Ye looked for much, and, lo, it came to little; and when ye brought it home, I did blow upon it. Why? saith the Lord of hosts. Because of mine house that is waste, and ye run every man unto his own house.

9. Respexistis ad multum, et ecce parum; et intulistis ad domum, et sufflavi in illud: cur hoc? dicit Iehova exercituum: Propter domum meam quae est deserta, et vos curritis (vel, addicti estis quisque domi suae) quisque in domum suam.

Here the Prophet relates again, that the Jews were deprived of support, and that they in a manner pined away in their distress, because they robbed God of the worship due to him. He first repeats the fact, Ye have looked for much, but behold little [138] It may happen that one is contented with a very slender portion, because much is not expected. They who are satisfied with their own penury are not anxious though their portion of food is but scanty, though they are constrained to feed on acorns. Those who are become hardened in enduring evils, do not seek much; but they who desire much, are more touched and vexed by their penury. This is the reason why the Prophet says, Ye have looked for much, and, behold, there was but little; that is, "Ye are not like the peasants, who satisfy themselves with any sort of food, and are not troubled on account of their straitened circumstances; but your desire has led you to seek abundance. Hence ye seek and greedily lay hold on things on every side; but, behold, it comes to little."

In the second place he adds, Ye have brought it home. He farther mentions another kind of evil — that when they gathered wine, and corn, and money, all these things immediately vanished. Ye have brought it home, and I have blown upon it. By saying that they brought it home, he intimates that what they had acquired was laid up, that it might be preserved safely; for they who had filled their storehouses, and wine-cellars, and bags, thought that they had no more to do with God. Hence it was that profane men securely indulged themselves; they thought that they were beyond the reach of danger, when their houses were well filled. God, on the contrary, shows that their houses became empty, when filled with treasures and provisions. But he speaks still more distinctly — that he had blown upon them, that is, that he had dissipated them by his breath: for the Prophet did not deem it enough historically to narrate what the Jews had experienced; but his purpose also was to point out the cause, as it were, by the finger. He therefore teaches us, that what they laid in store in their houses did not without a cause vanish away; but that this happened through the blowing of God, even because he cursed their blessing, according to what we shall hereafter see in the Prophet Malachi.

He then adds, Why is this? saith Jehovah of hosts. God here asks, not because he had any doubts on the subject, but that he might by this sort of goading rouse the Jews from their lethargy, — "Think of the cause, and know that my hand is not guided by a blind impulse when it strikes you. You ought, then, to consider the reason why all things thus decay and perish." Here again is sharply reproved the stupidity of the people, because they attended not to the cause of their evils; for they ought to have known this of themselves.

But God gives the answer, because he saw that they remained stupefied — On account of my house, he says, because it is waste [139] God here assigns the cause; he shows that though no one of them considered why they were so famished, the judgement of his curse was yet sufficiently manifest, on account of the Temple remaining a waste. And you, he says, run, every one to his own house. Some read, You take delight, every one in his own house; for it is the verb הצר, retse, which we have lately noticed; and it means either to take pleasure in a thing, or to run. Every one, then, runs to his house, or, Every one delights in his house. But it is more suitable to the context to give this rendering, Every one runs to his house. For the Prophet here reminds the Jews that they were slow and slothful in the work of building the Temple, because they hastened to their private houses. He then reproves here their ardor in being intent on building their own houses, so that they had no leisure to build the Temple. This is the hastening which the Prophet blames and condemns in the Jews.

We may hence learn again, that they had long delayed to build the sanctuary after the time had arrived: for, as we have mentioned yesterday, they who think the Jews returned in the fifty-eighth year, and that they had not then undergone the punishment denounced by Jeremiah, are very deluded; for they thus obscure the favor of God; nay, they wholly subvert the truth of the promises, as though they had returned contrary to God's will, through the permission of Cyrus, when yet Isaiah says, that Cyrus would be the instrument of their promised redemption. (Isa 45:5.) Surely, then, Cyrus must have been dead before the time was fulfilled! and in that case God could not have been the redeemer of his people. Therefore Eusebius, and those who agree with him, did thus most absurdly confound the order of time. It now follows —

Hag. 1:10, 11

10. Therefore the heaven over you is stayed from dew, and the earth is stayed from her fruit.

10. Propterea prohibiti super vos sunt coeli a rore, et terra a proventu suo prohibita est.

11. And I called for a drought upon the land, and upon the mountains, and upon the corn, and upon the new wine, and upon the oil, and upon that which the ground bringeth forth, and upon men, and upon cattle, and upon all the labour of the hands.

11. Et vocavi siccitatem super terram, et super montes, et super triticum, et super mustum (aut, vinium,) et super omne quod profert terra, et super hominem, et super animal, et super omnem laborem manuum.

He confirms what the last verse contains — that God had made it evident that he was displeased with the people because their zeal for religion had become cold, and, especially, because they were all strangely devoted to their own interest and manifested no concern for building the Temple. Hence, he says, therefore the heavens are shut up and withhold the dew; that is, they distil no dew on the earth; and he adds, that the earth was closed that it produced no fruit; it yielded no increase, and disappointed its cultivators. As to the particle כן-על, ol-can, we must bear in mind what I have stated, that God did not regard the external and visible Temple, but rather the end for which it was designed; for it was his will then that he should be worshipped under the ceremonies of the law. When, therefore, the Jews offered mutilated, lame, or diseased sacrifices, they manifested impiety and contempt of God. It is yet true, that it was the same thing as to God; but he had not commanded sacrifices to be offered to him for his own sake, but that by such services they might foster true religion. When, therefore, he says now, that he punished their neglect of the Temple, we ought ever to regard that as a pattern of heavenly things, so that we may understand that the coldness and indifference of the Jews were reproved; because it hence evidently appeared that they had no care for the worship of God.

With respect to the withholding of dew and of produce, we know that the Prophets took from the law what served to teach the people, and accommodated it to their own purposes. The curses of the law are general. (De 11:17.) It is therefore the same thing as though the Prophet had said, that what God had threatened by Moses was really fulfilled. It ought not to have been to them a new thing, that whenever heaven denied its dew and rain it was a sign of God's wrath. But as, at this day, during, wars, or famine, or pestilence, men do not regard this general truth, it is necessary to make the application: and godly teachers ought wisely to attend to this point, that is, to remind men, according to what the state of things and circumstances may require, that God proves by facts what he has testified in his word. This is what is done by our Prophet now, withheld have the heavens the dew and the earth its produce [140]

In a word, God intimates, that the heavens leave no care to provide for us, and to distil dew so that the earth may bring forth fruit, and that the earth also, though called the mother of men, does not of itself open its bowels, but that the heavens as well as the earth bear a sure testimony to his paternal love, and also to the care which he exercises over us. God then shows, both by the heavens and the earth, that he provides for us; for when the heavens and the earth administer and supply us with the blessings of God, they thus declare his love towards us. So also, when the heaven is, as it were, iron, and when the earth with closed bowels refuses us food, we ought to know that they are commissioned to execute on us the vengeance of God. For they are not only the instruments of his bounty, but, when it is necessary, God employs them for the purpose of punishing us. This is briefly the meaning.

PRAYER

Grant, Almighty God, that since thou kindly and graciously invites us to thyself, we may not wait until thou stimulates us with goads, but cast aside our sloth and run quickly to thee. And when our torpor so possesses us as to render punishment necessary, permit us not to harden ourselves; but being at length effectually warned, and we return to the right way, and strive so to render all we do approved by thee, that we may find a door opened to thy grace and favor: and being made partakers of those blessed, by which thou affordest a taste of that goodness which we shall enjoy in heaven, may we ever aspire thither, and be satisfied with the abundant blessings which we daily and even continually receive from thine hand, in such a manner as not to be detained by this world; but may we, with minds raised up to heaven, ever tend upwards, and labor for that perfect happiness which is there laid up fur us by Christ our Lord. Amen.

LECTURE ONE HUNDRED AND THIRTIETH

Haggai 1:12

12. Then Zerubbabel the son of Shealtiel, and Joshua the son of Josedech, the high priest, with all the remnant of the people, obeyed the voice of the Lord their God, and the words of Haggai the prophet, as the Lord their God had sent him, and the people did fear before the Lord.

12. Et audivit Zerubbabel, filius Sealtiel, et Jehoasua, filius Jehosadak, sacerdos magnus, et omnes reliquiae populi vocem Iehovae Dei sui, et ad verba Chaggai Prophetae; quemadmodum miserat ipsum Iehova Deus eorum; et timuerunt populus a conspectu Iehovae.

The Prophet here declares that his message had not been without fruit, for shortly after the whole people prepared themselves for the work. And he names both Zerubbabel and Joshua; for it behaved them to lead the way, and, as it were, to extend a hand to others. For, had there been no leaders, no one of the common people would have pointed out the way to the rest. We know what usually happens when a word is addressed indiscriminately to all the people: they wait for one another. But when Joshua and Zerubbabel attended to the commands of the Prophet, the others followed them: for they were dominant, not only in power, but also in authority, so that they induced the people willingly to do their duty. One was the governor of the people, the other was the high priest; but the honesty and faithfulness of both were well known, so that the people spontaneously followed their example.

And this passage teaches us that though God invites all to his service, yet as any one excels in honor or in other respects, so the more promptly he ought to undertake what is proposed by the authority of God. Our Prophet, no doubt, meant to point out this due order of things, by saying, that he was heard first by Zerubbabel and Joshua, and then by the whole people.

But as all had not returned from exile, but a small portion, compared with that great number, which, we know, had not availed themselves of the kindness allowed them — this is the reason why the Prophet does not simply name the people, but the remnant of the people, שארית העם, sharit eom. As also the gift of prophecy had been for a long time more rare, and few appeared among the people who had any decided evidence of their call, such as Samuel, Isaiah, David, and others possessed, the Prophet, for this reason, does here more carefully commend and honor his own office: he says that the people attended to the voice of Jehovah — How? By attending, he says, to the words of Haggai the Prophet, inasmuch as Jehovah their God had sent him. He might have said more shortly that his labor had not been without fruit; but he used this circuitous mode of speaking, that he might confirm his own call; and he did this designedly, because the people had for a long time been without the opportunity of hearing God's Prophets, for there were none among them.

But Haggai says nothing here but what belongs in common to all teachers in the Church: for we know that men are not sent by divine authority to speak that God himself may be silent. As then the ministers of the word derogate nothing from the authority of God, it follows that none except the only true God ought to be heard. It is not then a peculiar expression, which is to be restricted to one man, when God is said to have spoken by the mouth of Haggai; for he thus declared that he was God's true and authorised Prophet. We may therefore gather from these words, that the

Church is not to be ruled by the outward preaching of the word, as though God had substituted men in his own place, and thus divested himself of his own office, but that he only speaks by their mouth. And this is the import of these words, The people attended to the voice of Jehovah their God, and to the words of Haggai the Prophet. For the word of God is not distinguished from the words of the Prophet, as though the Prophet had added anything of his own. Haggai then ascribed these words to himself, not that he devised anything himself, so as to corrupt the pure doctrine which had been delivered to him by God, but that he only distinguished between God, the author of the doctrine, and his minister, as when it is said,

"The sword of God and of Gideon," (Jud 7:20,)

and also,

"The people believed God and Moses his servant." (Ex 14:31.)

nothing is ascribed to Moses or to Gideon apart from God; but God himself is placed in the highest honor, and then Moses and Gideon are joined to him. In the same sense do the Apostles write, when they say, that "it had pleased the Holy spirit" and themselves. (Ac 15:22.)

And hence it is evident how foolish and ridiculous are the Papists, who hence conclude that it is lawful for men to add their own inventions to the word of God. For the Apostles, they say, not only alleged the authority of the Holy Spirit, but also say, that it seemed good to themselves. God then does not so claim, they say, all things for himself, as not to leave some things to the decision of his Church, as though indeed the Apostles meant something different from what our Prophet means here; that is, that they truly and faithfully delivered what their had received from the spirit of God.

It is therefore a mode of speaking which ought to be carefully marked, when we hear, that the voice of God and the words of Haggai were reverently attended to by the people. — Why? Inasmuch, he says, as God had sent him; as though he had said, that God was heard when he spoke by the mouth of man. And this is also worthy of being noticed, because many fanatics boast, that they allow regard to the word of the Lord, but are unwilling to give credit to men, as that would be even preposterous; and they pretend, that in this way what belongs to the only true God is transferred to creatures. But the Holy Spirit most easily reconciles these two things — that the voice of God is heard when the people embrace what they hear from the mouth of a Prophet. Why so? because it pleases God thus to try the obedience of our faith, while he commits to man this office. For if the Lord was pleased to speak himself, then justly might men be neglected: but as he has chosen this mode, whosoever reject God's Prophets, clearly show that they despise God himself. There is no need of inquiring here, why it is that we ought to obey the word preached or the external voice of men, rather than revelations; it is enough for us to know that this is the will of God. When therefore he sends Prophets to us, we ought unquestionably to receive what they bring.

And Haggai says also expressly, that he was sent by the God of Israel; as though he had said, that the people had testified their true piety when they acknowledged God's Prophet in his legitimate vocation. For he who clamorously objects, and says that he knows not whether it pleases God or not to send forth men to announce his word, shows himself to be wholly alienated from God: for it ought to be sufficiently evident to us that this is one of our first principles.

He afterwards adds, that the people feared before Jehovah [141] Haggai confirms here the same truth — that the people received not what they heard from the mouth of mortal man, otherwise than if the majesty of God had openly appeared. For there was no ocular view of God given; but the message of the Prophet obtained as much power as though God had descended from heaven, and had given manifest tokens of his presence. We may then conclude from these words, that the glory of God so shines in his word, that we ought to be so much affected by it, whenever he speaks by his servants, as though he were nigh to us, face to face, as the Scripture says in another place. It now follows —

Hag. 1:13, 14

13. Then spake Haggai the Lord's messenger in the LORD'S message unto the people, saying, I am with you, saith the Lord

13. Et dicit Chaggai, legatus Iehovae in legatione Iehovae, dicendo (vel, dicens) populo, Ego vobiscum sum, dicit Iehova.

14. And the Lord stirred up the spirit of Zerubbabel the son of Shealtiel, governor of Judah, and the spirit of Joshua the son of Josedech, the high priest, and the spirit of all the remnant of the people; and they came and did work in the house of the Lord of hosts, their God,

14. Et excitavit Iehova spiritum Zerubbabel, filii Sealtiel, ducis Jehudah, et spiritum Jehosuae, filii Jehozadak, sacerdotis magni, et spiritum omnium reliquiarum (hoc est, totius residuae multitudinis) populi; et venerunt et fecerunt opus in templo (in domo, ad verbum) Iehovae exercituum Dei sui.

The Prophet tells us here, that he had again roused the leaders as well as the common people; for except God frequently repeats his exhortations, our alacrity relaxes. Though then they had all attended to God's command, it was yet necessary that they should be strengthened by a new promise: for men can be encouraged, and their indifference can be corrected, by no other means, to such a degree, as when God offers and promises his help. This, then, was the way in which they were now encouraged, I am with you. And experience sufficiently shows, that we never really and from the heart obey, except when we rely on his promises and hope for a happy success. For were God only to call us to our work, and were our hope doubtful, all our zeal would doubtless die away. We cannot then devote our services to God, except he supports and encourages us by promises. We also see, that it is not enough that God should speak once, and that we should once receive his word, but there is need that he should rouse us again and again; for the greatest ardor grows cold when no goads are applied.

And the Prophet makes known again his vocation, for he says, that he spake in the message of Jehovah, for he was his messenger. The word ראלמ, malak, means a messenger; and as angels are called מיכאלם, melakim, some foolish men have thought that Haggai was one of the celestial angels, clothed with the form of man: but this is a most frivolous conjecture; for priests, we know, are honored with this title in the second chapter of Malachi, Mal 2:1, and God in many other places calls his Prophets messengers or ambassadors. There is, therefore, no doubt but that Haggai meant simply to testify, that he brought forward nothing presumptuously, but was a faithful dispenser of the word; for he knew that he was sent by God; and that he might attain attention, he was able justly to testify that his message came from heaven.

Hence he says, that he spake as a messenger of Jehovah in the message of Jehovah; that is, he spoke according to his calling, and not as a private individual, but as one who derived his authority from heaven, and could call to order the whole people; for he was to give way neither to the chief priest nor to Zerubbabel the ruler of the people, inasmuch as he was superior to them on this account, because he had a message which had been committed to him by God. [142] We now then understand the design of the Prophet.

And we hence learn that there is no dignity which exempts us from obedience common to all, when God's word is addressed to us. Doubtless Joshua the high priest was superior to all the rest in matters of religion, and he was the chief angel or messenger of the God of hosts; and yet he refused not to submit himself to God's Prophet, for he understood that he was in a special manner appointed by God to this office. Zerubbabel, the governor of the people, followed also his example. Let us, then, know that God's word is proclaimed under this condition, that no eminence, either in honor or in dignity, exempts us, as it were, by a sort of privilege, from the obligation of receiving it.

The Prophet at length adds, that the people hastened quickly to the work, because God had given encouragement to them all. He had lately spoken of the fruit of his doctrine; but he now declares that his voice had not so penetrated into the hearts of all, as though it had been of itself efficacious, but that it had been connected with the hidden influence of the Spirit.

And this passage is remarkable; for the Prophet includes both these things — that God allows not his word to be useless or unfruitful — and yet that this proceeds not from the diligence of men, but from the hidden power of the Spirit. The Prophet, then, did not fail in his efforts; for his labor was not in vain, but brought forth fruit. At the same time, that that saying might remain true,

'He who plants and he who waters is nothing,' (1Co 3:7,)

he says, that the Israelites were ready for the work, because the Lord roused them; Jehovah, he says, stirred up the spirit of Zerubbabel, the spirit of Joshua, and of the whole people. It is not right to restrict the influence of the Spirit to one thing only, as some do, who imagine that the Israelites were confirmed in their good resolution, as they say, having before spontaneously obeyed the word of God. These separate, without reason, what ought to be read in the Prophet as connected together. For God roused the spirit of Zerubbabel and of the whole people; and hence it was that they received the message of the Prophet, and were attentive to his words. Foolishly, then, do they imagine that the Israelites were led by their own free-will to obey the word of God, and then that some aid of the Holy Spirit followed, to make them firmly to persevere in their course. But the Prophet declared, in the first place, that his message was respectfully received by the people; and now he explains how it was, even because God had touched the hearts of the whole people. [143]

And we ought to notice the expression, when it is said that the spirit of Zerubbabel and of all the people was stirred up. For much sloth, we know, prevailed, especially among the multitude. But as to Zerubbabel and Joshua, they were, as we have said, already willing, but delayed until the coldness under which they labored was reproved. But the Prophet here simply means, that they became thus obedient through the hidden impulse of God, and also that they were made firm in their purpose. God does not form new souls in us, when he draws us to his service; but changes what is wrong in us: for we should never be attentive to his word, were he not to open our ears; and there would be no inclination to obey, were he not to turn our hearts; in a word, both will and effort would immediately fail in us, were he not to add his gift of perseverance. Let us, then, know that Haggai's labors produced fruits, because the Lord effectually touched the hearts of the people; for we indeed know that it is his special gift, that the elect are made disciples, according to that declaration,

'No one comes to me, except my Father draw him.' (Joh 6:24.)

It is therefore said that they came and did the work in the house of Jehovah We may also hence learn, that no one is fit to offer sacrifices to God, or to do any other service, but he who has been moulded by the hidden operation of the Spirit. Willingly, indeed, we offer ourselves and our all to God, and build his temple; but whence is this voluntary action, except that the Lord subdues us, and thus renders us teachable and obedient? It is afterwards added —

Haggai 1:15

15. In the four and twentieth day of the sixth month, in the second year of Darius the king.

15. In die vicesimo quarto mensis sexti, anno secundo Darii regis.

The Prophet mentions even the time when they commenced the building of the temple. Three-and-twenty days interposed between the first message and the beginning of the work. It hence appears how ignorant he was who divided the chapters, having begun the second chapter at this verse, where the Prophet shows, as it were by his finger, how much was the distance between the day in which he began to exhort the people, and the success of which he speaks. He then simply tells us here when the Temple began to be built — that is, in the second year of Darius the king, and in the twenty-fourth day of the sixth month. He had previously said that a message was given to him in the second year of Darius the king, and in the sixth month, and on the first day. Then from that day to the twenty-fourth the people delayed; not that they disregarded the command of the Prophet, but because it was not so easy a thing to persuade them all, that they might unanimously undertake the work. Though then the promptitude of the people is commended, we must yet observe that there was some mixture of weakness; for the effect of the doctrine did not appear till the twenty-fourth day. [144] It afterwards follows —

CHAPTER 2

Haggai 2:1-5

1. 1 In the seventh month, in the one and twentieth day of the month, came the word of the Lord by the prophet Haggai, saying,

2. Speak now to Zerubbabel the son of Shealtiel, governor of Judah, and to Joshua the son of Josedech, the high priest, and to the residue of the people, saying,

2. Dic nunc ad Zerubbabel, filium Sealtiel, ducem Jehudah, et ad Jehosuah, filium Jehosadak, sacerdotem magnum, et ad reliquias populi, dicendo.

3. Quis in vobis superstes (vel, residuus, ad verbum) qui viderit domum hanc in gloria sua priore, et quam vos videtis hanc nunc, annon prae illa sicut nihilum in oculis vestris?

4. Yet now be strong, O Zerubbabel, saith the LORD; and be strong, O Joshua, son of Josedech, the high priest; and be strong, all ye people of the land, saith the Lord, and work: for I am with you, saith the Lord of hosts:

5. According to the word that I covenanted with you when ye came out of Egypt, so my spirit remaineth among you: fear ye not.

5. Secundum verbum quod pepigi vobiscum dum egressi estis ex Egypto; et spiritus meus stabit (vel, perseverabit) in medio vestri, ne timeatis.

The Prophet now states another reason why he had been sent by God, in order that he might obviate a temptation which might have hindered the work that was begun. We have seen that they were all stirred up by the celestial spirit to undertake the building of the Temple. But as Satan, by his many arts, attempts to turn back the godly from their course, so he had devised a reason by which the desire of the people might have been checked. Inasmuch as the old people, who had seen the splendor of the former temple, considered this temple no better than a cottage, all their zeal evaporated; for, as we have said, without a promise there will continue in men no ardor, no perseverance. Now we know what had been predicted by Ezekiel, and what all the other Prophets had testified, especially Isaiah, who had spoken highly of the excellency of the Church, and shown that it was to be superior to its ancient state. (Isa 33:21.) Besides, Ezekiel describes the form of the Temple, and states its dimensions. (Eze 41:1.) As then the faithful had learnt from these prophecies that the new Temple would be more splendid than the ancient, they were in danger, not only of becoming cold in the business, but also of being wholly discouraged, when they perceived that the new Temple in no respect reached the excellency and grandeur of the ancient Temple. And these things are described at large by Josephus.

But we may easily conclude, from the words of the Prophet, that there was then a danger lest they should lay aside the work they had begun, except they were encouraged by a new exhortation. And he says that this happened in the seventh month, and on the first day of the month.

Here arises a question, How was it that they so soon compared the new with the old building. Seven or eight days had passed since the work was begun: nothing, doubtless, could have been then constructed, which might have afforded a ground of comparison. It seems then strange, that the Prophet had been so soon sent to them. An answer to this will be easily found, if we bear in mind. that what I have stated at the beginning of the first chapter, that the foundations of the Temple had been previously laid, but that there had been a long interruption: for the people had turned to their own private concerns, and all had become so devoted to their own advantages, that they neglected the building of the Temple. For it is wholly a false notion, that the people had returned from exile before the appointed time, and it has been sufficiently refuted by clear proofs; for scripture expressly declares, that both Cyrus and Darius had been led by a divine impulse to allow the return of the people. Hence, when the Jews returned to their country, they immediately began to build the Temple; but afterwards, as I have said, either avarice, or too anxious a desire for their own private benefit, laid hold on their minds. As then the building of the Temple had been for some time neglected, they were again encouraged, as our Prophet has shown to us. They had now hardly applied their hands to the work, when, through the artifice of Satan, such suggestions as these crept in — "What are ye doing, ye miserable men! Ye wish to build a Temple to your God; but what sort of Temple will it be? Certainly it will not be that which all the Prophets have celebrated. For what do we read in Isaiah, Jeremiah, and Ezekiel? Have not all these testified that the Temple which would be rebuilt after our return from Babylonian exile would be more splendid than the other? But we now build a shed. Surely this is done without authority. We do not then fight under the guidance of God; and it would be better for us to leave off the work; for our service cannot be approved of God, except it be founded on his Word. And we see how far this Temple comes short of what God has promised."

We now hence learn, that it was not without reason that Haggai was sent on the eighth day to recover the people from their indifference. And hence also we may learn how necessary it is for us to be constantly stimulated; for Satan can easily find out a thousand impediments, by which he may turn us aside from the right course, except God often repeats his exhortations to keep us awake. Eight days only have elapsed, and the people would have ceased from their work, had not Haggai been sent to encourage them again.

Now the cause of this cessation, which the Prophet designed to obviate and to remove, ought to be especially noticed. The people had before ceased to work, because they were immoderately devoted to their own interest, which was a proof of base ingratitude and of profane impiety: for those who had no care for building the Temple were most ungrateful to God; and then their impiety was intolerable, inasmuch as they sought boarded houses to dwell in, being not content with decent houses without having them adorned, while the Temple was left, as it were, a wilderness. But the cause was different, when Haggai was sent the second time; for their indifference then arose from a good principle and a genuine feeling of religion. But we hence see what a subtle contriver Satan is, who not only draws us away openly from God's service, but insinuates himself in a clandestine manner, so as to turn us aside, under the cover of zeal, from the course of our vocation. How was it that the people became negligent after they had begun the work? even because it grieved the old men to see the glory of the second, so far inferior to the first Temple. For though the people animated themselves by the sound of trumpets, yet the old among them drowned the sound by their lamentations. Whence was this? even because they saw, as I have said, that this Temple was in no way equal to the ancient one; and hence they thought that God was not as yet reconciled to them. Had they said, that so great an expense was not necessary, that God did not require much money to be laid out, their impiety should have been openly manifested; but when they especially wished that the splendor of the Temple would be such, as might surely prove that the restoration of the Church was come, such as had been promised by all the Prophets, we doubtless perceive their pious feeling.

But we are thus reminded, that we ought always to beware of the intrigues of Satan, when they appear under the cover of truth. When, therefore, our minds are disposed to piety, Satan is ever to be feared, lest he should stealthily suggest to us what may turn us aside from our duty; for we see that some leave the Church because they require in it the highest perfection. They are indignant at vices which they deem intolerable, when they cannot be corrected: and thus, under the pretext of zeal, they separate themselves and seek to form for themselves a new world, in which there is to be a perfect Church; and they lay hold on those passages in which the Holy Spirit recommends purity to the Church, as when Paul says, that it was purchased by Christ, that it might be without spot or wrinkle. As then these are inflamed with a zeal so rigid that they depart from God himself and violate the unity of the Church; so also there are many proud men who despise the Church of God, because it shines not forth among them in great pomp; and they think that God does not dwell in the midst of us, because we are obscure and of no great importance, and also because they regard our few number with contempt.

In all these there is some appearance of piety. How so? Because they would have God to be reverenced, so that they would have the whole world to be filled with the fear of his majesty; or they would have much wealth to be gathered, so that sumptuous offerings might be made. But, as I have already said, Satan thus cunningly insinuates himself; and hence we ought to fear his intrigues, lest, under plausible pretences, he should dazzle our eyes. But the best way of caution is to regard what God commands, and so to rely on his promises as to proceed steadily in our course, though the accomplishment of the promises does not immediately correspond with our desires; for God designedly keeps us in suspense in order to try our faith. Though then he may not as yet fulfill what he has promised, let it yet be our course to attempt nothing rashly, while we are obeying his command. It will then be our chief wisdom, by which we may escape all the crafts of Satan, simply to obey God's word, and to exercise our hope so as patiently to wait the seasonable time, when he will fulfill what he now promises.

PRAYER

Grant Almighty God, that as we are not only alienated in mind from thee, but also often relapse after having been once stirred up by thee, either into perverseness, or into our own vanity, or are led astray by various things, so that nothing is more difficult than to pursue our course until we reach the end of our race, — O grant that we may not confide in our own strength, nor claim for ourselves more than what is right, but, with our hearts raised above, depend on thee alone, and constantly call on thee to supply us with new strength, and so to confirm us that we may persevere to the end in the discharge of our duty, until we shall at length attain the true and perfect form of that temple which thou commandest us to build, in which thy perfect glory shines forth, and into which we are to be transformed by Christ our Lord. Amen.

LECTURE ONE HUNDRED AND THIRTY-FIRST

The Prophet, after having declared why it was necessary to add new stimulants, now exhorts Zerubbabel and Joshua, and also the people, to be courageous, and thus to proceed with the work. And he again repeats what he had said, that the Lord was with them; I am with you, he says. Now this one thing is enough for us, that is, when God declares that he is with us; for his aid, we know, is stronger than the whole world, however Satan may on every side attempt to resist us.

He also adds, that his Spirit would be in the midst of them; and then he says, that there was no reason for them to fear. By his Spirit God means the power by which he strengthened their minds, that they might not give way to their trials, or, that fear might not hinder them. And what is particular is joined to what is general; for God is present with his own in various ways: but he especially shows, that he is present when, by his Spirit, he confirms weak minds. He then bids them all to be of a courageous mind. This is one thing. But he also shows whence this courage proceeded; for he sustained them by his Spirit when they were growing faint, or when they were not able to resist fears. The Prophet reminds them by these words, that courage was to be sought from God.

We hence learn that what belongs to our calling and duty is not required from us as though we were able to perform everything; but when the Lord, according to his own right, commands, he offers the help of his Spirit; and thus we ought to connect the promise of grace with the precept, of which foolish men take no notice, who deduce free will from what is commanded: for they thus reason — that it is in vain to require from us what is above our ability, and that as God requires us to form our life according to the rule of the highest perfection, it is therefore in our power to perform the highest justice. But the Prophet here, in the first place, exhorts Joshua and Zerubbabel, and the whole people, to be courageous, and then, he immediately adds, that the Spirit of God would be in the midst of them; as though he had said, that there was no reason for them to despond, though they had not sufficient strength in themselves; for courage was to be sought from the Spirit of God, who would dwell among them. In short, the Prophet teaches us that the faithful are so to strive as not to arrogate anything to themselves, but to offer themselves to be ruled by the Lord, that he may supply them with weapons as well as with strength, and thus conquer in them; for though the victory is ascribed to us it is yet certain that God conquers in us.

He then adds, According to the word; for so I render the particle את, at [145] They who think that the Jews are here reminded that it was their duty to obey God, and purely to serve him, and truly to keep his law, according to what he had commanded them when he brought them out of the land of Egypt, far depart from the design of the Prophet; for the Prophet pursues the same subject; and in the latter clause he confirms what I have just mentioned — that the Spirit of God would be in the midst of them. He therefore shows that he promises nothing new, but what God had formerly engaged to give to their fathers. If any one prefers taking the particle את, at in an explicative sense, I do not object; for the meaning would be the same — that this is the word which he had promised. The object of the Prophet is by no means doubtful; for he means to teach us that God is faithful and constant in his promises, and that the Jews would find this to be the case, for he would perform what he had formerly promised to their fathers. The word, he says, which I had covenanted with you when I brought you out of Egypt. For the Prophets were wont to remind the faithful of the ancient covenant, that they might gain more credit to their special prophecies. We indeed know that whatever God had promised to the Jews, was founded on their first adoption. When, therefore, the Prophets brought forward the ancient covenant, it was the same as though they led the Jews back to the fountain itself; for the promises, which now and then occurred, were like streams which flowed from the first spring, even their gratuitous covenant.

We now then see why an express mention is made of the ancient compact which God had made with the chosen people at their departure out of Egypt.

It must also be observed, that God became then the Redeemer of his people, in order to be their eternal Father, and thus to be the perpetual guardian of their safety. Hence the design of what the Prophet says is to show that their fathers were not formerly redeemed, that their children might reject God, but that he might continue his favor to his people to the end. But the ultimate issue is to be found in Christ, that is, the full accomplishment; for God does not cease to show kindness in him to his chosen people, but performs much more fully and abundantly what he had previously exhibited under types and shadows. For whatever he conferred on his ancient Church, was, as it were, a prelude of his vast bounty, which was at length made known by the coming of Christ.

We now clearly apprehend what the Prophet meant: For he upbraided the Jews for their stupidity, because they did not consider that their fathers were formerly delivered from Egypt, that God might defend them to the end. Hence he bids them maturely to examine the design and character of the covenant which God made at their departure from Egypt; for he entered into covenant with them, that he might be their Redeemer, and confer on them the fullness of all blessings. Since it is so, he says, the time is now come when God will perform what he then promised to your fathers; and whatever faithfulness ye have hitherto found in God, ought to be applied for this end — that ye may feel assured that ye have been now restored to your country, in order that he might re-establish his Church, and that ye might not continue in that low condition, which now depresses your minds. As then ye ought to look for that fullness of happiness which God formerly promised, either his covenant is void and he unfaithful, or ye ought with cheerfulness and alacrity to proceed with the work. It follows —

Haggai 2:6-9

6. For thus saith the LORD of hosts; Yet once, it is a little while, and I will shake the heavens, and the earth, and the sea, and the dry land;

6. Quia sit dicit Iehova exercituum, Adhuc unum modicum hoc, et ego commovebo coelos et terram et mare et aridam;

7. And I will shake all nations, and the desire of all nations shall come: and I will fill this house with glory, saith the LORD of hosts.

7. Et commovebo omnes gentes, et venient, desiderium omnium gentium; et implebo domum hance gloria, dicit Iehova exercituum.

8. The silver is mine, and the gold is mine, saith the LORD of hosts.

8. Meum argentum, et meum aurum, dicit Iehova exercituum.

9. The glory of this latter house shall be greater than of the former, saith the LORD of hosts: and in this place will I give peace, saith the LORD of hosts.

9. Major erit gloria domus hujus secundae (posterioris, ad verbum,) quam prioris dicit Iehova exercituum: et in loco hoc dabo pacem, dicit Iehova exercituum.

Here the Prophet expresses more clearly, and confirms more fully, what I have said — that God would in time bring help to the miserable Jews, because he would not disappoint the assurance given to the fathers. This declaration, then, depends on the covenant before mentioned; and hence the causative particle is used, For thus saith Jehovah of hosts, as yet a small one it is, or, yet shortly, I will fill this house with glory. The expression a small thing, most interpreters aptly to time. Yet there are those who think the subject itself is denoted. The more received opinion is, that it means a small duration, a short time, because God would soon make a change for the better. "Though then there does not as yet appear the accomplishment of the promises, by which ye have hitherto supported your faith and your hope, yet after a short time God will really prove that he has spoken nothing falsely to you."

There are yet some, as I have said, who think that the matter itself is denoted by the Prophet, even that the Temple did not yet appear in splendor before the eyes of men, a small one it is, that is, Ye see not indeed a building such as that was, before the Assyrians and the Chaldeans took possession of the city; but let not your eyes remain fixed on the appearance of this Temple. Let then this small one as yet pass by; but in a short time this house will be filled with glory

With regard to the main object, it was the Prophet's design to strengthen the minds of the godly, that they might not think that the power of God was inefficient, though he had not as yet performed what they had hoped. In short, they were not to judge by present appearances of what had been previously said of their redemption. We said yesterday that the minds of the godly were heavily depressed, because the Prophets had spoken in high terms of the Temple as well as of the kingdom: the kingdom was as yet nothing; and the temple was more like a shed than what might have been compared in glory with the former Temple. It was hence necessary for the Prophet to meet this objection; and this is the reason why he bids them to overlook the present appearance, and to think of the glory which was yet hidden. As yet, he says, it is a small one; that is, "There is no reason for you to despair, though the grandeur of the Temple does not as yet appear to be so great as you have conceived; but, on the contrary, let your minds pass over to that restoration which is still far distant. As yet then a small one it is; and I will move the heavens and the earth." [146]

In a word, God here bids them to exercise patience, until he should put forth the ineffable power of his hand to restore fully his Church; and this is what is meant by the shaking of the heaven and the earth.

But this is a remarkable passage. The Jews indeed, who are very absurd in everything connected with the kingdom of Christ, pervert what is here said by the Prophet, and even reduce it to nothing. But the Apostle in Heb 12:1 reminds us of what God means here. For this passage contains an implied contrast between the law and the gospel, between redemption, just mentioned here, and that which was to be expected, and was at length made known by the coming of Christ. God, then, when he redeemed his people from Egypt, as well as from Babylon, moved the earth: but the Prophet announces here something greater — that God would shake the heaven and the earth. But that the meaning of the Prophet may appear more evident, each sentence must be examined in order.

He says first, this once, shortly. I am inclined to apply this to time, that I may not depart from what is commonly received. But there is no reason for us to contend on the subject, because it makes little or no difference as to the main point. For we have said that what the Prophet had in view was to show that the Jews were not to fix their eyes and their minds on the appearance of the Temple at the time: "Allow," he says, "and give place to hope, because your present state shall not long remain; for the Lord will shake the heaven and the earth; think then of God's power, how great it is; does he not by his providence rule both the earth and the heaven? And he will shake all things above and below, rather than not to restore his Church; he will rather change the appearance of the whole world, than that redemption should not be fully accomplished. Be not then unwilling to be satisfied with these preludes, but know what God's power can do: for though it may be necessary to throw the heaven and the earth into confusions, yet this shall be done, rather than that your enemies should prevent that full restoration, of which the Prophets have so often spoken." But the Apostle very justly says, that the gospel is here set in contrast with the law; for God exhibited his wonderful power, when the law was promulgated on mount Sinai; but a fuller power shone forth at the coming of Christ, for then the heaven, as well as the earth, was shaken. It is not, then, without reason that the Apostle concludes that God speaks now to us from heaven, for his majesty appears more splendid in the gospel than formerly in the law: and hence we are less excusable, if we despise him now speaking in the person of his only begotten Son, and thus speaking to show to us that the whole world is subject to him.

He then adds, I will move all the nations, and they shall come. After having mentioned the heaven and the earth, he now shows that he would arrest the attention of all mortals, so as to turn them according to his will, in any way it may please him: Come, he says, shall all nations — How? because I shall shake them. Here again the Prophet teaches us that men come not to Christ except through the wonderful agency of God. He might have spoken more simply, I will lead all nations, as it is said elsewhere; but his purpose was to express something more, even that the impulse by which God moves his elect to betake themselves to the fold of Christ is supernatural. Shaking seems a forcible act. Lest men, then, should obscure the power of God, by which they are roused that they may obey Christ, and submit to his authority, it is here by the Prophet expressed by this term, in order that they might understand that the Lord does not work in an usual or common manner, when they are thus changed.

But it must be also observed, that men are thus powerfully, and in an extraordinary or supernatural manner influenced, so that they follow spontaneously at the same time. The operation of God is then twofold; for it is first necessary to shake men, that they may unlearn their whole character, that is, that forgetting their former nature, they may willingly receive the yoke of Christ. We indeed know how great is our perverseness, and how unnameable we are, until God subdues us by his Spirit. There is need in such a case of a violent shaking. But we are not forced to obey Christ, as lions and wild beasts are, who indeed yield, but still retain their inward ferocity, and roar, though led in chains and subdued by scourges and beatings. We are not, then, so shaken, that our inward rebellion remains in us; but we are shaken, so that our disposition is changed, and we receive willingly the yoke of Christ. This is the reason why the Prophet says, I will shake all nations, and they shall come; that is, there will be indeed a wonderful conversion, when the nations who previously despised God, and regarded true religion and piety with the utmost hatred, shall habituate themselves to the ruling power of God: and they shall come, because they shall be so drawn by his hidden influence, that the obedience they shall render will be voluntary. We now perceive the meaning of the Prophet.

He afterwards adds, The desire of all nations. This admits of two explanations. The first is, that nations shall come and bring with them everything that is precious, in order to consecrate it to the service of God; for the Hebrews call whatever is valuable a desire; so that under this term they include all riches, honors, pleasures, and everything of this kind. Hence some render the passage thus, I will shake all nations, and come shall the desire of all nations. As there is a change of number; others will have ב, beth, or מ, mem, to be understood, They shall come with what they desire; that is, the nations shall not come empty, but shall gather all their treasures to be a holy oblation to God. But we may understand what he says of Christ, Come shall the desire of all nations, and I will fill this house with glory. We indeed know that Christ was the expectation of the whole world, according to what is said by Isaiah. And it may be properly said, that when the desire of all nations shall come, that is, when Christ shall be manifested, in whom the wishes of all ought to center, the glory of the second Temple shall then be illustrious; but as it immediately follows, Mine is the silver, and mine is the gold, the more simple meaning is that which I first stated — that the nations would come, bringing with them all their riches, that they might offer themselves and all their possessions as a sacrifice to God.

It is, then, better to read what follows as an explanation, Mine is the silver, mine is the gold, saith Jehovah; that is, "I have not through want of money deferred hitherto the complete building of the Temple; for what can hinder me from amassing gold and silver from all quarters? Should it so please me,

I could in a short time build a Temple by all the wealth of the world. Is it not indeed in my power to create mountains of gold and silver, by which I might erect for myself a Temple? Ye hence see that wealth is not wanting to me to build the Temple which I have promised; but the time is not arrived. Therefore they who believe the preceding predictions, ought to wait and to look forward, until the suitable time shall come." This is the import of the passage. [147]

He at length declares that the glory of the second Temple would be greater than that of the first, and that there would be peace in that place. As to the words there is nothing obscure; but we ought especially to attend to what is said.

It must, indeed, be first observed, that what is said here of the future glory of the Temple is to be applied to the excellency of those spiritual blessings which appeared when Christ was revealed, and are still conspicuous to us through faith; for ungodly men are so blind that they see them not. And this we must bear in mind, lest we dream like some gross interpreters, who think that what is here said was in part fulfilled when Herod reconstructed the Temple. For though that was a sumptuous building, yet there is no doubt but that it was an attempt of the Devil to delude the Jews, that they might cease to hope for Christ. Such was also, probably, the craft of Herod. We indeed know that he was only a half-Jew. He professed himself to be one of Abraham's children; but he accommodated his habits, we know, to those of the Jews, oddly for his own advantage. That they might not look for Christ, this delusive and empty spectacle was presented to them, so as almost to astound them. Though this, however, may not have entered into the mind of Herod, it is yet certain that the Devil's design was to present to the Jews this deceptive shade, that they might not raise up their thoughts to look for the coming of Christ, as the time was then near at hand.

God might, indeed, immediately at the beginning have caused a magnificent temple to be built: as he had allowed a return to the people, so he might have given them courage, and supplied them with materials, to render the latter Temple equal or even superior to the Temple of Solomon. But Cyrus prohibited by an edict the Temple to be built so high, and he also made its length somewhat smaller: Why was this done? and why also did Darius do the same, who yet liberally helped the Jews, and spared no expense in building the Temple? How was it that both these kings, though guided by the Spirit of God, did not allow the Temple to be built with the same splendor with which it had been previously erected? This did not happen without the wonderful counsel of God; for we know how gross in their notions the Jews had been, and we see that even the Apostles were entangled in the same error; for they expected that the kingdom of Christ would be no other than an earthly one. Had then this Temple been equally magnificent with the former, and had the kingdom become such as it had been, the Jews would have acquiesced in these outward pomps; so that Christ would have been despised, and God's spiritual favor would have been esteemed as nothing. Since, then, they were so bent on earthly happiness, it was necessary for them to be awakened; and the Lord had regard to their weakness, by not allowing a splendid Temple to be built. But in suffering a counterfeit Temple to be built by Herod, when the manifestation of Christ was nigh, he manifested his vengeance by punishing their ingratitude, rather than his favor; and I call it counterfeit, because its splendor was never approved by God. Though Herod spent great treasures on that building, he yet profaned rather than adorned the Temple. Foolishly, then, do some commemorate what Helena, queen of Adiabenians, had laid out, and think that thus a credit is in some measure secured to this prophecy. But it was on the contrary Satan who attempted to deceive by such impostures and crafts, that he might draw away the minds of the godly from the beauty of the spiritual Temple.

But why does the prophet mention gold and silver? He did this in conformity with what was usual and common; for whenever the Prophets speak of the kingdom of Christ, they delineate or describe its splendor in figurative terms, suitable to their own age. When Isaiah foretells the restoration of the Church, he declares that the Church would be all gold and silver, and whatever glittered with precious stones; and in Isa 60:1 he especially sets forth the magnificence of the Temple, as though nations from all parts were to bring for sacrifice all their precious things. But Isaiah speaks figuratively, as all the other Prophets do. So then what we read of gold and of silver ought to be so explained as to be applied mystically to the kingdom of Christ; as we have already observed respecting Mal 1:11 —

'They shall offer to me, saith the Lord,
pure sacrifices from the rising to the setting of the sun.'

What are these sacrifices? Are heifers yet to be offered, or lambs, or other animals? By no means; but we must regard the spiritual character of the priesthood; for as the gold of which the Prophet now speaks, and the silver, ought to be taken in a spiritual sense; for since Christ has appeared in the world, it is not God's will to be served with gold and silver vessels; so also there is no altar on which victims are to be sacrificed, and no candlestick; in a word, all the symbols of the law have ceased. It hence follows that the Prophet speaks of the spiritual ornaments of the Temple. And thus we perceive how the glory of the second Temple is to be greater than that of the first.

It then follows, that God would give peace in this place; as though he had said that it would be well with the Jews if they only waited patiently for the complete fulfillment of redemption. But it must be observed, that this peace was not so evident to them that they could enjoy it according to the perception of the flesh; but it was that kind of peace of which Paul speaks, and which, he says, exceeds all understanding (Php 4:7.) In short, the people could not have comprehended what the Prophet teaches here respecting the future splendor of the Temple, except they leaped over all the obstacles which seemed to obstruct the progress of complete redemption; and so it was ever necessary for them to have recourse to this truth — yet a little while; as though he said that they were patiently to endure while God was exercising their faith: but that the time would come, and that shortly, when the Lord would fill that house with glory that is, when Christ would bring witch him all fullness of glory; for though they were to gather the treasures of a thousand worlds into one mass, such a glory would yet be corruptible; but when God the Father appeared in the person of his own Son, he then glorified indeed his Temple; and his majesty shone forth so much that there was nothing wanting to a complete perfection.

PRAYER

Grant, Almighty God, that since we are by nature extremely prone to superstition, we may carefully consider what is the true and right way of serving thee, such as thou dost desire and approve, even that we offer ourselves spiritually to thee, and seek no other altar but Christ, and relying on no other priest, hope to be acceptable and devoted to thee, that he may imbue us with the Spirit which has been fully poured on him, so that we may from the heart devote ourselves to thee, and thus proceed patiently in our course, that with minds raised upwards we may ever go on towards that glory which is as yet hid under hope, until it shall at length be manifested in due time, when thine only-begotten Son shall appear with the elect angels for our final redemption. Amen.

LECTURE ONE HUNDRED AND THIRTY-SECOND

Haggai 2:10-14

10. In the four and twentieth day of the ninth month, in the second year of Darius, came the word of the LORD by Haggai the prophet, saying,

10. Vicesimo quarto noni (mensis, subaudiendum,) anno secundo Darii, fuit sermo Iehovae ad Chaggai Prophetam, dicendo.

11. Thus saith the LORD of hosts; Ask now the priests concerning the law, saying,

11. Sic dicit Iehova exercituum, Interroga Sacerdotes de Lege, dicendo,

12. If one bear holy flesh in the skirt of his garment, and with his skirt do touch bread, or pottage, or wine, or oil, or any meat, shall it be holy? And the priests answered and said, No.

12. Si sustulerit vir (quispiam) carnem sanctam in ala vestis suae, et tetegerit ala sua panem, et coctionem, et vinum, et olcum, et quodvis edulium, an sanctificabitur? Et responderunt Sacerdotes et dixerunt, Non.

13. Then said Haggai, If one that is unclean by a dead body touch any of these, shall it be unclean? And the priests answered and said, It shall be unclean.

13. Et dixit Chaggai, Si tetegerit pollutus in anima omne hoc, an polluetur? Responderunt Sacerdotes, et dixerunt, Polluetur.

14. Then answered Haggai, and said, So is this people, and so is this nation before me, saith the LORD; and so is every work of their hands; and that which they offer there is unclean.

14. Et respondi Chaggai et dixit, Sic populus iste, et sic gens ista in conspectu meo, dicit Iehova: et sic omne opus manuum ipsorum, et quod obtulerint illic, pollutum erit.

Though interpreters seem to perceive the meaning of the Prophet, yet no one really and clearly expresses what he means and intends to teach us: nay, they adduce nothing but what is jejune and frigid; for they refer all these things to this point, — that sacrifices were not acceptable to God before the people had begun to build the Temple, but that from that time they were pleasing to God, because the people, in offering sacrifices in a waste place, proved by such negligence that they disregarded the command of God: but when their hands were applied to the work, God was appeased, and thus he began to accept their sacrifices which before he had rejected. This is, indeed, a part of what is meant, but not the whole; and the Prophet's main object seems to me to be wholly different. He has been hitherto exhorting the people to build the Temple; he now exhorts them to build from a pure motive, and not to think that they had done everything when the Temple assumed a fine appearance before the eyes of men, for God required something else. Hence, I have no doubt but that the Prophet intended here to raise up the minds of the people to the spiritual worship of God.

It was, indeed, necessary diligently to build the Temple, but the end was also to be regarded; for God never cared for external ceremonies; nor was he delighted with that building as men are with their splendid houses. As the Jews absurdly ascribed these gross feelings to God, the Prophet here shows why so strict a command had been given as to the building of the Temple; and the reason was, — that God might be worshipped in a pure and holy manner.

I will repeat again what I have said, that the explanation may be more familiar to you. When the people neglected the building of the Temple, they manifested their in-piety and their contempt of Divine worship: for what was the cause of their delay and tardiness, except that each of them regarded nothing but just his own private interest? Now, when all of them strenuously undertook the work of building the Temple, their industry was indeed laudable, for it was a proof of their piety: but when the people thought that God required nothing more than a splendid Temple, it was manifest superstition: for the worship of God, we know, is corrupted when it is confined to external things; for, in this manner God is transformed into a nature not his own: as he is a Spirit, so he must be spiritually worshipped by us. Whosoever then obtrudes on him only external pomps in order to pacify him, most childishly trifles with him. This second part, in my view, is what the Prophet now undertakes to handle. From the seventh to the ninth month they had been diligently engaged in the work which the Lord had commanded them to do: but men, as we know, busy themselves with external things and neglect spiritual worship; hence it was necessary to join what is said here, that the people might understand, that it was not enough to satisfy God, though they spared neither expense nor labor in building the Temple; but that something greater was required, even to worship God in it in a pure and holy manner. This is the design of the whole passage. But we must first examine the Prophet's words, and then it will be easier to gather the whole import of his doctrine.

He says then that he was ordered by God, on the twenty fourth day of the month, in the same year, in the second year of Darius, to ask the priests concerning the law [148] Haggai is not bid to inquire respecting the whole law, but only that the priests should answer a question according to the Word of God, or the doctrine of the law according to what is commonly said — What is law, is the question: for it was not allowed to the priests to allege anything they pleased indiscriminately; but they were only interpreters of the law. This is the reason why God bids his Prophet to inquire what the law of Moses defines as to the ceremony mentioned here. And the design was, that the people, being convinced as to the legal ceremonies, might not contend nor glamour, but acknowledge that all socks are condemned as sinful which flow not from a pure and sincere heart.

Haggai asks first, If a man takes holy flesh — that is, some part of the sacrifice, — if any one takes and carries it in a sleeve or skirt, that is, in any part of his vestment, and then touches bread, or oil, or any eatable thing, will anything connected with that holy flesh be sanctified by mere touch? The priests answer, No. Here also interpreters grossly mistake: for they take sanctified as meaning polluted, altogether falsely; for there is here a twofold question proposed. Whether holy flesh sanctifies anything it may touch? and then, whether an impure and a polluted man contaminates whatever he may touch? As to the first question, the priests wisely and truly answer, that there is no such efficacy in sacrifices, as that they can sanctify what they may touch: and this is true. The second definition is also most proper, that whatever is touched by an unclean man is polluted, as the law everywhere declares.

The Prophet then accommodates this to his present case, So, he says, is this people, and this nation, and the work of their hands. For as long as they are polluted, however they may spend money in sacrifices, and greatly weary themselves in worshipping God, not only is their labor vain, but whatever they offer is polluted, and is an abomination only. We now understand the words of the Prophet, and so we may now consider the subject.

But before I speak generally of the present subject, I shall first notice what the Prophet says here, that he inquired respecting the law; for it was not allowed to the priests to allege anything they pleased. We indeed know, that they had advanced into such licentiousness, as arbitrarily to demand what God had never commanded, and also to forbid the people what was lawful, the use of which had been permitted by God's law. But Haggai does not here allow such a liberty to the priests; he does not ask what they thought, but what was required by the law of the Lord. And this is worthy of being noticed; for it is a pernicious evil to exercise an arbitrary control over the conscience. And yet the devil has ever corrupted the worship of God, and the whole system of religion, under the pretense of extolling the authority of the Church. It is indeed true, that the sacerdotal office was very honorable and worthy of respect; but we must ever take heed lest men assume too much, and lest what is thoughtlessly conceded to them should deprive God of what belongs to him; as the case is, we know, under the Papacy. When the Pope seeks to show that all his commands ought without any dispute to be obeyed, he quotes what is found in De 17:8 —

'If a question arises about the law,
the high priest shall judge between what is sacred and profane.'

This is indeed true; but was it permitted to the high priest to disregard God's law, and foolishly to allege this or that according to his own judgement? Nay, the priest was only an interpreter of the law. Whenever then God bids those pastors to be heard whom he sets over his Church, his will is, as it has been before stated, that he himself should be heard through their mouth. In short, whatever authority is exercised in the Church ought to be subjected to this rule — that God's law is to retain its own pre-eminence, and that men blend nothing of their own, but only define what is right according to the Word of the Lord. Now this is by the way; I come now to the main point.

The priests answered, that neither flesh, nor oil, nor wine, was sanctified by touching a piece or part of a sacrifice. Why? because a sacrifice sanctifies not things unclean, except by way of expiation; for this, we know, was the design of sacrifices — that men who were polluted might reconcile themselves to God. A right answer was then given by the priests, that unclean flesh or unclean oil is not sanctified by the touch of holy flesh. Why? because the flesh itself was not dedicated to God for this end — to purify what was unclean by a mere touch. Yet, on the other hand, it is most true, that when a man was unclean he polluted whatever he touched. It is commonly thought, that he is said to be unclean in his soul who had defiled himself by touching a corpse; but I differ from this. The word soul is often taken in the law for man himself. —

'The soul that eats of what died of itself is polluted;
the soul that touches a corpse is polluted.'
(Le 17:15.)

Hence he is here said to be polluted in his soul, who had an outward uncleanness, as we say in French, Pollu en sa personne. Whosoever then is unclean pollutes by touch only whatever might have been otherwise clean; and the conclusion sufficiently proves that this is the purport of this passage. [149] I have said enough of what the design of the Prophet is, but the subject must be more fully explained.

We know how heedlessly men are wont to deal with God; for they trifle with him like children with their puppets. And this presumption has been condemned, as it is well known, even by heathens. Hardly a Prophet could have inveighed more severely against this gross superstition than Persius, who compares sacrifices, so much thought of by all, to puppets, and shows that other things are required by God, even

A well ordered condition and piety of soul, and an inward purity of mind, and a heart imbued with generous virtue [150]

He means then that men ought to be imbued with true holiness, and that inwardly, so that there should be nothing fictitious or feigned. He says that they who are such, that is, who have imbibed the true fear of God, do rightly serve him, thought they may bring only a crumb of incense, and that others only profane the worship of God, though they may bring many oxen; for whatever they think avails to cover their filth is polluted by new and repeated filth. And this is what has been expressed by heathen authors: another poet says, -

An impious right hand does not rightly worship the celestials [151]

So they spoke according to the common judgement of natural knowledge. As to the Philosophers, they ever hold this principle — that no sacrifice is rightly offered to God except the mind be right and pure. But yet the Philosophers, as well as the Poets, adopted this false notion, by which Satan beguiled all men, from the least to the greatest — that God is pacified by ceremonies: hence have proceeded so many expiations, in which foolish men trusted, and by which they thought that God would be propitious to them, thought they obstinately continued daily to procure for themselves new punishments, and, as it were, avowedly to carry on war with God himself.

They admit at this day, under the Papacy, this principle that the true fear of God is necessary, as hypocrisy contaminates all the works of men; nor will they indeed dare to commend those who seek feignedly and triflingly to satisfy God, when they are filled with pride, contempt, and impiety. And yet they will never receive what the Prophet says here — that men not only lose all their labor, but also contract new pollution, when they seek to pacify God by their sacrifices, unaccompanied by inward purity. For whence is that partial righteousness which the Papists imagine? For they say, that if one does not keep the whole law, yet obedience in part is approved by God; and nothing is more common among them than this expression, partial righteousness. If then an adulterer refrains from theft, and lays out in alms some of his wealth, they will have this to be charity, and declare it to be acceptable. Though it proceeds from an unclean man, it is yet made a covering, which is deemed sufficient in some way or another to pacify God. Thus the Papists seek, without exercising any discrimination, to render God bound to them by their works, though they may be full of all uncleanness. We hence see that this error has not sprung up today or yesterday for the first time; but it is inherent in the bones and marrows of men; for they have ever thought that their services please God, though they may be unclean themselves.

Hence this definition must be borne in mind — that works, however splendid they may appear before our eyes, are of no value or importance before God, except they flow from a pure heart. Augustine has very wisely explained this in his fourth book against Julia. He says, that it would be an absurd thing for the faithful to judge of works by the outward appearance;

but that they ought to be estimated according to the fountain from which they proceed, and also according to their design. Now the fountain of works I consider to be integrity of heart, and the design or end is, when the object of men is to obey God and to consecrate their life to him. Hence then we learn the difference between good and evil works, between vices and virtues, that is, from the inward state of the mind, and from the object in view. This is the subject of the Prophet in the first clause; and he drew an answer from the priests, which was wholly consistent with the law; and it amounted to this, that no work, however praised and applauded by the world, is valued before God's tribunal, except it proceeds from a pure heart.

Now as to the second part, it is no less difficult to convince men of its truth — that whatever they touch is contaminated, when they are themselves unclean; and yet this is what God had plainly made known to the Jews: and the priests hesitated not nor doubted, but immediately returned an answer, as though the matter was well known — that an unclean man contaminates whatever thing he touches. But when we come to apply the subject, men then reject what they had been clearly taught; nay, what they are forced to confess, until they see the matter brought home to them, and then they begin to accuse God of too much rigour: "Why is this, that whatever we touch is polluted, though we might leave some defilement? Are not our works still deserving of some praise, as they are good works?" And hence also is the common saying, That works, which are in their kind good, are always in a measure meritorious, and though they are without faith, they yet avail to merit the gift of faith, inasmuch as they are in themselves praiseworthy, as chastity, liberality, sobriety, temperance, beneficence, and all alms giving. But God declares that these virtues are polluted, though men may admire them, and that they are only abominable filth, except the heart be really cleansed and purified. Why so? because nothing can flow from an impure and polluted fountain but what is impure and polluted.

It is now easy to understand how suitably the Prophet had led the priests and the whole people to see this difference. For if he had abruptly said this to them — that no work pleased God, except the doer himself had been cleansed from every defilement, there would have arisen immediately many disputations: "Why will God reject what is in itself worthy of praise? When one observes chastity, when another liberally lays out a part of his property, when a third devotes himself wholly to promote the good of the public, when magnanimity and firmness shine forth in one, when another cultivates the liberal arts — are not these such virtues as deserve some measure of praise!" Thus a great glamour would have been raised among the people, had not Haggai made this kind of preface — that according to the law what is unclean is not sanctified by the touch of holy flesh, and also that whatever is touched by an unclean person is polluted. What the law then prescribed in its rituals silenced all those clamours, which might have immediately arisen among the people. Moreover, though ceremonies have now ceased and are no longer in use, yet what God has once declared still retains its force — that whatever we touch is polluted by us, except there be a real purity of heart to sanctify our works.

Let us now inquire how our works please God: for no one is ever found to be pure and perfect, as the most perfect are defiled with some vices; so that their works are always sprinkled with some spots and blemishes, and contract some uncleanness from the hidden filth of their hearts. In answer to this, I say first, that all our works are corrupt before God and abominable in his sight, for the heart is naturally corrupt: but when God purifies our hearts by faith, then our works begin to be approved, and obtain praise before him; for the heart is cleansed by faith, and purity is diffused over our works, so that they begin to be pleasing to God. For this reason Moses says, that Abel pleased God with his sacrifices,

"The Lord had respect to Abel and to his gifts." (Ge 4:4.)

Had Moses said only, that the sacrifices of Abel were approved by God, he would have spoken unadvisedly, or at least obscurely; for he would have been silent on the main thing. But he begins with the person, as though he had said, that Abel pleased God, because he worshipped him with an upright and sincere heart. He afterwards adds, that his sacrifices were approved, for they proceeded from the true fear of God and sincere piety. So Paul, when speaking of the real keeping of the law, says, that the end of the law is love from a pure heart and faith unfeigned. (1Ti 1:5.) He shows then that no work is deemed right before God, except it proceeds from that fountain, even faith unfeigned, which is always connected with an upright and sincere heart. This is one thing.

Secondly, we must bear in mind how God purifies our hearts by faith. There is indeed a twofold purification: He first forms us in his image, and engraves on us true and real fear, and an obedient disposition. This purity of the heart diffuses itself over our works; for when we are imbued with true piety, we have no other object but to offer ourselves and all we have to God. Far indeed are they who are hypocrites and profane men from having this feeling; nay, they are wholly alienated from it: they offer liberally their own things to God, but they wish to be their own masters; for a hypocrite will never give up himself as a spiritual sacrifice to God. We hence see how faith purifies our hearts, and also purifies our works: for having been regenerated by the Spirit of God, we offer to him first ourselves and then all that we have. But as this purgation is never found complete in man, it is therefore necessary that there should come an aid from gratuitous acceptance. Our hearts then are purified by faith, because God imputes not to us that uncleanness which remains, and which defiles our works. As then God regards with gracious acceptance that purity which is not as yet perfect, so he causes that its contagion should not reach to our works. When Abel offered sacrifices to God, he was indeed perfect, inasmuch as there was nothing feigned or hypocritical in him: but he was a man, we know, encompassed with infirmity. It was therefore necessary for his remaining pollution to have been purified by the grace of Christ. Hence it was that his sacrifices were accepted: for as he was accepted, so God graciously received whatever proceeded from him.

We now then see how men, while in a state of nature, displease God by their works, and can bring nothing but what is corrupt, filthy, and abominable. We farther see how the children of God, after having been renewed by his Spirit, come pure to him and offer him pure sacrifices: they come pure, because it is their object to devote themselves to God without any dissimulation; but as this devotedness is never perfect, God supplies the defect by a gratuitous imputation, for he embraces them as his servants in the same manner as though they were entirely formed in all righteousness. And in the same way he approves of their works, for all their spots are wiped away, yea, those very spots, which might justly prevent all favor; were not all uncleanness washed away by the blood of Christ, and that through faith.

We hence learn, that there is no ground for any one to deceive himself with vain delusions, by attempting to please God with great pomp: for the first thing of which the Prophet treats here is always required, that is, that a person must be pure in his heart, that inward purity must precede every work. And though this truth meets us everywhere in all the Prophets, yet as hypocrisy dazzles our eyes and blinds all our senses, it ought to be seriously considered by us; and we ought to notice in an especial manner not only this passage but other similar passages where the Prophets ridicule the solicitude of the people, when they busied themselves with sacrifices and outward observances, and neglected the principal thing — real purity of heart.

We must also take notice of what the Prophet says in the last verse, that so was every work of their hand and whatever they offered [152] It seems apparently a hard matter, that the very sacrifices were condemned as polluted. But it is no wonder that fictitious modes of worship, by which profane men dishonor God, should be repudiated by him; for they seek to transform him according to their own fancy, as though he might be soothed by playthings or such trifles. It is therefore a most disgraceful mockery when men deal thus with God, offering him only external ceremonies, and disregarding his nature: for they make no account of spiritual worship, and yet think that they please him. We must then, in a word, make this remark — that the Prophet teaches us here, that it is not enough for men to show obedience to God, to offer sacrifices, to spend labor in building the Temple, except these things were rightly done — and how rightly? by a sincere heart, so there should be no dissimulation, no duplicity.

PRAYER

Grant, Almighty God, that inasmuch as we come from our mother's womb wholly impure and polluted, and afterwards continually contract so many new defilements, — O grant that we may flee to the fountain, which alone can cleanse us. And as there is no other way by which we can be cleansed from all the defilements of the flesh, except we be sprinkled by the blood of thy only begotten Son, and that by the hidden power of thy Spirit, and thus renounce all our vices, — O grant that we may so strive truly and sincerely to devote ourselves to thee, as daily to renounce more and more all our evil affections, and to have nothing else as our object, but to submit our minds and all our affections to thee, by really denying ourselves, and to exercise ourselves in this strenuous effort as long as we are in this world, until we attain to that true and perfect purity, which is laid up for us in thine only-begotten Son, when we shall be fully united to him, having been transformed into that glory into which he has been received. Amen.

LECTURE ONE HUNDRED AND THIRTY-THIRD

Haggai 2:15-19

15. And now, I pray you, consider from this day and upward, from before a stone was laid upon a stone in the temple of the LORD:

15. Et nunc ponite quaeso (vel, agedum) super cor vestrum a die hac et supra, antequam poneretur lapis super lapidem in templo Iehovae:

16. Since those days were, when one came to an heap of twenty measures, there were but ten: when one came to the pressfat for to draw out fifty vessels out of the press, there were but twenty.

16. Ante haec quum veniret quis ad acervum viginti, fuit decem; quum veniret ad torcular ut hauriret quinquaginta e torculari, fuit summa viginti.

17. I smote you with blasting and with mildew and with hail in all the labours of your hands; yet ye turned not to me, saith the LORD.

17. Percussi vos orientali vento (vel, urente) et rubigene, et grandine in omni opere manuum vestrarum (alii vertunt, et omne opus, sed male, et potius hic debet resolvi quemadmodum dictum est, in omni ergo opere) et vos non ad me, dicit Iehova.

18. Consider now from this day and upward, from the four and twentieth day of the ninth month, even from the day that the foundation of the LORD'S temple was laid, consider it

18. Ponite quaeso super cor vestrum a die hac et supra, a die vicesimo quarto noni mensis, a die quo fundatum fuit templum Iehovae, ponite super cor vestrum.

19. Is the seed yet in the barn? yea, as yet the vine, and the fig tree, and the pomegranate, and the olive tree, hath not brought forth: from this day will I bless you

19. An adhuc semen in horreo? et adhuc vitis, et ficus, et malusgranata, et arbor olivae non protulit; a die hac benedicam vobis.

I am under the necessity of joining all these verses together, for the Prophet treats of the same thing: and the import of the whole is this — that the Lord had then openly punished the tardiness of the people, so that every one might have easily known that they acted very inconsistently in attending only to their private concerns, so as to neglect the Temple. The Prophet indeed speaks here in a homely manner to earthly men, addicted to their own appetites: had they really become wiser, or made greater progress in true religion, he might have addressed them differently, and would have no doubt followed the rule mentioned by Paul,

'We speak wisdom among those who are perfect.' (1Co 2:6.)

But as they had their thoughts fixed on meat and drink, and were intent on their private advantages, the Prophet tells them what they could comprehend that God was angry with them, and that the proofs of his curse were evident, as the earth did not produce fruit, and they themselves were reduced to want. We hence perceive the object of the Prophet: but I shall run over the words, that the subject may become more evident.

Lay it, he says, on your heart. Here the Prophet indirectly condemns their insensibility, as they were blind in things quite manifest; for he does not here direct their thoughts to heaven, nor announce deep mysteries, but only speaks of food and daily support. Since God, then, impressed clear marks of his wrath on their common sustenance, it was an intolerable stupidity in them to disregard these. And the Prophet often repeats the same thing, in order to shame the Jews; for their tardiness being so often reproved, ought to have made them ashamed. Lay it on the heart, he says; that is, Consider what I am going to say; from this day and heretofore, [153] he says, before a stone was laid on a stone; that is, from that day when I began to exhort you to build the Temple, consider what has happened to this very day.

Then he adds, Before ye began, he says, to build the Temple, was it not that every one who came to a heap of twenty measures found only ten? that is, was it not, that when the husband men expected that there would be twenty measures in the storehouse or on the floor, they were disappointed? because God had dried up the ears, so they yielded not what they used to do; for husband men, by long experience, can easily conjecture what they may expect when they see the gathered harvest; but this prospect had disappointed the husband men. God, then, had in this case given proofs of his curse. Farther; when any one came to the vat, and expected a large vintage, had he not also been disappointed? for instead of fifty casks he found only twenty.

He afterwards adds, I have smitten you with the east wind: for שדפון, shidafun, is to be taken for a scorching wind; and the east wind proved injurious to Judea by its dryness. So also וירקון, irkun, is mildew, or a moist wind, from which mildew proceeds; for we know that corn, when it has much wet, contracts mildew when the sun emits its heat. As to the meaning of the Prophet there is no ambiguity, for he intended to teach them that they were in various ways visited, that they might clearly perceive that God was displeased with them. He then mentions the hail: for when famine happens only from the cold or from the heat, it may be ascribed to chance or to the stars: but when God employs various scourges, we are then constrained to acknowledge his wrath, as though he were determined to awaken us. This is the reason why the Prophet records here various kinds of judgements. And he says, In every work of your hands. Some read, And every work, etc., which is improper; for they were not smitten in their own bodies, but in the produce of the earth. Then he adds, And you returned not to me, that is, "During the whole of that time I effected nothing, while I was so often and in such various ways chastising you. And yet what good has the obduracy of your hearts done you? ye have not returned to me."

Lay it, he says, on your heart from this day, and heretofore, etc. He repeats what he had said, even from the twenty-fourth day of the ninth month. We have seen before, that the Prophet was sent on that day to reprove the people for their sins. Lay it then on your heart, he says, from this day, etc. We see how emphatical is this repetition, because in things evident the Jews were so insensible that their want and famine could not touch them: and we know that there is no sharper goad to stimulate men than famine. Since then the Lord snatched away their food from their mouth, and they remained inattentive to such a judgement, it was a sure evidence of extreme stupidity. It is on this account that the Prophet often declares, that the Jews were extremely insensible; for they did not consider the judgements of God, which were so manifest. He now subjoins, Is there yet seed in the barn? Jerome reads, in the bud; and the probable reason why he thus rendered the word was, that he thought that the clauses would not correspond without giving the meaning of bud to מגורה, megure; but, as I think, he was mistaken. The Hebrews propose what I cannot approve, for some of them read the sentence as an affirmation, For there is seed in the barn; because they dared not to commit the seed to the ground in their state of want. And others read it as a question, as though he had said, that the time of harvest was far off, and that what they had remaining was so small that it was not enough to support them. But, in my judgement, the seed refers not to what had been gathered, but to what had been sown. I therefore doubt not but that he speaks of God's blessing on the harvest which was to come after five months, to which I shall presently refer. Some, indeed, render the words in the past tense, as though the Prophet had said, that the Jews had already experienced how great the curse of God was; but this is a forced view. The real meaning of the Prophet is this, Is there yet seed in the barn? that is, Is the seed, as yet hid in the ground, gathered?

He then adds affirmatively, neither the vine, nor the fig tree, nor the pomegranate, nor the olive had yet produced any thing; for it was the ninth month of the year; and the beginning of the year, we know, was in the month of March. Though then they were nearly in the midst of winter, they remained uncertain as to what the produce would be. In the month of November no opinion could be formed, even by the most skillful, what produce they were to expect. As then they were still in suspense, the Prophet says, that God's blessing was in readiness for them. What he had in view was, to show that he brought a sure message from God; for he speaks not of a vintage the prospect of which had already appeared, nor of a harvest when the ears had already made their appearance. As then there was still danger from the hail, from scorching winds, and also from rains and other things injurious to fruit and produce of the land, he says, that the harvest would be most abundant, the vintage large, that, in a word, the produce of the olive and the fig tree would be most exuberant. The truth of the prophecy might now be surely known, when God fulfilled what he had spoken by the mouth of his servant. I now return to the subject itself

As I have before observed, the Prophet deals with the Jews here according to their gross disposition: for he might in a more refined manner have taught the godly, who were not so entangled with, or devoted to, earthly concerns. It was then necessary for him to speak in a manner suitable to the comprehension of the people, as a skillful teacher who instructs children and those of riper age in a different manner. And he shows by evidences that the Jews were unthankful to God, for they neglected the building of the Temple, and every one was diligently and earnestly engaged in building his own house. He shows by proofs their conduct, — How? Whence has it happened, he says, that at one time your fruit has been destroyed by mildew, at another by heat, and then by the hail, except that the Lord intended thus to correct your neglect? It then follows, that you are convicted of ingratitude by these judgements; for you have neglected God's worship, and only pursued your own private advantages. This is one thing.

The latter clause contains a promise; and by it the instruction given was more confirmed, when the people saw that things suddenly and unexpectedly took a better turn. They had been for many years distressed with want of sustenance; but, when fruitfulness of a sudden followed, did not this change manifest something worthy of their consideration? especially when it was foretold before it happened, and before any such thing could have been foreseen by human conjectures? We see then, that the Prophet dwells on two things, — he condemns the Jews for their neglect, and proves that they were impious and ungrateful towards God, for they disregarded the building of the Temple; and them, in order to animate them and render them more active in the work they had begun, he sets before them, as I have said, what had taken place. God had, indeed, abundantly testified, by various kinds of punishment that he was displeased with them: but when he now promises that he would deal differently with them, there hence arises a new and a stronger evidence.

But some one may here raise an objection and say, that these evidences are not sure or unvaried; since it often happens, that when people devote themselves faithfully to the service of God they are pressed down by adverse events; yea, that God very often designedly tries their faith by withholding from them for a time his blessing. But the answer to this may be readily given: I indeed allow that it often happens that those who sincerely and from the heart serve God, are deprived of earthly blessings, because God intends to elevate their minds to the hope of eternal reward. God then designedly withdraws his blessing often from the faithful, that they may hunger and thirst in this world; as though they lost all their labor in serving him. But it was not the Prophet's design to propound here an evidence of an unvarying character, as he counted it sufficient to convince the Jews by experience, that nothing prevented them from acknowledging that their avarice displeased God, except their extreme stupidity. The Prophet then does here reprove their insensibility; for, while they greatly labored in enriching themselves, they did not observe that their labor was in vain, because God from heaven poured his curse on them. This then might have been easily known by them had they not hardened themselves in their vices. And what the Prophet testifies here respecting the fruitful produce of wine, and corn, and oil, and of other things, was still, as I have said, a stronger confirmation.

Now, if any one objects again and says — that this was of no value, because a servile and mercenary service does not please God: to this I answer — that God does often by such means stimulate men, when he sees them to be extremely tardy and slothful, and that he afterwards leads them by other means to serve him truly and from the heart. When therefore any one obeys God, only that he may satisfy his appetite, it is as though one labored from day to day for the sake of wages, and then disregards him by whom he has been hired. It is certain that such a service is counted as nothing before God; but he would have himself to be generously worshipped by us; and he loves, as Paul says, a cheerful giver. (2Co 6:7.) But as men, for the most part, on account of their ignorance, cannot be led at first to this generous state of mind, so as to devote themselves willingly to God, it is necessary to begin by using other means, as the Prophet does here, who promises earthly and daily sustenance to the Jews, for he saw that they could not immediately, at the first step, ascend upwards to heaven; but it was not his purpose to stop short, until he elevated their minds higher. Let us then know, that this was only the beginning, that they might learn to fear God and to expect whatever they wanted from his blessing, and also that they might shake off their stupor, under which they had previously labored. In short, God deals in one way with the rude and ignorant, who are not yet imbued with true religion; and he deals in another way with his own disciples, who are instructed in sound doctrine. When I say that the Prophet acted thus towards the Jews, I speak not of the whole nation; but I regard what we have observed at the beginning of this book — that the Jews cared for nothing then but to build their own houses, and that there was no zeal for religion among them. As then the recollection of God was nigh buried among them, the Temple being neglected, and every one's anxiety being concentrated in building his own house, we hence learn how grossly earthly their affections were. It is therefore no wonder that the Prophet treated them in the manner stated here. Let us proceed -

Haggai 2:20-23

20. And again the word of the LORD came unto Haggai in the four and twentieth day of the month, saying,

20. Et fuit (postea fuit) sermo Iehovae secundo ad Chaggai vicesimo quarto mensis, dicendo,

21. Speak to Zerubbabel, governor of Judah, saying, I will shake the heavens and the earth;

21. Dic ad Zerubbabel, ducens Iehudah, dicendo, Ego concutiam coelos et terram;

22. And I will overthrow the throne of kingdoms, and I will destroy the strength of the kingdoms of the heathen; and I will overthrow the chariots, and those that ride in them; and the horses and their riders shall come down, every one by the sword of his brother.

22. Et evertam solium regnorum, et perdam robur regnorum gentium; et evertam quadrigam et sessores ejus evertam quadrigam et sessores ejus; et descendent equi et sessores eorum, quisque in gladio fratris sui.

23. In that day, saith the LORD of hosts, will I take thee, O Zerubbabel, my servant, the son of Shealtiel, saith the LORD, and will make thee as a signet: for I have chosen thee, saith the LORD of hosts.

23. In die illa, dicit Iehova exercituum, sumam te Zerubbabel, fili Sealtiel, serve mi, dicit Iehova; et ponam to quasi annulum, quia elegi te, dicit Iehova exercituum.

The Prophet now proceeds still farther; for there is here a really gratuitous and spiritual promise, by which God affirms that he will have a care for his people to the end. He does not now speak of wine and corn, in order to feed the hungry; but he shows that he would be an eternal Father to that people; for he could not and would not forget the covenant he made with their fathers. There is no doubt but he points out Christ in the person of Zerubbabel, as we shall presently see. So that it is right to distinguish this prophecy from the last; for God has before shown, that the worship which the Jews had for a time disregarded was pleasing to him, as a reward was in readiness, and also that he was offended with the negligence previously reproved, as he had inflicted manifest punishment, not once, nor for a short time, but for many years, and in various ways. What then does follow? In this second prophecy he addresses Zerubbabel, and promises to be a Savior to the people under his authority.

With regard to these words, some think that a continued act is signified when he says, I shake the heavens and the earth; and they give this explanation — That though it belongs to me to shake the heaven and the earth, and I am wont to subvert kingdoms, yet I will render firm the sacred kingdom which I have raised among my people. But this view is very frigid: and we see even from this chapter what is meant by the shaking of the heaven and of the earth, of which mention is made. The Apostle also rightly interprets this passage, when he teaches us, that this prophecy properly belongs to the kingdom of Christ. (Heb 12:26.) There is therefore no doubt, but that the Prophet means here something special, when he introduces God as saying, Behold, I shake the heavens and the earth. God then does not speak of his ordinary providence, nor simply claim to himself the government of the heaven and of the earth, nor teach us that he raises on high the humble and the low, and also brings down the high and the elevated; but he intimates, that he has some memorable work in contemplation, which, when done, would shake men with fear, and make heaven and earth to tremble. Hence, the Prophet no doubt intended here to lead the Jews to the hope of that redemption, some prelude of which God had then given them; but its fullness could not as yet be seen — nay, it was hid from the view of men: for who could have expected such a renovation of the world as was effected by the coming of Christ? When the Jews found themselves exposed to the wrongs of all men, when so small a number returned, and there was no kingdom and no power, they thought themselves to have been as it were deceived. Hence the Prophet affirms here, that there would be a wonderful work of God, which would shake the heaven and the earth. It is therefore necessary that this should be applied to Christ; for it was, as it were, a new creation of the world, when Christ gathered together the things scattered, as the Apostle says, in the heaven and in the earth. (Col 1:20.) When he reconciled men to God and to angels, when he conquered the devil and restored life to the dead, when he shone forth with his own righteousness, then indeed God shook the heaven and the earth; and he still shakes them at this day, when the gospel is preached; for he forms anew the children of Adam after his own image. This spiritual regeneration then is such an evidence of God's power and grace, that he may justly be said to shake the heaven and the earth. The import of the passage is, that it behaved the Jews to form a conception in their minds of something greater than could be seen by their eyes; for their redemption was not yet completed.

Hence he subjoins — I will overthrow the throne of kingdoms; I will destroy the strength of the kingdoms of the nations; and I will overthrow the chariot and him who sits in it; come down shall the horses and their riders; every one shall fall by the sword of his brother. He confirms here the former sentence — that nothing would be an hindrance that God should not renew his Church. And rightly he adds this by way of anticipation; for the Jews were surrounded on all sides by inveterate enemies; they had as many enemies as they had neighbors; and they were hated even by the whole world. How then could they emerge into that dignity which was then promised to them, except God overturned the rest of the world? But the Prophet here meets this objection, and briefly shows that God would rather that all the nations should perish, than that his Church should remain in that dishonorable state. We then see that the Prophet here means no other thing then that God would overcome all those impediments, which Satan and the whole world may throw in the way, when it is his purpose to restore his Church.

We now perceive the Prophet's designs, and we also perceive the application of his doctrine. For whenever impediments and difficulties come in our way, calculated to drive us to despair, when we think of the restoration of the Church, this prophecy ought to come to our minds, which shows that it is in God's power, and that it is his purpose to overturn all the kingdoms of the earth, to break chariots in pieces, to cast down and lay prostrate all riders, rather then to allow them to prevent the restoration of his Church.

But in the last verse the Prophet shows why God would do this — even that Zerubbabel might prosper together with the whole people. Hence he says — In that day saith Jehovah, I will take thee, Zerubbabel, and will set thee as a signet, for I have chosen thee. As we have before said, God addresses Zerubbabel here, that in his person he might testify that he would bless the people whom he intended to gather under that sacred leader; for though Zerubbabel never had a kingdom, nor ever wore a crown, he was yet of the tribe of Judah; and God designed that some spark of that kingdom should exist, which he had raised in the family of David. Since, then, Zerubbabel was at that time a type of Christ, God declares here that he would be to him as a signet — that is, that his dignity would be esteemed by him. This comparison of a signet is found also in other places. It is said in Jer 22:24 — "Though this Coniah were a signet on my right hand I would pluck him thence." But here God says that Zerubbabel would be to him a signet — that is, Thou shalt be with me in high esteem. For a sealing signet is wont to be carefully preserved, as kings seek in this way to secure to themselves the highest authority, so that more trust may be placed in their seal than in the greatest princes. The meaning, then, of the similitude is, that Zerubbabel, though despised by the world, was yet highly esteemed by God. But it is evident that this was never fulfilled in the person of Zerubbabel. It hence follows that it is to be applied to Christ. God, in short, shows, that that people gathered under one head would be accepted by him; for Christ was at length to rise, as it is evident, from the seed of Zerubbabel.

But this reason is to be especially noticed — Because I have chosen thee. For God does not here ascribe excellencies or merits to Zerubbabel, when he says that he would hold him in great esteem; but he attributes this to his own election. If, then, the reason be asked why God had so much exalted Zerubbabel, and bestowed on him favors so illustrious, it can be found in nothing else but in the goodness of God alone. God had made a covenant with David, and promised that his kingdom would be eternal; hence it was that he chose Zerubbabel after the people had returned from exile; and this election was the reason why God exalted Zerubbabel, though his power at that time was but small. We indeed know that he was exposed to the contempt of all nations; but God invites here the attention of the faithful to their election, so that they might hope for more than what the perception of the flesh could conceive or apprehend; for what he has decreed cannot be made void; and in the person of Zerubbabel he had determined to save a chosen people; for from him, as it has been said, Christ was to come.

PRAYER

Grant, Almighty God, that as we are still restrained by our earthly cares, and cannot ascend upward to heaven with so much readiness and alacrity as we ought — O grant, that since thou extendest to us daily so liberal a supply for the present life, we may at least learn that thou art our Father, and that we may not at the same time fix our thoughts on these perishable things, but learn to elevate our minds higher, and so make continual advances in thy spiritual service, until at length we come to the full and complete fruition of that blessed and celestial life which thou hast promised to us, and procured for us by the blood of thy only begotten Son. Amen.

SCRIPTURE TRANSLATIONS

HABBAKUK

CHAPTER 1

1 the burden which Habakkuk the Prophet saw:

2 How long, Jehovah, shall I cry, And thou wilt not hear? And cry aloud to thee of violence, And thou wilt not save?

3 Why showest thou me iniquity, And makest me to see trouble? And why are violence and plunder in my sight, And he who excites strife and contention? (19)

4 Therefore dissolved is the law, And judgment does not continually go forth; For the wicked surrounds the just, Therefor go forth does perverted judgment. (21)

5 Look ye among the Gentiles and see, And be astonished, be astonished; For a work will I work in your days, Which ye will not believe, though it be told you:

6 For behold, I will rouse the Chaldeans — A nation bitter and hasty, Which shall march through the breadths of the earth, To possess habitations not its own:

7 Terrible and fearful shall it be, From itself shall its judgment and its dignity proceed:

8 And swifter than leopards shall be its horses, And fiercer than the evening wolves; And numerous shall be its horsemen; And its horsemen from far shall come, They shall fly as an eagle hastening to devour: (30)

9 The whole of it for booty shall come; The aspect of their faces will be like the east-wind; And he will gather captives like the sand:

10 And at kings he will laugh, And princes shall be a scorn to him: Every fortress he will scorn, He will gather dust and take it:

11 Then will be change his spirit, And pass through and act impiously, Ascribing this his power to his god. (37)

12 Art not thou, Jehovah, from the beginning, my God? My holy One! we shall not die: Thou, Jehovah, for judgment hast set him; And thou strong One, for correction hast established him.

13 Pure art thou of eyes, so as not to behold evil, And on trouble thou canst not look: — Why lookest thou on transgressors, And takest no notice, when the ungodly devours One more righteous than himself?

14 Thou makest man like the fish of the sea, Like the reptile, which is without a leader: (46)

15 The whole by his hook will he draw up, Collect into his drag, and gather into his net; He will therefore rejoice and exult: (48)

16 Hence sacrifice will he to his drag, And incense will he offer to his net; For through them fat will be his portion, And his meat will be rich. —

17 Shall he therefore extend his drag, And continue to slay the nations, so as not to spare them?

CHAPTER 2

1 On my watch-tower will I stand, And set myself on a citadel; And I will watch to see what he may say to me, And what I may answer to the reproof given me.

2 Then answer me did Jehovah and said, Write the vision, and make it plain on tables, That run may he who reads it;

3 For yet the vision shall be for an appointed time, And will speak at the end, and will not deceive: If it tarry, wait for it; (66) for coming it will come, and will not delay.

4 Behold the elated! not right is his soul within him; But the just, by his faith, shall he live." (72)

5 Yea, truly! as by wine, transgress does the proud man, And he will not rest; (87) For he enlarges as the grave his soul, And is like to death, and is not satisfied; Yea, he collects to himself all nations, And heaps together for himself all the people.

6 Shall not all these take up against him a parable, And against him an enigmatical taunt, and say, — "Ho! he multiplies what is not his own! how long! And he accumulates on himself thick clay!

7 Shall they not suddenly rise up who shall bite thee, And awake, who shall torment thee? And shalt not thou become tramplings to them?

8 As thou has spoiled many nations, Spoil thee shall all the remnant of the people, On account of men's blood, and of violence To the land, to the city and to all its inhabitants.

9 Ho! he covets an evil covetousness to his house, In order to set on high his nest, That he may keep himself from the hand of evil!

10 Thou hast provided shame for thine own house, By cutting off many nations, And thou hast sinned against thine own soul."

11 For the stone from the wall shall cry, [154] And the wood from the chamber shall answer it, —

12 "Ho! he builds a town by blood, And sets up a city by iniquity!"

13 Behold, shall nothing be from Jehovah of hosts? Hence labour shall the people in the fire, And weary themselves in vain;

14 For filled shall be earth with the knowledge of the glory of Jehovah, As the waters cover the sea.

15 Wo to him who gives his friend drink! — Uniting thy heat, thou makes them also to drink, That thou mayest look on their nakedness. (112)

16 Thou art filled with shame for the sake of glory; Drink thou also, and be thou uncovered: Poured forth to thee shall be the cup of Jehovah's right hand, And shameful spewing shall be on thy glory:

17 For overwhelm thee shall the violence done to Lebanon, And the spoiling of beasts, which terrified them; On account of men's blood, and of violence To the land, to the city, and to all its inhabitants.

18 What avails the graven image? For graven it hath its framer, Even the molten image and the teacher of falsehood; For trust does the framer in his own work, when he makes dumb idols. (122)

CHAPTER 3

1 The prayer of Habakkuk the Prophet respecting ignorances:

2 Jehovah! I heard thy voice, and was terrified; Jehovah! thy work in the midst of the years, revive it; In the midst of the years, make it know; In wrath thy mercy remember. (137)

3 God! from Teman he came; And the holy One from mount Paran: Selah: Cover the heaven did his glory; Of his praise full was the earth:

4 And brightness, — as the light it was; Horns, — from his hands they were; (143) And there was the hiding of his strength:

5 Before his face walked the pestilence, And come forth did burning coals at his feet:

6 He stood, and he measured the earth; He looked, and he dissolved nations; Yea, shattered were perennial mountains, Bent down were hills of antiquity; The ways of ages were his.

7 For iniquity saw I the tents of Chusan; (150) Tremble did the curtains of the land of Madian.

8 Wert thou angry with rivers, O Jehovah? Was thine indignation against rivers? Was thy wrath against the sea? For thou didst ride on thy horses, Thy chariots were salvation.

9 Quite bare was made thy bow: The oaths to the tribes was thy word: Selah: (155) With rivers didst thou cleave the earth.

10 See thee did mountains, they fell down; The stream of waters passed away; Utter its voice did the deep, On high did it raise its hands. (158)

11 The sun and moon stood still in their habitation; At the light of thy arrows did they proceed, At the brightness of the glittering of thy spear. (160)

12 In wrath didst thou tread on the land, In anger didst thou thresh the nations:

13 Go forth didst thou for the salvation of thy people, For their salvation, with thy Christ: Strike didst thou the head From the house of the wicked, Making bare the foundation even to the neck: (164)

14 Smite didst thou with his own staffs The head of his villages: They rushed as a whirlwind to drive me away; Their joy was to devour the poor in secret:

15 A way hast thou made in the sea for thy horses, Through the heap of great waters. (168)

16 I heard, — and tremble did my bowels, At thy voice quiver did my lips; Enter did rottenness into my bones, And within me I made a great noise; That I might rest in the day of affliction, When he ascends against the people, Who shall cut them off. (171)

17 For the fig-tree shall not flourish, And no fruit shall be on the vines, Fail shall the produce of the olive, And the fields shall not bring forth food; cut off from the fold shall be the flock, And there shall be no ox in the stalls:

18 But I — in Jehovah will I exult, I will rejoice in the God of my salvation:

19 Jehovah, the Lord, is my strength; And he will set my feet as those of hinds, And on my high places will he make me to walk — To the leader on my beatings.

ZEPHANIAH

CHAPTER 1

1 The word of Jehovah, which came to Zephaniah, the son of Cushi, the son of Gedaliah, the son of Amariah, the son of Hizkiah, in the days of Josiah, the son of Amon, king of Judah.

2 By removing I will remover all things From the face of the land, saith Jehovah; I will remove man and beast;

3 And I will remove the bird of heaven, And the fishes of the sea: And stumblingblocks shall be to the ungodly! And I will cut off man From the face of the land, saith Jehovah: (190)

4 Yea, I will extend my hand upon Judah, And upon all the inhabitants of Je; And will cut off from this place the remnants of Baal, The name of its worshippers with the priests;

5 And those who worship, On their roofs, the host of heaven; And those who worship and swear by Jehovah, And swear by their own king;

6 And who turn back from following Jehovah, And who seek not Jehovah, And do not inquire of him.

7 Be silent at the presence of the Lord Jehovah! For nigh is the day of Jehovah; Yea, prepared hath Jehovah a sacrifice, He hath prepared his guests:

8 And it shall be in the day of Jehovah's sacrifice, That I will visit the princes and the king's sons, And all who wear foreign apparel;

9 And I will visit all those who dance on the threshold in that day, Who fill the house of their masters By means of rapine and fraud. (204)

10 And there shall be in that day, saith Jehovah, The voice of crying from the fish-gate, and howling from the second gate, And great breach from the hills. (212)

11 Howl ye, inhabitants of the lower part, For exterminated are the people of traffic, Cut off are all loaded with money.

12 And it shall be in that day, That I will search Jerusalem with candles, And visit the men, congealed on their lees, Who say in their hearts, — "Good will not Jehovah do, Nor will he do evil:"

13 And their substance shall be a spoil, And their house a water; And houses shall they build and not inhabit; And plant shall they vineyards, And shall not drink the wine of them.

14 Nigh is the great day of Jehovah, Nigh and hastening quickly; The voice of Jehovah's day Will cry out bitterly, — then will he be strong; (222)

15 A day of wrath shall be that day, A day of distress and of affliction, A day of tumult and of desolation, A day of darkness and of thick darkness, A day of clouds and of mist;

16 A day of trumpet and of shouting Over the fortified cities And over the lofty citadels.

17 And I will straiten men, And they shall walk as the blind, Because they have done wickedly against Jehovah; And poured out shall be their blood as dust,

18 Even their silver and their gold shall not avail To deliver them, in the day of Jehovah's wrath; And by the fire of his indignation shall their land be consumed; For a consummation, and a speedy one, Will be made of all the inhabitants of the land.

CHAPTER 2

1 Gather yourselves, gather, Ye nation, not worthy of being loved;

2 Before the decree brings forth, — (As chaff shall they pass away in a day) Before it comes upon you, The fury of Jehovah's anger, — Before it comes upon you, The day of the anger of Jehovah. (232)

3 Seek Jehovah all ye meek of the land, who his judgment have sought; Seek righteousness, seek humility, It may be that ye shall be concealed In the day of Jehovah's anger.

4 For Gaza, it shall be forsaken, And Ashkelon shall be a waste; Ashod shall they at mid-day drive out, And Ekron shall be rooted up.

5 Ho! the inhabitants of the line of the sea, The nation of the Cherethites! The word of Jehovah is against you; Cannaan! the land of the Philistines! I will also exterminate thee, That there may be no inhabitant:

6 And the coast of the sea shall be a habitation For sheepcots of shepherds and folds for sheep; (242)

7 And that coast shall be For the residence of the house of Judah; Among them shall they feed; In the houses of Ashkelon Shall they in the evening lie down; For visit them shall Jehovah their God, and he will restore their captivity.

8 Heard have I the reproach of Moab, And the revilings of the children of Ammon; By which they have upbraided my people; And they have extended themselves over their border: (247)

9 Therefore as I live, Saith Jehovah of hosts, the God of Israel, — Surely Moab like Sodom shall be, And the children of Ammon like Gomorrah, A soil for the nettle and a mine for salt, And a waste for ever; The residue of my people shall plunder them, And the remnant of my nation shall possess them.

10 This shall be to them for their pride; Because they have reproached, And exulted over the people of Jehovah of hosts.

11 Terrible will Jehovah be to them; For he will consume all the gods of the earth, And worship him shall each from his place, All the islands of the nations. —

12 Ye also Ethiopians! — Slain by my sword shall they be.

13 And extend will he his hand to the north, And he will destroy Assyria, And set Nineveh a waste, A desolation like the desert:

14 And lie down within it shall flocks, All the beasts of the nations; Even the bittern and the owl Shall on its pillars pass the night; A voice shall sing in the window, In the door-way there shall be desolation, For he will make bare the cedar.

15 This is the exulting city! Which sat in confidence, Which said in her heart, — "I am, and there is besides me no other." How is she become a waste, A resting-place for beasts! Every one who shall pass by Will hiss at her, he will shake his hand.

CHAPTER 3

1 Wo to the polluted and the filthy — The city which is an oppressor! (261)

2 She has not attended to the voice, She has not received correction, In Jehovah has she not trusted, To her God she has not drawn nigh!

3 Her princes within her are roaring lions, Her judges, the wolves of the evening; They break not the bones in the morning!

4 Her Prophets are vain, men of deceits; (268) Her Priests have polluted what is holy, They have subverted the law. (269)

5 Jehovah is just in the midst of her, He will not do iniquity; Every morning his judgment He brings to light, — he fails not: Yet the unjust knoweth no shame.

6 I have cut off nations, Waste have become their citadels, I have destroyed their streets, So that no one passes through; Wasted have become their cities, That there is not a man, not an inhabitant: (275)

7 I said, "surely, thou wilt fear me, Thou wilt receive instruction;" Then cut off should not be her habitation, However I might have visited her: — (279) Truly! they have hastened, They have corrupted all their doings!

8 Therefore look for me, saith Jehovah, Till the day when I shall rise up for the prey; For my purpose is, To gather nations, to assemble kingdoms, That I may pour upon them my wrath, The whole fury of mine anger; For with the fire of my indignation Shall be devoured the whole earth. (281)

9 But I will then turn to the people a pure lip, That they may all call on the name of Jehovah, That they may serve him with one consent. (283)

10 Beyond the rivers of Ethiopia shall be my suppliants; The daughter of my dispersed shall bring mine offering.

11 In that day thou shalt not be ashamed On account of all thy doings, By which thou hast transgressed against me; For then will I remove from the midst of thee Those who rejoice in thy pride, And thou shalt not take pride any more In my holy mountain. (292)

12 And I will cause to remain in the midst of thee, A people afflicted and poor; And they shall trust in the name of Jehovah.

13 The remnant of Israel shall not do iniquity, And they shall not speak falsehood, And not found in their mouth Shall be a deceitful tongue; And they shall feed and lie down, And there shall be none to terrify them

14 Exult thou daughter of Sion, Exult thou Israel; Rejoice, exult with thy whole heart, Thou daughter of je: (299)

15 Removed has Jehovah thy judgments, He has turned aside thine enemies; The King of Israel, Jehovah, is in the midst of thee, Thou shalt see evil no more.

16 In that day it shall be said to je, Fear not; Sion! relaxed let not thine hands be.

17 Jehovah thy God is in the midst of thee, He is strong, he will save; He will exult over thee with joy, He will rest in his love, (304) He will exult over thee with triumph.

18 The afflicted, at the appointed time, Will I gather, — who shall be of thee; Who sustained for her reproach. (308)

19 Behold, I will destroy all thine oppressors at that time, And I will save the halting, And restore the driven away, To make them a praise and a name In the land of their reproach.

20 At that time will I restore you, At that time will I gather you; For I will make you a name and a praise Among all the nations of the earth; When I shall restore your captivities, Before your eyes saith Jehovah.

HAGGAI

CHAPTER 1

1 In the second year of Darius the king, in the sixth month, on the first day of the month, came the word of Jehovah by Haggai the Prophet, to Zerubbabel, the son of Shealtiel, the governor of Judah, and to Joshua, the son of Josedech, the high priest, saying —

2 Thus saith Jehovah of hosts, saying — This people say, "The time is not come To build the house of Jehovah."

3 Then came the word of Jehovah, By Haggai, the Prophet, saying —

4 "Is it time for you To dwell yourselves in your boarded houses, And this house a waste!"

5 And now thus saith Jehovah of hosts, — Apply your heart to your ways:

6 Ye have sown much, and brought in little; Ye have eaten, and were not satisfied; Ye have drank, and were not replenished; Ye have clothed yourselves, and were not warmed; And he who gains wages, Gains wages for a perforated bag. (330)

7 Thus saith Jehovah of hosts, — Apply your heart to your ways;

8 Ascend unto the mountain and bring wood, And build the house; And I will be to you propitious in it, And glorified shall I be, saith Jehovah. (333)

9 Ye have looked for much, but behold little! And ye brought it home, and I blew on it: Why is this? saith Jehovah; On account of my house, because it is waste, And ye run, each of you to his own house.

10 Therefore restrained over you Are the heavens from dew; And the earth from producing is restrained:

11 Yea, I have called for drought On the land and on the mountains, And on the corn and the wine and the oil, And on everything which the earth produces, On man and on beast, And on every labour of the hands. (338)

12 And Zerubbabel, the son of Shealtiel, the governor of Judah, and to Joshua, the son of Josedech, the high priest, and all the residue of the people, attended to the voice of Jehovah, their God, and to the words of Haggai, the Prophet, as Jehovah their God had sent him; and the people feared Jehovah.

13 Then said Haggai, the messenger of Jehovah, according to Jehovah's message, saying to the people, "With you am I," saith Jehovah.

14 And Jehovah stirred up the spirit of Zerubbabel, the son of Shealtiel, the governor of Judah, and to Joshua, the son of Josedech, the high priest, and the spirit of all the people; and the came and carried on the work in the Temple of Jehovah of hosts, their God,

15 on the twenty-fourth day of the sixth month, in the second year of Darius the king. [155]

CHAPTER 2

1 In the seventh month, and on the twenty-first day, came the word of Jehovah to Haggai, the Prophet, saying, —

2 Speak now to Zerubbabel, the son of Shealtiel, the governor of Judah, and to Joshua, the son of Josedech, the high priest, and to all the residue of the people, saying, —

3 Who among you is alive, Who saw this house in its former glory, And how do ye see it now? Is it not to that as nothing in your eyes?

4 Yet now strong be thou Zerubbabel, saith Jehovah; And strong be all the people of the land; And work, for with you am I, Saith Jehovah of hosts,

5 According to the word I covenanted with you, When ye came forth from Egypt, And my Spirit shall be in the midst of you, fear ye not. (354)

6 For thus saith Jehovah of hosts, — Yet for a little while shall be this,

7 And I will shake the heavens and the earth, Also the sea and the dry land: Yea, I will shake all nations, And come shall the choice things of all nations; And I will fill this house with glory, Saith Jehovah of hosts:

8 Mine the silver and mine the gold, Saith Jehovah of hosts:

9 Greater shall be the glory Of this latter house than that of the former, Saith Jehovah of hosts; And in this place will I give peace, Saith Jehovah of hosts.

10 On the twenty-fourth of the ninth month, in the second year of Darius, came the word of Jehovah to Haggai, the Prophet, saying, —

11 Thus saith Jehovah of hosts, Ask the priests respecting the law, saying, —

12 If a man carry holy flesh in the skirt of his garment, and with his skirt touch bread, or pottage, or wine, or oil, or any eatable, shall it be made holy? And the priests answered and said, No.

13 Then said Haggai, If any one polluted in his person touch any of these things, shall it be polluted? The priests answered and said, It shall be polluted.

14 Then answered Haggai, and said, — So is this people, and so is this nation, In my sight, saith Jehovah; And so is every work of their hands, And what they offer, — it is polluted.

15 And now I pray, lay it to heart, — From this day and beyond it, Before a stone was laid on a stone In the temple of Jehovah, —

16 Before this time, when one came To a heap of twenty, there were but ten measures, When he came to the vat to draw fifty, There were from the vat but twenty vessels:

17 I smote you with blasting and mildew and hail, As to every work of you hands; And ye turned not to me, saith Jehovah.

18 Lay it, I pray, to your heart, — From this day and beyond it, From the twenty-fourth day of the ninth month, From the day the temple of Jehovah was founded; — Lay it to your heart, —

19 Is there now seed in the barn? And as yet the vine and the fig tree, And the pomegranate and the olive, Have produced nothing; — From this day will I bless you. (378)

20 And the word of Jehovah came again to Haggai, on the twenty-fourth of the month, saying, —

21 Speak to Zerubbabel, the governor of Judah, saying, —

22 I will shake the heavens and the earth, And will overthrow the throne of kingdoms, And destroy the strength of the kingdoms of the nations; Yea, I will overthrow chariots and their riders, And down shall come the horses and their riders, Every one by the sword of his brother:

23 In that day, saith Jehovah of hosts, I will take the Zerubbabel, The son of Shealtiel, my servant, saith Jehovah, And I will make thee as a signet, For I have chosen thee, saith Jehovah of hosts.

ENDNOTES

[1] Poeticus est Habbaccuci stylus; sed maxime in Oda, quae inter absolutissimas in eo genere merito numerari potest — Proel, 21. (p. 1)

[2] Equidem totum hunc locum pari qua ingressus est magnificentia exornat vates; ex tanta rerum admirandarum copia nobilissima quaeque seligens, eaque coloribus splendidissimis, imaginibus, figuris, dictione elatissima illustrans; quorum summam sublimitatem cumulat et commendat singu-laris clausulae elegantia: ita ut, nisi una atque altera ei insideret obscuri-tatis nebula vetustate, ut videtur, inducta, vix quidquam hoc poemate in suo genere extaret luculentius aut perfectius. — Proel. 28. (p. 2)

[3] Is nihil videtur hahere singulare aut eximium, in dispositione rerum, vel colore dictionis. — Proel, 21. (p. 2)

[4] Est vaticiniorum ejus argumentum Deo dignissimum, sive serias ejus redargutiones, sive severas comminationes, sive amicas monitiones, sive blandas promissiones, ad gratiam N. T. quam maxime protensas, spectemus. In quabus omnibus non tantum quoad rem consentientes alios habet vates, sed et phrases adhibuit — Anal. Tseph. Exeg. (p. 2)

[5] I. Haggai 1:1-11.
II. Haggai 1:12-15.
III. Haggai 2:1-9.
IV. Haggai 2:10-19.
V. Haggai 2:20-23. (p. 3)

[6] Who Habakkuk was is uncertain. Some have concluded, from chapter 3:19, that he was of the tribe of Levi; but the premises do not warrant the conclusion. "He was probably," says Adam Clarke, "of the tribe of Simeon, and a native of Bethzacar." The grounds for this probability are not stated. — Ed. (p. 6)

[7] Newcome's opinion is the following: — "It seems probable that Habakkuk lived after the taking of Nineveh, as he prophesies of the Chaldeans, and is silent on the subject of the Assyrians. We have also reason to conclude that he prophesied not long before the Jewish captivity. See chapter 1:5; 2:3; 3:2,6-19. He may therefore be placed in the reign of Jehoiakim, between the years 606 and 598 before Christ."

Henderson agrees with this view.

"Hunc librum canonicum esse constat," — tum 1. quia in Bibliis Hebrais extat; tum 2. quia in N.T. allegatum, Ac 13:41; Ro 1:17; Ga 3:11; Heb 10:38. It appears that this book is canonical, 1., because it is extant in Hebrew; 2., because it is quoted in the New Testament," etc. — Tarnovius. (p. 6)

[8] Rather, a causative meaning; for so does Calvin take it; and Junius and Tremelius, Piscator, Grotius, and Newcome, agree with him: but Drusius, Marckius, Henderson, and others, consider it simply in the sense of seeing or beholding, and say with truth, that there is no other instance in which it has, though it be often found, as here, in Hiphil, a causative sense. The context, as Calvin says, seems certainly to favor this meaning; and we might suppose that Habakkuk used it in a sense different from others, were it not that he uses it at least twice in this very chapter, verses 5 and 13, simply in the sense of seeing or beholding.

In these two verses there is no need of continuing the interrogatory form throughout, nor is this justified by the original. A strictly literal rendering, such as the following, would be the most appropriate:

2. How long, Jehovah, have I cried, and thou hearest not? I cry aloud to thee, "oppression," and thou savest not:

3. Why showest thou to me iniquity? Yea, wickedness is what thou seest; Even wasting and oppression are before me; Then there is strife, and contention arises.

Some think that there is to be understood a preposition before [חמם], which I render "oppression," in the second line; but there is no need of it. The word means outrage, wrong forcibly done, violent injustice. [למע], wickedness, in the second line of the third verse, in its primary sense, is labor, toil; it means also what produces toil, mischief, wickedness. Henderson renders it misery; but it is not so suitable; for it must be something that corresponds with iniquity in the previous line. Wickedness is the word adopted by Newcome. [ביר], strife, is a verbal contention or quarrel; and [זודמ] contention, is a judicial contest, or a trial by law. Then in the next verse we see how unjustly this trial was conducted. — Ed. (p. 10)

[9] Calvin omits to notice "therefore," [על-כז], at the beginning of the verse. Henderson says, that the connection is with the second verse: but this can hardly be the case; and certainly what this verse contains is no reason for what is stated in the previous verse. [זכל], a similar proposition with this, when followed by [יכ], as the case is here, refers sometimes to what follows and not to what precedes. See Ps. 16:10, 11, Ps. 78:21, 22. The meaning of the verse will be elicited, as I can conceive, by the following version: —

On this account the law fails,

And judgment goeth not forth to victory, —

Because wickedness surrounds the righteous;
Yea, on this account perverted judgment goeth forth.

The expression, [אל נצח], is rendered "never" in our version, and by Newcome; but it never means this: "not for ever, or not always," it is rendered in other places. See Ps. 9:19, Ps. 74:19. But [נצח] means as a noun, superiority, excellency, strength, victory; and this, according to Parkhurst, is what it means here. It seems better to render [רשע], wickedness, than wicked. It means injustice, the perversion of right, and by this the just man was surrounded or completely beset, so that he had no chance of having justice done to him. — Ed. (p. 12)

[10] This may perhaps be considered one of the very few instances in which the Septuagint seems to have retained the true reading without the countenance of a single MS.; for the word "despisers" is more suitable to the context. The very same word is found in the 13th verse of this chapter. The omission is very trifling, only of the letter [ד], and Paul in quoting this passage, in Ac 13:41, retains this word, while in the other clauses he departs from the Septuagint, and comes nearer to the Hebrew text. Pocock thought that [בוגים] is a noun from the Arabic [אגב], which means to be unjust or injurious; and thus the Hebrew is made the same with the Septuagint, and St. Paul, καταφρονηται, despisers — the insolent; but the former supposition seems the more probable — that the letter [ד] has been omitted. Dathius renders the word "perfidi — perfidious," and Newcome "transgressors." — Ed. (p. 14)

[11] This is the proper rendering, and not as in our version. It is not the usual mode in Hebrew to enhance the meaning by connecting two verbs together; but the two other verbs here are in the imperative mood, only the first is in Niphal and the other in Kal. Parkhurst very properly renders them, and be ye astonished, wonder, etc. The repetition, says Drusius, is for the sake of emphasis. — Ed. (p. 14)

[12] "Bitter" rendered "cruel" by Drusius. To be "bitter" in mind means passively, to be grieved, or distressed, or discontented, 1Sa 22:2; and actively, to be revengeful, cruel, or inhuman, Jude 18:25 — "Hasty" signifies to be rash, inconsiderate, or soon excited and made angry. It is obvious that the order is reversed; what follows is mentioned first, and then what precedes it; for to be hasty in entertaining anger is first, and then follows cruelty in executing it. A similar order is found in the next verse; the worst feature is mentioned first, that the nation would be "terrible;" and then what is less, that it would be "fearful." This is what is often doen by the writers of both of the Old and New Testament. — Ed. (p. 17)

[13] The word, [מרהביםׁ], means "breadths" or broad places, or wide regions, as Henderson renders it. — Ed. (p. 17)

[14] Multiples, various: but this is not the meaning of the verb [פשׁה]; it signifies to range at large, or to spread far and wide. The whole verse may be thus rendered, —

And swifter than leopards shall be its horses,
And more eager than the wolves of the evening;
Spread far and wide shall its horsemen;
Yea, its horsemen from far shall come,
And fly as an eagle hastening to devour.

The horsemen are represented as sweeping the whole country, spreading themselves in all directions; and when espying a prey at a distance, they are said to fly to it like an eagle. The idea of being "numerous" or "abundant," as Junius and Tremelius render the verb, is derived from the Rabbins, and is not sanctioned by examples in Scripture. The rendering of the Septuagint is ἐξιππάσονται, shall ride forth, and of Jerome, diffundentur, shall spread themselves. There is no occasion to borrow a meaning from Arabic, as Henderson does, and to render it "spread proudly along." Newcome follows our common version. — Ed. (p. 19)

[15] This clause has been variously interpreted. The Targum, Vulgate, and Symmachus, countenance the view given here. There is no help from the Septuagint, as no sense is given. The word [מגמח], only found here, is rendered by Symmachus, πρόσοψις, sight, aspect. Targum explains it by a word which signifies "front." Henderson and Lee regard this as its meaning. Others, as Newcome and Drusius render it, supping up, or absorption, and derive it from [גמא], to drink up, to absorb; and they regard the idea to be, that the very presence of the Chaldeans would absorb every thing like a scorching wind. But "the supping up of their faces shall be as the east wind," which is Newcome's version, is an odd phrase. The last word has [ה] affixed to it, which is never the case when it means the east wind. It is by all admitted, that "towards the east" is its proper construction. Hence the most probable rendering of this passage is, "The aspect of their faces shall be towards the east;" and with this corresponds what follows, that they should "gather captives as the sand;" that is, that they might carry them away to the place where they turned their faces.

The version of Henderson, which is essentially that of Symmachus, is the following, —

The aspect of their faces is like the east wind.

He owns the difficulty as to the last word, and views it here as in an irregular form. Dathius gives this paraphrase, —

It will have its face direct towards the east.

He says that the word [םודק], by itself never means the pestilential wind from the east; but that when it means this, it has another word attached to it. — Ed. (p. 21)

[16] The foregoing verse is one on which no satisfactory explanation has been given. The one adopted here has been materially followed by Vatablus, Druius, and Dathius, except as to the last clause. As to the first part of the verse Henderson gives the best sense, for it corresponds with "changing" to [ףלח] and "courage" to [חור], (see Josh. 2:11, Josh. 5:1;) and of "passing onward" to [רבע], and not of "passing over," i.e. bounds or moderation, which it seems not to have, when used, as here, intransitively. The passing here is evidently what is referred to in verse 6, as the renewing of courage would arise, from the success mentioned in verse 10.

The best exposition of the last clause is what Grotius has suggested, and has been followed by Marckius and Dathius — that the Chaldeans made their own strength their God; (see verse 16;) the rendering then would be this, —

Then will it renew courage, And pass through,
and become guilty; — This is strength being its god,
or literally, This is strength for its god.

There is an inconsistency in our version, and also in Calvin, as to this passage, from verse 6 to the end of this verse. The number is changed. The "bitter nation," mentioned in verse 6, is meant throughout; and we ought to adopt the plural number throughout, as Newcome does, or, according to Henderson, the singular. There is no change of person, as some suppose, at the beginning of verse 10; for [אוה], there, and [אוה] in verse 6 is the same — the "bitter nation." — Ed. (p. 25)

[17] Most commentators agree with our version in connecting "from the beginning," or "from eternity," with Jehovah, and not as Calvin seems to do, with "God." His view is evidently the most consonant with the design of the passage, and countenanced by the Septuagint, for Jehovah is rendered κυριε, in the vocative case. To assert the eternity of God seems not to be necessary here; but to say that he had been from old times the God of Israel is what is suitable to the context. The Prophet in saying "my God," identifies himself with the people; for he says afterwards, "we shall not die." Viewed in this light the former part of the verse may be thus rendered, —

Art not thou from of old, O Jehovah,
my God! My holy one, we shall not die.

The reason for which he calls him "holy" will appear from what the next verse contains. The Prophet seems to sustain himself by two considerations — that Jehovah was the God of Israel, and that he was a holy God. When he says "we shall not die," he means, no doubt, as Marckius observes, that the people as a nation would not be destroyed, for he had prophesied of their subjugation and captivity by the Chaldeans. What he had in view was the Church of God, respecting which promises had been made. — Ed. (p. 26)

[18] It seems that Calvin regarded "my holy one," as equivalent to "my sanctifier;" he who had separated the people from others to be his own. The primary meaning of [שדק] is no doubt to separate a thing from a common use to a sacred one; but whether in this connection it has this meaning is not quite certain. "The holy one of Israel" is a phrase several times used by Isaiah, see Isa. 30:11, Isa. 43:3, etc. The sentence here may be rendered, "God of my holiness," or "My God, my holiness." — Ed. (p. 28)

[19] Many agree in this view, Drusius, Piscator, Marckius, Henderson, etc. The Septuagint affords no help. The rendering of Symmachus is κραταιον, strong, and of Aquila, στερεον, firm; then it would be, "and strong (or firm) for correction hast thou established him." Grotius, and also Newcome, adopt this meaning.

And thous hast founded them on a rock to chasten us

This is, no doubt, the easiest and most natural construction. See Eze 3:9. God rendered the Chaldean nation firm, and strong, and resolute, to punish the Jews. — Ed. (p. 29)

[20] Adjectives and participles in Hebrew commonly take a plural form, but not always, as evidently in the present case; for the word for "pure," though singular, will admit of a better construction with "eyes" than in any other way; and so Grotius renders the clause, "Purer are thine eyes," etc.; which is better than our version, followed by Newcome and Henderson. The whole passage will thus read better: —

Purer are thine eyes than to behold evil,
And to look on wickedness thou art not able:
Why then lookest thou on the perfidious,
And art still when the wicked swallows up
One more righteous than himself?
And makest man to be like the fish of the sea,
Like the reptile which has no ruler?

"Evil" means here wrong, injustice; the corresponding clause is "the wicked" swallowing up or oppressing his better. The Jews were bad, but better than the Chaldeans. "Wickedness," [למע], is such a mischief as is done through treachery: hence in the next line, which, according to the style of the Prophets, corresponds with this, "the perfidious" are mentioned, improperly rendered "plunderers" by Henderson, and "transgressors" by Newcome. The Chaldeans had been the allies of the Jews.

With respect to the reptile or the crawling fish, such as keep to the bottom of the waters, why is it said to be without a ruler? Is it more insulated and less gregarious, so to speak, than other fish? If so, "without a ruler" has an obvious meaning. — Ed. (p. 31)

[21] The construction of this verse can only be understood by a reference to the preceeding verse; where two things are mentioned, the fish of the sea and the reptile: as it is customary with the Prophets, the first clause was rasied up by a hook, and the fish were enclosed in a net, or collected by a drag. The reptile, [שמר], is in the singular number, and used in a collective sense, and [הלכ], every one, at the beginning of this verse, is in the same number. This entirely removes the difficulty which critics have felt, and made them to propose emendations. The verse then would read thus: —

Every one (i.e. every reptile) by a hook he raises up
He draws them out (i.e. the fish) by his net,
And collects them by his drag;
He therefore rejoices, and exults.

To "gather then into the net" can hardly be sense; nor is "in the net" much better. The drawing out and the collecting were evidently by the net and the drag; the preposition, [ב], has very commonly this meaning, as ἐν in Greek.

The representation here is, that every means would be employed: men being compared to fishes, some are set forth as creeping along the bottom, and others as swimming at large at all depths; and then the fisherman, the Chaldean comes, and draws out the first by a fishing-hook, and the rest by a net and a ddrag; so that he takes them all. — Ed. (p. 33)

[22] "His fat portion and rich meat" were the people whom he conquered. The words verbatim are these, —

For through them abundant his portion,
And his meat well-fed.

The comparison of the drag and net is continued; by which is signified military strength and power. See Isa 10:13. — Ed. (p. 37)

[23] The verb is [קיריק], a hiphil form, and means, to evacuate, to empty, to empty out, and this is the sense in which it is taken here by Drusius, Marckius, Newcome, and Henderson. But the verb means also to draw out, i.e., a sword, Ex 15:9, Le 26:33, and to draw forth, i.e., an army, Ge 14:14, and this is the meaning given to it by Grotius, Junius, and the Septuagint. To draw forth, to extend, or to expand, seems most in accordance with the drift of the passage. To empty his net, and that for the sake of filling it again, which must be what is implied, is rather a farfetched notion. — Ed. (p. 37)

[24] On my watch-tower, [ימשמרתי]; the word means commonly the office, or the act of watching, but here it means evidently the place; the verb "stand" and the corresponding word [מצור] fortress, or citadel, in the next line, prove clearly that this is its meaning here. The metaphor is taken from the practice of ascending a high tower, when any messenger was expected with news. That any locality is meant here is supported by nothing in the passage. The Prophet puts himself in an attitude of waiting for an answer from God to the complaints which he had made: and the metaphor of "tower and citadel" is most beautifully applied by Calvin, and in a very instructive and striking manner. I give this version —

On my watch-tower will I stand,
And I will set myself on a citadel;
That I may look out to see what he will say to me,
And what I shall answer to the reproof given to me;
Literally, to my reproof.
— Ed. (p. 40)

[25] That is, to the chiding, rebuke, or reproof, given to me. Both Newcome and Henderson give a version of this line, which is nearly the same, but seems incongruous, though Grotius agrees with them. The version of the former is as follows: —

And what I should reply to my arguing with him.
The latter renders the line thus: —
And what I shall reply in regard to my argument.

The phrase is, [על-תוכחתי] upon, (to, says Drusius) my reproof, or rebuke, or chiding. This is the current meaning of the word, see 2Ki 19:3; Prov. 10:17, Prov. 12:1; Isa 37:3. He calls it "my," because given him, either by his enemies, as Calvin thinks, or by God, as some others suppose. The view of Piscator and Junius is, that it is the reproof or correction he administered to the people in chapter 1:2-12. He was waiting to know what he might have to give as a reply in defense of that reproof. "And what I may reply as to my reproof," i.e., the reproof given by him. In this case, the preceding clause, "What he may or will say to me," refers to his complaint respecting the Chaldeans. This is altogether consistent with the mode in which the Prophets usually write: reversing the order, they take up first the last subject, and then refer to the first. He then waited to know two things, how to solve his difficulties respecting the conduct of the Chaldeans, and how to reply to his own people for the severe rebuke he gave them. There is much in this view to recommend it. — Ed. (p. 41)

[26] The word means, to open, or make open. It was to be written in open and plain letters, and on tables or tablets. These were either of wood or stone, made smooth. The Septuagint render the word πυξιον, a smooth plank of boxwood, and give the whole sentence thus: "Write the vision and openly (or plainly — σαφῶς,) on boxwood." See De 27:8. So Junius takes the word as an adverb, perspicue, perspicuously. — Ed. (p. 45)

[27] It is not a common word that is used: [חפי], "it will breathe." When transitively, it signifies, to breathe out or forth, and is rendered often in our version, to speak; see Prov. 6:19, Prov. 12:17. The idea here seems to be the restoration, as it were, of a suspended life. The vision was to be for a time like a body without any symptom of life: but "it will breathe," he says, "at last," or at the end; that is, it will live, and manifest life and vigor. This breathing, or this life, would be its accomplishment. Corresponding with this idea is ἀνατελι, "it will rise," by the Septuagint. — Ed. (p. 46)

[28] [בזכ], its primary meaning, is to fail, Isa 63:11; and to fail, in a moral sense, is to lie, and also to deceive; and the latter meaning is attached to it here by Drusius, Piscator, and Grotius, non fallet, it will not deceive, i.e., disappoint. — Ed. (p. 46)

[29] What is here said is very true; but the words are not the same in Hebrew. The first signifies delay, [המהמתי] rendered "linger" in Gen. 19:16, Gen. 43:10. The other verb, [רחאי], means, to put off, to postpone: and the sense is, that the vision will not be after the appointed time. So the two lines may be thus rendered:

If it will delay, wait for it,
For coming it will come, it will not be postponed;
or, be after, i.e., the appointed time.
Dr. Wheeler, quoted by Newcome, give the right idea, by the following paraphrase:
It shall not be later than its season.

Both Jerome and Marckius have found a grammatical difficulty in this verse from a mistake as to the gender of [חזון], vision; and they had been evidently led astray by the Septuagint; in which the gender is changed, and the phrase, "wait for it," is rendered, "wait for him," ὑπόμεινον αὐτον; and so as to what follows, "for he that cometh (ἐρχομενος) shall come." But [חזון] is the masculine gender; it is elsewhere connected with verbs in that gender. See 1Sa 3:1; Eze 12:22. Indeed the whole tenor of the passage admits not of any other construction. It is probable that this mistake made Eusebius and Augustine to apply this verse to Christ, and some to Nebuchadnezzar, in a typical sense. — Ed. (p. 47)

[30] Most authors agree in the main with Calvin in his exposition of this clause. The whole verse is quoted by Paul in Heb 10:39, nearly verbatim from the Scriptures; only he inverts the clauses, and leaves out the pronoun, "my," connected with "faith." But this clause, as quoted by him, is materially different from the Hebrew text, as it now exists, though the chief difference relates to the word [הלפע], rendered elation, or pride, by Calvin and many others. Two MSS. give another reading; one has [הפלוע], and the other, [הפלע], which means to swoon, or to faint, or to fail.

This reading would essentially harmonize the passage, and the context evidently favors it, as well as the antithesis in the verse itself. As to the rest of the clause the meaning is same with the Septuagint version, as cited by Paul, though the words are different; and there are other examples in which the apostle did not alter that version, though varying in words, when the sense was preserved. To say that man's soul is not right in him amounts to the same thing as to say that God is not pleased with him. There is indeed one MS. which has [ישפנ], "my soul," and not "his soul;" and then [הרשי] is often rendered ἀρεσκειν, to please, by the Septuagint. See Nu 23:27; 2Ch 30:4. There would in this case be a complete identity of words as well as of meaning.

What especially countenances these readings is, that the alteration would agree better with the preceding verse. There is an exhortation to wait for the vision, i.e., its fulfillment. To refer to pride in this connection seems not suitable; but to mention fainting or failing through unbelief is quite appropriate; and then as a contrast to this state of mind, the latter clause is added. Adopting the main alteration, [הפלע] instead of [הלפע], (only a transposition of two letters,) I would render the verse thus —

Behold the fainting! not right is his soul within him;
But the righteous, by his faith shall he live.

The word for "fainting" is in the feminine gender, either on account of the word "soul" in what follows, or [שיא] is understood, the "man of fainting," instances of which are adduced by Henderson on this verse, though he retains the word of the present text; as [הלפת ינא], "I am prayer," instead of "I am a man of prayer." — Ps. 109:4, Jer. 50:31, 32, Dan. 9:23

Now not only the antithesis is here complete, but the order also in which it occurs corresponds with what is often the style of the Prophets; the first part of the first clause corresponds with the last part of the second, and the last of the former with the first of the latter; and not according to Dr. Henderson, who represents the clauses as regularly antithetic. See a similar instance in Hab 1:13, and also in the first verse of this chapter. The man who faints, and he who lives by faith, form the contrast; and the addition "by faith" in the latter clause implies the fainting to be through want of faith, or through unbelief. Then the soul that is not right stands in contrast with the righteous, or the just in the second line. Thus every thing in the verse itself, and in its connection with what precedes it, is in favor of what has been proposed. And Grotius and Newcome seemed disposed to adopt this reading. — Ed. (p. 52)

[31] Though the general meaning of the beginning of this verse is what most critics agree in, yet the construction is difficult. The only difference as to the meaning is, whether the proud man is said to be given to wine, or is compared to such an one, or to wine itself. Newcome takes the first, and gives this version —

Moreover, as a mighty man transgresseth through wine,
He is proud, and remaineth not at rest.
Henderson, agreeing with Grotius and Mede, takes the latter sense, and renders the line as follows: —
Moreoever wine is treacherous;
The haughty man stayeth not at home.

This is rather a paraphrase than a version; but this is the meaning of which the words are most capable. The two first participles need not be connected according to what Calvin proposes. Then the distich may be thus rendered —

And truly, as wine is treacherous,
So is the proud man, and he will not rest.
Then follows a delineation of his character —
Because he enlarges as the grave his desire,
And he is like death and cannot be satisfied;
For he gathers to himself all the nations,
And collects to himself all the people.

As to wine being treacherous, see Pr 30:1. Wine is pleasant to the taste and inviting in its color, but degrading, when taken immoderately, in its effects; so a proud and arrogant man is at first glittering and plausible, and splendid in his

appearance, but afterwards cruel and oppressive. This seems to be the most obvious similitude, as contained in the passage.
Parkhurst renders the two first lines as follows —
Yea, as when wine deceiveth a man,
So he is proud, and is not at rest.
He interprets "proud," as meaning "intoxicated with power and dominion," and refers to Da 4:30. — Ed. (p. 64)

[32] This can hardly be allowed; for in this case the final letter of the previous word must have been [ת] and not [ה]. It is a word evidently in apposition, designing the character of the proverb and the taunt, they being enigmas, conveyed in a highly figurative language. The whole verse may be thus rendered —

Shall not these, all of them,
Raise against him a proverb and a taunt —
Enigmas for him;
Yea, say will every one —
"Woe to him who multiplies what is not his own! how long!
"And to him who accumulates on himself thick clay!"

To render the last word [טיטבע], (or [טיט בע], apart, as given by ten MSS.,) "pledges," as it is done by Newcome and Henderson, does not comport at all with the rest of the passage. The Septuagint favor the common explanation, and also the Vulgate, and most commentators. — Ed. (p. 66)

[33] It is rendered impersonally by Jerome "et dicetur — and it shall be said." Junius introduces a question, and supposed the just, who lives by faith to be referred to — "And shall not he, i.e., the just, say?" But Marckius considers that God is the speaker — "And he, i.e., God, shall say." But the most obvious construction is, that each one of the nations previously mentioned is introduced as speaking — "Unusquisque illorum — every one of them," is understood, says Piscator. — Ed. (p. 67)

[34] This is rendered by Henderson, "that have lent thee on usury;" but incorrectly, as the corresponding clause is found in the following, and not, as he ays, in the preceding line. The literal version is as follows, —

Shall not suddenly arise thy biters,
And awake thy tormentors,
And thou become for spoils to them?
Now, the two corresponding words are "biters" and "tormentors;" and the idea of lending on usury cannot be admitted; and the common meaning of the word [נשׁך],

is to bite, and means lending on usury only in Hiphil. What the Septuagint gives is δακνοντες — biters.

Here is an instance of the peculiar manner of the Prophets, and also of the writers of the New Testament; the most obvious act is mentioned first "arise," and then what is previous to it, "awake." There is also a similar difference in "biters" and "tormentors," or those who vex and harass: to torment or vex is not so great an evil as to bite, as it were, like a serpent; for such is the biting meant here. — Ed. (p. 71)

[35] So Grotius, Drusius, and Henderson regard the passage: the land, and the city, are supposed to have been used poetically for lands and cities. The word rendered "violence," [חמס], means an unjust or wrong act done by force, an outrage, a violent injustice: hence Grotius rightly renders it here, "direptionem — robbing, pillaging, or plundering." While Newcome and others apply the passage to Judea and Jerusalem, the Septuagint version would lead us to suppose that Babylon was intended. The view taken here would be the most probable, were it not that the words are repeated at the end of verse 17; and there clearly they refer to the land of Judea and Jerusalem. — Ed. (p. 73)

[36] Literally, "sinning thy soul." We have in Pr 8:36, [יאטה], "my sinner," rendered no doubt correctly, "he that sinneth against me." So here "sinning thy soul," means "sinning against thy soul." See the same words in Pr 20:2. In Nu 16:38, the preposition [ב] is before "souls." "Thy soul hath sinned," as given by the Septuagint, and adopted by Newcome, does not convey the meaning; for to sin against our souls, is to injure ourselves so as to bring down judgment, as in the case mentioned in Nu 16:38, while the other phrase conveys only the idea of doing what is wrong. — Ed. (p. 76)

[37] The word rendered here "Wood," lignum, is [כפיס], and only found here. The Septuagint has κανθαρος, a beetle, — Sym. συνδεσμος, bond, tie, or joint, — Theod. ἔνδεσμος, bandage or jointing. The context shows that it must be something connected with wood-building. Parkhurst says, that it is a verb in Syriac, and means to connect, to fasten together, and he renders it a beam or a rafter, which would exactly suit this place. The word, [מעץ], "from the wood," evidently means the wood-building or wood-work. So that tabulatum, a story or a chamber in a building, as rendered by Calvin, is not amiss. Perhaps the best version would be, —

And the beam from the wood-work answers it.

Bochart says, that [כפיס], in Rabbinical writings, means a brick, and that it was usual formerly, as it was in this country not long ago, to build with bricks and wood or timber together; and Henderson has adopted this meaning, but the other is more satisfactory. — Ed. (p. 78)

[38] The construction of the first line of this verse, as given by Calvin, is stiff and unnatural. There is no doubt but that [הנה] is a pronoun in the plural number, and so it has been taken by the Septuagint, ταυτα, these things, and such is the rendering of the Syriac and Arabic versions. No improvement, perhaps, can be made on Newcome's rendering of this verse, —

Are not these things from Jehovah God of hosts,
That people should labor for the fire,
And nations should weary themselves for a vain thing?

The intimation is, that all the buildings erected by blood and prepared by iniquity, were destined for the fire. "For the fire," [שא ידב], literally is, for the supply of fire, as Parkhurst renders the phrase: then it is, for the supply of emptiness or vacuity, [קיר ירב].

The last two lines, with some variety, are found in Jer 51:58, and applied to Babylon. In Jeremiah, "for a vain thing," is in the first line, and "for the fire" is in the second. Jeremiah puts the less evil first, and the greatest last; but Habakkuk's usual manner is the reverse, which has been before noticed, and we find an instance in the preceding verse, where he mentions "blood" first, and in the next line, "iniquity."

That the destination of Babylon for the fire is here meant, seems evident from the following verse. See Jer 51:25. — Ed. (p. 79)

[39] The idea is nearly the same, though not the words. The verse in Isaiah is literally this —

For fill the earth shall the knowledge of Jehovah,
Like the waters spreading over the sea.

The verb rendered "cover" here and in Isaiah is, [הסכ], which means first to spread, and in the second place to cover, as the effect of spreading. It is followed here by [לע], over, and by [ל], over, in Isaiah; and so spreading must be the idea included in the verb. The comparison in Isaiah is between knowledge and waters, and the earth and the sea. Hence the common version does not properly present the comparison. The verb [אלמ], is used in a passive and active sense. See Ge 6:13, and Gen. 1:22, Gen. 24:16. This verse may be rendered in Welsh word for word, without changing the order in one instance: —

Canys henwa y ddaear wybodaeth o Jehova,
Vel y dyvroedd dros y more yn ymdaenu.

"The knowledge of Jeohovah," [הוהי-תא העד], is not an instance of a genitive case by juxtaposition, which is common both in Hebrew and in Welsh; for [תא] here must be a preposition, "from," for it is sometimes used for [תאמ]. It is a knowledge that was to come from Jehovah, and not a knowledge of Jehovah. — Ed. (p. 81)

[40] There is no reason to doubt but that this is the meaning of the sentence here: and it is a striking instance of the variety of meaning which belongs to similar expressions, when differently connected. The glory of God is manifested by judgments as well as by mercies. In Isaiah it is "the knowledge of or from Jehovah;" here the expression is, "the knowledge of the glory of Jehovah." By "the knowledge of Jehovah" is to be understood the revelation made by the gospel. But by "the knowledge of his glory" is meant evidently the display of his power in destroying Babylon, as power is often signified by glory. — Ed. (p. 81)

[41] The rendering of this verse has been various, though most agree as to its import. Grotius, Marckius, and Henderson, take nearly the same view of its meaning as Calvin, regarding it as metaphorical. But Marckius thinks that the drunkenness which the king of Babylon produced, means the evils which he inflicted on other nations. To make a nation drunk was to subdue and oppress it. See Isa. 51:17, 22; Jer. 25:15, 16, 27, 28, Jer. 51:7, 39, 57. This view is confirmed by the following verse, where the king of Babylon is threatened with a similar judgment; he was also to drink of the cup of Jehovah's right hand. As he made other nations drunk, so the Lord threatens him with a like visitation.

The verse will admit of a much simpler rendering than what has been commonly offered, such as the following: —

Woe to him who makes his neighbor to drink,
Who adds his bottle, and also strong drink,
In order that he may look on their nakedness.

To render [המח], wrath, or heat, or gall, or poison, as some have done, is to introduce an idea foreign to the context, and the word is often found to signify the bottle of skin in which wine was kept. Newcome renders it "flagon." By mentioning bottle, abundance of wine was probably intended, and to this abundance was added the strong drink, [רכש], intoxicating liquor. It is commonly rendered as though it were a verb in Hiphil; but it is not so. It means here no doubt, as in other places, strong drink. This line is only an application, as we find often in the Prophets, of the preceding line.

Though there is no MS. which has "his" instead of "thy" connected with "bottle," yet the preceding and the following lines seem to require it; and this is the reading of Symmachus and of the Vulgate. The change of persons, it is true, is very common in the Prophets, but not in such a way as we find here, the third person being adopted both in the preceding and in the following line.

The idea of drinking as a judgment may have arisen from the cup of malediction given to criminals before their execution. See also Ps 75:8. Babylon is in Jer 51:7, represented as "a golden cup" in God's hand to make the nations drunken. It was "golden" to signify an outward appearance that was plausible, and alluring. So the mystic Babylon is said to have a golden cup, which was full of all abominations, Re 17:4. — Ed. (p. 83)

[42] The view presented here of the first clause of the verse is striking, and such as the words may admit. But most commentators attach to them another meaning. Newcome's version is —

Thou art filled with shame instead of glory.
Henderson's rendering is —
Thou art filled with shame, not with glory.

The verb being in the past tense seems to favor Calvin's view — "Thou hast been satiated with shame from glory," that is, thou hast been filled to satiety with the shame occasioned to others, arising from the pursuit of thine own glory. And then, as Calvin justly observes, his punishment is denounced. — "Drink thou also." — Ed. (p. 86)

[43] The verb [בוסת], loosely expressed here, is very correctly rendered by Henderson "shall come round;" and this is the idea which Calvin suggests in the following explanation. — Ed. (p. 87)

[44] It is commonly derived from [קי], a contraction of [איק], a vomit or spewing, and [זולק], shame. Compounds are no common things in Hebrew; and these are found separate in nine MSS. The Septuagint have ἀτιμια, reproach only; and the Vulgate, "vomitus ignominiae — the spewing of shame." Newcome renders it "foul shame," and Henderson "great ignominy," regarding it as a reduplicate noun for [זולקלק]. But as drunkenness is the metaphor used, "shameful spewing," or the spewing of shame or of reproach is most suitable to the passage. — Ed. (p. 87)

[45] It is commonly agreed, that Libanus here means either the temple or the land of Judah; most probably the last, according to the opinion of Jerome, Drusius, and others. The "violence," or outrage, of Libanus, means the violence done to it, as Newcome and others render the clause. The next line is more difficult: if the verb

be retained as it is, we must either adopt what Calvin has proposed, and after him Drusius, or take the [ו] at the beginning as a particle of comparison, according to what is done by Henderson, "As the destruction of beasts terrifieth them." But to preserve the parallelism of the two lines, it would be better to adopt the correction of all the early versions, Sept. Arab. Syr. and also of the Chald. par.; which substitute [ד] for [ר] and make the verb to be [דתיחי]: and there are two MSS. which have [יתת]. In this case the rendering would be the following —

Because the violence done to Libanus shall overwhelm thee;
And the depredation done to the beasts shall rend thee;
On account of the blood of men, and of violence to the land,
To the city, and to all who dwelt in it.

The reason men are called "beasts" is because Libanus is mentioned which was inhabited by beasts; and in the two following lines the statement is more clear, and according to the order usually observed, "the depredation done to beasts" is "the blood of men;" and "the violence to Libanus" is "violence to the land." And then, as it is often the case in the Prophets, there is an addition made to the two last lines, "To the city," etc. — Ed. (p. 89)

[46] Rightly to understand this verse, it is necessary to remember that the graven and the molten image was the same; it was first graven and then covered with some metal, either of gold or of silver. See Note on Micah 1:7, vol. 3, p. 167.

This verse, as given in our version and in that of Newcome, presents hardly a meaning; and Henderson is not justified in the peculiar sense he gives to the particle [יכ], taking it as a relative pronoun. The rendering of Calvin gives an evident and a striking sense. The verse may be thus literally rendered —

18. What avails the graven image? —
For its graver has formed it, —
The molten image and the teacher of falsehood?
For trust in it does the former of its form,
After having made dumb idols.

The last line show that the singular number before used is to be taken in a collective sense: and the preposition [ל] before an infinitive has sometimes the meaning of "after." See Ex 19:1, "When he has made," etc., is the rendering of Grotius. — Ed. (p. 90)

[47] With the exception of the clause, "It will teach," there is a general agreement in the mode of rendering this verse. "Shall it teach," is Newcome's version. Henderson considers it to be ironical, "It teach!" Grotius agrees with Calvin, "It will

itself teach thee," that is, that it is deaf, and no god. I regard the verse as capable of a simpler and more literal rendering, as follows:

19. Woe to him who saith to the wood, "Awake, Arise;"
To the dumb stone, "It will teach:"
Behold, it is covered with gold and silver!
Yet there is no breath within it.

The two verbs, "Awake, Arise," stand connected with "wood," and they are so given in the Septuagint; and there is a striking contrast between the dumb stone and teaching. — Ed. (p. 92)

[48] The more correct rendering here would be, "A Prayer (or rather, An Intercession) by Habakkuk the Prophet;" that is, It was a prayer composed by him. The preposition [ל] before Habakkuk, as often before David in the Psalms, would be better rendered in this way, than by "of;" for the meaning is, not that it was his prayer, that is, one offered up by him, but that it was composed by him. "A Psalm of David," ought to be, "A Psalm by David." — Ed. (p. 100)

[49] This explanation, adopted by Calvin, is derived originally from Aquila and Symmachus, who rendered the phrase, ἐπι ἀγοηματων, — respecting oversights or errors: and they have been followed by Jerome, Vulgate, etc. The prior version of the Septuagint is, μετ᾽ ᾠδδης, — with an ode that this prayer is composed in metre, is evident from the word, "Selah," and from the conclusion of the chapter. The most probable meaning of the word is what Drusius has suggested, and adopted by Grotius, Marckius, and Henderson, and that is, that it refers to a peculiar metre, a kind of composition, which from its irregularity is called erratica cantio, an erratic verse. "The prayer of Habakkuk," says Drusius, "was to be sung according to the odes which they called Sigionoth." To the same purpose is what Grotius says, that is, it is "a song according to the notes of an ancient ode which began with this word." It is derived from [הגש], to go astray, to wander, that is, in this instance, from the regular metre of an ode. It is an erratic ode, that is, one containing varieties. It may be thus paraphrastically expressed, "According to the notes of the irregular ode;" or, as it is in the margin of our Bibles, "According to variable songs or tunes." — Ed. (p. 101)

[50] The verb, "territus sum, — I feared," has been omitted. It is even omitted in the French version. — Ed. (p. 102)

[51] The view given of "the middle of the years," is ingenious and striking; but the common interpretation is, that "the years" of calamity, allotted to the Jews, are meant. The Septuagint version of this verse is so extremely wide of the original, that none can account for the differences. There are no various readings of any

moment; and the literal rendering of this verse, and of the former part of the following, I consider to be this, —

2. O Jehovah! I have heard thy report;
I feared, O Jehovah!
Thy work! in the midst of the years revive it;
In the midst of the years make it known;
In anger remember mercy:
3. May God from Teman come
And the Holy One from mount Paran. Selah.

It is called "thy report," as it was a report which came from God; the allusion is to the threatenings in chapter 1. "The report from thee," would convey the sense. The third line is a prayer; and so are the following lines, though all the verbs are in the future tense, while that for "revive" is in the imperative mood. The third verse ought to end with the word "Selah." What follows in the other part and in the subsequent verses, is a relation of what took place when God had formerly interfered in behalf of Israel; while here, and in the latter part of the preceding verse, the Prophet expresses a prayer to God in reference to his people, and borrows his language from the past interpositions of God. — Ed. (p. 104)

[52] The word [הלס] is found 70 times, as Parkhurst says, in the Psalms, and thrice in this chapter. "It was most probably," he adds, "a note of music, or a direction to the singers in the temple service to raise their voices or instruments where it is inserted." The opinion of Gesenius is the same, it being a direction, as he says, "to repeat the preceding verse in a louder strain." It is always rendered by the Septuagint Διαψαλμα, which means a variation in singing.

Some have rendered the word pause, but it cannot be so considered, for it occurs at the end of at least three of the Psalms. There seems to be no regularity in its adoption in some of the Psalms it occurs once, in some twice, in others thrice, and in one psalm four times.

Calvin has not referred, in his comment, to the latter part of this verse, which, according to his Latin, may be thus translated, —

Cover the heavens did his glory;
With his praise full was the earth.

Both glory and praise here are to be taken as signifying their manifestations. The reference is made to the displays of divine majesty on mount Sinai. The original may be thus rendered —

Cover the heavens did his shining,
And his lustre filled the earth. — Ed. (p. 105)

[53] That [זרק] means to irradiate or to shine, is clear from Exod. 34:29, 30, 35; "for shine did the skin of his face," [ויינפ רוע זרק יכ]. Most critics consider that the noun here, though in this sense in no other instance, means rays, or beams of light; and this corresponds with the description given elsewhere of God's appearance on mount Sinai. Drusius, Marckius, Newcome, and Henderson, render it "rays." The line then would literally be —

Rays from his hand were to him.
or, to retain the English idiom.
He had rays from his hand.

To render the line, "Rays streamed from his hand," is to give a paraphrase.

The objection of Calvin as to the next line, seems not valid; for the hiding of strength may refer to the hand, or to the place, Sinai, whether we render the previous word, rays or horns; — to the place, if we retain our present reading, [הזע], "of its strength;" but to the hand, if we adopt the reading of many copies, [וזע] "of his strength," which is perhaps the most accordant with the passage. — Ed. (p. 108)

[54] Most agree in the view given of this verse, only there is some shade of difference as to the word [ףשר]; but though Calvin renders it carbo ignitus — ignited coals, yet in his exposition he seems to regard it with many others as a burning disease. In the six other instances in which the word occurs, it certainly has not this sense, except it be in De 32:24, which is doubtful. It signifies not a burning coal, but a glowing fire, burning or lightening. Compare Exod. 9:23, 25, with Ps 78:48; where it designates the fires or lightnings produced by thunder, which accompanied the hail. Lightning would be its mot proper rendering here; for instead of referring this verse to the plagues in Egypt, it may be considered as a continuation of what is contained in the foregoing verse; and the Septuagint and Theodotion have rendered [רבד] in the preceding clause, not pestilence, but word — λογος, its most usual meaning. This makes the whole to comport to what we read of God's appearance on mount Sinai. See Ex 19:16; De 33:2. The version then would be this —

From before him proceeded the word (i.e. the law;)
And forth came lightning at his feet.

Most of the ideas in this, and in the two preceding verses, seem to be similar to those we find in Deut. 33:2, 3. — Ed. (p. 109)

[55] This verse is explained in a very striking manner, but the version is not so strictly correct It may be thus rendered: —

6. He stood, and measure the earth;
He looked, and agitated the earth;
And burst themselves open did the perpetual mountains,
Bend down did the hills of ages;
The going of ages were his.

"The perpetual mountains" are literally "the mountains of perpetuity," which had remained the same from the beginning. "The hills of ages" might be rendered the hills of antiquity or of old time, [עולם], an indefinite past time. "The goings of ages," are God's proceedings, that is, in his works, and may therefore be rendered "deeds;" and they are said to be deeds "of ages," i.e., of old time, with reference probably to the creation of the world: for he who makes perennial mountains to burst, and perpetual hills to bend downwards, must be their first creator. — Ed. (p. 112)

[56] The word [און] not only means iniquity, but also what iniquity produces, labor, trouble, affliction; and this latter meaning, as allowed by Newcome and Henderson, is most suitable to it here. The word is so taken in Ge 35:18; De 26:14; Ho 9:4. Besides, this meaning makes a correspondence between this and the following line, as will be seen by the following version —

Under trouble have I seen the tents of Cushan,
Tremble did the curtains of the land of Madian.

The "curtains" were those used in forming tents, and are used here to designate them. The most obvious reference here is to Cushan, mentioned in Judg. 3:8, 10, as Calvin states; yet some consider that it stands for Cush, as Lotan, in Ge 26:20, is put for Lot: and some, as Gesenius, say, that the African Cush is meant, and others, as Henderson, think, that it is the Arabian Cush, especially as Madian is also mentioned. Still the events recorded in Judges, nearly connected together, favor the opinion adopted by Calvin. — Ed. (p. 113)

[57] The two first lines present a difficulty in their construction. The most literal is this rendering of Junius —

Did against rivers kindle, O Jehovah —
Against rivers, thy wrath;

Our language will admit of a similar construction in another form, by inverting the order —

Did thy wrath against rivers, O Jehovah,
Did it kindle against rivers?

Some connect the two last lines of the verse with the previous one, thus —
Was thine indignation against the sea,
When thou didst ride on thy horses,
On thy chariots of salvation?
But Calvin considers them rather as an answer to the previous questions, or as explanatory; and they may be thus rendered —
When thou didst ride on thy horses,
Thy chariots were those of salvation.

It is observed by Henderson, that "there is no necessity for our understanding either the angels or thunder and lightning by 'horses' and 'chariots.' They are," he adds, "merely figurative expressions, designed to carry out the metaphor adopted from military operations." Or it may be, that the horses and chariots of the Israelites are here meant, as in the 11th verse, the arrows and spears of the people are spoken of as those of God. — Ed. (p. 114)

[58] This clause has been variously explained: the interpretation here given has been mostly adopted. In the Barberinean manuscript the whole of this prayer is given in many respects different from the present received text of the Septuagint, and this clause is thus found in it — ἐχορτασας βολιδας της φαρετρας ἀυτου. It is evident that this idea falls in more with the preceding clause than any other; and the Hebrew will admit of a sense bordering on this with less alteration than any other that has been offered. No version has been given without supposing somethin to be understood. Newcome says, that sixteen MSS. read [תעובש]; by leaving out the [ו], it may be a verb in Kal in the past tense, as rendered above, and writers might have easily put down [רמא] for [רוזא]. Then the line in Hebrew would be,
[רוזא תוטם תעבש]
"Thou hast filled with arrows the girdle."

It is a description of one equipped for battle; his bow was made ready, and he had filled his girdle, that is, his military guide, with arrows; for this girdle the preceding Greek version introduced the quiver, in which arrows were commonly carried. The word [תוטם], means rods or staves, that is, of arrows, as we may take it here. This is the most satisfactory solution of the difficulties connected with this line, of which there have been, as Henderson says, more than a hundred interpretations.

The last clause of the verse is thus rendered by Newcome, —

Thou didst cleave the streams of the land;
and by Henderson, —
Thou didst cleave the earth into rivers.

The words will not admit the first version; the genitive case in Hebrew is always by juxtaposition; here "streams" and "earth" are separated by the verb. The other version contains hardly a meaning. The most literal rendering is that given by Calvin, and it affords the best sense. The words will admit of the following, which is materially the same, —
By streams didst thou cleavest the earth.

The allusion evidently to the streams of that water which miraculously issued from the smitten rock, and followed the Israelites in the wilderness. — Ed. (p. 117)

[59] Most critics have overlooked the peculiar construction of this verse; but it presents a striking instant of the order in which the Prophets often arrange their ideas. There are two things referred to — the mountains and the waters — and the first verb regards both; the nominative case being anticipated, and the first of the two last lines refers to the waters, and the last to the mountains. This is the literal version, —

They saw thee, — in pain were the mountains,
The flood of waters passed away,
Utter did the deep its voice,
The height its hands lifted up.

To construe [רוֹם] adverbially, "on high," does not so well comport with the characters of the Hebrew language; and it evidently here refers to the "mountains," as the "deep" refers to the water. — Ed. (p. 119)

[60] There is much beauty and force in this explanation: and accordant with it is the version of Henderson. But that of Newcome is somewhat different —

The sun and the moon stood still in their habitation:
By their light thine arrows went abroad;
By their brightness, the lightning of thy spear.
To avoid the insertion of so many words in italics which are not in the original, I would render the verse thus —
The sun! the moon! — it stood — she remained stationary,
For light to thine arrows which went forth,
For brightness to the flashing of thy spear.

The genitive case is often to be rendered as a dative, as in Jer 31:35, [הליל רואל], "for the light of the night;" that is, "for light to the night."

There are twelve MSS. which have "and," [ו], before "moon:" but it is not wanted, the verb "stood" being singular; and it is followed, as I conceive, by another verb in the singular number, and in the feminine gender, while "stood" is in the masculine, and refers to the moon, and the last refers to the sun; which is sometimes feminine, while moon is ever the masculine. The verb [לבז] is not properly to dwell, but to continue fixed, or to remain stationary. The order in our language would be this —
The sun remained stationary, the moon stood.
— Ed. (p. 121)

[61] However true is what is said here, it seems not to be the doctrine of this text. The version of Aquila and the Vulgate have been followed as to the second clause of the verse. The Septuagint read, του σωσαι τον χριστον σου — to save thy Christ;" or, according to Alex. cod., "thy Christs — τους χριστους σου;" or, according to Barb. MS., "thine elect — τους εκλεκτους σου." Five Hebrew MSS. have [משיחיד], "thine anointed ones." But if "people" in the preceding line; or it may refer to Joshua and his successors, the singular being used, as it is often done by the Prophets, in the collective sense. The particle [את] before it is not often used as a preposition; and the word [ישע] may better be taken here as a verb, according to the Septuagint, than as a noun, though as a verb it most commonly occurs in Hiphil: but see 1Sa 23:5; 2Sa 8:6. The following would then be the version —

Go forth didst thou to save thy people,
To save thine anointed:
Thou didst smite the head from the house of the wicked,
Emptying out the foundation even to the neck.

The reference in the two lines is evidently to the rooting out of the Canaanites, and not, as Newcome thinks, to the destruction of the firstborn in Egypt. The singular is poetically used for the plural: "head," instead of heads, or chiefs, etc. The last line seems to be a proverbial saying, signifying an entire demolition, the very foundation being dug up, though so deep as to reach up to man's neck. There is no MSS. nor version to countenance [צור], "rock," which Houbigant and Newcome adopt. — Ed. (p. 124)

[62] The Keri and many MSS. read [ופרזו], "his villages;" but there is no need of this change, for the singular is used throughout instead of the plural, until we come to the two following lines; and this proves that the singular is to be taken in a collective sense. Henderson renders it "captains," contrary to the meaning of the

word in other parts. It means an open unfortified village, as it were scattered, and without any boundaries. — Ed. (p. 125)

[63] Newcome and some others, without any authority, read "thy rod;" but conjecture, without some solid reason, cannot be allowed. — Ed. (p. 126)

[64] "To devour the poor in secret," seems to have an allusion to the practice of wild beasts, who take there prey to their dens to devour it there. The poor her, as in many other places, mean the helpless, such as are destitute of aid or power to resist their enemies. The line may be thus rendered —
Their joy was, as it were, to devour the helpless in secret.
— Ed. (p. 127)

[65] The word is [רמח], which many have rendered acervus — heap; but there is no clear instance in which it has such a meaning. It is without a preposition, and the Septuagint render it by a participle, ταρασσοντας, which agrees with "horses." It is singular in Hebrew, and, if a particple, it agrees with the nominative case to the preceding verb, [תכרד], "thou didst guide" or direct. The two lines might then be rendered thus, —

Thou didst guide through the sea thy horses,
Disturbing mighty waters.

Both Marckius and Henderson think that the passage through the Red Sea is not what is meant; but the subjugation of the Canaanites, conveyed in a language derived from that event. — Ed. (p. 127)

[66] The word [רשא], which Calvin renders ut, "that," has occasioned great trouble to critics. Marckius reads qui — "who," "Who shall rest," etc.; Henderson, "yet," "Yet I shall have rest," etc. But it is never found as an adversative. The construction of this line and the following is very difficult; and many have been the forms in which they have been rendered. The verb [נוח] means not only to rest from action or labor, but also to rest in the sense of remaining or continuing. See 2Ki 2:15, and Isa 2:2. And were it taken in this latter sense here, there would be a consistency in the whole passage. The Prophet describes first the dread which seized him on hearing the report of God's vengeance; and then in the two last lines he accounts for his consternation, because he should remain to witness this vengeance; and he proceeds in verse 17 to set forth the effects of it, and in verse 18 he states that he would still rejoice in the God of his salvation. The three verses may be thus rendered, —

16. I heard, — and tremble did my bowels;
At the voice my lips quivered;

Enter does rottenness into my bones,
And on my own account I tremble;
Because I shall remain to the day of distress,
To his coming up to the people, who shall invade me.
17. For the fig-tree shall not shoot forth,
And no produce shall be on the vines;
Fail shall the fruit of the olive,
And the fields, none shall yield food;
Cut off from the fold shall be the sheep,
And no ox shall be in the stalls:
18. But as for me, in Jehovah will I rejoice,
I will exult in the God of my salvation.

"On my own account," or for myself, [יתחת]: the preposition, [תחת], is often taken in this sense; See 2Sa 19:21, Pr 30:21. "Invade us" or assault us, or them, the people, [ונדוגי]; for [גו] is either us or him, but in our language them, for so we speak of people. "And the fields, none," etc. There are instances of [אל], as here, in which it may be rendered "none" and "nothing." See Eze 20:38, Job 6:21, Job 8:9. "In the God," etc.; it may be rendered, "In my God, my Savior," as it is in the Septuagint and the Vulgate. — Ed. (p. 129)

[67] The verb means to break forth either in buds, or germs, or shoots, and so to germinate, or to blossom. It is rendered by the Septuagint καρποφορησει, shall bear fruit. — Ed. (p. 131)

[68] No satisfactory conjectures have been made by any as to the my added to this word. Hezekiah says at the end of his prayer, Isa 38:20, [יתוניגנו זגננ], "and my neginoth will we sing," or play, etc. Our version makes this my to refer to the ode or song he made to be played on the neginoth, supposed to have been a stringed instrument. In this case, "my neginoth" means the song he made for the neginoth. Then we might render the words, —

For the leader; my song on the stringed instruments.
— Ed. (p. 134)

[69] This clause stands connected with the preceding words; "the stumblingblocks" were the idols, and they were to be taken away "along with the wicked," according to Henderson, and according to the version of Symmachus, συν ἀσεβέσι, though Newcome, with less accuracy, renders the words thus, —

And the stumblingblocks of the wicked.

The whole verse is poetical in its language; the collective singular, and not the plural, is used; and the first verb, [אסף], in its most common meaning, is very expressive, and denotes the manner of the ruin that awaited the Jews. They were "gathered" and led into captivity. The two verses may be thus literally rendered, —

2. Gatherings I will gather everything
From off the face of the land, saith Jehovah;
3. I will gather man and best;
I will gather the bird of heaven and the fish of the sea,
And the stumblingblocks together with the wicked;
And I will cut them off, together with man,
From the face of the land, saith Jehovah.
— Ed. (p. 143)

[70] The word is found in two other places, 2Ki 23:5, and Ho 10:5. In the latter text the priests of the calf of Bethaven are thus called; in the former, they are said to be those who "burnt incense in the high places." From this fact, Parkhurst concludes, that they were called scorched, as the word means, by their fumigating fires.

The "priests" mentioned here were the sacrifices, while the "Camerim" were the incense-burners. There were "altars" (not an altar) reared for Baal in the temple; one, as it seems, for sacrifices, and the other for incense. See 2Ki 21:3. In 2 Chr. 34:4, 5, the priests and sacrificers are alone mentioned; but in 2Ki 23:5, where the same things are recorded, the Camerim and incense are alone named. The Prophet in this passage mentions both.

Some, as Cocceius and Henderson, have been disposed to think that the unfaithful priests of the true God are here meant. But the other view is more consistent with the whole passage. If we retain not the original word, we may thus render the line, —

The name of the incense-burners with the priests;

That is, those who burnt incense and those who offered sacrifices to Baal. — Ed. (p. 146)

[71] It appears that this idol had two names, Moloc and Milcom, or Molcam. It is called Moloc, or Molec, in Le 20:5, and in seven other places; but Milcom in 1 Kings 11:5, 33; 2Ki 23:14; as well as here, and also in Jer. 49:1, 3, though improperly rendered in our version, "their king." The Ammonites are the people spoken of.

The swearing is here differently expressed: it is to [(ל)] Jehovah; and by [(ב)] Milcam. To swear to, is to make a promise to another by an oath, or, in this instance, to swear allegiance to God: but to swear by, is to appeal to another as witness to an engagement. We have the two forms together in Jos 9:19. The Jews made a solemn profession of obedience to God, and yet they acknowledged Melcam as God, by appealing to him as a witness to the truth. It is called the abomination of the Ammonites, 1Ki 11:33

The image of this god, according to the Rabbins, was hollow, made of brass, and had seven compartments. In the first, they put flour — in the second, turtles — in the third, an ewe — in the fourth, a ram — in the fifth, a calf — in the sixth, an ox — and in the seventh, a child! All these were burnt together by heating the image in the inside! To drown the cries and noises that might be made, they used drums and other instruments. See [רלמ] in Parkhurst. How cruel is superstition! and yet how wedded to it is man by nature! Though the Jews had knowledge of the religion of him who is the God of love and mercy; yet they preferred the religion of savages and barbarians. How strongly does this fact prove man's natural antipathy to God! — Ed. (p. 151)

[72] Calvin has omitted to notice the last words in the verse, "Nor enquire of him;" which Henderson, adopting a modern phraseology, has rendered, "nor apply to him." The reading ought to be, as many MSS. have it, [והושרד]. The verb means to enquire of, to consult, and also to regard or to care for. They did not enquire of God as to his will, or they did not show any regard for him. See Genesis 25: 22; Eze 20:1; and also De 11:12; Job 3:4. To seek the Lord is to seek his favor and communion with him; to enquire of the Lord is to seek the knowledge of his will in any difficulty. — Ed. (p. 153)

[73] The word is [הט], and is evidently an interjection enjoining silence, Hush! or, Silence!

7. Silence at the presence of the Lord Jehovah!
For nigh is the day of Jehovah,
For prepared hath Jehovah a sacrifice,
Selected hath he his guests!

The passage is remarkably forcible and striking. Jehovah was coming, and everything was prepared, and all were to be silent. And then follows what is no less striking and expressive, —

8. And it shall be in the day of Jehovah's sacrifice,
That I will visit the princes and the king's sons,
And all who wear foreign apparel.
9. I will also visit, in that day,
Every one who leaps on the threshold,

Who fill the house of their master
By plunder and by fraud.

There is in the last line a metonymy; the act is put for what was acquired by it: they filled the house of their master by spoils gained by plunder or violence, and by fraud or cheating. — Ed. (p. 155)

[74] The first idea of the verb [שדק], is evidently to set apart, to separate either men or things for a certain purpose. For this meaning Parkhurst refers to Le 20:24, compared with version 26, and to Deut. 19:2, 7, compared with Jos 20:7. This idea seems the most suitable here, "I have set apart (or selected) my guests." Newcome renders it "appointed," and Henderson, "consecrated," as Calvin does. "Segregavit — set apart," is the version of Drusius, and Junius has "preparavit — prepared." When the verb is followed by "war," it is rendered "prepare" in our version. See Jer 6:4; Joe 3:9; Mic 3:5. The explanation given by Theodosius is ἀφώρισε — he separated or selected. — Ed. (p. 157)

[75] This was a prophecy: though the king Josiah had no children at this time, yet he had some afterwards; and they proved themselves deserving of the judgment here announced, and it was inflicted on them. Henderson's objection, that as Josiah had then no children, the prophecy could not apply to them personally, seems wholly inadmissable: it was a prophecy. — Ed. (p. 157)

[76] Or, literally, "the garment of a foreigner or stranger," [ירכנ]. The singular is used poetically for the plural, instead of "the garments of foreigners." — Ed. (p. 157)

[77] Marckius, following the Septuagint, and some of the fathers, Cyril, Theodoret, Jerome, etc., think that the thoughless intruders into the temple are here meant, and such as brought there as sacrifices and gifts the fruits of plunder and fraud. But the passage cannot possibly bear this meaning according to the Hebrew text: nor is such a meaning consistent with the context. The view given here is that of Kimki, Drusius, Newcome, and Henderson. — Ed. (p. 159)

[78] Junius, Piscator, Newcome, and Henderson think that it means the second city, a part of Jerusalem, being so called, as they supposed, in Ne 11:9: where our version is considered to be wrong, and the clause ought to be, "and Judah, the son of Jeruiah, was over the second city" — [ריעה-לע הנשמ]. So it is deemed improperly rendered "college" in 2Ki 22:14 and 2Ch 34:22; where it ought to be "in the second city." But the passage in Nehemiah is not decisive on the subject; and our version is countenanced by the former part of the verse, where "Joel" is said to be the "overseer," and "Judah" is mentioned as being next to him, the second in office: and it is so rendered in the Septuagint. As to the other text, the word is by itself as

here. What Calvin, after Cyril and Theodoret, suggests, is the most probable solution.

The word rendered by Calvin "contritio — breach," and by Henderson, "destruction," is [רבש]. As "crying" and "howling" are said to proceed from the other parts, so something similar must have proceeded from "the hills." The word means breaking, and it is often applied to the heart — "a broken heart," Ps. 34:18, Ps. 51:19, etc. It seems to mean here the breaking out into weeping and wailing. The parallelism of the verse would thus be complete —
And there shall be in that day, saith Jehovah,
The voice of crying from the fish-gate,
And howling from the second gate,
And great wailing from the hills.

Wailing is the breaking out of anguish and pangs. The word is used in Eze 21:6, for acute pain in the loins, and may be considered as used here metonymically. — Ed. (p. 161)

[79] This original meaning of the word is much more probable than what lexicographers generally give. The braying or pounding is evidently derived from the noun, and the noun from the form of the mortar. Most agree that the word here means the lower part of the city — the hollow, from the circumstance of being surrounded by hills. The "hills" were those on which a part of the city was built, such as Zion, Moriah and Ophal. — Ed. (p. 161)

[80] This opinion has been entertained, because the Jews are so called in Ho 12:8. That the word means a trader or merchant is evident from Job 41:6, (in the Hebrew Bibles, 40:30;) Isa 23:8; Eze 17:4. In the last passage it is rendered "traffic" in our version; and it may be so rendered here — "all the people of traffic," or of trade. The version of Newcome is, "all the trafficking people." The verse may be thus literally rendered, —
Howl ye, the inhabitants of the lower part,
For reduced to silence have been all the people of trade,
Cut off have been all the laden with silver.

They are called to howl, as though their calamity had already taken place, a mode of speaking often used by the Prophets. That the event was future is clear from the context, especially from the next verse. "Reduced to silence" — [המדן], is literally the meaning, not "destroyed;" and appropriate is the term, as people of trade create much bustle and noise. "The laden with silver," may be rendered, as Newcome does, "the bearers of silver:" and silver is here for money. — Ed. (p. 162)

[81] There is a similar meaning in Jer 48:11; but the verb is different, [טקש], which means to be still, to rest, to settle, while the verb here is [אפק], which signifies to be condensed, or to be congealed, Ex 15:8. But as things congelaed become fixed, the verb seems to have the meaning of fixedness here; as wines on the lees, to which allusion is made, do not become congealed, the comparison seems to be, that as wine kept still on the lees increases in strength and flavor so the Jews, settling on their dregs — their sins — became strengthened and confirmed in their wickedness and atheistic notions. But Newcome and Henderson take another view of the metaphor, and consider that "the thoughtless tranquillity of the rich is compared to the fixed unbroken surface of fermented liquors." Our version favors the former idea, as the verb is rendered "settled." — Ed. (p. 163)

[82] The Rabbinical punctuation has destroyed the simplicity of this passage by connecting "bitter" with the latter clause. Jerome, Pagninus, Newcome, as well as the Septuagint, connect it with the former clause. The literal rendering of the two lines is as follows —
The voice of the day of Jehovah shall be grievous;
Roar out there (or then) shall the brave.

"The voice of the day," etc., means the voice uttered on that day, as Drusius explains it. [רמ] is no doubt "bitter;" but it is often applied in scripture to express what is grievous, afflictive, or sorrowful. If we render [שט], "there," it refers to Jerusalem, verse 12; but it is sometimes used as an adverb of time, "then," see Ps 14:5; Ne 3:15. "The meaning is," says Drusius, "that the voice of that day, which they who excel in strength of mind and body shall utter, shall be bitter." The whole verse is remarkably concise and emphatical, —

14. Nigh is the great day of Jehovah,
Nigh and hastening quickly:
The voice of the day of Jehovah shall be grievous;
Roar out then shall the brave.

Then the following verse is not to begin, as in our version, which as been followed by Newcome and Henderson, "That day is a day of wrath," but thus —
A day of wrath shall be that day.

This is the order of the original, and as there is no verb, it must be supplied and regulated as to its tense by the context. — Ed. (p. 168)

[83] The original words are similar in sound and meaning; the first, [הרצ], comes from a verb which means to inclose, to confine, to straiten, and it may be rendered, narrowness, confinement, straitness, distress. The other, [הקוצמ], is oppression, as the verb means to press down, to press close. (p. 170)

[84] Waste or confusion is, [האש, האושמ], derived from the same root, may be rendered desolation. The two next words, "darkness" and "thick darkness," occur in Joe 2:2. In the same passage we have also "the day of cloudiness and of entire darkness," literally, bare or naked darkness; for the word is, [לפרע], derived, as I conceive, from [רע], bare, and [לפא], thick darkness. There is a gradation in the words used in each line; the second word is stronger than the first. — Ed. (p. 170)

[85] Rather "acclamation," the triumphant voice of conquerors. As an attempt to preserve the distinctive character of each word in this singular passage, I offer the following version —

15. A day of extreme wrath shall be that day,
A day of distress and oppression,
A day of waste and of desolation,
A day of darkness and of thick darkness,
A day of cloudiness and of entire darkness;
16. A day of the trumpet and of acclamation
Over the cities that are inclosed,
And over the towers which are lofty.

The word [הרבע], "extreme wrath," means such wrath as passes over all bounds — overflowing wrath. We are obliged to use the word darkness three times for lack of suitable terms. The first is the common darkness of the night, the second is a grosser darkness, and the third is complete darkness. The words "gloominess" and "obscurity," used by Newcome and Henderson, are not sufficiently strong, and convey not the meaning. — Ed. (p. 170)

[86] The Hebrew words are literally,
For against Jehovah have they sinned.
— Ed. (p. 171)

[87] "Copiously and in contempt," says Marckius; "as a thing of no value," says Grotius; "as worthless as dust," says Drusius. The comparison is evidently intended to show that their blood, or their life, would be treated with contempt, and no more regarded than dust. — Ed. (p. 172)

[88] The word is [טחל], usually rendered food; here it means what is fed, the carcass, the body. It is rendered "flesh" by the Septuagint. — Ed. (p. 172)

[89] Quickness rather than terror is what is evidently meant. See version 14. Most agree in this respect. Newcome renders it "speedy," and Henderson "sudden." The word "riddance," for [הלכ], in our version, is improper. It is rendered "full end" by

Newcome, and "consummation" by Henderson, and "συντέλειαν — end" by the Septuagint. The particle [אך] does not mean "altogether," as rendered by Henderson, but it is an asseveration — surely, indeed, certainly, doubtless. The [את] before "inhabitants" has evidently here the meaning of κατα, with regard to. It is rendered επι, upon, in the Septuagint, and "with" by Marckius and Newcome. The whole verse is as follows, —

18. Neither their silver nor their gold
Shall be able to deliver them
In the day of the extreme-wrath of Jehovah;
By the fire of his jealousy
Shall be consumed the whole land;
For an end, doubtless sudden, will he make,
As to all the inhabitants of the land. (p. 173)

[90] The verb, found only in five other places — Exod. 5:7, 12; Num. 15:32, 33; and 1 Kings 17:10, 12, means to collect, to gather, and not "to search," as said by Kimchi, and adopted by Marckius; nor "to bind," as rendered by Henderson. The import of the passage is considered by all to be an invitation to repentance, though the words are differently rendered. It is difficult to see the meaning when it is said — "Gather yourselves, yea, gather," etc, except such an assembly is meant as is recommended by Joe 1:14; the kind of gathering being well understood, it is not mentioned. "Gather yourselves," that is, to offer prayers, says Grotius. "Be ye assembled — συνάχθητε," is the rendering of the Septuagint. — Ed. (p. 175)

[91] [כסף] is found as a verb in four other places, Ge 31:30; Job 14:15; Ps 17:12; and Ps 84:3. It means to be or to grow pale, either through love, as in Genesis and Job, or through hunger, as in the first Psalm referred to, or through longing for God's house, as in the last, or through shame, as some — such as Grotius, Dathius, and Gesenius, suppose to be the case here; and they therefore give this rendering — "O nation without shame;" or, "not ashamed." This idea is favored by the Septuagint — "unteachable — ἀπαίδευτον." In no instance is it found in a passive sense as to the feeling through which the paleness is occasioned, and therefore "worthy of love," or "desired," cannot be its proper rendering. Buxtorf give its meaning in Niphal — "desiderio affici — to be touched with or to feel a desire." Hence the person spoken of is the subject, not the object, of the desire. According, then, to the use of the verb, the rendering here is to be — "Ye nation that feels no desire," that is, for God and his law, or, "that feels no shame," that is, for its sins. The paraphrase of the Targum is — "not willing to be converted to the law," which corresponds with the idea which has been stated.

Marckius considers that the nation is here described as having "no desire," that is for that which was good, and that its torpidity and indifference as to religion is what is set forth. And such is the view of Cocceius; it had no thirst for righteousness, no desire for the kingdom of God — the mark of an unregenerated mind. — Ed. (p. 176)

[92] It is difficult to make the words bear this sense. Hardly a sentence has been more variously rendered. The most satisfactory solution perhaps is to regard it parenthetic, and to consider "the day" as that allowed for repentance: it was to pass away quickly, like the chaff carried away by the wind —
As the chaff passing away will be the day:

Both Marckius and Henderson regard this as the meaning. Then the whole verse might be thus translated —

2. Before the bringing forth of the decree,
(As the chaff passing away will be the day,)
Before it shall come upon you,
The burning of Jehovah's anger;
Before it shall come upon you,
The day of the anger of Jehovah.

Literally it is, "Before it shall not come," etc., or, "During the time when it shall not come," etc. [בטרם] may be rendered "while;" then the version would be —

While it shall not come upon you,
The burning of Jehovah's anger;
While it shall not come upon you,
The day of the anger of Jehovah.

There are several MSS. which omit the two first lines; but evidently without reason. They are retained in the Septuagint.

Possibly the second line may refer to the speedy execution of "the decree," that its day would pass quickly. Its birth, or its bringing forth was its commencement; and the second line may express its speedy execution: it would be carried into effect with the quickness by which the chaff is carried away by the wind —

As the chaff passing away will be its day.

The word [עבר] is, in either case, a participle, and the auxiliary verb is understood, as often is the case in Hebrew, and must partake of the tense of the context. — Ed. (p. 176)

[93] Newcome renders the adjective "lowly," and the noun "lowliness;" but Marckius and Henderson render the first "humble," as the Septuagint do — ταπεινοι, and the second "humility." They were those who had been made humble by affliction. The design of affliction is to make us humble, submissive to God's will; and this is the effect of sanctified affliction. It is somewhat singular that the verb means to afflict and to be humble, as though affliction were needful to render us humble. The word [תונע], occurs in 2Sa 22:36, and Ps 18:35, and is rendered "gentleness" in our common version, but more correctly in our Prayer-book version "loving correction." Perhaps the best rendering would be "humbling affliction;" and the idea of humbling affliction making great is very striking. The word used by the Septuagint is παιδεια — discipline; and the Vulgate is the same. — Ed. (p. 178)

[94] The idea is not "protected," as given by Newcome, but "secreted" or concealed as in a hiding-place. "Hid" is the version of Henderson, and also of Marckius. — Ed. (p. 181)

[95] This verse, literally rendered, retains more of its poetic character, —

4. For Gaza, forsaken shall she be,
And Ashkelon shall be a desolation;
Ashdod, at mid-day shall they drive it out,
And Ekron shall be rooted up.
In the first and the last line there is a correspondence in the sound of the words.

The following presents another instance of the nominative case absolute, —

5. Woe to the dwellers of the line of the sea,
The nation of the Kerethites!
The word of Jehovah is against you:
Canaan, the land of the Philistines,
I will even destroy thee, that there shall be no inhabitant.

The line of the sea, meaning the coast along the shore, is so called, says Henderson, "from the custom of using a cord or line in measuring off or dividing a territory."

Some derive "Kerethites" from [כרת], to cut off, to destroy; and so they were cutters off or destroyers. They were celebrated men of war in the time of David, 2Sa 8:18. "Philistines" mean emigrants, says Henderson; the word being derived from a verb, which signifies, in the Ethiopic language, to rove, to migrate. — Ed. (p. 183)

[96] The words, [םיער תרכ תונ], are rendered by Calvin, "habitaculum caulis pastorum — an habitation (or a dwelling) for the sheepcots of shepherds." The Targum takes the two first words in the singular number; the second is evidently so, and the first may be so also: and [תרכ] certainly does not mean sheepcots, but digging, from [הרכ], to dig. The reference is either to the pits dug for watering the flock, as Piscator thinks, o rto the subterraneous huts, or caves, dug for the purpose of shelter, as Drusius and Bochart suppose. Junius and Tremelius render the words, "sheepcots, the delvings of shepherds;" and Drusius, "dwellings of the digging out of shepherds," i.e., dwellings dug out by shepherds. The most literal and the easiest construction is, "dwellings, the digging of shepherds." Then the verse might be thus rendered, —

And the line of the sea shall be dwellings,
Dug out by shepherds, and folds for sheep.

Parkhurst quotes Harmer, who says, "the Eastern shepherds make use of caves very frequently, sleeping in them and driving their flocks into them at night. The mountains bordering on the Syrian coast are remarkable for the number of caves, and are found particularly in the neighborhood of Ashkelon." How fully then was this prophecy fulfilled. — Ed. (p. 185)

[97] That is, the reproach cast by Moab, and the revilings uttered by Ammon. — Ed. (p. 187)

[98] There is a difference as to the meaning of the last line. Newcome adopts our common version, —

And magnified themselves against their border
Henderson's rendering is essentially the same —
And carried themselves haughtily against their border.

The verb [לדנ] is transitive and intransitive in Kal — to make great and to be great; it seems to partake of a similar character in Hiphil, as it is found here, to magnify, and to grow great or proud, and hence to exult or to triumph; and when followed by [לע], as here, to exult over a person or a country, — see Job 19:5; Ps. 35:26, Ps. 38:17; Eze 35:13. In these verses "to exult over" would be the best rendering; as also in 10th verse of this chapter. The idea of enlarging or extending over, as adopted by Jerome and Dathius, as well as by Calvin, is not countenanced by any other passage. The best rendering here is —

And exulted over their border.

This line corresponds with the revilings of Ammon, as the preceding does with the reproach of Moab. That it was the triumphant and exulting language of Ammon is evident, because it was what was heard — "I have heard," etc. The particle [רשא], rendered here "quibus — by which," and "wherewith" by Newcome, is rendered "who" by Marckius and Henderson — "who have reproached on my people;" and this is the most natural construction. Some have rendered it "because." — Ed. (p. 188)

[99] This clause is rendered differently by some. The word [קשממ] occurs only here. It is rendered by the Targum by a word which means a "deserted place," and so Newcome renders it, "A deserted place for the thorn:" so also do Drusius, Grotius, Piscator, and Marckius. The Septuagint have mistaken the word for "Damascus," and give a version of the whole clause wholly foreign to the context. Henderson thinks that the word has the same meaning with [רשמ], to draw out, to extend, and gives this version, "A region of overrunning brambles." This is far-fetched. The word, [לורח], rendered "nettle" by Calvin, Grotius, and others, cannot be so taken, according to Drusius and Bochart, for in Job 30:7, men are said to gather under it. It is found besides only in Pr 24:31. It may be rendered either a thorn or a bramble. The other part of the sentence is literally "a digging place for salt."
Moab was to be like Sodom, and Ammon like Gommorah, not as to the manner of their ruin, but as to the extent of it. It was to be an entire overthrow. Their habitation was not to become a pool of water like Sodom and Gommorah, but a place where the bramble was to grow, and salt might be dug. And it was to be "a desolation," [םלוע-דע], "for ages;" for the word means an indefinite time. So Drusius regards it here as meaning a long time. But some consider the "desolation," as having reference to the people and not to the place. If so, the rendering were wholly obliterated. Moab and Ammon, as a separate people, are altogether extinct. The whole verse is as follows —

9. Therefore, as I live,
Saith Jehovah of hosts, the God of Israel,
Surely Moab like Sodom shall be,
And the children of Ammon like Gomorrah,
The desert of the thorn and the excavation of salt,
Yea, a desolation for ages;
The remnant of my people shall plunder them,
And the residue of my nation shall possess them.

The two last lines refer to the children of Ammon, as the two preceding especially to Moab. The country of Moab was on the eastern side of the Dead Sea, and that of Ammon was north-east, of Moab. Both were subdued and led captive by Nebuchadnezzar about four or six years after the captivity of Judah. They were afterwards partially restored, especially the children of Ammon, as Tobiah was their chief in the time of Nehemiah. Ne 4:3. They were "plundered," as recorded in 1 Macc. 5:35, 51, by Judas Maccabeus. Of Moab we read nothing at that time: but it appears, that for ages it has been desolate. "Not one," says Burckhart, the traveler, "of the ancient cities of Moab exists as tenanted by man," and he speaks of "their entire desolation." Another modern traveler, Seetzen, a Russian, speaking of Ammon, says, "All this country, formerly so populous, is now changed into a vast desert." — Ed. (p. 189)

[100] The word, [ארון], is rendered "to be feared," by Cocceius and Henderson, and [מהילע], "above them," that is, "the gods of the earth," mentioned in the next line; it being considered an instance of a pronoun preceding its noun. But this is forced; and it is not necessary. Moab and Ammon are evidently referred to; and what is said is, that God would be terrible to them, as well as to others, for he would famish or destroy all the gods of the earth. And then in the next verse he mentions other nations. Some extend what is here said to gospel-times; but there seems no reason for this, inasmuch as God's judgment is the subject of the Prophet. — Ed. (p. 191)

[101] Literally —
And bow down to him, every one from his place,
Shall all the islands of the nations. (p. 191)

[102] By the earth the Jews understood the great continent of all Asia and Africa, to which they had acces by land; and by the isles of the sea they understood the places to which they sailed by sea, particularly all Europe. Sir I. Newton on Daniel, p. 276." — Newcome. (p. 191)

[103] Newcome cuts the knot, here by an emendation, by [מתא], ye, for [המה], they; and Houbigant, by [ויהת], ye shall be, — "the wounded of my sword shall ye be." This is according to the Septuagint; but the former is more in accordance with the Hebrew idiom; for the pronoun is often used without the auxiliary verb. Some take [המה] as ipsi in Latin, connected with vos, ye yourselves. Then the rendering would be —

Also ye Cushites,
The slain of my sword shall ye yourselves be.
But what Calvin says is not uncommon in the Prophet, the abrupt change of persons. — Ed. (p. 192)

[104] It is literally, "every wild beast of the nation," — [ווי], — "of the land," in the Septuagint. What is meant is, every wild beast that beloned to that country. — Ed. (p. 194)

[105] Both Newcome and Henderson render the two words, "the pelican and the porcupine." The former says that [תאק], "pelican," comes from [האק], to vomit, because it casts up fish or water from its membranaceous bag; and [דפק], "porcupine," according to Bochart, is from the verb, which means to cut off as by a bite, or rather, he says, from its Syriac meaning, to dread, for it is a solitary animal. See Newcome. But Parkhurst contends that it is the hedgehog, and both the Septuagint and Vulgate render it so.

What Calvin translates "in postibus ejus," [היותפכב], is rendered by Newcome, "in the carved lintels thereof," by Henderson, "in her capitals," and by Parkhurst, "in her door-porches," i.e. when thrown down. — Ed. (p. 194)

[106] The first word, [הארומ], is rendered "rebellions" by Newcome and Henderson. The Vulgate is nearly the same, "provocatrix — provoking." The verb is [ארמ], once in Hiphil in Job 39:8; and to take it to be the same with [הרמ], to rebel, is gratuitous. The context in Job shows its idea to be that of raising up or swelling; and Parkhurst very properly renders the participle here, swelling, arrogant, insolent; and this notion entirely corresponds with the character given of the city in the next verse; being arrogant, it did "not hear the voice" of God. The verse may be rendered thus —

Woe to the arrogant and polluted,
The city, which is an oppressor!
Then follows a specification as to her conduct, —
She has not hearkened to the voice,
She has not received instruction;
In Jehovah has she not trusted,
To her God has she not drawn nigh.

To "obey the voice," as given in our version and by Newcome, is not quite correct; she was too arrogant even to hear or attend to the voice. "Correction," as in our version, and by Calvin, is rendered "instruction" by Newcome and Henderson; for [רסומ] has often this meaning. The Septuagint have παιδαιαν — discipline. But the same phrase occurs in verse 7, where the word necessarily means instruction, by way of warning, communicated by the example of others. — Ed. (p. 200)

[107] This is the explanation of Grotius, Mede, and Henderson. The latter's version is — "They gnaw no bones in the morning;" i.e., all is devoured in the night. Newcome, adopting the conjecture of Houbigant, supposes the true reading to be [ומדי], and gives this rendering — "They wait not until the morning," which seems to have no meaning in this connection. What Cocceius proposes is more probable — "Who have not gnawed in the morning;" and on this account they were exceedingly voracious in the evening. But the idea of our common version is very

appropriate; it implies that they were like wild beasts prowling all night, and carrying as it were their prey to their dens, that they might devour it there in the morning. This is the view taken by Henry. "They devour the flesh," says Adam Clarke, "in the night, and gnaw the bones, and extract the marrow afterwards." — Ed. (p. 204)

[108] Her prophets are light, they are treacherous men. — Newcome.
Her prophets are vainglorious, hypocritical men. — Henderson.

The word rendered "light," as a river, and not "unstable," as in our version. It is applied as a participle in Jud 9:4, to designate persons overflowing in wickedness, dissolute, licentious, dissipated; and as a noun in Jer 23:32, to set forth the licentious conduct of the false prophets, who like the priests under the Papacy, were given to lasciviousness, and "committed adultery with their neighbors' wives," Jer 29:23. See also Jer 23:14. As Zephaniah was cotemporary with Jeremiah, his description of the Prophets is thus seen to be the same, "Her Prophets are licentious," or lascivious.

Men of dissimulations or deceits, [תודגב ישנא], signify, that under the pretense of telling the truth, they delivered what was false; or in the words of Jeremiah, they "caused the people to err by their lies," while they pretended to deliver true messages from God: so that Jer 23:32, contains an explanation of this clause. "Deceiving men" would perhaps be the best rendering. Though they were licentious, yet they deceived men, and made them to believe that they were true Prophets. They were impostors, and notwithstanding their immoral character, they persuaded deluded men that they were true and faithful. — Ed. (p. 205)

[109] The word, [שדק], as Calvin intimates, does not specifically mean the sanctuary, but holiness, or, as Henderson renders it, "what is sacred," or holy. Both our version and Newcome improperly render it "the sanctuary." The explanation of what is meant may be found in Eze 12:26. The word for sanctuary is [שדקמ]. See Ezek. 23:38, 39

The words, [הרות וסמח], have been taken to mean, — either, "They violated the law," as the words are rendered in Eze 12:26, that is, transgressed it by acting contrary to it; or, "They perverted the law," forcing it, as it were, out of its plain meaning by subtle glosses. The Septuagint render the verb ηθετησαν — set aside or abolished, in Ezekiel, and here άσεβουσι — act impiously. "Trangressed," says Grotius; "Do violence to," say Piscator and Drusius, that is, by wresting its words. It occurs much oftener as a noun than as a verb, and it commonly means a wrong or injustice done in an outrageous and violent manner. According to this general idea, we may render the phrase here, "they have outraged the law," either by their conduct, or by their comments. It was in either case a wrong done to the law, that was enormous, passing all reason and decency. So that to transgress or to violate, or to do violence to, or to pervert the law, does not convey the full meaning. — Ed. (p. 206)

[110] The verbs here are in the future tense, but evidently express, as Calvin observes, a continued act. The same is exactly the case in Welsh; the verbs are in the future tense, but are understood as expressing a present act or a continued act, or what is continually or habitually done. In English the present must be adopted —

The righteous Jehovah is in the midst of her,
He doeth no injustice:
Every morning his judgment
He bringeth to light — it fails not;
Yet the unjust knoweth no shame.

"Injustice" in the second, and "unjust" in the fifth line, come from the same root. "Judgment" here is what God judges and determines to be right and just; and it is set forth here as the sun rising every day from morning to morning, and as never failing to appear. — Ed. (p. 210)

[111] This verse, literally rendered, is as follows, —
I have cut off nations;
Desolate are become their towers;
I have made solitary their streets, without a passenger;
Deserted are become their cities,
Without a man, without an inhabitant.

It is not the destruction. The nations being cut off, then the towers became desolate, the streets empty, and the cities forsaken. The last line but one is literally — "Hunted have been their cities," so that no man was left behind. — Ed. (p. 211)

[112] The last clause has been variously rendered. There is no assistance from the Septuagint, as the whole text is very different. Marckius, after Drusius, connects it, not with the preceding, but with the following line, in this sense, that how much soever God had punished the city, yet its inhabitants were the more best to corrupt their ways. But the words can hardly admit of this meaning. Henderson supposes [כ] to be understood before [לל], and gives this rendering of the two lines —

That her habitation might not be cut off,
According to all that I had appointed concerning her.
Newcome differs as to the last line —

After all the punishment with which I had visited her.

None of these are satisfactory. Grotius, taking the sense of the Targum, means to have given the best meaning. He says that [דקפ], followed by [לע], means sometimes to appoint or constitute, and refers to 2Ch 36:23, "All the good which I have appointed to her," or promised; but he unnecessarily supposes "shall come" to be understood; for the word, "all which," may be considered to be in apposition with "habitation." I give the following version of this whole verse —

I said, "Surely thou wilt fear me,
Thou wilt receive instruction;"
Then cut off should not be her habitation —
All that I have committed to her:
Yet they rose up early, they corrupted all their doings.

To rise up early is a Hebrew phrase, which means a resolved and diligent attention to a thing. The import of the line is, that they with full-bent purpose and activity corrupted all their doings. — Ed. (p. 214)

[113] This verse is considered by Newcome and Henderson to be addressed to the godly, to encourage them at the approaching calamities, while Piscator, Grotius, Marckius, and Dathius, agree with Calvin that it is an awful warning to the wicked Jews, spoken of in the preceding verse. Differing somewhat from Calvin, they regard the "nations" and "kingdoms" to be the Babylonians, who were composed of various nations and kingdoms, and "upon them" to be the Jews, and "the whole land" to be that of Judea. This view, no doubt, is the most consistent with the context. The objection made by Henderson, that the words expect, or wait for me, are ever used in a good sense, seems to have no force, for these words by themselves can mean neither what is good nor what is bad, the whole depends on the context. The verb [הכח] simply means to tarry, to wait — μενειν. The word "therefore" seems to connect this with the preceding verse, and there is nothing in the foregoing part of the chapter that alludes to the godly. Besides, the words which follow "wait for me" explain them, as will be seen by the following literal rendering of the whole verse —

8. Therefore wait for me, saith Jehovah,
For the day of my rising to the prey!
For my purpose is to gather nations,
To assemble kingdoms,
In order to pour on them my indignation,
All the heat of my anger;
For by the fire of my jealousy
Shall be consumed the whole land.

The "fire of God's jealousy" sufficiently proves that what is meant is the land of Judea. (See chapter 1:18.) — Ed. (p. 216)

[114] [כי אז], "For then," Henderson; "Surely then," Newcome; "Postea vero — but afterwards," Dathius and Grotius. And Newcome says, that [אז] is used here largely, for "afterwards." It refers to the time after the execution of the judgments previously mentioned.

"The pure lip" is evidently not the language which God would adopt in addressing the nations, but the language they would adopt in addressing him. What is meant is a pure heart; what gives utterance to the heart is mentioned for the heart itself; as the "shoulder" is afterwards used for the service that is rendered to God.

The verb [הפך], to turn, means to change the form, condition, or course of a thing, conveying perhaps here the idea, that the pure lip is substituted for that which is impure: "I will give them as a change, instead of what they have, a pure lip." Μεταστρεψω — "I will change," Sept. and Sym.; στρεψω — "I will turn," Aq. and Theod. It is rendered "reddam" and "restituam" by Drusius and Grotius

Newcome, following the conjecture of Houbigant, reads [רפשא], "I will pour out," contrary to all the ancient versions, and without the countenance of a single MS.

Though the word, [עמים], peoples, most frequently means the nations, yet there are instances in which it means the people of Israel, inasmuch as they were composed of various tribes. See 1Ki 22:28; Joe 2:6. And if we render the verb, "restore," with Drusius and Grotius, then we must adopt this meaning. Eleven MSS. have "and," [ו], before the verb to "serve:" and as there is no preposition before "shoulder," we may render the verse —

But I will then restore to the people a pure lip,
That they may, all of them, call on the name of Jehovah, —
And one shoulder, that they may serve him.
— Ed. (p. 217)

[115] The expression "with one shoulder" is rendered by the Septuagint, "under one yoke" — ὑπὸ ζυγὸν ἕνα. The idea is that of oxen drawing together. To serve God under one yoke, is to do the same service unitedly. "A metaphor," says Newcome, "from the joint efforts of yoked beasts." — Ed. (p. 218)

[116] It is more consonant with the style of the Prophets to render the clauses apart, as Calvin does, than as it is done in our version, and by Newcome and Henderson. The auxiliary verb, as is often the case, is to be understood in the first clause, —

From beyond the rivers of Cush shall be my suppliants;
The daughter of my dispersed shall bring my offering. (p. 220)

[117] This may be rendered, "Those who exult in thy exaltation:" the Targum has it, "in thy glory." This "glory" or "exaltation," as explained in the next verse, was Mount Sion. There was a preeminence, but it was made an object of unholy boasting. The paraphrase of Henderson, "thy proud exulters," completely leaves out the character of their exultation. The whole verse may be thus rendered, —

In that day thou shalt not be ashamed of thy doings,
By which thou hast transgressed against me;
For then will I remove from the midst of thee
Those who exult in thy exaltation;
And thou shalt no more be elevated
On account of the mount of my holiness.

The word [גאות] means exaltation or glory in a good as well as in a bad sense. See Ps 93:1; Isa 12:5. What they exulted in was in itself good, but they exulted only in an outward privilege, without connecting it with God, as many have done in all ages. This is the essence of Pharisaism. Vatables and Drusius regard the word as having this sense here. — Ed. (p. 224)

[118] The first word, [עני], means one made humble by distress or affliction, the humbled, rather than the humble. The second word, [דל], is one exhausted, or reduced in number, or reduced to poverty. Newcome renders it "lowly," but improperly. Jerome has "pauperem et egenum — poor and needy;" the Septuagint, "πραυν και ταπεινον — meek and humble;" Marckius, "afflictum et attenuatum — afflicted and diminished." Perhaps the best rendering would be, "a people humbled and reduced." The idea of being "afflicted" or distressed, is excluded by what is expressed at the end of the next verse, and also that of being "poor" in a worldly respect. The reference seems to be to a humbled state of mind, occasioned by calamities, and to a reduced number — a remnant.

"I will leave" for [יתראשה], as in our version, is not its full meaning. It means to reserve as a remnant. "I will cause to remain," or, "I will reserve," would be the proper rendering. — Ed. (p. 226)

[119] To give the words their specific meaning, they may be thus rendered, —
Cry aloud thou daughter of Zion,
Shout ye Israel;
Rejoice and exult with all thine heart,
Thou daughter of Jerusalem.

The first two lines encourage the fullest expression of feelings, loud crying, and shouting like a trumpet; and then is set forth the character of these feelings; they were to be those of job and exultation. Our version, Newcome and Henderson, render the second line correctly, but not the first; and "Be glad and rejoice" are too feeble to express what the third line contains: for the exhortation is to "rejoice" and to "exult." It was to be the loud cry of joy, and the shouting of exultation or triumph. — Ed. (p. 230)

[120] Turned aside hath Jehovah thy judgments. — Ed. (p. 231)

[121] The words are, [רְבִיא הנפ], "he hath turned away thine enemy." Many copies have [רְיבִיא], "thine enemies;" but it may be regarded as the poetical singular. — Ed. (p. 231)

[122] This is a very remarkable passage. Perhaps the more literal version would be the following, —

16. In that day he will say to Jerusalem, "Fear thou not;
Sion! relaxed let not thy hands be:
17. He will rejoice over thee with joy;
He will renew thee in his love,
He will exult over thee with acclamation."

The verb [רמאי] is rendered as above by the Septuagint, ερει, meaning the Lord. The last line but one is according to the Septuagint and the Syriac; and this sense has been adopted by Houbigant, Dathius, and Newcome. There is the difference only of one letter, [ד] for [ר], which are very like. The law of parallelism is in favor of this meaning. The verse contains four lines: there is an evident correspondence of meaning in the second and the last line; and so there is between the first and the third according to the preceding version, but not otherwise. The word rendered "acclamation" is a noun from the verb [הכר], to cry aloud, used at the beginning of verse 14. — Ed. (p. 234)

[123] This verse presents considerable difficulties, and has been variously rendered. The Septuagint and the Targum differ as much from one another, as they do from the Hebrew. None regard the former as at all suitable; but some, as Grotius and Dathius, take the meaning of the latter, though to reconcile it with the Hebrew is difficult. Marckius seems to have given the most probable meaning —

Remotos a festivitate collegi,
Ex to sunt, onus super eam opprobrium.
Those driven away from festivity have I gathered,
From thee they are — a burden on her is reproach.

The word [יָגוֹן], he derives from [הגה]. In this case it is literally, "my driven away," or, "my removed" ones. [דעומ] is assembling or meeting, as well as a fixed time or season; and the assembling was that on festal days: it may therefore be rendered, "festivals." "From thee" is "Sion" in verse 16. Instead of "on her," more than ten copies, as well as the Targum, have "on thee," [עָלֶיךָ]; but an abrupt change of person is of frequent occurrence in the Prophets.

Following the sense of the Targum, we may, perhaps, give the following version —
The grieved for the festivals have I gathered from thee;
They were a burden on thee, a reproach.
The paraphrase of the Targum, as given by Dathius, is the following —
Those who among thee have impeded the seasons of thy festivity,
I will expel from thee; wo to them who have carried arms against thee, and loaded thee with reproaches.

The "grieved for the festivals" were those who disliked them, who grudged the offerings that were to be made. The words are in the past tense, but future as to what is said; for the Prophets declare things as exhibited to them in a vision. — Ed. (p. 237)

[124] The first clause in this verse is amended by Newcome and some other in conformity with the Septuagint: but this is a very unsafe process. Henderson's version is —Behold, I will deal with all thine oppressors at that time. "Deal," [עשה]; "interficiam — I will slay," Vulg.; "conficiam — I will make an end," Drusius; but to "deal with," or "act against," is the literal rendering. More is implied than what is expressed, which is often the case with words used in every language. — Ed. (p. 238)

[125] "Prophecy ceased with these Prophets until the time of Christ. For it was God's purpose, by this famine of the word, (according to the prophetic language,) to render the Jews more desirous (appetentiores) of the Messiah, who was to surpass all the Prophets in the power of doing miracles." — Grotius. (p. 242)

[126] "We know nothing of the parentage of Haggai. He was probably born in Babylon during the captivity. He was sent particularly to encourage the Jews to proceed with the building of the temple, which had been interrupted for about fourteen years." — Adam Clarke. (p. 242)

[127] According to the opinions of Plato and Cicero, the Cyropaedia of Xenophon was a moral romance; and these venerable philosophers suppose, that the historian did not so much write what Cyrus had been, as what every true, good, and virtuous monarch ought to be." — Lempriere's Class. Dict. (p. 245)

[128] The account of the Magi is briefly this: — Cyrus had two sons, Cambyses and Smerdis. When Cambyses ascended the throne, suspecting the fidelity of his brother, he caused him to be secretly put to death. This was known to some of the Magi. On the death of Cambyses, one of them, named Smerdis, who resembled the deceased prince, was by the Magi declared king, under the pretense of being the brother of Cambyses. The imposition was detected, and seven of the nobles of Persia dethroned him after six months' reign, and on themselves, Darius Hystaspes, was made king, in the year before Christ 521. — Ed. (p. 245)

[129] Adam Clark says, that is was in the sixteenth year after their return from Babylon. — Ed. (p. 246)

[130] The reference in John 2:19, 20, seems to have been made not to the time in which it was built then, but to the time in which it was built or rebuilt by Herod the Great. For this temple was finished in the sixth year of Darius (see Ezr 6:15,) and about twenty-one years after the temple was finished in 515. It was about four years in building under Darius. — Ed. (p. 247)

[131] [החפ]; it is a word currect in several languages, Chaldee, Persic, etc. Parkhurst derives it from [הפ], to extend. Theod. Aq. and Syn. render it ἡγούμενον, governor. He is called Sheshbazzar in Ezr 5:14; and Cyrus is said to have made him [החפ], governor or deputy. It is the name of a person endued with authority by a sovereign. Zerubbabel, [לבברז], has been derived from [רז], a stranger, and [נבב], Babylon, a stranger or sojourner at Babylon. It deserves to be noticed, that the civil governor is put here before the chief priest; and we find from Ezra that it was to the civil governor that Cyrus delivered the holy vessels of the temple. See Ezr 5:14. — Ed. (p. 248)

[132] The words literally are, —
This people say, Not come is the time,
The time for the house of Jehovah to be built.
— Ed. (p. 250)

[133] There is a double pronoun, [מתא סכל תעה], "Is it time for you, even you," or, "you yourselves?" The Welsh often use two pronouns in this way, for the sake of emphasis. The rendering is very flat, as in our version, and adopted by Henderson, "Is it time for you, O ye?" etc. Houbigant, who always amends, proposes [התא], to come, "Is the time come for you?" etc. This is suitable, but without authority. Dathius suggests the place, but it is no more than a conjecture. There is no doubt an emphasis is intended by the repetition. — Ed. (p. 252)

[134] It is rendered "wainscoted" by Henderson; "κοιλοστάθμοις — ceiled," by the Sept.; "ωροφωμενοις — roofed," by Aquila. It was the custom in the east, says Parkhurst, to cover or line the roof with boards or wainscot. — Ed. (p. 252)

[135] Literally it is, "Set your heart on your ways." An idiomatic phrase, but very expressive. They were to fix their attention on their conduct, not merely to take a glance, but seriously and steadily to reflect on their ways. (p. 253)

[136] There seems to be an irregularity in the construction of the whole verse. Literally it is as follows —

Ye have sown much, but the coming in is little;
There is eating, but not to satisfaction;
They drink, but not to fullness;
There is clothing, but there is no warmth in it;
And earn does the earner for a perforated bag.
This change in the mode of construction takes away the monotony which would have otherwise appeared. The word [אבה], [לוכא], and [שובל], are not infinitives, as some suppose, but participles used as nouns; which is often the case in Hebrew, as well as in Welsh, and often to in English, such as teaching, drinking, clothing, etc. — Ed. (p. 254)

[137] The whole verse may be thus rendered —
Ascend the mountains, for ye have brought wood;
And build the house, that I may delight in it,
That I may be glorified, saith Jehovah.

The [I], vau, here in two instance may have the meaning of ut, that; but before [מתאבה], a verb in the perfect tense, it must be rendered "for," or, "as;" and the clause seems to be a parenthesis. The [I], vau, is not conversive when preceded by a verb in the imperative mood, as it appears from the end of the verse. The mount was not Libanus, as many have supposed, but Sion, where wood had been previously brought, but was not used. See Ezr 3:7. As to the verb [הצר], followed by [ב], it means to approve, to be pleased with, or to take pleasure or delight in, a thing. See 2Ch 29:3; Ps 147:10; Mic 6:7. Probably the best rendering of the two last lines is the following —

And build the house, and I shall delight in it
And render it glorious, saith Jehovah.

To take the last verb in a causative sense is more consistent with the tenor of the passage. This is the meaning given by the Targum, and is adopted by Dathius. — Ed. (p. 257)

[138] The first word in this verse, [הנפ], is evidently a participle noun; similar instances we find in verse 6. The verse, literally rendered, is as follows —

Looking for much, and behold little!
And you brought it home, and I blew upon it;
On what account this, saith Jehovah of hosts?
On account of my house, because it is waste,
And ye are running, each to his own house.

The first line is put in an absolute form, as is sometimes the case in Hebrew; "There has been," or some such words being understood. Both the Targum and the Septuagint read [היה] instead of [הנה], which would be more suitable to the word which follows, which has [ל] before it. The line would then be —

There has been looking for much, but it came to little.
The "blowing" seems to be a metaphor taken from scorching wind, blowing on vegetation, and causing it to wither. The last line may be thus rendered —
And ye are delighted, each with his own house.
— Ed. (p. 257)

[139] This is the literal rendering — "On account of my house, because it is waste." [רשא] is not "which" here, for it is followed by [אוה], "it;" but a conjunction, "because." The word quod, in Latin, admits of two similar meanings. — Ed. (p. 258)

[140] Calvin seems to have overlooked [מכילע], "on your account." The verse is —
Therefore, on your account, withheld have the heavens from dew,
And the earth has withheld its produce.

The verb [אלכ], to restrain, to keep back, to withhold, is used here twice, and in the first line in an intransitive sense, and in the second in a transitive sense, as it is often the case in other languages, when the same verb is both neuter and active.

The 11th verse is passed by without any particular remarks. The word [ברח] is rendered "Siccitas — drought," as Jerome does, and also our version, as well as Newcome and Henderson; but Grotius and also Marckius very justly observe, that it means here "waste," or "desolation," it being the same word as is applied to God's house in verse 9. They left his house a waste; by a just retribution he had brought or called for a waste on the land, etc. The contrast is so evident that it cannot be denied. The ideal meanings of the word is to be waste or desolate: it is then applied to various things which produce desolation, the sword, drought, pestilence, etc.; but it is used here in its primary sense, and the contrast is very striking: "My house has been left waste; I have caused a waste to come upon every thing else." The verse may be thus rendered —

And I have called for a waste
On the land and on the mountains,
And on the corn and on the wine and on the oil,
And on whatever the ground produces,
And on man and on the cattle,
And on all the labor of the hands.
— Ed. (p. 260)

[141] This clause may be thus rendered, —
And fear him did the people on account of Jehovah.

This comports better with the previous clause, that Jehovah had sent him. The [ו] affixed to "fear" is a pronoun, otherwise the verb is plural; and "people" seldom, if ever, has a verb in the plural number. To fear sometimes means to respect, to reverence: the people honored him as God's servant, by obeying his message. — Ed. (p. 264)

[142] The verse literally is —
Then said Haggai, the messenger of Jehovah in the message of
Jehovah to the people, saying,
I am with you, saith Jehovah.

The word for "messages" is in the plural number, preceded by the preposition [ב]. Why commentators have generally rendered it in the singular number, does not appear. Haggai is expressly said to be God's messenger in, or with regard to, the messages or communications he made to the people. To connect the word, as some do, with "said," hardly gives a meaning, except the clause be rendered, as it is done by Newcome, "by the message of Jehovah," that is, by his command; but then a plural word is made singular. — Ed. (p. 266)

[143] It is sometimes the case, that a doctrine is illegitimately drawn from a passage, and then that it is unfairly opposed. The building of the Temple had nothing to do with the first movement of the spiritual life: and therefore to draw an argument from the willingness of the people to undertake that work in favor of free-will in the great business of salvation, is by no means legitimate. It would have been, then, better to deny the application, than to turn the passage from its regular course. But we shall not do violence to the passage, if we render the [ו] at the beginning of this verse, "Thus," and refer "the stirring up" to the threatening and the promise previously announced. The object seems not to have been to set forth the direct influence of the Spirit on the minds of the people, but to show the effect

produced on them by the message conveyed to them from the Lord by the Prophet. God stirs up the minds of men both by his word and by his Spirit, both outwardly and inwardly. The former may more properly be meant here. — Ed. (p. 267)

[144] The reasons assigned here for a different division is by no means satisfactory. The fact is that this verse necessarily belongs to the last of the previous chapter, as it specifies the time when the people began the work as there mentioned; and what follows this verse is another message, and at another time. The usual division is no doubt the best. (p. 268)

[145] This is the most approved manner. There is no instance in which it means "according." It may be rendered — "This is the word," etc. There were two things which were intended to dispel their fear — the covenant made with the fathers, and the Spirit of God — the spirit of prophecy, "standing," or existing among them. The Chaldee Paraphrase is — "My Prophets are teaching among you." The verse may be thus translated —

This is the word which I covenanted with you
At your comming forth from Egypt,
And my Spirit is continuing among you; fear not.
Junius and Tremelius render the [את], "with," and the verse thus —
With the word (i.e., having the word) which I covenanted with you
When ye came forth from Egypt,
And with my Spirit standing among you, fear not.

Henderson considers "the word," and "my Spirit," to be nominatives to the particle "standing," or rather to the auxiliary verb which is to be understood before it, and that "standing" is in the singular number, on account of the nearer nominative "my Spirit." Newcome follows our version, and views [את] as a preposition — "according to." — Ed. (p. 274)

[146] Our common version is no doubt the best, and is materially followed by Newcome, Henderson, and many others. Retaining the tense of the passage, I would render the clause thus,

Yet once, shortly will it be,
And I will shake, etc.
"Shortly will it be," [עמט היא] (shortly it) may be taken as a parenthesis.
Yet once more, in a short time — Newcome.
Yet once, within a little, — Henderson.

The shaking of the heavens, earth, sea, and dry land is explained, according to the common manner of the Prophets, in the next verse, by shaking of all nations: the material world is named in the first instance, while its inhabitants are intended. So Henderson very properly renders the [מ] at the beginning of the seventh verse, "Yea." — Ed. (p. 277)

[147] Many have been the criticisms on this clause, both as to its grammatical construction and as to the import of the word rendered "desire." The verb "come" is plural, and the word for "desire" is singular. The easiest solution, and countenanced by the Septuagint, where the word is rendered τὰ ἐκλεκτὰ — "choice things," is to consider [תדמח] as a plural, the [ו] being omitted. This would remove the grammatical anomaly, and the sentiment, as Calvin says, woud be more consonant with the context.

And come shall the choice things of all nations.

There is no ground for the objection which Bishop Chandler states, that to "come" is in this case an improper expression; for there are other similar instances. See Jos 6:12; Isa 60:5. It is also applied to trees, Isa 60:13; and to incense, Jer 6:20. Newcome takes the word as a plural, but applies it as deliciae in Latin to a person, and refers to Da 9:23; where Daniel is called [תודמח], rendered in our version "greatly beloved."

The version of Henderson is the following —
And the things desired by all nations shall come.

He considers that they are the blessings of the kingdom of Christ, and thinks that the Prophet refers to the general expectation which pervaded the world of some better state of things, and especially of some deliverer.

But the most tenable is the view of Calvin, which has been held by Kimchi, Drusius, Vitringa, and others. — Ed. (p. 280)

[148] This clause is literally rendered by Newcome — "Ask now the law from the priests;" or, according to the order of the words, "Ask now from the priests the law." — Ed. (p. 285)

[149] The words are [שפנ-אמט], polluted of soul, or polluted soul. When pollution by a carcase or a dead body is meant, the preposition [ל] is put before [שפנ]. See Num. 5:2, Num. 9:6, 7, 10. A polluted person seems to be intended here, without any reference to the way in which he became so; and this is sufficient for the purpose of the Prophet. Theodoret takes this sense — ἀκάθαρτόν τινα — "an

unclean person." But most agree with our version; so do Jerome, Dathius, Newcome, Henderson, and others — "the polluted by a dead body." — Ed. (p. 287)

[150] Compositum jus, fasque animi, sanctosque recesssus Mentis, et incoctum generoso pectus honesto. — Per. Sat. 2. 74. (p. 287)

[151] Non ben celestes impia dextra colit. (p. 288)

[152] The literal rendering of the verse would be as follows, —
Then answered Haggai and said, —
Such is this people and such is this nation,
Before me, saith Jehovah;
Yea, such is every work of their hands,
And what they offer there, polluted it is.

The Prophet seems to have pointed to the altar on which they offered their sacrifices, when he says, "What they offer there." Both Newcome and Henderson are evidently wrong in rendering the passage in the past tense. The last verb is future, used, as it is often, as a present. So we render it in Welsh, yr hyn a aberthant yna; but we understand it as a present act. We may notice here what is often the character of the Prophetic style; the two last lines explain more particularly what the two first contain. — Ed. (p. 292)

[153] Supra, [הלעמ]; "upward," Newcome; "backward," Henderson; "forward," Secker. The last refers to 1Sa 16:13, and 30:25, as the only places besides here and in verse 18, where it is applied to time: and clearly in Samuel it means "forward," or hereafter. It means the same when applied to age, Nu 1:20, and when applied to place, De 28:43

If we retain this meaning, we must consider this verse, and its repetition in verse 18, as the commencement of a sentence, which is completed at the end of verse 19, as intervening clauses. Then the passage would be as follows —

15. And now take, I pray, notice;
From this day and forward,
From the time of setting a stone on a stone
In the Temple of Jehovah,
16. From the time you came to a heap of twenty,
And it was ten,
And came to the vat to draw fifty measures,
And there were twenty;
17. I smote you with blight, and with mildew,
And with hail, even all the work of your hands;

But ye turned not to me, saith Jehovah; —
18. Take, I pray, notice;
From this day and forward,
From the twenty-fourth day of the ninth month,
From the day in which was founded
The Temple of Jehovah; — take notice;
19. Is yet the seed in the granary? —
And as yet the vine and the fig tree,
And the pomegranate and the olive, it hath not borne; —
From this day will I bless you.

I prefer "Take notice," or, "mark," to "consider," as the meaning of [ומיש סכבבל], "set or fix your heart." In favor of "your" instead of "their" in verse 16, there are three MSS.; and it is more consistent with the context. The expression literally is, "From your being to come," i.e from the time in which you came, and found out the deficiency. "Fifty measures;" [הרופ] is rendered by the Septuagint μετρητὰς — "baths;" by Jerome, "Lagenas — flagons." The word means here evidently a vessel to measure the wine from the vat; what quantity it contained is not known. It is here in the singular number, while the numeral, "fifty," is in the plural; deugain, which literally in English is, "ten measure and forty." In verse 17, "even all the work of your hands," is in apposition with "you," and explanatory of it, according to what we often find in the Prophets; for by "you" was meant their "work," and not themselves personally. "But ye turned not to me," literally, "But ye not to me;" perhaps the meaning is, "Ye ascribed it not to me," that is, the judgment previously mentioned, or, "Ye attended not to me:" but the verb [סתבש] is commonly thought to be understood. See Am 4:9. The question in verse 19 is to be taken negatively, to correspond with the negative declaration in what follows. — Ed. (p. 294)

[154] Calvin makes here a change in the discourse; but the whole to the end of the chapter may be viewed as the parable or the taunt mentioned in verse 6, and the particle Ho! may be retained instead of Wo. The taunt seems to have been formed so as to have been especially suitable to be used by the Jews.

By regarding the passage in this light, we can understand the sudden change off person in verse 16, if the proposed emendation be disapproved; for we see the same in the former portions of the "taunt." See 6 and 7, and also 9 and 10. That the reader may see the whole of this passage, containing the "taunt," in the light in which I am now fully inclined to regard it, it shall be presented to him complete: —

6. Will not these, every one of them, Raise up a proverb concerning him, And a taunt, enigmas for him, and say, — "Ho! He increases what is not his! how long! And he accumulates on himself thick clay! —

7. Will they not suddenly rise up — thy biters, And awake — thy tormentors, And thou become booties to them?

8. For thou hast spoiled many nation, And spoil thee shall all the remnant of the people, On account of men's blood, and of violence To the land, to the city, and to all its inhabitants."

9. "Ho! he has coveted an evil covetousness to his house, To set on high his nest, In order to save himself from the hand of evil! —

10. Thou hast consulted shame to thine house, By cutting off many nations And by sinning against thine own soul:

11. For the stone — from the wall it cries, And the beam — from the woodwork it answers it, —

12. 'Ho! he builds a town by blood, And sets up a city by oppression!' —

13. Shall nothing be, lo! From Jehovah of hosts? Yea, labor shall the people for the fire, And nations — for vanity shall they weary themselves:

14. For filled shall be the earth With the knowledge of the glory of Jehovah, Like the waters which spread over the sea."

15. "Ho! he gives drink to his neighbour! — Thou addest thy bottle and also strong drink, In order to look on their nakedness!

16. Thou hast been filled with reproach rather than with glory: Drink thou also, and be uncovered; Come round to thee shall the cup Of the right hand of Jehovah; And shameful spewing shall be on thy glory:

17. For the violence done to Lebanon — it shall overwhelm thee, And the plunder of beasts — it shall rend thee; On account of men's blood, and of violence To the land, to the city, and to all its inhabitants."

18. "What avails the graven image! For its graver — he forms it — Even the molten image and the teacher of falsehood: Yea, trust in it does the former of its form, After having made dumb idols!

19. Ho! he saith to the wood, 'Arise, Awake;' To the dumb stone, 'It will teach?' Behold it! covered it is with gold and silver, Yet there is no spirit within it! But Jehovah is in his holy temple: Silent at his presence let the whole earth be."

The "taunt" may be deemed as terminating at the end of the 17th verse; but I regard it as continuing to the end of the chapter. The word "neighbour," in the 15th verse, is a collective singular, meaning every neighbour: hence "their" at the end of the verse. The same may be said of "image" in verse 18, which means every image or images, as "idols" are mentioned afterwards. Such are common instances in the Prophets. "It will teach," in verse 19, most evidently refers to "the dumb stone" — the idol; for it is expressly called "the teacher of falsehood" in verse 17. — Ed (p. 307)

[155] What is said in a Note in p. 347 does not apply to what Calvin says. He refers not, as I inadvertently apprehended, to the present division of the chapter, but to that adopted in the Septuagint; for this verse in that version forms the beginning of the next chapter. — Ed (p. 317)

www.ingramcontent.com/pod-product-compliance
Lightning Source LLC
Chambersburg PA
CBHW051604010526
44119CB00056B/778

I dedicate this book to my mother,
who always encouraged me
to organize my mind by creating lists.
Which I never did
until I stopped drinking alcohol.
I love you.

Books by Wing Williams

The Bear Within
As a Wolf Breathes
Owl of The Moon
Grand Father Tree

PART ONE
The Howling Twenties

An Opening Analogy	9
The Beginning of My Oregon Trail	11
Haunts of the East	22
Grand Teton National Park	26
The Appalachian Trail	45
A Long Chapter for a Long State	73
PNW on the PCT	119
There Must Be a Plan	151
Colorado Rocky Mountain High	167
Gamble Gulch	181
Lump Gulch	225
The Unsettling & The Decision	249

PART TWO
From Death to Life

Fierce Brown Liquor	277
Beast with Many Heads	295
The Dark Ages	314
What Matters Most	333
A Worthy First Step	338
Turbulence	361
Would You?	377
If He, Then I	384
Angels, Demons & The Lion	398
The Writing Shed	407
The Purpose of Life	424

Acknowledgments	430

This memoir contains traumatic content
that may be disturbing or emotionally challenging
for some readers. Assaults, alcohol and drug abuse,
spiritual warfare and other mature themes are explored.
However, despite any darkness, it all ends with light.

Part I
The Howling Twenties

An Opening Analogy

It can all become quite complicated. A chaotic mess so dense the notion of inner peace seems impossible. One can push on living in mental mayhem until the darkness wins or slow down to confront and untangle it all. The latter is the journey I began in December 2022. If I had not embarked at the time I did, I would not be alive today. If I stray from this endeavor without seeing it through, it shall be what kills me.

I do not ask for compassion. I never seek pity. Give your measure of sympathy to someone more in need. This is a redemption story. I take full responsibility for all that has transpired. What I ask is that you listen. I impart to you the full, unaltered saga so that beyond the thrills of wild amusement perhaps it may uplift and encourage, providing strength, renewing life and offering direction to a weary soul.

As I sit here and write, in my sturdy chair upon level ground, I am on a boat. A boat in the brain, rising and falling, tumbling as the sea. Incessant neurological instability is the baseline for a now-normal day. The most stable day is a calm sea, rolling as I exist. An awful day is a vertigo-induced tempest, swirling into hellish bedlam where only sleep can mimic a tranquil breath. I recognize a boat as the truest analogy I can provide because long before the traumatic brain injury I lived it.

At the fresh age of twenty-one, I commandeered a job as a photographer on a cruise ship amidst the islands of Hawaii. I called myself a ship-paparazzi. If you have ever partaken in a vacation cruise, you understand photographers show up at each meal, gangplank and event, attempting to siphon more pictures and money out of you. The oceanic shimmer of this adventure spiraled into a shade of ill mental health, yet it supplied me with the analogy I now share.

Night one on the grand ship was an event to celebrate. Many alcoholic beverages were drunk while making a variety of acquaintances. My colleagues treated my induction into the contractual rotating crop of employees as a party on land with no regard for the heaving roll of a ship at sea. The amount I could imbibe on solid ground was the amount I consumed aboard The Pride of Aloha. Thus, the stumble back to my metal bunk below water line was a battle against the forces of balance and narrow, yawing hallways. Once horizontal in my berth, I could not contain the liquor. Rising and falling over each wave forced me into a dizziness I had yet to experience. Profusely, I vomited until fading into a tremulant sleep. Yet we adapt. By the end of the first week, my equilibrium returned. I gained my sea legs.

The employment contract I signed lasted nine months. During the first three and a half months I thrived, but by the fourth month I began descending into a claustrophobic, rebellious, tumultuous mindset. After seven months of cruise ship life, authorities threw me into the brig, detained me until the Port of Hilo, then escorted me off handcuffed and crazed, parading me in front of my peers as no pride of aloha. During those seven months, the unsteady footing on a vessel at sea had become the standard. Upon returning to land, the earth undulated beneath my feet, as if it was our planet rhythmically exhaling and inhaling.

Now, on the scale of a calm sea to a tempest, upon a foundation which should remain steadfast, is the sensation of imbalance I carry every day. My brain rises and falls, spins and shudders each moment and second ever since my traumatic brain injury on January 17, 2020.

CINEREAL

The Beginning of My Oregon Trail

My primary commitment is to God. Second commitment is to a life of writing. The third till-death-do-us-part, I shall no longer drink alcohol. I suppose if I ever get married, that will become my fourth lifelong commitment. However, this is the story of how I descended into alcohol addiction, what led to my conviction for alcohol sobriety and how freedom was achieved.

The adolescence of this saga wears the American cloak of being born into a culture that celebrates booze. I had my first beer, marijuana toke and cigarette smoke all within twenty minutes behind the high school at age fifteen. The season was autumn, the year 2000, and my birthday recently observed. A brewing rebellion within was ready to blossom. My friend, a year older than I and a sophomore, showed me how. We first swigged a Budweiser, then turned the empty beer can into a smoking device for the pot, inhaled, passed it to the other, exhaled and repeated until we burned the green sticky bud into ash. To cap it all off, we smoked the harshly magnificent Marlboro Red. "A hat trick," he joked, playing to my love for scoring goals on the soccer field. I coughed a lot, gained both a head and body buzz, and declared it felt like flying to the moon. It was a good start.

Simultaneously, at age fifteen, my sturdy, seemingly moral family was falling apart. The seeds of destruction had been growing for years, but in this new era, the sin breached the soil. Thus began my education and confusion in learning that life is often not as it seems. Then, as a switch turned off, all authority's glow and trusted role were severed. I leaned into selfish indulging, trading my previous obedience for rampant rebellion. I transformed from a boy with a passionate heart for God into an unmanageable wildling in New Hampshire. With this, I developed into yet another problem my mother did not deserve.

As a teenager, I mostly hot-boxed cars and partied in the woods. Drinking booze and smoking became routine after athletic matches were complete. Occasionally we'd steal something, like a marble statue out of

CINEREAL

some rich guy's front-yard, or a six-liter bottle of Belvedere vodka on prom night. My friends carried me in from the rain as I cradled the liquor-loot in a dumb, poisoned stupor from the brick pathway between puddles. Alcohol was easy to procure, always scuttling one step ahead of police and parents. I maintained high scholastic grades in class while excelling at sports on the field, revealing few visible red flags to be concerned about. However, after high school graduation, my teenage mischievousness turned into a season of crime, descending into despicable felonious activity. With no moral guidance and a growing disdain for hypocrites declaring, "This is right, and that is wrong," I tumbled into a world of selfish actions which harmed others and myself, flirting with a life of ultimate disaster.

University life was like when a team wins the big game, and the players pour a giant cooler of hydration liquid all over the coach in celebration. Except in college, it was booze. Alcohol saturated every day. I never missed a step between the gym, the cafeteria and the parties. Each night, a stale barley malt stench filled the rooms, soles of shoes sticking and ripping with each sneaker'd step. Girls, intoxicants, greasy food and raucous pranks were the primary objectives until the sun rose. With this mindset, living in an autonomous environment, unlike in high school, I only earned the minimum grades to remain. Rarely did I go to class. Instead, I got arrested for my first time.

I deserved the arrest, and although it seemed like a life interruption, it saved me from the plummeting direction I had been embracing. At the age of nineteen, my year became divided into two parts. First half, paying for my societal transgressions. Second half, volunteering with the Red Cross in Louisiana amid the aftermath of Hurricane Katrina. I arrived in the balmy state two days after the tragedy occurred. Despite my moral conflicts, my heart remained intensely compassionate for those suffering. Foregoing the first semester of my sophomore year, I leaned into serving others. Post-Katrina southern Louisiana was a raw immersion into a world far beyond the northern lifestyle I had known. This selfless season following my criminal one stitched back a few open wounds, for when you give, you receive. And yet, the receiving is not what I sought. The era resulted in an influential, emotional story I might someday divulge in another book. After Louisiana, as October fourteen and my twentieth birthday approached, I returned north to spend the holidays in New England and potentially pick up where I had left off in my formal scholastic endeavors. Yet during the winter of my sophomore year, I pivoted away from school and towards the future I would only achieve if I started immediately.

I never intended to stick with college. Subconsciously, I knew that going in. My parents wanted me to pursue a proper education, or so they had encouraged. Dad took me to visit my supposed schools of choice, such as Columbia, NYU and Juilliard. But I was no urban city boy. Nor could I afford to attend such lofty institutions. Both Pepperdine in California and Ithaca in upstate New York I applied to and considered. However, despite my acceptance, financial abilities remained the same. When it came down to it, the in-state University of New Hampshire was the cheaper and proper fit. As my chance of graduating was minimal, spending less and avoiding debt proved the best course. In the winter at age twenty, all it took was for one professor to pull me aside after a creative writing class, look me in the eye and demand, "What are you doing here?"

I sputtered without a rudder. "Well, I'm not sure. Learning, practicing?"

He placed his hand on my shoulder, which I shrugged off. "Young man, you," he nearly tapped my chest indicating me specifically, "will never be a writer like this. You need to go live the hungry, dirty life of experiences out there," he waved his hand gallantly. "These classroom lessons are not for someone like you! I see the wild yearning explorer within. I read it in your essays, see it in your vapid gazes out the window, so go, live dang-it, live!"

That was all I needed to hear. I dropped out of school and followed his advice.

~~~

To begin my third decade alive, following my leave from university, I set off on a grand American road trip. New England to California, Northeast to Southwest, Atlantic to Pacific Ocean, with my friend Andrew by my side. A rumble brewed in my soul. I had earned back the freedom I craved, which I had lost following my arrest. The time to dive into a landscape of untamed adventure was upon me. Southern California lay as a jungle of flavors, of which I was determined to taste as many as I could. The opportunity to mess around and find out was unlimited. In Los Angeles, I met and became quite fond of drugs a tad heavier than marijuana. While booze remained the staple of my diet, always serving as my reckless guide, I careened through each day, projecting vomit along the outside of an exotic lady's exotic car, howling, speeding, lights but lines, colors and orbs, swerving, dancing, and spewing along the Hollywood freeway. Though I worked as an extra on a few television shows, I maintained no firm foundation to stand upon. I abandoned all morals and clung only to the savagery of each moment. Within less than a year, this abominable adventure crumbled beneath fists, intoxicants and irresponsible financial decisions. The world quickly chewed me up and spat me out. A year later, I returned to New Hampshire with no money and much chagrin.

If my plan, which I had indeed set as my plan, to live a wild decade of adventures and experiences was to succeed, I was going to need to get creative with how I earned an income. Signing up for a soul-sucking nine-to-five job somewhere remained not an option. I was determined to earn money in epic places. Jobs that provided room and board were ideal. My first step back in my home state was to buy a few ounces of marijuana, break it down into grams and sell it all for profit on the campus I dropped out of school from. Once the first batch sold, I could afford to buy more, steadily building modest savings. I returned to classes, not as an enrolled student, but as an opportunistic auditor. Here I created a comprehensive client list both for illegal cannabis sales and for writing other student's assigned papers. While maintaining my cover jobs such as landscaping and food and beverage to limit questions, roaming the campus appearing as if I had never left with a backpack full of illegal medicine and scholastic papers captivated my focus. I handed these out to all those who paid my price. At night I slept on couches and partied. Life was risky and grand.

On the nights I did not party, I would stay with my dad in an apartment he rented nearby. He and I had not repaired our relationship following the damage leading to the family's dissolution, but he did desire for me to have a safe place to stay. He knew I disregarded my mother's rules, and thus her home was not an option. He also knew I strove to live as I wanted, choosing streets and couches instead. Despite Dad and I's fractures, I agreed to make a room in his apartment my temporary abode. After all, he kept the kitchen stocked with food, beer and wine. During the evenings when he was home and not traveling for work, we watched old movies and ballgames together, played chess, ate whatever meal he concocted from the cookbook he was working through, and always drank our wine. The alcohol kept us both in the same room together. It allowed us not to think about the deep pain from all the unresolved soul wounds. The alcohol helped us to rebuild our relationship, not yet as a dad and son but as friends.

CINEREAL

Following my twenty-first birthday, I announced to him I secured a job as a photographer on a cruise ship in Hawaii. Soon I was to be sent to Annapolis, Maryland, to be trained and earn the required Merchant Marine Document. Within a few months, I stood victoriously on the bow of the large ship. I watched Honolulu fade into the oceanic horizon and then turned to tackle new challenges in my fresh environment. I alluded to what became of that job, and you will know more soon, but for now this nautical venture only serves as part of the contextual life-timeline. After the drama ensued, and the police escorted me to the airport gate to kick me out of Hawaii, Dad welcomed me home without judgment or anger. We, as on each occasion, drank to the occasion.

Before I proceed with the raucous twenties, I must first explain where the relationship with my dad stood. My dad was the first person to break my heart. He broke the hearts of everyone in my direct family the awful year I was fifteen. But this is not an account of family sins, yet necessary background to the story of my descent into alcoholism and battle to crawl through and onward. I love my dad, and he loves me. The way he lived back then, when our entire world turned upside down and scattered, does not reflect the man he is now, the man he matured to become. He, like me, was living life to his fullest and in time took humble accountability for his actions. Despite his repentance, it would not be until later in my twenties that I truly forgave him. For far too long I harbored resentment, which, though the world may deem understandable, was wrong of me to do. No matter what inane situation I got myself into in life, he always offered a place to live. Although he knew I was angry and hurt, he provided unconditional love and forgiveness as I raucously navigated the gauntlet of life. He understood he had lost the patriarchal bond with his children, and yet faithfully he remained there for us.

While much of our time together included drinking alcohol, Dad himself is not an alcoholic. Nor did we see anything wrong or dangerous in how we then imbibed. A young adult son and a young healthy dad sharing a few drinks was a way to rebuild our fractured bond. My later actions are not a product of our time drinking together. He impressed responsibility on me. He educated me about the potential dangers of alcohol. All the actions that would lead to my demise were choices I alone made.

Occasionally I wondered, during the feats of my twenties, if I was constantly attempting to earn his respect, while he, in his efforts, was

CINEREAL

attempting to earn back mine. However, as I developed, I realized that in our own ways we were just trying to show how much we loved each other. Today, my dad and I have a repaired, rehabilitated, healthy relationship, and for that I am grateful.

~~~

At age twenty-two, I settled into my adventurous stride. Following a blooming May in New Hampshire, I was ready to launch toward new horizons again. I headed south to stay with a surfer pal I'd made on the cruise ship, to explore the beaches and islands outside of Charleston, South Carolina. For this trip, I did not have a vehicle, but one does not need a vehicle on Folly Island. My immature-self had sold the dependable, gas-efficient, modest Honda Civic Dad had gifted for my eighteenth birthday. After it carried Andrew and me across the country to California, I assumed I was upgrading by turning it in for a Nissan 300ZX Turbo. I drove the champagne speedster like a maniac all over the greater Los Angeles region until the bank repossessed it in the middle of a warm, alcohol-saturated night because of my delinquency.

With no vehicle, only a beach cruiser bicycle down among the long Carolina sands, I continued with my dependable side hustle of selling marijuana. Purchase the ounce, break it down, sell for profit, buy more. The easiest gig in the early 2000s USA. We imbibed every day. When money could afford it, I purchased cocaine. My body functioned on little food or sleep, consuming MDMA, LSD, rowdy powders, booze, cigarettes and "medicinal" although illegal marijuana. Amidst this behavioral and moral depravity, there still existed a responsible side to me. I understood I needed a legal occupation, so I scoured the same website I had found the cruise ship job listing on.

Within a few days of my hunt, I secured employment after a successful telephone interview. I had been targeting all the western national parks, a location where I could live, work and hike. Excitedly, I told my beach-bungalow mates the news. "The Grand Canyon! North Rim. They say it's far more remote than the South Rim. Despite the minimal wages, I will also receive room and board, like on the cruise ship. And I will be immersed in one of our nation's most beautiful wildernesses." They feigned sadness to see me go between checking wave reports and microwaving instant meals. I didn't care if they cared. I didn't care if anyone cared. This was my life and the East Coast liberation I desperately craved.

CINEREAL

My journey to the Grand Canyon would lead through Savannah, Georgia. I was eager to visit as I had never been there. A lovely friend of mine, with whom I had shared a romantic week during a prior season, was attending Savannah College of Art and Design. I would stay with her for sixteen hours and then fly to Las Vegas.

On the train from one southeastern coastal city to another, I relaxed into dreams of the west. I was born in San Diego, La Jolla to be exact, where the naval officer Scripps Memorial Hospital was located, and though raised in the east, the magnificent, rugged lands beyond the prairies always called to me. As a boy, the historic phrase "go west young man" seemed directed at me. My soul sensed its own call of the wild. My heart desired its own Oregon Trail. "This is the beginning of that trail," I whispered into the stuffy Amtrak air. The move to California when I was twenty had failed. The disaster in Hawaii scarred my mind, and this presented as another fresh chance. I swigged from my brown-bag beer, drank a gulp of whiskey from my flask, and peered out the window at the sodden world speeding by until the train slowed to a halt and a recorded drawl announced our arrival. "Welcome to the Hostess City of the South."

The following sixteen hours featured cobblestones, cigarette smoke, biking through ornate parks, admiring old mansions, basking beneath southern live oaks draped with marvelous grey moss, a beautiful woman with blonde hair, blue eyes, and a boisterous night of partying. As sticky bodies mashed around us in a nightclub, she shouted, asking if I wanted to stay awhile longer, "My dog loves you after all!" But I declined, for although our embraces suggested they should have one hundred more, I could not ignore the beckoning west.

For the first time in my young life, I recognized the destruction the poisonous drink could summon. With my flight scheduled for a dawn departure, she promised to deliver me on time, "but first we must soak up Savannah." Until the bars and nightclubs locked their doors, we danced and imbibed. When closing time came, they allowed us to carry our beverages out onto the street. Excitedly, we loaded up with a few extra to-go drinks. Southern rain poured with fervor, a deluge upon our passions, so we danced on, drenched from our skin to our blood. Promiscuously, we defied the late night's restful intentions, only to perceive the sun was soon to rise. We sped to the airport, shared one last farewell squeeze, and then she and I continued in our different directions.

CINEREAL

Upon landing in Las Vegas and turning on my cellphone, I listened to a chilling voicemail. She was in the hospital. After our wild, sleepless, boozy night, after delivering me to the airport, an 18-wheeler big-mac truck struck her vehicle. With her car destroyed, it seemed like a miracle that she was still alive. From the on-ramp to the highway, merging into traffic, a giant mass of extreme lethal force had barreled into her.

My heart dropped upon hearing the news. My mind spun into a scramble. Delirium interrupted calm thinking. *Why did we stay up partying all night? Why, then, had I let her still drive me? What the hell is wrong with me? What a selfish, thoughtless mindset, that I would put her in such grave danger. She easily could have been killed...* Not for a second until listening to the voicemail had I considered our intoxication. I acted as nothing but a blind drunk fool.

Upon calling her back, it went to voicemail. I would have to wait. I wanted nothing more than to sit by her, hold her hand, turn back time and spend the evening differently, but I could not. *Get on the bus to St. George. Get on the shuttle to the Grand Canyon. Go to work and pray she recovers.* My heart hurt, but calm thinking returned. *Just get to the Grand Canyon.*

St. George, Utah, offered an opportunity to rest. The shuttle to the North Rim wouldn't arrive until the following morning. All I could think about was her, but I needed to eat and sleep. I had little money, and after booking a room in the cheapest motel I could find, only thirteen dollars in change remained. Out of cash, no credit card, only coins. The change afforded two tall-boy Tecate beers, a pack of cigarettes, two small bags of spicy peanuts and a banana. I ate my meager meal, drank the cold beer and smoked a few cigarettes outside the door of my room. Exhausted, staring beyond the highway into the expanse of the western sky, I could still smell her on my skin. My mind fumbled with a meager prayer. *Please, Lord, let her recover. Do not punish her for my foolishness...* I wondered what she was thinking, so far away in a hospital bed. I looked inside my room at the polyester blanket. When the sun finally set, so did I.

~~~

Working at the Grand Canyon North Rim resembled an adult summer camp. Two hundred and fifty employees of eighteen to seventy-year-olds, representing a plethora of countries and backgrounds, catered to and dealt with the eager mass of tourists flooding the forested Kaibab Plateau. Down the one-lane wilderness highway to the edge of this wonder of the world, thousands clogged and chattered. They arrived from all over the world. We,

CINEREAL

the employees, provided them with smiles, sustenance, sarcasm, eye-rolls and genuine interaction. But when we finished our shifts for the day, we partied like it was our last day on earth.

Each employee was an important cog in the tourism wheel. From dishwashers to banquet managers, housekeepers to barbecue pit masters, we put on our hats and kept the show rolling forward, spring into autumn. My job was that of an inventory worker. The department comprised three. Twenty-two-year young me, a sixty-six-year-old half-blind man, then the inventory manager, a forty-year-old wild ole boy from Arkansas. Two weeks into the season, they promoted me to inventory manager. And Chris, well, he could stay if we swapped roles. Chris agreed.

I loved my job. I drove a clunky white box-truck from dry dock to dry dock along the rim of the canyon, one mile, back and forth, all day long. The sum of the resort's food, beverages and paper goods delivered to me, checked by us three and then distributed in our truck to each corner of the small North Rim resort. Although the truck did not have a working radio, it had a compact disc player and two CDs, Willie Nelson's greatest hits and Led Zeppelin's Mothership. We sang out each word in our beautiful green, blue and orange world. Often, I drove with a cold beer safe in its cupholder. No one cared. Few knew. If the job was completed without incident, why would anyone gripe or investigate such trivial things? Out here in the far reaches of southwestern topography, life and work ran a bit more casually than back in civilization.

On days off or mornings before work shifts, I hiked and explored the Grand Canyon and Kaibab Plateau. I grew to love the remote wilderness. I walked among a history erased by much of the country. The land of the Anasazi and Havasupai. A landscape of howls. My second psilocybin mushroom trip occurred in the same cave Teddy Roosevelt and renowned cougar hunter Uncle Jim Owen had spent a season living in, along with an orphaned mountain lion cub. Surrounded by the echoes of long-ago legends, I melted into an environment that finally felt like a home.

At each day's end, the employees returned to our little village away from tourist's eyes. With a small gathering of cabins, dorms, an RV park, a rustic lodge, bathrooms, a cafeteria, an employee bar complete with a billiard table, big screen television, computers, laundry and more, we had all we needed. The resort's 250 employees became a familial, quirky community. We drank, gamed, dated, fought, bon-fired, danced, drugged and hugged.

CINEREAL

Cocaine had been an acquaintance of mine for years by the Grand Canyon season, yet it was there I first met oxycodone. A typical Wednesday night had ensued. A few of us, after closing out the employee bar, continued the party at the RV park. One brought the weed, another brought a case of beer, I brought a whiskey gallon, and another guy busted out some pills and started chopping them up into appealing ivory lines, just like the powder I knew.

"You ever snorted oxy, New Hampshire kid?" He sneered like a frenemy.

"No, just blow, and well I've smoked opium, that was certainly an effervescent dream…" I replied, confident that I could handle any substance.

"Ah, well, you are in for a treat, my friend. Pass the whiskey and I'll trade ya." He snorted. I handed him the whiskey. He handed me the drugs, and I snorted.

We sailed, we laughed, we drank and smoked and ingested more. In levitation's fade, we smoked cigarettes and stared at the stars. The vinyl record in the background ended. In the still-swigging silence, I stumbled away with the whiskey gallon towards my room, but I could not make it.

I could not see where my bed might be, just trees and darkness. I lay down on pine needles, where I began to quiver and vomit. My body tingled with horripilation, then sweat, then cold again, sticking to dirt and cradling the earth. I curled into the fetal position and fought the lure of disintegration. I recognized this feeling from an incident I had in California. A toxic heavy cocktail of drugs had sent me into a darkness I barely crawled through then. My friend Andrew's dad, a doctor, had instructed us what to do over the telephone. Now, all I could do was stay awake. Under no circumstances could I let myself sleep. Hardly could I breathe. I didn't even know if I was breathing. Hardly could I move, but I didn't even want to move. I just wanted to close my eyes and fade, fade, fade away from this, this, *what even is this…*

Snapping myself into a hazy focus, I considered crawling inside the dorm to my bed, but I knew I would fall asleep there and probably die. The cool air was helping me stay alert enough not to succumb to the danger of slumber. The temperature was in the low sixties. Even at nearly 9,000 feet above sea level, it was still August in Arizona. *I will not catch hypothermia.* My head lay sideways on a rock. I searched for God, the God I loved but had

CINEREAL

abandoned, and wondered why I only considered Him when I did not feel safe. My thoughts drifted to the mountain lions that slunk through camp each night, then to my mother and how much I had let her down. *Why did I make her heartbreak more difficult? Why had I been a destructive tumor upon my already hurting family?* The minutes crawled by like a molasses drip. It would be hours until sunrise, but I must not let go of life, not for one sighing second. *I must not let go.*

~~~

The Grand Canyon summer turned into autumn. I hiked my first North Rim to South Rim trek in September. Down the North Kaibab Trail, across the Colorado River, up the Bright Angel Trail to the other more populated side. A drunk tourist fell off the canyon's edge and died that day. Aspen leaves turned from green to gold. I slowed down on my partying, filling time with long jogs through the Ponderosa Pines. An ache in my soul grew, yet I did not know why. I wondered if it was God disapproving of my frivolities.

In October I turned twenty-three, so we dressed in our ridiculous best and hoisted one last Grand Canyon gala. Wary from the awful drug experience prior, I stuck to only the intoxicants I was confident with. The time to try anything new had passed. We were all about to move on. A few days later, the season ended. The employees of the GCNR exchanged goodbyes and then, just as we arrived, only in reverse, we rolled down our sleeves and left. Each on their own way, each toward new horizons, each an adventure older.

I took my time heading home, stopping by San Diego for a few days, dragging my feet, drinking lagers with limes and eating chips with salsa. My heart did not want to leave the west, but for now it must be so. By Thanksgiving, I returned to my East Coast liquor stores, to the Atlantic beaches, to my ex-girlfriend if she would have me and to the frigid, dim season of long shadows. I returned to the land of my haunts.

CINEREAL

Haunts of the East

Before I continue with the adventures of the west, I must address the haunts of the east. This is where it gets odd. A living oddity I had been experiencing since childhood. Peculiarities that seem other-dimensional. Sinister saps of darkness that cling to the skin. Receive my account of sensations, observations and knowledge, without the need to comprehend. As a child, I did not understand it all, although I do now, but what I knew is that it terrorized my soul.

For years before and shortly after my parent's divorce, we lived in a basic colonial-style house on five acres in the rural hills of central New Hampshire. A land of birch trees, hemlocks, oaks and maples. Our town boasted no stoplights, with many of the roads remaining unpaved. In the winter, snow piled high above the mailbox, trees stood as skeletons, and the roads that were paved, heaved upwards creating bumps, cracks and a jostling ride.

In my young teenage years, leading up to the family dissolution, I was haunted in the clapboard house. At night I would wake to voices whispering my name, encouraging me to harm myself. Sharp lights shone intrusively through my window from the forest. Piercing the darkness, these lights would follow me about the house as I crept down into the living room, peeking out windows, searching for the source. Dark shadows and occasional faces, unrecognizable as humans, roamed around our home. In trepidation, I would sit in a living room corner chair with a knife in each hand, staring at the doorknobs as they rattled, attempting to turn. Each successive day, when scouring the mud or snow for proof, there were never any footprints. The haunts never entered the house until one January afternoon.

Home alone in the winter of eighth grade, having been expelled from school at the beginning of the year, I sat on my bedroom bunk completing the assignments Mother now structured. My family's two cats were upstairs. The dog down in the kitchen. At three in the afternoon, a torrential gust of

CINEREAL

force entered the upstairs hallway, carrying a shrieking audible scream. This long-tailed burst poured from the door connecting to an unfinished storage room on the same level. A room with only one small window never unlocked nor opened. I had always feared this room, so for my awareness I maintained a rolled-up towel at its base flush to the door, so that if anything entered and shut the door behind, the displaced towel would signal its occupancy. Instantly, in-sync with the menacing blast, I sensed the scream and slither of this invisible beast flood each upstairs crevice with the strength of a burst dam. One cat started clawing frantically at the bathroom window, attempting to escape. The other cat darted under my bed. The dog downstairs howled and whimpered. Overcome with a fear I had never experienced, my body leapt into action, thrusting open the bedroom window two stories above frozen snowy ground, punching out the window screen and jumping out, twenty feet down, barefoot, wearing no proper clothes into the snow. I sprinted to my neighbor's house a few telephone poles away.

When my mother returned, she met me at the neighbor's home. We all went to investigate the event of terror I described to them. At first, downstairs on the main level, the setting we observed appeared to be a normal one, except for the dog and two cats hiding and shivering in fear. Upstairs, the bathroom's wooden window frame wore deep gashes from the cat's frantic claw scrapes. The entrance to the attic was shut. The one window within remained locked. But the rolled-up towel had moved, as if the door had been violently flung open. No human or beast was discovered, but the fear within my and the animal's bodies could not be quelled.

After the family divorce, as soon as able, Mother moved us out of the colonial Deerfield home. With my younger brother, sister, mother and me now living an hour away from the haunts, we rested and proceeded, seemingly safe in a new home on the seacoast of New Hampshire.

Although life moved forward normally, with a new high school, new athletic teams, new friends and community involvements, the living darkness was not ready to leave me alone. My divorced parents did not know what to do with me, or how to handle my confusing terrors. Therefore, psychotherapy became a top priority. I hated and fought against each remedy, revolting with a vehement animosity. Seven therapists gave up on me, not willing to deal with my spectrum of sass to sheer obstinate anger. The eighth, a psychiatrist, labeled me schizophrenic with severe depression, or something along those lines. The former was not an accurate diagnosis, I knew, but it gave my parents something to hold in their intellectual hand. Each night and day I remained tormented by the living darkness, my mental health continuing to deteriorate. The only solace I could find in life was being alone in the forest, writing poems, playing sports, taking drugs and ultimately, drinking alcohol.

Despite beginning my drinking career in the curious manner many pleasure-seeking teenagers do, I discovered that when I drank, the living darkness did not feel as hostile. Instead of fighting against the enemy, I could commune with it. During my young twenties, when at home in New Hampshire, I would often separate myself, tuck away into different outdoor nooks, to drink and secretly share fellowship with this beast. These nooks were pleasant places, where the end of roads met water, many rocky steps away from sight, beneath an overhanging tree. There, I would sit on the earth, drink my alcohol, stare out into the distant horizon and they would appear, entering through my peripherals. Like drifting wisps, sauntering, with visible bodies yet concealed faces. Occasionally, long lines of them approached, never-ending footless walkers dominating the full scope of my vision, gently greeting me, rarely uttering a sound. Not these silent forms, at least. There were many kinds I came to learn.

I knew Mom and Dad understood I saw these beings, Mom with more comprehension, but I don't believe I talked about it much once I'd begun my young adult adventures. During these long sits, my mind was usually far away. Staring at the horizons, letting my smoke drift into my comrades, they both of similar shape and color, *like that brackish water out there…* It became something of a Stockholm syndrome, for when I opened myself to allowing time with them, by drinking alcohol and accepting their summons, they did not infiltrate my mind with the desire to hurt myself as often. Perhaps this is because I was harming myself. Only when I'd fight against this darkness would they tear me down within, and I'd be warmly swaddled by the seducing pull of death.

For this reason, my job on the cruise-ship had come to a forceful end. After a few months of work life, the exotic makeup of adventure wore off. Beneath was the simple truth of being stuck on a giant metal box at sea with 3,000 unruly vacationers and 1,500 dutiful staff. Claustrophobia set in. Few locations offered refuge from the perpetual noise and crowds. I rebelled against my "authorities," smoking cigarettes on public decks, snapping back when reprimanded. My attitude switched from a cheerfully obedient employee to a "don't tell me what to do" deviant. The living darkness' voices persisted, following me from New England out to the center of the Pacific Ocean. At night when storms ravaged the water, and no one was permitted on the decks, I would sneak out regardless, to rise and fall upon the crest of giant waves, smoking defiantly, laughing maniacally.

Seven months into my contract, as I was trying to sleep in the lights-out obscurity of my below sea level berth, the voices of the living darkness escalated, calling my name audibly with sharply mocking, heinous intention, baiting me into reaction. At first, I placed a pillow over my head, but they only summoned louder. Then, I took a few swigs of whiskey from my bottle, but this did not help. Finally, in a fed-up rage, I started beating the metal standing bureau. I pounded and pounded, screaming back while ravaging the metal until they stopped. Thirty minutes later, exhausted and wearing no clothes other than boxer-brief underwear, I sat on the lower bunk in the dark. I lit a cigarette and smoked. My body ran wet with perspiration, so I wiped my skin with damaged hands, unaware of the blood pouring out of my fists. All I could feel was the numb of silence. Abruptly, my roommate opened the door and turned on the light. With a gasp, he shuddered at my sight, sitting there, crazed, covered in red vital fluid, the metal dresser now adorned and speckled with hundreds of fist-shaped dents all battered in gore.

Within thirty minutes, they threw me into the brig. Law-enforcement and the ship's doctor asked demeaning questions for hours, then left me for the night to stew in my madness. During the entire interaction, I did not cooperate peacefully. I fumed like a rabid animal about to be shot. Around noon the next day, having docked in Hilo, Hawaii, they led me handcuffed through the ship and down the gangplank to a police car, driven to a psych-ward and detained for the afternoon. Although the hospital was hesitant to let me go, two phone-calls and two guarantees from both my New England psychiatrist and my dad convinced them to hand me over. An officer then finally transported me to the airport, escorted me onto the airplane, and I flew to Los Angeles. The days at sea on a ship of jesters were finally complete.

CINEREAL

Grand Teton National Park

Early in the spring of 2009, at age twenty-three, I fulfilled my promise to return to the Grand Canyon North Rim to help clean, set-up and prepare for the new season. I had purchased a used evergreen '98 Jeep Wrangler hardtop in New Hampshire that winter, so I drove solo across the country, returning to the lands I love. Park gates were closed, the snow was still high, but as I was there for duty the rangers let me in. The weeks picked up where autumn had left off. A reunion with co-workers, spring bonfires, hikes to Anasazi ruins and awe-inspiring vistas, but once the doors opened to tourists, I was determined to move on. Obtaining a job working with horses in Grand Teton National Park was my goal. Prior to the summer surge I told my boss I quit, trekked one last Grand Canyon rim-to-rim hike, played poker all night, won 200 dollars, threw my duffle bag into my Jeep "Izzy Roadhouse" and rode out at dawn.

    The morning wore a magical, familiar sensation. The first step of a new, wild adventure. Deprived of sleep, I pushed on until reaching the small community of Jacob Lake, where there stood a store, restaurant and gas station. A location I imagine Edward Abbey had appreciated as well. I loaded up on supplies, such as cigarettes, beer, water gallons, beef jerky and apples, filled my gas tank, then located a nook in the trees in which to sleep for a few necessary hours. Acquiring rest proved difficult. Despite completing a twenty-four-mile rugged hike a day earlier and persevering without sleep for almost forty-eight hours, all I could think about was exploring the expansive west. Once restored enough to drive, I purchased a large coffee and then pushed north into the massive maroon lands of Utah.

    As far as my vision allowed, dramatic horizons surrounded my rattling green box. Powerful gusts of wind pushed my sharply shaped vehicle back and forth across the road. Strenuously, I held onto the steering wheel with a lean into its charge, until passing through a slot canyon and having to correct back because of the sudden absence of the blow. Then, upon exiting into vast orange and brown space again, I clutched the wheel with both hands,

CINEREAL

ready to receive the next blasts to come. I imagined what I looked like to a condor above peering down upon my travel. Spotting the one wobbly motor on this lengthy thoroughfare, from his wingspan drift, cackling at my green speck being bashed about, attempting to hold the thin gray line in a land constantly forced to battle against a society which attempts to tame. "May the land win!" I shouted, raising my hand out the window into the dry rushing air.

In the afternoon, with the sun beating on my left cheek, I came upon a ranch and inquired about horseback riding lessons. I had ridden often in my youth, my grandfather made sure of that, but to earn a western horseback job in Jackson Hole, I knew I'd better practice. It seemed my request was an odd one, for there was no inviting sign, but the ranchers chuckled and obliged, waving me in and pointing where to park. They mounted me on a horse within fifteen minutes. We rode across the raw earth and talked about all things equestrian. Occasionally we picked up speed, causing spring sagebrush to zip by in a pale verdant gush. When we returned to the ranch, I mucked a few stalls and helped feed the steeds. We all ate dinner outside as the sun set beneath a celestial canopy of developing colorful hues. The kind folks told me that my visit had been a pleasant surprise. "We don't get many visitors out here," the gray-haired lady with a button-nose chimed between chews. They offered me a bunk and stay for breakfast, which I thanked them for, but I must continue following the North Star to Wyoming.

"When else does a young man get to experience the pull of Polaris like this, other than on his first drive north through Utah beneath this wide-open sky? I haven't slept much in a long while, and that while isn't quite over yet. I'll pull over and sleep when I need to. Don't worry, I will be better than fine." I smiled gratefully at them all. From their nods and extended head-lifts to the heavens, I knew they understood.

~~~

I had never been in the presence of the Grand Teton Mountains before. This would be my first venture into Wyoming. Approaching from the south, crossing state lines with the exquisite Utah in my rear-view mirror, I turned up the Jeep compact disc player's volume of Johnny Cash. "I'm going to Jackson," I bellowed and sang along, never caring that he might have meant Jackson, Mississippi, and not this one. "I'm gonna mess around, yeah I'm going to Jackson, look out Jackson town!" With adrenaline thrills, I rolled into the wealthy municipality, parked Izzy Roadhouse and commenced a bar-hopping day. *This is the best way to know a place,* I then believed. *Drink everywhere, talk to the locals, get a feel, learn the vibe, ask questions that lead to answers.* After five or six drinks, I made friends, who invited me to a party and even offered a couch to sleep on. *A proper start to a new chapter,* I thought, clinking my beer with others, laughing late into the night. I partied for a few days, but as my limited Grand Canyon money dried up, I knew it was time to get out of town, drive up into the park, and go find that job.

Wyoming contains thousands of ranches, the Jackson Hole area harboring hundreds, yet one stood out as it was more than just a ranch; it was a whole resort. This appealed to me, for my goal wasn't to be a cattle hand, but more of a paid interactive personality atop a horse. Structured much like the Grand Canyon North Rim, only much larger, the Grand Teton Lodge Company employed around 1,000 people, offering room and board as part of its compensation package. The facilities comprised lodges, restaurants, cabins, spas, the dude-ranch, swimming pools, non-motorized boat services, white-water rafting, camping and more, all the typical park-resort services. *This will be adult summer camp varsity edition,* I considered gleefully.

The drive north out of Jackson town into GTNP, on US Highway 89, is a stunning bride in a royal's dress. The weight of the mountain range's beauty isn't truly experienced until surpassing the town's surrounding modest hills and buttes. Then it hits you, with the same impact of gargantuan space and allure as standing on the rim of the Grand Canyon, only it isn't looking across and down, it is looking up and into. The mountains rise as magnificent granite cathedrals, a western wall of jagged teeth gnashing upward from the wide flat valley floor, as if from a folklore land, with naked necks, ivory corseted waists, donning forested skirts draping hems into diamond lakes. Bejeweled by the sun or silhouetted by its set, steadfast thrones in airspace-fires, silent seers in midnight skies. The Grand Teton Mountain range is a voluptuous giant.

Upon arrival at the resort, I put on my best unwashed outfit, combed my messy hair with calloused fingers and confidently walked into the main Jackson Lake Lodge. I was feeling extra savvy as my adventurous work-life resume had been advancing. I had finessed how to talk and present myself from the Hawaii and Arizona jobs. *Look them in the eye, maintain posture, present a firm handshake, enunciate, secure the job.*

CINEREAL

The lodge boasted a spacious room that continued onto a wide veranda. Baring tall ceilings and massive windows looking out upon Willow Flats, Jackson Lake and the mountains, it appeared more prestigious than any other room I had ever entered. Leather couches, an impressive fireplace, a stuffed upright grizzly bear, a snarling mountain lion and even a grand piano decorated the space. Because I had been a classically trained pianist for over a decade in my youth, this fine instrument enticed me. *I will play that piano soon*, I decided. Tucked in the northwestern corner of the lodge was a clean little tavern, my first point of contact.

As soon as I sat on a barstool, two staff members welcomed me. It was clear they weren't busy. The season was still young, and the time was merely two in the afternoon. I smiled at the girls working and ordered a beer. I thought they were cute and fancied maybe they thought the same of me. She placed my cold, tall, golden ale center to my shoulders and elevated the conversation as I peered around the room.

"Welcome to Jackson Lake Lodge. Is this your first time here?" She could tell I was new to the area.

"It is, and I must say I am impressed thus far." Sipping my beer, we laughed at the foam mustache it left on my lip.

"Good. I'm glad you like us, like it… welcome to the Grand Tetons." She fluttered her arm in the mountain range's direction clearly visible through the tall clean windows. "Well, what's your plan? Are you going to go hiking?"

I looked her in the eye as I made quick progress with my drink. "Most certainly, but first I am going to snag a job." Her eyes lit up inquisitively as she watched me chug and set my empty glass down. I grinned and continued, "In fact, would you be so kind as to point me toward the human resources office?"

It seemed I had made an impression, for she giggled and replied, "I can do you one better, I will walk you there." Turning to her coworker she informed, "Sadie, I'll be back in a few minutes," to me, "come on cowboy, wipe your mouth and follow." I obeyed her command. Internally reiterating, *cowboy*, with a gentle smirk.

The human resources office was down in the basement recesses of the resort. The first lady I spoke with appeared less charmed than the sparkling-eyed bartender. "Have you filled out an application online? All our available job listings are on there."

CINEREAL

"No, no, I have not. I haven't been on a computer, let alone the internet, for some time. But I am here now and am happy to fill out a paper application. I am ready to work." The lady did not seem enthused.

"You must fill out an online application first. That is how we do things around here."

"Well, maybe it's time to mix things up. I am here, ready, available. I am not online." Standing my ground, she did not look me in the eye, only glanced at my dirty black jeans and returned to her paperwork. "Is there someone else I can talk to, someone more helpful?" At this slightly impervious request, a lady from an adjacent office emerged with a much more welcoming shine.

"Hi Wing, come on in here. I am Lisa, Cathy's boss. Let's discuss job options and see if we can't sign you to the team."

Happily, I obliged. I gave Cathy a wink. She rolled her eyes as I joined Lisa in the back office. Lisa shook my hand, made me feel worthy, and we began by discussing my employment history. "We are mostly staffed for the season. We just opened, as you know, but we incur a decent amount of turnover through the year. What is the job that you are looking for?"

"I would like to ride and work with the horses on the ranch. I know how to ride. I always hustle, embrace dirty work, learn quickly, and am confident I will be an asset to the equestrian sector."

She chuckled at my enthusiasm. She didn't laugh at me, or maybe she did, but I did not mind. "Well Wing, I can tell you this, I would love to hire you for a job, but the wrangler positions are highly sought after, filled, and most of the candidates were raised on real ranches, working cattle in Texas, Idaho, Montana, they are not hobby riders. It is also a position that requires first aid certification and involves daily interpretive interaction with guests, for it is more than caring for horses; they act as storytelling guides. Our wrangler position must keep guests safe in the backcountry, guide them on horseback plus educate and entertain them with interesting facts of the mountains, flora, fauna, history, all of that, you understand?"

"Ah yes, that sounds perfect for me! But I understand they are filled, and I imagine my riding is novice compared to them all. However, I do have my current first aid certification, and if a wrangler position opens, I am confident I will learn to fill the role with exceeded expectations." I grinned. She paused, smiling as if to set the horse focus aside.

CINEREAL

"What I have available and am happy to offer you right now is newsstand cashier." She noticed my excitement fade and continued. "It isn't a glamorous position, and it only pays minimum wage, but it is full-time and comes with room and board. A bed in a two-person room and three meals a day."

This was all I needed to hear. *Get my foot in the door, prove myself, secure a place to live in the park and daily food to eat.* "I'll take it, Lisa! Thank you, and when or if a wrangling position becomes available…"

"We shall see, Wing, we shall see. I will prepare the new-hire paperwork. Come back tomorrow morning at nine, and we'll get you all set up. And Wing, shave your face. Every day you must be clean-shaven. A mustache is fine, but the cheeks, chin and neck." Lisa rubbed her chin, indicating smoothness. I understood.

"Yes ma'am. See you tomorrow morning!" I strode out elated, buzzing with an eager heart and staccato steps. This new opportunity was worth celebrating. One more night in Jackson town and then a new life chapter at Jackson Lake Lodge.

~~~

I did not entirely enjoy my job at the newsstand, but I embraced it. I knew it was an opportunity to prove myself, to learn and to connect. Most importantly, it allowed me to live and play in the glorious national park. All my life I needed challenges to grow, from the athletic fields, school and beyond. When I did not feel challenged, I would seek outlets that provided such. *This Wyoming season will provide unique opportunities for development*, I acknowledged.

The newsstand was a small store in the lodge's main lobby. I could see the front doors from my post behind the register. It sold magazines, newspapers, candy bars, chips, drinks and the like. I and co-worker Don, an older, slower man, split the shifts and created our own schedule. Initially, I overwhelmed Don, because I had many ideas on how to run the store properly, but after a few stubborn days, he relented and let me take over. "These are the ways to make this store run more efficiently, Don, trust me."

"I'm starting to grasp the reasons behind your ways, Wing. You remind me of my grandson, the good one." Gray-haired Don leaned with his elbows on the countertop.

"Thank you, Don, well my grandfather always told me, 'There is a right way to do things, and a wrong way,' and to that I add, sometimes there is more than one right way, however that doesn't apply to everything. Currently, this is a jumbled mess, so we shall adjust accordingly. No leaning at work, Don. Please bring this overstock to the back room. I am going to reorganize these shelves." Don chuckled, shrugged and obeyed.

When I wasn't on paid duty, I used my time exploring all of Jackson Hole in my Izzy Roadhouse. The wild land was full of bears, both grizzly and black, mountain lions, wolves, coyotes, elk, moose, bison and a plethora of other local critters. Throughout the season I observed them all. I would set out at dawn and place myself somewhere ideal for such interactions. One morning, from only 100 yards away, I witnessed a grizzly bear kill an elk calf.

I climbed many of the Grand Teton peaks with new acquaintances, then hustled down before the afternoon thunderstorms. At night I competed in billiard tournaments in the employee bar, drank cheap beer and whiskey, flirted with girls, smoked marijuana behind the dorms, then retired to bed and did it all over again. Employees from many countries were present. International work visas were popular among young people like me. I made friends with the Ukrainians, Filipinos, Latinos, Germans, Australians, Italians, Brits, Native Americans, and Serap. She was one of the beautiful Turkish women. Serap spoke little English, and I did not speak any Turkish, so I purchased a translation dictionary and asked her roommate to help me learn. Beginning with "merhaba" and progressing to "bugün çok güzel görünüyorsun," Serap and I quickly became adult-summer-camp companions.

Amid all the good-times and newsstand work shifts, I did not forget my goal. Often, I visited the horses, examined the wranglers in action, studying how they worked the ranch. My understanding for the flow of their day grew as I observed their chores and how they pulled horses for the tourists to ride. Twelve guests and two employees would head out on backcountry tours daily. They would leave with smiles and return appearing exhausted. Despite the interpretive guide's humor, it looked to be very stressful dealing with the often-clueless city slickers. On one day off, I purchased a ride for myself, implementing my earned employee discount. I blended in with the guests, followed the wrangler's commands and listened to the stories they expressed on the excursion. There was much to know, so I applied myself to learning it all. I purchased books specific to the greater Wyoming and Montana wildernesses. Birds, plants, animals, local legends, geological history and more, I read and soaked it all up. I understood that one must go out and earn life's opportunities, as they are not readily offered. Position and prepare to make each dream come true. After one month of flawlessly running the newsstand, keeping the money till always exact, and each guest leaving with an informed smile, the day finally arrived. A wrangler had broken their leg on duty. The team needed a new wrangler as soon as possible, and though I never wished harm to anyone, I was ambitiously prepared.

First thing in the morning, I returned to Lisa's office in human resources and proclaimed I desired the wrangler position. She smiled charmingly and agreed I had a chance. "You have done well in the newsstand, Wing. The cash is always correct. The shop always opened on time. And the guests rave about you, saying you know all about the park already, providing informative advice and directions."

"Thank you, Lisa. Everything I do, I give it my best. I will do the same with the wrangler position."

"You will need to speak with the general manager concerning this. I will give you a chance, but the confirmation must come from him." She spoke seriously. I understood why. It was a serious job, and I had seen him around; he was an austere man.

~~~

"This is not a job to take light-heartedly Mr. Wing? Williams." Reuben Goldberg looked at me with no hint of a smile from across the organized boss-sized desk.

"Yes, sir, I understand, and I take this all with the utmost respect and preparation. I am committed to keeping everyone safe and doing the job well." I felt uneasy in my large, squeaky leather chair, but I maintained confidence.

"Yes, safety is the most important priority, but we must also give the guests a grand experience." His mustache seemed to tickle his nose, hairs pointed errantly, as if tines on a cactus, yet he did not sneeze.

"A Grand Teton experience!" *I shouldn't have chimed in with that...* He did not find it amusing and continued.

"This is the most demanding job on the resort, well, this and the white-water raft guides, and neither do I delegate lightly. All our wranglers, and we understand it isn't your typical wrangler job, but nonetheless it is what we call it, all our wranglers have been raised with horses, lived on real working ranches, and applied for their jobs months before the season began. It is not a job we just hand out, Mr. Williams." Reuben Goldberg seemed quite reluctant to offer me a chance. He seemed set on scaring me away, as if he wouldn't give me a direct no, yet wanted me to withdraw my interest. *I must step up, take control, and convince him I am worthy.*

"Mr. Goldberg, I agree with you. If any part of me believed I was not a valid candidate, I would not be here. Although I did not grow up on working ranches, I was first placed on horseback as a young child by my grandfather and took riding lessons in Florida, Georgia and New Hampshire. Mucking stalls, properly caring for tack, reading the animal, listening, understanding their language, knowing how to form a trustworthy relationship with each horse is a skill I have been taught and know well. To keep the guests safe, we must keep the horse safe, understand the horse, not push it into or beyond what it desires. I trust horses, and they trust me. When it comes to the rigors of the work, I am not scared by any of it. I was taught to hustle, to never give up an inch, to push through exhaustion, to persevere. Pain is not an enemy. It is a guide and a teacher. When it comes to the knowledge needed to be a good interpretive leader, that I have been studying. I know the western meadowlark is Wyoming's state bird. I can identify every avian, animal, flower and tree in the park. Did you know Aspen bark wears a gentle white powder? Rub it, see it on your hand, that is SPF 5, natural sunscreen! Sagebrush, once considered cowboy cologne, was used to mask body odor and emit fresher of a scent after long journeys through the wilderness. Did you know that when the sunlight hits the Skillet Glacier on Mount Moran just so, you can spot the glint of the aircraft that crashed there on November 21, 1950, which killed all twenty-one people on board? I know the stories, the history, I have the skills, temperament, motivation, patience, persistence and grit for this job, Mr. Goldberg. You just need to give me a chance to prove myself." I was no longer smiling, and I had much more I could say, but I shut up, looked him in the eye with the power of a determined young man.

Mr. Goldberg leaned back in his chair and, for the first time I had ever witnessed, he smiled. "Alright, Wing, I like you. Finish up your last shift at the newsstand tomorrow and on Monday report to the stables. Five-thirty in the morning. Do not be late. I will inform Mary, the manager, today. She will conduct your training and report any mishaps back to me, but I must say, this just might be the right job for you." He tapped his finger on the desk, finally wiggled his pestered nose and gave a nod of affirmation.

"Thank you, sir." My heart soared, my soul fluttered, yet my face remained mostly stoic, displaying only a hint of glee. It was time to prove my assertion.

~~~

My new co-workers on the dude ranch did not seem to like me much. Which was fine. I'd made enough friends at GTLC. That's not what I was searching for. I desired to work and learn. I preferred to earn their trust and respect than their friendship. First, Mary informed me it was called a dude ranch because "dude" referred to the city-slickers, the paying guests, or the "idiots," as Oren put it. "They come in here and hurt the horses more than anything else, 'cuz they don't know how to ride. But sometimes they tip ya fat." He rubbed his thumb and pointer finger together, indicating cash-money.

Oren was the most talkative to me and to everyone, it seemed. He was twenty-one, grew up ranching in Oklahoma, and was the "best damn rider on the ranch," he winked and declared. He knew I was a greenhorn, but at least he took the time to explain the procedures and tricks of the trade. Mary, the boss, was kind, but short with her explanations. She expected me to figure things out on my own. Only if I was about to attempt something incorrectly would she interfere, do it herself effortlessly with a few huffs of guidance, then leave me to it. Dallas was a few years older than I, the most capable but reticent one. I observed him often. Everything he did, each knot tied, each horse handled, each whisper of direction, each smooth sweep, brush and effortless mounting, he performed as a born natural. Once, to be helpful, I put his saddle away in the tack room. He was feeding the horses, so I figured it would be a friendly gesture.

"Never touch my saddle again, Wing," Dallas snapped. "Never touch another man's saddle or horse."

Noted. His short, direct words stuck with me.

There were sixty-five "dude-horses" and one diminutive cranky pony at the ranch. Everyone called the pony Sixes because, well, he was number sixty-six and exuded the personality of a little devil. The dude-horses were calmer, older, well trained. They were supposed to put up with the city-slickers' naivety. This was usually the case, but not always. Beyond these sixty-six horses, each wrangler, I made number seven, had two designated chargers of their own. No one else would ride another wrangler's steed. These majestic animals were not always well-mannered, nor even very well broken in. That was one of our duties. We were to bond with them and help them mellow into calm, trusted rides. Eventually, in the years to come, ours would then most likely be added to the herd of "dudes." The two horses designated for me were Pigeon and Jalapeño.

Pigeon was a beautiful dappled grey Arabian. She was the older of my two, at the adult age of seven, yet she showed no signs of slowing down. "Newly acquired by the ranch only a few days ago," Mary informed me. Pigeon was the equivalent of a Porsche company-car. She was remarkably nimble, could turn on a dime and run from morning until sunset.

Jalapeño was her counterpart, not a sports car but more of a compact Ford Ranger truck. As a mixed breed of Mustang and Quarter-horse, she was sure-footed, strong, rugged, intelligent, and in-tune with the western country. Her dark brown coat glistened red in the sun. Her long dark mane covered her eyes when she was stationary and moved like the Colorado River when she galloped. She was young, age two, and was also recently acquired by the dude ranch. Because of her history and age, Jalapeño had not been ridden many times. "Give him Jalapeño. That'll teach Wing," Oren loudly suggested to Mary my first day on the job.

I took the time to become friends with my mares. Instead of directly jumping on and riding, I whispered to them, letting them smell my breath, neck and hands, desiring they grow familiar with me. I sang to them as I'd brush, saddle and feed. Every moment with my horses was an opportunity to strengthen trust. We became fond of each other swiftly. As we rode and experienced the nuances of each day, we learned to understand how each other thought and moved. Although Jalapeño bucked me off three times in the first two days, we were just figuring each other out. They each exuded their own unique personalities. Pigeon, my emotional spitfire, and Jalapeño, my intrepid steed.

The days on the ranch were growing into weeks, and while I looked the part, I was still in training. My riding had been improving, but I knew I wasn't there yet. One day Reuben Goldberg stopped by the ranch seeking a report on my performance to determine whether I should keep the position. I was in the tack room sweeping and heard the conversation with Mary. She had left her office door open. "Well, he has the proper teachable attitude, a hard worker," she spoke, "but he is still adapting to the intricacies of the job. We

CINEREAL

keep him busy here, make him do the tasks we don't want to and let him ride daily for practice, but we haven't sent him into the backcountry with guests yet. Hey Dallas, what do we think of Wing?"

Dallas poked his head into the office and solely stated, "He'll do." I smiled upon hearing this. I must continue to improve, but I would be permitted to stay.

The workday started promptly at 5:30. Wake and arrive at the stables with twilight. We fed the horses before we'd feed ourselves. The six of us worked six days a week, revolving the seventh hand on one day off. Breakfast was 6:30 to 7:15. By 7:30, the four wranglers who were taking guests out on the day-long rides would begin to pick and pull the dude-horses. This selection process depended on a few factors: the type of guest, whether it was a rest day or workday for the horse, and which horses cooperated with the others. Some horses we would never place next to each other, as they would always fight.

One morning Tilly, a tough wrangler from Montana, hollered at me, "Wing! Go pull and saddle Foghorn, Iris, Red Lady, Mama Bee, Thunder and Seldom."

"You got it, Tilly! Which one is Mama Bee again?" I inquired.

"You should know each horse by now. Go figure it out." She retorted.

Alright. I grabbed the six horses' halters from the tack room and proceeded into the paddocks. My presence still being fresh to this herd caused each beast to turn heads and stare me down, shuffling and romping about without a care for my goal. I pulled two horses at a time, starting with the ones I knew. The other wranglers jeered at my rookie ways. "Two at a time, eh," smirked Dallas as he led six horses at once, three sets of reins in each hand, all six horses calmly bunched and submissively walking behind him. I ignored him. *I'll rise to that soon, but first I need to remember who the hell Mama Bee is.* After securing my fifth horse, Red Lady, I cornered who I believed was Mama Bee. On my walk to the line with the final two steeds, "not Mama Bee" reared up and started kicking Red Lady, causing the mare to spin and fight back. Suddenly, I found myself in the middle of a dust storm with hooves and necks flailing about. A hoof crashed down upon my foot, shooting lightning pain through my entire body, but I held on to the reins. In the mayhem, the wranglers laughed hysterically, and I knew, *this is not Mama Bee.*

CINEREAL

Guests arrived for their backcountry excursions at eight-thirty and nine-thirty, timed for the rides departing at nine and ten. Two wranglers rode out with each ride of twelve guests. The lead wrangler determined the exact route, adjusting direction from the usual trail for wild animals or weather. This wrangler would also act as the interpretive guide, pausing the caravan at vistas or meadows to tell stories and facts of history and fauna. The second wrangler rode in the far back, monitoring each horse and guest, making sure saddles, girths, bridles, and reins were all properly used and secure. As the caboose of the cavalcade, they would trot up to guests when needed, help them adjust stirrups, or advise on how to ride more comfortably. Each wrangler had an important role to fulfill to maintain order, ensuring every rider and horse remained safe.

Mary had made it clear I was not ready to work on one of these rides yet. So, during the day I remained on the grounds at the ranch. She always possessed a radio attached to her belt to communicate with each wrangler in the backcountry as needed. Occasionally emergencies transpired, such as horses bucking off tourists, or even just tourists quitting on the ride out in the middle of the backcountry. Meanwhile, between eavesdropping on the radio calls, I kept myself busy with the many tasks at the stables and paddocks. Cleaning up manure, fixing fence posts horses kicked down, chasing and catching the defiant pony Sixes each time he escaped, sweeping, moving and stacking hay bales, all needed to be accomplished daily, plus any other job Mary delegated. I did not mind being the grunt, for everything I accomplished was of value. My time to join the expeditions would come. Often, Mary emerged from her office and guided me through the process of administering medicine to the animals in need. Be it from wounds or illness, this was a priority task. This part of the job was especially enjoyable for me, operating as direct loving care. I adored the horses. Spending my days among them nourished my soul.

In the afternoon, at three-thirty and four-thirty, the twenty-eight dusty horses and riders would return. Guests shared laughs and photographs, the wranglers received their cash-money, and everyone bid their grateful farewells. The adventure had come to an end. In the morning's reverse, we'd then cooperate in putting away all the guest's saddles, brush and tend to each steed, then slap their rumps and send them romping into the large paddocks. Feeding the horses would always be the day's last chore, wrapping up our work around five or six in the evening. The twelve-hour shifts produced

CINEREAL

robust appetites, and a hearty dinner often encouraged early sleep. But regardless of the long days, my twenty-three-year youthful body still prioritized time to drink alcohol.

~~~

In late June, when spring shifted into summer and the mountain snow melted into torrential cascades, leaving only glaciers to shine white, I was finally called upon for my first working backcountry ride. I would be the wrangler in the back. Oren would lead as an interpretive guide. Although thrilled to learn of this opportunity, I acted as if it were not a big deal. *I deserve it. I am ready for this.* In all areas I had improved, and though I still felt like an outsider amongst the posse of wranglers, I wasn't being treated as much of a rookie anymore. Every day I now administered each horse's medicine without Mary's help. Each horse I knew by name and personality. I pulled and led six steeds at a time, and no animal rebelled against my commands. My riding had matured, performing naturally in the saddle, walking, cantering, galloping and communicating in symbiosis with both Pigeon and Jalapeño. I'd been bucked, bitten, kicked, and stepped on, and with thirty days of long, hard, fulfilling work under my belt, I knew the ranch and its routines as a home.

Oren was a goofball. While his twenty-one-year-old mind radiated through an exuberant smile, it also added to his marginally reckless decision making. I experienced this as soon as we left sight of the ranch, entering the backcountry and spotting a black bear sow with cubs. Oren ordered the guests to stay put as he then chased after the bears, causing the mother to curse him in bear's words. He returned laughing, claiming he pulled the stunt for the guest's safety, although both he and I knew that wasn't the reason. Most of his stories and interpretive skills were jokes only he found humorous. Often, he spoke over the shoulder in a manner which caused most of his words to be lost in the wind. I observed diligently from the rear, occasionally trotting up to a guest and repeating to them what he had most likely proclaimed.

At the Oxbow Bend overlook, a wide vista thrust above the Snake River, I launched into a story for the guests as Oren urinated in a distant bush. I explained how Oxbow Bend received its name, about the Snake River's origins and destination, and how a healthy wolf population contributed to maintaining firm riverbanks. The guests listened engaged, following up my speech with a few questions. Oren had returned during the talk, and once I completed my lesson, he let out a whoop and holler, saying, "That's my boy Wing! He knows more about that stuff than I do!" We continued, with Oren in the front, but at each pause and photo opportunity, I now spoke first. Oren strode about with boots on the ground, taking pictures of each guest on their mount as I propelled into another unique fact or story. Oren did not seem to mind that I commandeered the interpretive guide duties. He listened intently and smiled in his jolly, good-natured way.

At dinner that night, Oren announced to the rest of the wranglers, "Wing made us more tips today than I've made any ride all season." They all raised heads from shoveling food into their mouths with either curious or surprised expressions. I didn't know about that, nor did I have another ride to compare it to, but I stated we did alright. "No, we did more than alright. This guy's a natural at talking to the guests," Oren wolfed down a forkful. "From now on, when Wing rides with me, I'm letting him tell the stories."

Everyone continued eating grilled chicken and green beans, letting the table to silence and the chattering background hum of the cafeteria take over. Next to speak was the man of few words. "Wing's riding with me tomorrow, and he can do all the talking." Dallas looked at Mary and then at me. She nodded. I nodded. The decision was made.

~~~

My second outing on an official trail ride, with Dallas leading the way, turned out to be the most pivotal episode of my Wyoming season. I had ridden Jalapeño the day before, so it was Pigeon's turn. My heart wore a smile as we clopped along, I in the back, tasting the dust, smelling the excrement and sweat of thirteen horses ahead. The morning cruised by with no stressful incidents, but by afternoon distant thunder rumbled. While this was a common occurrence, these atmospheric snarls appeared foreboding. The mountains wore an ominous cloak of dark clouds, as if the severity of those sharp gothic peaks might spill out into the sky directly above our heads. Dallas and I each had a radio to communicate as needed. Back at the ranch, Mary was keeping an astute eye on the weather's developments. If we needed to divert from the typical trail, we would do so.

As our line of riders approached Elk Flats, Dallas and I received an urgent message from Mary. "Bring the ride back to the ranch immediately! Do you copy? Return to the ranch ASAP!!" It was apparent this was the correct decision, for within moments the storm spilled into the valley. Lightning bolts struck the ground less than a mile away. Hail unleashed from

CINEREAL

the heavens and shot down in a rampage. Our location upon Elk Flats, which is an aptly named swath of land, flat and wide, ideal for elk congregation, was especially treacherous in a storm like this, for its exposed ground of sagebrush, native grasses and rocks left our convoy vulnerable to the violence above. Only a few lone trees dotted this expanse, some of them already shattered from lightning bolts in the past.

The danger escalated on the highlands. We must descend at once. As the storm approached, Dallas and I attempted to keep the horses and guests calm. Lightning flashed with immediate booming thunder. Wind knocked hats off heads, prompting Dallas to exhibit rare emotion, yelling, "Leave it!" The usually mellow dude-horses acted scared and agitated. Sidestepping and spinning, taking advantage of the novice rein-holders, the guests were losing control of their steeds. One horse bucked and threw an adult onto the ground. Dallas jumped off his steed to help. Her horse shot across the acreage with the saddle sliding low around the belly. Another horse bucked slightly, but the rider held. Another lightning bolt shattered the sky. Horses continued to fall out of line as all spiraled into risky disorder. As I was holding the reins of one of the guest's horses, attempting to calm his nerves, a brown gelding with a young twelve-year-old rider bucked up and took off like an arrow across Elk Flats. The boy was nearly tossed from the horse, but his ankle became caught in the saddle's stirrup. His body flailed to the side, and his top crashed to the ground while the horse sped away from us. Helplessly, the animal dragged the boy as it galloped. His head hung dangerously close to the horse's frantic hooves. His face bashed against sagebrush and dirt. It was evident his ankle would not slip free from the stirrup, which had become twisted up and held him prisoner.

Within one second of seeing this hazard unfold, I reacted. Dallas was on the ground helping others, so I spurred Pigeon into a gallop and rushed after the brown gelding and flailing pre-teen. I must stop them, but to do so I must not approach from behind, for this would only goad the escaper to flee faster. I arched Pigeon's course, creating a curved approach intended to cut them off. Pigeon's speed accelerated as I leaned in. She understood the assignment. Her Arabian ancestry naturalized her for this. While she covered ground faster than the brown gelding and boy, we had further to go, a calculated arch versus the torrid line. Sagebrush whooshed by while a deluge of heavy raindrops replaced the hail. To my right, the boy was still being dragged. He cried out fearfully. His voice, though frantic, signaled that he was still conscious. We continued our gallop, cutting right and ahead, edging into the angle, determined to come down on the gelding's chaotic efforts. Once we had cut them off, we decelerated our speed, now riding down into the face of the runaways. I watched the gelding's reaction to our presence, judging for any new erratic movements. Terror exuded from the bulging whites of his eyes.

"Whoa, whoa boy, whoa," I tried to soothe his speed once I was within arm's reach. His gallop sputtered into a jumbled canter. I reached out and grabbed the loose, unmanned reins, jumping from Pigeon. She veered away from the tackle. My boots hit the dirt, then I leaned back into my heels, pulling the lively mass to a halt. The boy sputtered a mixture of tears, dirt and sobs as I rushed to his side. I held up his torso with one arm and untangled his ankle with my other. I let go of his horse and tenderly set him flat upon the ground. His eyes locked with mine. He was alive, but the brutal dragging cut and slashed his face. Blood trickled down to his lips while his entire body quivered with pain, terror and adrenaline. His ankle was mangled and broken. "It's okay, bud, I'm here. We got you." I tried to calm and assure him as I looked back at the distance we'd covered, at the tiny horses and humans scattered across Elk Flats, at his mother screaming above the now deescalating winds, at Dallas who was trying to gather them all back together.

I radioed Mary and Dallas. "I've got him. He's alive but needs medical attention as soon as possible. He won't be riding back. He can't walk, fractured ankle. We will probably need a helicopter to evacuate him out of here." To the boy I smiled, "You doing alright, kid? That was some tough stuff you went through, but you held on strong." The boy tried to smile back, but his flesh and mind seemed to fade into shock from the wild event. I held him as he trembled. "It's going to be alright, bud. Match my breathing, in deep, out deep, I've got you. Everything is alright."

The storm passed as quickly as it had ravaged. Dallas and I gathered all the loose pieces and put them back together as we waited for the helicopter to arrive. We retrieved hats and horses and assured everyone they were now safe. The sun bore down upon us again, causing illuminated steam to rise from each drenched body. I kept my eye out for any other danger that might occur, like a curious grizzly bear. The potential of such was always out here. The boy now lay beside his mother. She rubbed his head while his dad paced back and forth. Once the tough kid was aboard the air-ambulance en route to the hospital, we escorted the somber troop home. The guests all sat slumped in their saddles. They were tired from the heightened commotion. It was not the adventure they signed up for, and yet, it was the adventure this land would occasionally provoke.

When the day was finally complete, the horses corralled and fed, all guests departed, with dinner but a short jaunt away, Dallas walked stride in stride with me. He placed his hand on my shoulder and spoke. "Had he been dragged much further, I'm not sure he would have made it. One kick to the head, or just one big rock. I think you saved that kid's life today, Wing. Good work."

I looked at Dallas and nodded but did not speak. *Yup,* I thought, *one kick to the head, or one big rock…*

~~~

The next morning at the ranch, I received a phone call from the boy and his parents. They had spent the evening at the hospital and were resting up. Doctors attended to his broken ankle and the cuts on his face, but everything would heal. They thanked me for what I had done. The seriousness of the situation had not escaped their minds. They joked maybe they were better off in the city. I wished them well and hung up the phone. We commenced our day as usual, with a calm, beautiful ride, followed by evening chores and feeding. As I was scooping up manure before last meal, I heard the rush of footsteps behind me. Before I could turn around, two people secured both my arms and dragged me backwards in a forceful motion. Fighting to get loose, Oren and Dallas gripped tighter. I kicked my boots, digging heels into the dirt. I jostled my limbs trying to break free, but the guys only stated, "You ain't gettin' outa this one, Wing." They hauled me across the paddock, stopping once we reached the edge of the large trough filled with water, the horse's drinking hole. *Oh no.* I fought and twisted and tried to swing my fists into their bodies, but I lost beneath their efforts. Up and into the water they lifted and dunked me. Their joyful faces were visible in my blurred vision as they submerged me in the cold, dirty water. Only then did they let go.

I stood up in the trough, drenched from my boots to my Stetson hat. My jeans and pearl-button shirt saturated with the saliva-filled murky hydration. Wiping my face and eyes, I could now clearly see each wrangler, including Mary, standing around me cheering. Oren and Dallas laughed in exultation. Everyone clapped as I stepped out of the trough, shaking my hat free of excess. I tossed a few harmless punches their way and laughed with them. *This is not being bullied; this is not a sign of dislike; this is love and acceptance. This is a "wrangler baptism."*

"Wing, you're all wet! Why'd you go swimming like that?!" Oren chimed with his big goofy grin. "Go get yourself cleaned up. We are going to eat steaks and then go to the rodeo tonight! I'm riding saddle-bronc, and then after we are all getting drunk!" He dragged out the last word, exciting all our boozy appetites.

And so, that is exactly what we did. For the first time since my arrival, I joined the wrangler gang on a wild night in Jackson town. All seven of us rolled out of the Hole, consumed a robust dinner of medium-rare ribeye steaks, then cheered on Oren as he lasted eight seconds at the rodeo. *Maybe he is the best rider of us all,* I proudly considered. After the event, we drank pints of beer and shots of whiskey while playing billiards at the Million Dollar Cowboy Bar and dancing with girls we'd just met. When last call arrived, our sober designated driver, Mary, drove us back to our bunks. After a mere few hours of sleep, the sun rose, and we gathered again to start our day. Hungover, we sat atop our sure-footed steeds, clomping through the dust, smiling at each other and the mountains. From then on, I led the rides regularly, and though there were more emergencies in the backcountry to come, involving bears, moose, stubborn tourists and medical episodes, we responsibly handled each one, keeping all the guests alive. Every day forth until the end of the season, we lived and worked together as a coherent family.

In late September, I drove the long way home. Izzy Roadhouse and I followed the Snake River from its Jackson Lake origin to its Columbia River destination. I spent an afternoon exploring Seattle, but the city only made me miss the mountains. The next day I visited Mount Rainier, then destined east, camping at Priest Lake in Idaho, gradually rolling through northern Montana, North Dakota, Minnesota, Wisconsin, around the Great Lakes, on through Pennsylvania, across upstate New York and finally into New England. It was time for another cold, dark season of the haunts.

CINEREAL

The Appalachian Trail

On October 14, 2009, having recently returned to the Northeast, I turned twenty-four years of age. My season working with horses in Wyoming inspired me to progress in this vocation. I found a stable/stable job in New Hampshire at Kensington Farm. Eastern horsemanship is a different style from the Western riding I preferred. In this "English" riding, equestrians wore helmets, tight pants, fancy clothes, and polished shiny boots. Everyone seemed to have plenty, if not too much, money. To me, the attitude of the horse owners appeared snobbish. Instead of rodeo, barrel, trail and such, they applied the terms dressage, fox hunt, show, and jump. A well-known Olympian, who trained others aspiring to compete at high levels, managed Kensington Farm. Wealthy folks boarded their expensive animals, and though I did not prefer the people as much, I swiftly bonded with all the steeds. The Quarter Horses, Mustangs and Saddlebreds of the west were replaced by Thoroughbreds, Morgans, and Warmbloods in the east.

Duplicor was a colt rated the top one-year-old Irish Warmblood in the nation. He was worth nearly a million dollars; I was told. However, Duplicor knew nothing about money, for he was just a curious kid. While I mucked his stall, he played with my hat, picking it off my head and tossing it against the wall, then emitting a joyous whinny. I taught him how to do basic math by stomping my foot on the ground the number of times each numeral was worth. Once he understood single-digit numbers, such as stomping his hoof with me three times for three, I'd ask him what the sum was of two plus two. We'd stomp four times together. I knew he probably didn't fully understand, but he certainly enjoyed the mental exercise.

My other favorite horse on the farm was Chaco. After my job interview and invitation to join the team, I'd asked if there were any horses I could ride. The owner laughed and said, "Well, there's Chaco." Curiosity beckoned me to know more, and so she continued. "Chaco is kind of my forgotten horse, poor boy. He's only four and hasn't been ridden in maybe three years. He lives out in the far paddock. Chaco doesn't really fit our lifestyle here, as he's not a show horse, but rather our black sheep of the family. But he has a strong Western pedigree. His sire was a barrel champion."

Chaco sounds a lot like me, I thought.

She continued. "He's a wild thing, not allowing anyone near him. He gets fed and mostly just does his own thing. If you can catch him, you can ride him all you want, but Wing, be careful." I assured her I would and looked forward to meeting the kindred animal.

During the first week of work, I made my way over to Chaco's corner on the wide-open meadows surrounded by the forest line. He was a handsome young brown horse. I didn't bother to wrangle him yet. This was just a meet, greet and opportunity to build familiarity. I meandered about the field while he frolicked around me, keeping a wide distance. The next day I returned and did the same thing, talking to him, assuring him we were going to become friends. He'd approach within fifty feet, attune his listening ears, then zestfully spin around and romp off to the far side of his acres. When wrangling day arrived, I brought a halter and rope, determined to catch him. He huffed a few snorts upon my entrance, keenly watching as I walked to the center of the field and sat down. That's all I did. I sat down on the grass. Positioned with my back to Chaco, I hoped it would trigger his curiosity. My strategy worked. Within a few minutes, the young brown horse felt impelled to inquire. Perhaps he wondered, *why did this human turn his back to me like that, and sit down on my grass? They always chase me and leave.* He then walked all the way over to me. I listened to his hooves clomp until they stopped. Now looming above, he sniffed my hat. He sniffed my ears and neck. I reached up and gently petted his muzzle, then rose to my feet since he was not jolting back. Chaco lifted his leg as if considering bolting, so I stood still and whispered to him. He remained calm but wary until he set his hoof down and sniffed my face. With ease, I slipped the harness over his head and began striding with him. That was all it took. The owner had one old western saddle she offered me to use. Graciously I accepted. The first time I placed it on him was a raucous event. Chaco bucked me twice before surrendering into a pleasant rhythm. Within a few weeks, we were galloping all over the farm. I taught him both direct reining and neck reining, while we preferred to implement the latter. We developed a trustworthy friendship as two loners who needed each other. In this, myself, Chaco and the owner were quite content.

CINEREAL

I remained a quiet, dependable farmhand, moving in the shadows and empty spaces between the activity of the rich folk. They paid little attention to me, which I preferred. I roamed the grounds on the farm tractor, tending to tasks, turning the horses out to their fenced paddocks in the morning and then leading them back into their stalls at day's end. I'd change their large wearable blankets, feed, water and brush them down and muck each stall daily, providing fresh sawdust for a clean, comfortable bed. When a horse broke out of its outdoor containment, I wrangled it up, guiding the heavy-breathing rascal home. Hay bale stacks and manure piles were rotated and tended by my hand. Occasionally my services were required to be more public, like when an impatient owner could not load their anxious Thoroughbred aboard their long, modern, lustrous trailer. The horse stomped obstinately, rebelling against the owner's sharp commands. So, I stepped in, leaned in, whispered, breathed with and then smoothly guided the horse inside the claustrophobic metal container. "It's gonna be alright, my friend. I don't know where they are taking you, but when you get back, I'll be here." I smirked at the owner, who thanked me with an insincere gruff, then continued with my duties.

The time I spent on the farm that winter kept me out of trouble, mostly. Although I was not out partying and wasting too many nights, I always kept a flask of whiskey in my boot. No one knew or cared because they rarely spoke to me, usually leaving me alone to do my job. I'd occasionally flirt with the rich girls, informing them of the sore hoof or leg their expensive animal was nursing, and sit out in the far meadow on the seat of the tractor, smoking and sipping, watching fancy people braid manes then jump over rails and logs, or shuffle back and forth to the large indoor riding facility. I soaked in the winter's low afternoon sun, observing the light shift across the land. It was a place I could think, allow my mind to focus and plan my next chapter. A new seed had been planted within me during the Wyoming summer, a seed which had grown into winter decision and preparation. I knew what I would do next, and come spring, I would be ready to announce it to my predecessor.

~~~

"Alright Dad, drum roll, please. Are you ready? Are you ready to hear what I'm going to do next!?" I piqued his attention as he uncorked another bottle of smooth Spanish Rioja.

CINEREAL

"I'm ready, son. Let's hear it. What is next for my firstborn?" I handed him my glass. He filled both his and mine to a hearty line just beneath the brim.

"I am going to hike the entire Appalachian Trail. From Georgia to Maine!" I beamed with excitement. Hearing the words out loud made it seem more real.

"You are going to what?!" He feigned disbelief. This was a step up from my previous working adventures.

"I am going to hike 2,179 miles, all by myself. I heard someone mention the Appalachian Trail when in Wyoming, and then I remembered we saw some thru-hikers, that's what they are called, the ones who go the distance in one season from beginning to end, on top of Mount Washington when we hiked it for my birthday a few years ago. Remember that?"

"I remember that, yes. The trail comes right through New Hampshire in the White Mountains, doesn't it? Up and over Mount Washington."

"It does, so if I start at the southern terminus in Georgia, atop Springer Mountain, it'll be like walking home." I smiled again. In fact, I was probably smiling the entire time, complete with wine-tinted teeth.

"Alright then. Have you gotten this all planned out? When are you going to start? What gear will you need?" He sat back down on the couch in front of our paused Humphrey Bogart and Lauren Bacall movie.

"Today is April 1st, and this is no fool's joke, I tell you, but I quit my job at the farm yesterday, and I am going to ride the Amtrak down next week with my goal to start hiking north on April 10th. As for gear, I have already gathered half of my supplies and will purchase the rest, such as a sleeping bag and backpack, before departure. I've written out a list so I know exactly what I will need. Also, I have opted not to bring a tent, just a hammock and tarp." I sipped and paced, eager to hear more of his opinion.

"I see, I see. Well, that doesn't leave you much time. Are you sure you will be ready by then?" Dad always kept matters realistic.

"Of course. I have been thoroughly preparing. I've researched each section, including what trail towns will be available for resupplies. As far as what I can learn beforehand, I feel confident in the logistics. There will be much to learn as I go, surely. This is no last-minute spontaneous idea. I am just telling you last minute." I laughed, knowing this might irk him slightly, but also, I did not care, for I always made my own plans, while he delighted in having such a unique adventurous son, or at least I hoped.

CINEREAL

Dad nodded, drinking wine in his dad sort of way, looking at me and then looking off, thinking to himself. When he spoke, he said words I did not expect. "I'll tell you what. How about I move my trips around some, I'll look and see, but it should work out, and I could drive you down to Georgia myself? We can leave on the seventh or early on the eighth and get you to the trailhead to hike the morning of the tenth."

"You'll do that for me!?" I couldn't believe what I was hearing. Sure, he had visited me in Hawaii and at the Grand Canyon, but this was next level and would simplify transportation significantly.

"Of course! I couldn't come see you in Wyoming, and you know I love the resume of unique experiences you have been building. I would be honored to be a part of helping you begin your next adventure." Dad beamed back at me. He loved me, I knew, despite all that had been. He wanted the best for me, and if that would not be college, it might as well be a grand life of exploration. We clinked our wine glasses together and cheered.

"Cheers, Dad. Cheers, Son. To the Appalachian Trail!"

Nine days later, on the night of April 9, 2010, Dad and I sat on the spacious stone patio of Amicalola Falls Lodge. We had our wine once again, and our feet up, for the drive to the trail's southern terminus was accomplished. Nothing more remained than to rest and say farewell in the morning. Before us lay the dark expanse of the Appalachian Trail. No visible lights shone to our north, only thick mountainous forest covering the rugged peaks of northwestern Georgia.

"It feels a little odd driving you down here just to drop you off in the woods and hope for the best." Dad cut through the silence with his gentle concern.

"It does feel a little odd, but I am prepared for whatever comes. I may not be prepared in the sense that things might arise I have never dealt with and did not expect, but mentally, I am prepared for anything. Plus, I have the gear to survive in any weather." I assured him. "Remember what you were doing when you were twenty-four? You were a Navy pilot exploring this planet in your own way, entering the unknown, facing obstacles, succeeding. Give me the same trust you gave yourself then."

Dad nodded and spoke. "Yes, you make an excellent point. We each are explorers in our own way. I know you will be alright, better than alright. You will, and do, succeed in whatever you set your mind to."

CINEREAL

"Thanks, Pops." We smiled and then sipped, returning to silence, savoring our northwestern Georgia evening together and the earthy notes in our glasses.

I did not sleep well that night, although Dad did. A few times I looked over at his chest rising with each chortled snore. But it wasn't the noise keeping me awake; it was the anticipation. In the morning, I could not eat breakfast. As Dad helped himself to another decadent round, I sat forcing small bites. We talked minimally, for my mind was full. He nodded, chewed and understood. *I am ready. I am here. There is nothing else to do but begin. I'll eat on the trail.*

~~~

One often thinks he or she is prepared, or that they know what to expect upon entering a massive new undertaking. Preparation is vital, but experience is where true learning takes place. I had read guidebooks on the Appalachian Trail, studied maps, backpacker articles, grew up hiking in the White Mountains of New England, logged solid miles and climbed many summits in the Grand Canyon and Grand Teton regions, but nothing could have prepared me fully for hiking 2,179 continual miles of rugged mountain terrain other than committed immersion. Start, and then you will come to know. All the fear I'd held to myself leading up to the hike melted away as soon as I took my first steps into the unknown. No longer was I waiting in anxious anticipation; I was there. I was in it. The dream had become a reality.

The Appalachian Trail's southern terminus is Springer Mountain. Its northern terminus is Mount Katahdin in Maine. The goal of accomplishing the entire hike seemed so massive it was difficult to wrap my mind around. Even the first day was brutal and exhausting. Therefore, I chose not to dwell on the entirety and instead focused on one day at a time. The Georgia mountains are nothing to scoff at, which I innocently thought prior. They aren't the tallest mountains on the trail, maxing out just above 4,000 feet in elevation above sea level, but they are harsh, steep and continual. They stretched to North Carolina as a rollercoaster 2,000 feet up, 2,000 feet down, repeatedly for horizons on end. I created a mental gauge of steepness based on elevation gained or lost over a mile. One thousand feet of change in a mile was average. Anything above that I considered potentially strenuous; anything less, easy. While being April, the flatlands below had welcomed warm spring weather, but up in the mountains it was still cold, wet and

CINEREAL

dreary. Leaves were barely starting to bud on the naked trees. Thus, my venture began with the birth of foliage.

When we begin something new, when we step into an environment we have never entered before, the community that world offers greets us. The trail community is a marvelously passionate one, and I joyfully realized I was now a participant. I had heard of things such as trail angels and trail magic, but I did not accurately know what that entailed. Every hiker who set out into the forest with the same goal became an active member of this loving community. Those who aided the hikers were considered trail angels. The help these angels provided was labeled magic. Trudging through the Georgia woods, facing bears, ghosts and harsh weather along the way, a most welcoming sight was a beverage cooler at a road crossing, with a note attached, encouraging the hiker to keep going. "Please help yourself" to a sports drink, water, beer, soda, fresh piece of fruit, or candy bar from inside the hospitable box. Each simple, thoughtful gift reinvigorated the soul. Sometimes the trail magic was far grander, such as a few kind people grilling burgers and hot dogs at a gap, notch, or pass on the trail, generously providing a full meal for the hikers. The magic came as rides offered to town, to resupply and skip the potentially sketchy hitchhiking process. While the occasional rides made for convenient municipal access, I preferred the enterprise of hitchhiking, for one must trust their instincts when accepting or declining a ride. Hitchhiking was much like bear encounters; I came to learn. Nine times out of ten, it was a safe, thrilling experience, but that tenth time, survival tactics might very well be needed to subsist.

Though there were many hikers who embarked from Springer Mountain, intent on reaching Mount Katahdin like me, many of them quickly became overwhelmed, injured, or simply exhausted by the magnitude of the goal. Scores of people quit in the unrelenting mountains of Georgia. We thru-hikers labeled them the "Georgia statistics." By the time the bubble, the hiker mass, had reached the North Carolina border a mere seventy-six miles in, almost half of the hikers surrendered and decided this undertaking was not for them. Georgia slashed the weak, as wind separates chaff from grain.

In the early days on the trail, each hiker in their rookie season receives a trail name. This name differs from their birth name, and someone usually gives it to the individual after a unique or ridiculous event. For example, some of my new friends were called Mohawk, Hand-Me-Down, 151,

CINEREAL

Jurassic, Flying Colors, and such. While Wing is not my birth name, it is the name I had been dubbed two years prior and called by many. And as Wing is already unique, I did not want this name to potentially hinder what could become my trail name, so during each introduction I told everyone to call me by my old sports moniker "Dubs." During the first few days, everyone tossed around ideas for each other. Some stuck, and for some the time had yet to come. My time arrived in the small town of Hiawassee.

Fresh out of the woods with only one more day of Georgia to go until reaching the North Carolina state line, we piled into eateries to fill our bellies with comfort food and beer. I, along with many other hikers, discovered a barbecue joint claiming to have the "hottest wings in Georgia." They offered a hot wing eating challenge, warning that very few could ever complete the task in the allotted time. The wings were so hot they supposedly left everyone suffering and surrendering in pain. Boldly, I announced I would partake in the endeavor. While an entire barbecue barn and porch full of hikers and locals looked on, I ate wing after wing, holding nothing back, leaving no meat on the bone and no hot sauce on the plate. The challenge required the participants to eat all twelve wings within an hour, a time that at first sounded generous, but with the fiery blazing heat of each wing, it became clear why the entire hour was provided. I did not care, one down in thirty seconds, mouth already on fire. Two down in one minute, my entire skin poured perspiration. Three down in two minutes, my vision blurred, and body trembled uncontrollably, yet I pressed on with a fury. By the time I passed six wings in ten minutes, pausing only to laugh maniacally and swig beer, the entire barbecue joint full of humans was cheering me on. Pints and fists pounded on tables. "Hot wing, hot wing, hot wing," was chanted in unison. I pushed on like a wild man, reaching the twelfth wing before twenty minutes had elapsed. I paused and stood up, lofting the excruciating piece of meat in the air, and to the raucous applauds of all, lifted by the loud chorus of cheering, I annihilated the final wing triumphantly. My body slumped back in my chair exhausted as if I had survived a mighty battle, sweat puddles had formed on the floor below me, my entire body felt as if it had been dipped into hell, but I had won, I did it, I ate them all. "Hot Winggg!" Mohawk yelled. "You are motha-freakin' Hot Wing!!!" And so, Hot Wing became my trail name, even though they did not know I was already called Wing at home (another wild story I will in due time share). I then realized, breathing slow soothing breaths, turning down the offered cup of milk, partaking in a cigarette and another pint of cold beer, *perhaps this confirms it, I was meant to become Wing all along.*

Although I and most others had entered the wilderness alone, there were so many hikers on the trail I did not feel alone. It was easy to make acquaintances and friends because we were all in this together, while each still hiking one's own hike. We shared meals by springs and rustic camping huts, reveled in fellowship, traded stories of our lives and days. Yet each hiker moves at different speeds, so after Georgia shattered many spirits, the early season masses known as the hiker bubble thinned out. Everyone grew more separated, spreading out along the trail heading north through the lush ranges of North Carolina and Tennessee. It was easy to settle into the long spaces ahead or behind and walk completely alone, listening only to the chatter of birds, groan of trees and the occasional crack of branches as a bear scampered across the trail.

Spring in the southern Appalachians was wet. Everything, everywhere. Snow melted in the highlands, causing the trail to be muddy and slippery, resulting in slow, arduous progress. Hikers took advantage of every chance to dry out in the sun. I would strip myself of all clothing and hang the drenched attire on branches or rocks in full shine, pull everything out of my backpack and let each piece steam until dry. While soaking up the sun's rays, with moisture steaming off my body as well, I ate my disfigured trail food, tended to new blisters or rashes, and observed the surrounding nature, attempting to ignore the aching pains in my feet and whole, all while laughing at how authentic and worthy the suffering was. "Embrace the brutality" is a phrase we thru-hikers cheerfully lived by. These breaks in the sun not only warmed the body and uplifted the spirit, but they also dropped pack weight, as moisture-logged items grow heavy. Once everything was dry, we placed all items back where they belonged and continued hiking, often into an afternoon rain shower or thunderstorm, wherein we would become saturated again.

The first month on the trail broke my entire body down into a struggling crawl of a pace. I was in strong physical shape when I started the hike, or so I believed. I'd always been an athlete, and would consistently workout in gyms, run and hike on trails back home, but nothing can prepare the physique for carrying a heavy pack up and down mountains every day, other than carrying a heavy pack up and down mountains every day. The first month was a period of extreme discouragement. Achilles tendons constantly throbbed in pain. Knees shook beneath exasperated use and weight. Feet were always cut and blistered. Rashes ravaged where my clothing and pack straps rubbed against skin. Swollen trench foot turned my lower extremities into mush, seemingly unable to heal. The body's shoulders and core felt like they could hold no more. Many times, upon hearing the hum of a road in the distance, growing louder the closer I approached, "veins of society" I called them, I considered quitting, knowing how easy that would be, how close comfort and the elimination of self-torture was. But deep in my heart, this was not an option. *I knew this would be difficult, maybe not this difficult, but I did not come out here to give up, ever.* So, I'd stand up, hoist the pack again, and keep going, slowly, one miserable, painful step at a time. Often, peering up steep ascents, I forced myself to count steps to one hundred, then take a break, to ten, break, one, break, another step, but under no circumstances abandon the goal.

After a month of hiking, everything changed. The troposphere thickened into a jungle-like humid air. The sun beat down hot, and the body strengthened. Each pain faded, and in place of the misery an armored power emerged. One I had never experienced in my entire short twenty-four-year life. No longer did I fall short of breath or my body desire a slower pace. No longer did I need to take a single break despite the grade and length of ascent. Descending mountains didn't shoot sharp pain into my knees anymore, nor did I need to nurse one leg or foot over the other. I was born anew, forged in the rigors of the Appalachian Trail, reconstructed into a wellspring of stamina. With this new potency, the entire experience became one of feeling superhuman. I ran up and down mountains. Daily mileage doubled. My mind no longer flirted with ideas of quitting, yet I rose each day fully rested, enthralled in the endless possibilities ahead. I did not feel like I was away from home on a grand adventure anymore, for the mountains had become home. Each day now wore the cloak of blessings, beauty, surmountable challenges, peace, the routine of walking and deep, sincere gratefulness.

As I trekked north, I realized I had not been hearing the voices of the living darkness for some time. I considered when and why that had changed. Though they were always prominent in New England, they were not contained to that corner of the country. *They had followed me to Hawaii and to the Grand Canyon, but they must have ceased in Wyoming.* This realization surged with elation in my soul, although its cessation held a much darker reason than I then understood. The previous winter in New Hampshire they had not returned, yet I had not recognized it until these forested steps. *Perhaps it is because I discovered a way to spend my days doing things I loved. Working with horses had been healing for me. Spending each day in the mountains is strengthening me,* and yet, perhaps their silence was because my focus and mind had grown so far away from obeying God... I haughtily laughed and pridefully shouted out loud as I roared up the long winding trail. "Demons no more! I am free!" Laughter quickly broke into tears, escalating into weeping sobs of confusion. Part of me celebrated the absence of the malevolent weight; another part wept in shame. Salty secretions forced dirt down my face as my legs quickened into an emotionally driven charge up the steep mountainside.

During these Appalachian days, I learned how to stride perfectly. Sure, I knew the basics of walking, in the way we all learned as babes, stand on two feet and move forward. But I realized I was refining how to walk for hiking. With my arms swaying, extended down at full length, and trekking poles balanced in my fingers parallel to the ground's contour, I settled into a pure flow of gentle mechanical pendulum action. This action propelled me forward. My posture adjusted, my stride focused on how far apart they must accurately be, keeping the weight of my core and backpack in my center. By month two, in every moment I knew exactly the speed I moved, such as 3.7 miles per hour, 4.1 miles per hour, 2.9 miles per hour. I counted steps, distance, calculating the math in my mind each day, gliding across the earth simply, fluidly, efficiently. Other hikers complained about seeing nothing but roots, rocks and dirt. A long hike staring at the ground was no way for me to live, so I trained my vision and mind. As I trekked day after day, I practiced looking at the earth ten steps ahead, memorizing each potential obstacle, aware of what was to come, then lifting chin to peer up at the trees, ridge lines and horizon. If I tripped or stubbed my toe, I had not memorized the earth ahead of me well enough. With each step of every mile, I practiced this, mile after mile until it worked its way into my subconscious and became a habit. Look ahead, observe the land without telling yourself to do so, then walk with head high, trusting that you know what is to come. This practice improved my entire hike. While other hikers hung their heads down in careful, limited vision, I soared, flying upon the highlands as a bird with wings emancipated.

As walking served as a form of meditation, so did my relationship with the millions of tiny, pesky airborne bugs. The surrounding hikers grumbled about mosquitoes, gnats and flies, swatting profusely at them, donning nets on their heads to keep them off their faces and necks. Many people wore ridiculous amounts of bug-repellant. I observed this constant losing battle everyone succumbed to each day, while dealing with the continual annoyance of the bugs myself, but in my observations, I mused there must be a better way. Instead of fighting the bugs, I made a treaty with them. On my walk amid a bug-infested spring, I started conversing with them telepathically. *Hello bugs. I am Hot Wing. It is nice to meet the multitude of you. I have come to a decision and a request. From now on, I will not swat at you, nor flinch when you zoom at me. No longer will I kill any of you out of frustration, nor fight the never-ending war against you. Instead, I am simply going to exist with you. My request is asking you to treat me the same. Let us form a symbiotic treaty. Tell your friends, spread the news, Hot Wing is not an enemy. I am your friend.* I continued to speak to them in this manner each day. They never spoke back, but the result was marvelous. While I sat and ate my lunch with no mosquito netting or any repellent, the swarm of bugs around my body ceased biting me. They were still there, but we began to peacefully occupy space together. I watched as they continued to bite all the other hikers, and the hikers all continued to fight back, but not me. Many of the hikers asked how I did it, and I told them, to which many sneered, but even though they too saw the continual results, they kept on swatting and living in the bug-biting hell I had escaped. To this day, I practice this successful method.

A few days after mastering the bug problem, as I was searching for some jewelweed, which is a natural remedy for the rash poison ivy causes and always grows near the other, I had another idea. *Since my plan with the bugs worked, couldn't my telepathic intentions also work for plants?* All living organisms carry defensive properties but utilizing these properties exhausts and depletes the organism to a degree. That is why a baby rattlesnake's bite is potentially more dangerous than a mature snake. The baby doesn't know when to hold back its venom, but the adult does, for releasing its venom requires a sort of restoration period. Therefore, the plants, in theory, should only use their defensive properties when they sense danger, when it is a necessary time to use such. As animals can detect fear and emotions, and then react in the appropriate manner, perhaps plants do as well. *From now on*, as I rubbed jewelweed onto my poison ivy rash, *I will project the same telepathy to plants as I do to bugs. I will tread intentionally, seeking never to harm, and they will know by my mindset and energy that I am not a threat.* "Save your defensive properties next time, poison ivy!" I bellowed into the forest. "I shall be more respectful of you." From that day onward, although my body still occasionally brushed against poisonous foliage, my skin never again developed an uncomfortable reaction.

While many of the hikers grouped into trail families, and many singles coupled up, I preferred to progress alone. We all knew and cared for each other. The trail community is a tight-knit one. News traveled swiftly up and down the brown ribbon, through the green tunnel. Each rustic camping hut or hostel along the way had a trail journal hikers could sign. This acted much like a news source, an account we would scour and add to. It was entertaining to see the unique signatures reappear, to become familiar with the hikers ahead, and to read accounts of what happened in the location prior, such as a resident bear harassing at night. I had my unique way of signing my trail name, Hot Wing, often with a tidbit of poetry. After each journal entry, I voyaged onward as a woodland creature, happy in my meditative steps but always eager to party and drink alcohol.

Trail towns are a hiker's vortex. Existing exactly as designated. They are usually modest mountain villages either directly on or near the Appalachian Trail. Hot Springs, North Carolina, is an example of the former. In these vortexes, hikers stay for a few hours to multiple days and reconnect with hikers that had been ahead or behind on the trail. Town days proved to be restful and peaceful, or occasionally downright wild. We called our non-hiking days "zero-days," as zero miles were hiked. Nero-days was slang for "nearly zero" miles hiked. Nero or zero-days amongst society comprised resupplying trail food and vices at the markets or picking up resupply boxes we'd mailed ahead to the post office. We washed our one small load of clothes at the laundromat, bathed our filthy bodies clean, and most important of all, ate and drank. A thru-hiker is always hungry and thirsty, and town offered all the delights to fulfill our woodland fantasies. With our daily caloric output so high, so too could our caloric intake be. Entire pizzas were consumed, burgers and milkshakes on double order. Beer was drunk in volume, pint after pint, for it was difficult to become inebriated with our metabolisms. I never understood why someone would want just one or two alcoholic drinks. To me, it seemed to fall short of the ideal goal, as I always drank to gain a solid buzz. At age twenty-four, I was oblivious to the notion of a red flag, naive to this omen of the future. The idea of alcohol addiction was alien to me, as I knew of no alcoholics in my family history. Since I could stop drinking whenever I chose with no withdrawal symptoms, there must be no problem with my actions.

Two rowdy days in Hot Springs consisted of arm wrestling and drinking games with the Aussies, Germans and locals. Once we'd had our fill of the taverns, we purchased racks of beer and headed to the riverside where we made camp and continued partying into the night. We whittled bows and arrows out of forest saplings, competed in fire-making contests, grilled steaks and fresh vegetables, cooked whole chickens underground, devoured copious amounts of junk food, and shared grand sagas until the sun began to lighten the sky. Despite our town parties, we would eventually hear the whisper of the trail calling us home. To this beckon we would submit, for our duty was not to stay, but to always trek onward.

~~~

Summertime in the Mid-Atlantic states felt as if the heat and humidity knobs were turned up to full blast. We continued to be drenched from sweat and rain. On top of the heat, snakes slithered and lounged everywhere. One morning, I had to maneuver around seven giant rattlesnakes in the first mile of hiking. Although we were passing through their territory, snakes had always been the only living creatures I felt uncomfortable around. Copperheads and rattlers bit a few hikers I knew. They were rushed to the hospital and then returned to their respective homelands. With each day and each step, I persevered mindfully. The serpents and weather must be endured; therefore, every chance to cool off was taken. The rivers, lakes, creeks, an occasional trail town swimming pool and slightly cooler air at night provided our only respites.

Another aspect of the trail I observed and pondered was the history of the land. From the formation of the ridges, valleys and peaks to humanity's usage upon it. As I approached the Mason-Dixon Line at the Maryland/Pennsylvania border, I considered all the runaway slaves who had fled through the same rugged lands I had just hiked. All that dense, exhausting way, fighting to reach the Mason-Dixon Line and hopeful safety. It caused my heart heavy sadness to consider this, of those treated as less because they differed from the white self-righteous colonials. It made me angry to think that those who claimed to love and follow God would subject others to such hatred. This always confused me. *How could God be their poster for such malice?* I knew it was not of God, but from the greedy evil distortion in humankind. Under the banner of God, crusades had wrought havoc,

CINEREAL

raping and killing thousands. Apartheid ravaged civilizations. Murderous dominions, all announcing, "This is the will of God." *Utter blasphemy*. I knew in my soul it was horribly, despicably wrong. Despite having been raised in a Christian home, now as I young man I was not sure what to do with what I believed. Although I had grown to be repelled by religion, angered by the distortion of purity, my soul could never shake the existence of the Almighty loving Father. That Jesus was indeed His resurrected Son. I believed in the Holy Trinity and recognized the Holy Spirit convicting me in my wayward actions, and yet I persisted in shoving these convictions away as it directly interfered with the wild ways I desired to indulge and live.

When I was twelve, I witnessed celestial beings as real as the trees and mountains. Not in a dream, but in the awake, unaltered, sober reality of tangible existence. I knew they were not of this world, not of our dimension, their supernatural abilities more powerful than anything on earth. When I experienced this event, I comprehended why and what they were doing. The terrifyingly glorious supernatural beings were shown intentionally to me, and though I understood their purpose, I was yet to fathom why I was allowed to witness such magnificence in action. The event became something I could never forget nor dismiss. In my lifetime, I had only explained the full details of this occurrence to a few people, for most considered my statements to be insane. Consequently, I guarded them, steadfastly believing in life's deeper significance, beyond societal fleeting, empty, egotistical emphasis, and ultimately in our universe's Creator.

Summer on the trail, amidst the steady progress of hiking north, had become far too many zero-days taken. The trail in the Mid-Atlantic region crossed so many roads, which led to so many possibilities, most of which I would investigate. I'd become quite fond of side-quests and hitchhiking. An adrenaline thrill arose when standing on the side of the road with my thumb out, not knowing who would pick me up. I hitchhiked to historic battlefields, towns and nearby cities, explored for a few days, then returned to where I'd left off and continued trekking onward. Virginia Beach was one such side-quest, yet I returned injured, having dislocated my shoulder body surfing the ocean waves naked and drunk at midnight with a group of women I met at a beachside tavern. Determined not to be deterred from the ultimate journey because of my idiocy, I fastened a crude sling formed from bandanas, adjusted my backpack's straps and continued in deserving pain.

CINEREAL

The Appalachian Trail crosses through fourteen states. The southern spring season was an arduous remote trek through grueling Georgia, blooming North Carolina, luscious Tennessee and highland Virginia. Upon completion, a muggy summer welcomed us thru-hikers into craggy West Virginia, moderate Maryland, rocky Pennsylvania, delightful New Jersey, and cluttered New York. In New York State, the trail crosses train tracks with a train stop leading straight into Manhattan for, in 2010, only thirteen dollars one way. I purchased that ticket and took a solo ride.

After spending months with few other humans in the forest, arriving in Grand Central Station, Manhattan, was an absolute mind-bender and culture shock. I had a friend, a girl I'd met at a woodland party back home a while prior, who lived in New York City. She was a well-to-do ballerina, and with her connections and prestige she showcased Manhattan in a fashion I could never have experienced alone. We attended the renowned Memphis play on Broadway and VIP parties, skipping each velvet rope and line at clubs, all with a hotel room overlooking Times Square as our home base. It was a whirlwind of sleepless, party-fueled nights, rendering me ragged and yearning to be back in the woods. The city was no place for me. I needed the mountains and trees. When I finally arrived back on the Appalachian Trail, my hunger for side-quests had been satiated. It was time to get back to work. It was time to make up for the slower trail progress afflicted by summer distractions. Despite our hiker credo "Last one to Katahdin wins," it was time to recalibrate and focus on the trek north. I was nearing my New England homeland. Only five states on the AT remained. Calm Connecticut, surging Massachusetts, mystical Vermont, formidable New Hampshire and finally, magnificent Maine lay ahead.

~~~

The mountains and forests of Connecticut and Massachusetts developed into the land I knew best, the land I had grown up hiking in. Even though it was still summer, the nights were growing much cooler, and the thick coniferous woodlands darker. I partied less and logged far more miles weekly than I did in the summer. Increasing excitement filled me atop each mountain peak as I gazed north. Eventually, on the distant horizon, Mount Katahdin would appear. To the south, farther than I once imagined I would ever have walked, is where it all began. The days were peaceful again, for the mayhem of the Mid-Atlantic was behind me. The New England townships I dipped into for resupplies wore a historic charm. Covered bridges and old

CINEREAL

stone walls appeared. This was no longer the beginning of the adventure, nor the middle; this was approaching the final stage. I often encountered hikers I had not seen for a thousand miles. We would walk for a day or two together, discussing what the trail had grown to mean to us. One dear friend I met way back at Neal's Gap on day three, named Wilbur, encouraged us to consider and prepare for what life might hold beyond the trail.

I had always sensed a kinship with Wilbur. Ever since our meeting in Georgia, we had spent many nights camping together, sharing many meaningful conversations along the way. He was older than I by a few decades, yet our relationship was one of brotherhood. Wilbur's trade and personality were those of a mental health counselor. He liked to joke that he earned his marriage counseling license the same year he got divorced. While this may have been true, he jested with a sadness I recognized behind his words. One day, deep in the forest of Vermont's Green Mountains, as Wilbur and a few of my similar-age comrades and I were lounging by a river smoking some marijuana, he posed a question. "What are your plans after this hike?" We all sat on rocks and dirt, a bit stoned, deep in thought until each responded with sincere thoughts on the matter.

When it was my turn, I stated, "I am finally going to share my writing. And I am going to write more dedicatedly than I have been. I've always aspired to be a writer, I mean, I have always actively been one, but it is time I start sharing it with others, write intentionally, and not keep it in a journal to myself." Wilbur and the boys nodded, with eyes settled on the river, observing the water flow by.

"Well, Hot Wing," Wilbur returned, as Baloo the husky licked its paws, his companion and our friend, "when you write and share, never say what you think they want to hear. Always write exactly what is in here." Wilbur pointed to his heart. I affirmed I understood.

We had many little meetings of this sort throughout New England. When we were all together, we would stop for lunch or an afternoon rest, smoke some of that fine backpacking smoke and discuss life. After our meaningful repartee, we hiked on into the golden hour as a team, in line, singing songs such as The Beatles' "Carry That Weight" loudly and proudly in unison. "Boy, you're gonna carry that weight, carry that weight a long time." Camaraderie and words drove us steadily forth. Our bellows filled the valleys and wafted along the treetops. When our voices grew tired and our minds yearned for solitude with the forest again, we would spread out on the trail, listening to the sublime song of the wood thrush, often not seeing each other again for many miles and days.

Upon reaching the New Hampshire border and checking Vermont off the fourteen Appalachian Trail states list, mixed emotions greeted me. On one hand, I was proud. I had walked "home" from Georgia just like I told my dad I would, at least to my home-state. I still had 161 miles atop the granite peaks, then 282 miles of Maine until I'd completed the trail, but this seemed quite monumental. On the other hand, I was anxious, as New Hampshire stirred a sting in my soul, always fearing that the living darkness might return. I never genuinely enjoyed returning to New Hampshire, but I always loved leaving it. The AT cuts right through the town of Hanover, where Dartmouth College is located. The aesthetically pleasing and comfortable brick-laden municipality offers many eating and drinking options. Hanover was considered a friendly trail town, as not all of them were, so I decided to take a few zero days to play and rest before tackling my home state's familiar White Mountains Range. This time would also allow the other hikers around me to disperse a bit on the trail. I desired to be alone in New Hampshire. After crossing the bridge that spans the Connecticut River and arriving during the sun's zenith, I resupplied and imbibed all afternoon, camped at the forest's edge in my hammock, then spent the next day imbibing again.

At midnight, when most were asleep or stumbling to their tents, I slunk out-of-town alone, returning deep into the mountains. I'd purchased fresh battery stock for my headlamp, ensuring confidence in carving a modest light line through the thick dark woods. The Velvet Rocks at one a.m. reminded me of my living haunts, and though I could sense the loom of their presence, I could not hear them. During the next few days of hiking, I strode at a pace and place between any other hikers, providing a few miles of buffer for solitude. A favorite sight of mine early in the morning on the dusky damp trail was the unbroken spiderwebs stretching grandly across the path. One must go through them, and since they remained intact, this sight acted as a sign, indicating I was the first to walk this way today. In this successful seclusion I progressed, basking in the sounds of the forest.

Atop Mount Moosilauke, the first above tree line summit ushering in New Hampshire's tremendous range, I sat on the granite, swaddled in my sleeping bag. It was the first genuinely cold weather I'd experienced since springtime, a harsh, seeping into bones kind of chill. The September winds

CINEREAL

had just begun. After soaking up the sentimental views, I hiked onward, immersed in stunted Krummholz forests of dwarfed spruce and firs. Sharply up and down the trail progressed, from grand bald rocky peaks and down again into highland trees. The White Mountains are magnificent, steep, slick, and demand mindful, accurate foot placement. Stormy weather with thick clouds frequently arrives rapidly, stealing the hiker's vision and orientation, yet one must attentively persevere, eyeing the white blaze which acts as a guide, painted upon boulders and cairns. Atop each summit I sat, listened, and simply existed. At night I hung my hammock in the short, bent coniferous trees just below the elevation where they grow no more, swaying to sleep cocooned in the wind. When I reached Lost River Road, Highway 112, I hitched a ride into the town of Lincoln. There was a hiker hostel I could stay at, a grocery store to resupply food, and hopefully, a local from whom I could buy some much needed marijuana for both my mental-medical and pleasure purposes.

My plan was to get in and out as efficiently as possible. Buying and possessing cannabis was still illegal everywhere in the country, other than in states allowing medically prescribed possession only. I understood that seeking it out in a town where I knew no one was risky, but regardless of the potential consequences, I was determined to locate a half ounce. This amount would last me the rest of my journey. Besides, covert operations enticed me. After signing my name on the hostel's garage wall and enjoying a hot shower, I commenced my side-quest. The first and safest point of contact is to ask other hikers. None of them had any green for sale, but two asked if I could find them some as well. They each wanted a quarter ounce, I the half, and so I was now on a hunt for one ounce total. Bar patrons and bartenders are usually a potential source. They often smoke weed themselves or know most of the people in town who do. Although I located a pub with a billiard table and jukebox, the bartender could not point me in any helpful direction. I realized I had raised some suspicion, for even though I was just a hiker passing through, he wore a furrowed brow as I inquired about my illegal request. "No man, none of that here, good luck though," was all he muttered before promptly turning his back.

I went about my day resupplying trail food and asking anyone who didn't look like a possible off-duty police officer or undercover cop. Every inquiry led to a dead end. Discouraged, I returned to the hostel and drank a few beers with the other hikers in the backyard. As I sat by the bonfire I'd assembled and lit, I noticed a neighbor in a tie-dye shirt. Her hair hung as a mighty mane of long dreads with colorful beads, which, although stereotyping, she appeared like someone worth asking. I made my way over with an extra beer in hand to offer and struck up a conversation. Her face brightened as I handed her the beverage. We dove into an earnest chat about trail life, the mountains and seasons. When the moment seemed appropriate, I divulged my intent. She leaned back and looked at the sky as if the answer might be up above. "Well, Hot Wing, I only keep on me what I smoke for myself, but I can ask my guy. He frequents the pub with the jukebox. Chances are you already asked him," she winked at me, "but he might be more inclined if I vouch for you."

Aha! I smiled and thought, *I knew I was hunting in the right place. Makes sense though, no one here has any idea who I am, other than an eager hiking pot seeker.* I thanked her as she instructed to check back in an hour.

The plan had been set. The guy with the ganja would drop off the goods at the pub around sunset. I just needed to be there, by the billiard table, and keep everything discreet. That I could do. I packed up my backpack with restocked supplies and headed to the location to challenge anyone and everyone to a game of eight-ball. After I'd received the marijuana and given the other two hikers their supply, I would hike out of town. There was no need to linger once I had achieved my goal.

Two pitchers of beer, two cheeseburgers and a dozen games later, after darkness had set in the valley, I knew the marijuana had arrived. I could smell it before I could see it. *This must be some quality bud.* A guy I had not met tapped me on the shoulder and gave the follow-me nod. I subtly obeyed. We went out back each lit a cigarette and stood between two trucks to complete the transaction. The flower was indoor-grown, medical grade. I thanked him genuinely. He shrugged, flicked his cigarette carelessly, then sauntered off into the night. I located the two other hikers, divided out their portions and began my hitchhiking journey back to the trail. Within thirty minutes, I was safe at home in the thick forest.

The next morning as I was sitting atop South Peak Kinsman Mountain smoking some fresh green from the tiny metal one-hitter cigarette-looking piece I used on the trail a grand idea entered my mind. Call my best friend Andrew from the high school and college days, the same one who joined me in California, and see if he wanted to drive up and meet me for a bit of the hike. I would be descending into Franconia Notch in a few hours, and if he was available, it would be the perfect time and location to meet. We could spend the afternoon climbing up Franconia Ridge together, a magnificent stretch of trail. My cellphone flickered with one timid bar of service. Fortunately, the call went through. *This is a good sign.* Andrew answered. He was free and ready for adventure. My delighted voice lifted off the summit. His exclamations bounced within the walls of his abode. He promised to meet me in four hours.

Franconia Notch is one of the most beautiful passages for vehicles through the White Mountains. It served as a direct commute up Highway 93 from our homeland down on the seacoast. I waited at the trailhead parking lot, which is where Andrew would be arriving. The area was quiet with only two empty cars. Therefore, it would be easy for him to see me. Our timing aligned. Less than thirty minutes after I had propped myself against the curb to snack and rest, he rumbled in on his motorcycle. We embraced as brothers do, beaming with grins of enthusiasm. Andrew was all packed and ready for the hike, but first we sat down on the curb by my temporary lounge and dove into the preliminary trail and summer questions. With pride, I pulled out the half ounce of marijuana I had procured in Lincoln. He examined the sticky bud, nodding his head, sniffing and agreeing, this was fine quality herb indeed.

"Let's smoke a J before we get moving." I suggested and started rolling the joint like a damned fool right there on the edge of society. My excitement had blinded me, my pride had stolen my usual caution, and in the parking lot, just twenty feet away from my forest sanctuary, I doomed myself. Within minutes, distinguishing no warning, a constable on patrol appeared in front of us. The vehicle proclaimed Town of Lincoln Sheriff on its flank. Enthusiasm sank in my chest. From my seat on the ground, his car loomed like a great white shark suddenly emerging in calm waters. There was nowhere we could go. The cop glared at us from ten feet away. There was nothing I could do. I should have prevented this, but I was caught sticky-fingered and red-handed with my jar of illegal plant lying out in the open and the joint rolling in my digits.

He opened his door, placing a boot on the asphalt. As he rose out of the shark-like vehicle, he sternly stated, "Young man, have you ever been arrested before? Because it looks like you are about to be."

Shit.

CINEREAL

Andrew was not arrested, and for that I was relieved. He had not acted irresponsibly, nor had he committed a crime. Andrew had just been sitting there with his own gear packed away, cheerfully observing his out-of-place-and-mind mountain friend. It was all my stuff spread out in the open. My marijuana. I was the one who deserved to be in handcuffs. Andrew promised to wait and see what would come of my debacle down at the station.

As we caravanned into town, I in the back of the Sheriff's car and Andrew following behind us, the lawman leaned back and spoke to me, "You know twenty feet back in the woods and I never would have seen ya."

I know. I thought, nodding my head in disbelief, that I was arrested and heading back into Lincoln. *The town provided, and then the town took it back. Freaking New Hampshire, you don't have to wear a seatbelt, but you can't smoke pot. Live free or die, my ass.*

By the time I had been processed, bail paid and finally released, it was too late to hike up Franconia Ridge. Andrew was waiting in the parking lot with a smirk on his face. He patted me on the back and agreed to just get pizza, beer and a cheap motel room for the night. I was grateful he was there. It was encouraging to spend time with a dear friend who knew me well. We spent the night laughing and sharing stories, filling our bellies with greasy food and booze. The next morning, we ventured onwards, both our separate ways. He rode south on his motorcycle, and I trekked up Franconia Ridge to the northeast on my feet.

~~~

Maine, the last frontier of my long pilgrimage, welcomed with deep boreal forests far away from civilization. Bogs that could swallow a human whole, and giant regal undulates dominated the land between its rocky peaks. Although it was only September, this far north the flora was quickly morphing into red and orange autumn hues. I walked silently and thoughtfully. Months of lessons and adventures filled my mind. It seemed as if I was in the final course of a graduating program, for life on the trail had been just that, an education of self, a journey into new awareness of the world. My court date for the marijuana incident was scheduled before my hike would be completed, and so, knowing I would not be leaving the wilderness until I had reached Mount Katahdin, I wrote the honorable judge a letter from the wet coniferous woodland. I explained to him what I was doing and respectfully asked him to allow me to repay my societal infraction on a later date. I would not know the answer to this until October, I imagined, and hoped he would understand and agree.

Maine vibrated as if it were a land described in fairy tales. Magnificent trees eyed my every move, draped with boreal slumber, the critters all fraught with attitude and actions of winter preparation. On the edges of lakes, I watched moose maneuver long limbs and mighty antlers around the brush, eating the foliage of their chosen vegetation. Beavers slapped their tails on the water tops when I approached too closely. Bald eagles hunted and soared victoriously with fish in their talons. Loons sang the melody of seclusion, and heavy mist clung to the glassy aqua pura when the sun rose each day. This was not a land to be raucous in, but a land to be muted and humble. All felt sacred.

I realized I was not the naive, foot-stomping human I had started the long hike as. But now I was integrated into organic truths, aware that I tread as a symbiotic part of the living natural world. I had come in as a fool of manufactured society, yet the honesty of nature had stripped that unnatural coating away from me, leaving me aligned, a creature of the land, living with, not living on. Although I looked forward to the culmination of the grand hike, I also carried melancholy in my heart. I did not want to go back there, to the land of cement, materialism, greed and noise. The wilderness had become my home, and I had become simplified, needing very little, using all I owned. I left no sign of my existence, no trash, no plastic, no trace, only a passive indent of my body upon the earthen floor.

Upon crossing a dirt track for vehicles in the density of evergreens, I heard the silence-shattering scream of dirt bikes somewhere nearby. I shuddered at the mechanical noise and scurried on until I could hear it no more. I chuckled remembering how this sound supplied me moonshine from woodland dwellers back in the southern Appalachians, but now I aspired to be like the fox and the lynx, like a lady slipper flower who exists without being seen. My soul was both at peace and unsettled, unsettled for returning to a world which seemed unnatural, at peace for not being there yet. I did my best to focus on the present and not worry about the future. Although my understanding for the value of all that transpired in the past five months was still developing, my long hike had created a structure I would live by for the rest of my life. A blueprint of perseverance was etched into my being. A foundation cemented in my soul. In times of suffering, no matter the pain, just keep going, grit and keep on. Approach each grand endeavor one mountain, one step at a time. When enough steps are taken, you will arrive at your goal. I remembered how daunting the magnitude of the whole had seemed at the beginning, but by breaking my macro-goal down into micro-goals, I had achieved it. *Well, a few more micro-goals to go, and then I will have achieved the macro*, I acknowledged, leaning forward into another uphill climb. I also considered, *live as the wild animals do, not as the civilized humans. The civilized keep believing they deserve more, fueled by greed not gratitude, but here, in this sanctuary, minimal is enough, with efficient intentional work providing exactly what is needed.*

As I pondered the animals, my gratitude grew for all the wildlife I had been privileged to experience on the trail. Twenty-two bear encounters, hundreds of deer, many moose, fox, skunk, porcupines, coyotes, bobcats, millions of birds, thousands of small critters, way too many snakes, and billions of bugs. Everything that lived in these wilds I communed with. I even had the blessing of riding horses twice in Virginia. This memory caused me to guffaw out loud. Both circumstances had been ridiculous events. *I wonder how Chaco was faring.* I overflowed with joy at every detail of my Appalachian Trail experience. *This is my church, this is my home, and if I could stay here forever, I would. However, I must finish this hike and then carry, practice and share these principles forth forevermore.*

~~~

Maine, and the Appalachian Trail's final northern stretch, is the 100 Mile Wilderness. The town of Monson serves as the gates for this remote land. My trail comrades and I reunited at the local hostel after being dispersed for a while. We resupplied, ate and drank, washed our ragged clothes one last time, and prepared our mental and physical sights on completing our worthy journey. Wilbur, the crew, and I set out into the last 100 miles at a staggered rate, for this wasn't the cavalcade of Mid-Atlantic anymore. We each carried meditations in our hearts that were meant for ourselves and the land only. At summits, lakesides and river crossings we reconvened our fellowship, sharing tokes of marijuana smoke, sips of whiskey and stories of our 2,000 miles over campfire. In the morning mist we persevered humbly, silently, each dissolving into the hues of Maine.

The last night we all camped together was before the final marathon to the base of Mount Katahdin. Seventy-four miles of the 100 Mile Wilderness were accomplished. Hiking over 2,000 miles from Georgia had occupied the time span of deciduous trees' foliar life. I watched a bright red maple leaf

CINEREAL

flutter to the forest floor, remembering when I watched the southern sprigs start to bud. The four of us, plus Wilbur's dog Baloo, prepared camp as we always did, stringing up hammocks and setting tents a distance from the others. Locating a strong, expansive branch that we would utilize to hang our food bags away from the reach of determined bears. I built the fire, as was always my self-declared task. We cooked our dinners, and for our last huddled evening, sipped only spring water and tea. Our conversation focused on the kindness extended by strangers along the trail. We took turns sharing the small and big things we had been given, each one an uplifting gift to our souls.

"Remember Ballhawk, you were there, in Salisbury Connecticut, when we were lounging under a tree outside the grocery store drinking beer, and a black SUV pulled up, rolled down the window, then a mother with kids hollered, 'Hey hiker trash,' with a smile, 'do you boys like steaks?'" Ballhawk's eyes lit up reminiscing the story as I continued, "to which we replied, 'of course, we love steaks!' And so, we followed her directions to a big house on the corner, where she and her husband concocted a lavish multi-course meal of eggplant parmesan, veggies, dips, deviled eggs, steaks and dessert. It was so incredibly kind of them. They provided their laundry machines, gave us sweatpants and t-shirts to wear while we washed our disintegrating clothes, and we played with the kids in the yard and treehouse, even inscribed our trail names in the wooden panels with a pocketknife."

Ballhawk added with a joyful grin, "That was so generous of them. They filled us up. That one kid was learning how to walk on stilts. Hot Wing, you tried the stilts and almost broke your leg!"

"Yup, my hike could have ended right there, broken legs and all, and I'd still have been the happiest I've ever been. They fed us and they provided a home-family-life for a night. That second part really meant a lot to me too." I sensed an ache in my heart. When I spoke the word "family," tears welled in my eyes.

Cous Cous, our other hiker family member for the 100 Mile Wilderness, stated with reverence, "Miss Janet." This name immediately caused a mighty reaction of gratitude from all of us.

"My goodness, Miss Janet, the greatest trail angel the Appalachian has ever known. Year after year she gives her all." I bobbed my head and pursed my lips together fervently.

CINEREAL

Ballhawk affirmed, "She was everywhere, especially down south. If you needed anything, a ride, food, shelter, a new backpack, boots, beer, literally anything, she would come find you and save you."

All four of us held up cups of water for a cheer. In unison we exclaimed, "To Miss Janet!"

With emotion in our hearts, we sat back and stared into the dark covering of tree limbs above. Firelight flickered, accentuating the underbelly details of our natural ceiling. Smoke rose, slithering through an evergreen web upward towards the stars. After a few moments, Wilbur broke the silence. "None of us deserved any of the kindness we were given, and now I believe we must pay it forward for the rest of our lives." We all nodded in agreement. For all the kindness we had received, we would pay it forward for the rest of our lives.

After a restless night of half-sleep, I awoke before the sun. I could not lie cocooned in the hammock any longer. No one else had emerged from their sleeping bags. Baloo only slightly lifted head at my movement, then tucked a damp nose back into a curled sleeping pose. I gathered the temperate coals from the night's fire and revived cackling flames. On them I boiled water for coffee and oatmeal, ate and drank my modest meal in five a.m. tranquility, packed my gear and headed north on the trail alone. Twenty-six miles to the base of Mount Katahdin. The last marathon of a mighty journey. My pace started slowly, ambling into the dark, damp gloss pressing upon trees and fallen leaves. When the sun rose, gliding its gentle autumn beams into the forest, the woodland erupted into a mosaic of colors. Amidst this iridescent caress I warmed, placing feet mindfully with both speed and precision upon the red, yellow, purple and orange carpet. Beneath grand green boughs I strode, subconsciously aware of each stone and root, peering into the sky's emboldening blue hues. Brown, gray and black pillars held the world aloft, while pastel variations of above and below levitated between. A moose raised his crowned head, observing me slide past his sky-mirroring lake wade. I gazed at him with admiration and proceeded, brimming with gratitude, hiking as a young man who had grown into a mountain man, a man who could not see himself aligning with the world outside of the wilderness ever again. The journey had reassembled me, molded me, transformed me.

September 27, 2010, was the last day of the mighty Appalachian Trail thru-hiking quest. Millinocket is a small town close to Baxter State Park, the

CINEREAL

land of Mount Katahdin. I met my dad in the morning. He was there to drive me back to where I had hitched in from the trail the night before, and then to greet me upon the trail's completion. When the day was finished, he would drive me back to my Jeep in New Hampshire. I spent the night in a hiker hostel and got raucously drunk in town one last time with my hiking buddies. My head throbbed, but I did not mind. *One last hangover for the trail, a worthy weight,* I considered. We had a weather window to summit Mount Katahdin, and while others had been waiting a week for the storms to break, my 100 Mile Wilderness peers had charged forth so as not to miss this chance. It was wonderful to see my dad. He had visited me a few times throughout the journey, but to see him at the end, just as he had dropped me off at the beginning, welled a feast of love and pride in my heart.

Wilbur, the crew, all other hikers who had waited for the capricious weather to abate, and I gathered at the Mount Katahdin trailhead. An aura of communal eagerness vibrated in the air. We all carried the struggles and resilience of a long journey, and unlike all other days when we walked onward alone, we would embark on this final mountain, our final mountain of the Appalachian Trail, together. Mount Katahdin itself is a massive beast rising prominently above the expansive woodland, but this mountain was more than a beast. It was the mountain we had held in our dreams, in our speech, in our proclaimed goals for 2,179 miles. Mount Katahdin appeared as a throne in a paradise, and with each step higher up its rocky shoulders, it seemed as if we were ascending to heaven.

At the last trickling spring of water emerging from the mountain, high above the tree line nearing the summit, I knelt and placed my lips in the cold, clean liquid and drank, savoring each sip. I thanked God for this journey, for the earth. I felt as if I had become the land, that the old me had bled and poured out, mixed into the soil, and that each cell of my new, of my now, were the molecules of the forests, streams and mountains. When I was ready, I arose and continued onward, joining the strides of my comrades. We cheered each other on, slapping backs, hugging hands, smiling until our faces froze in joyous grins. We could see the top. The summit's famous sign awaited us. Trekking the final paces, pushing ourselves upward on the culminating ascent, our emotions erupted as we moved into our ultimate steps. We cheered victoriously, howling into the sky. The time was finally here. We had done it. I had done it. Each of us standing atop Mount Katahdin had accomplished the goal. The journey was complete. Two-

CINEREAL

thousand one-hundred and seventy-nine miles of wondrous planet Earth walked. The invisible badge now earned and worn. I had completed hiking the entire Appalachian Trail.

CINEREAL

A Long Chapter for a Long State

Shortly after returning to New Hampshire, I turned twenty-five years of age. With a quarter of a century lived, I realized I didn't know where "home" truly was. New England no longer felt like a true home, for returning to the land of my haunts always depressed and darkened me. My family didn't have a proper home, as they were all spread out. Mom had a quality roof over her head, Dad did too, but buildings lived in do not instantly qualify as homes. My brother and sister now seemed estranged. They were busy, and for years I had usually been gone. I realized when I was in New Hampshire, I isolated myself more than I took part, lost in my own disturbances and vices. The trail was the place I had been most challenged, alive and content. It was in the mountainous forests that I could genuinely connect with my surroundings. I'd bonded closely with a like-minded community in the woods. That was the most home I knew. But the trail was complete, and like on the trail, I must move forward.

Until winter arrived, I slept outside. I could not sleep under a ceiling. Claustrophobia wreaked havoc on my mind each time I was within four walls. The stagnant air indoors, the lack of evening and morning birdsongs, no owl hoots at night, it was not the environment I had grown accustomed to. I returned to Kensington Farm and inquired about my old job, but everything there had changed. Everything everywhere had changed, or maybe it was just I that had changed. My friends treated me as an adventuring hero, but they did not understand. It wasn't a big deal. There were many others out there too, many other adventurers far more traveled than me.

I tried my hand at a few jobs that intrigued me, such as working on a lobster boat at sea, mushing dogsleds further north, but nothing stuck. I seemed incapable of fully applying my heart to anything new. *How did I discover so much of myself out there, only to feel so lost now?* I mulled and paced and spiraled into deep depression. Loneliness set in and grew. *No one understands, and no one ever will,* or so it seemed in my disdainful over-emphasizing ways.

CINEREAL

During long sits of drinking alcohol alone, I missed the voices of the living darkness. I wondered where they had gone and why they had forsaken me.

Despite my desire to leave New Hampshire altogether, I was bound by the need to make money and rebuild my adventure fund. I remembered what I had told Wilbur in the forest and set my goals on writing and beginning to share my stories. This small motivation inspired me to wrangle the basics. I secured a job serving tables at an old Italian restaurant in downtown Portsmouth and signed a lease to an apartment nearby. *A different kind of adventure. A town life quest, just for one year, where I can smell the ocean's salty air.*

Portsmouth, New Hampshire, is a darling town. And one of the nation's oldest colonial settlements, dating back to the year 1630, incorporated in 1653. Portsmouth is a port town, as the name aptly suggests, nestled by the Piscataqua River and the Atlantic Ocean. Streets, alleys and many of the buildings still wear the same old brick and cobblestones from original construction, providing a quaint and historic charm of yesteryear. Foghorns and bells of ships entering the harbor sound regularly, with seagulls adding their calls to the audible atmosphere of the small city. Portsmouth is considered a foodie town, with many fine restaurants, while a plethora of taverns stir the vibrant nightlife until past midnight. My third-floor apartment was nestled amid this haven, complete with a small porch on which I could sit and stare out across the rooftops. In the winter, I found solace in viewing the many chimneys emitting smoke across the horizon. During the early morning hours, after the taverns had closed and before the coffee shops opened, all looked and smelled of simpler times.

To most observers outside myself, it appeared as if my twenty-five-year-old life was a pleasant and positive one. But that couldn't be further from the truth. While I performed well at my job, lived alone in an ideal location, had friends and took beautiful daily walks, my soul was aching. I continued to rebel against God, ignoring His constant convictions. I made many terrible choices that year, most of them stemming from seeking affection in the wrong places. There was one young woman I briefly invited into my life, while sharing space and my heart with another. Torn between two kinds of love, I did not know what was right or wrong. My actions under the darkness of night, though masqueraded as romantic youthful delights, unraveled into havoc and pain. I hurt others because of my selfish decisions and hurt myself by allowing my soul to flail. Emotional weakness ruled my movements, not yet to learn and earn the strength and value of emotional maturity. Much of that year does not need to be told in this book, other than with all I did, the saturation of alcohol was a constant, and while manageable in my young age, a destructive and deceptive companion.

Positively, amidst the social and daily chaos, I started writing a blog online. I posted many of my short stories, gaining numerous readers around the globe. This process both invigorated and humbled me. Quickly I learned how harsh the world can be towards a young artist. I received comments and messages from strangers abroad and local acquaintances declaring how pitiful my life and adventures were. Many people mocked me for some of the events I wrote about and shared. While such feedback stung my heart at first, it ultimately served as a motivator. I decided I would not care whether people liked me. Each malicious comment meant that they were in fact reading my writings. That mattered. I was living a bold, untraditional life, and for that I would always be judged. I began to revel in being disliked and misunderstood. Yet, despite the hate, I also received kindness and love. My grandmother read each story about my adventures on the Appalachian Trail to my grandfather. Gratefully, I imagined what this looked and sounded like down in Georgia. She, speaking with animation in her Southern accented voice from her computer in the living room, and he, listening with wide-eared joy in his big lounge chair, while dabbing each cigarette into his ashtray. I loved my grandmother and grandfather dearly. As the parents of my dad, they always supported me from afar, and while their affection for my writing may have been biased, it still warmed my heart.

Sharing my writing helped me progress in my craft. I was unconcerned if anyone considered my creations well written or of interesting material, for the process of writing and vulnerably putting it out there allowed me to connect with others and be myself in a way, and in a time, I so direly needed. Away from the forest, living in a busy town, writing provided me an anchor and a purpose. Writing with intention was and always will function as a conduit toward healing. The public distribution allowed those who wanted to read it the ability to do so. This combination provided a ledger for personal development. I could look back upon old writings and see how far I'd come, or in what areas I needed to improve. To this day, with this book I now write, I care not for perfection, only soul-flowing truth.

During my year on the New Hampshire seacoast, I harbored no plans to retire from my life of adventure. While I was often questioned about what was next, or when I would settle down and work a proper job, a seed planted within had been growing strong roots. I knew what I was going to do, but I needed to save money. A documentary I watched at a hiker-feed in Duncannon, Pennsylvania, on the Appalachian Trail, had determined my next backcountry adventure. When the time approached, at twenty-six years of age, I sold my weary Jeep Wrangler, Izzy Roadhouse, shutdown my raucous townie life and announced my plan. I was going to thru-hike the Pacific Crest Trail from Mexico to Canada. Two-thousand six-hundred and fifty miles of California, Oregon and Washington's roughest and most remote terrain. The East Coast was no place for me. I had done my time. It was time to return home to the wilderness, to my favorite land, the west.

~~~

On April 10, 2012, I stood at the southern terminus of the Pacific Crest Trail. Outside the small border town of Campo, California, nestled in the desert next to a tall metal wall separating the United States and Mexico is a monument announcing the trail's terminus. It was the same day I had started my Appalachian Trail journey, separated by exactly two years. My dad stood by me, taking pictures to document the birth of this new adventure. We both surged with the eager anticipation each new chapter brings. Although I could have made my way to this arid, faraway nook of the country on my own, having him with me once again was a precious gift of life. We flew from Logan Airport in Boston to San Diego, revisited the city where I was born, rented a vehicle, and eased our way into the desert, taking the time to acquire proper gear, and consume multiple fattening meals. For this trail, I purchased a proper one-person tent, forgoing the hammock and tarp setup I carried through the Appalachians. The last night before embarking into the desert, we dined on steaks and wine. In the morning, I was able to eat a full breakfast, unlike that dawn in Georgia. The time had come. *I am here.*

"On to another one, Hot Wing. This may be your biggest quest yet. You stay safe out here." My supportive dad chuckled as he pronounced my trail name, swiveling his head south to Mexico, north to the vast United States of America, then back at me with a proud grin.

"It is certainly my longest venture yet." Sighing with satisfaction, I smiled at him in return. "It feels so good to be home." I lifted my head and drew long breaths of desert air. We laughed for different reasons. To him, this was not my home, and to me, it was a new environment, yet I was back on a long trail, ready to stride into the unknown with purpose, and to me that was home. After shaking hands and embracing, we kept our words brief, for all that needed to be said had been spoken already. He watched as I walked north alone, disappearing into hills the color of mountain lions, speckled with pale green accents of sagebrush.

As I hiked into the serene land, I realized I had not felt anxious as I had before the Appalachian Trail. I was at ease, confident, strong, my body and mind remembering the pace I had already learned. The routine of two feet. I was not a rookie thru-hiker anymore. Acknowledging that this trail would differ from the east, I believed I was prepared for all to come. The Pacific Crest Trail would provide new challenges I had not faced in the Appalachians. While the hiking itself might be less challenging than my eastern pilgrimage, everything else would be more difficult. The PCT is graded for horses. Therefore, the ascents and descents are not as steep. There are no rock-fastened ladders to climb up and down like in New England. However, in the west, exposure to the weather is far greater, for there is little shade from the unforgiving sun, and wind ravages the landscape with few trees to aid in relief. Water sources are far fewer with long stretches of barren land between, and the trail towns, my resupply points, would be less frequent and often more difficult to reach. The aridity would require me to carry much water, adding to the weight of my overall load. On some days in the southern 700 miles of desert, I would need to carry water for thirty-plus mile stretches. Springs often dried up, and the only option would be murky still-liquids from cattle troughs along the way.

In the middle of day three on my trek north from the Mexico border, I climbed into the Laguna Mountains. The area was reminiscent of the North Kaibab Plateau at the Grand Canyon, laden with tall Jeffrey pines. The familiar scent of conifers was a welcome relief after the first days down on the desert floor. Cool mountain air at 6,000 feet elevation foretold of changing weather soon to come. Storm clouds formed as I made my first contact with civilization. The modest settlement of Laguna comprises log-style buildings, vacation cabins, a general store, a small tavern and one simple motel. I sat on the general store porch drinking a beer and eating a carne asada burrito, listening to the gray-bearded locals discuss the weather. One man inquired about my plans.

"Young man, you're hiking the PCT, correct?" He spoke over to me as if he knew I had been eavesdropping.

"Yes, sir. Today is day three, but I haven't walked far today, slept at the base of this mountain." I responded mid-chew.

CINEREAL

"That's a good starting pace, two strong days. However, you're going to need to slow down for now. A big storm is rolling in, possibly bringing a couple of feet of snow tonight into tomorrow. Would be wise to lie low until it passes. The motel has plenty of reasonably priced rooms available." He advised as if he were the motel proprietor himself. It turned out he wasn't, but his brother was.

"Thanks for the concern, mister..." He cut me off before I could continue.

"Just call me Barney, book a room inside the store with Bobby. He'll give you a hiker discount, I'm sure." Barney returned to his conversation as if his duty with me was complete.

Barney and Bobby, I thought to myself gleefully, completing my meal and beer. *I wonder if Bonny and Betty are here too.* I chuckled at my thoughts and decided I would in fact book a room and sit the storm out. *More time to drink and maybe meet some other hikers.*

After procuring a room at the motel 100 yards away from the general store, I returned freshly showered and purchased a six-pack of lagers and a bag of chips to continue my leisurely sit on the porch's wooden chairs. I liked that they didn't care if I smoked cigarettes close to others, so I rolled a few and puffed away. I had met only a few other hikers in the past days on the trail, a stark difference from the crowds of the Appalachians. There was no bubble out here. Everyone seemed far more spread out and reserved, *but the snowstorm might change that,* I considered. Around beer four, I hollered at Barney, who had been meandering about. *Not far for him to go in this small community,* I observed. "Hey Barney, my name is Hot Wing." I stood, and we shook hands. "Say, Barney, you wouldn't know where I could buy a little marijuana, do you?"

Barney didn't smile, but he didn't frown either. In fact, he was as unfazed as anyone I'd ever offered the question to. He responded practically. "Did you book a motel room, or are you hiking on?"

"I booked a room with your brother Bobby. Staying until the storm rolls through."

"Smart man. Sure, Hot Wing, I can make that happen. I'll go grab a few nugs from home and be back in about thirty minutes."

I sat back down, amazed and tickled by the ease of it all. *Freakin' California, I ain't in the East anymore!* While I continued my sit, sip and smoke session, I watched as a group of three hikers approached the store from the direction I had arrived. We made eyes and nodded heads at each other. I listened as the three of them discussed booking a two-bed motel room for the night, then had an idea.

"Yo, hiker trash!" They looked my way, offended by my slang. With a laugh I assured them, "Ya'll must be rookies. Hiker trash is what we are known as. Wear the label with pride. I heard you talking, and I got a room with an extra bed, so if one of you wants to split with me, then we each can have one." This idea made sense to all, and within a few minutes I'd gained a bunkmate from New Mexico named Scott, who hadn't earned a trail name yet. Barney returned at that moment with some kindly delivered green marijuana. I handed some of the cash my new hiker acquaintance provided for his bed to Barney. I thanked the gray-bearded man and winked at Scott, who watched the simple transaction go down. Back in my chair, I sat to roll a joint and remain basking in my mellow woodland buzz. The temperature continued to plummet, snow started to fall, and Jeffrey Pine needles turned from a dark green to laced in a powdery white. I was happy, for I was home. Forty-two miles into my trek, and all seemed right in my world.

The next morning, we awoke to a foot of snow on the ground, with blizzard conditions still in full effect. More hikers had arrived, the motel was now fully booked, and a small community of us gathered around the general store. We shared names and swapped stories, sipping coffee and throwing snowballs. Although we were all meeting for the first time, a comfortable camaraderie emanated. We were all out here with similar goals, braving the same terrain and logistical obstacles. After our morning coffee happy hour, we decided to all reconvene at the tavern at six p.m. for a grand hiker trash bash.

As soon as I entered, I knew I liked the tavern. My first delight was spotting a brown upright piano in the corner. My second approval was of a well-maintained billiard table. Mountain bar decor covered the walls, including pronghorn and deer mounts, a prowling taxidermic mountain lion, rattlesnake skins, and vintage alcohol brand signs. The establishment provided a full dinner menu, along with many beer-taps and liquor options. Hikers scuttled in, shaking off snow, adding upbeat energy to the casual locals sitting on and in their preferred stools and booths. I ordered a shot of whiskey with a cold pint of beer and racked up the billiard balls for a game with anyone who dared play me. The blizzard raged outside, threatening to exceed two feet of snow accumulation. Windows looking out upon

CINEREAL

lamppost lights illuminating the brumal bluster added to the warm and cozy atmosphere indoors. *This is going to be a rowdy, fun evening,* I enthusiastically thought.

Indeed, it was. Nearly twenty hikers and twenty locals ate and imbibed late into the night. We meshed and surged together as each pint was drunk and set down. Cooks in the kitchen chimed out names of dishes and table numbers ready to serve. The smack of billiard balls crashing into each other added a sharp tone. Bells on the tavern door frequently chimed as latecomers and smokers scurried in and out. I jumped onto the piano and played a song. Everyone cheered, and some sang along. The hum of humanity had grown to a roar, everyone tipsy and asking for more. Many faces glowed with a reddish hue from laughing heartily, while others wore frosted eyebrows dripping into spongy wet beards. The bartender acted as the master of ceremonies. She commanded, dashing and flirting like both a mother and a Mrs. Claus. An introverted couple from Germany also hiking the trail erupted into extroverts, bellowing a drinking ballad from their homeland. After the makeshift bar choir subsided, I needed to cool down, so I retreated outside beyond the lamppost's umbrella light reach. Sending my spliff smoke signals upward, I observed the gallantry of our party. Even though the building was a sturdy log-cabin structure, it seemed to pulse and dance along with the boisterous glee within. Snow had piled up so high on the roof, ground and trees it looked like a fairytale-land full of golden characters defeating any old whispers of discouragement. My heart and soul grinned. In time, I stubbed out my smoke and returned straight to the piano to play another song. After the night waltzed through last call, and all bar-tabs and food-bills paid, we each gathered our items, layered our coats, hugged and waved goodnight. As we stumbled towards our bunks, I noticed the snowfall had ceased. Above the thick white blanket swaddling Laguna, stars shone crisply in the sky. The storm had passed. *Tomorrow I will continue hiking north.*

~~~

The next day I was the first to break trail, the first to put boots to snow. It was impossible to know exactly where the path was because of the massive drifts and overall accumulation, but I had my map, compass skills and sensibility. I was to follow the ridge northwest and then drop into the desert to the northeast. I felt like a true pioneer, comparing the lay of the iridescent land to my paper topography map, trusting the sun, full of vigor, alone in a new-to-me wilderness. The goal orientated explorer within had to quell the

CINEREAL

also-child explorer within as my curiosity to where mountain lion tracks crossing my direction led. I compared my hand to the feline's giant prints. Considering the depth of the pawmarks and no sign of exposed claws, it seemed to have been walking without a worry. I could also distinguish where its long tail had brushed the snow. *Wider than my hand. That is a big cat. It appears to have climbed right up into those cliffs. Keep the course, Wing, keep your course.*

The sun glared, casting its completeness onto the land. The only shadows were crooked lines beneath sporadic brush. It was high noon. Two thousand feet below, I spotted orange ground with no snow. As the day matured, and I hiked into lower elevations, the orange dirt appeared gradually around me. When I finally found the Pacific Crest Trail's exact path, it resembled melted sherbet cream. Everything glimmered as a new slippery planet. Snow was melting rapidly now, and the rocks beneath showed face, like white hairdos and white beards sliding down sandstone boulders. I still had not seen another human footprint, and despite a few long breaks to observe, listen and eat, no other hiker had caught up behind me. *Perhaps everyone else stayed for another day.* If that were the case, I would be miles from anyone until I reached the town of Julian. The trail descended sharply, requiring me to take short, careful steps, engage my core muscles, and hold back the weight of my pack from tumbling me forward. Despite my caution, I placed my foot on some slush that covered a few round slick rocks. Before I could catch myself, my right foot shot out over the cliff's edge, forcing me to throw my upper torso and shoulders away from the inertia, attempting to save my body from a deadly fall. Awkwardly, I rolled down the trail, skirting the edge of the precipice yet smashing hard and fast upon the slick rocky ground. I wound up forty feet below where the danger had begun, finally coming to a painful halt. My right knee twisted in this action and now lay mangled beneath my mass. I forced myself to breathe deliberately, encouraging the spiked adrenaline to temper. As I tried to stand and steady myself back into walking position, I realized I could not place any weight on my right knee. The sharp discomfort and inability to use my leg indicated I was in real trouble. This far away from civilization was no place to be injured alone. About 300 feet below lay a flat patch of muddy soil surrounded by chest-high manzanitas. I needed to make it there, hobble down, scoot on my butt, roll, whatever it took, then camp for the night and figure out a plan.

CINEREAL

Once cozy in my little makeshift camp, peering upwards to the stars and dark ridge-tops around me, I thought of the cougar prints I had observed earlier in the day. I wondered whether the lion was watching me. After boiling some water, I made a simple dinner of noodles and pre-cooked chicken, adding olive oil for calories and red-hot pepper flakes for flavor. I played my harmonica and rolled a joint. My knee had swollen up tripling its original size, so I searched for any remaining snow I could reach to combat the inflammation, but down here in this canyon it had all melted away. Only mud remained. I couldn't bend my right leg. Pain throbbed throughout my entire lower side. Smoking a bit of Barney's herb helped, and I was alive. *All will be well. I just need to get out of here.*

I sipped tea and examined the map. It was clear the trail continued an up-and-down meandering trajectory, dipping slightly lower than I currently sat, then gradually back up following the ridgeline. My knee would not be able to handle that terrain. At the trail's lowest point, there appeared to be a dry creek bed. *Perhaps some water will be gathered there from the melting snow.* The PCT's ultimate route led to Scissors Crossing, a road leading into the small town of Julian, California, to the west. The creek route seemed to head in the same direction, only more direct with much flatter topography. I still had water in my canteens. More than I needed if I had hiked without an injury, but now it may be just enough. *My pace will be a handicapped trudge, but I'll use my trekking poles as a crutch for my right and follow the creek bed to the junction. It will be hotter down in the gorge, but at least I will not get lost or risk another accident.* I decided to act on this plan. After an hour of playing the harmonica and stargazing, I finally fell asleep.

It took me two days of slow, painful hobbling using my trekking poles in place of my right leg to reach Scissors Crossing. Because of the route I chose, I saw no other humans during my stagger. The mountain lions had seen me, of that, I could almost be sure. I'd heard and attempted to communicate with an owl in the night. Large cottonwood trees occasionally offered generous shade, and the critters that crawl on the ground were abundant, but no sign of humans, not one footprint. When I finally reached the hazy asphalt road, the temperature was higher than 100 degrees. The snow afore seemed like a holiday dream. Relieved and exhausted, I found a place to hitchhike into town. While normally I would stand and walk in the intended direction with my thumb out, this occasional called for a laze. I settled into a sit on my pack with my right leg and swollen knee extended out. When a car pulled over to help, I smiled at the clean lady in the driver's seat. Although I hadn't made the trail progress I originally desired, I was ready for Julian-town.

"Dear, you need to get some ice for that knee immediately." Sandra rolled down the windows and turned up the air conditioning. My body odor was raw; I knew it. The frigid blast from the car paired with the hot wind from outside coalesced into immediate relief.

"I know. I will. Need to get a motel room and rest this one out, I fear. Hopefully, I'll be better soon." I responded, trying not to sound discouraged.

"I don't know about soon. You should probably go to a doctor, but then again, they might just give you news you don't want to hear!" She was right, nor could I afford a doctor. I shouldn't be spending my budget on another motel room yet either. And for how many nights I did not yet know. Sandra continued. "Well, I'm glad you made it, Hot Wing. Welcome to Julian. We are an apple town, and I am the apple pie queen here." She looked at me and smiled sweetly. I observed apple orchards as we wound uphill into an oasis away from the oven below. "I am going to drop you off at my restaurant. You go in, get a free sandwich and a slice of apple pie on the house. If you need anything while you recover, you know where to find me." As we rolled into town, Sandra pointed out the motel where all the hikers stayed, explained where the doctor was located and patted my dirty shoulder with the tenderness of a mother whose kids have grown and moved away.

I thanked Sandra for her kindness and followed her orders, hobbling into the quaint eatery on Main Street. Salivating from the aromas wafting in the air, I washed my hands, forearms and face in the bathroom while awaiting my lunch, then ate my fill of a delicious sandwich and the best slice of apple pie I had ever tasted.

~~~

Julian, California, was never supposed to be a layover. An apple pie pit-stop perhaps, but certainly not an overnight. Nor was I ever planning on staying two nights in Laguna. However, circumstances had forced such, and as always, I was determined to make the best of it. The motel was buzzing with hikers. As I approached, I heard my name hollered from someone I had known on the Appalachian Trail. My heart warmed as I limped towards hugs, reuniting with old friends and meeting many new, yet a discouragement lingered within, concerned the knee injury might derail the entire season. If I could not heal, I could not hike. The rooms were small and cheap, so I paid for my one-bedroom and locked myself away to rest and think. Hikers were busy drinking beer and laughing noisily outside, but I did not share the same jovial mood. Once the party sounds diminished and I had iced my knee for a while, I hobbled downtown and weighed my options. Although painful to move, I could not lay in the small box any longer. I needed air, the sky and proactivity.

Downtown comprised one main street, and that was about it. Simple shops, a few eateries including Sandra's place, many apple signs, the liquor store, a small library, the town hall, and down a side avenue was the doctor. I did not want to go there. I already knew what would come of that. Instead, I found a bench in the middle of it all and sat down to contemplate. My knee throbbed. The entire right side, which supported the weight on my trekking-pole-crutch, pulsed with exhaustion. I could feel additional pain creeping towards my left, for its imbalanced overuse was now opening the way for fresh injury. That is not what I needed, and though I would not accept it yet, I knew that if a few days of rest exhibited no signs of progress, my Pacific Crest Trail hike might already be over.

As I mused on the bench for maybe an hour, zoning out into a melancholic daze, sipping some whiskey I'd just purchased, smoking cigarettes I'd just rolled with tidbits of fallen tobacco sticking to my legs, I sensed another beside me. To my right now sat an older woman, with a cowboy hat decorated with feathers. She wore a multi-colored pearl-snap collared shirt and a jade necklace. Bold red cowgirl boots adorned her feet. Her fine gray hair was pulled back and laid long in one thick braid. She smiled at me as I looked over but said nothing until I dabbed out my cigarette, considering she may not like the smoke.

"It's okay. I don't mind." She spoke kindly, nodding at my gesture, then returning her gaze gracefully forward. We sat in silence for a few more minutes until I took a sip and offered her some of my liquor. "No, none for me anymore. My husband and I retired from drinking many years ago."

"Ah, that's good of both of you," I muttered, not realizing until I opened my mouth that my words had become lethargic. "Maybe I will stop drinking someday, but for now it seems alright."

"It's not alright for that swollen knee," she said lightly, recognizing my swollen limb. "Alcohol increases inflammation. It may mask the pain, but it is only hurting your body more." Her admonishment didn't sound judgmental, but it did sound caring.

CINEREAL

 We introduced ourselves and talked about why she quit drinking, about life in Julian, and about shedding the things that do not serve us anymore. The colorful lady's name was Margaret, to which I replied, "That's my grandmother's name." In time I added, "I don't think I have shed anything yet. I'm still adding." Margaret chuckled, affirming that someday I would understand. When my knee indicated it was time for more care, I bid her farewell and hobbled back to the ice machine and my room.

 The next day I turned my hobble and downtown sit into a routine. Margaret joined me on the bench again, concurrently as on the previous day, and we chatted for over an hour. For four days in a row, it went like this, discussing hobbies, family, theism, and tragedy. Though the inflammation in my knee subsided, I didn't sense or observe any healing. I believed I had torn a ligament, and I slowly began to accept that my short Pacific Crest Trail hike would end in Julian.

 "Sometimes, we are forced to slow down for reasons we don't comprehend." Margaret said one day, "Your plans are not always His plans."

 "What do you mean by that?" I inquired, feeling uneasy, knowing she was alluding to God, a topic I was open to discussing more of, yet unwilling to unveil my full stubbornness against. He was always near, convicting me to return to Him, but I continued to close my heart and ears.

 "Well, Wing, you say you are an adventurer and a writer, but perhaps you are supposed to write about more than just adventure. Take this town for instance, and myself and my husband, this is a modest place, we live a simple life, but I have discovered more truth in the silence, in the mundane, than I ever found when we lived fast, exciting lives. We didn't plan to move to Julian when we did, but life told us to slow down and be present. I had been living for the thrill for too long, and in that thrill, I was rarely present. You understand?" I nodded, listening, not sure I fully understood, but I knew she spoke from what she had learned. Margaret rested her hand on mine, closed her eyes and spoke a gentle prayer. "Lord, guide Hot Wing to where You want him, please heal his body and his mind, keep him from despair, open his heart to You."

 A flash of anger bolted within as she said this, but also, I felt loved. She cared in a way that was bigger than her. She was not just Margaret; she was more. As sudden as my flash of anger, so too arrived a flash of need, a need to convey something to her that perhaps she would understand. "Margaret?" I paused. "May I tell you about something I saw? About an event I witnessed as a child that, well, holds no earthly sense. To be honest, I know I rebel against God. I accepted His salvation, placing my faith in Jesus and all He has done for us when I was young, and I still believe in Him, but for a long time I have pushed Him so far away. I told you a little about that, about the family stuff... However, something occurred when I was twelve, after my faith and before my rebellion began, something I can never shake. Most people whom I have told this to think I am crazy. I think only my mother understood, but maybe you will as well."

Margaret pushed up the tip of her hat a tad, focused her eyes on me and settled into the gentle smile she often wore between words. Her eyes tacitly welcomed the account of this unique event. So, there on the bench, between sips of whiskey, while the citizens of Julian ambled by, I told her all that had happened on that supernatural night in the woods of Maine. When I was done, she reached over and squeezed my hand tenderly. She believed me. I could sense this, but also, she now tipped her hat low closer to her eyes. It was time for me to take my leave.

As I stood up to hobble back to ice my knee again, Margaret told me she would not be here tomorrow, but the day after she would return. "Still, Hot Wing, come sit on our bench for the both of us."

"Okay, I will. I'll see you in two days." I then joked, "unless I'm miraculously healed and off bounding up the trail again! But I doubt that..." With this jest, Margaret winked at me, causing me to smile as I turned towards my motel room.

The next day I returned to our bench, knowing it would be just me. I didn't want to be around the other hikers anyway, for they merrily came and merrily went, healthy and focused on the thousands of miles of trail north to Canada. The crew I had spent the snow days with at Laguna had already passed on by. They wished me well and assured me they'd see me again, but the look in their eyes did not match their words. It was becoming quite clear; *I should go home or just stay in Julian forever.* I hated this thought. I hated it all. Even apple pie was beginning to taste like mockery. As I sat in my gloom, brooding, falling into the despair Margaret had prayed against, I noticed the eyes of a stranger looking at me from across the street.

I looked up at a woman I had never seen before. In my five days of observing this town, I believed I had seen everyone, for I saw the same faces every single day. She looked more than at me, but into me as if she was about to communicate telepathically from thirty feet away. Instead, she raised her hand and waved. I waved back, and the short, plump, blond, middle-aged lady dashed across the street and sat right next to me in Margaret's spot. "Hi," is all I said.

"Hi, you are injured, yes?" She spoke with an accent I had never heard. *And how and why did she know I was injured? I've just been sitting here, and if I have not seen her before, surely, she has not seen me.*

"I am, but how did you know that?" I looked at my knee, and though the icing routine decreased the swelling, it was discolored and looked awful. *Ah yes, maybe it was obvious.*

"I am here to heal you." She stated this as a fact, causing me to wonder what was going on. "You will not be hiking anymore unless I heal you, yes? You have a motel room. I have the medicine. We go to your room. You do not need to be afraid of me. I have come to heal you."

My mind was completely baffled, and though I did not fear the woman, for something about her seemed genuine and not insane, I did not know how or why or where she had gained this knowledge. "Did Margaret send you?" I asked, thinking surely this must be some kind of small-town holistic doctor friend of my new colorful acquaintance. To my question, this lady looked puzzled. It was clear she did not know Margaret.

"No, Margaret, I am Katya. Come, we go to your room, and I will heal you." She stood up and reached out her hand as if I must join her, and oddly, I felt compelled to obey and trust her. If anything, this would be an experience I could not pass up. *If she is a looney, I will kick her out or yell for help.* I stood up, touched her hand in return, and told her I would go to my room on my own, but she could meet me there. I didn't want to get into this stranger's vehicle, if she had one hidden somewhere, and at least I could tell some other hikers about my weird visitor in case danger should arise. Katya agreed to meet me in thirty minutes.

Back at the motel room, Katya arrived carrying a folded massage table and a bag with unknown contents. I met her outside, so other hikers could observe who was about to enter my room. One hiker jeered as if this was some sort of impromptu romantic meetup, but as far as I was concerned, it was no such thing. I certainly hoped it was not. Katya remained focused, acting as if this was not an odd interaction, just another day for her. Once inside my room, she unfolded the massage table, told me to undress down to my underwear, assuring me, "No need to worry, everything is connected, I must massage your whole body." She pointed to my whiskey bottle on the dresser. "No more alcohol today, Wing." I nodded, agreeing that I would not drink for the remainder of the day. I watched as she emptied her mysterious bag, extracting long white linens and green leaves from a plant I did not recognize. "These are comfrey leaves." She held one up. "I will make a poultice, which will heal any tears in your knee."

At this point, despite not knowing where she had come from, nor how she knew I was injured, I decided to submit to the treatment. I could tell she was not here to take advantage of me or harm me, and maybe she knew something I did not. I attempted to shut my brain down and relax, lying on the table and following Katya's orders. First, she administered a full-body massage. I melted into the luxury and winced with the pain. For two full hours, she gently and vigorously rubbed each muscle. When that was complete, she pulled out a stone bowl and rod and muddled some of the comfrey leaves, along with some water and another powdery ingredient I did not know, into a thick green paste. "Before the poultice application, you must go to the bathroom," she instructed. "For you will rest all night once the comfrey mixture is adhered." As I stood urinating with most of my weight on my left leg, I noticed through the small window it was already dark outside. I chuckled at the peculiarity of the day, cleaned my hands and then returned to Katya. Upon the linen, she placed the paste she had mixed and wrapped my knee securely with the poultice. "Complete," she stated. "Here, you take this pill and drink some water. It will help you sleep. Leave the poultice on until you wake in the morning and then go easy on your knee for the day. However, by then, you should be healed. Some light walking and a nutritious meal will strengthen you again."

I thanked her sincerely, although I remained baffled by who she was and where she had come from. She had brought comfort, deep care and hope, and for that I was grateful. Despite my skepticism, I wanted to believe her, and so as she gathered her items, presented one last kind smile and then disappeared, I decided I would try to have faith that all would be well. Easily, I drifted into a deep sleep.

When I awoke, the sun was lighting the sky. I felt groggy and unsure of exactly all that had transpired the afternoon and evening before, but something in my body seemed different. My memory was clear, but my understanding of how it had come about remained a mystery. I delicately unwrapped the poultice from my knee and realized I could bend it without pain. Elated, I stood up and timidly walked about the room. I could place

CINEREAL

full weight on my right leg. Everything was tender, but nothing felt undone, broken, or torn. Amazed, I hydrated, showered and continued walking about. *Did it really work? Had Katya healed my knee just like that!?* My soul lifted enthusiastically, realizing my hike may not be over barely after it had begun. *Is my optimism warranted? Should I be celebrating already? Surely, I need to be careful, as Katya instructed, and take it easy today.* I followed her orders but also ventured into town for food and ultimately, my bench sit with Margaret. *She must know who this Katya is. I am sure she sent her.*

Throughout the day without utilizing my trekking poles as a crutch, confidence in the healing increased. Reveling in this seemingly miraculous mystery, I ate my last apple pie slice at Sandra's shop, resupplied trail food at the grocery store, then topped off tobacco and whiskey from the liquor store. After securing my necessities, I packed my backpack with the plan of hitchhiking back to Scissors Crossing and the Pacific Crest Trail that evening, but first I must meet with Margaret.

I did not bring whiskey to my bench sit that afternoon, only my excited self, ready to tell my elder cowgirl lady-friend the entire event. She arrived at her usual time. Margaret cooly apologized for her absence the day before, then energetically exclaimed at my missing crutch. "Hot Wing, what happened yesterday!?" Ready for this question, I unloaded all the details to her with animated hands, an upbeat voice, all while standing and even demonstrating a few hops and dancing steps to prove how far and quickly my knee had healed. Margaret beamed, smiling with my joy, but also encouraging me to still take it easy.

"Margaret, you must have sent this lady, Katya. You did, didn't you? How else did Katya know me and what I needed? How Margaret, it makes no sense otherwise."

Margaret seemed less surprised than I was, and assured, "Wing, I do not know this lady. Other than talking with my husband, I told no one about your knee or our sit and chats. In fact, I do not believe there is a Katya who lives in Julian, none that I have known in my eighteen years here."

"Well then, how did this happen? How did she know me, and heal me?" I inquired perplexed, as if Margaret must know the answer.

With patience in her eyes, Margaret calmly and seriously stated, "Wing, I believe she might have been an angel."

"No…" my retort faded into silence. "Trail angel yes but" Margaret cut me off.

CINEREAL

"Wing, those vivid, magnificent celestial beings you told me you saw when you were twelve. Of how they protected that boy who was in danger. Of the terror and harm, they shielded him from, which you could see, but those beasts he could not see. He was helpless, a feather on the earth in those moments. I know you know what they all were, and yet maybe you do not fully comprehend it all. I cannot give you the answer to your healing, but we do not need to fathom something for it to be true. Sure, people have used comfrey leaves for healing, but not in the overnight miraculous way you received them. So, I encourage you to lean into the mystery, into His power, seek Him, listen for Him, lean in, not away. Perhaps someday you will understand." Margaret stood up and wrapped her arms around my thrilled, confused, healed body. She looked me in the eye and spoke as if sending me on my way. "Hike on Hot Wing but remember this. Never forget all that has been given to you, what He has given and shown to you, and someday, write about it all."

~~~

I hiked north from Scissors Crossing through the San Felipe hills of hell. Although taking it easy on my knee was an objective, this stretch of trail was extremely hot and dry, with no ideal places to camp. One must hike a marathon to reach the next water source and suitable resting spot. The trek was laborious and full of rattlesnakes, so I stepped mindfully, maintaining a minimum pace of two miles per hour. I arrived at the glorious, clean spring and camp after dark, grateful to lie down and rest. The day was a success. My knee throbbed only slightly. Though healed, it was still regaining strength, but it had held strong across a rugged tract of wilderness. A sense of wonder lingered within, recognizing that in just two days, I went from barely being able to walk to hiking a strenuous marathon. *Perhaps Katya was more than a trail angel. A real one. An angel in disguise as a human.* Quickly, I brushed this thought from my mind. The mighty depths of the supernatural world were not a reality I wanted to face. Everywhere I walked, I often met strangers who tried to point me towards the Almighty. God this and God that, and yet I just wanted to turn my way, drink another whiskey, wine or beer without conviction from these messengers. Whoever Katya was, I was now healed, and it was heartening to be making progress, to be actively a part of this long migration, in stride with other hikers instead of waving to them from a bench in town.

CINEREAL

In the southern desert days, I made two friends who would become my brothers of the Pacific Crest Trail. I met G at Scissors Crossing and then started hiking with him the following day from Warner Springs. G, with his curly brown hair and my same medium stature, was from "the valley" near Los Angeles. He reminded me of a guy whose parents wanted him to become a lawyer, and yet he was in revolt. Safari, I met further up the trail deep in the California desert. Safari looked like a young Ryan Gosling, born with a charm he had yet to recognize himself. G, Safari and I were of similar mindsets. We enjoyed living each day to the fullest. They were both calmer than I was, but they cheered on my antics and joined in on many of the side-quests I concocted. We rejoiced in the beautiful adventure together, diving into every possibility trail life offered. G was about my age. Safari turned twenty-one on the trail in May. His birthday we celebrated by wolfing down a batch of marijuana cookies gifted to us in a trail town. While G matched my drinking habits, Safari was the first person to admonish my lifestyle. He placed his hand on my shoulder in a mountain village tavern and stated with a straight face, "Both of you drink too much." G and I laughed him off and ordered more cold India Pale Ales. Safari declined to join us for another round of beers that night. Instead, he rolled a spliff and stepped outside to smoke away from our raucous behavior. While watching him walk out the door, I pulled the house ashtray towards me and lit another cigarette. For him, drinking excessively was rare, but for me it had become every opportunity. Safari might have thought his stern observation and concern were lost in the haze of smoke and booze, but they were not. I appreciated him, even admired my new younger friend. His words remained catalogued in my mind, seeded as a subconscious warning I may someday consider.

As we progressed up the trail and in our developing brotherhoods, I began to realize that at times I could become a bit much to handle. My heart always brimmed with loyal adoration for those I grew close with and held loving kindness for each living being on the planet, yet my temperament could also exhaust others after extended periods shared. For a while, G matched my competitive nature well. We pushed each other to hike faster, further, drink more and carpe diem with escalating intensity. We engaged in push-up and pull-up competitions, races to summits, and billiard games. Nearly every day for 400 consecutive miles of trail, we continually battled head-to-head in some sort of self-concocted competition. When I came up with a wild idea, he would join in, at first with doubts, then after with the guffawed statement, "How the hell did we survive, Hot Wing?" To this I would provide him a grin and a shrug, then barrel forth seeking new unknowns. Everywhere we ventured, I sought a party in even the most obscure nooks, a party I would go out, wrangle, and proudly bring back to share.

On one such time in the desert, we came upon a rare well-flowing creek. Capacious trees surrounded this oasis, offering cool air and shade. A small group of hikers had gathered, for the days before and days to come would be subject to only night's relief from the sun. A rugged dirt road with old, faded tire tracks lay on the shelf above the creek. I knew it must lead somewhere that had alcohol. G shook his head as he observed my mind considering a plan.

"This road has got to lead to beer, eventually." I spoke decidedly. "I will walk until some old desert runaway-kind-of-fellow picks me up, convince him to take me to a store, buy as much beer as I have cash, then make my way back and we can have a real party by this creek!" Speaking to the small mass of hikers. "If you all promise to camp here tonight, I think I can be back by dark. If you give me cash, I will bring more beer." The time of day was only noon.

G quickly retorted. "Not going to happen, Hot Wing. There are no fresh tire tracks on that barely-a-road. You'll walk all day and never see another soul. It's a waste of time, I tell you." The other hikers listened, waiting to see what my verdict would be.

"No man, it will not be a waste of time. For even if I don't see anyone and I find no beer, it will be a new land walked, a new side-quest explored, and side-quests don't need to have the outcome desired to be a success!" A few hikers chuckled. "And who knows, maybe it works! Then you'll all be regretting doubting me when I come back with cold brews. Come on, who's got cash? You add to my twenty bucks, and I'll be able to buy more."

G watched as a few other hikers jumped onto my ludicrous plan. They probably mused, *if Hot Wing is the one going on this mission and they were not, they might as well lounge by the creek with some money in the pot and relax the afternoon away. In the best-case scenario, they would get beer. Worst case, Hot Wing would die and not return.* I managed to raise about sixty dollars to add to my twenty. Eighty dollars should buy plenty of beers. G understood I was going to go on this quest with or without him, so at the last minute he joined. "Just to make sure you don't get murdered," he affirmed. I squeezed his shoulder with my dirty hand, grateful to have him by my side.

G was almost right, for we walked about three miles down the long, winding dirt road and never saw a sign of anyone. He tried to convince me it was time to turn back. I kept urging him to walk further, for I had a feeling we were close. G rolled his eyes, and we persisted with our dusty steps.

"Do you hear that?" I stopped walking and listened.

"Hear what?" G muttered slightly peeved.

"Shhh." An engine rumbled ahead around the bend. "That!" I took off running to see a car slowly pulling out of a trailhead parking spot and driving away from us. I sprinted after the car with my backpack smacking against my core and trekking poles tucked under my arm, yelling for the car to stop. The vehicle applied its brakes. Red taillights strengthened my hope. The driver stopped, rolled down his window and asked if we were alright.

"Oh yes, we are alright, thank you for stopping," I spoke, and winked at G encouraging him to follow my lead. "We are just extremely thirsty and were hoping you could drive us to the nearest store so we can resupply our beverages."

The driver was a man perhaps a decade older than us, with a wife in the passenger seat. He looked over at her. She shrugged, and he consented. "Jump in, guys, but it's like twenty miles to the nearest store. We've been hiking all day and are very ready to get home."

G gave me the look. He was amazed we secured a ride, but now we would be twenty plus miles from the trail. I gave him the chin tilt, tacitly relaying, *whatever man, we are already on a long walk. Don't worry. It'll work out somehow.*

As we rumbled our way further west from the Pacific Crest Trail, from home, away from our line of duty, I struck up a conversation with the kind couple. I knew that if I had any chance to convince them against their desire to wait for us in the store, and then drive us all the way back, I would need to strike a chord of friendship, create a bond, give them a reason to want to spend more of their tired afternoon helping me fulfill my party-by-the-creek dream.

"You both are truly trail angels," I began. "Thank you so much. We have been so parched in this desert heat, and it is because of people like you we can do what we do. Truly, thank you."

CINEREAL

"Do you not have water out there?" The wife turned her shoulders with genuine concern. It was clear they did not know we were buying alcohol.

I spoke, for G liked to remain silent with strangers. He always let me do the talking. "We do, but dirty desert water can become so drab, and even dangerous. I plan to buy enough for other hikers as well, so you aren't just helping me and G; you are helping a lot of us." She smiled. The husband rolled on.

As simple signs of civilization appeared, such as a mailbox in front of a gate, and the remnants of a bicycle in the brush, I did my best to allude to our need for a return ride. Without directly asking, I planted the seed. We finally arrived at a small country store, the first and seemingly only establishment around. At the store, a sign declared that this clapboard building also served as a post office. As I exited the car, I asked the husband and wife if I could buy them anything for their trouble. They declined, but I decided they would appreciate a few cold sports drinks after their day-hike. "We'll be right back. Quick, I promise. I'm going to leave my backpack in your car, so please don't leave yet. And I'll get you both something refreshing to drink!" G and I rushed inside before they could change their minds.

G laughed as we stood in front of a large cooler with racks of beer. He muttered in a tone of both moderate awe and relief, "I can't freaking believe it."

"Told you." I beamed smugly.

"What if they just leave, and steal your pack?" G asked, wisely wearing his.

"They won't, did you see the look on their faces as I told them stories from our hike? We are the most interesting people they've ever met. Did you see what they were wearing? He probably works in tech. He's a tech bro, yo. And she feels bad for us that we are now so far away from the trail. They are hooked, trust me." I did the beer math in my head while pulling racks out of the fridge. "Five eighteen-packs of beer and two sports drinks, we have just enough cash."

G and I continued smiling and chuckling at the cash register. We chuckled and beamed some more while we loaded the ninety beers in our arms and walked out to the car. The man and his wife's jaws dropped when they saw what we purchased. I handed them their non-alcoholic drinks and stated with a certain pitch of intention. "Well, folks, I suppose this is where we part ways…"

CINEREAL

"Get in the car. We've decided to drive you guys back. We can't make you carry all those, ahem, proper hydration beverages, twenty miles." The wife spoke, as she was evidently the decider in this decision. She gazed at us with wondrous eyes, not in a flirty way, but in a strange sort of admiration, as one may look upon a pair of Bigfoot creatures ambling up a distant hill. The man just nodded in agreement. They would drive us back.

After a slow drive an hour later, and a heavily loaded walk the rest of the way, G and I arrived back at the PCT and our peers lounging in the shade. I let out a loud whoop, kooie, and a holler. Everyone looked up and cheered, seeing G and me standing victoriously with a plethora of beer in our arms. Some hikers rose from their lounges and clapped. "A standing ovation, how about that, G!?" I tossed this comment to my friend as we stepped carefully down the steep bank to the desert beach. A fire was lit, and shortly after, so were we. With nine people including Washout from Alberta, Cactus from Colorado, and Trip from New Zealand, we each were allotted ten beers. It was a night to behold. Our unexpected party in the desert. In the morning, I picked up all the empty beer cans, crushed them into tiny disks and stashed them in my pack. The beer boxes we had burned to ash the night before. Everyone moved a little slower as the sun rose, but everyone smiled with satisfaction.

While cleaning camp, determined to leave no trace, G commended my efforts. "You pulled it off, Hot Wing. Did you know it would work out like that?"

"Of course I didn't know, bud." I spoke, a tad hungover. "But I needed to act as if it would for it to happen. Big things never become if we do not give it a go with belief."

G returned, "Not going to lie, Wing, but I kind of doubted you at first."

"G, people have doubted me my whole life, and they will probably always doubt me to some extent, but that only motivates me more. I thrive on it. Now come on. We've got more blistering desert miles to eat if we are going to reach those tree-haven mountains anytime soon."

~~~

In those California Pacific Crest Trail days, I was a fool. I did not recognize this then, but in my growing bravado, tenacious daily ambition, party-wilding ways, I was developing into someone I would look back on with shame.

Hot Wing, G and Safari were a force to be reckoned with, or so we believed. On the trail, we often ran up mountains, passing every other hiker, then sat atop summit boulders while smoking and drinking, feeling like heroes of the earth. When we rolled into trail towns, we arrived with dust plumes behind us, ready to feast, imbibe and mingle. Three good-looking, fit, life-zealous young men ready to engage in every pleasure a town could offer. The town-girls liked us. The town-guys did not. Our brash attitudes often got us in trouble. We rumbled into a fistfight over a billiard game with some townies in Wrightwood, slipped into a verbal spat which teetered on the edge of altercation in Big Bear, and almost got arrested in Idyllwild. Bar patrons smoking cigarettes in a parking lot in Tehachapi witnessed me get maliciously jumped, which I narrowly escaped. At each southern California town we arrived at, we left as desperados desperately returning to the range. We weren't breaking any laws, other than drinking in public, or purchasing unregulated marijuana from the streets, but we weren't living gently or humbly either. To be fair, Safari was often elsewhere when such clashes occurred, and though he too could heat into a temper, his presence usually calmed us down, while his absence allowed G and I's egos to rage.

Our lifestyle affected each of us differently, yet around our rowdy selves existed natural purity. The journey itself was intoxicating in its own wholesome way. The land provided organic splendor. Each day offered long ascents and descents, grand horizons, inspiring sunrises, and enriching sunsets. Unlike the Appalachian Trail, which existed mostly in a green tunnel, allowing only occasional long views, the Pacific Crest was a wilderness of enormous mountains and sky. Trail angels such as Donna Saufley and the Andersons poured love into each hiker. Nearly every turn brought kindness from strangers. And yet despite each nourishing hug and gifted meal, I would not allow my escalating sins to cease. With a bottle of whiskey in hand, held to my lips, I stood upon mountains as if I were a king. A dangerous scorn to the One who is true. To the One I had once given my heart and submission. My prideful actions were stirring the darkness within. Compounded upon my God-ignoring life chapters, bathing in filth, flying too high on adrenaline, I constantly sought each impure gratification of society. I wasn't hurting anyone, or so I told myself. I loved and treated everyone with kindness, and yet it was myself I did not love nor treat kindly. In no single day, but in the crescendo of years, I had become a moral taint upon honest land. The earth was beautiful, but I was not. Thus, a deepening chasm of darkness and emptiness infected my soul.

~~~

CINEREAL

Kennedy Meadows, a small settlement comprising a few rustic homes and one seasonal restaurant, sits at mile 702 on the Pacific Crest Trail. It is the gateway to a land of magnificence. Nestled in the foothills at the southern end of the Sierra Mountains, this small remote community camp is the last location to complete resupply and hiking logistics before ascending into a high elevation trek through what John Muir called "the range of light." Here at Kennedy Meadows, G had patiently waited for me for days. We had become separated after Tehachapi. I'd received news that a dear friend had died of a drug overdose. While reeling on the side of a desert hill, getting drunk on morning wine beneath a Joshua Tree, my mind was consumed with grief. I wondered what she had looked like after she had died. I thought of my best friend Trey, who was killed when we were thirteen, just minutes after we'd argued on the phone. My dad had taken me to his funeral. Trey lay there with makeup covering his ashen skin in an open casket. I pushed the thoughts of him away and returned my morbid mind to her. *It didn't matter what she looked like,* I told myself. *Dead is dead. Her soul is no longer in her body.* And where her soul may have gone, I would not allow myself to consider. After finishing the bottle of wine, I tried to turn my body north and continue hiking, but something would not let me. I was not ready or willing to quit. I just could not put one foot in front of the other in the direction I must go. So, I did what I had to do, disappearing to a place where no one would find me.

After a few days of leaning into darkness and comfort away from the trail, I returned to the spot I had left. From there until Kennedy Meadows, I hiked alone for the first time in a long while. Although I moved in sadness, I also sensed rejuvenation. Following 700 miles of persevering through the deserts and southern mountain ranges, the tide was shifting. A new ecosystem, the grand High Sierra, lay before me.

G and I greeted each other warmly, embracing and shaking our heads at some situations we had gotten ourselves into down south. Despite it all, here we were, still alive, entering a new chapter of the trail.

"Where the heck have you been, Hot Wing?" G grinned while he sipped on a soda.

"Eh," I paused, "some things went down. So, I met up with that lady I met in Tehachapi. Don't worry about it."

"You and your ladies." G chuckled. "What went down?"

CINEREAL

"Can't a guy have secrets!? I said don't worry about it. And no, it wasn't like that." I snapped back sharper than I wanted to, causing G to raise his eyebrows. I softened my tone and tried to divert the topic. "But hey, I brought us a fresh batch of pot cookies she baked in her fancy kitchen! Is Safari around?"

"Naw, haven't seen him in a bit. He'll pop up somewhere again, I'm sure. Give me one of those cookies." G put out his hand with a silly hungry beckon, while turning to lead me to where he had been camping.

I was thankful to be reunited with my trail brother again, and hoped Safari would indeed pop up soon, but currently I needed to reset my mind. We lounged in the shade and munched on peanut butter THC delights. I taught G how to play chess, amazed he had never learned before. After beating him multiple games in a row, G dispiritedly admitted defeat. Understanding his frustration, I spoke, "Hey man, don't let it get to you. You are only learning. To lose 100 games and then win one is to win 101 games of knowledge." G chuckled, understanding my universal point.

He set aside his discouragement, offering, "We'll play more next time we find a board. Heck, maybe we should buy one in a town sometime to carry with us." I happily agreed with his idea.

After returning the chess set to the nearby makeshift hostel, we continued talking about everything recent other than my friend's death. We agreed to shed all past follies and move forward with a refreshed focus on safe, mindfully present, possibly even sober mountain miles. At dusk we commenced our hike into the Sierras together with no whiskey in our packs, and for a few days and nights, we lived peacefully again, rejoicing in the sheer granite rise and 5,000-year-old bristlecone pines. At night we conversed calmly, watching our fire cast a dancing light upon large boulders, digging into why and how our desert mentalities had spiraled into chaos.

"I was scared of you the first night we camped together, Hot Wing," G spoke sincerely. "Not scared like you were going to attack me but, you were just so much. Waving your arms around, telling stories like a madman, drunk on whiskey and raging like the fire. You are an intense dude. Kinda freaked me out. I like you, but shit." He snickered in the I'm sorry but not sorry sort of way.

"I know, man..." I mused soberly, save for a toke of medicinal marijuana. No booze pulsed through my body. "It's the alcohol that gets me going like that. I don't know why I drink so much. It didn't always get me so damn high and so damn low. But I feel like my control over alcohol is slipping a bit."

"Without alcohol we can talk like this," G stated, "but when we are drinking together, especially whiskey, we just push each other into two Hydes. I fear they may turn on each other eventually."

"I hope not. I love you like a brother, man."

"I know. Love you too, Wing. But let's just try to drink less."

"Alright G, agreed. Less booze is best." I held a pinecone in my hand and slowly turned it, looking at each detail but also thinking about everything we discussed. After a few moments of silence, G stood and nodded to me, indicating the end of his day.

The next morning, as we strode across the ridges and highlands of the Southern Sierras, progressing deeper into the mighty spires of granite treeless rock, I announced to G that I would climb Mount Whitney, the tallest mountain in the lower forty-eight states, the more difficult way, up the steep mountaineer's route from the east side accessed by Whitney Portal. Most hikers would climb from the west, where the Pacific Crest Trail provided an easier approach to the summit, but that was just a long series of boring switchbacks, so I had decided to do it the other, far more exciting and dangerous way. G loved my plan and decided to join.

We consulted our map and navigated accordingly. First, we stopped in Lone Pine, a small town at the eastern base of the Sierras in Owens Valley on US 395, where we loaded our packs to the brim. With all our daily trail food and as many extras as we could fit, including a pint of whiskey each, our pack-weight topped 50 pounds. I was proud of this "only a pint" fact, for I usually carried a fifth of whiskey out with each resupply. To G I stated, "See, I'm buying less, so I will drink less." He apathetically shrugged.

Once we arrived at Whitney Portal, the trailhead for entry, or in our case, re-entry into the Sierras, including the harrowing mountaineer's route, we settled beneath a colossal Ponderosa pine tree before the big climb. Our packs were far heavier than anyone else attempting to navigate the mountaineer's route, as they were only outfitted with a day or two of supplies, not a week of food and all the extras we carried. We also noticed we were the only thru-hikers at the Whitney Portal. Regardless of this, most thru-hikers on the trail leaned into the idealism of ultralightweight backpacking, carrying minimal as possible, the lightest meal options, and obsessively shaving off fractions of ounces. Yet we were not of this mindset.

CINEREAL

We proudly referred to ourselves as middleweights. Those who could enjoy alcohol in the wild, a harmonica around the fire, an entire hunk of salami and block of aged cheddar for lunch, and a journal in which to sketch and write.

An example of the unconventional things we, or in this case I carried, was my ice axe. While many hikers brought this vital piece of gear during the sections requiring it, then mailed it home or ahead when they did not need it, I lugged my ice axe throughout the entire journey. From the beginning to the end, through deserts, dusty highlands, dense forests and certainly in steep ice and snow, my trusty mountaineer's axe, weighing only a pound, always wielded on my pack. Many ridiculed my unnecessary load, yet I ignored them all, knowing that in fact my axe was only an ice axe in such conditions. Otherwise, it remained a comprehensively helpful tool.

"Why do you carry that thing in the desert?" G reasonably asked one hot California day.

"To dig holes for my bathroom breaks. Or to scavenge firewood easily in a dense thicket. To protect myself from predators, or maybe you..." I winked at him while speaking confidently about my tool's many uses. "Also, I just like it. Watch this." I reached over my shoulder and pulled out the Black Diamond aluminum sharp shaft swiftly, twirling it in my hand then swinging it smoothly and violently into the neck of an imaginary cougar or wanna-be-murderer. "See," I stated, "this thing is the best."

G laughed, delighted by my eccentric ways. "I dig my poop holes with this little trowel." He pulled a pathetic plastic thing out of his backpack's side pocket.

"Yeah, I'm sure it provides just as much amusement as it does efficiency, huh?" I jeered at the item, which looked like a toy.

"Actually," G admitted, "it's awful. I must lean way over and scrape on the hard ground with it. Every day, it gets closer to breaking in half."

"Yup, not this smashing thing." I casually slid my implement back over my shoulder into its pack-spot without breaking stride. "All you have to do with this not-always-just-an-ice-axe, is slam the steel head on the ground and you've got a hole ready to go. Then when you're done, it makes it easy to cover back up. I tell you what, next time you need to do your business, borrow my axe, and try it. You'll see."

The next time G had to defecate he indeed borrowed it. From that day on, every morning when I heard his tent unzip, without a word I would slide my axe out to him. He would pick it up, and when he was done, return the multi-use item. And though for the rest of the long trail other hikers continued to question this item I carried, the two who mattered the most to me, my dear friends G and Safari, understood.

As G and I smoked and lounged before beginning our steep ascent, we noticed a small store selling grilled cheeseburgers and beer. I told G I was going to buy one of each. He hesitantly joined in. We ended up eating two and drinking three or four and smoking many rolled cigarettes while tourists and clean mountaineers looked on. Finally, with full bellies, we started our progress back to the Pacific Crest Trail via climbing up and over Mount Whitney. The day was nearing sunset, and tomorrow would be June 21, the summer solstice. A perfect day to summit the tallest mountain in the contiguous United States of America. After climbing 500 feet of elevation, we improvised a cozy stealth camp nestled between large boulders off the route where we would not be seen. Despite camping not being permitted in this location, we were thru-hikers, and that is what we would do. Already we had stealth camped in many areas we were not allowed, such as atop mountain summits, or in wooded town lots behind stores. Once settled in for the evening, I pulled out my pint of whiskey. G suggested we each drink only one swig as a nightcap and save the rest for later. At this I chuckled. After I drank one, I drank another, and so did G. G then suggested we have no more than half our pint, but once we reached half, I continued, and so did he. After many more rolled cigarettes smoked, and savage howls to the non-judgmental moon, all our whiskey had been consumed. Drunkenly, deep in the night, after pretending to be outlaws on the run, we finally succumbed to sleep. At nearly noon we awoke to the harsh summer solstice sun, raggedly hungover, thirsting for water.

"Well," I mumbled, "at least we won't get drunk again tonight. Come on, G, let's get to our climb. We'll sweat that shit out in no time." G cursed at me. I laughed. I cursed at him. He laughed. Up the steep mountain we hiked.

Although our banter produced smiles and revelry, even when we marinated in self-caused misery, I could sense that because of the booze our friendship was deteriorating. Perhaps not deteriorating, but stalling, stuck in a stagnant, unhealthy murk. He enjoyed partying and getting wild occasionally, but not all the time, and it was clear he was growing weary of it. I, however, was not. Going wild until it knocked me unconscious was the

CINEREAL

only speed I knew. *It was not always that way,* I considered... *or had it?* In my heart, I knew I was losing control, and the only way I could keep myself from drinking was to be in the mountains far away from any booze. *Like now. It's a good thing I drank all my whiskey last night. Mother always warned me about others being a bad influence on me, but it is I. I am a bad influence on others.*

Once G and I perspired the alcohol, our day climbing Mount Whitney up the mountaineer's route was marvelous. Our packs were heavy, and the route was steep. There were no boring switchbacks or a defined trail to elevate casually up the side of the massif. We embraced the solstice, navigated the ascent, and released the fog alcohol intoxication creates. Pausing only to hydrate and eat, we bid farewell to the trees while inhaling the crisp, clean air of high elevation. With each upward step, the Gothic-spired summit drew closer. I'd grown to love the air at 10,000 feet. It had become my preferred elevation. Anything below seemed too thick, and anything above, well, *perhaps too thin to build a cabin at someday.* Using calm minds, we chose our steps through massive talus fields and slippery slopes of scree. At the last lake before the final 2,000 feet of elevation, we noticed others setting up camp for the night. The sun had set behind the mountain's sheer, austere walls towered above. G and I observed the other hiker's climbing ropes. We had none. They were going to ascend the last steepest pitch in the morning with the eastern rising sun warming their backs. We were not. The time was now. Onward, in all conditions, as thru-hikers do.

The campers hollered multiple cheers to us as we continued upward in the cold gray dusk. We waved but did not turn our backs. The weight of our heavy packs forced us to constantly, deliberately lean forward. One slight erratic movement in the wrong direction would pull us backwards, resulting in a tumble to our deaths. G and I moved slowly and steadily. At 14,000 feet, a small saddle on the northern flank of the mountain, just 505 feet below the summit, provided a shelf suitable for camping. Here, we left the eastern cold gray and bathed in the sunset. We had climbed high enough just in time to see the fiery sphere shooting sunbeams across the broad wild land. Each peak illuminated as if dipped in gold. We sat in awe, looking into the shimmering belly of the High Sierras. *John Muir was accurate in calling this the Range of Light.* We marveled, exhausted and humbled, struck by the raw, harsh beauty. It was one of the most astounding horizons I had ever witnessed. Once the sun slipped below the far west, a harsh chill blanketed the wilderness. All golden hues were replaced with unforgivable blues, creeping with the wind into the depths of our skin.

"That was one of the most dynamic sunsets I have ever witnessed. I'm grateful we are here together, G." I spoke still looking west. G returned my comment with only a murmuring shiver. His mutter forced me to look urgently his way, suddenly recognizing he was struggling. His body and mind appeared to be shutting down. I realized we had not eaten enough that day. Coming off a heavy night of drinking and ascending over 7,000 feet in one afternoon had taken a toll on him. The thin air was making it difficult for him to breathe. G was suffering a panic attack at 14,000 feet above sea-level.

Immediately I faced him and instructed him to mimic my deep slow breaths. "Sit right here, G," tucking him against the corner of the wall, attempting to protect him from the stiff wind. "Point out choice rocks for building a wall with," I shouted above the intensifying gusts. He needed a task to distract him from anxiety, but also, he shouldn't be moving rocks himself right now. Hastily, I erected a horseshoe-shaped stone barrier two feet high, which we could lie in away from the gusts. He followed my instructions and kept trying to breathe deeply and slowly. We needed to eat, but neither of us had any appetite at this elevation. I had an idea that might motivate him. "Alright, G, we need calories. Your body needs energy to warm itself. Take this pack of Pop-Tarts. Whoever can finish them first will buy the next lunch in town." G chuckled anxiously knowing what I was doing, but he didn't want to lose any competition to me, so we both started gnashing on the dry crushed tarts. They were difficult to swallow, but small sips of water and another bite made progress on the food that didn't want to go down. We lay on the cold stone ground encased in our sleeping bags atop our hiking pads. Darkness was setting in. The wind whistled fiercely above our heads. I continued encouraging him to take another bite, then one more. Eventually, we finished the meager meal.

The calories helped, G caught his breath, and in time, when the urgency of the hour had passed, he finally looked over to me and articulated. "Thanks, brother." I smiled at him. He added, "yeah man, that was one beautiful sunset."

"Sure was G. Alright, let's try to get some sleep. We'll finish the last 500 feet in the morning."

At dawn, the final ascent up Mount Whitney was a steep, icy wall. Not intended for guys with heavy packs and no ropes. Death looked up at us

CINEREAL

from below, but we succeeded, and celebrated with pushups, rolled cigarettes, cheers, jumping jacks to warm our joints, and embraces of triumphant joy. The summit belonged only to us that gorgeous June 22, 2012, morning. Down below at Iceberg Lake, we could spot the mountain climbers beginning to pack their tents. We "kooied" loudly down to them. They watched as we danced like cocky ants at the top. I encouraged G we must force-feed ourselves a bit more food and hike down. His panic attack still loomed worrisome in my mind. We could rest and relax for as long as we desired once we reached Guitar Lake, a few thousand feet below on the west side of Mount Whitney. "Let's get back to the trail, G." I reiterated as he dragged his feet, our successful morning adrenaline having worn off. "PCT, we are coming home!"

Two hours later, we lounged in the grass by a lake which, from above, did indeed resemble the shape of a guitar. The sun warmed our faces affectionately. All was well. The mountaineer's route was accomplished. We napped in the grass, ate a full lunch, refilled our water supplies, snickered at how we had made the journey more difficult than it needed to be, but mostly, we rejoiced in the reality of being alive on the Pacific Crest Trail.

~~~

G and I persevered through the Sierra Nevada mountains. G's mother, brother, and sister-in-law were set to visit us on the trail while on a brief trip of their own. They would hike south towards our north. His mother had asked if we needed anything. I suggested whiskey. Reluctantly, with an eye-roll, G sarcastically repeated my request to her, a request I should never have made. With their arrival nearing, we charged onward. Up and over Forrester Pass, the highest point on the PCT at 13,153 feet, then down into talus fields surrounded by snow. In the gray and white exposed landscape, two hours before noon, we encountered them. Our assembly was brief but lively. G's mother generously presented two individual pints of whiskey. G laughed and placed one inside his pack, while I thanked her and opened mine immediately. To the shock of all, I lifted it upwards, tilting it back and drinking long gulps. With a refreshed tingling "Ahhh," I smirked. While wiping and licking dribbling excess booze from my beard, I added a "Why not?" The judgement on everyone's faces faded, but the reality remained clear. Hot Wing might have a drinking problem.

After parting ways, G and I got drunk in the shadows of the pyramidal East Vidette, down in the thalweg of Kings Canyon. The mountain winds

CINEREAL

and the winds within us raged late into the night. My darkness seemed contagious. In this disease, we broiled together. Come morning, we shook off our mental murky cobwebs by stomping up to Kearsarge Pass, where day-hikers sat eating sandwiches like a flock of hunched seabirds on sun-drenched islands. They had approached from a five-mile trail we must now traverse. These side trails, which connected the Pacific Crest to civilization, were always littered with tourists who asked too many questions and made predictable comments such as, "Now that is a beard." By each slow traveler we flew, running and jumping beyond everyone in our way. Down with thru-hiker speed to a parking lot where we could hitch from the village of Independence into the municipality of Bishop.

    The once jovial zero days of town now wore a tense frigidity, born from my uncontrolled drinking. My dad visited, treating us both to dinner as he had done prior in Palm Springs. He greeted G as a son, observed the growing angst in our brotherhood, then drove us back to the trailhead. There, by a trail angel's cooler full of beer, G and I parted ways. "Until Mammoth, on the fourth of July. A little space for our own walk and thoughts. Travel well, brother." G spoke these words to me with a tinge of shared melancholy. I knew he needed to get away from me for a while, and I, well, I was going to sit by the cooler of free beer and gain a buzz before I continued my hike. *Let him get a head start.*

    I took my time progressing north, immersing myself in the beauty of the High Sierra wilderness while sipping on whiskey without the judgement of another. At Rae Lakes, I paused and fished alone using a sapling for a rod, floss as line, and a kernel of corn as bait on a hook I'd concocted from the tab of a beer can. I found a neglected firepit far from the trail, nestled among flora, about fifty feet away from a creek. After reassembling the stone heap into proper order, I made a fire to cook my rainbow trout on, feasted, then laid back to stare at the sky. I wondered how far G was ahead and knew that if I was going to meet him in Mammoth on the fourth of July, I would soon need to log solid miles. The brush by the creek rustled. Fearing a bear had smelled my meal, I looked up to see a massive black-tailed deer with large antlers lingering for a drink. This calmed me, for the buck would know if a predator was nearby. Neither of us was concerned with the other. After the deer drank, he laid down in the dirt, just like me. We shared a peaceful space as the sun drifted further west. At dusk, I hiked a few miles north to sleep far beyond the scent of my cooked fish.

CINEREAL

On the night of July 3rd, I consulted my map to see how far I was from Mammoth. I still had forty-six rigorous miles of terrain to go. Therefore, I did what must be done. I awoke at three in the morning and started walking, hiking all day without a break. I ate as I strode, urinated to my side as I progressed, pausing only to refill my water jug. Up and over Muir Pass, persevering at a minimum pace of three miles per hour. I was determined to reach Mammoth that day. By evening, I had succeeded. My body shuffled along the streets of the new-to-me bustling town, exhausted from a grueling day. Locals dashed around wearing red, white and blue, waving sizzle-sticks and drinks, celebrating the holiday. When I asked other thru-hikers if they had seen G, everyone said no. He had not made it to town yet. This saddened me, but I knew he had a reason. *I must have passed him in the night before he awoke, or perhaps he had taken a side-quest to Vermillion Valley Resort. Since he had not seen me catch up, he must have assumed I would not arrive on our determined day.* Either way, I had painfully held up my end of the bargain and hoped he was alright.

That night, while stealth camping in a grove of trees between motels, I punched a bear in the snout. I awoke from a whiskey-drenched evening as he was sniffing the mesh of my tent. There was no need for my rain fly; therefore, his large black body hovered like a hazy mass nearly on top of me. Upon contact, he reacted with a surprised woof and bounded off to find an easier meal. *Freaking town bears,* I mused while drunkenly gathering up my food I had foolishly strewn around the inside of my tent. Once I stashed all bear-attracting items into my pack, I shuffled barefoot to the rear of the nearest motel and threw it over a tall, chain-link fence. *He won't get my food there, hopefully. I'll retrieve it in the morning.*

As I waited for breakfast at a cafe, I met a lovely young woman named Elora. In the afternoon, she took me horseback riding around Mono Lake. She owned one horse and had access to a second, yet she only had one saddle. Happily, I rode almost bareback upon a saddle pad. I liked Elora. Her genuine smile, witty mind, and long blonde hair distracted me from my concern about G. Thirsty from our long ride, we ambled the horses to a gas station where I jumped off Mellow Martin and hustled inside to purchase cold beers. Back on the horse, clomping out of town, side by side we rode in delight, sipping brews and chatting with each other. When I returned to Mammoth, G had finally arrived. The edge of our frustrations had softened with time apart, so we paid for a two-bed motel room, ordered two large pizzas, split a case of beer, and shared all our recent stories. My heart was content again, but I knew I must not let my growing alcohol issue interfere with our friendship. The next day we returned to the trail at Reds Meadow and continued north towards Yosemite. I promised Elora we would meet in a few days to climb Half Dome together.

Elora and I were to convene at the Clouds Rest trailhead. However, the trailhead was on the other side of Yosemite from where I had hiked in at Tuolumne Meadows. At dawn I awoke to ensure being first in line to secure Half Dome permits. Successful in this, I attempted to hitch a ride over to meet her. The park bus system was down for the day, and tourists were hesitant to pick up unkempt travelers. This obstacle resulted in added road-walking miles and my very late arrival. Elora was nowhere to be seen. I worried she thought I had stood her up, so I ran through the parking lot searching for her vehicle. When I spotted what I presumed to be hers, I decided she must have hiked up Clouds Rest without me. *Why wouldn't she? She'd come all this way.* Motivated by this assumption, I started running up the trail. As I ran the entire distance, up 2,000 feet of elevation, I asked each day-hiker descending if they had seen a woman of her description. Finally, one answered with the question, "Are you Hot Wing?"

"I am!" I exclaimed hopefully.

"Well, Hot Wing, the woman you describe is indeed up the trail. She's been asking about you too!"

With this encouraging information, I ran even faster, despite my heavy pack, onward and upward, for I had a woman to meet on the mountain. When I breached the trees and stood below the rocky summit, I spotted Elora standing on top waiting for me. We waved with elation. I continued my gallop, and within minutes we embraced overlooking El Capitan, Half Dome, and the entire marvelous national park.

That night we camped in Little Yosemite Valley. I cooked her one of my favorite trail dinners, chicken broccoli Alfredo with penne pasta. Not the freeze-dried pre-made type, but fresh, each ingredient in separate pieces, garlic cloves, and rustic bread. A fine dine. Since we were in the thick of tourist land, the park authorities prohibited fires except for one communal campground firepit. Consequently, it was there, in front of sixty family folks, as they poured hot water into their meal pouches and waited, that I grilled, diced, sauteed, boiled, combined and seasoned, all while telling everyone grand stories of my exploits. Little children sat forward in astonishment. Parents gasped and laughed. Elora watched gleefully while I put on a show.

CINEREAL

Beaming at her through the flame's illuminating dance, our purple-tinted teeth mirrored each other. I drank only wine that night, for whiskey would have fueled me differently, but Spanish Rioja, now that is the lover and storyteller's vine.

Elora had never cowboy camped before. After our grand meal, I introduced her to this practice. As we lay on the earth of Little Yosemite Valley observing the stars, in a nook I discovered away from the official campground, with no tent to hide us from the trees, sky, breeze and eyes of all animals, we listened to bears shuffle from one locked metal food storage box to another. We cuddled closer with excitement. Black bears roam boldly in Yosemite, but they just want food. There was little danger to us, I knew. In the morning, we approached the famous Half Dome cables, conquered the rock, and rejoiced in the incredible gift of a day. Our adventure was triumphant. We stretched each hour and mile back to the valley floor as long as we could, then parted ways thinking we would never see each other again. It was time for her to return home to Mammoth, and for me to continue hiking north on the Pacific Crest Trail.

~~~

A few days later in northern Yosemite, I contracted the horrible illness of giardia. After swimming, and accidentally swallowing from the idyllic, but stagnant water of Benson (Riviera) Lake, I awoke with no appetite, feeling abnormal. I knew something was amiss. The absence of any hunger was a telling sign. Trusting my intuition, I pushed on and then hitchhiked into Bridgeport from Sonora Pass. I arrived just in time, as my body erupted into a disgusting creature of symptoms on the front lawn of a motel. All the rooms were booked, but the explosive diarrhea, vomiting and spiking fever would not wait. Succumbing to each symptom simultaneously, I wretchedly suffered on the grass in daylight for many to see. I did not know what to do. G was probably somewhere ahead, and Safari somewhere behind, but they wouldn't be able to help. I didn't need a buddy, or money; I needed shelter with a toilet and a sink. Lying in excrement and pushing buttons on my cellphone with trembling fingers, I called the only human who could save me. Within three hours, Elora arrived, tenderly guiding me to her vehicle, compassionately setting my filthy body on her clean leather seat. I curled into a leaning fetal position with my head hanging out the window all the way back to the town I had recently departed. When we arrived at her home, she led me to her bedroom. She shut the curtains, patted my skin with a cold

CINEREAL

damp cloth, and placed a bucket by my side. It was a Friday. For three days I could hold nothing in my body, and even when I had nothing left to expel, I continued to dry-heave from both ends. On Monday, when Elora drove me to the doctor, I had lost fourteen pounds from an already lean frame. The physician provided medicine, and on Wednesday my body began to hold fluids, rehydrate, accept gentle food, and slowly regain strength.

In a strange turn of events, while I was healing, Elora fell ill with an unrelated malady. After I had been bedridden and she had taken care of me, it was now her writhing horizontally in the dark room. As she suffered, I took care of her, her dog, the errands and chores. When she recovered, and our two combined miseries had finally passed, we gratefully and humorously remarked how much we had needed each other. With echoed words we agreed, "It was meant to be. If not for a lifetime, our companionship was for a brief chapter, that we may take care of each other." Elora drove me north back to the trail, where I hiked onward into Northern California.

Once my boots hit the ground, I charged forth like a madman. Eating as much food as possible, I swiftly strengthened. Remembering the success of my heroic hike into Mammoth, I leaned boldly into this speed, slashing away miles from early in the morning until late at night. Many thirty and forty-mile days piled into giant swaths of wilderness rapidly covered. It seemed as if I were turning the globe with my feet, pressing back, pushing forward. One night, a fox trotted parallel to my stride. The next morning, five deer hastened in my wake. At dusk, a bear walking towards me pivoted and sprinted away. A mountain lion screamed at me in the dark. Owl's heads rotated, bird songs morphed into anthems, and with each step I accelerated. I wasted no time in trail towns, and cowboy camped only, exposed to the stars. Utilizing my tent was a luxury I eliminated, a time-consuming chore in which I chose not to partake. Progressing, eating miles for breakfast, lunch and dinner is all I cared about. Amid this mighty push across the land, within my heart and soul, darkness festered. It had gone nowhere, only paused for the time with Elora. Perhaps it had even emboldened as it waited, applying interest to the darkness I owed. Mentally, I was unraveling, yet one fact held me together. In three days, my brother Michael was getting married in Virginia, and to this I must go as a steady minded strong older brother.

~~~

After my torrent of hiking gusto, I caught up to both Safari and G. We spent some time together, but I had an airplane to catch. I hitchhiked to the city of Redding and flew across the country. My ride from the wilderness to a land of asphalt was driven by a cigarette-smoking teenager. His toothless mother slurped warm beer in the passenger seat. I was a bit scared as he swerved and regularly looked away from the road but knew I shouldn't judge. *Who am I other than a God-rebelling, chain-smoking, drunk?* I chuckled a sincere thank you when they dropped me off. It might have been bizarre, but after miles of road-walking with my thumb out, they were the only ones who offered me a ride.

From the West to the East, I whooshed through the sky. Stepping out of the terminal, I first noticed the drastic difference in humidity. The land I loved was now far away, my body now in thick moist air. Dad stood waiting with a grin. He slapped my back with a "There's my boy. Last I saw you was in the Sierras! Let's go get your brother married." To this I nodded, lit a cigarette and sighed. It was time to go celebrate love.

On top of a grassy hill, dotted with white chairs and a white arch, my brother and his bride united in marriage. I was proud of Michael and his new wife and applauded them for choosing such a lovely, lofted site near the Appalachian Trail. Between the vows and hurrahs, I gazed at the surrounding mountains, remembering my time walking through the terrain. Everything about the wedding was flawless. A clean, beautiful event, including a wholesome, lively reception in a church. During prayer, I bowed my head reverently and went through the motions, but within, guilt constricted my heart. I truly missed having a relationship with God, but it was now so far away... I knew what I should do, but somehow, I could not. It was pleasing to spend time with family, and play the part of the older brother, but even as I stood with my arm around Mother, and embraced my siblings, I also felt distant from them. After dinner, my dad's predecessor and I smoked our cigarettes on the manicured lawn. We talked about horses and long journeys. My brother and I drank beer together for the first time, and with everything the day involved, I realized he had grown up.

As I departed Virginia and sat in the airport waiting for my flight back west, the loneliness in my heart grew. I had G and Safari, a plethora of other hiker friends, and my family who still loved me, but it was the kind of loneliness not softened by the company of another.

~~~

With boots on western ground, having returned to the preferred arid air of the Pacific Crest Trail, I contacted G and Safari to inform them of my new

CINEREAL

plan. An epic side-quest a short distance away from our long path, I hoped they would both partake in. Enthusiastically, they hitched a ride from their respective locations to join me. We hoisted cold beers and eagerly cheered to the task at hand, summit Mount Shasta.

California had been a long state to hike through. Each of us had grown weary in our own way. I do not know everything that festered in G or Safari's heads, other than what they told me and the actions I observed. Nor did they know of the escalating lonely depression and spiritual rebellion I walked with, although they certainly witnessed some of my darkness seep out. But none of that currently mattered, for we were on vacation. A hiking vacation away from our hiking life. All our demons were set on pause. We had a mystical volcano to climb.

"I'll be honest with you. I wouldn't go up there this time of year." G, Safari and I held a silent stare at the Mount Shasta Base Camp store manager, prompting him to elaborate upon his statement. "It has been so hot lately that the rocks above tree line are dangerously loose. Lightning storms form out of nowhere, and most of the people who die on Shasta die this time of year." We sustained our silent stares with climbing helmets, crampons and ice axes in our hands, as if his opinion wasn't acceptable to us. He then added, "That being said, you guys are strong and knowledgeable. You have been hiking for a long time. You have more wilderness experience than most. I understand you are here and want to summit now. I believe you can. Just please be very careful."

After listening to this news and securing the necessary gear, we discussed the local's opinion over some alcoholic beverages. Our decision was this. We would, as always, closely monitor the weather, watch for falling rocks, loose glacial ice, melting shifty snow and ultimately make our decision on the mountain. His warning would not deter us. Mount Shasta had reunited the three of us. We knew how each other hiked, our strengths and weaknesses, and as a team we believed a successful summit expedition was achievable.

On Friday evening, August 17, 2012, we walked out of the town of Mount Shasta to the Bunny Flats trailhead. The sky was clear, and the air was brutally hot. Three in a row we ascended through resinous forest, singing, kooie-ing and grinning. In less than an hour we arrived at the Shasta Alpine Hut, an old stone structure at 7,884 feet elevation. Here the tall pine

CINEREAL

trees thinned out, forest lay below, and above us rose the massive gray, white and red peak. We stared up towards the summit at 14,179 feet.

"Now that's a mountain." Safari declared.

"Indeed. She's a beauty." I concurred.

"Hell yeah." G stated.

We leaned forward into movement, rising higher with each step. A few other humans moved slowly as dots above. The dots quickly grew larger until we passed the heavy-breathing hikers who stepped to the side. To them, we grunted, smirked and winked our versions of hello and thank you. As we paced, I considered the words of a friend from New England. "When you're out west, if you have the chance," Mit had said, "go climb Mount Shasta." He spoke with such earnestness that it had planted a seed within me and grown into a determined goal. *Well, buddy,* I thought, striding vigorously upward, *I'm doing it. I'm climbing Mount Shasta.*

Once we reached Helen Lake at 10,400 feet, we scoped out the crude landscape to pick a spot for our camp. About ten other hikers lingered around, creating a mini tent city. They cheered when they saw us and encouraged us to join them. Without hesitation, we shook our heads and shifted to the far side. Low stone walls lay in rings around the flat plateau of a dried-up Helen Lake, providing windbreaks for tents. We each chose an empty plot and set down our packs. Standing and stretching as tall as I could, I breathed in the pure air.

With emboldened excitement, I shouted to my comrades. "Mount Shasta boys! We are here!" Safari and G laughed, sharing my amusement. We set up our tents as we had done 100 times, unable to wipe elated smiles from our faces. As evening set in, the sky morphed from a calm, wispy blue into an awakened color palette. Passive sky-sloths transformed into energetic, majestic clouds. The great mountain walls breathed. Rocks occasionally tumbled from above with smashing, errant roars. They bounded down her flanks with tremendous power and then crashed to a thunderous stop. The wide landscape around the mighty pinnacle seemed to snarl, ushering in the night. The descending sun slithered behind Casaval Ridge, firing off cannons of sun rays behind her strong, silent black appendages. Purple, pink and orange hues filled the sky. A color-snaring haze of wildfire smoke hung on the distant horizon. Developing clouds awakened from their dull gray rest paraded upward into illuminated billowing castles. Beneath the show, Mount Shasta undulated methodically, as if she brewed ominous, secret plans. Every mountaineer was at her mercy, seduced by the beauty that boasted above. As her stony mass pulsed under our feet, I observed the varying shades of white that swaddled her shoulders. A snowy sea of pearls shimmered in the fading light, growing tired one by one, until the sun laid down to sleep beneath the black blankets of volcanic rock. G, Safari and I prepared dinner, keeping our eyes affixed to this wondrous display. We set alarms on our cellphones for four in the morning, to awaken and commence our 4,000-foot climb before any other hiker had disturbed the shifty earth. After one more cheer and swig of whiskey each, we parted to our separate tents and lay down, to drift into sleep, and dream of the morning to come.

I awoke to a threatening flash of light. Three seconds later, a long rumble of thunder shook the mountain. Another flash of lightning lit the sky. I sat up, realizing *this is not a dream*. A storm had formed in the night and was expeditiously strengthening above us. *This might be very dangerous*. As thunder shook the mountain again, I threw my ice axe and crampons away from my tent. Metal would only attract the lightning. More violent electricity flashed. Thunder now boomed only two seconds away. G and Safari yelled back and forth through the loud rumbles and increasing wind. "We are just going to have to ride this one out!" One of them shouted. The wind died to an eerie silence, leading to another immense roar as hail began to pummel our tents. Lightning and thunder became one. *Death could come at any second.* The mountain screamed above as rocks plummeted down into Avalanche Gulch where we lay. Everything shuddered viciously. I lay in my tent sharpening my courage, gritting through each second. The phone alarm sounded softly amidst the warlike clashes. It was now our intended time to start the climb, but Mount Shasta had other plans. *We must wait.*

After two hours passed, hail and wind had battered our tents into a sunken, dilapidated mess. We crawled out from beneath our collapsed shelters. Daylight had emerged. Mount Shasta's summit remained shielded from view in a thick lenticular cloud. Yet beyond this cloud, gentle blue skies offered hope. We had survived the storm. All other hikers camped on the Helen Lake plateau packed up their camps and hustled down the mountain, forfeiting their summit plans. G, Safari and I stayed put. Smiling as we watched them depart, I spoke. "The mountain has separated the boys from the men." My comrades chuckled and nodded. Calmly, we drank coffee and ate breakfast, absorbed in the environment we preferred, a mountain to ourselves. We would wait and observe the signs in the sky. Too late of a start would create too late of a summit, which would not do, for the afternoon heat and unpredictable weather might create dangerous chaos again. However, it was still early, we still had time, so we hadn't ruled out the objective yet. As we ate, journaled, chatted and prepared, the lenticular summit cloud faded. At eight-thirty we received our opportunity.

The first stretch was a 1,000-foot climb up steep, loose shale to the base of a vast snowfield. One by one we progressed, allowing ample space between, shouting to the others when rocks tumbled through. Multiple times we had to dodge these falling death bombs. With sturdy legs and lungs, we never stopped, moving steadily higher. Once we reached the edge of the snow, we strapped on crampons and assessed the routes before us. The Heart loomed another 1,000 feet in elevation above us. This "heart" was a large sheer wall we must navigate around. Our next aim, the base of the Red Rocks. On either side of The Heart lay narrow ice chutes, which we must reach. Carefully, we climbed the steep, icy snowfield towards these precarious passageways. This portion we accomplished as the previous. Remaining spread out, warning of falling rocks, persevering upward. Once at the base of the wall, we climbed straight up the center of the steepest snow chute to the right of The Heart. Sunrays reflected off the dirty ice as we ascended higher. Sunglasses shielded us from the sharp luster, while bandanas veiled our grins. Safari in the lead shouted down to me again. My helmet sat strapped to my head. Quickly, I looked up from my focus and shifted my spikes to the right. Clinging to the wall of the chute, small rocks struck my helmet as a giant rock somersaulted by. I yelled to G, advising him of this. He evaded the danger, and we returned to our progress. One step, set spikes securely in the ice, bury the axe deep, step. We gained elevation quickly, never growing tired or out of breath, only occasionally peering behind us in awe. As the chute narrowed, we approached the Red Rocks. Water gushed beneath the ice, forcing us to choose our steps with extra caution to avoid breaking through, lest we be swallowed into the mountain forever.

Atop the chute, the Red Rocks menaced above. These would have to be traversed around or over and included some of the steepest climbs and loosest crumbling rock. We tackled them aggressively through a vertical crack, a precarious thrill we accomplished without ropes. There was no assurance of success, for as we moved upward, it seemed as if the mountain

CINEREAL

was falling beneath us. Red soot shot downward with every move. With each mindful hand and foot placement, more of the mountain shifted. Our breathing remained calm, yet adrenaline stirred within. Hanging on the side of this majestic mountain, our hearts beat like loud metronomes. Onward towards the summit.

Upon succeeding up and past the Red Rocks, we approached a tall, snowless Misery Hill. This steep hill high on the mountain is aptly named for its laborious trudge, and from below it falsely appears to be the summit. However, we knew better, and noted with confident tones as we continued our rise, "Misery Hill ain't that bad." Atop Misery Hill we could finally see the sharp, craggy true summit of Mount Shasta. A crown above Northern California, a lady of mystery, Mount Shasta and we were finally face to face. Her beauty sparkled. She pulled us toward her. To the base of this final pinnacle, we crossed a wide, lightly inclining snowfield. Once across, we stood below the culminating ascent. To reach the top, there were multiple routes we could choose from. Each route contained one key possibility. If you fall, you die. And yet, that is how the entire climb had been. Safari, G and I discussed and decided. We chose our route, and I led the charge. Gripping cold stone walls and teetering boulders, wind tore at our limbs, pummeling our jackets and packs. With deep breaths, quick committed jumps, staunch holds and daring scrambles, we pulled ourselves higher until there was no more rock above, only the sky and the vertical stance of sweet accomplishment. A metal register attached to the summit sat waiting for us to sign, declaring our victory.

Intoxicated with triumph, we howled and hugged, dropped to our hands and performed our traditional summit pushups. We exulted in the beauty of standing on top of the world. Despite our joy, we understood the battle had only been half won. We had survived the storm. We had climbed up the snow and ice, dodged falling boulders and conquered the apex, but still had to descend the wilderness crown. After nourishing our bodies with water, almonds and cigarettes, examining the horizon in all directions, signing the register and latching it shut, we eyed the clouds, tightened our minds and proceeded. We chose alternative routes, scaled down precipices and glissaded across the snowfields. Loose shale followed in our wake as we flew. It was as if we were surfing the mountain, much like a snowboarder but with legs like goats. Once back at the tree line, we looked upwards at the mountain we had conquered. Safari stated in a narrator's voice, "On the date of August 17, 2012, only three humans summit Mount Shasta. Their names were Hot Wing, G and Safari." We laughed and agreed that indeed it was so. With this, we turned our faces toward the forest. The day had been a monumental one, a day we would never forget. It was time to go get drunk.

~~~

On one of California's last afternoons, deep in the rugged Trinity Alps, I trudged along dehydrated. The evening prior, I became fiercely drunk on whiskey, alone at the base of a cliff and on the precipice of another. Between these sheer heights, in an air thick with wildfire smoke, I drank, carousing with demons. The dark loneliness had returned after Mount Shasta. A loneliness that hisses vehemently and wails insufferably within, echoing in the hollow chasm of soul. When I awoke from my drunken murk, covered in scratches and dried blood for reasons I could not remember, I chugged far too much water than I should have. There would be no spring, creek, spigot or cattle-trough for thirty miles, and what water I still had, I must conserve. A distance later, after the sun had drifted low to my left, creating golden corridors through the coniferous forest, I plodded along, dragging my spirits in the dusty cloud my feet stirred behind me. I sliced perpendicularly through the shafts of light, my wafting hazy remnants striped with illumination and forgotten hues. Although dehydrated, I still had nine more miles to hike until water. Periodically, I sipped my rations, mindfully persevering, chewing on a stick.

Abruptly, in front of me, only fifty feet up the trail, a large mammal pounced onto the path. It was descending the steep mountain flank from my right, scampering down heading west. Its eyes locked with mine, but only for a second as it bounded onward into thick brush. Curiously, I lightened my steps, forgot my angst, approaching where it had crossed in the shadows. *If only it had stopped in one of the beams of light*, I considered. *It was smaller than a bear, yet far bigger than a raccoon, low, dark and long, a bit humped and muscular, not a mountain lion, wolf or coyote, but unless I see it again, I will not be sure what animal it was.* As I reached where it had crossed, I looked down to my left. *And there!* At the northern base of a mossy tree-trunk, in the brilliant warmth of sunrays, was a mighty male wolverine peering up at me. My breath gasped, but he did not run off, nor act alarmed. He gazed kindly up into my eyes without fear or aggression.

Smoothly, the wolverine descended a few more feet on giant paws to the base of another tree and peered back up at me again. He almost seemed to be intentionally conveying something, wanting me to follow him. I knew it was outrageous, and my tired, thirsty mind might be delusional, and yet the way he stepped, turned and pleaded his eyes into mine, exuded communication. Compelled, I stepped off the trail and followed him. As the wolverine proceeded to descend the side of the mountain, lowering into the flora beneath a clustered canopy, I continued to follow. Every few yards he turned his head and looked at me again as if making sure I was still behind him. Frequently, I observed where I had veered from the PCT, memorizing landmarks, ensuring I would not get lost.

Far down away from the trail, the wolverine looked at me one last time before hustling away. After the shuffling noise of his departing body dissipated, I heard a faint trickle. It was a sound I knew well. A sound all living beings desire to hear in a hot, dry land. Just a few paces from me, tucked on the side of the mountain, was a freshwater spring. There was no creek, nor a gush, just tiny droplets falling out of a rock onto lush, spongy, verdant ground. Amazed, overwhelmed with joy and awe, realizing that this wolverine had led me to water, I sat down by the spring and filled my water containers. Joyfully, I sang a made-up song out loud for the wolverine, hoping he would hear and understand my sincere gratefulness. Drinking bountifully with each slow bottle fill, I sat in the heavenly nook for an hour. The water tasted pure, cold and delicious. *In fact, this may be the tastiest water I have ever drunk!* I determined, then wondered if the noble animal was still watching me, or if it was off to save another. *For all I know, or rather don't know, that wolverine might have saved my life. So easily I could have tripped in my dehydration and fallen down the mountain.* No longer did I need to force another nine stumbling miles to the next water source. I had received an incredible gift. I could rest and contemplate all that had happened in California. Reminisce upon all the miles and mountains I had hiked to reach this magical seat in the forest.

As I sat blissfully sipping the magical life source, I recognized the darkness I battled the night before now seemed to be an immature distant dream. At this, I chuckled pitifully and shook my head. Gentle teardrops started to well and slip out of my eyes. Not from sadness, depression or loneliness, but from an overwhelming awe that I was being looked out for. *Maybe I am not alone. The wolverine was certainly caring for me.* "Thank you," I whispered. While viewing the sun slowly dip towards the horizon, more so, sitting on a globe turning away from the sun's stead, I remembered I was

CINEREAL

about to arrive in Oregon for the first time in my life. With renewed energy, I rose and climbed back up to my trail and continued hiking north. *Onward, to the state I have dreamed of since I was a child.*

PNW on the PCT

I stepped into Oregon mentally exhausted yet filled with euphoria. Turning towards the south, acknowledging the 1,700 miles hiked on the Pacific Crest Trail, plus hundreds of additional side-quest miles accomplished, I offered the land a grand bow and brief speech. "It's been a wild journey, California," I proclaimed. "I have loved you and hated you. I have been loved in you, by you, while also tested and battered. You pushed my limits, yet here I stand triumphantly upon the land of my dreams, Oregon! California, you welcomed my birth and considered my death, and for all that your wild land is, and for the kindness bestowed upon me by your people, animals and trees, I thank you. Now, I happily bid you farewell."

With this, I embarked into the state of the western meadowlark, examining each tree, smelling and tasting the soil, humming a fresh tune, marveling at each turn in the trail. Everything still smelled the same as northern California, of cedars, pines and forest fires, but my arrival conjured the eager anticipation of a new chapter. Oregon may be the land of my dreams, but I did not know what it held. As an adolescent, the name Oregon shimmered mysteriously in my mind. It was the state I would name as my destination when I played games in the eastern woods concocting pretend adventures. To me, it was where "Go west young man" always meant. The region sang stories to my heart and mind of Native Americans, hunters, trappers, mountain men and famous grizzly bears like Ol' Reelfoot. It was the countryside in which to build a cabin and call home. Beyond the great plains, beyond the Rocky Mountains, Oregon purred as a magical nook of endless possibilities. This land of volcanoes, dinosaur tracks, woolly mammoth bones and diverse ecosystems beckoned to me as a boy and now too as a modern explorer.

Pilot Rock greeted me on the first day in Oregon. Because the stone mass had been rooted in my mind long ago, I trekked a short side trail, craving to be closer to its lore. *This is where Ol' Reelfoot tread, and near where he was killed,* I mused to myself, remembering the legendary account. I camped and slept on the same soil the infamous bear once walked and languished upon. That night while peering at the stars, soberly comfortable upon the earth with no whiskey in my pack or belly, I wrote a poem about the grizzly bear and his plight. As a boy who studied books of the West, I was now immersed in the places I once could only imagine. It was all real to me now. *I am here. Oregon is starting out well*, I concluded. *Tomorrow I will reach its first trail town for rest and resupply, and I will not bring my California blues with me.*

Ashland buzzed with energy. I sensed a dynamism pulsating into the forest before I even strode into town. The large Interstate 5 hummed with engines, reminding that a busy America beyond my forest and mountain world was always churning on. Once I reached the heart of town, filled with hippies and travelers, I located G, who was preparing to return to the trail. He had already spent a few days in Ashland and was reluctant to humor me for long. "Alright, one beer, Hot Wing, then I must be on my way." He smiled, knowing one beer might end up being three or four, but he was determined not to stay another night.

I assured G not to hold him back long this time, and added, "Safari should be here or rolling in shortly. We weren't very far apart out there. I had to take a personal mini side-quest to start this state off right." G nodded understanding my ways while also delighting to receive news of Safari. Sure enough, our youthful comrade's smiling face soon bounded our way.

"It's a reunion!" Safari exclaimed.

"Yes, but a short reunion this time," G reminded. "I have been here too long already. You guys take over the Ashland shift, and I'll be on my way."

We cheered with cold beers and swapped stories of our days since Mount Shasta. I bathed in a creek next to the pub in the center of town. We laughed at the tourists who pointed at us. They were sighting wild mountain men, astonished by our brass behavior. And yet, we were simply being ourselves, the selves we had become.

Although we all became slightly inebriated that afternoon, G remained true to his word and hiked onward at dusk. Safari and I toured all the drinking spots in town. As two wildings in a new land, we romped ourselves into a grand party of a night.

The next day, Safari hugged me goodbye. I was not sure whether he was continuing his hike north. Something about him seemed different from before. *Perhaps his mind and desires about the trail have secretly changed.* California was tough on all of us, and I knew he lived with his sisters up in Portland. *Maybe stepping foot into Oregon was enough for him.* If his time on our long path was complete, I would miss him, but we were each out here to hike our own hike, however that may unfold. I spent my day amassing a major resupply, procuring food for multiple boxes and mailing them further up the trail, to places such as Elk Lake and Mount Hood. I knew my opportunities to hitchhike into towns were minimal the further north I progressed. Once I left Ashland, I imagined I would spend most of my time in the wilderness. Bend and Portland were the only two Oregon urban locations I was resolved upon investigating. My intention was to view these municipalities as potential places to move to in my near future.

After a few days of social, logistical and restful activity, I shot like a ball from a cannon out of town. My mind and body were eager and replenished. Inspired by this new-to-me land, my spirit soared on my own wings, ready to fly into the interior of the Beaver State. Quickly I accumulated distance, surpassing thirty miles a day for several consecutive days. I hustled beyond Mount McLoughlin, hungry to explore the famous national treasure of Oregon.

Through thick forests of firs, hemlocks, sugar pines and scrub oaks, past lakes and rugged vistas, my soul surged with excitement as I approached Crater Lake. I marveled at the copper-colored lava rock earth, the soil nearly weightless and unique. Climbing up to the crater's rim, I considered all the changes in geology. There had been an incredible variety of landscapes I had traversed on the Pacific Crest Trail. Although I had been hiking in volcano-land since northern California, Oregon genuinely appeared as the ring of fire. Scaling a crater provides a unique experience. Unlike a distant mountain, which looms steadily larger as one gets closer, it is merely another ascent until, upon reaching the rim, you gaze across and down into a vast blue splendor. Crater Lake's magnitude struck my eyes much like the Grand Canyon's expansive power. Spanning five miles across, with Wizard Island dotting its interior, Crater Lake pulsates as a true gem of Oregon. I sat on the rim and ate a second breakfast, my soul vibrating with delight.

After feasting on food and views, I worked my way over to the simple Crater Lake Village for a pint of beer. Once there, amid the swarm of tourists, full parking-lots and bustle of society spilling into my peaceful wilderness-world, I decided to delve into another side-quest for the afternoon. The plan, hitch a ride down to the small town of Shady Cove, buy a bottle of whiskey, and return. My map showed it would be a long hitch, probably a multiple-vehicle endeavor, but it was possible. Anything was possible with the right attitude and steps taken. *This venture will allow me to experience more of Oregon,* I concluded.

Attaining a ride southwest from the rim to the bottom of Crater Lake Highway was easy, but they dropped me off at the intersection of Highway 230 and 62, in the middle of Umpqua National Forest. They were heading north on 230, and I must continue south on 62. This proved to be a difficult location to secure a ride. I was now far away from my trail, on the side of a busy road where few cars were willing, or even able, to pull over. I walked towards my destination, holding out my thumb to show objectivity and make gentle progress. Despite the large trucks and fast cars whooshing by at high speeds, uncomfortably close with little of a road shoulder to tread upon, I chuckled at the precarious situation I had placed myself in. *Here I am once again, many miles away from the PCT, all alone, where no one knows my name. And anyone who does know my name does not know where I went.* A wayward traveler in an unfamiliar land, all because of whiskey.

After more than an hour passed, my stomach rumbled with hunger, and my mind grew concerned. Shady Cove was too far away to reach in one day by walking. I depended on a hitch for this plan to succeed, and even if I were to get lucky, the journey back to Crater Lake would be even more difficult. Just when I was doubting my decision, I heard a truck roll up behind me and brake to a halt. Turning with a smile of relief, I saw a welcoming grin in return. In an old tan Ford pickup truck, a man approaching my grandfather's age sat with a young girl. He was beaming as if picking up hitchhikers was his favorite pastime. The young girl spryly jumped into the back cab seat. As I motioned to throw my sweaty backpack into the bed of the truck, I noticed the bed of the truck was already full, with a large dead elk.

"Oh yeah, don't mind the bull! There's room for your pack here in the cab, by my granddaughter. This is Emma, and I am Larry." Larry reset his ragged navy-blue ball cap on his head, pushing back gray hairs.

"Hi Larry and Emma, I am Hot Wing, but you can just call me Wing. Thank you for picking me up!" I hopped in the old Ford truck, making myself comfortable on the spacious passenger seat.

"No problem, Hot Wing. Have you been out here trying to catch a ride for a long while?" Larry steered his rig back onto the highway and continued south at a speed that made my thirty-mile hiking days seem like a slow crawl.

CINEREAL

"A bit, yeah. I was dropped off at the Crater Lake turnoff maybe three, four, miles back. I'm heading to Shady Cove. Figured I'd take an afternoon away from the PCT. Call it a field trip," I joked.

"Well, Hot Wing, I'll tell you what, we live just north of Shady Cove. There is a fine little market for your resupply. We were on our way home, but how about…" Turning to his granddaughter, "Emma, should we go get some ice cream?"

Emma smiled shyly but nodded her head enthusiastically. Yes, she absolutely wanted ice cream.

Larry continued, "Perfect plan, we'll get some ice cream while you shop in the market, and Hot Wing, if you will oblige an old grandfather like me for the afternoon, I will drive you all the way back to the Crater Lake rim this evening."

Oblige him? I was not sure what he meant, but he seemed kind and genuine. His granddaughter wasn't scared of him, and a ride all the way back would be marvelous. "I am happy to oblige you, Larry. What do you have in mind? A ride all the way back would be so very helpful, thank you. I didn't realize quite how far my journey was until I was on it."

Larry chuckled. "Sometimes it will be like that. Oblige me, Hot Wing, by spending the afternoon with me. You see, I live with my wife, daughter and Emma here, so I don't get much guy time in my life unless I am hunting with some old pals, whom I'll introduce you to." Larry winked back at Emma, reaching his arm around and squeezing her knee. She put her hand on his and gave him a squeeze in return.

"Let's do it, Larry. Show me your world and I'll tell you stories of mine." I started by sharing with him my hike through California, and how I had always dreamed of Oregon as a boy. Larry nodded, occasionally exclaiming at my ventures, then informed details about the elk he had harvested that morning. The miles on the road evaporated. Amidst the thick of conversation, we rolled into Shady Cove. He parked between the market and a small ice cream shack.

Larry pointed to the cold-snack shack. "We'll be over by those picnic tables, Hot Wing. Take all the time you need."

For the first time in my entire life, I felt ashamed and uneasy about purchasing whiskey. It seemed dirty in the presence of this clean, kind grandfather and granddaughter. *Take all the time I need? I was already carrying plenty of food. Well, since it doesn't take long to buy one bottle of whiskey, I suppose I*

CINEREAL

will buy a few extra items to camouflage the original intent. I added chips, summer sausage, cheese, extra tobacco, a baguette and a few fresh pieces of fruit, filling out the brown paper market bag enough not to look so suspicious, in case Larry should see or inquire. After transferring everything into my backpack, I joined Larry and Emma at the ice cream stand, where I purchased a chocolate peanut butter milkshake to-go.

"Alright, Hot Wing, let's take this elk home. I need your hands to help me hang the bull. Since I plan to shoulder mount him, we'll hoist him up by the head." Larry knew what he was doing. He didn't need my help, but he saw me as a friend for the day, and I was alright with that. He seemed to be a decent man, and he was helping me.

Just a few miles north of Shady Cove, down a dirt road into thick forest, we arrived at his compound by a creek. "I got one, Hunny!" Larry shouted to his wife, who came out when the truck rolled onto the gravel driveway.

"You got one what! An elk or a hiker?" She had long gray hair and eyes that sparkled as a woman content with life. Emma ran to her enthusiastically, ecstatically informing her about the ice cream she'd just eaten.

"Both!" Larry smiled and winked at me. "Matha, meet Wing. Wing, meet Martha." I shook her hand and smiled. Larry jumped back into his Ford and motioned where he wanted me to stand.

Larry backed the truck up to his animal hanging and dressing location, a large shed with tall ceilings, insulated walls, stalwart beams and a thick cement floor. There appeared to be a plethora of structures on the property other than the main cabin. I imagined he had built them all himself. We pulled the bull out, taking the time to hang the heavy creature from the beam where Larry had evidently hung many animals before. I had never moved 700 pounds of dead weight, but Larry had a hook and pulley system set in place, so it turned out to be straightforward. *Larry could have done this on his own*, I thought, *but I can tell he is enjoying showing me how he lives.* Once the elk was hung, no longer filling the bed of the truck, it appeared even larger all stretched out. Its rack of antlers sprawled upwards like a mighty crown. I had seen thousands of elk in the wild, but this was my first time handling one. My palms on its hide produced the memories of touching many animal furs in places like the Boston Museum of Science and the Audubon Center as a kid. The natural history section was always my favorite to explore in any museum or learning center.

CINEREAL

Larry slapped the brown body and spoke to the large, dead mammal, "I'll be back." He shut the shed doors and walked me around his property, explaining previous kills while pointing to mounted antlers adorning various structures. Once we arrived at a large garden, he claimed was his wife's pride and joy, we sat on wooden Adirondack-style chairs for a few moments. I wanted to roll a cigarette and have a sip of my whiskey, but I knew this was neither the time nor place, so I gratefully sipped the ice water with lemon Martha provided. *Larry and Martha*, I considered. *A match made for heaven on earth.* After a five-minute break, Larry signaled our next move. "Come inside, Hot Wing, I have a gift for you."

The indoors of the fine Oregon family's home was just as country and cozy as the entire yard. An enormous stone fireplace graced the center of a wood-paneled living room. I looked at the framed photographs that hung on the wall while Larry shuffled in the kitchen. There were Larry and Martha at their wedding, looking young and finely fit for each other. His daughter and her husband, whom I was hesitant to ask about. Something in my heart insinuated he was no longer with them. Emma graced many of the newer pictures, smiling through all her young ages. I couldn't help but grin at the family love on proud display.

"Alright, Hot Wing, you will not go hungry in Oregon, I promise you." Larry returned from the kitchen with a full bag of food, but not just any food. "I got you an elk back-strap wrapped up in here, some dried trout, venison jerky, and here, try this." Larry handed me a stick of oily meat resembling beef jerky. "Bear." He grinned and chomped a bite of his own. I did the same and nodded as I chewed.

"Dang, Larry, this is kind of spicy, and delicious! I've never eaten bear before. Wow!" I exclaimed, peeking into the generously filled bag. "This is all just so kind and so much food. Elk back-strap! Now that's about the best eatin' I could ever wish for." I marveled at the bounty he gave me. "And all of it harvested from the Oregon woods." Larry enjoyed my enthusiasm and nodded with bright eyes as he chewed on his stick of bear.

"Certainly is, bud. Elk back-strap, make sure you cook it all the way through, and probably eat it sooner rather than later. The predators will know what you are carrying out there." He made an excellent point. I would be a choice target for the bears and lions with all this meat.

"Martha dear," Larry walked into the kitchen as he cooed her name. His words were easy to hear through the spacious openings separating the

CINEREAL

rooms. "I'm going to take Hot Wing down to the hunting camp, show him a few things, but then I promised I'd return him to the Crater Lake rim. I'll be back, hopefully not too long after dark." Returning to the living room, he then said to me, "Come on, mountain man, bring that meat and let's go for a drive." After saying my goodbyes to Martha and Emma, with Martha remarking she wished I could have met Emma's mother as well, Larry and I rolled out of the driveway in his sturdy Ford.

We zipped along with a lighter load without the elk in the truck-bed. We drove all over the forest, through mazes of worn dirt roads. He showed me where he'd shot animals over the years, including the morning's kill. We walked along a river, where he pointed out an elk trail on the opposite bank. He talked about hunting mostly, but I sensed there was more than small talk he wanted to convey to me.

Back in the truck, Larry revealed he was taking me to a hunting camp where a group of his friends were processing wild animals they had harvested. "They've been there and will be there for weeks." It was early September, and this was a tradition they followed every year. On the way down another rough forest road, my hunter-host turned to me and asked candidly, "Hot Wing, do you drink and smoke?" This direct question surprised me, for it seemed almost like an interrogation.

"I do." I looked forward into the woodland tunnel we slowly navigated.

Larry responded gently, "I thought so, Hot Wing. I can tell you've been on edge this afternoon. You have been nothing but considerate, good company, but I can sense these things. Have a cigarette if you want to." Larry nodded to the window, indicating it was alright if I smoked in his truck.

Relieved, ready to take the edge off, I rolled down the window fully and rolled up a cigarette from my kit, which was always placed close to me in my pocket. As I smoked, Larry talked.

"This camp we are going to, they party hard out here. I don't mind if you drink and smoke with them, but I must tell you, I had to retire from drinking years ago. I had lost control. It was either continue drinking and wither away until death, or to reform my habits and live for my family, and ultimately, for God." Larry paused. I nodded, and he resumed. "I see a lot of my young self in you, Hot Wing. Pride, that is what I see. Stubborn, obstinate, selfish pride. I know you are strong, resilient, possibly angry at the world in a way, but that strength will eventually run out, and the alcohol will drag you down into a pit you won't be able to get out of, not on your own."

Larry paused again, perhaps to make sure I was still listening. What he was saying struck a truth deep within me, at least the pride and angry at the world part. I sensed I should say something so he wouldn't think I was shutting my mind off to his words.

"What you are saying rings true to me, Larry. But I will not let the alcohol take over my life." It seemed foolish to say these words, for what did I know? Other than the faint knowledge deep within my heart that maybe the alcohol had already taken over my life.

"Pride, Hot Wing," Larry continued. "It will destroy you. It was destroying me. For most of my life, I rebelled against God, for I believed I could do all things on my own, but I urge you, that strength will run out, and there is only one with a strength that will save you."

"I'm guessing you mean God, huh, Larry?" I glanced at him and then back ahead into the forest, for I did not want to enter the God conversation right now. It struck too close. The things I had seen and heard, the rejection of Him I was living in. The perpetual torment my rebellion created... I knew the truth. I knew Larry was right. I knew I was in the wrong, but I wasn't ready to face that yet.

"Yes, Hot Wing. I know it may sound ridiculous and far-fetched, and the world hates even thinking about Him, because the world is full of pride and their own 'godship' they don't want to let go of. But submitting, surrendering the pride in yourself, is the only way. I say this because I know it, because I lived it, because I fought against it for so long and it nearly destroyed me. The only way out and up from that pit I had created was God. In Him exists eternal strength."

"Larry," I paused, choosing my words carefully, "I comprehend more of this than you may realize. I do believe in Jesus. I once had an active relationship with God through Him, but some messed up things went down, a lot of trust and perhaps even faith in my faith was shattered, or jumbled, shaken, confused. A lot of darkness, man..." My voice trailed off. I didn't want to talk about any of it. Resuming with words more present, "Honestly, I've kind of been running far away from all of that for a long time. It is a battle I fight, but someday maybe I'll return. I don't know."

Larry reached over and gave me a gentle thump on the chest with his fist, like a coach might do with his star-player after a hard-fought loss. "Pride, Hot Wing. There is nothing more dangerous than rejecting God. Especially when you know the truth. Even Satan and the demons believe.

CINEREAL

You have something the world wants, but God wants you more. The world does not love you, but He does." Larry paused, straightened his posture and spoke again. "Do not let the sins of others keep you from an eternity with Him. It does not matter who sinned or hurt you or hurt others. All have sinned and fallen short of the glory of God. This is a fallen world, Hot Wing. Even if the sin came from those close to you, perhaps even from others who claim to love God, that sin is not from God. Grace, love, forgiveness and healing are from God, as well as judgement for sin. Satan will twist anything to keep you in his grasp. Yet our heavenly Father has dominion over sin, over death." Larry peered at me, assessing my attentiveness. "As you move forward on the Pacific Crest Trail and the trail of your life, never forget that. And hopefully, when and if you are ever ready, you will return fully to Him, Hot Wing. Why hold on to pride when eternal life with Him or being cast away from Him are at stake? Why ignore that so adamantly, as so many do, as I did? Humble yourself. Submit every anger, fear, prideful notion, confusion, every broken piece, sadness, loneliness, surrender all of yourself to Him. The fight you feel within, give that to Him. Do not let the darkness win. In Jesus' name the darkness trembles, for He is the Light. He is the Way, the Truth, and the Life. Give it all to Him."

We rode in silence for another bumpy mile. He was right. I knew it. I could even feel the darkness within me shudder, my heart convicted. Larry's words struck at my deepest essence. Through his words, it was as if God was banging on the door of my soul. I glared at the trees, staring defiantly beyond all invisible truths. I did not want to dwell on any of it.

The reformed hunter finally put the subject to rest. "Alright, my friend. I won't bring up the God stuff anymore. But I had to say it! Just know I will pray for you." Larry smiled at me as I extinguished my cigarette in the palm of my hand, right into the callous I had formed. I rubbed the embers into the fabric of my shorts.

"Hunting camp, eh?" I smiled back at him gratefully. Larry was showing me his world, and a big part of his world was his relationship with God. He spoke out of love, even if I did not want to hear it. This was not the day I had envisioned when I began my side-quest from Crater Lake, but perhaps it was the day I needed.

"Hunting camp!" Larry returned my question excitedly. "We are almost there."

CINEREAL

The hunting camp was indeed a wild scene. There were at least four mobile truck campers, ten dirty men, a few bright-eyed women, and many children running amok. Dead bears, deer, and elk hung while even more filled the back of pickup trucks. Three bonfires blazed. A stench of death and meat filled the air. Many people's sweatshirts and hands were stained with blood. The sun was setting, and the forest camp appeared to be straight out of an apocalypse movie. Every greasy human embraced me and instantly provided a beer to chug. So, I followed orders, downing the alcohol happily with a few young men my age. After the cold brew's completion amid multiple hurrahs, someone handed me a bottle of whiskey and another beer. The energy was kinetic. No one other than an old lady sat still. Everyone wanted to tell me about their hunt and ask questions about my hike. I kept my eye on Larry. He remained sober and laughed with his friends. He watched me as if he were protecting me, making sure I was alright. I was more than alright, for this was my kind of environment, gaining a buzz with wild folk. They passed around a marijuana joint, which I took a few tokes from. When it was delivered to Larry, he politely declined. *He might not imbibe anymore, but he also doesn't seem to care that everyone else is.* I liked that he didn't judge others. He was kind and strong in what he had become. I admired him. The sparks from the fire danced into the woodland ceiling. Night had arrived, and though I enjoyed being engaged in this rowdy Oregon community, I needed to get back to the Pacific Crest Trail. As if Larry could read my mind, he announced to everyone that it was time for us to leave.

"I promised Hot Wing I would return him to the trail tonight, and so, my friends, I must complete my end of our verbal contract. Hot Wing did his part." Larry winked at me while the crew gathered to say farewell. Everyone gave us one last hug, and someone handed me one last beer for the road. I declined this beer, for something in me didn't feel it would be honorable to be drinking in Larry's truck. An hour later, Larry fulfilled his agreement. We parted ways in the crisp air back up at mountain elevation. A waxing moon dominated the sky, its luminescence reaching the dark waters of Crater Lake. Larry and I shook hands and exchanged our last words.

"Thank you for all you have shown and given me today, Larry. The elk meat, the trout, the venison, your words of wisdom, hosting me, taking me to your home and bringing me back to mine." I waved my hand in the direction beyond the parking lot where we idled. Larry understood. "Your kindness shall not be forgotten."

CINEREAL

"It has been my pleasure, Hot Wing. You made my day as well. I am proud to have met you. Remember what I said."

"I know, cook the elk meat soon and all the way through," I assured him. Larry interrupted with a laugh.

"Yes, that, but also," Larry placed his hand on his heart, then pointed to the sky.

"Yes, Larry, and especially that too. Thank you. Off I go, truly, thank you." With one last handshake, I walked toward the crater's rim. Larry got into his truck and drove away.

Silence fell over the land once again, like a comforting blanket. No more rumble of engines, no more cacophony of drunken hunters, no more being told what I should and should not do, just the wilderness, the moon and me. There is an old photograph from 1923 I had always loved, of a Native American Klamath chief standing regally on the rim of the crater. By the positioning of Wizard Island in the photo, I could identify proximity to that very spot. In the moonlight, I walked along the edge of the curving precipice until I was confident of the location. "This will do," I whispered with the trees, "to the best of my memory, perhaps the very place." I did not set up my tent that night. Instead, I lay on the dirt, finally opening and sipping the fifth of whiskey I had purchased at the Shady Cove market. I smoked a few cigarettes, tapping their ash and disposing of each ember into muddy spit in my palm. Deeply, I considered all Larry had said. I could not deny the fact that I was living in rebellion against God. And yet, it wasn't with an attitude of animosity. I honestly couldn't face Him, yet... In the moon-moving time, I drifted into sleep beneath the grand Oregon sky.

The next day I extended my walk along the Crater Lake Rim Trail until dipping back onto the Pacific Crest Trail. *I walk to return to my walk,* cheerfully I acknowledged. *I sure have become a pro at walking, haven't I, Wing?* Zany laughter rippled from my lips. Oregon had been treating me well so far. I moved with vigor despite my loaded backpack. *I certainly have enough food to feast for many days.* By afternoon I left the busy park road and tourist crowds behind, settling into mellow, forested miles. The kind of trail and miles I preferred. I made camp but did not cook the elk meat yet, for that I wanted unlimited access to water by a creek. According to my map, Mount Thielsen and then Thielsen Creek would be tomorrow. *Perhaps I will grill it over a fire then.*

~~~

CINEREAL

When I awoke in the forest, I did not know how memorable a day it would become. I stretched my limbs, pumped out a few sets of push-ups, whistled a melody with the birds, added instant coffee and chocolate protein powder to my overnight water-soaked oats, and started walking. With a heavy pack full of food and water, I progressed further into Central Oregon. The trail was very dusty, as rain had not fallen in a long while. It was Mount Thielsen day, a Matterhorn-like peak I eagerly expected to see for my first time. People often referred to this mountain as the lightning rod of Oregon because it stands sharply exposed in the sky and lightning often strikes it. Mount Thielsen was another volcano, as most of the mountains in the Cascade Range are, an extinct shield volcano which had lost its cylinder shape because of an explosion long ago. A prominent horn thrust towards the heavens. According to my map, the Pacific Crest Trail would lead me up to the tree line on its western flanks, then onward down to Thielsen Creek. I was not planning to summit this peak, but a full lunch staring up at its sheer pinnacle would serve as a worthy midday break.

The walk towards Mount Thielsen was another idyllic stroll through Oregon timberland. The dirt contributed to a more strenuous exertion of the legs. Some of the terra was almost a beach-like texture, unlike down in the Sierras. The volcanic soil does not pack down as firmly as soil in other ecosystems. With each brush of my hand and pester of my tread, a beige and reddish-hued haze lofted in the air. I trudged along content beneath the weight of elk and bear meat, plus multiple gallons of water, humming the tune of The Beatles' song I used to sing with comrades in the Appalachians. Looking upon each tree with admiration, listening to each bird, considering the mountain lions who were likely watching me, I strode serenely, hoping I might glimpse another one. So far, I had encountered one mountain lion who stalked me in California, and two others screamed at me on separate nights, yet even with these tense interactions, I always sought to observe more. Onward at a leisurely pace, I consulted my map. According to the contour lines and the way the trail was trending, I would soon spot Mount Thielsen on my horizon, miles before arriving at its base.

As I continued along the ridge, gradually gaining elevation, I suddenly heard a sound I did not recognize. This sound was coming from ahead, in the mountain's direction. While still surrounded by thick forest, the unique resonance was not clear to me yet. I picked up my pace and hustled towards the foreign chorus. Within half a mile, I finally reached a vista. As I first gazed upon Mount Thielsen, the music enveloped me. The mountain was magnificent, sharp and dominant as I had imagined, but the escalating sonority was a hundred times more so. The loudest, grandest choir I had ever heard sang a coherent song. It seemed to rise out of the forest surrounding the mountain while also pouring like shimmers from a chandelier above. I had heard nothing more glorious in my entire life. It was as if the Choir of King's College in Cambridge had been transported into the Oregon woods. This exquisitely blended hymn radiated and hovered above the forest, amplified by voices stronger, smoother, sweeter than I knew could exist. *But where and what is this assemblage?* I did not understand what was going on. They sang words in a silky continuous melody, yet these words were of a language I did not recognize. It was not Greek, Latin, Hebrew or Arabic, certainly not English, nor Spanish, Italian or Portuguese. It sounded ancient. *Is this Aramaic? Adamic?* There was no way for me to know. However, the words were unquestionably of profound purpose and meaning. Thousands of these voices, louder than any speaker at any concert I had ever attended, ascended and descended, filling the surrounding wilderness. So shocked, soothed and inspired by the music, it summoned tears into my eyes. My skin immediately was brought to horripilation. Hair stood on end. I felt compelled to bow in reverence but also dash toward the source. The sound was music of joy, a fruit of the most immense purity and peace, yet it was also strong, as stalwart as the lightning rod mountain rising mightily before me. Since I did not fathom what was going on, I stood and listened, bathing in it, tears streaming down my face as if I were witnessing the very songs of heaven. The how and why and what I did not know, and yet somehow, I did know. There was only one explanation. Music such as this was undeniable, even if it didn't make scientific sense. After standing in wonder for some time, I snapped out of my awestruck gape and ran towards the mountain. As I sprinted into the realm where the music emanated, the sounds grew even louder. I continued running all the way to the tree line on the western base of Mount Thielsen. Once there, I paused, as the choir suddenly faded and disappeared, leaving behind an echoing resonance that evaporated into the sky. I did not want it to stop, and yet it slipped away like a rainbow, beheld and the next moment is not.

    Surely everyone else near this place must have heard the music as well. I looked around hoping to see another human so I could ask them. At this spot, the Pacific Crest Trail continues north, but on the western flank of the mountain, it intersects with a trail to the west. My map showed this trail led toward Diamond Lake and the parking lot for those who are day-hiking to Mount Thielsen. To my right, the trail progressed towards the summit. When I looked that way, up and to the east, I saw two people sitting beneath one of the last trees until the elevation held only rock. Hustling over to the two humans, I made it clear I intended to talk to them. They lifted their heads from meals in their laps and offered a welcoming wave.

With a rushed breath and fervor in my tone, I asked them this absurd, unique question. "Did you two hear the incredible choir of voices singing the most beautiful music just now, or in the past half hour? It just ended, but I have been hearing it for the last two miles!"

They both looked at me as if I were insane, and shook their heads no. Not speaking even one word. They must have thought I was crazy.

Taking a deep breath, I then asked them a calmer question. "I'm sorry. I know that sounds ridiculous. But maybe, well, did you hear any singing, music or noise at all?"

The lady of the couple chewed her sandwich and stated, "No unique noise or music, just the chipmunks and a hawk overhead."

"Uh huh." I glanced around bewildered, shifting from the surrounding horizon until staring up at the mountain summit thrust above. "Well, maybe I've just gone mad. I have been walking since the Mexico border, so… I am sorry to bother you. Enjoy your lunch."

I didn't understand. *How could they not have heard? It is clear they have been here longer than I, at least in this vicinity beneath the umbrella of magnificent music. How did they not hear it? Am I going mad, or was this something like those other times, when I was allowed to see and hear things others were not? This was not the voices of living darkness I have been cursed with for much of my life. In fact, it was exactly the opposite. The voices of living darkness were a haunting, sadistic hatred encouraging me to hurt myself and degrade my soul, but this, these voices, the music they sang, were the sounds of the purest greatest feelings known to humankind, or I must say, beyond those even known to humankind. I've heard weird screams and strange shrill pitches on my long hikes. Even heard unique pings and alien-like resonances on Mount Shasta. Once I listened to the gentle notes of a not-human-being singing in the southern Appalachians, like a siren of the sea, luring me to a place I knew I did not want to go. But this, this was completely different. If heaven's songs could be heard on earth, what I just heard would be it.*

I did not plan to climb the sharp, steep mountain, but as I sat on a rock pondering everything that had occurred, I looked upwards to the 9,184-foot summit and realized, *I must climb Mount Thielsen.* The climb was almost as steep as the mountaineer's route up Mount Whitney. To make it easier on my body, I relinquished my pack and stashed it beneath a boulder. From there, free climbing the last few hundred feet felt like ascending into the space from which the music had come. Atop the summit, blackened and burned by the lightning bolts that strike it, I sat on the tiny island in the sky, observing the expansive Oregon forest brimming with evergreens. The words of a Bible verse I had not considered for many years entered my mind. Psalm 19:1 (NKJV) "The heavens declare the glory of God; and the firmament shows His handiwork."

Yes, Lord, the music I heard was worship from the heavens, and this beautiful land is Your handiwork. Trembling in awe, for the first time in a long while, I prayed to God. Although I praised His glory, His dominion and His name, I foolishly could not submit. All I could do was tell Him I still believed, and that I knew He was always there. That I heard and recognized His hand in my life. He was calling my heart, but I did not know if I could face what He wanted of me. I did not want to change my ways, my drinking, partying, wild, passionately frivolous ways. *But please, Father,* I begged, *do not give up on me yet. I hear you.*

After a moment, the moment I should have exceeded a prayer of recognition and sorrowfully, thoroughly, reverently repented of my rebellious ways and surrendered my all to Him, I feared I would be struck by a bolt of lightning and killed. There was no storm, no ominous clouds in the sky, but I knew in my heart He was angry with me. His righteous wrath that I deserved for my cemented obstinacy left me more frightened than I had ever been. *Am I spitting in the face of God? Am I being offered every chance to live for Him, and yet I deny them all?* Out of fear of the Almighty Creator, I hastily climbed down the mountain with a shudder in my soul.

Once I'd returned to my backpack, I snagged my bottle of whiskey and took a drink. I needed to quell the squall of emotions within. As I stepped back onto the Pacific Crest Trail, a group of four hikers approached from Diamond Lake. With the comfort of liquor in my body, I asked, "Hey guys, did you hear any music or singing on your way up the trail today?" They all replied with strange glances and shakes of their heads. *Nope, they all did not. Of course they did not. Alright, I must have been the only one to hear it,* and by this point, I was not surprised.

CINEREAL

Mount Thielsen Creek, just a few miles north, provided the second most delicious water I encountered on my entire long journey. Perhaps the whiskey buzz and dehydration played an influence in this evaluation, but I had drunk from many clean mountain sources in my thousands of miles and only one had satisfied me more. That one was the satiating spring the wolverine led me to. With a hint of humble fear lingering within, I made camp near the creek and cooked my gifted meal. *There is no better spot for my elk feast than this.* I dug a small pit, lined it with flat rocks and sparked a modest cooking fire, rolled a marijuana joint, a few tobacco cigarettes, and settled into the soil with my back to the northwest and my face set upon Mount Thielsen. Allowing the meat to cook while enjoying my vices, I observed the sun's setting rays light up the sharp stone horn of the volcano. *I sat up there today*, I reflected. *After listening to the greatest music, I've ever heard. Wow, just wow, what a wondrous and terrifying day.* To cap off the splendor, the elk back-strap was the finest meal I ever ate on the trail. "Thank you, Hunter Larry!" I bellowed out loud, swigging my whiskey and blowing my smoke out like a steam engine. "Thank you, Oregon, and thank you, God." My voice lowered to a whisper as I spoke to Him. After a few seconds of silent reverence, I swigged from my bottle and elevated my head and attitude again. "And for all you mountain lions watching me, this bite is for you!" I chewed, smoked and drank until darkness consumed the forest. When I finally slept, it was a whiskey and guilt saturated exhaustion which pressed my body down into the cool volcanic soil.

~~~

As I continued hiking north, progressing into the heart of Central Oregon, I pondered what all I had been experiencing meant. On one hand, I had been partaking in an intimate connection with the earth. On the other hand, I experienced another supernatural occurrence. While walking and communing with the land, observing how all living beings went about their days and seasons, the ethereal realm beyond the tangible was calling me. As if commanding, "Here, look at this. See this? This is bigger, this is more, this is most important." *But what is real when it is not tangible? The rocks are real, but they are not timeless in their stead. Trees are real and kind, knowledgeable in patience and community, but they too have a beginning and an end. Birds see the land from above and descend into chosen places to eat and rest. The mammals have their own trails and make their own homes. They know where the water is and where danger lurks, but all of this is temporary and created by the Creator. All of this did not randomly come about, with prior species evolving into new species, like the deceiver has caused so many to believe. The evidence for creation is overwhelming, albeit shoved aside, while the false evidence for a big bang and evolution is fallible, built on assumptions, twisted to fit the framework they want it to fit and forced into our minds. Humans have developed the Earth, constructed cities and manipulated the planet's resources for survival and gain. But they too shall pass away. Their supposed strength is their dooming weakness. Larry was right. Pride before God is worthy of judgement. Pride may even be the root of all sin. Rejection of Him is worthy of eternal death. Human's decided self-importance does not disqualify the truth. It is He who is beyond the immense scope of the entire universe. It is He who is calling me. And yet here I am, clinging to my pride. Why? I cannot deny what I have seen and heard, such as the angels and demons I witnessed in action as a youth. I cannot deny the lion that peered deeply into my soul in Maine, which according to science and humanly limited sense could not have been. The voices of the living darkness and their power I cannot refute, nor the miraculous healing from the lady in Julian, nor the choir of music on the mountain. I cannot deny the existence of these things just as I cannot deny the existence of the forest. In fact, no matter how much I resist God, I can never deny Him, or His triumvirate Son and the Holy Spirit, who all together are one, are God. The Holy Trinity, which again most humans cannot seem to accept. But I can. He is truer than everything I can touch. Deep in my soul, I believe in Jesus' resurrection, in His words, actions and love. Without a single doubt. Something must not need to be tangible for me to see its truth, for as humans we can only see a sliver of what exists. Then, with this knowledge, am I denying Him by continuing to live the way I want to? Am I scared of what He will call me to do? Am I fearful of what He wants from me? For surely, He only gives us goodness, and I should not be fearful of being rejected by a fallen world. What I should only fear is rejecting Him and the deserving consequences of such.*

What I found to be discouraging was how adamantly most humans denied my knowledge, or to them my supposed knowledge of supernatural happenings. Anytime I even brought up such topics to most, they scoffed, laughed, decided I was an idiot, a fool, sick in the head, or straight up deranged. "It is from the drugs and drinking," they would say, but I knew this was not true. Or, "I was a dreamer and did not live in the real world," but again, this was not why nor how. At my core, I did not care what they thought. Yes, I enjoyed being liked and included, but I genuinely did not care if they believed me or not. I knew what I had experienced. I knew who was Truth.

But what am I to do with this? Seek and ye shall find? Must I learn how to open my heart to God in a way that yearns to know Him? "If you love me, you will obey me."

CINEREAL

But do I love Him? I should since His love is real, for what He gave and who He is. Ahh, I do know in my mind. But is it in my heart? That if I surrender myself to Him, He will do the work in me. It is not I, but Him. What am I to do with this? There I go again… I seem to question and turn to my own desires every chance I get instead of seeking first the kingdom of righteousness. I do need to seek Him. Why am I asking myself questions I know the answers to? Why, why, why am I so damn wretchedly pathetic in this?

    Deep in the Oregon forest, I lifted the depleted bottle of whiskey to my lips. I guzzled warm, gushing gulps until only a few swigs remained. The alcohol coursed through my body and into my bloodstream. Emitting a frustrated primal howl into the air, my body convulsed in its stead like a beast about to transform. When the silence returned to the air, I continued walking. I could not ignore the conviction in my soul. But I did not know if I could ignore the gratifications of the world either. I was stuck in the middle as both a slave to the darkness and a young man with a heart who knew what must be done. But which way I would go was yet to be decided.

~~~

I dominated the Pacific Crest Trail in Oregon. From the beginning of the Beaver State until the end, I averaged over thirty miles a day. When I reached Elk Lake Resort, I gratified my appetite with a bacon cheeseburger and beer. The rustic lodge sat nestled among Ponderosa pines next to the lake by its resort's name. Mount Bachelor and South Sister commanded the horizon. A lodge such as this was one of my favorite kinds of places. I relaxed all afternoon socializing with other thru-hikers. We traded stories of our journeys, discussing wildlife encounters and our excitement for what lay ahead. I did not disclose the music I had heard around Mount Thielsen. For the time being, it seemed like a treasure meant only for me.

    Hiking onward with a fresh resupply, I thoroughly enjoyed the natural beauty of Central Oregon. The Three Sisters Wilderness inspired the solution for my future home. *This is the place I want to live;* I mused. With lava fields, obsidian falls, clear blue lakes, vast forests and picturesque mountains, it was a land I must someday return to. When I arrived at Santiam Pass, I caught up with a kind woman and her giant malamute dog. We strode the last bit of trail towards the pass together. She owned a small shop in the town of Bend and invited me to stay in a furnished apartment above her garage for the night. She would feed me, provide laundry and a shower, and then drive me into town in the morning. I accepted her generous offer, so

CINEREAL

we jumped into her vintage Volkswagen van and barreled our way through the town of Sisters, south to her abode on the outskirts of Bend. The idea of a brief rest from the trail was appealing, for though I had allowed a few zero days in Ashland and spent an afternoon with Larry, so much had already happened in Oregon that my body and soul needed to slow down. Together we grilled chicken and vegetables on her patio, drank hearty red wine, smoked cannabis, almost kissed but then both pulled back, laughing at our tipsiness and turning in for the night. In the morning, she delivered me to Bend. She dropped me off downtown, where we hugged goodbye, wished each other well and parted ways.

Instantly I adored Bend, Oregon. It had a quaint yet bustling ambiance, which I preferred. *This is my kind of town,* I deliberated, while walking up and down Wall and Bond Streets. I first visited the famous Deschutes Brewery and drank a pint of West Coast India Pale Ale. Next, I grabbed a sandwich to-go at a little shop called Great Harvest Bakery. Across the street, I purchased a new pair of cheap sunglasses and plenty of loose tobacco with rolling papers from Bond Street Market. Donning my new shades while rolling a cigarette between my fingers, I then walked down to Drake Park to eat my lunch. In this green, clean community haven by the Deschutes River, I called G hoping he would answer his phone. *Probably not,* I thought. *We turn our phones on only in town or on top of mountains, but it's worth a shot.*

To my delight, the phone rang, and G answered. With a reserved, almost cautious tone, he spoke. "Oh man. We got a wild Hot Wing calling, eh?" As my elated socializing fortunes would have it, I had caught up to G on the trail. We were both set to resume our hike at Santiam Pass, and he was currently sitting at a McDonald's gas station combo in Sisters, north on Highway 97. The very road I had been driven down the previous night.

"Dude, Hot Wing, I've spent the night in Sisters and am all packed and ready to keep hiking," G warned as if he thought I might try to keep him in town any longer.

"Yeah, bud, that's great, but don't you want to see me?! We caught up only briefly in Ashland, and we haven't hiked together since, well, since Mount Shasta. That's a long-time man! I miss you, brother. Just wait for me there. I'll hitch up to you now." While encouraging G to stall, I jumped up from my Drake Park grassy lounge and hustled across town to Highway 20.

"Wing, I'll be here until my phone is fully charged. If you make it that quickly, great. If not, I'm hiking on."

CINEREAL

I caught a hitch before I even reached the highway. A cheerful young couple in a Subaru with Maine license plates picked me up with grins on their faces. It was their first experience with a thru-hiker, so I provided the full personality, showering them with wild stories of my adventures. They asked all the questions I was accustomed to being asked. My answers were ready like a loaded six-shooter. Wild animals, mountain miles, diet, trail names, trail towns, resupplies, favorite vistas, sunsets, sunrises, harrowing encounters and much more were all discussed on the quick ride up to the quaint western town. They dropped me off at the McDonald's gas station combo, where I left them inspired by the brimming possibilities of life.

Inside I spotted G sitting like a lonely grump hovered over his phone at a table. He hadn't seen me yet, so I purchased two tall beers and approached from the side. Sliding into the opposite chair and setting the tall beer cans between us, I addressed him coolly. "Been a while, buddy." I waited with a smirk, eager for his reaction.

G looked up, set his phone down, shook his head and grinned. "Well, I'll be. If it isn't Hot Wing again. You made it, and in a timely manner, I see." His reception seemed genuinely delighted, causing my heart to swell with happiness.

"Obviously I made it. When my trail brother is nearby, I waste no time. And do I have some wild stories to tell you." I cracked my beer and pushed his closer towards him. "Come on now, you said if your phone wasn't done charging, and it appears to be at," looking at his cellular device, "only eighty-seven percent, perfect."

"Of course you have wild stories." G cracked his beer. We clinked the cans together and gulped down the gas station's finest. "My hike has been uneventful lately. I suppose it's a good thing you are here."

"That's what I do, mate, liven things up. Come on, let's get out of here and go smoke some ganja in the woods behind the store." I picked up my pack, G grabbed his phone, charger and gear and followed with a fresh hop in his steps.

Two of the three wild men were back together again. We had heard Safari had gone home to Portland, Oregon, and considered going to see him when we reached the Columbia River. Once the cold brew had loosened my lips, I told G about the heavenly choir of singing voices I'd heard at Mount Thielsen. He just listened and looked off towards the horizon. After a few beers and smokes were imbibed in the discreet wooded lot, convincing G to take part in one night of partying together before hiking out in the morning was easy. We rallied like the desert days, bar hopping to each of the few spots in the small country municipality. Our evening ended at Hardtails, a rowdy biker bar that accepted us openly as fellow travelers. Amidst the black leather jackets with patches, we pounded beers, played billiards and drank whiskey. We met two sisters in Sisters that night, sweet ladies visiting from Portland who owned a family cabin in Camp Sherman on the Metolius River outside of town. They invited us to stay on the pretext of no funny business. To this, we graciously promised. Late into the night, the four of us reveled around a bonfire in the forest, the river murmuring its tune just paces away. The girls slept inside, and we mountain men slept around the coals, waking to a peaceful morning beneath a grand coniferous canopy. After coffee and breakfast, the sisters we met in Sisters returned us to the Pacific Crest Trail at Santiam Pass. They continued to Portland while G and I walked north amid our wilderness homeland once again.

Torrential rain greeted us in the Mount Jefferson Wilderness. For days it poured, washing away any remnants of summer in the mountains. As it was now mid-September, every day forth would be wet, dark and cold. We hiked on, briskly in the morning, drying out the best we could in midday sunbeams, then onward into evergreen twilights. These days of hiking together in the northern half of Oregon were calm and pleasant. We talked peacefully, not raging beneath the gasoline of booze, eating pistachios and meat jerkies, laughing at our slides and slips through mountain snow fields. We admired each view ahead and behind while reveling in a brotherhood that had grown through many miles and trail chapters. Mount Hood capped our trek through the Oregon volcanoes. All was healthy and wholesome until we hitched a ride into the city of Portland.

~~~

Oregon had been a riveting conductor of inspiration on my long hike. After the trials of California, Oregon had lifted me back up, allowing remembrance of why I had embarked on this grand adventure. I regained wonder, awe, joy, and deep appreciation for life. As well as a conviction I wasn't sure I was ready to face. I didn't want to leave the state I had romanticized so much as a youth, but the trail led north, and so I must hike on. Before crossing the Bridge of the Gods, the 1,854-foot steel-truss passage across the Columbia River into Washington, G and I decided to explore the City of Roses, locate our trail brother Safari, and hopefully return him to the long brown

CINEREAL

wilderness path we called home. Although our plan was one of adventure and reunion, a mixture of emotions stirred within me as we rolled into Portland. I was eager to party and run amok in this new-to-me metropolis, but I could also sense the darkness in my soul surging again. Like gurgling lava deep within the Cascade Mountains, the wretched man within me was awakening.

G and I wasted no time in getting drunk on alcohol. After spending our months in the wilderness and occasional small mountain towns, being dropped off in the city with no guardians or guides was like releasing two wild animals into a jungle. We knew the name of the neighborhood Safari lived in with his sisters, so we pub crawled our way there. When we found him, and greeted him in his civilian clothes, we rallied to bring him out into the dense urban land of human and alcohol saturation. It was indeed a night I cannot remember, but we survived and slept in his garage when sleep or death became our only two options. His sisters did not want their brother's mangy, drunk trail friends inside the main house, which we understood and respected. It was clear even to us how starkly different we were from the cleaner, civilized city folk. To them, we must have seemed like aliens given permission to roam Portland for but a few days.

Between the bars and bottles, G and I slowed down to accomplish the few resupply chores we must attend to. During the lull of these few hours, while organizing our hauls in Safari's garage, I was permitted to use the kitchen, and there in the tender touches of pink and floral hues, I met one of Safari's sisters. I shall call her Lily. Her beauty immediately struck me, but also the aura of her presence. She was not like the women I met on the trail, or even in the societal nooks we would hike through. Instead, she exuded a wholesome and stylishly creative energy. I was pleased when she let me sit at the kitchen table and talk with her for a few minutes. Her life was a book from a different library than I had ever known to exist. Her eyes were sincere, and unlike Safari's other sisters, she didn't seem to oppose my existence in her home.

To my delight, Lily also enjoyed smoking marijuana. Along with her dear-to-me brother, we ground up some herb, rolled it into a joint, and lit it in the kitchen. Between puffs and passes, we laughed about life's frivolities without the crude edge I had become accustomed to. When smoking pot, there is a way every person transforms slightly as they inhale their first toke and shift from being not stoned to being moderately high. Every person is different. As I witnessed the way her eyes lightly glossed, the way her smile developed from polite to almost mischievous, the way her humor emboldened from educated to educated with zest, the way she naturally conducted her mannerisms, the effortless ease of her charm, I became enamored with her. To me, she was the classiest young woman I had ever met. Sitting there with a silly smile, now in my own slightly stoned state, I could sense my skin turning rouge. Every time she smiled and looked at me, I blushed. I was not sure if Safari noticed, but I think maybe Lily could, that I, Hot Wing, without being able to help it, had developed an instant crush on her. After a blissful time, our social segment came to an end. G was done with his hygiene routines, all three of us young men were clean and ready to hit the streets of the city once again. I must go on and leave the kitchen, departing the company of Safari's sister. I wanted to tell her I liked her. That her loveliness roared as an ocean to me. But I could not bring myself to declare such. It was not my place, and I probably would never see her again. With one last smile, I thanked her for spending time with me and followed the pulling gesture from Safari to move along. It was time to go.

Our hour in the kitchen was the most wholesome human hour I had while in Portland, Oregon. When we returned to the streets, I returned to my wild partying habits. *I would end all my filthy ways and become a proper man*, I thought to myself as we rushed from drinking whiskey downtown towards consuming whiskey on Hawthorne. *To be worthy of someone like her, I would finally grow up.* After a mental pause, I considered. *Why would I do that for her and not for God? What the hell is wrong with me...* With this, I remembered how I considered myself. Deep down I knew, despite the adventures, skills, and unique experiences, I was becoming a horrible drunken waste. And in this moment, I leaned in the wrong direction. I buried God away and let the darkness win.

That night I spiraled into self-loathing and anger. Safari returned home in the evening, but G and I continued to roam and rage. Around midnight at a bar called the Dig a Pony, my bankcard, which the bartender held for my tab, went missing. In a drunken fury, I concluded the bartender, who I believed had been presenting me demeaning stares ever since we walked in the door, must have stolen it. Yelling over the loud music, I called him out on his alleged theft, which escalated into an argument as he denied responsibility. Since he would not return my card, I lit a cigarette, jumped onto the bar top, kicking over empty pint glasses while running back and forth from one end of the counter to the other, eluding the security men who chased me, while bellowing an embittered lofted speech for all to hear. Everyone paused their socializing and dancing to witness the savage creature I turned into. Inebriated with indignation and booze, I screamed at the masses, pointing condemningly at the suspect, causing a reckless, monstrous scene. The bouncers finally caught me, dragged me out the door and threw me down onto the asphalt sidewalk. And yet my vehemence was not ready to concede. Repeatedly, I attempted to charge through the big men and return inside. Finally, with fists and through fists I broke the barrier and barreled to a piano sitting tucked in the corner. While I pounded ferociously on the keys, the bouncers placed arms around my neck and dragged me back outside again. Seconds later, I found myself face down in a puddle, with blood trickling out of my nose. Still unwilling to surrender, I stood and rammed the doormen. While they battled to block my seething attempts at another reentry, G stood by the bar top shocked, unsure of how to handle his deranged friend. I shouted at him to grab any shot of whiskey and beer near him and bring them outside to me. He did, tucking the drinks inside his jacket, then sidling past the security, to whom I held up both my middle fingers. He handed me a whiskey, which I slammed down my throat and then smashed the glass on the sidewalk, and again charged at the bouncers. G caught my shirt and wrapped his arms around me until I stopped struggling. He encouraged me to leave, pulling my body away. "They are one second away from calling the cops, Hot Wing," he urged. Once my body stopped resisting, G let go and lifted two pints of beer off the ground where he had set them. The glasses would have been full if not for all the turbulence. His eyes pleaded, his face smiled as my rabid vision finally recognized my friend, causing my craze to fade. I relented. Away from the chaos, we walked towards a park to drink our beer. As we approached the edge of the Willamette River, I broke down in wasted, messy, loathsome, pathetic tears.

"What is wrong with me, G?" I sobbed. "What is my problem? Why do I keep drinking like this and spiraling like this and pushing harder and harder like this? Who am I? Why am I even like this?"

G sat next to me, letting all my alcohol-fueled emotions pour out, until I stood and hovered above the edge of the river with my arms spread wide, peering down into the black water through hazy eyes, screaming into the night for the living voices of darkness to tempt me. I wanted to jump in, to die, and end it all. I was a wretched man, not even a man, a wretched child who would never grow to be a man.

G drew me away from the water and encouraged our shuffle towards a place we could sleep. While dodging pestering drug addicts, jumping over fences and cutting through alleyways, G stated, "Hey, Hot Wing, I've never seen you like this."

"Like what?" I snapped back. "Drunk? You always see me drunk."

"No, no, aware of your drunkenness. Aware of your mess. I've never seen you care that you get this way." G was honestly trying to be tender with me. I recognized his sincerity, so I forced a smile and shrugged while G continued gently. "You are a soul of strength and fire, Hot Wing. I have met no one like you, for both the joy you can ignite and the passion which can burn you, but you need to learn how to handle it."

"I know, brother, I know, but I am just a damn wreck inside and out, all the time..." My voice trailed.

"Hey, look at me." G stopped walking and stood still with an earnest face. "Wing, we are only twenty-six years young. Others might be getting married and sitting miserably in an office somewhere, but we are free out here. We have what most do not. Give yourself a break. You will figure yourself out."

I looked at my loving friend and thought, *he may not understand, but he does genuinely care*. With a playful smirk and words tangled in both candor and sarcasm, I stated. "I will fight you, G."

"I will fight you, Hot Wing." G returned with no smirk and no sarcasm.

At this, my cheeks finally turned up into a beaming grin. "I know, I know you would. I fight myself every day. I love you, man, and sure, we are only twenty-six, but that is no excuse. I cannot give myself any excuses. Despite dramatizing my inability to pull myself together in my heightened drunk emotions, I know exactly what I'm doing wrong." My rejection of God and growing slavery to the bottle loomed in my thoughts. Brushing this aside, forcing my mind into a proactive mentality, I altered my voice and declared. "We must get out of this damn city. We need to get back to the wilderness."

G nodded his head and strode forth with deliberate paces. "Love you too, man, and you are right. We need to get out of here and go back to the woods."

~~~

CINEREAL

After five eventful months south of the Columbia River, having convinced Safari in Portland to rejoin us on the Pacific Crest Trail, we walked across the Bridge of the Gods into Washington. Our journeys to arrive in the northwesternmost state of our country, all the way from the Mexico border, had been unique for each of us. Yet despite the miles, mountains and internal angsts which had separated us many times before, the three Shasta summiteers were reunited in the wilderness again. Many other hikers, including Funk, Chef, Trooper and the rest of their rowdy gang, joined the jubilant transition across the river that had once served as a passageway for Lewis and Clark. Cascade Locks, the small trail town on the Oregon side of the bridge, had been a vortex for many. And though a rambunctious group of us ascended the steep slopes from the river into Washington's rugged, lush mountains, we would not walk as a caravan for long.

The discord of ten hikers coughing themselves awake shattered the serenity of dawn. Everyone lay strewn a few feet apart from the other, no tents, only sleeping bags on soil, with empty cans of beer lying between. Chef and I were the first to light cigarettes while still horizontal inside our sacks. He looked across the ground at me and lifted his crudely crafted stick in the motion of a cheers then declared, "I roll enough at night and set them next to me so I can smoke every time I wake up to pee."

With a chuckle, I responded, "Chefs do love their prep work. I roll two as soon my brain turns on before I even open my eyes, at the same time, one in each hand." I blew some of my smoke in his direction. He guffawed amusedly. G waddled over and picked up my ice axe, emitted a gruff then shuffled into a dense thicket. Funk sat up and pulled out his pouch of marijuana.

We all sounded haggard, except for Safari, who did not cough but jested at our hiker trash ways. To a drowsy owl peering down, we might have looked like a rough band of desperadoes, but we were merely a temporary gathering of benevolent nonconformists who preferred to party in the mountains more than anywhere else. I grinned at the scene unfolding. Funk stood in his underwear and passed around his unnecessarily bulky glass marijuana pipe he kept in a padded case. *I love that he carries that.* After Safari received his toke of green smoke, he shook his head at the rest of us and sauntered away to sit by a nearby pond with his morning instant coffee. After I inhaled my hit, I joined him while the rest of the gang inadvertently scared all the birds away.

CINEREAL

"Instant coffee always tastes like the good stuff when we are out here," I said softly while sitting down next to Safari.

"Yeah, everything is better out here. It is good to be back." Safari lifted his camp mug to mine. We clinked more gently than the voices of the crew behind us then sat in stillness for a few minutes observing otters swim in the calm, glassy water. Steam fog hung above the surface, while dense clouds filled with moisture threatened to conquer the hazy hover soon. Once the playful critters dove out of sight, my younger trail brother spoke again. "I appreciate you guys coming to get me, and snapping me out of my city slumber, but I'm not sure how long I'll stay. I've gotta figure some things out."

I nodded while sipping the brown sludge from my tarnished vessel. "Same, man. Something in me has changed. I'll keep walking north for now, but an internal darkness has awakened. I think I left my sanity in the bars of Portland. So, I suppose I also need to figure some things out." We smiled at each other with a mutual understanding and returned to silence. The two otters resurfaced. Only their heads poked above the smooth sheen. Small wakes shaped as Vs followed their movements. When the undulations of their actions reached the shore by our feet, I posed a question. "What do you want in life, Safari?"

He tilted his head, thinking, as if his mind hadn't considered it much before. "I'm not sure exactly yet, but certainly adventure, a lot of it. But not the same thing repeatedly. This one has lost its luster for me. I really liked the desert, so probably will head south when I can." He smirked and added, "but it certainly has been a wild one! Mount Shasta was the cap for me." We shared a proud grin of agreement. "What about you, Hot Wing? What do you want out of life?"

I turned my gaze from my friend to peer across the pond again. The otters now played on the far bank. After another sip of my coffee, I stated, "I just want peace. Peace in my mind, peace in my heart, peace in my soul."

Safari pursed his lips together solemnly. The contemplative pauses between our exchanges were interrupted by G yelling to us that he was ready to hike on, "With or without ya!"

"Guess it's time to clean our stuff up and walk again," Safari muttered with acceptance.

Forcing an enthusiastic tone, I encouraged, "Breakfast first. We'll catch G. One step at a time."

CINEREAL

~~~

The first week in Washington was filled with fog and elk bellowing in rut. The land sounded ancient, as if dinosaur ghosts traveled on the wind. Long silences were filled with hurling whispers of autumn pulsing in. Autumn knocked persistently and blew the door wide open. On a morning of the newly arrived season, while walking alone through the thick layer of vapor levitating in the forest, my narrow path took a sharp left. When I breached the trail's elbow, I came face to face with a massive creature. A mature bull elk with sabers for antlers was confidently striding south to my north, and due to our blind curve, we suddenly stood three feet apart. My body flinched beneath his shocked eyes. His nostrils shot snot onto my face as he raised his towering head in dominion. Slowly I stepped backwards, but it was too late. He lowered his rack of swords while stomping a hoof and then charged. Instinctively, without half a second to waste, I dropped my pack at his feet to create a stumbling block, grasped my ice axe, and scuttled up a thin pine tree faster than my personal record speed. A blade of his antlers pierced the trunk below my rising foot. The entire tree shuddered. Then, just as suddenly as we had alarmed each other with our happenstance, we were both shocked as to the shift in position. I did not know how I reacted and climbed so fast, and he did not know how this human rapidly scored the higher ground. The bull tried to maintain his grimace, yet my axe slashed at brittle branches, causing a shower of shattered wood to descend onto his head. With an imposing voice I informed him, "I'll stay up here all day, bud, I know you just want to mate or fight, but I'd much rather do neither!" With this, the elk accepted defeat and casually sauntered south. His head turned back at me one more time before disappearing around the curve. I clung to my roost for another few minutes, not wanting to risk another confrontation. As I clutched the timber, rich laughter emanated from my body, picturing how I looked. *Here I am, hugging this tree for dear life, fifteen feet off the ground. If only someone could see me now...* I knew it was pathetic, but I didn't care. It had worked. When I was sure he was long gone, I jumped down to the earth, hoisted my pack and continued silently persevering north, eager to relay my story to the others at camp that night.

After 100 miles in our northernmost state, we each departed into the fog at different intervals. Our group of many dissolved into smaller groups of few. Camaraderie had carried me forth, although my soul felt pulled back towards Oregon. The wilderness was beautiful. The wildlife in abundance.

CINEREAL

Almost every day I spotted more elk, bears and foxes. One afternoon I walked past a little meadow, and on its edge were a bull and cow elk consummating their desires. I didn't stare, rather hustled beyond, but I admired each animal encounter. Yet none of nature's splendor could brighten the darkness in my soul. Much of me had changed. Everything was different now. This was not like the final state of Maine on the Appalachian Trail when I stirred with joy, pushing stalwartly to the finish line. No, each step here now seemed out of sync with my heart and soul. My pride wanted to proceed forth, but every other part of me had drained empty. The darkness consumed. I was ready to end my long walk.

Two weeks into Washington, G announced it was his birthday. We came upon a dirt road, and since our group had run out of alcohol, G decided he would follow the lane until he found beer. If we waited for him, we could celebrate together when he returned. Proud of my friend for taking the side-quest initiative, I offered to join, but he stated, "Today, I must do this alone." I understood. Safari, our quirky friend Chameleon and I waited for him in the lush thick forest beneath towering evergreens. We smoked marijuana, lying on a mossy floor, staring up into the verdant canopy, which blocked every ray of sunshine. When G returned with enough beers for the four of us to get merrily drunk, we did so with hurrahs and reinvigorated glee. On the earth we continued our lounge, as the hiker trash we were, crushing each empty can into a compact disc to stuff into the recesses of our backpacks. G beamed warmly. *He is having a suitable birthday with his brothers of this long journey;* I considered while smiling back at him.

When we awoke where we had partied the evening before, our group of four scattered north into the woods alone, one by one. I would not know for some time what became of Safari or Chameleon, for it was the last time I saw them on the Pacific Crest Trail. G was gone before the dawn, but I would catch up to him one more time. I took up the rear and trekked apathetically. About a quarter mile up the trail, I turned around and returned to the dirt road G had used to find his birthday beer. I trudged until arriving at a small town and a tavern, where I filled my heavy soul with the warm blanket of whiskey. When numb and ready, I forced myself to resume hiking north on the trail. Isolated from all other human beings, deep in the wilderness, I faced and communed with the aches in my soul, knowing my journey's end would come in only a matter of mountains and miles. *Canada may not be the ultimate destination for me after all.*

CINEREAL

In this last stretch, I intentionally basked in the land's magnificent beauty, soaking it up as a solemn farewell. The Goat Rocks Wilderness, often touted as one of the most scenic stretches of Washington, was shrouded in clouds. Snow started to fall. In the morning, midday, afternoon and night I bathed in the wet cold which would not dry nor warm my shivering body and soul. All temporary joy faded. All ambition died. My purpose no longer existed. I walked because it was the only thing I knew how to do.

Mount Rainier guided me north, dominant on the horizon. The grand mountain symbolized the pillar of my end. Despite this, I trudged on until the active volcano disappeared to my south. When I reached Stevens Pass, at the entrance to the renown North Cascades National Park, I knew it was time. From a distance, I sat and watched other hikers, including my trail brother G, hoist their packs with vigor and disappear into the forest. The weight of the decision lay upon me. A decision I had never considered seriously until the darkness of my soul had triumphed over my determination during that awful scourge in Portland. I too had always hoisted my pack and persevered through pain and displeasure, but now, now it was not so. I was empty. At mile 2,462 on the Pacific Crest Trail, with only 188 miles to the Canadian border, I quit. For the first time in my life, I gave up. I wasn't sure whether I was doing the right thing. But what I knew was that I had squeezed every ounce of vigor I once held, and now I was as arid as desert air. I looked up into the drizzle and announced to the sky, "I am dry, I have no more, no matter the rain and snow that you pour, I am done."

I took my time, lying in the dirt under an evergreen, away from where anyone would notice me, smoking one last marijuana joint, and one last trail cigarette. I then stood and walked down the road to the west, with my thumb out, to hitch a ride toward Seattle, and ultimately south to Portland. It was not long before a vehicle stopped to ask if I was okay. "Am I okay?" I repeated to the polite older man. Tears trickled down my cheeks. "I just need to get out of here, and yes, I will be alright." The man obliged and, in a whoosh of speed and demoralizing urban lights, like a dream which has no considerate feelings for the past, I was gone.

In just a few days' time, after hiding away in the garden of an acquaintance in Portland, I found myself in the bustle of an airport, then squeezed into an airplane. As I flew to Boston and stared down at the planet below, my mind reeled in turmoil. *What is this awful burden growing heavier with each second? It is a burden beyond any I have ever known.* The feeling I presumed was of allowing the darkness to win. *Did I make the right choice? Or have I failed in a way I will never forgive myself for?* I did not know. All I knew was I had given up, or given in, or given all… I was lost and had no home to return to. My only home was the trail, and that home I traded away for the tormenting relief of despair.

CINEREAL

There Must Be a Plan

When I returned to New Hampshire after my Pacific Crest Trail hike, there was no plan. My friends wanted to hear the stories, celebrate the adventure, glorify my explorations, but I only wanted to drink alcohol and disappear. Once again, I perceived they did not understand. No one in the world knew how I felt. Each time I returned to New England, I returned differently from when I had left, which confused everyone who thought they knew me. I did not enjoy the things I once had, nor did I want to explain any of my reasons or darkness to them.

My plan after the Appalachian Trail had been to hike all three of the major long-distance trails in the United States of America. Together, the AT, the PCT and the CDT (Continental Divide Trail) are hailed as the Triple Crown. Quest for the triple crown had been my goal, but now, after losing grip on my soul out west, I no longer cared to continue this pursuit. Each day on the long hikes had provided unique experiences and taught valuable lessons, but now I desired to use what I had been learning towards building a stable future. I did not want to turn into a professional hiker as some of my peers were progressing to become. I wanted more. But what this more was, I did not yet know.

The internet blog on which I had been writing and sharing stories of my adventures became an outlet I'd grown tired of utilizing. Instead, I wrote intensively in my notebooks. My rigorous daily writing developed into poetry, for poetry seemed to be the only way I could ease my troubled soul. As an adolescent, poetry proved to be a valuable outlet for me, even more so now. Wherever I roamed, I carried a small notebook in my pocket or satchel. Each day I scribbled lines, images, thoughts, concocting poems often only I could comprehend. *They don't need to understand;* I told myself. *No one needs to understand what and why I do what I do.* With this defiance, I veiled the fact that I also did not entirely grasp my misguided movements. For whom can, when alcohol has become the driving force of one's actions?

CINEREAL

I simply knew I must escape New Hampshire immediately. I could not spend another winter in the haunting towns of old, traveling the same streets, sitting in the same bars, facing the same friends who had been fading into strangers. After celebrating my 27th birthday in October, sleeping on couches and in a friend's bed for November, I reached out to G on Thanksgiving Day, imploring him to meet me in Colorado.

"Let's reunite in the Rocky Mountains!" I urged with an impatient tone, promising the grandeur of a new mountain season. Post-trail life was also tormenting him. Returning to a preferred elevation in the mountains seemed to be our answer. "It essentially splits our distance. We can meet in the middle." I added, as he lived in Southern California and I in New England. "We'll each fly to Denver, take a bus and meet in Boulder, then go work and ski in Vail."

"Why Vail?" G responded.

"I don't know, because it's fancy, plenty of money floating around, close to other resorts up there, and we've never been to Vail. We can figure it out as we go. We'll find work there no problem."

"Alright, screw it," G agreed. "I'm not doing anything of value here, so we might as well keep our mountain party going. See you soon, Hot Wing."

Our plan was flimsy at best, as we had minimal money left after the PCT, nor did we have any jobs secured in the Rocky Mountains. What I did have was a close friend from the college days, Mit Willard, who lived in Boulder, Colorado. Mit agreed that G and I could crash on his living-room floor and when we were ready, he would drive us up to Vail. I did not have a vehicle, having sold my Jeep before the trail, but I decided I did not need one. *Besides, both G and I have grown quite adept at walking and hitchhiking.* With our dwindling dollars, we flew from our opposite sides of the country to start a new adventure. G and Mit met and quickly hit it off. Their comfortable banter caused my heart to happily swell. Merging my dear friends from different life chapters always conjured joy. With the thrill of a new chapter upon us, we dove into the Boulder bars for a rowdy night of pints, whiskey and wild conversations.

I had always loved Mit. He was one of my favorite friends from New Hampshire. Mit was also close with Andrew, the comrade who had met me at Franconia Notch where I was arrested for marijuana possession. On dark winter evenings during the college years, Mit often hosted a make-your-own-soup and bread night at his abode. Both his gatherings and his personality

CINEREAL

exuded serenity. The year prior, Andrew was married in St. Louis to which Mit, my unruly but lovable friend Stenny and I road-tripped from New England to partake in. Andrew had bestowed upon me the great honor of operating as his best man at the wedding, a role I applied myself to with my full personality and sincere brotherly love. Once the marriage and weekend of celebration were complete, Mit drove Stenny and me to the airport, then he proceeded to Boulder, Colorado, to build his adult life. Mit was a no-drama, genuine soul. He valued gardening and all things organic. His smile brightened every heart he met, and all that he did was done with focus, joy and efficiency.

After a few days of gallivanting, the three of us zoomed up into the Rocky Mountains in Mit's old Honda. Vail glistened beneath fresh white powdery snow and ornamental holiday lights. Our kind courier admitted he wasn't sure how comfortable he was leaving G and me up in the zero-degree temperatures. After all, we had nowhere to stay, and no jobs secured, but we assured him, or rather I assured him, "We will be alright." G scanned our new environment, bewildered by the posh luxury and opulent structures. Yet again, I assured G, "We will figure it out." Mit drove off in the night back down the mountains to his home, and G and I started texting hiker friends from the trails who hopefully, possibly, might live nearby.

Once Mit was gone, G spoke with a tone I did not appreciate. "How the heck did I let you convince me to come here? This isn't our kind of town. And it's freaking cold!"

"I promise you, dude, Size-Up, 151, and McCaw are all working in Vail this winter." I ushered G towards a tavern, ordered us each a pint, then moved over to a large blazing indoor fireplace. We sipped the soothing alcohol while warming up. I did not appreciate G's sudden doubt about my plan. My flimsy plan.

"Well, they better get back to you soon because we have no plan. No proper plan, Hot Wing!" G drank his beer and slouched into an oversized leather chair.

"Does my boy need a blanket too?" I joked with a bit of stab, pointing to the blankets piled for patrons nearby. G held up his middle finger, so I refocused and resumed. "We have a bit of a plan," I smiled encouragingly. "Come on, we need to remain confident. Think with intentional positivity. We made it here. That is a checkpoint success. We will look for jobs tomorrow. It is all going to work out. If one of us snags a job from the resort, they will provide us with employee housing, and then we won't be homeless in Vail. Trust me, I know how these companies work. Let's go explore the town while we wait to hear from our potential couch-for-the-night leads."

G shrugged and followed me back out into the cold. I offered him a cigarette, which he declined, so I ignited my own and marched from one decorative ice sculpture to another. Vail was so finely manicured, underneath and between large mounds of snow, it nearly convinced us we were exploring Santa's village in the North Pole. I delighted in every twist and turn. G did not. Despite his occasional mumble, he hung close until finally, around midnight, one of our hiker acquaintances texted back. They were just getting off work and were both surprised and hesitant at our request. G glared at me. "You mean you didn't warn them we were coming?"

"I did. They knew. They just didn't know when, or if it was going to happen, I suppose." I gave G a smirk and a shrug, to which he rolled his eyes. "Hey, who cares if we inconvenience Size-Up and her roommates a bit? They are offering their floor for two nights, in and out. We'll thank them with a case of beer and find a job that offers us lodging by then."

"Alright, whatever, let's go. It's already one in the morning, and I am tired. We'd better get some sleep if we are going to find jobs tomorrow." G picked up his backpack, just like we had on the trail, and onward we trudged across town.

I knew G wasn't happy with me. It seemed he was already regretting coming to Vail, but I was determined to remain positive. "The quality of our outlook and focus will determine the quality of our results G."

"Shut up, Wing." G hustled a few steps in front and put on his headphones over his winter hat. This did not bother me; I understood he needed space. I wouldn't let his discouragement infect my attitude. If anything, his gentle tantrum was a comfort, for we were together again. I knew him well, and deep in his heart I imagined he was excited. *We both just need to get some sleep.*

The next day, G and I tromped down to the nucleus of resort operations, human resources. We spent hours proceeding through the steps of a resort hiring process. G, to his satisfaction, swiftly obtained a job. His employment included being paid to ski on the mountain, and he would receive employee housing as well. This provided us both with a warm room, shielding us from the winter temperatures. It brought me pleasure to see him elated. The resort's regulations did not allow me to live in this room as well, but we did not care about such rules. In the meantime, I attended an interview for a lucrative position working with an elite club of wealthy Vail members.

"Congratulations, Wing, we think you are perfect for this position and would like to offer you employment." The stiff, clean-cut man in a suit spoke to me after I swooned them with an hour of outrageous stories about my unique resume.

"Ah, thank you, Mr. Pauly. When shall you have me begin, tomorrow?" I asked, staring into the boring man's eyes.

"Yes, we can start your training tomorrow afternoon, but first you must go get a haircut and shave your face. You can do that in the morning. Once you are all cleaned up, we may proceed." The shorn man applied a balm to his lips after speaking.

"I see." I recognized a defiance awakening beneath my beard. "So, you say I am perfect for this job, but you want me to change the way I am. Therefore, you do not think I am perfect for this job."

"Well, you seem to be a great fit. Your personality and hard-working resume show this. You talk very well, and you have an exceptionally charismatic way with people. But we have a dress-code and appearance policy here at Vail that all company employees must adhere to."

Now, younger me might have been fine with shaving my face and cutting my long hair, but the me who had hiked the Appalachian Trail and Pacific Crest Trail (minus the last 188 miles) would not change my appearance to work for some rich pricks who cater to even richer pricks.

"Mr. Pauly," I spoke firmly. "That is a shame. I believe we are at an impasse here, for I will not change the way I look to cater to your, or anyone's, code of appearance. Thank you for your time and best wishes on finding someone you can conform to your corporate mold, which I am sure will not be difficult." I stood up, tossed my hair about like a lion's mane, offered my hand out for a firm shake, which he returned limply, and then strolled out the door leaving Mr. Pauly speechless.

I knew G wouldn't be thrilled with my decision, but at least he had secured a room for the two of us. I would continue looking for employment with a business not owned by Vail operations, although here in Vail, I knew my options would be limited. For now, I could hustle rich tourists out of their money by playing billiards. With this plan in mind, I walked to the nearest bar with a billiard table to do exactly that.

As Christmas approached, all of Vail glistened as a curated, tinseled wonderland. While G worked during the day, I spent much of my time in the Vail library reading books and staying warm. I read ten books in those weeks, revisiting favorites by Jack Kerouac and nourishing my mind with many new ones. When I grew tired of reading, I drank alcohol and challenged plush travelers to billiards matches. My strategy was as old as the West. First, I approached my target, set a twenty-dollar bill on the table, placing the game offer which they usually accepted. I would then deliberately lose the match, acting like a bumbling fool, only making the easy shots, missing the mediocre ones and leaving my cue ball in spots I pretended were poor luck. I would always lose the twenty-dollar game, then immediately challenge them to play for one-hundred dollars or more. In this second game, I would play precisely, leaving my cue ball in wise locations and ultimately, quickly, win the lot. They could have my first twenty. It was the hundred I was after. When G got off work in the afternoon, we would meet up, and I would proudly buy him a whiskey or dinner from the money I had earned.

"A profitable day for you, eh, Wing?" G sipped on his frosty cold beer.

"Indeed. I used some of my earnings to buy a half ounce of marijuana too. Which I'll break down into grams and sell it well above market price to tourists. I've got this town figured out." Winking at G, picking up my cold pint again, lifting the golden goodness to my lips causing a layer of foam to remain in my beard, I added, "Oh, and I scored us some mushrooms today too."

"Oh, did you now?" G spooned out a gob of his chili with melted cheese trailing a long string to the bowl.

"I did. Tonight?" I suggested.

G chuckled and affirmed, "Tonight."

Between my unemployment side hustles and G's daily work routine, we ravaged the town like two outlaws on a mission. We knew when and where every happy-hour deal was and what bars sold the best and cheapest food. We memorized the layouts of Vail's extravagant villages, the trail systems around the forests, the bus schedules, and how to recognize when a tourist needed marijuana and when they needed directions. For the few weeks until

CINEREAL

Christmas, G and I were on the brink of thriving, until our attitudes and bravados eventually clashed and a nasty argument ensued.

By December 23rd, 2012, G had grown tired of my wild ways. "That's enough, Wing. You can't sleep on my floor anymore. My roommates said, you must go, and honestly, I agree with them."

"Your roommates!? Those assholes? What did they say?" I retorted, hurt by my trail brother's rejection.

"They say you are a ridiculous person, and you scare them." G spoke firmly.

"Scare them? I wouldn't hurt anyone unless I was defending myself or you."

"I know you wouldn't Wing, but your antics have gotten out of hand, and honestly, I think you are going to get jumped and beaten up, possibly killed, any day now. The way you gallivant around and hustle people for money over billiards. I'm just trying to do honest work. I can't do this, this buddy-support thing anymore, not right now." G vented sincerely, and maybe he was right.

Although receiving this admonishing reality stung, I would not show how much it hurt me. Instead, I attempted to understand his perspective and shifted my sight elsewhere. There were many Colorado mountain resorts to explore. There was no point in trying to convince G to let me stay with him if he was so set against it. So, I packed up my backpack and sadly hitched a ride down to the small town of Frisco.

That afternoon, I explored Copper Mountain resort, but my deflated heart lacked motivation. Because of our conflict, I did not have any gumption to score a proper job. *They'll just want me to shave and cut my hair anyway*, I supposed, kicking strewn snowballs with my boot. *Maybe I will try Breckenridge next. Hustle the tourists there. But no, G is right. I deserve to get my ass kicked. What have I become? And why in the last year have I perpetually been needing to ask myself that question? I used to be an honest person, and in some ways, I still am, but this hustling ruse is deceitful. That is not who I aspire to be. I got lost in the escapade of it all, but if something is born from a dishonorable place, then it is not morally right.* Distraught by my actions and in dire need of warm rest, I booked the cheapest motel room I could find. *Tomorrow is Christmas Eve, so I might as well get drunk by myself and take a hot shower. But no Wing! No*, I immediately retorted within. *This is not a time to get drunk. It is a time to refocus, seriously consider how I veered off course, and return to honest living.*

CINEREAL

The next day, the loneliness in my heart ached. But I understood the timeout was necessary. I had fallen away from all that was ethical. My actions had exhausted G and even exhausted myself. *No more billiard hustles ever again. Or any cons to disgracefully make money. From now on, if I want competition at the game, I will enter tournaments. And I need to apologize to G. If he lets me come back, which I hope he does, I will return to our friendship but not my out-of-control ways. If he does not want me to come back, so be it. Nevertheless, he deserves an apology.*

Before I could call, G called me. Seeing his name on my phone ignited hope in my heart. I answered, and he spoke the words I had wished for.

"Hey Hot Wing, I'm sorry. I just needed a break, some personal space." His voice sounded as if life might be glowing a tad dimmer without me.

"No, no, G. You don't need to apologize for a single thing. I am the sorry one. I recognize how out of hand I can get, and how I let my emotions and zest for life pour erratically without thinking about consequences. The money hustling was extremely wrong of me. I will not do that anymore. It is time I slowed down, refocused my energy towards something stable, towards honest work. I know my energy can escalate too much, but I will try to be less and tame that side of me. I promise, no more of the old wild Wing. Mellow Wing from now on."

"Dude, it's okay. You are not too much, nor do you need to be less. You just need to recognize when you get out of control. That awareness is the first step in mellowing it. I don't want you to be something you are not, Wing, just... controlled. It sounds like you've done some serious thinking, a step towards maturing. It's Christmas Eve. Where are you? Are you close? Will you come back?" G's voice resonated tenderly once again.

"I'm in Frisco. I'll hitch back right now. Call you when I'm there. I'll find you wherever you are." Excitement and relief stirred within. *He is giving me another chance.* Instantly, I started packing my few belongings.

"Alright, my friend, have a safe hitch. I'll see you soon." G hung up the phone.

Eagerly, I returned the motel room key and paraded through the snow up to the highway's edge. A large, hoisted thermometer in town displayed -7 degrees Fahrenheit. *This must be the coldest weather I have ever hitchhiked in, and on Christmas Eve no less. I am heading back to G!* My thoughts returned to glee-filled motivation, not minding the cold one bit, elated to be returning to my friend for Christmas.

CINEREAL

Upon arriving back in Vail, with the song "I'll Be Home for Christmas" singing in my mind, I found G at a bar we enjoyed playing billiards at. He was in the middle of a game with a few of his co-workers. I felt like the odd man out, but he gave me a hug and a warm smile. Consciously, I attempted to remain calm, although my heart wanted to sing and dance and do so perhaps on a bar top. *But no, I must keep it mellow.* While watching G and his new friends play the game, I sipped on my beer and listened to the music. I wasn't used to being on the sidelines like this, but at least I was here. After they finished their match, G looked over to me and hollered.

"Hey Hot Wing! Do you want to be my partner for this next game?" G extended a peaceful offering.

Leaping off my barstool and skipping to the table, I replied, "Of course I do. Are we playing for money or just for fun?"

"Just for fun, Wing, come on now…" G side-eyed me.

I laughed at his retort, knowing I deserved it. "G, I was kidding! Too soon for that joke? I'm not going to play for money anymore. Tomorrow, well tomorrow is Christmas, the next day then, I will go look for a normal job again. I promise, no more dishonorable hustles." As I spoke, the song Stand by Me by Ben E. King played on the jukebox. G and I stood next to each other while the opposing team racked the billiard balls. The song described one of the things I craved. "This is all I ever needed, G. Just a friend to stand by me, like this." I spoke sincerely, with no humor in my voice. Tears welled in my eyes. G peered at me and saw the emotion I struggled to hide. He placed his arm around my shoulders and smiled.

"I know Wing. Everything is alright. We are doing the best we can. You want to break and start the game?" G nodded to the billiard table.

"Yeah, man, I got this. And thank you, brother." I rubbed my damp eyes, drying the welling tear ducts, stepped up to the table and delivered a shattering, resounding strike.

~~~

On Christmas Day, G and I sat at the bar of a pub eating our "good-deal meal" of elk chili. The hot sauce bottle passed frequently between the two of us. Although we had been scrapping and earning just enough to get by, we were most likely the two poorest people in Vail. In fact, we may have been the only two poor people in Vail. We sipped on our beers instead of chugging them, and discussed simple things, such as trail memories and the purpose of life. Mid-conversation, when the bartender asked if we needed

CINEREAL

anything, I half-joked and stated, "Just a job." It was a good thing I said this, for the bartender responded that the pub was hiring a doorman for the security team. I told him I'd do it. He sized me up. I lifted my chin. He grabbed the manager. We talked and decided I would start work the next day. G chuckled as we accepted a round of beers on the house after I shook hands and concluded with the manager. I didn't need to shave or cut my hair, and I could smoke. It was a new, rowdy challenge, one I could not have been more delighted about.

"Merry Christmas to us," I chuckled with glee, picking up my pint glass to clink in cheers with G.

"Merry Christmas to us," my comrade grinned in return.

During those dark, odd end-of-year December days before the new year, G and I worked daily and lived somewhat calmly. G skied on the mountain doing whatever it is he did up there, and I checked tourist's identification cards and broke up fights at Garfinkle's. My job was simple. Protect the liquor license and don't allow the underage inside. The pub was a popular late-night hangout in Lionshead Village, next to the ski-slopes and a busy chairlift. It was always busy, and I always had international IDs to analyze. I remained confident in detecting a fake USA ID from any state, but other country's passports proved to be tricky. The boss paid us an extra twenty-five dollars for each fake ID we confiscated as motivation towards perfection. I meticulously studied an identification guide of global IDs, which helped me to identify and secure multiple fraudulent IDs per shift quickly. Along with my hourly wage, cash tips and ID bonuses, I also sold marijuana to tourists at a steep price. It turned out to be quite a lucrative little job. I had the pleasure of breaking up multiple fights, rumbling into a few myself, appropriating any drugs being ingested in the bathroom, and gathering all the broken glasses and bottles at the end of the night. The energy of a wild night invigorated me. Willingly, I slithered through the tight crowd, demanding out-of-line drunks to behave, dunking punches and then dragging the fool by his neck back through the crowd, to toss him out the door into the white world of brumal Vail. It felt great being the one to do the expelling, as I had been on the receiving end many times in my young life. Since my job went until two or three in the morning, and G worked in the daytime, we rarely got to see each other anymore. After New Year's Eve raved, raged and passed, G and I had our first time to relax together since Christmas. Although it had only been a week, it had been an action-packed week apart, leaving us both to miss our billiard game fellowship nights and colorful conversations.

"Happy New Year, Hot Wing." G hoisted his glass first this time.

"Happy New Year, G! Look at us, we made it to 2013." I lifted my glass in return and clinked his.

"It's going to be a big year." He nodded, using a phrase we frequently stated, no matter the day.

"Indeed, it is. Closing out a big one and stepping into another grand one. I sense good things to come this year." Between sips of our beers, we grinned together. With a proud guffaw, I stated. "Well, man, we did it. We conquered Vail. I'd call this a success."

G gave me a look as if I were a madman and then spoke. "We've only been here for a month, Hot Wing. Less than a month, like twenty-six days."

"Twenty-five days. Yes, but we came to a new land with little plan, made a heck of an impression, and both got jobs. And we haven't died! I'd call that a success." I put emphasis on the word success, my eyes glinting to G as if I had another idea brewing.

"We did. No, we didn't. And yes, we did…" G's voice trailed, allowing me room to complete my thought.

"I wonder how Mit is doing… Boulder sounds nice about now." I beamed, unveiling our near future.

"It is freaking cold up here, and no one likes us." G dropped two truths with this line, a line I immediately laughed to.

"It is so true! No one likes us up here. We are too much for them." My amusement escalated.

G added to the truth and joined in the laughter. "We are like two renegades, outlaws, rowdy kids from the woods, and they just don't know what to do with us."

My hand was nearly slapping my knee by now. "They do not know what to do with us! Maybe we should go hang out with Mitty and kick it in Boulder for a bit. I'm over Vail. We did the damn thing." As I spoke these words, G's face lit up brighter than I had seen since the summit of Mount Shasta.

"I hate the cold. You know that. My Southern California blood is exhausted. Yes, let's go see Mit." G agreed.

"Alright then, it's settled. We'll quit our jobs and hitchhike back down to Boulder. Cheers, brother, to conquering Vail and a brand-new year. Let's go get it." And so, much like that, we concluded.

CINEREAL

 Mit was delightfully surprised to see us when we returned to Boulder. Hitchhiking out of the mountains hadn't been too difficult. It was a cold hitch, one we both did under the strain of fevers, having fallen achingly ill because of our lifestyle, but a successful one. But now that we were back in the flatlands peering upon the mighty Flatirons, which rose like angled knife blades complementing the rocky horizon of Boulder, G's spirits seemed less stressed. We rested, healed, and thanks to the nurturing warmth of whiskey in my belly, I decided I was content enough for the time being.

 We returned to our favorite billiard bar and discussed the near future. Mit told us about his new job building gardens at schools come spring, while still working shifts at an upscale restaurant. He was very busy and could offer us only a sliver of his time. Another friend of mine from back east, Frank, an Army veteran, now lived in town as well. I always thought Frank resembled a junior senator from the Roman Republic until he opened his mouth and said something inherently goofy. He would occasionally fill the third barstool when Mit worked. G promised to stay a few days, but then he must return to the west coast, and I, well I didn't want to go anywhere. I aspired to be done with New Hampshire entirely, although I must go close out loose ends, purchase a vehicle, and then stop meandering about. When the time arrived, I escorted my trail brother to the bus station. Amidst screeches, churns, and the intrusive scent of exhaust fumes, we bid our farewells. As he signaled his last wave and disappeared into his travels, a vast sadness and void settled into my heart. I shuffled away from the cacophony alone, seeking the solace of booze.

 From the pub with a piano, I called Frank. He arrived amid the boisterous clamor of my fingers pounding upon ivory keys. Due to the "no playing piano" sign, I had drawn the ire of the owner, softened only by the entertained faces on collared drunks. Men in mahogany booths roared along with my clanging howls. When I looked up and witnessed Frank's laughter at the scene I produced, I tipped my hat to the crowd and hustled out the front door. He drove me in his obnoxiously loud Firebird to the top of a local vista where we sat in silence on the rocks and smoked. I stared beyond the town below us, far into the east, and considered all that had recently been. *Perhaps I was never content after all. I had been merely distracted.* Mit was focused on a proper life, G was returning to family and purpose, and my existence seemed lacking. *I never used to feel this way, for I always knew what I was doing and why I did it, until the end of the PCT of course...* The obvious reason glared at me. *I need to stop treating life as a trail town. The long hikes are behind me. It is time to step forward intentionally. It is time for a proper plan.*

A few days prior, my dad had informed me he was moving all his belongings from New Hampshire to Florida, where he planned to purchase a house. He had asked for my help instead of hiring expensive movers. Sitting there on the boulders above Boulder, with only the ashes of motivation in Colorado, his request seemed to be my next best move. *It would be an excellent way to spend time with my pops and do something worthwhile.* Between drags of my smoke, I called him and announced I would do it, aid in his move from the north to the south. When I hung up the phone, I winked over at Frank. A new smile emerged on my face. "Onward I go, my friend. The trail goes on forever, and the party never ends."

~~~

In the spring, Dad and I set off on our drive down the east coast. We stopped to visit my grandmother and grandfather at their home in Georgia. We relaxed by throwing the football in the yard like old times, feasting on ham and Grandma's delectable banana pudding. I smoked cigarettes with Granddad and listened to the hounds' bays in the evening across the cotton fields. We ate pecans and sat in rocking chairs until watching Steve McQueen and John Wayne movies. Our beds held the scent of memories. At sunrise we all drank coffee together. Observing my dad around his parents entertained me, for around them he acted like a mischievous teenager.

On the last night in Georgia, my grandfather and I shared what would become our last moments one on one, although I did not know it then. I sat outside at the end of the driveway, smoking, drinking, observing the stars and listening to the sounds of the country. Gunshots from the field where they trained the hounds jarred the air, followed by incoherent hollers of drunk men. Despite the distance, there were few other sounds or trees to inhibit their voices. Granddad was very strict about returning inside after the sunset, promptly locking the doors and windows. I brushed this off as old-man paranoia, as he was born in a different generation and always carried his military mindset. My solo nightly musings beneath the sky were of value to me. I still had trouble feeling comfortable indoors, yet beneath the stars I could serenely process each day.

During this sit, I heard the front door creak open. I sensed his presence peering out at me from the house behind. At first his voice sounded almost kind, although firm. "Son, it is time to come in for the night. I am going to lock up the house now."

It was only nine-thirty in the evening, so I turned around slightly and responded with a compromise. "Alright, Granddad, I'll be in by ten. Just another cigarette or two out here." I heard him close the door, assuming he was fine with my answer, for I meant what I said, and my calm, introspective rest resumed. *I will follow his command within thirty minutes, which seems very reasonable.* Lighting another cigarette, I leaned back in the lawn chair.

Not half-way through my freshly lit smoke, I heard the house door open again. Granddad leaned out, and this time his voice boomed with an authority and anger he rarely voiced to me. "Son, you get your ass in here now! I am not giving you a suggestion. I am giving you an order! This is my property, and you will do as I say." My spine shivered at hearing him yell with such force. And so, I, who rarely responds to any human authority with submission, instantly snubbed out the cigarette, gathered the beer cans, folded the lawn chair and hustled inside. I was in the kitchen within thirty seconds. As I locked the door behind me and looked at my grandfather, his eyes blazed.

He nodded for me to sit down opposite him at the kitchen table. When I obeyed, he stood up, grabbed a clean ashtray from the cupboard, placed it in front of me on the table, then sat back down and lit his own cigarette. He had his own ashtray, and I now had my own, so I also lit a cigarette awaiting what he had to say.

Granddad looked at me long and hard. He dragged on his smoke for a few seconds, exhaled, then took his dentures out of his mouth, set them on the kitchen table, and spoke. "Son, do you know why I needed you to come inside when I told you to?"

Respectfully, I shook my head no, glancing at the gums of his mouth, which I rarely saw. I wasn't about to suggest any kind of sarcastic comment or play a guessing game. My attitude was now humility and readiness to listen.

He continued with an answer. "It is for two reasons. One, I am your grandfather, and you must do as I say here on my land. I know you lost respect for authority when you were younger, and I will not discuss that, only explain the reason for obeying me. I gave you an order not to hurt you, but to protect you." He dragged on his cigarette.

"Yes, sir." I dragged on my cigarette.

CINEREAL

He continued, "The people across the field there, shooting their guns, they are drunks, and they are not always careful with where the bullets go. It would take one badly aimed shot, or one errant, negligent pull of a trigger, and that bullet would pop you right in the head." Granddad snapped his fingers, as if portraying how quickly I would be dead.

"Yes, sir, I understand." I responded again.

"Do you understand?" And right then, his aging eyes and tone shifted from lava stern to an imparting gentleness. "I am not strict with you to be mean; I am strict with you to protect you." Granddad himself, a pillar of a man, within seconds had tears welling in his eyes. This affected my heart, and my emotions started to show. With a whisper, he stated. "I am strict with you because I love you."

"I understand, sir. I am sorry, I..." My voice trailed, we both stubbed out the butts of our cigarettes in our ashtrays. "Truly, I am sorry, Granddad. I love you, too. I did not mean to brush off your order; I was just in my head out there."

He brushed the damp away from his eyes, and I did the same. He lit another cigarette, and so I did as well. "I know. I know you think long and deeply. You are an adventurer, a traveler, a creative. You know your grandmother reads all your stories to me about your hikes. I hear your words and know you better than you might think. I love who you are becoming, but you need to stay alive and gain some maturity."

"Yes, I love you too, Granddad, so much, you know that, and I am sorry for not obeying your loving command. I honestly never considered an errant bullet, or any of it." I spoke sincerely, moved by his care for me.

"Well, we have that understood. Now tell me, what is your next adventure plan?" Granddad brightened with a toothless smile.

My grandfather, whom I verbalized as Granddad, and I sat and talked at the table, smoking and laughing for another hour. Our ashtrays filled up with cigarette butts while the kitchen filled with smoke. At eleven, the latest I had ever witnessed him still awake, he stood, opened the door allowing fresh air in, and declared it was time for bed. He locked the door and double-checked the windows. We shook hands and retired to our separate rooms. I fell asleep without knowing it would be the last time I would ever be alone with him. This both tough and yet compassionate man, whom I had loved dearly my whole life, had always been there for me, from playing baseball in the yard when I was a young boy, to being the first to place me upon a horse.

CINEREAL

He taught me woodworking and tractor skills, and once killed a rattlesnake, coiled and ready to strike me inside the garden shed when my height only reached his waist. I remember my fear and his decisive action. We shared numerous talks at dawn when my dad was away at sea for the navy. He always with his coffee and cigarettes, and I with eager ears and glazed doughnuts. In my adulthood, our conversations developed, focusing on the deeper aspects of life. At my brother's hilltop wedding, it was only us who smoked. Our cigarettes represented a special bond, a pastime I never considered unhealthy. It was simply what we did together.

After a hearty breakfast, and one last photograph of three Williams' generations, I embraced Grandma and Granddad, then my dad and I continued south to Florida. We unloaded his truck and observed the sultry environment. Tiny lizards dashed across the driveway. Ivy wrapped around tree trunks. Although beautiful with its dense fauna and beaches, Florida was no place for me. I had lived in the Sunshine State for a few years as a child, but much had changed. Heat and humidity irritated me. Cool and dry is what I had grown to prefer. I needed higher elevations. "Do you think anyone here has ever climbed a mountain, or walked uphill?" My question to Dad conjured an eye-roll paired with a chuckle. He waved it off as if it were not worth answering. I knew my comment was unnecessary, so I lifted the next box and continued our duty.

When the job was complete, I boarded an airplane and flew back to New England. A lovely friend picked me up in the cool of the night. I grinned when I saw her comely doe eyes and smirking grin. We drove to the oceanside in New Hampshire and lounged on a seawall. The Atlantic waves crashed beneath our feet. We sat shoulder to shoulder, arm in arm, cozy in the salt air. There was much to like about my land of the haunts, especially after being in Florida, but not enough to sustain me. I shuddered remembering the past, a past that felt present beyond the wisp of an invisible veil. She squeezed my arm tighter. *I must try to relax for now.* Within days I purchased an old red Subaru Legacy wagon. It was time to formulate my new life-chapter's plan.

Colorado Rocky Mountain High

Following a few months of wild New England excursions, I left New Hampshire for the last time, determined never to return. I did not part on solid terms with the state, its inhabitants, or my family, instead leaving in a black cloud of confusion and rage. *West was where I was born, west is where I prefer, so to the west I must return.* Although my short winter in Vail, Colorado, had been a unique adventure, I had simply been "winging it," filling the void of unsettlement with a purposeless existence. One thing I learned in my young life of working adventures is that I thrive with a plan, and I spiral without one. So, I created a new plan. With a weary soul, a nearly empty wallet and an emboldened fire of determination, I returned to Colorado to create a new life for myself.

The plan was, move to a town called Nederland, get a job, any foot-in-the-door job, become a part of the community and grow. By grow I meant this in multiple parts, foremost mature as a young man in all ways, and learn to cultivate marijuana. Colorado had passed the law as the first state in the nation to legalize recreational marijuana, which for me meant no longer needing to look over my shoulder or hide my affection for this medicinal plant in the shadows. I aspired to learn everything I could about marijuana from the old hippie outlaws who had been growing it for decades. I desired to learn from the masters.

I had never been to the small town of Nederland before, but I had heard about it often. In my traveling ventures, many people had encouraged me to go check out this mountain town. "If there is anywhere in this country for you, Wing, it is Nederland." Ned intrigued me, appearing to have the qualities I was searching for. It was a high-elevation town sitting at 8,235 feet above sea-level, check. I needed to be in the mountains. It was also a small town boasting a tight-knit community assembled with various types of people. As someone who did not like to be labeled, put into a box, or expected to follow certain societal guidelines, this too made Ned appealing. I was not a hippy, although it was friendly to hippies, I was not a punk, or a hipster, not a conservative, a liberal, nor a judgmental pious hypocrite, I was simply a passionate for life mountain man with kindness in my heart for all. Although my soul often exhibited the shards of confusion, my actions intense, and my ardor misguided, I craved a peaceful home and community, the suitable home for a young man like me seeking to improve.

When I finally drove into the state of Colorado, culminating a road trip filled with a cornucopia of emotions, elation overflowed from my fluttering soul. The large I70 Colorado sign announcing I wasn't in Kansas anymore surged excitement within. I had made it, or I had almost made it. There was no looking back, only forward. The eastern portion of the state still resembled the Midwest prairies, verdant hues fading into late summer tawny waves, but the vibe was immediately different. I pulled off into the first rest stop at the welcome center, admired the Native American teepee, consulted my paper map, and rolled a marijuana joint. Miles beyond the horizon, I knew the Rockies loomed, awaiting in their patient magnificence. Once my parking lot victory dance was complete, I continued into my new state with a sparked joint hanging from my lips. Turning up the music on my janky radio in my old Subaru Legacy red wagon, I drove forth smoking with glee. I didn't have many belongings or much money, but I had everything I needed. I carried my sleeping bag, a tent, a hammock, a large tarp, the old trusty backpack, a few pairs of clothes, an axe, a hatchet, a few suitable knives, a basic toolkit, unlimited confidence and vital personal guidelines. These treasures were enough for me to start a new life.

My guidelines were simple. I believed they would help me become a worthy part of any community. Foremost, I would not date or fraternize with the mountain town girls in any romantic or physical manner, not for a while at least. I knew well from previous experiences and observations that jumping into the dating pool too soon could cause a lot of problems and create unnecessary enemies. My encounters had taught me that women in a small town are often interested in the new guy, thus the men are wary and sometimes even vile towards the fresh arrival. I would not let this happen, for I did not want to step on any toes, accidentally cross any unknown boundaries or conjure any antagonists. I would be friends first and friends only until I knew the lay of the social landscape. It behooved me to become like a brother to all and not to create rifts. I did not want or need a new fling. I strove only to become an appreciated citizen of Nederland. *If I must flirt, keep it with the Boulder women down in the flatlands,* I decided.

CINEREAL

Another guideline, immediately search for and accept any job available. I did not care if the work was not glamorous. What mattered, especially considering I was very low on money, was that some money would be coming in. I needed a paycheck. By working a humble position promptly, I would have co-workers and opportunities to make friends. This would help me find a place to live and provide me with a chance to prove my work ethic. No matter what job I found, I was determined to commit my all. There would be zero cons or billiard hustles. Just because I had turned away from God, temporarily slipped into hustling tourists out of money, and loved to party did not mean, in my misguided young mind, that I was a complete delinquent. Apart from my messy side, I strove to live by the following standards. Devote one hundred percent to everything I did, be humble, take initiative, hustle (but not immorally), listen, be teachable, apply each lesson learned and more opportunities will be provided. When someone can be responsible with little, they can be responsible for much. Do not steal, do not lie, do not snitch, hold every secret anyone shares in an internal vault, be kind to others, sow good and good will grow. The guilt of how I strayed and chose to earn money dishonestly in Vail prodded sharply within, but I knew there would be no more of that.

When I reached Denver, I called a graduate of Colorado University I had befriended in Boulder following my Vail flail. She was delighted to see me and generously offered lodging for the night. I accepted, direly needing to relax and clean my body before advancing into the mountains. I had slept very little on my road trip. My only chance for rest was at a stopover at Andrew's in St. Louis, but even then, I drank beer on the porch all night instead of sleeping or showering.

The city of Denver pulsated like a playground I did not need to explore yet. I had seen plenty of it before. My focus was on Nederland. Although my kind friend provided comfortable bedding indoors, I opted to sleep on her outdoor apartment patio hoisted on the seventh floor. She found this to be eccentric, but I found it necessary and much more comfortable. I still had trouble sleeping inside, and since I was finally back in Colorado, all I wanted to do was observe the sky, breathe the air without interferences, even if it was city air, and peer upon the colossal Rocky Mountains to the west. *Tomorrow,* I knew, *tomorrow I will be up there.*

After wine, weed, tacos and sleep, tomorrow arrived. I thanked my friend for her hospitality, declined her offer to revive our little party with

CINEREAL

lunch in the city, and rolled onward toward Boulder. Even though Mit lived in Boulder and I looked forward to seeing him again, I decided that would have to wait. *Boulder will be my flatland playground, but I am going up, towards the stars, into the snow, into the aspen groves, into the eagle's nest, to the ridge tops where I belong.* Nederland is only a sixteen-mile drive at the end of Boulder Canyon Road from Mit's town below. Depending on the weather, the winding steep route can be a crawl, or even a potentially lethal hazard, but that day in the summer it was an expedited path towards paradise. Carving upwards through the canyon, adjacent to a bubbling creek which flowed from the mountains down into Boulder, my whole body shimmered with excitement. When I arrived at the crown jewel of my recent dreams, I bellowed, "Nederland, Colorado, please welcome Wing graciously, for I am here!"

It is important to understand that my experience in and around the land of Ned was twofold. I existed with dual parts to my whole, as both a positive and a negative. The positive was the enigmatic character I was, the person I gave to others and poured into everything I did. I could commune with anyone, listen to another tell their story and glean from it both entertainment and wisdom. I turned every conversation on park benches and barstools into worthy moments of being alive. The self I gave to others was uplifting, cheerful, sincere, teeming with zest. But the other side of me, the one I kept to myself, was dark, terrorized, a soul in suffering, or as some may say, one who is waging war against demons. For that war, Nederland became the battleground I needed, a community near expansive wildernesses with mountains and remote waters, a realm where I could be alone or, when I needed it, commune with a friend.

When I was a young boy, before my family fell apart and the voices of the living darkness inflicted havoc in my mind, I already carried a foundation of sadness. I never understood why, but each day my burden was the weight of feeling too much. Our family had pets, cats and dogs, but there was one cat I adored. For this anecdote, I shall call him Bond. In the New Hampshire house, which would eventually be the casing of my haunts, existed a closet beneath the stairwell. A small, dark room with no windows, only boxes and dust. My young self would take Bond, hold him in my arms in this closet, and cry heavy, weeping tears into his black and white fur. The cat was kind and loved me in return. Therefore, he tolerated my emotions. To me, Bond was the only beating heart that seemed to allow the oceanic amount of emotion I needed to expel from my body. I always cried until I had exhausted the internal well. Upon doing so, I would then open the door, let Bond scamper on his way and rejoin the family, finally empty and numb to the confused me I was.

In the state of Georgia, when I was in first grade, I got into a fight with a big bully in the second grade. We were all at recess, playing basketball on the court. The bully kept knocking my fellow first-grade comrade down, attempting to break his spirit. His attempt was working, and while my peer walked off the court about to cry, I snapped. Fearlessly, I approached the much bigger boy, towering above my medium frame. I called out the bully for his actions, demanding that he apologize or fight, and thus a rumble of fists ensued. Teachers broke up our scuffle and disciplined us both, but it was worth it, for my acquaintance, the victim of harassment and jabs, now felt safe. He had me, a new friend who would stand up for him. At the end of the school day, the fellow first grader gave me a gift, a token which to him was a prize, a vintage bullet. He pulled it out of a small box where he stored his favorite things and thanked me for what I had done. When I got home, all the strength I had paraded at school dissolved into a river of emotion. I hid away with Bond, crying out those tears that always returned. This time, I mourned with anger. I could not understand why humans could be so horrible to others. Why must people put others down? Why must we create and act with so much harm? My view of an innocent world was changing, and yet my sensitivity to it never did.

One autumn day in New Hampshire, Bond disappeared, a frequent occurrence for our free-ranging animal. After many days went by without seeing Bond, the family grew concerned. As I was raking leaves in the large backyard, I discovered him. He was torn apart, shredded, half eaten and buried by a bobcat. Bond was very much dead. It had fallen upon me to discover him in his mangled state. I did not produce a single tear for Bond, perhaps because I did not have him to cry with. Instead, I wrote a poem about his companionship, his violent death, and then read the poem in front of my school class. Each student listened with horrified expressions as I depicted the gruesome events. After reading this poetic eulogy, I sat down and tried never to think about Bond again. As a young man arriving in Nederland, Colorado, my heart still welled like the boy who mourned with his cat in the closet. Although I attempted not to exhibit this pain to the world, every day my soul suffered for reasons I seldom understood.

CINEREAL

For a few hours, the melancholy part of me was distracted. Nederland commanded my attention. My first order of action, as determined, was to find employment. So, I got a beer in every tavern and asked each barkeep if they were hiring. None claimed to be looking for an additional worker, but this allowed me to start surveying the town and land. I learned that only around 1,400 people lived in the immediate community, while many more dwelled in the surrounding forests. Small boroughs such as Ward, Rollinsville, and Eldora, contributed to the region's general population. With each cold pint of beer and each curious glance from locals, I observed and grinned back. It did not dawn on me then that the people I nodded to and smiled at would soon become friends or acquaintances. Everyone in the small town knew each other. Therefore, I surely stuck out like an alien.

I asked the bartender of the Pioneer Inn, the main saloon with an infamous history, referred to by locals as the PI, where would be a safe place to camp as I eased my way into the fabric of mountain society. He directed me towards Magnolia Road. "That's where all the travelers and hobos camp," he stated. "No one will bother you there. Well, the cops won't, but the vagrants might. Just keep your wits about you." I assured him I understood. I had experience in such situations. He added, "All the campers clear out in the fall. It gets snowy up here early." Perhaps he thought I would travel on myself. I thanked him for the information, paid for my one beer and left to search for Magnolia Road.

As I slowly rolled through Nederland in my red Subi, which I had started to call Rubi, I noticed a hitchhiker walking along the side of the main road dubbed the Peak-to-Peak Highway. I smiled at seeing him and pulled over to offer a ride. The young mountain man thanked me and said he was heading home. "I always hitchhike to and from work," he added. "Sometimes I get picked up, sometimes I don't. Either way, it's no bother, only five miles." I very much appreciated this man's mentality. We rumbled down a dirt course further west towards the Continental Divide. During our few minutes, I asked him where a decent place might be to apply for work. He thought for a moment, and then spoke two words, "Sundance Lodge."

"Alright then, I'll check out that place tomorrow, thanks, man." I pulled over to the mailbox he motioned to. He gave a grunted nod while hopping out of Rubi and then strolled down another dirt path towards a lodging not visible beyond aspen groves.

CINEREAL

As the sun lowered further west, disappearing behind the treeless mountaintops of the Indian Peaks Wilderness, casting the whole town in a brisk blue-gray shadow, I located Magnolia Road. Like most of the roads up here, other than the principal thoroughfare, it was dirt and bumpy, my favorite kind of lane. I could smell the campfires of others, recognized the tarps and tents of small encampments, discovered a quiet spot of my own, and rolled a joint. Lazing into the first night in my new town, high in the Rocky Mountains of Colorado, for a short while my soul seemed at peace. *Tomorrow I will go to the Sundance Lodge and, hopefully, secure a job.*

In the morning, I met Tilly. Tornado Tilly is what she was called, and it didn't take me long to understand why. Tilly owned the Sundance Lodge, a quaint motel and restaurant boasting a grand lofted view of the Arapaho and Roosevelt National Forests. I walked in, prompting a bell on the door to chime, and there in the restaurant by a small bar was Tilly surrounded by, who I would come to know, many of her employees. It didn't look like a work meeting, as everyone was taking shots of some clear alcohol, but indeed the gathering was one of officiality, and this is how they were conducted. Drinking, yelling, discussing and then doing. Upon asking for the manager or owner and introducing myself, Tilly raised her hand, looked me up and down, then curtly spoke, "What do you want? Wing? Is that your name? Winggg…" Her eyes sparkled with goodwill, although her tone came off a bit intense. But this was of no matter. I could handle it.

"Yes, that is me, and I would like a job, Tilly. Any job. I just arrived in town yesterday and would like to work as soon as possible." I held my ground amidst the stares of seven pairs of glossy eyes.

Tilly stood up, rising to her menacing height of five feet, bore her eyes up into mine and then asked me one direct question. "Wing, are you going to the Phish concert?" She referred to the popular jam band, a band I had never cared for much although many humans were quite obsessed with them.

"I am more of a Bob Dylan, John Prine, and even A$AP Rocky guy myself, so no, I will not be going to the Phish concert." I didn't even know Phish was playing nearby soon.

Tilly smiled upon hearing this and responded, "Well, that is an excellent start, Wing, because all of my employees seem to be quitting on me for the show!" She looked around at her crew with a playful glare. "No, no, they aren't quitting, but I do need someone to wash dishes so that others can go have their fun. Can you wash dishes, Wing?"

"Absolutely, Tilly, I can be the best damn dishwasher you've ever had. When do you want me to start?" Eagerness grew within me, for here I was, getting a job just like that. In my head, I snapped my fingers.

"Ha! Best damn dishwasher I ever had will not be difficult, Wing, a bunch of stoners and drunks around these parts. Do you smoke pot and drink the poison, Mister Wing?" Tilly was already pouring another round of the clear liquid into her employees' shot glasses. She grabbed another one and set it in front of me.

"I sure do, Tilly, but I don't let my vices get in the way of my responsibilities." I smiled at the others and lifted my now-full shot glass up for a group cheer.

"Well, here," Tilly stated proudly as she held her liquid in the air, "here we do both. Work and play, both just as hard. Welcome to the team, Wing. You start tomorrow at seven in the morning sharp. I will need you to work a double on your first day. Minimum wage plus some cash tips."

I clinked my shot glass with the others. "Seven sharp, I will be here. A double shift does not scare me!" We each tipped our liquor back into our throats, breathed deeply after our swallow allowing the schnapps to tingle pleasantly, then everyone scurried off to their places and duties within the restaurant.

I officially had a job, and it was only my first morning in Nederland. My primary objective was complete. Thus, I had an entire day to explore the town and its grounds before reporting for duty. I parked Rubi the Subi in a central parking lot, manually locked the doors and set out to explore. An old train car converted into a cafe caught my eye, so I purchased a coffee and bagel and sat outside observing the locals. A few guys with long hair and tattered western hats sat by me. We nodded to each other and dipped our chins into the steam rising from our cups. A carousel, the vintage kind with ornate horses painted colorfully, sat still and patient nearby. I asked the guys next to me if it still worked. It does, they assured, and many a tourist keeps that thing in business. I nodded and sipped. After eating my bagel, I strolled down to the water, passing a small hotel and the post office.

Barker Reservoir sits on the eastern side of town. I noticed a trail along the shoreline and followed it, observing the contour of the land. At the far end, the closest edge facing Boulder Canyon, a large dam harnessed the reservoir, creating a lake effect. Here the water trickled through, sourcing Middle Boulder Creek, the creek I had driven along on my way up to Nederland. I hiked back around and made my way into town again, ambling by the Pioneer Inn where I had drunk my first local beer the evening before, continuing past a few artsy shops, a co-op, some small restaurants such as a barbecue and a Deli. There was a gas station, a few more taverns, and a large old mining machine sitting rusty and unused. A modest mining museum sat next to the retired metal apparatus. There was one small church and what appeared to be a marijuana dispensary. I had never seen a legal marijuana store before. A neon green cross hanging in the tinted window delighted me. However, spotting the church shot a pang of guilt into my soul. I knew I should go to church, but I brushed the conviction out of my mind. Proceeding, I crossed a classic covered wooden bridge decorated with local art. A creek that flowed from the mountains down into Barker Reservoir gurgled underneath. Lush verdant willows rose on either side of the creek. Porches attached to small homes reaching to these willows dotted the landscape. Onward through a patchwork of dirt roads separating blocks of cottages and A-frame abodes, including log cabins and funky shacks, filling the layout of small neighborhoods. Subarus, Toyota trucks and Volkswagen vans appeared to be the vehicles of choice by those who lived here. *This is real-life, not the opulent, shallow, boastful world of Vail,* I thought, pleased to be in a land of humble living. Many multicolored-clothed individuals with long hair and dogs walked about. Most dogs were not on leashes yet roamed both considerately and playfully. Some dogs looked like wolves, giants among the normal canines. Small flocks of children roamed near their mothers, like little wildings buzzing around their personal queens. Everyone who beheld me waved or nodded, accepting my presence. No one ignored each other, with everyone interacting genially and welcoming.

    As I continued exploring, I perceived the scent of marijuana everywhere. People smoked openly. No one was hiding the natural herb or fearful of consequences. In one such hello outside of the local grocery store, I was offered a hit from some old-timer's joint. He asserted that it was homegrown. I happily accepted and giggled, sensing my eyes turn a tad hazy. "This surely is some fine flower," I assured him, then strolled on with a fresh hop in my step. Up and around the edge of town, I reached another trail. I followed this path into craggy rocks and lodgepole pines, which dominated the forest. The trail led me atop a hill, providing a generous vista facing the expansive mountains to the west. Plump clouds settled leisurely above the peaks. I reached out my hand and tried to pet the wooly billows, laughing at my behavior. The trail continued around the back of the Sundance Lodge, where I had scored employment that morning, and onward all the way towards the unofficial campgrounds around Magnolia Road. Now here without Rubi, I trekked through the forest, noting the many encampments of travelers. A few guys and girls, many with their hair formed into long dreads, invited me to join them by a small fire. This invite I accepted. We smoked a joint and talked about where we had come from and maybe where we would go. They were leaving once the snow arrived. I told them I planned to stay.

My stomach started to grumble. Hunger was stirring. So, I hiked the main road, returning towards the center of town. I had little money left to spend until receiving my first paycheck; therefore, I explored the co-op and purchased some frugal items that must carry me over. Bread, meat, cheese and fruit would need to last me a few days. I made a simple sandwich and ate an apple by the creek. A sprawling aspen grove and community park provided me with the environment for an afternoon of leisure. Some people played on the grass with their dogs. Others sat in a meditative position. A few humans practiced yoga, while one man painted a canvas propped on an easel. Everything about Nederland felt and looked idyllic. I had spotted a bookstore earlier, so after concluding my park relaxation, I went to investigate. Inside the bookstore, I perused the shelves, opened some pages, and read some poetry in a big rocking chair by a woodstove that was currently dormant. It was August after all, but summertime in Ned remained mild, a pleasant seventy-something degrees.

My exploration continued into the evening. I discovered a nook outside to sit and watch the sun lower towards the Arapaho Peaks. High in the hills further above my perch, I could see houses with large windows reflecting the sun's golden rays. Here, I pulled out my leather-bound journal filled with poems and drawings. I added to this, scribbling some thoughts and sketches on paper. The surrounding town began to bustle with an awakening energy. I listened to the whoops and hollers of jovial souls dancing between bars. Drinks were being clinked, joints were being smoked, billiard games were being played, and fiddles were singing. *Soon I will join them,* I gratefully acknowledged, *but not yet. I must rest and work, save money and find a place to live.*

CINEREAL

The forest will be a perfect home for now, but perhaps soon I might find a room in one of the cabins.

~~~

I arrived at my new job fifteen minutes before seven the following morning. A heavy-eyed server sauntered up to the backdoor where I smoked and waited. She forced a cheerful smirk onto her face. "You must be Wing," she mumbled, not yet fully awake, her hand shaking a bit as she unlocked the door. I had not seen her among the crew of morning drinkers the day before.

"I am." I acknowledged.

"What'd you do, sleep out back? You sure are early." She opened the kitchen door, letting us both in.

"Hah, no, I slept up the hill by Magnolia. Early is on time, I was always told." My hand was not shaking, but I recognized that as a sign of perhaps over-drinking for too long. She looked older than I imagined her age to be. *I hope that never happens to me*, I thought.

She started the coffee machine and responded a few minutes later. "Yes, Magnolia is where many of us began here, ten years ago for me. You plan on sticking around for a while?" Her words stabilized into a daytime caliber.

I glanced around the kitchen, poking my head into different doors to gain a grasp of the layout. "Yes, that is my goal. I moved here from New England, and I have no plans of going back."

"Alright, Wing, welcome to Nederland. If you have questions, don't hesitate to ask. My name is Molly, and since it is Saturday, we have Bloody Mary races at eight. Can you drink? If so, want to be my partner for this one?" Molly poured a cup of coffee and turned her smirk into a smile.

"I do drink. Bloody Mary races, eh? I'll be your partner. Count me in!"

"I love it, partner," Molly winked. "The others will be in soon. They should have already been here by now, but some days it starts a little slow." Molly disappeared into the front of the restaurant, leaving me to my back-of-house exploration.

Within thirty minutes, the mellow morning roared into escalating clangs and sizzles. The breakfast shift had begun. The two cooks, Berengar and Jarl, danced the line in full symbiotic swing. Jarl reached over and turned the radio music up. I busied about following orders, grabbing ingredients from the refrigerated walk-in and washing dishes as they arrived. At eight, all the servers, Tornado Tilly, the cooks and some other guy I'd seen the previous day gathered around pint glasses full of Bloody Marys with two straws in each. Molly reminded me I was on her team, pointing to my straw, and habitually everyone counted down from three then sucked as hard as they could. Molly and I tied for first, igniting the sound of straws inhaling moist air from the emptied glass containers.

"Ah," everyone exclaimed, each of us experiencing the sensation of spicy tomato juice and vodka rushing to our brains, bloodstream and bellies. Then, just as quickly as the Bloody Mary races took place, everyone returned to their duties.

Once the busy day began, time seemed to fly by. Sundance Lodge was apparently a very popular breakfast joint. As soon as one table left, a server wiped it clean, placed fresh settings and more people filled its seats. There was a gentle lull before lunch, during which I smoked marijuana and tobacco with my new co-workers out back. Jarl joked loudly and often, his big belly jiggled, and his face shone bright red from his jolly nature and the kitchen's heat. I liked Jarl immediately. He exuded the air of a philosopher. We jived during talks about literature, art, and anthropology. Jarl flicked out his smoke and jumped back indoors as someone bellowed a new food ticket was up. His long hair and long beard moved in the air as he retreated from our small smoking circle.

Berengar, the other cook, was quieter than Jarl, but held a composed strength about him. He reminded me of a German American alpine version of a samurai warrior. Berengar, like Jarl, also had long hair and a beard. His long blonde locks tied up in a bun next to Jarl's wild reds. And then there was me, my brown hair and beard slowly growing into the Nederland dress code. I regretted cutting my hair earlier that spring, *for if they had seen the way I looked in Vail, I surely would have fit in here and now! Alas, my hair shall equal theirs soon.* The three of us young men ran the kitchen as a well-oiled machine through lunch and into the early afternoon. Around three-thirty, Tilly told us we could wrap it up for the day. They were rarely open for the dinner shift, only on special occasions, I was told. Apparently, a double shift here meant only breakfast and lunch, and for someone like me, who had frequently worked in multiple restaurants and bars late into the night, the long day at Sundance Lodge was not bad at all. *Kind of like Misery Hill, it ain't that miserable.*

"Sign me up for all the double shifts!" I told Tilly, tossing my soiled apron into the hamper. She smiled and asked me what I wanted to drink.

CINEREAL

Everyone who worked the day now lounged in the small bar, the same spot where I drank schnapps with them the day before.

"A whiskey for me, please."

"And...?" Tilly added.

"And well, a pint of IPA if it's free." Disclosing I was out of funds until my first paycheck, requiring me to be cognizant of how much money I poured down my throat.

Following our shift drinks, Tilly pulled me aside and handed me 129 dollars in cash. "Great work today, Wing, keep that up. Here are your portions of the tips today. Twenty-nine dollars and the extra hundred is to hold you over until your first paycheck." She promised me a shift meal each workday and as many workdays as I desired. I was humbled and beholden for her kindness. It quickly became clear that although Tilly may be a tornado, she was a generous and thoughtful matriarch to her Sundance family.

After work, sticky, dirty, tipsy, stoned and a little tired, I retreated to my camp in the forest where I settled in a bit more. I arranged my tent and tarps in a more homely fashion, constructed a safe firepit, then leaned back satisfied in my orderly woodland home. I did not know how long I would live in the woods, but my plan was to save a few paychecks and then search for a room to rent. *Perhaps after a month of this, I will have a cabin roof over my head,* I reasonably hoped.

~~~

The next day at work, Berengar, the kind blonde cook, approached me with a surprising offer. "Wing!" He hollered, walking up with familiarity.

"Berengar! Good morning, how're you today?" It felt good to have this welcome, to hear my name from a Nederland local.

"I am great, man. Another day in paradise. I have an offer for you." He stood straight and tall, smiling almost as wide as his hair was long. "At home last night, I discussed an idea with my housemates, and, well, we have a room available. I am officially offering you the bedroom. You can move in tonight after work if you want."

I couldn't believe what I was hearing. *Already being offered a place to live!?* "Wow man, that is so very generous! I'd love to take you up on that, but I don't have any money saved for rent yet." I held the brim of my cap on my head as a gust of mountain wind threatened to send it flying.

CINEREAL

Berengar responded as if he knew what I was going to say. "Not a problem, I already discussed that with them as well. We have already paid the rent for this month, so don't worry about that. You can pay your portion next month. You'll have money soon. There's no need to stress about finances. Really, we'd just love to have you there. It's a four-bedroom cabin about seven miles from Ned, uphill near Rollinsville. We grow ganja, have about 100 plants, can teach you everything and be grateful for your help. It is a beautiful, rugged place, man. Three of us live there now. Myself, my buddy Mike about our age who moved with me here from California, and an old guy named Sam. He is quite a character, you'll see. You will have your own room all to yourself."

Enthusiasm developed within. *Berengar is serious. This is real. A new home, a family, a new life in Nederland is coming together easier than I imagined, and they grow marijuana!* "Yes, let's do it. I am honored, Berengar, thank you. Really, truly, thank you." We shook hands, moved with a lighthearted skip on our way to the kitchen, and worked energetically through breakfast and lunch.

Once the workday was complete, I drove Berengar to my camp on Magnolia Road and packed up my temporary abode. We purchased a few groceries at the market, plus a beer and a slice of pizza each at a cool little bar called Backcountry Pizza, where I met many wonderful mountain folks. As the sun set behind the mountains and darkness crawled into the high elevation land, Berengar directed me as I drove us both up dirt roads I had never travelled. We turned onto our lane and rolled along, rising higher with each tire rotation. Wonder and gratefulness filled my heart. Steep slopes and conifers rose on either side of us, limiting the night sky and causing stars to shine in a speckled corridor. When we reached a rustic log cabin with a single light on a small porch, Berengar showed me where to park.

My new brother beamed with the same excitement I also felt. I held back thankful tears threatening to escape my eyes. Berengar placed his hand on my shoulder and spoke with sincerity. "Welcome home, Wing. Welcome to Gamble Gulch."

Gamble Gulch

As history would have it, Gamble Gulch was a premier location for gold discovery in the local region of the Rocky Mountains in 1859. Gamble was one miner who struck it rich out of the creek that flows through the gulch. He built and resided in the very structure I was walking into. The cabin sat close to the dirt road but higher up, for everything was higher than the rough road parallel to the creek. From the front, it looked like a spacious abode, albeit sunken into the earth a bit, like the shoulders of an aged, exhausted man. It comprised two levels, with the rear second story appearing to be a ground-level floor due to how steeply the land ascended. Cement steps led to a small porch. There was no chair on the porch, but I would fix that. The scent of marijuana emanated from the bright slivers surrounding the wooden front entrance. Large windows showed a large room, and with a whoosh the door flung open and light cast upon Berengar and me.

A cheery face of a ninja-looking guy held the door ajar. He had long black hair with a bandana wrapped around his head and paired with his lanky build, resembled an emo band guitarist.

"Hey Wing, welcome! I am Mike!" His upbeat voice deserved exclamation marks after everything he spoke.

"Hey Mike, I am Wing." I reached out my hand to shake his, but he wrapped me up in a hug instead.

"We hug here, brother, welcome home!" Mike moved to the side to let me walk through the door upon Berengar's chuckling encouragement. Although I usually preferred handshakes over hugs, I instantly liked Mike and his positive demeanor.

To the right of the door was a desk by a window, and sitting at the desk in a well-used office chair on wheels was a stout man with a gray beard, portly belly, and a smile beaming even larger than Mike's, if that was possible. Upon the desk were large jars full of marijuana, and loose on the desk was a cluster of the herbaceous flower. The man's fingers were rolling a joint, fingers which stuck to my hand as we firmly shook.

CINEREAL

"Hey mon" (for mon is how he said man, his voice always laden with a Jah Mon inflection). "Hey mon, welcome to the cabin. I am Samuel Libby, but you can call me Sam."

"It is a pleasure to meet you Sam. Thank you for having me. I promise to be a worthy addition to the home and family." I asked Sam what he was rolling, and he informed me it was Blueberry Kush, a strain recently cured and ready for smoking.

I looked around the open concept of the downstairs cabin. The large living room featured a stone slab in the corner, where a woodstove should go, yet there was no stove. Also, in this room sat a long black leather couch and a man painting on the couch. He was not sitting on the couch and painting a canvas; rather, he held his brush to the black leather and was painting the actual couch. He looked about Sam's age, donning a cartoonish grin on his face as he looked up from his work. "Hey Wing, I'm Art. I live in my van outside with my parrot, but we are patching up and insulating the side shed. I'll move in there soon."

"Ah, I see. Nice to meet you, Art. What is your parrot's name?" I walked around to observe the spectacular space galaxy he was painting on the out of commission seating area.

"Colors." Art spoke, holding his gaze to his palette of paints and dipping his brush. "The parrot's name is Colors."

I nodded at this, muttering in my mind, *that tracks*.

A gray tabby cat slithered through our legs in the crowded room. "That's Dao," Berengar spoke. "He comes and goes as he pleases." I leaned down to pet the feline, thought of Bond, and continued my eyeful exploration.

"So, Wing," Sam stood up slowly, slightly struggling to get out of his marijuana desk throne. When he was upright, he stood shorter than the rest of us, yet his presence seemed larger than his mass. "Wing, is that your real name? What's the story there?"

"Oh man, Sam," I chuckled, "we are going to go there right from the start, eh? Well, it is a heck of a story. People always ask, and I often just tell them that my dad was a pilot, and my mother was a hippie. Thus, they decided on Wing. However, that isn't quite accurate. Dad was and still is a pilot. My mother was never a hippie, and though they did not name me Wing, neither did I name myself. I was dubbed Wing when I was twenty-two, and it stuck. This is one of those, the truth is stranger than fiction scenarios. I say that usually because the truth only leads to more questions, and it becomes a whole thing. But, since we are to be a family here, you all deserve to hear the story."

Berengar chimed in, "Wing, well, Hot Wing, right?" My new brother turned to the others, announcing his knowledge. "He earned his trail-name on the Appalachian Trail and then continued on as Hot Wing on the Pacific Crest Trail."

"Yes, this is true," I verified. "However, I was Wing before the hikes, but I didn't want the other hikers to know that is what I was called back home, to see what trail name I would earn. Like I said, the way 'Wing' came to be is ridiculous but so has been most of my life."

Sam shuffled into the kitchen to fill his glass with water. "Wing, we are going to need to hear this ridiculous story. While you get settled in, I'll roll some more joints, and then we'll have a safety meeting. You can explain the history of your dubbing."

"Sounds good to me, Sam." I lifted my modest bag of belongings.

"Come on, Wing, I'll give you the house tour and show you your room." Berengar led the way.

First, he showed me the basement full of marijuana plants. It looked like a bit of a build-as-you-go operation. The basement's main room was being used for plants in the vegetation stage, with an additional annex room for plants in the flowering stage. Hanging lights, buckets, ventilation tubes, fans, plant food and extra soil were hoisted and crammed wherever they could fit. All the things needed to cultivate cannabis from start to finish were packed into the constricted area. Although I had never been inside a marijuana grow room before, I could sense they were doing the best with the accommodations they had available. Berengar remarked on this, admitting it could be better with more space and higher quality ventilation. He added, "We aren't even supposed to be growing here. The landlord does not like it. She keeps threatening to kick us out, but we keep trying to hide and deny that we even have plants down here." We chuckled together.

Along with the main grow rooms, there was also a large cabinet in the living room with another grow light inside. Here they stored smaller plants, adolescent clones from mothers and babies sprouted from seed. Besides the main living area, the kitchen, plus the four bedrooms and two bathrooms, marijuana production occupied all the usable square footage in the old miner's cabin.

CINEREAL

"If the landlord is always on y'all's ass about this, and it isn't ideal anyway, perhaps we can find a more suitable grow location nearby?" I suggested to Berengar. To this he nodded and admitted that money was the major factor in an upgrade. "Well, that is something we will figure out." I encouraged him. "I am here to help in every aspect. Teach me all that goes into it. I can provide muscle, my car, adding to your and Mike's shared vehicle, and I plan to obtain another job on top of the Sundance. Therefore, more money will flow in soon. Put me to work, brother!" We smiled, sensing the potential in our new combined efforts.

Upstairs, my new bedroom was simple but perfect. The small room held a futon bed and a closet full of items I was told belonged to Bee and Chops, other members of the mountain family who were away on artistic endeavors. Bee had a dog named Basil, and when they returned, I would still have this room as my own. I lay down on the bed and peered at two large windows overlooking the steeply ascending forest. As it was dark outside, all I could see was my reflection, but I could hear the wind howling through the lodgepole pines and the shifting of branches scraping upon the cabin's exterior. A surge of happiness washed over me. *I finally have a home, my own room, in a cabin up in the mountains, with kind folk who have welcomed me with open arms.* Feeling blessed and relieved for having arrived in the environment I desired to be in, I whispered to the window, "I can now build the life I crave."

Downstairs, a gruff but loving voice bellowed my name. "Hot Wing!" Sam called. "Safety meeting story time, mon!"

A safety meeting is a code phrase used by marijuana smokers for a smoke session. Downstairs everyone gathered and sat, except on the wet paint of the galaxy couch. Sam, whom I had already begun respectfully referring to in my mind as Ol' Man Sam, held three freshly rolled joints in his hand. Everyone looked at me with anticipation, hungry for the Wing origin story. I grabbed a beer from the six-pack I had purchased in town, smoothly popped the cap off the glass bottle with my teeth causing all family members to wince and cheer, and stood before them as if on a stage ready to deliver the information they craved.

"All right, gang. As Berengar correctly informed us, yes, I earned the trail-name Hot Wing on the Appalachian Trail. In Hiawassee, Georgia, I dominated a hot wing eating competition to the pounding fists on tables of

CINEREAL

enthusiastic hikers chanting 'hot wing hot wing hot wing,' but that is not where 'Wing' originated."

Ol' Man Sam lit a joint, dragged and passed it to Mike on his left. Then he lit another, inhaled and passed it to Berengar on his right. He then lit the third joint and handed it to me. I took a long drag, inhaling the goodness, coughed slightly, sensed a gentle glaze set into my eyes, and passed it onward to Art. As I talked, the three joints circled around the small room, filling the cabin with a luscious, silky, skunky, blueberry aroma.

"Wing began in May 2008, when I was twenty-two years of age. Shortly after I had returned from Hawaii but before Charleston, South Carolina, and the Grand Canyon." I paused and looked at them, knowing they were not ready, despite thinking they were ready, for me to drop this ridiculous bomb of fact. I chuckled and let it fly. "I did not name myself. It was Snoop Dogg who dubbed me Wing."

"What?!" Mike nearly spit the joint he held in his mouth across the room. "Snoop Dogg!? Like the one and only D-O-double G?"

"Yes, the very one." I affirmed, ready for the usual carousel of bewilderment, disbelief and questions that follow. I held up my hand as mouths started to form inquisitive words and assured, "I shall now explain how this came to be in detail."

Art shook his head in disbelief. Ol' Man Sam sat up straight. Berengar grinned like he had brought home the perfect missing piece of the family.

"Now, to understand this thoroughly, we must go back to the origins of my government name. It is important to know that ever since my family split up, and that is a story for another time, ever since I was fifteen and throughout all my teenage years to follow, I hated my given name. It was not me. Then when I was eighteen, I committed some horrible atrocities, which I paid society back for, felony things. David things. My mother named me David Kelly Williams after King David in the Bible. A man after God's own heart. But since I no longer felt that was me, my friends always called me DKDubs, or Dubs, and such, not David. To elaborate, I did not deserve the birth name unless things changed, but that does not matter for now…" My voice trailed upon this thought.

Ol' Man Sam interjected, "King David to Wing David, eh. As a Jewish man, I always loved the wild but God-loving heart of King David."

CINEREAL

I acknowledged, "Yes, I agree, Sam. But in my case, drop the David. And yeah, man, we will have to talk Bible stuff soon. We'll talk about everything in time."

Ol' Man Sam smiled and responded, "Sounds good, mon. Alright, let's hear how this Snoop Dogg situation went down."

I continued. "To sum it up as concisely as I can, it was a right time, right place, yet seizing hold of opportunity type of scenario. Which, fairly, I believe I am and strive to always be adept at doing." I smoked again on the third joint, each of the three smoke-sticks arriving one after the other. I was higher than the trees at this point. Everyone chuckled, feeling much like I did. After a throat-clearing rumble, I proceeded. "In the small town of Durham, New Hampshire, deep in a spring night's laze, Snoop Dogg was to perform a show at the University. I currently worked the front desk of the only local hotel, where Snoop and his entourage would be staying. They had booked the entire third floor, which was the top floor, and Snoop had requested the hotel provide him with an old-school boombox and an Xbox in his suite. Why he wasn't supplying his own, I don't know. Those were his only two requests. The hotel secured him an Xbox, but they didn't have a boombox, and the general manager said he would not bother with that. Well, at my lodging in Dad's space, I had my old-school big clunky boombox, fit for both CDs and cassettes, and so on the day of Snoop's arrival I placed it in my vehicle and brought it to the hotel with me. Snoop and his crew were to arrive late, around midnight, a shift only the night auditor worked. I knew this employee. She was lazy, always doing the minimum, and if I wanted to meet Snoop, I knew I would need to be present. Thus, I offered to work my normal three-to-eleven shift and then continue until after the Snoop party arrived and checked in. To this, the manager and the night auditor agreed." I paused, taking a long swig of my crisp Colorado beer.

Mike spoke up as he finished the end of a joint and discarded the short filter into an empty bottle. "You were taking initiative here, eh?"

"I was, yes, I was determined to lend Snoop Dogg my boombox, but I wasn't going to just leave it in the room, as the boombox might be my ticket to meeting him. Alright, so late that night, around one in the morning, two long black window-tinted tour buses arrived. I manned the front desk hoping Snoop would walk through the lobby; however, he did not. His manager and entire entourage of nine big guys all entered the lobby, filling it wall to wall, but Snoop was escorted to his room through a back door and up the elevator, incognito. Upon checking in, Snoop Dogg's manager and the big men announced Snoop was starving, they all were starving and inquired where they could get food in the small town. The problem was that there was nowhere open. I mean, come on. It is little Durham, New Hampshire! Aside from the gas station across the street, nothing stayed open late. One bar called Libby's (I nodded to Sam, recognizing his last name) was open until one, but that was now closed, and so no, there were no options. The nine big men were not happy about it."

Dao the cat gingerly walked across the wooden floor and jumped onto Berengar's lap. Mike and Art leaned forward on elbows and the edge of their seats. Ol' Man Sam sat back deep into the couch, forgetting it had just been painted. Their faces urged me to continue.

"I realized I had to figure something out quickly. The men all glared at me as if it was up to me to somehow miraculously conjure the feast they desired. So, to assume control of the chaos and create possible momentum, I asked the manager what kind of food they wanted. The manager looked at me directly, leaning on his palms upon the hotel countertop and without skipping a beat he stated, 'Snoop wants wings. Hot wings.' He looked over his shoulder to the rest of the guys, lifting the question 'hot wings?' All the men agreed with grunts and nods. I struggled to think clearly under the escalating pressure for hot wings. There I stood in a small town, alone behind a hotel desk, now after one in the morning, with everything long closed, and yet I must do something. Breakfast was almost closer to being opened than the local wing shop had been shut for the night. That is when it hit me. The Wing Spot! My eyes lit up. The manager observed this beat of hope. I alerted Snoop's manager. 'Hold on, man, I have an idea.' I pulled out my cellphone, for the owner of The Wing Spot was a guy who regularly bought marijuana from me, and I called him. I winked at the men as the phone rang. The rings went to voicemail, no answer. Dang it, but of course, it is late. He is surely asleep. However, I called again, and again, and again. All of Snoop's men waited anxiously with bated breath. All eyes were on me. Although the owner did not answer his phone after five calls, I persisted repeatedly until finally, on the tenth call, he answered."

"Oh, sheeiit!" Berengar projected a drawled exclamation.

I smiled at him while diving deeper into the story. "So, The Wing Spot guy Matt finally answers with the words 'What the hell, Dubs, this better be an emergency.' And with all eighteen eyes on me, I launched into an epic motivational speech. I said, 'Matt, yes, this is an emergency. Snoop Dogg is in town for his show tomorrow. I am here with his manager and entourage, and they all want hot wings.' Matt tried to interject and shut down my plea, but I did not let him. 'This is a call to greatness, Matt. Who cares if the shop is closed or this is not normal protocol? So, what if this is unusual or you are tired? This is an opportunity to rise to greatness and satisfy not just Snoop and crew but also the whole town! How do you think Snoop Dogg will perform tomorrow if he is unhappy and left hungry? The town will not receive a top-quality show. But how do you think Snoop will perform tomorrow if we come together to make his hot wing dreams come true!? With gratitude, showmanship and passion most certainly! Now, Matt, get out of bed, go fire those vats of oil, pull out all the wings you have and call me when you are ready. No, I will call you back in thirty minutes with the full order, and you be ready! You got this, Matt? You got this? Will you rise and be great, or roll over and be lame?' With a chuckle in his voice, realizing he could not say no to this opportunity, Matt agreed. I hung up the phone and announced to Snoop's men, 'We are in business, boys!' Everyone cheered. My motivational speech impressed everyone. I pulled out a piece of paper and began writing the massive multi-part hot wing order. By the time it was complete, there were 204 wings, with multiple kinds of sauces, some tossed, some naked with sauces on the side. The last person who added to the order was Snoop Dogg. He wanted hot buffalo wings tossed in the sauce with blue cheese on the side, carrots and celery too, of course. This order came to the manager's phone from Snoop himself, and as I wrote it down, I mentioned that is exactly how I order my wings as well. 'Add yours to the list.' The manager spoke and nodded to me. So, I added my Snoop order replica to the long list, bringing the complete total of wings to 216. Everyone was about to have an early-morning feast." I paused for a moment to catch my breath.

"This is outrageous." Ol' Man Sam spoke with a shake of his head. I nodded in agreement.

"Once the order was compiled, everyone checked into their rooms upstairs. I called Matt, placed the order, ignored his whining about the amount of wings, reminded him why he was doing this, told him he would probably be tipped well in cash, and then sat back and waited. When the food arrived, the manager came down with another guy to purchase and carry the many bags full of to-go containers back up to the rooms. Matt gave me a bewildered look. I witnessed the manager tip him generously in cash, so I gave Matt a thumbs up. We could talk more about this on another day. The deed was complete. The manager handed me my container of buffalo hot wings and told me the words I hoped to hear. 'I'll call down to you after we eat. I told Snoop about your speech, and he wants to meet you. He instructed to bring the boombox with you as well.' As you can imagine, I was teeming with excitement, subtly though, I didn't want to display it."

Mike chimed in excitedly from his seat. "Dude, you are about to meet Snoop Dogg! Were you nervous?"

"Exactly, no, not nervous, but certainly eager. So, I went outside, retrieved the boombox, ate my hot wings and waited. But I didn't have to wait long. When the front desk telephone rang, I picked it up. Snoop's manager said he would meet me by the elevator and escort me to the room, 'bring the boombox.' I gathered my nerves and the bulky music player and walked down the hall. At the elevator, the manager grinned, placed his hand on my shoulder and asked if I was ready. 'Sure am,' I replied, grinning in return. When we reached the third floor, the entire hallway smelled of marijuana smoke. I could see it spilling out of the suite at the end of the hall. That was Snoop's room and where most of the guys were currently gathered. At the door, the manager knocked, and I heard Snoop's voice tell us to enter. The door opened, and just like that, right there in the lanky flesh was the rap mogul and smiling man just as I had seen him on TV, in his music videos, and every media outlet of my youth. He was sitting on a couch playing Madden Football on the Xbox and held a fat blunt in his hand. As I entered, Snoop stood up to greet me. The first words out of his mouth were, 'Oh shit, it's the wingman.' He looked at the boombox, thanked me for bringing it by, motioned to the manager to set it up in the corner and patted the couch seat next to him, encouraging me to sit down, so I did. Snoop asked if I smoked and offered me the blunt, to which I said yes and received it from him, then pulled a nice long drag off the fire stick. The whole time we chatted, Snoop just kept calling me 'Wing.' He asked whether I had tickets to his show. I said my budget was tight these days, so no. He asked whether I had a girlfriend. I said I did. Then he turned to the manager and commanded, 'Make sure Wing and his girlfriend have tickets for my show tomorrow night.' Then he turned back and informed me, 'Two tickets will be waiting for you at the entrance under the name Wing.' The entire room was full of the guys finishing their meal, smoking blunts and chatting. Music was quickly turned on my boombox, and Snoop and I smoked our blunt and chatted for a while. When the time seemed right, I stood up, told Snoop I must be on my way but that I would see him the next night. Snoop stood up with me, gave me a big hug, thanked me for making the hot wing feast happen, and invited me to come by again after the show. He promised his manager would let me in for the after-party. As I left Snoop again said, 'thank you Wing!' After that I clocked out and rushed home to tell my girlfriend Suzana about the night and our new plans."

"So, you went to his concert, right?" Berengar spoke as Dao the cat jumped off his lap.

"We did yes. Just as Snoop had promised, there were two tickets waiting for us under the name Wing. The show was fantastically vivacious. Afterward, we went back to the hotel for the party. By this point everyone on campus had learned where he was staying, so the hotel parking lot became crowded, the masses wanting to meet or see him. But the security was tight, and they were only letting a few people, mostly pretty ladies, into the after party. When Suzana and I walked up, the manager hollered, 'Wing, come through here!' Everyone gathered around heard this invite and saw us quickly escorted inside. Suzana and I hung out for a while. She met Snoop, I smoked and drank a bit, and when it was time, we left and went home, feeling overwhelmed and exhausted. But the next day, word of Wing had spread like wildfire around campus, as the guy who lent Snoop Dogg a boombox and become Snoop's VIP. From then on, most everyone just kept calling me Wing." I gave a little bow to indicate the story was complete. Art let out a whoop as the cabin living room erupted in exclamations.

"That is freaking legendary." Mike spoke with astonishment. We all laughed in agreement about how truly ridiculous it all was.

Ol' Man Sam, now easing into standing position, asked, "So do you think Snoop would remember you if he saw you again?"

I paused, considered, and replied, "Maybe. He meets so many people all over the world, you know, so I'm not sure my face would stick out. But I bet he would remember the scenario. Small-town New Hampshire, hot wings, the guy who made it happen, the boombox. Those details I think he would remember. I doubt he knows it was he who dubbed me Wing, for he was probably just calling me that as an association nickname. He probably doesn't know that it caught on, and that I grew into the name. Someday perhaps I will tell him and thank him."

CINEREAL

"That is one wild story, Wing, and the fact you turned around and earned the trail-name Hot Wing a few years after Snoop only solidified it." Berengar remarked, which I heartily agreed with.

"All right, new mountain fam," I spoke, my voice tiring from the long monologues, "I'm about ready for sleep. Berengar, we have work in," I checked the time. "Dang, in only five hours!"

"Yeah, we better turn in," Berengar agreed. "Your first night in the Gamble Gulch cabin, Wing!"

"I know, thank you, from the fullness of my heart, thank you, guys. This is the dawn of a new chapter." Mike and Berengar retreated to their rooms for the night, Art went out to his van and parrot, and Ol' Man Sam sat back down at his desk. I stepped outside to sit on the front porch, smoke a cigarette, and reflect upon my day. Every night, no matter where I was, I would do exactly that. I could never go from action to sleep without winding down alone, without time to process and think. I must always do this outside, no matter the weather. On the cabin porch my first night in the gulch, I allowed my eyes to adjust to the dark and observed all I could see from my new sitting spot. The creek below, just beyond the dirt road's edge, gurgled its timeless lullaby. The wind had relented, trees all wore the cloak of tranquility, and the mountain floor carpeting the earthen folds now softened into methodical resting breaths.

When I was ready for sleep, I opened the door and stepped into the cabin. Ol' Man Sam looked up from his desk and smiled. I asked him what he was doing, for the marijuana was now set aside and he sat hunched over his laptop.

"I am writing, mon." He responded with a tired drawl, then cleared his throat and sat up.

I sat down next to him. "Writing, eh? I am a writer as well. What are you writing about?"

"Well, Wing," the husky man looked at his laptop and then back at me and snickered. "This is a mad piece about the Morning Glory flower, and how the Aztec priests would utilize its hallucinogenic properties. A plant to connect with the beyond. I used to write for The New York Times long ago, but now I just write for my blog, and maybe another book someday." Ol' Man Sam opened his desk drawer and pulled out a copy of his book The Jah Department of Environmental Protection (D.E.P.). "Read this, mon."

"I will, Sam." I looked over the book, thumbing through the pages.

CINEREAL

"What do you write, Wing?" He asked as I read the first page of his book.

"I write poems and short stories about the places I have explored, the people I have met, things I have observed, sensed and learned. I have a blog too, but I stopped adding to that, just writing for myself in notebooks currently. In time, I will write books. I guarantee you that." I stated this last fact with fervor.

Ol' Man Sam nodded and grinned. "We have much to talk about, and like you said, we will talk about everything."

"Indeed." I stood to walk upstairs then added, "That porch out there, Sam, one of these nights, I am going to see a mountain lion from that perch."

He laughed at my wildlife optimism. "They are out there but rarely seen."

"Aye, but one thing I have learned is one finds what they seek. I'm telling you, man, one of these nights. Goodnight Sam."

"Goodnight, Wing." Ol' Man Sam turned back to his laptop. Though it was past two in the morning, it didn't appear as if he was ready to close his eyes just yet. I crawled into my sleeping bag atop my new-to-me bed and drifted into a peaceful rest, my soul both excited and humbled, deeply grateful for a mountain family and home.

~~~

Life at Gamble Gulch was busy and pleasant. I worked mornings washing dishes at the Sundance with Berengar, made friends with locals in town, becoming a regular at the taverns and saloons of Nederland, but in the gulch, we focused on tending to our mountain projects. The first step, in my eyes, was to clean up the outdoor area and construct a comfortable firepit and gathering space. Next, secure a woodstove for the indoor living room. Winter would wait for no one, so we needed the proper heat for the approaching season. Stove and wood must be the priority.

I started by cleaning up the side yard, leveled a bit of land with a shovel, fashioned a large firepit, and carved earth benches into the surrounding mountain. I also cleared brush next to this leveled outdoor gathering zone as space for stacking logs and chopping wood. Berengar, Mike and I were gifted a used chainsaw which we cleaned and sharpened, and each day we hiked up the steep slope behind the cabin to harvest dead still-standing trees. In the thick of the tilted forest, with one leg positioned higher than the other,

CINEREAL

we mapped our lines and then fell each deceased lodgepole pine one by one with the shrill sharp whine of our reconditioned saw. Up high, hundreds of feet above the cabin, 9,000 feet above sea-level, we would then dissect the fallen giants into approximately eight-foot-long logs. The timberland filled with scattered logs bucked into manageable lengths. We then used our own body power and gravity to roll and lift each one end over end, all the way down the steep slope to our small, leveled yard. We amassed many logs, stacking them taller than our height, sawing the bounty into eighteen-inch rounds, and finally chopping them into suitable pieces for the woodstove with an axe. It was a physically strenuous process we loved. There is no greater mountain man workout than ascending a mountainside, harvesting a tree, moving the dead mass from forest to home, and hacking it into pieces ready for burning. In the evening, we beamed with pride, cheered our beers, sat, smoked and acknowledged our progress of the day.

Ol' Man Sam and I embarked on a woodstove hunt in Rubi. There was a fellow he had observed who lived in a cabin down another gulch nearby with a plethora of old stoves littered about the yard. Sam did not remember which gulch or which cabin, and with no cell phone service in our part of the mountains, phone calls were not an option. Hunting with wheels and eyes was our endeavor for the afternoon. I turned down each dirt road Sam pointed to, swiftly growing familiar with the forested maze. There were many traces of gold mining through each gulch and in the hills between them, from historic ruins to modern, ambiguous home operations. No one drove these back roads unless they lived here. This was not an area for tourists. Eventually, after creeping by cabins in the beat-up red wagon, Sam exclaimed, "That's the spot!"

Sure enough, there were at least four woodstoves lying in the earth with grass grown tall around each one, as if the metal boxes were but forgotten relics. We parked and approached the cabin. A man with a shotgun met us on his porch. Once we explained our intent and where we lived, the man generously offered one. "Choose from those two over yonder," he pointed with the barrel of his gun and slurred. "The others have holes in 'em, no good anymore. Good luck gettin' it in that wagon of yours, heavy son-of-a-bitch those metal boxes." We proposed to trade the man an ounce of homegrown marijuana for the stove, but he declined, stating that he also grew his own. It seemed everyone in the highlands practiced the art of cultivation. Cannabis was so prevalent in Colorado one couldn't even use it as currency. He then admitted that our taking the old junk off his hands was helpful and agreed to a swig from my whiskey flask. After a satisfied grunt and wiping a few droplets of the brown liquor from his untamed facial hair, he disappeared into his cabin.

The kind gaffer was correct. The woodstoves were heavy. But this did not surprise us. Once we decided which of the two to bring home, and I backed up Rubi as close to the unit as possible, Sam and I managed to roll it into the back of my wagon utilizing two wooden planks as a ramp. Ol' Man Sam cussed and wiped his hands on his faded blue t-shirt after the grueling lift was complete. Rubi the Subi sank lower to the ground than I'd ever seen her sag. We rolled back to Gamble Gulch slowly, cautiously navigating each bump and pothole.

When Berengar and Mike returned from their afternoon, all four of us lifted and dragged the cumbersome box step by step up the cement stairs and into the cabin. We set it on the foundation in the living room corner and measured the dimensions for the chimney pipe. A hole in the ceiling where a smokestack had once been set already existed; therefore, our last step would be easy. To us, the woodstove's addition felt like resurrecting the old home to its former glory. However, according to Ol' Man Sam, who applied choice words to describe the landlord, she had forbidden installing a woodstove. "But that was madness!" Berengar chimed in. "How else will we survive the winter in this drafty cabin?" A reasoning we all agreed upon.

Berengar and I drove into town to the hardware store, purchased the pipes and installed them the next day. Although we blatantly ignored the landlord's rules and possibly the building codes, we made certain to install everything safely. Within a week of my arrival, the cabin brimmed with a cozy warmth, and the side yard was full of split and stacked wood for burning. We would continue harvesting dead trees from the forest, bucking logs and chopping timber deep into autumn, but for our mountain family of four, it was a good start.

Ol' Man Sam, Berengar and Mike taught me everything they knew about cultivating marijuana. Sam had grown for many decades, and though he complained about the limitations the basement provided, including our inability to stand straight up, I could practice, apply and understand how it all worked. With determination and hard work, we believed that in due time we would discover a more suitable space nearby for the operation. In the meantime, we would make the most of what we had.

CINEREAL

Along with my daily work on the indoor farm, I read manuals that were for or related to the art of growing cannabis. Ed Rosenthal's Marijuana Grower's Handbook, Teaming with Microbes and The Living Organics became three volumes I intensively studied. Since I had learned the basics of gardening from my mother, including seed to harvest cycles, the importance of soil composition, organic feeding, and the values light or its absence provides, the current agronomy involved a language I was familiar with. Rapidly my studies and application matured into thorough understanding. Despite my inner depression and silent battles, I nourished my mind with as much mountain education and active enterprise that I could, living the life I desired to live. For my first month in the mountains, as summer dwindled towards autumn, I felt nearly content.

Another priority I promptly accomplished was switching my driver's license from New Hampshire to Colorado, registering my Subaru wagon and obtaining Colorado plates. I looked and moved forward. No longer would I return to New England, for I had finally found a home. The day I received my new state ID, I celebrated in Nederland-town. From the Pioneer Inn to Backcountry Pizza, I played billiards and drank liquor, reveling in life with my new mountain comrades. In the same manner that I had secured a job in Vail at Garfinkle's, I secured a new job at Backcountry Pizza. There was no need to fill out an application, for they required a barman, and I declared I would give the job my all if they would let me work. Keith looked me up and down. I lifted my chin, and he asked if I could start the next day at four in the afternoon. To him I replied, "Absolutely." And just like that, my Nederland-world became elevated. I had successfully woven myself into the fabric of the community. One of the local's favorite watering holes, Backcountry Pizza, would become the epicenter of my life.

~~~

Backcountry Pizza is no ordinary town pizza shop, although at first glance it may appear as one. It is a small establishment, with an open kitchen, seven square-shaped tables, and a bar top with stools to seat eight people. BCP boasted a generous selection of quality beers on tap, rotating regularly. A deck next to the front door provided more room for those wanting to hang out with a cold beer in hand. It served as a normal restaurant for anyone to grab a pizza slice and beer, or a whole pie to go, but it also served as a community rowdy wind-down and smoke-up. It was not an ordinary town pizza shop, for Nederland is not an ordinary town. BCP in those days always catered to residents first and tourists second. The locals enjoyed smoking their homegrown marijuana on the deck, dancing to loud music, getting tipsy and chummy, cussing, occasionally fighting, and ultimately uniting as a raucous clan of societal misfits. Frequently, a family of tourists would approach with smiles and quickly depart disgruntled. Tourist mothers complained about the plethora of both marijuana and tobacco fumes drifting in the open door, which the mountain mamas added to. Tourist dads would cover their children's ears at the choice of conversations the residents bellowed. While local patriarchs provided their children with a homemade knife and a piece of wood to carve while he imbibed and swapped stories with his friends.

My job as the barman, was to serve pints of beer and glasses of wine, receive all the food orders, from those in person and those who called on the phone, manage crowd control, act as bouncer if anyone got out of line, and always, put on a show. I was the emcee of the daily party. We opened at eleven in the morning and closed at nine at night, or so the sign on the door suggested. Sometimes we opened late and stayed open late. Sometimes we closed it down to tourists and had ourselves a Ned-head only party. It all depended on the BCP staff and the locals, not the owner, who lived down in the flatlands of Boulder. Although the owner cared about his small pizza bar, he usually stayed at the parent restaurant below. The Boulder BCP was a well-behaved establishment, but the one up in Ned, he called the wild west. The Wild West it was indeed. "Leave us alone. We'll run it our way and make you plenty of money, boss!"

I swiftly grew familiar with all the regulars. The regulars became my friends, as did everyone in town who drank beer and ate pizza. When happy hour started at three, the mountain men and marijuana growers all poured in the door. I began pouring their pints, having learned what and usually how much each of them drank. From three o'clock on, well through the end of the happy hour at six, Backcountry Pizza erupted into a high-elevation gala, complete with buckskin suits and homemade dresses. All the resident growers brought samples of their recent ganja harvests, passing them around, first in raw, trichome-sparkling bud form, and then ground and rolled atop the bar to be ready for smoking. As I worked, I sampled all the strains. Smoke slipped out of my nose as I poured another pint of beer, accepted a pizza order and turned up the music simultaneously. Chris and Liz, Frank and Andy, Geno and Geno, Arnie and Mitul, Loopy and Sue,

CINEREAL

Jess, Sarah, Fritz, Billy, Deb, John, Jen, Nick, Theo, Shane, Neil, Margot, Risi, Stevie, Uriah, the list goes on for everyone was usually present and ready to share their joyful spirit of life with everyone who would reciprocate. Working at Backcountry Pizza was an opportunity for me to serve the community, and in return, they too served me. It was a world of love, a job of love, and ultimately, a rugged golden nook in paradise.

After a few weeks of working at both BCP and washing dishes at the Sundance Lodge, I submitted my two-week notice of retiring from dishwasher to dedicate my full employment attention to the pizza-bar. Tilly understood, informing me she had plenty of other dishwashers she could call, releasing me with no need to remain until she hired someone new. We embraced each other, drank a shot of tequila and then carried on. We would still see each other often, for the town was small, Berengar remained a full-time cook at the Sundance, and Tilly frequented BCP for the same reasons as everyone else. She had provided my first job in Nederland, opening a door which led to many more open doors, and for that I would forever be grateful.

Upon completing my short tenure at Sundance, I could commit mornings to working with Ol' Man Sam on the marijuana grow while Berengar and Mike operated at their respective jobs in Nederland. My life shifted into the later hours. After closing shop at BCP, I often imbibed in town, played billiards at the PI or visited the homes and grows of other masters of the craft. I saturated all the information and lessons available. I usually drove home a tad inebriated, often arriving when Berengar and Mike were going to sleep. Ol' Man Sam and I would then stay up late into the night talking, smoking, writing, thinking, existing and consciously being. My new dear friend rarely drank alcohol. I admired this about him, and though I always had a bottle of whiskey to pour from, and wine or beer in my hand, he never disputed my vices. All he said on the matter one especially wild night was, "Someday Wing, you might feel differently about the drink than you do now."

Ol' Man Sam and I discussed everything under and above the sun and moon. We debated God, Jesus, the Holy Spirit, the Old Testament, the New Testament, and Satan. We talked about angels and demons, faith and atheism, science and women. From nihilism, anarchy, socialism, capitalism, stoicism, love and beyond, we debated philosophy, mindsets, beliefs, Buddhism, Islam, creation, evolution, facts, myths, ideas, and living truths.

CINEREAL

We shared a fond curiosity about the ways of the world, history, nature, music, writing, and what drives man to do what he does. While Ol' Man Sam was a Jew by birth, but not so much by practice, we discussed every element of all faiths and religions. He listened and attempted to understand all my encounters with the supernatural, both the demonic and the celestial. As we communicated, we never sought to discourage or judge, only to examine. There was much we disagreed on, an aspect we enjoyed, for our conversations were a form of exploration. We were travelers seeking to uncover every hidden crevice in both the ethereal world and the tangible. "It would be of little value if we agreed on everything," Ol' Man Sam stated between coughs on a Strawberry Cough joint.

"Aye, my friend. Would be as profitable as talking to a mirror." I replied, grabbing the joint he dropped onto the floor.

On a typical evening, I walked in the door, said goodnight to Berengar and Mike, appreciated the new painting Art had hung on the wall that day, while Ol' Man Sam bellowed, "Welcome home Wing, I'm rolling up a joint. Let's pick back up where we left off."

I'd then pour myself a mug of red wine, sit beside him, and reply, "Let's see where we were... oh yes, the European wars of religion. Up to the 17th century on this I believe, correct?"

To the judging eyes of society, Ol' Man Sam was a funny bloke that many discarded as a washed-up hippie-type. I lovingly considered his appearance to resemble that of a retired Ninja Turtle. With his gray beard, sharp eyes, pullover hooded drug-rug, slow shuffling walk, hair not always in order, harmonica in pocket to play when the moment arose and a smile that could pierce hatred paired with a fist that could drop any man to his grave, he emanated authenticity. He was himself, and to me that mattered. His writings were self-described as gonzo journalism. A brutally honest portrayal of humanity that anyone too sensitive could not handle. Between our marijuana work and nightly discussions, we ambled on mountain paths, observing the way each specimen adapted to the mountain seasons, and studied the stars and moon. We were quite the pair, Ol' Man Sam and I, he with his long wooden staff and I twirling my infamous ice axe, loafing around the dramatic landscape. Each day ended the same, involving our talks and marijuana tokes, then my silent sit on the cabin porch, always watching for the elusive mountain lion.

CINEREAL

"Alright, Sam, I need to turn in. It is five in the morning. You still want a ride into town tomorrow? I leave at three-thirty." I poured myself a glass of water to wash down the night.

"Yeah mon. You be at BCP tomorrow?"

"I am. The day after that, I am off though. Berengar and I are going to climb South Arapaho Peak."

"Good, mon, good. Yeah, I'll take a ride. Can you give me a slice of pizza and a soda cup when I stop by?" He tossed playful eyes, already knowing my answer.

"Of course, Sam. Anytime, every time." I patted his shoulder lovingly and then ascended the cabin stairs to my room, cheerfully chuckling at my friend. Like clockwork, he came into BCP almost every day that I worked. Around five he would appear, and always I had a slice of cheese pizza and a soda cup ready for him free of charge. Keith, the manager, never cared. No one cared. It was for Ol' Man Sam.

~~~

Summer shed its verdant dress as autumn crawled in. Green shimmering aspens transformed into magnificent living golden earth-shawls. The once-bare Rocky Mountains now wore blankets of fresh snow. The Gamble Gulch family piled into the Rubi-mobile, and we barreled down the mountain with my hands on the wheel. Dear friends of Ol' Man Sam's were playing a show in Boulder, and he wanted to introduce me to them. Elephant Revival was the name of a Colorado bluegrass/folk band led by D. Ro and Bonny, with whom Sam shared a thorough history. He had been friends with D. Ro for many years and was instrumental in the band's formation and national tours. I was quite eager to meet the melodious bunch and listen to their music live.

As "Sing to the Mountain" bellowed from the outdoor arena, I swayed and stomped, letting the words and notes seep into my heart. Ned-heads from our uphill home speckled the Boulder crowd, each one standing out as a mountain man or woman amongst the cleaner-cut population. A haze of marijuana smoke hung in the air, illuminated by the setting sun above dancing bodies. Each soul filled with the joy live music creates. Our eyes shone with stoned euphoria as we embraced being alive. After the show, Ol' Man Sam introduced me to the tall D. Ro, sweet as honey Bonny and the rest of the band. Unanimously, we decided to assemble for a Thanksgiving Day feast up at the Gamble Gulch cabin in two months' time. With enriched

CINEREAL

gusto and toes still tapping we rumbled back up Boulder Canyon Drive, through the town of Nederland, onward upon the Peak-to-Peak Highway, until stopping for a pint of beer at the closest bar to our home, The Stage Stop Saloon in Rollinsville.

Rollinsville, the census-designated home of our gulch, can easily be missed if one were to blink their eyes while driving through. The small borough comprised one dirt road, harboring the saloon, a post office, and a modest number of small homes and businesses. It sat next to the train tracks, leading west towards and into the tunnel that runs through the Continental Divide. Near the top of our world, the large, red, old, haunted barn serving as Rollinsville's only drinking establishment became one of our favorite hangouts. It often provided live music, and many of the mountain folk who lived deep in the hills would leave their cabins to sit on barstools and commune with mountain comrades. We played billiards and discussed the upcoming Thanksgiving holiday. I promised to cook the turkey, as I had a unique way to prepare a bird I wished to demonstrate. After our bellies were full, the tabs paid and so-longs-for-now announced, we exited the saloon to be greeted by cold mountain gusts. A squall of snow whirled across the land, reminding us of the season's change. Gleefully, we completed the last mile home. Another magical Colorado day lived and concluded. That night while I observed the world from my porch sit, although a neighbor's dog had recently been killed by one, the elusive mountain lion remained unseen.

~~~

Autumn in the Colorado Rockies is the most splendid season of land I had ever witnessed in my young life. Surely, New England at such a time is celebrated for its prestigious deciduous tree colors, but at high elevation in the west exists an unequaled sensation. The sky looms with gray and blue power, crisp clean air nourishes, aspen trees amplify golden hour with angelic spines, and the sun draping its southern drift reaches out to kiss coniferous spires. The mountains submit their bold summer staunches into the slumber snow presents. From the tip of the peaks dripping down into the gurgle of gulches and valleys, all is laden with slower, meaningful breaths. The magic in the atmosphere is that of a vibrant natural gratitude. In every direction, one can imagine oil paintings coming alive. All animals are preparing for winter, just as a soul prepares for the first note of an orchestra's magnum opus. Multiple shades of brown, from light beige grasses bent in the wind, to the stalwart deep dark trunks of trees lifting evergreen canopies towards the heavens, sweep across the range with a gallant praise. In this sprinkle of enchantment, I celebrated my birthday and turned twenty-eight. I had not had a birthday in the West since I turned twenty-three at the end of my Grand Canyon season. Most birthdays had occurred in New Hampshire shortly after returning from my adventures. But now, finally, far away from those haunts of the East, I turned a year older in a land I loved, with a family who understood me. Basking in an ecstasy that outweighed my internal angsts, we lifted our drinks together and sang in my new year. Onward, into life, into winter, but first, with appreciation, the holiday of Thanksgiving.

On Thanksgiving Day, we divided responsibilities for the feast and party in the evening. Elephant Revival would arrive in the afternoon. Therefore, preparation started early. I cracked a beer with my breakfast as the family completed plans. Berengar and Mike would bake and cook in the kitchen, some food with standard butter and some food with our fresh batch of marijuana butter. Art would paint with his parrot, Ol' Man Sam would roll joints and encourage us on, and I would prepare and cook the turkey outdoors, in my underground oven.

I learned how to cook birds by this method on the Appalachian Trail hike. Although I had experience with chickens, geese, and ducks, this would be my first time cooking a turkey underground. Digging a deep hole in the earth was the first step, but since the earth had already frozen and been covered with snow, I lit two fires to begin. The primary fire would be my supply source. This blaze I stoked in our firepit. I placed the second on the spot where I would dig the hole, to thaw out the frozen ground. Once this heat had softened the earth, I dug a hollow deep enough for the large turkey. I prepared the turkey with stuffing, olive oil and seasonings, wrapping it with multiple layers of aluminum foil. Next, I lined the hole with rocks and transferred hot coals from the primary fire into the pit. The fire here needed a few logs to create a thick layer of fierce embers. Once the logs burned into substantial coals, I placed the foil-wrapped turkey into the hole, setting it atop the heat, then buried it with dirt. With the hollow suitably filled, now appearing as a patch of level brown earth, I built another fire on top. Down there, under this third fire was the turkey, cooking between two fires, shrouded between intensities. According to my calculations, a turkey of its size must cook for about six hours.

CINEREAL

D. Ro, Bonny and company arrived, and the party officially commenced. Many shades of green, multiple kinds of beans, casseroles, and sweets occupied the countertops. The kitchen smelled of cinnamon, fruit pies and baked bread. The woodstove roared, emanating warmth throughout the old goldminer's cabin. As the bird cooked, we played music together. Bongos and guitars filled the gulch with lively percussion. Ol' Man Sam let his harmonica sing to the trees, and each of us danced on mountain legs. Around the fires, we lifted cacophonous melodies, breaking our strums and beats only to embrace and grab another drink to imbibe. Whiskey and wine stained our tongues and bellies, preparing the way for another course, another song, another romp on the mountain's arm. When the turkey was ready, I announced, "The unearthing is upon us!" Everyone gathered around the soiled belly broil and exclaimed as I stuck the shovel deep beneath the top coals, down into the innards of the pit. With the leverage of my tool emerged the dead beast wrapped in foil. I pulled it to level ground with the help of my ice axe. D. Ro admitted from his almost seven-foot height that he had never seen such a spectacle. At this we laughed and salivated, smelling the juices oozing from its swaddle. Like mammals who had yet to invent forks and only recognized knives, we ate with our hands. Downing the moist bird with savory mumbles from our full mouths, we stuffed ourselves with all we had gathered and prepared. Staving off the slumber of tryptophan, we continued to imbibe with more booze, and smoke more of the aromatic homegrown herb. We picked up the musical instruments and prolonged our songs until dessert. Sweets piled high on plates until these too we downed in our bellies, leaving empty platters with only crumbs. Decarboxylated marijuana cooked long into butter and then used in the brownies and pies sank into our psyches, contributing to the escalating silliness in our melodies. The moon was aware we were celebrating life, and the mountain echoed our songs. Our day was long, and our night even longer, but as always it must roll forward into a new day. As dawn tenderly announced its arrival, we relinquished our vices, returned to silence and submitted to sleep with thankfulness in our hearts and bones.

~~~

For Christmas, I announced that my dear friend and trail brother G would visit for the holiday. Having him meet my new mountain family filled me with glee. Ol' Man Sam, Berengar, Mike and Art were curious as to what kind of hooligan their wild Hot Wing loved so much. As Art put it, "Things keep getting more colorful around here every day, despite all the snow!"

A few days before December 25th, I proudly picked G up at the same spot I had left him eleven months prior, the Boulder bus station. Like before, he flew from Los Angeles to Denver, then rode the airport bus to Boulder. Yet unlike his previous Colorado trip, he now arrived at an established plan.

"Freaking Hot Wing, look at you!" G exclaimed, opening his arms for a brotherly embrace.

"Oh my, it is invigorating to see you, G. Welcome back. Colorado 2.0!" I hugged my friend enthusiastically and walked him to Rubi the Subi, motioning with a gallant open-palmed sweep as if the red mediocre vehicle was a royal chariot.

I called Mit, informing him of G's return. The three of us rendezvoused at a Boulder pub to drink a few pints and catch up on G's warm-weather life. Once our innards were cozy from the whiskey and beer, we bid Mit farewell and drove into the mountains. I pointed everything out to G as we drove through Nederland, explaining to him what each building, mountain and dirt road meant to me. "Don't worry G, these next few days you will experience it all firsthand, but for now let's go meet the family at our home in Gamble Gulch."

G beamed the smile I remembered well, his not yet exhausted grin. The expression I received at the beginning of our ventures together. "It looks like you have really carved yourself out a life up here, Wing. I am proud of you. Last time we saw each other, you were drowning in some kind of darkness. I know you never wanted to admit it, but I could see it."

I gripped the steering wheel with one hand and cracked a beer open with the other. I handed the beer to G, opened another for myself and lit a cigarette. "Yeah, well, the darkness is always there, but I have found some light as well. It's all about the balance, you know."

"I see you still drink and smoke a lot though." G lifted his beer for a cheer. We clinked cans and gulped down the frothy goodness.

I chuckled, wiping foam from my beard and tapping the cigarette refuse into my cupholder ashtray my grandfather had given me. "Eh, what is beer anyway, other than hydration with an extra nourishing kick? I'll be fine. Don't you worry about my drinking, pal. We are on vacation."

When we pulled up to the cabin home, Berengar and Mike were practicing sword fighting techniques with long sticks in the side yard. Art hobbled by in paint-stained sweatpants carrying his parrot. Ol' Man Sam sat on the porch chair I had installed, smoking a joint. G presented a wide-eyed tacit statement to which I replied, "Yup. This is how we roll up here, brother. Ain't no point living the way they think is normal down there. No television, no societal distractions, we create our own fun up here. Come on and meet the fam."

As G and my mountain family exchanged handshakes, hugs and hellos, I stood back and soaked it all in. Tears welled in my eyes, but I brushed them away before anyone could spot them. My heart surged with happiness at having everyone together. Two of my many worlds were meshing, and though G appeared a tad overwhelmed by it all, I knew he was also pleased. Upstairs, I unrolled a yoga mat onto my bedroom floor for G to use as a bed, then stepped out, allowing him a few moments to himself. When he was ready, we would all climb the backyard mountain to the ridgeline and watch the sunset with marijuana and whiskey, then rumble back down in the dark for dinner. A cauldron of homemade soup simmered in the kitchen.

The few days before our Nederland Christmas comprised peaceful, homely days. G and I partook in our usual trail town routines of playing billiards and socializing with locals. We ventured on short hikes in the snow and long high-country drives. I showed him Caribou Hill, Ward, Eldora, and brought him to the train tunnel at Rollins Pass. We absorbed the mountain skies and ate sandwiches by the creek. He got to see me in action as I manned the bar and hosted the daily party at Backcountry Pizza, meeting all the regulars and grasping the essence of our marvelous land and its inhabitants. It stirred my delight when G looked around and nodded, agreeing that this truly is a magnificent place. "You've discovered a slice of heaven here, Wing." He gave a brotherly one-armed side hug after his genuine comment. Together as a family, we harvested a small woodland evergreen to use as a Christmas tree. In our living room, we decorated it with beer bottles and extraneous unique items we marijuana growers had lying around. Our holiday decor looked far from traditional, which to us was exactly the point. After attending to the cannabis plants and gathering all the holiday supplies, we bundled in layers and embarked towards Chris and Liz's annual Christmas Eve bash.

I was already intoxicated by the time the sun was setting on December 24th. As I hopped into the driver's seat of Rubi to escort us all into town, G noted my inebriation. "Dude, Hot Wing, you are drunk. Are you sure you'll be fine driving?"

Ol' Man Sam eased himself into the passenger seat and stated, "Ah G, don't you worry, Hot Wing is the best drunk driver I have ever seen. In my six decades of life on this planet, I haven't ever seen a better drunk driver than this man."

My rosy cheeks lifted, showing my teeth as I twiddled a cigarette playfully between them. I beamed at Sam and G. "Thank you, Sam. Hear that, G? We will be just fine. Berengar and Mike are going to another party. I'll drop them off, and then the three of us are going to Chris and Liz's! Chris is a mighty fine grower. He has taught me much, just like the fam here. His house is rad, dude, custom-built out of multiple large shipping containers. You're going to dig it."

Begrudgingly G squeezed into the back with Berengar and Mike. I turned and assured him we would be fine. "Now off to the big city of Nederland, my gentle-wild-men!" I exclaimed, sliding down the snowy road, guiding my wagon into the tracks. A blizzard poured from the sky, affecting every sensation. Although the roads were a menace to traverse, it only added to the adventure. "Besides," continuing to rationalize my condition, "it is Christmas, everyone is drunk." The boys in the back sat quietly, hopeful we would be safe. Ol' Man Sam started whistling a holiday tune without a worry in the world. Once I dropped Berengar and Mike off at their destination, G had more room in the back, which I hoped would help ease his anxiety. Onward to the Christmas party we progressed.

I had only been to Chris's home once, and with darkness setting in, snow blinding the roads, and whiskey coursing through my veins, I wasn't sure which driveway was his. Ol' Man Sam couldn't remember either, and G just sat clueless and stressed. I chose one driveway, but once I reached the house, I realized it was the wrong one. Haphazardly, I whipped Rubi around, but in doing so, I accidentally backed into a small tree, knocking it flat to the ground. The homeowner erupted from his den. He hustled towards us with a disgruntled face, spewing angry words. I revved Rubi's engine, spinning the tires as they caught a grip, and right before he could reach the car we lurched out of his yard. G mumbled words in the back, to the effect of, "This is ridiculous. Hot Wing shouldn't be driving. We are all going to die."

"That isn't helping, bud!" I looked over my shoulder back to G.

CINEREAL

"Dammit, Wing, just keep looking forward!" G finally calmed down once I pulled into the proper driveway, brought the car to a halt and turned off the ignition.

"Safe and sound." I smiled. Ol' Man Sam remained undisturbed. G scowled.

Locals packed the party indoors. A sweet aroma of a fruity marijuana strain poured out the front door as Chris and Liz welcomed us in. I carried a large box full of alcohol. It was heavy with two six-packs of glass-bottled beers, a large handle of whiskey and two bottles of red wine as gifts for the hosts. The kitchen island countertop was full of booze the other guests had brought, so I carelessly pushed half of the box onto the edge. It stayed where I set it, and from the back of the box I grabbed the whiskey, causing the shift in weight to crash the entire package onto the hard floor. Both wine bottles and all twelve beers shattered violently, scattering glass and a pond of alcohol. Everyone shouted, "Hot Winggg!!" G glared at me and my mess. Ol' Man Sam patted me on the shoulder. Feeling genuinely awful about my mishap, I started collecting up the broken glass. Chris and Liz reassured me it was a common accident and laid down towels to sop up the boozy puddle. However, everyone at the party recognized that I, Wing, was already drunk. After cleaning up my mess, someone, perhaps Andy, placed a well-rolled blunt in my grasp. I took a long drag of sweet smoke, swigged more from the whiskey bottle, and that was it. Other than a few hazy memories, such as dancing around the Christmas tree, the double visioned faces of jolly friends cheering me on, crashing down backwards over a chair and looking up at the ceiling, I could remember no more.

A few hours later, I awoke shivering in the cold. After a few moments of attempting to understand where I was, my foggy wits cleared. I realized I was in the back seat of my Subaru, still parked in Chris and Liz's driveway, alone. *I must have placed myself in a napping timeout,* something I tended to do when I caroused too wildly at a party. *But where is G? Where is Ol' Man Sam? I need water. I need to locate my family.* Returning to the house intending to rejoin the party, I turned the doorknob, but it was locked. As I peered into the window, I realized it was dark inside. Everyone had left. My cellphone remained in my pocket. "At least I didn't lose this," I murmured, while checking the clock. *Four minutes until midnight. Four minutes until Christmas. The party must have migrated to other homes.* Fortunately, in this part of town, I had one bar of cellphone service. I listened to a voicemail from Ol' Man Sam that he had recorded an hour prior.

"Wing, mon! Where are you? You disappeared." Sam's voice sounded a little tipsy. "G and I got a ride to a party behind the church. Big white house. It is wild here, man, but G ain't doing good, mon. I hope you are alright, but we need your help. No one here is helping us, mon. Everyone is hammered out of their minds. As soon as you hear this message, come find us."

Hearing this call for help caused my dizzy state to click into full attention. I ate a handful of snow, jumped into my driver's seat and turned on Rubi. I knew exactly the house he was talking about. If I could traverse through the blizzard and down the long hill, I just might find them. In the hour since Ol' Man Sam had left the voicemail everything could have grown much worse. I worried about G but drove as carefully as I could. There was no time to be concerned about police cars. I needed only to stay on the road. My vision blurred, some things still appeared double, my head pounded, but I still had my whiskey bottle with me. I took a swig of the potent drink, reached out and grabbed another handful of snow at a stop sign, shoveled the cold into my mouth and rolled onward, determined to find my friends.

After fifteen minutes of slipping and sliding, I arrived at the white house behind the church. *This is certainly the place,* I acknowledged, observing the many parked trucks and cars covered with fresh snowfall. The large yard had at least 200 feet of expanse I must traverse to reach the distant porch. The murmur of human activity from the party barely reached my ears amidst the turbulent wind. Hoping G and Sam would be inside, I lowered my head and charged into the bluster. Snow pounded on my face as I pushed through the deep accumulation towards the yellow lights. Standing in the weather was difficult. Moving, even more so. My body weakened from being too drunk, from forcing myself to operate when all I wanted to do was sleep. Yet I persevered, determined, and finally reached the house. A few figures loitered on the porch with large parkas and hoods over their heads. "Is Ol' Man Sam here?!" I shouted. Most of them ignored me, or didn't hear me, and one just shrugged. *Thanks a lot, guys,* I sarcastically thought, pushing through to the door.

Once inside, I was greeted by wild glossy eyes and apathetic turns of bodies that were too messed up to offer a proper hello. It was challenging to observe anything clearly myself, and though I had made it, I needed a sharp snap of energy to locate Ol' Man Sam and G in the crowded maze of debauchery. I noticed a pile of cocaine on the glass table in the living room. A few people stood around it, some with the white still on their noses. I recognized them but did not know their names. *Surely, I have served them beer at BCP before.* Urgently, I asked if I could have some of the drug, to which they garbled, "Sure thing, Wing." *Well, they knew my name. That is good, I suppose.* I grabbed one of the short straws strewn on the table and snorted up a long, fat line of the intoxicating powder. *Woowee!* My brain started doing jumping jacks. I snorted another fat line into my other nostril. *Oh man, that'll do it.* Audacious energy and stabilizing clarity washed through my body, as if a new life had been brazenly instilled into a dying corpse. *I must find Ol' Man Sam and G.*

I roamed the house, rushing around like a maniac, ignoring all beckons of my name. In each room I scanned, asking if they had seen Ol' Man Sam or G, but everyone failed to provide adequate information. Some mentioned things like, "Yeah, we saw them, I don't know when though, I don't know where though." I ran up the stairs, checked every bedroom, every bathroom, pushed through crowds and checked under bodies on couches, checked in closets, checked on the back porch. Finally, in the pantry behind the kitchen, slumped in the corner, I found G passed out. No one seemed to care that he looked dead. I checked his pulse. He was still alive. I slapped his face lightly and noticed his eyeballs trying to flutter open. At that moment I heard Ol' Man Sam's gruff voice in the other room. I shouted his name persistently until the stout geezer appeared. The old man's face brightened when he saw me. He tried to talk, but he was also drunk and slurring his words. I interrupted him with instructions.

"Sam, grab two red cups from that stack there and fill them with water. We are getting out of here now."

"Okay mon. You made it, mon! But how did you…" Sam fumbled around looking for the water cups I had pointed to while trying to interact with me simultaneously. I snapped back my instructions with an extended finger at the cups and returned my focus to G.

"G, wake up, brother. It's Wing. I am going to get you home." I talked to G closely so he could hear me among the raucous sounds of the party.

G managed to open his eyes slightly and recognized my presence. "Wing, you are here." He could barely talk, but at least he recognized me.

CINEREAL

His eyes closed again. He tried to raise his arm but gave up. That was too difficult for him. His appendage slumped back down onto the sticky floor.

"Yes, buddy, I am here. I need you to work with me. I am going to lift you up, and we are going to the car. Can you do that with me?" G nodded just enough, so I knew he understood. His eyes continued to waver between open and closed. I put my arms around his waist and pulled him upwards, then wrapped my arm around his upright position and tried to walk forward, but G's body remained drooped, his weight pulling us down.

"Sam! Where are you? Did you get the two water cups? One for each hand. Sam, come on now! We are leaving pronto!" I realized I was going to need to carry G with no help, so I hoisted his body up onto my left shoulder with a strength only adrenaline and cocaine could offer. G's feet dragged along the floor. Ol' Man Sam followed closely, carrying two red plastic vessels with water splashing out onto his belly.

As we barreled our way through the party, people moved out of the way, responding to my sharp commands. A few even understood our endeavor. I kicked open the front door, looked over my shoulder to make sure Sam was still with us, and pushed outside into the snowstorm. My car appeared far away across the brumal front yard. Its red body was already covered with a few inches of fresh snow. As I pulled G down the porch, with him still hoisted on my shoulder, I felt and heard him beginning to cough, so I steadied him upright in front of me. G opened his eyes, then opened his mouth, and vomited all over my chest. I did not care. *This is good. He needs to expel some of the poison.* After he finished retching on the front of my coat, his eyes remained open with more stability. Suddenly he understood what we were doing. Although he still could not walk on his own, with my arm firmly around his waist, he started intentionally moving his feet.

"We just need to make it 200 feet to the car, G. Here, drink some of this water." I grabbed a now half-empty cup from Ol' Man Sam and held it up to G's mouth. Gently, he gulped. "Good, G, good. Okay, let's walk. You've got this. I've got you. I won't let you go. Walk with me. One, two, good, another step. Good, another one."

It was a difficult and blizzardy trudge to the red wagon, but with one valuable step at a time, we made it. I laid G on his side in the back. Ol' Man Sam slumped into the passenger seat. Sam handed me the last half-empty cup of water, which I poured down my throat. *Now, I just need to drive safely for seven miles in the storm to get us home.* I rubbed my face vigorously and slapped my cheeks harshly, attempting to snap some clarity into my vision, to align my eyesight in the kaleidoscope bluster of snowfall. The world around me and within me roared. *Calm it down, Wing. Only seven miles. You've got this.*

We made it through town, and then we made it up and past Magnolia Drive. On the flats, Rubi threatened to slide off the road. I coolly turned into the skid, recognizing we were about to crash, but a controlled crash would be better than an uncontrolled one. Successfully, we hit the snowbank on Rubi's flank and not her front. The old red wagon shuddered to a temporary stop. All was well. We could continue driving towards home. G finally sat up in the back. Ol' Man Sam cheered me on with colorful encouragement. Beyond Eldora, up and around and towards Rollinsville, advancing past the Stage Stop Saloon, just a bit more until finally turning a right onto Gamble Gulch Road. Up the slope, slowly enough not to slide into the creek but with enough speed not to stall in the deep snow accumulation. Onward, onward, onward, and finally, home.

As I turned the car off in my parking spot at the cabin, G had now revived from near-death and bellowed with loud glee. "Goodness gracious, Sam!" G hollered. "You were right! Hot Wing is the best drunk driver I have ever known."

As G sang out his praises, relieved chuckles guffawed from my lips. "I must admit that was not my best performance. I mean, I crashed into the snowbank!"

G added, "Yeah, dude, you crashed twice. Earlier tonight, you took out an entire tree."

At this we all laughed, not only at the truth of the statements, but out of pure exhausted relief to be home. It had been a wild night fueled by whiskey and questionable decisions, but somehow, we had survived. Home sweet Gamble Gulch home, and Merry Christmas.

In the morning, we eased about the cabin in rough condition, but that was alright because it was Christmas. We were alive and grateful. It certainly wasn't the first time G and I had been hungover together. It was in fact, as I reminded G, our second Christmas spent together. "Two in a row!" I declared while drinking coconut water. We all ate chocolate cake in the living room by the woodstove and shared our stories from the night. Berengar and Mike had caught a ride home from their event and gleaned much entertainment listening to the harrowing account of our night. After a slow day of recovery, we bundled up and climbed the ridge through waist-deep snow. The storm had passed, the sky had cleared, and a tremendous sunset mirrored the bonfire we set ablaze high in our Colorado mountains. G's visit had been a success. Soon I would drive him down to the Boulder bus station, and he would return to Southern California. No matter what might become of our friendship in life, whether we walked together as on the trail or in opposite directions, he would always remain a brother in my heart.

"The road goes on forever, but the party never ends," Robert Earl Keen aptly sang. In our mountain life, this surely seemed to be the case. New Year's Eve was upon us. Life had returned to its normal routine of running the bar at BCP, working with the marijuana plants, late-night talks with Ol' Man Sam, and chopping wood with the brothers. It had been another wild year, and we were ready to close it out in such a manner. Elephant Revival was performing a New Year's Eve show at the Stage Stop Saloon. All the mountain folk masses were sure to attend.

We donned our finest jackets and hats and rolled down the hill to the infamous establishment by the train tracks. The night indeed brimmed with all the authentic wildness the highlands could conjure. Everyone danced and stomped the wooden floor, bending the floorboards which held us aloft, howling and singing along with D. Ro, Bonny and company, drinking and embracing until the lights were turned off well after midnight. The community arrived in a thousand pieces, yet all left as one. One magnificent beating heart of love. Back at home at three in the morning, when all but Ol' Man Sam had gone to bed, I sat on the cabin porch observing the night and considering my life. For the first time in far too long, I prayed to God, citing each thing I was grateful for. It was a long prayer, for my gratitude inventory was as the road. I had not reverently addressed God for over a year, ever since foolishly rejecting His convictions in Oregon. But some things in life are just too good, sweet euphoric gifts, such as time with friends in the mountains, that even in my darkness I needed to acknowledge The I Am Who Is. Despite my gratitude, defiance still coated my soul. I would not repent. When I was ready, I stood up and returned inside, packed the woodstove full of logs, patted my elder author friend on his shoulder, then ascended the stairs to drift into a long sleep.

~~~

On February 7, 2014, my grandfather died. My dad called and told me the news. His voice cracked, struggling to maintain his usual strong, levered tone. I knew that in recent months Granddad had received a lung cancer diagnosis. Despite his health deteriorating quickly, it was not the cancer that ended his life; it was a sudden brain aneurysm. Perhaps he suffered less than he would have otherwise. Although he passed away in southern Georgia, his funeral would be in Gainesville, Florida, where he grew up and married my grandmother. He was to be buried in the military section of Forest Meadows Cemetery on February 12th.

Berengar drove me to the Denver airport in my car. He could hold on to and use Rubi until I returned. I flew to Orlando and met up with Dad. We then travelled to Gainesville together. The pale green warm winter flatlands of Florida did not faze me. Nothing fazed me. All I could think about was Granddad, the one who had loved me unconditionally since the day I was born. I loved him just as much in return, and the fact he was gone did not yet seem real.

In Gainesville, we checked into the hotel and reunited with family. I held my grandmother in my arms as she spoke only of the good things. "He made his soul right with God before he passed away, Wing. He is with God in heaven now." It was good to hear her speak these words, for I knew how he too had rebelled against God for much of his life. When I was an adolescent, before turning away from God myself, I loved Jesus so deeply I remembered begging my grandfather to love him too. I just wanted Granddad to hold the same love that my ten-year-old self held, but when I grew older and confused, having witnessed terrible sins in the church and family, when my heart turned away, I understood how my grandfather felt. We shared a similar stubborn defiance. To learn that my grandfather had shed his pride and submitted his heart to God, knowing his earthen days would soon end, filled me with both gratitude and shame. I acknowledged that was right of him, and that I was choosing to live in darkness.

My brother, sister and mother did not come to the funeral, which stung in my heart, but I chose not to dwell on that. *Surely, they have their reasons.* My dad's sister, Aunt B, and her children, cousins Steph and Jeff, were there. With melancholic joy, we reunited and shared our stories of grandfather together. I had not seen Jeff since we were young lads, and now as adults we embraced sincerely, sizing each other up with a few laughs, recognizing that even though our beloved grandfather was gone, his death had brought us back together.

Jeff and I were sharing a two-bedroom hotel room, so once everyone settled in for the evening, he and I sauntered into the center of Gainesville

CINEREAL

in search of alcohol to quench our grieving hearts. My cousin and I drank whiskey and beer, played billiards and talked about Granddad until we were too drunk to be served any more. We stumbled back to our hotel and sat outside on the parking lot curb, smoking cigarettes, drinking more beer we purchased from a gas station, and with tears streaming down our cheeks, shared story after story of our memories with the beloved Marion Kelly Williams.

In the morning, Dad banged on our hotel door. He knew we would be hungover, and as I opened it, he threw water bottles at both of us. "Get up, you bums! It is time to go lay your grandfather to rest."

The day was gray, threatening to rain, which seemed appropriate, for my heart felt gray, my eyes gray, threatening to rain tears. At the funeral home, many people who loved my grandfather gathered. The tone was hushed, but the interrogation was constant. Many relatives or friends of relatives who had met me as a boy but never seen me as an adult asked questions about my life, about my hikes and adventures. I tried to smile back at them, to the humans I could not remember, attempting to answer the inquiries with some genuine anecdotes to fulfill their curiosities, but my mind was not in it. I could think of nothing other than the man we were laying to rest. Old hymns played softly in the room we gathered. Pictures of Granddad's life and loved ones sat propped up around his closed casket. I watched as my dad struggled like I was, fielding all the questions and hugs, smiling back and responding, but his mind was also on his dad, not on updating every relative about his flights and travels. But that is the thing about funerals. No one really knows what to say to those who are living. They feel the need to fill silence with chatter, as if the chatter will somehow ease a griever's pain. But it does not, not for me. I needed silence.

When it was time to transfer my grandfather in his casket out to the hearse, they were to roll it through a large gathering room that was not being used for our event. In this room, there was a piano. I sat down at the piano and played Granddad one last song. His casket rolled by. I wept. Tears reached my chin and dripped onto the keys. As a young boy, when I was first learning to play the piano, Grandma had an upright much like this one in their home. During all those years, on each visit, Granddad would listen to me play. *A last song for him now. "In the Sweet By and B," one of his favorites.*

At the cemetery, it was my duty, along with Jeff and two others, to carry my grandfather from the hearse to the grave as we were the pallbearers. I held the casket firmly, each of us with our posture straight, faces firm and chins held high, just as grandfather would expect from us. When we reached his resting place, we set the casket down onto a platform that they would later lower into the ground. I stood under the gloomy sky next to my grandfather as we prayed. A man I had never seen spoke a short sermon. As I stood next to the casket, facing all who had come to the funeral, I investigated each of their faces. My eyes paused tenderly on my grandmother. A mighty surge of love for her filled my heart. As I continued scrutinizing the others, a mild tinge of satisfaction ensued, because it was obvious everyone in attendance loved him.

My dad delivered the eulogy. As I watched him, something clicked within me I had never experienced before. *Here is my dad, speaking about his dad, at his dad's funeral. The generations of time are ticking forward.* My grandfather's life on earth had ended, while my predecessor had recently become a grandfather, for my brother and family had just welcomed their first child. Dad was stepping into his dad's shoes, and I, well, I was not a boy, or a teenager, or even in my young twenties anymore. A weight of realization settled upon my mind. *Although I stand here as a twenty-eight-year-old man, am I living as a twenty-eight-year-old should?* This I did not know. All I knew was I needed to mature.

To conclude the funeral, there ensued a military salute, for Granddad had spent many of his years serving in the navy. My dad had followed in his footsteps and joined the navy as an officer and pilot, but I had always chosen the opposite. Granddad, Dad and I all shared the same middle and last name, Kelly Williams, which is perhaps all I shared with them… Grief and guilt brewed severely within, and on that somber day in Gainesville Florida, although I loved my family fervently, I hated who I had become.

~~~

In the months that followed, I did not mature. Instead, I drank alcohol more heavily than I ever had before. I had already been drinking every day for many years, but now I consistently started earlier in the day and with more ferocity. Although I wore a grin in front of each human, within I raged. Each work shift, I forcefully turned on the charismatic personality, like a switch, to provide each character the fun-timing me they desired. After work, I turned off the switch and bathed in the bosom of a boozy dark bottle, soaking up poisons of the earth. Ol' Man Sam watched it all unfold. He sat

CINEREAL

at his desk in the living room, warmed by the woodstove and his sweater, observing my soul spiral deeper into darkness.

Never in my life had I known a friend like Ol' Man Sam. Never had I met someone who took the time to understand me, even when they did not like what they were growing to know. Ol' Man Sam never judged me. Other than mentoring in the ways of marijuana, he was not a mentor or father-figure. I didn't need a dad; I had one I loved dearly. He became more like an older brother. I revealed to him all my darkness, honestly disclosing my anger and confusion. I confessed to him the pain in my soul. Together, we endeavored to peel back each layer and discover the source. And yet, the opposite of healing escalated, I wallowed in torment. As we contemplated all the elements of life during our nightly talks, including the Almighty God, I did not grow closer to the Creator, but continued to drift even further away. As I voluntarily exposed each painful layer, I consumed more drugs.

The marijuana did not hurt, but the cocaine did, and the occasional new experimentation with meth and crack. Despite Nederland being the haven, I had desired, it also provided every substance I chose to ingest. In that grievous late winter of all-consuming horrors, Ol' Man Sam witnessed my emboldening degradation. He viewed me as I wailed tears of anguish. As I snorted powder atop mirrors or shoveled it into my nose with a little spoon. He watched as I drank myself into demonic heaps and madly bawled to the brink of insanity. He looked on while I dared the depths of hell to vanquish me from the earth. Back and forth across the cabin wooden floor my booted footsteps paced, my hands waving maniacally in the air. I muttered long absurdities to myself, then howled and seethed until there was no drop of moisture left within me. Picking the bottle back up to replenish my tears, I cried and continued ranting. Outside I smoked, cigarette after cigarette, chaining them down into my lungs then pushing the fumes aloft into an unsympathetic sky. During these tempestuous torments, in moments of drug-induced exhaustion, I read to Ol' Man Sam from my notebooks, sharing poems I had not and would never share with others. I inflicted my insanity on a compassionate old man. Yet even in anguish, I recognized his kindness. He willingly entered the room of my mind, which, until him, had been a war-room for only me and the devil. A room that God would not enter.

Berengar and Mike were gracious and patient with me. They also let me be as I must. Art, however, grew frustrated with my antics and outbursts.

CINEREAL

He'd had enough of my morning booze and four in the morning wine. On one such morning, as I was chopping wood and crushing cans of beer down my gullet and then throwing them against a tree trunk, Art slung the words at me I had not heard before. For the first time in my life, and not the last time, I was called an alcoholic. "You are an alcoholic, Wing." Just like that. With a firm, straightforward, sharp, bitter face, he said it just like that. "You are an alcoholic, Wing." I yelled back at him some words I would come to regret, infuriated by his audacity. *Even G had not gone that far.* Art promptly marched away.

I continued chopping wood, chugging beers and chucking cans, but I could not wrap my mind around the notion that I might be an alcoholic. *Alcoholism happened out there, to other people, or they were born into it, or it became like some decrepit fall that would never happen to me. Just because I drink every day does not make me an alcoholic. I can stop if I want to. I just don't want to. This is just a phase.* I lied to myself repeatedly, stunned at the thought that someone believed I was an alcoholic. *Twenty-eight-year-olds are not alcoholics. This is normal, that asshole lonely man calling me that,* I spat. With the self-destruction fueled, I pounded another beer, hurled the empty can at the tree trunk, grabbed the whiskey bottle and poured the brown liquor down my throat.

Despite my vicious drinking, much of our mountain life seemed to progress as normal. My body was strong, and other than the all-consuming mental and spiritual darkness, the drinking and drugs didn't seem to affect the day-to-day routines. We each kept living our lives. Everyone fulfilled the responsibilities. Everyone played their role. Winter was long and cold, but we persevered.

On one early March day, Berengar and I rolled down the mountain to Boulder in Rubi. We had errands that required more services than small town Nederland offered. At lunch I consumed whiskey with my beer, but Berengar only drank a mellow dark stout. After lunch I wanted to keep imbibing, so between errands I jumped into pubs to grab a shot of whiskey, pound a pint of beer, then resume our mini missions. When the day's duties were complete and we returned to the car, I realized the keys were not in my pocket. I had accidentally locked them inside Rubi, and all the windows were closed.

The sun had not yet set, potential witnesses roamed the downtown parking lot, and I was almost drunk. I knew we could not linger, nor place ourselves in jeopardy of alerting the law enforcement's attention. I needed to unlock the car and drive away as soon as possible. Despite being more inebriated than Berengar, I would not let him drive. Although I loved and trusted him, this was my car and my mess. As Berengar vocally brainstormed ideas on how we might remedy the situation, such as perhaps unlocking the car with a metal wire, calling AAA, or I don't really know because I wasn't listening to him, I walked over to the edge of the parking lot and picked up a dense rock the size of a grapefruit. Without hesitation, I approached Rubi and hurled the rock through the window behind the driver's seat. Berengar watched with wide, stunned eyes. Glass shattered and scattered everywhere. An unhoused man sitting nearby commented, "That was gnarly, man." After the violent blast, the rock lay in the back seat of the car, along with thousands of tiny shards of glass. As if it were a routine occurrence, I reached inside carefully, unlocked the front door, casually sat on the glass-filled seat and started the car.

"Get in." I said to Berengar. "We need to get out of here pronto." I looked back at the faces of the citizens who stared and pointed. They probably thought I was stealing this vehicle, but no, I was simply doing what needed to be done. Driving out of the parking lot and leaving a plethora of glass in our wake, I smiled and gave a thumbs up to the unhoused man. He nodded his head with amusement. Careful not to exceed the speed limit, we drove up Boulder Canyon Drive as if nothing unusual had happened. When we breached the top of the canyon, cold air from Barker Reservoir filled the vehicle through its new gaping hole. Neither of us had spoken the entire ascent, but with our mountain town in our sights, I looked over to Berengar and calmly stated, "I was planning on getting a truck soon anyway."

~~~

A few weeks later, I did get a truck. My replacement for Rubi the Subi was slightly newer but still a used Toyota Tacoma. This upgrade pleased me. I named my new truck Rhino, for it was gray and, to me, resembled a rhinoceros. That night I sat on the cabin porch smoking cigarettes, admiring my steed, patiently waiting in its stall for whenever I needed it. It was the 241st night of my nocturnal gulch observation, the night my seek was finally fulfilled. The first noise I heard was a sharp call interrupting the gulch's usual lullaby. Followed up with another somewhat chirping call. Down to the right, a few hundred feet away in the darkness, the noise sporadically persisted. At first, I thought it was a fox, but after some silence, as the animal moved closer in the darkness, the voice returned with more of a shrill drawl.

CINEREAL

I called back from the porch with a similar tone. My call to the animal caused its silence, and perhaps to hold off on its next step. I could see nothing down near the creek, but it seemed as if the animal was standing still and staring at me. I called again with a tone mimicking the one it had exuded. This time it responded to me. *Oh, my goodness*, I thought. *Is it communicating with me?* I called again, and this time the animal responded from a different location in the dark. It had traveled from deeper right to close right, a decent space in a brief time. Our unique conversation continued for another few minutes. This exchange helped me perceive how close the animal was and where it softly strode. It seemed to have moved near the road, very close to where the moonlight reached and illuminated the ground. It called again, less than 100 feet away. I stood up calmly, stepped over to the cabin door, opened it lightly, leaned in, and urgently whispered to Ol' Man Sam, who was sitting in his spot, "Sam, I think it's happening."

"What is happening, mon?" He glanced up curiously from his craft.

"A mountain lion. I think there is a mountain lion out here. I have been chatting with it." Faintly, I chuckled at the ridiculousness of my statement. "Come out here, man, check it out."

Ol' Man Sam stood up gradually, as if his knees disagreed, and leaned out the doorway to watch where I directed with my point.

"It was right over there last, listen." I gave the call it had been responding to, but now there was no response. Surely the animal must be watching us. It was no fool. "Just stand out here with me, Sam. Let's watch that swath of snow in the moonlight there. I think it is..." before I could finish my sentence, it happened.

Less than 100 feet away, to the right of our porch, where the dirt road meets the mouth of a neighbor's long driveway, where the moon could reach the ground between lodgepole pines, there in that lit up glorious space, a massive mountain lion strode majestically through to the darkness on the other side. For a few precious seconds, our vision captured its entire tawny body, from its head to the tip of its long tail, in the moonlight upon a backdrop of snow.

Ol' Man Sam and I both stood in wonder, holding our breaths. Once the large feline had slipped into the forest, onward up the mountain behind our cabin, we erupted with exclamations. We couldn't believe it, and yet we could believe it, for we had just seen it. After the moments of elation subsided, Ol' Man Sam returned to his seat at his desk, and I to my seat

CINEREAL

outside. *Wow,* is nearly all I could speechlessly think. *Truly wow, what a magnificent creature. It had happened.* I had finally seen a mountain lion from our cabin's front porch, and it only took 241 nights of dedicated sentinel observation. In the morning, I examined the area for any paw prints it may have left. Despite a few vehicles having left recent tire marks, there were still a few large, clear mountain lion tracks on the edge of the road. Exactly like the many I observed on the Pacific Crest Trail.

~~~

Spring arrived timidly in the mountains. Down in Boulder, the weather prompted sundresses and shorts, but up in Nederland and Gamble Gulch, snow persisted well into June. In April, the aspen trees began to bud their small green leaves, but another foot of snow on Mother's Day held all full blossoms at bay. We did not mind the long winter. It was a worthy price we happily paid to live at a high elevation. We continued to shovel our parking spots and pathways, slosh around in the afternoon mud, tread cautiously on the morning ice, turn our faces towards the sun when it shined, and merrily huddle around the woodstove in the evening.

Often, I ventured out on my own. My truck facilitated reaching all my favorite highland nooks. I sat beneath fiery sunsets, far away from all other humans, to cry and pray. I did not know exactly why I was crying. It was not the death of my grandfather. I understood and accepted his passing. It was something deeper. Akin to the confused pain I suffered as a child. The inner angst I had always carried unrelentingly intensified. Anguish oozed from an unfathomable source. Despite my friends and mountain family, I felt utterly alone. A desolate, sinful speck upon the earth pouring an eternal river of loathsome distress. After the expunge, I would dry my face and return to civilization with a forced smile. I started to think God had given up on me. I would call out to Him, begging Him to forgive me, and yet I would not repent of my rebellious, rejecting, destructive ways.

I formed a brief relationship with a college graduate from Louisiana. We met when I poured her a beer at BCP while she was on vacation. She had never been sledding in the snow before, so I took her to Caribou Hill and introduced her to the wintry pastime. After my grandfather's funeral, I visited her in the Pelican State before returning to the mountains. We rode horses through warm hardwood forests and partied in Baton Rouge. A month later, she prolonged our affair by surprising me in Colorado. In still moments together, with moisture from hot springs lingering on our skin, our brief romance seemed real, until she left the mountains and returned to her home again.

After my southern belle, I occasionally drove down to Boulder seeking a woman away from the tight-knit community of Ned. When I grew tired of flirting, I would compete in billiard tournaments, then rage upon pianos in bars until they forced me to leave. My dear Mit, while flourishing in his gardening career, was a stable friend. He became a keel to the volatile boat I acted as, helping to keep me from completely capsizing. At the cabin, the mountain family grew with the return of Chops, Bee and her dog Basil, lovely souls who had lived in the gulch before me. Berengar and Mike performed their daily routines. Working in the morning and attending to the marijuana grow in the evening. I continued staying up late with Ol' Man Sam after Backcountry Pizza, then attending to my shift with the marijuana plants around noon. Art and I kept our distance from each other. We exchanged no more words. I was nothing but a damn alcoholic anyway. A high-functioning bitter alcoholic still angered by the accusation. The rift irked me, for although my pride kept a wall between us, something in me knew he was right, and I still loved the kooky, talented painter.

In June, I realized I must leave Colorado soon for a family celebration. Not all the way to New Hampshire, but to Wheaton, Illinois. My darling sister Carmen was set to get married. As the day approached, I experienced a turmoil of emotions. On one hand, I was thrilled for her and eager to see my family. I craved some alone time with each of them, especially my mother. But on the other hand, I must temporarily leave my mountain haven and venture out into what others call the real world.

~~~

I decided to drive to the wedding. It was only fourteen highway hours away. Although Dad was a Delta Airlines pilot and plane tickets were easy for the family to obtain, the idea of a road trip in my Rhino allowed more freedom than air travel would. Down the mountain, into the mile-high flatlands of Colorado, descending onward into the breadbasket of America, I progressed. It seemed odd driving east, nearly wrong. Driving into the morning sun felt backwards, against the grain of my soul. I kept reminding myself; *I am not going all the way to New England. No further east than Chicago. Stay the course, Wing.* I slept in Omaha, Nebraska, and when I awoke before the sun, a refreshed excitement occupied me. Golden rays of a new day flooded the rolling hills of Iowa, illuminating bluffs of midwestern trees and the tips of verdant grasses. Now that I was a day removed from my mountains, the small adventure didn't seem so bad after all. My family awaited my arrival just one state away.

I arrived at a large house in a well-manicured neighborhood my mother had rented for Carmen and all the bridesmaids. The aura was one of busy, upbeat preparation. Carmen greeted me as a beautiful young woman I barely knew. In my mind, she was still the little sister I had grown up with, but she had matured and glowed like an angel. Her eyes were full of graceful confidence. It was delightful to see my brother. He and his wife introduced me to my first and brand-new niece Aleah. I gifted her a tiny pair of stylish sunglasses. Michael smiled and amusedly spoke, "Her first shades." My mother hugged me affectionately, but she had much to do and fluttered off into the floating bustle of all the butterflies that were my sister's bridesmaids. Stepping into the clean, refined, wedding preparation environment was overwhelming, but there was a piano in the house, so I sat on the bench and played for an hour. I patterned my songs after the surrounding energy, upbeat, a little jazzy, full of color, and wholesome. When my soul grew tired, I took a long break to smoke outside in the yard and commune passively from a distance.

Relieved I would not be lodging at the lively Victorian home, I made my way to the hotel where I would stay with Dad and Grandma. I had exhausted all I could exert in my sister's world. It was time to retreat to the Williams' world. The one with a bar, where I could shower, drink whiskey and sneak hits of marijuana to ease my anxiety. The day was June 26th. Tomorrow would be Dad's birthday, his first since his dad's death and a long day full of pre-wedding activities. On June 28th, my sister and her husband to be, the tall David, would unite in marriage at the church she and he had attended while at Wheaton College.

Seeing my dad and grandmother relaxed me. I could always be myself with them. I didn't need to walk on eggshells, or pretend, constantly trying not to knock over the allegorical delicate vase of expected behavior. The last thing I wanted was to be a stain on my sister's weekend, so when I was around them, I gripped my emotions and words together securely. My existence to them (in my muddled mind) was a curse word, a blotch, a long-haired smear.

The events of the next day, the pre-wedding day, were as lovely as Georges Seurat's painting A Sunday Afternoon on the Island of La Grande

CINEREAL

Jatte. My sister and I had stood in front of that painting, the real one, in Paris a decade before. I allowed the peace and community of the day to flow as she desired, forcing the dragon of my soul to remain hushed within. I lay in the grass and let Aleah crawl on me. She curiously pulled on my beard while wearing her new first pair of sunglasses. I smiled graciously with my brother and mother and held my grandmother's hand when her gaze looked like she was thinking about Granddad. When the youngsters started playing frisbee, I jumped in and ran the field with them. Frequently, I peered over at the rest of the group. Carmen merrily socialized in the shadow of a tree beside her fiancé. I believed tall-David to be a respectable man. I could see that he loved her, and as long as he always protected her and remained honorable to her, all would be well.

The day of the wedding was a grand event. The church was a noble, wide brick building with stately white pillars and trim. As everyone gradually gathered inside, I smoked on the terrace wearing the suit I had been provided. While everyone else wore fine dress shoes, I rocked canvas Converse sneakers. Despite all the other men displaying shiny cufflinks on ironed shirts by their wrists, I had both my jacket and white shirt sleeves rolled up like a rugged flannel. I hated being stuffed in a suit, but it is what my sister wanted, so I cheerfully complied. I flicked out my cigarette and smiled at some folk frowning at me as they walked in.

When my sister floated down the aisle in her wedding dress, she radiated pure joy. I had never felt prouder in my life. Tears welled in my eyes, and not the kind I shed in the mountains. She smiled at me lovingly as she glided by and approached tall-David at the altar. Under God, in the eyes of the government, with family and her friends as witnesses, she was married to her husband, and he to her.

A jubilant celebration followed at an outdoor venue in a commodious garden. An immense tent provided decorated space for the feasting and dancing. It was mostly a dry party, with no liquor or beer, but there was champagne for toasting. I watched Carmen and David dance in an energetic swing fashion. She tittered and grinned with each pull, spin, dip, lift and twirl. Memories of our times together as children washed through me, my little sister now a wife. As the floor filled with her friends, I retreated to the tables where the attendants had poured the champagne. Upon conversing with a lady who was working the event and convincing her to find me some whiskey, I stood on the outskirts, smoking and sipping, occasionally

CINEREAL

wrapping an arm around my mother. She could not talk long, for she frequently needed to dash off, rightfully ensconced in the role of mother of the bride. I was pleased to be with my family of birth, but ready to return to the mountains.

After the festivities ended and everyone parted to their respective lodgings, the emotions I had been suppressing spilled out for my dad and grandmother to witness. I drank whiskey and chain-smoked on the hotel outdoor patio while gushing out all the dark tears I'd held. The dam broke. They could be held no longer. Grandma assured me all would be well. Dad sat without judgement, yet I could not pull myself together. Late into the night, when everyone had gone to bed, I sat alone. I texted my mother, pleading to spend some time together before everyone traveled away the next day. It was late, and I received no response. In the morning, the rush of arrival was rewound backward, everyone too busy to be slow. Again, I asked Mother, "May we please get lunch, just the two of us before you go?" But she had to drive Cindy to the airport early, and by then she would soon have her flight. Dismayed, I shook hands with Dad, embraced Grandma, hopped in my truck and left. If I could not have a proper goodbye with Mom, there was no point in sticking around any longer.

I drove back with a tumultuous range of emotions. Speeding my way through the monotonous land of Nebraska, slicing a line beneath all-seeing skies, I ached for home again. Returning to the mountains was all that mattered. I slept for a few hours in the truck once I crossed into Colorado, and in the morning pushed on up to Nederland. When I reached town, I drove straight to the bar and ordered a shot of whiskey. Next, I drove to the Sundance to greet Berengar and promptly drank two shots of tequila and two IPA beers. Then I purchased a six-pack for the truck and rolled a joint. I agreed to drive two of my friends into Rollinsville, where we peeled off onto a side-quest cruise down the long, remote dirt road to Rollins Pass, all the way to the foreboding train tunnel which bore into the Continental Divide. There, as high on the earth and as far away from society as I could possibly place myself, I was pulled over by one random police car that also was taking a joyride that very day, hour and minute. Immediately, the officer arrested me.

It all happened rapidly, unexpectedly and deservedly. My awful, selfish, mindless habits of drinking and driving had finally caught up with me. Less

CINEREAL

than forty-eight hours after my sister's wedding in Illinois, I sat in a jail cell in Gilpin County, Colorado.

When they allowed my phone call, I called the one number I had memorized, my dad's. The call went to voicemail. *Surely, he is flying an airplane.* I left him a detailed message, asking him to call Berengar and inform him of my circumstances and the box of cash I kept under my bed. I needed my mountain family to bail me out. When Dad had visited the previous autumn, he had met my eclectic household and saved their phone numbers. *Perhaps in the case of a situation like this.* Since we did not have cellphone service at the cabin, I did not know when anyone would show up to help me. *I must accept this forced timeout.* After leaving Dad a message, all I could do was sit back and wait. Twenty-six hours later, the police announced someone had paid my bail. Waiting for me outside the jail was my brother Berengar with a beaming smile. My heart welled with relief and gratitude to see him. On the ride home, he told me some big news the mountain family had received while I was away at the wedding. The landlord had become factually aware of our marijuana grow in the house and the illegally installed woodstove. Thus, we were expeditiously getting evicted.

I leaned back in the passenger seat, breathed out a long sigh and lit a cigarette. It appeared two significant changes were upon us. The consequences my unlawful actions would bring, and the end of our home at the Gamble Gulch.

Lump Gulch

Moving out of the Gamble Gulch cabin occurred so quickly there was little time for ceremony or emotion. We focused on what must be done. Our plethora of marijuana plants was the priority. One we promptly discovered a solution to. Sue, a hardy widow and friend who frequented Backcountry Pizza, lived deeper west in the crevices of Gamble Gulch. She owned a large garage completely outfitted for indoor grow rooms. Instead of spending our money on renting a new place to live, we decided to rent a new place for our plants to thrive. The equipped space proved to be a valuable upgrade from our subpar cabin operation. Out of necessity, we hustled to relocate all 100 plants.

As for ourselves, and where we would lay our heads at night, we preferred roughing it outdoors. There were ample options for each of us to rent a bedroom in other houses, but that would force our mountain family to separate. Following a safety meeting, we agreed we would rather stay together, build a mountain camp for the summer, save money, and wait for a proper new home. Berengar and I would lead this operation. We remained confident we could locate an appropriate abode before the brumal weather arrived in the autumn.

Besides the shift in our domestic living, I had to alter my lifestyle drastically. Immediately I started dealing with the ramifications of my DUI arrest. In the blink of a shimmering aspen leaf, I went from drinking alcohol every day to drinking none. At first, this abrupt modification generated inner distress, as I had been managing all my inner darkness with alcohol for so long. Not once had I seriously considered whether my body and brain were addicted to alcohol. With its sudden absence, I swiftly realized how accustomed I had become to being saturated with booze. Two years prior on the Pacific Crest Trail, I often went days without any of the poison, and I was only twenty-eight years old, therefore no life-threatening withdrawal symptoms loomed. However, for the first week I felt on edge, irritable, murky beneath persisting headaches. The main withdrawal symptom was extreme, energetic anxiety. I could not sit still, so I filled my time with running. Between waking and work, I ran everyday all over town and the surrounding mountain trails. Not being permitted to consume the socially acceptable liquid forced me to miss out on all the community fun Nederland offered, or so it seemed, enhancing my melancholy. To avoid facing such depression, I continued jogging and sprinting. Rapidly my mountain body transformed into a lean, vibrant specimen. Push-ups and miles became my drug. Each day upon waking, I would run five miles, work the marijuana grow, run five more miles, go serve the alcohol I could not drink, run five more miles, engage in multiple sets of push-ups throughout the day, go to sleep and then do it all over again.

Part of the DUI consequences was providing regular urinalysis drug-tests. Colorado enacted a unique system for this, seemingly created to wreak inconvenience and frustration. They did not organize it the way I had heard it to be in other states, from friends who shared their DUI experiences. Elsewhere an individual may need to drug test every Monday, for example, but in Colorado, I needed to call in daily by eleven in the morning, and, like Russian roulette, I may or may not need to drug test that day. On any day, my name might be pulled, possibly three days in a row, or none for a week. When it was called, I must get down to Boulder, urinate in a cup while being supervised by a government stranger, then return to Nederland in time for my four o'clock work shift. According to the court, it was mandatory that I maintain employment and still make it down the mountain for drug testing. One added difficulty to this was the absence of cellphone service where I lived. Each morning, I would drive to a place where I could call by eleven, and if my name was pulled, do what must be done. Exercising, pouring beer and drug testing became the sum of my life. For a brief period, I could drive to the drug tests until the courts confiscated my license, a date which was quickly approaching.

In addition to the frequent drug testing, I had alcohol education classes to attend, courses to complete, and exams to pass. Although it was not mandatory to start fulfilling such stipulations until after court sentencing in early August, I prioritized these obligations, enrolling in the classes immediately. I wanted to complete every step the legal system required with a humble, genuine attitude, progress through the process smoothly, then put it behind me and move forward. Utilizing the forced sobriety time, I seriously examined the way I had been living. I understood I was guilty and genuinely did not desire to remain living unlawfully. I sincerely regretted my deeply irresponsible behavior, not because I was caught, but because it could have harmed or even killed someone else. No part of me, despite the inner angsts, ever wished damage on another soul. No one ever deserved my physical and emotional collateral destruction. With no alcohol in my system, the horrendously callous selfishness of my actions became clear. I deeply desired to change.

As we chose a location for our mountain summer camp, we took my limitations into consideration. Close to cellphone service and our work would be ideal, yet far enough away from other transient camps or the watchful eye of local police was necessary. Berengar discovered the perfect site. Down a trail, a little less than half a mile from the Sundance Lodge, existed a secluded flat woodland plot among large boulders and lodgepole pines. The large rocks would serve well to protect us from the wind. We could park our two vehicles behind the lodge and then discreetly trek into our camp. The location was deep enough into the forest, away from the fringes of town, to remain undiscovered by the hobos, hippies and vagrants who flocked and camped all around Nederland during the warmer season. Berengar beamed proudly as he guided us all to his discovery, to which we immediately agreed, this shall be our summer home.

We each chose a nook in our new plot and set up our tents, tarps, and hammocks. I dug in and built a proper hazard-free firepit in the center, creating our new living room. Once camp had been built, it resembled a little village. The rustic abodes amounted to five, with Berengar, Mike, Ol' Man Sam, Bee with her dog Basil, and me all arranged in a spacious circle around the firepit. We were very pleased with the isolation. No one could see us from even 100 feet away because of the large boulders surrounding the encampment. It would take an intentional search to be detected. Each of us had plenty of experience with remote camping and nomadic living. The practice of leaving no trace was our primary principle. We would not leave any trash strewn about and no fire or embers unattended. When we needed to use the bathroom or shower, we would utilize our friend's facilities in town and occasionally be permitted access at the Sundance Lodge. The family would import only necessary supplies to camp, such as water and daily meals. Cooking would remain limited so as not to attract animals. All our stipulations were set to live respectfully at mountain summer camp.

CINEREAL

Once we had established camp, life flowed with its new daily routines. Berengar and Mike worked in the mornings and then attended to the marijuana grow in the evenings. Bee and Basil flit freely. I went to Boulder during the day for alcohol classes and drug-testing, exercised every opportunity I had, operated BCP in the evenings, and Sam would do whatever Ol' Man Sam pleased. Including his daily free slice of cheese pizza and soda cup. Since I was not partying and drinking after work anymore, we spent our nights together sitting in the dirt around our fire discussing the day. The family smoked joints of marijuana, and I smoked the only thing I had left, my tobacco. Although I missed the alcohol, after a few sober weeks, I did not mind too much, for without the booze I was less anxious and emotional. The absence of marijuana was not a hindrance. I loved smoking cannabis, but it was always a take it or leave it kind of thing, never addictive, simply pleasant, helpful in lessening bodily aches and enhancing creativity. As we let the night coals simmer into sleep, we lay on the cool mountain soil and gazed at the stars.

The few summer days when I did not have to drug test and neither Berengar nor I were scheduled to work were glorious. Both of us shared a passion for pushing our physical and mental selves. We would drop and do 100 pushups and then run up a mountain. On the summit, we continued our pushups followed by jubilant laughter with the sky. We ate picnic lunches by high-elevation lakes, swam in clear, cool emerald waters, then ran onward as uninhibited creatures. Our talks focused on the Zen of being, shedding all that held us back and clearing our minds towards enlightenment. Deep within I knew that even this was a defiance toward God. The Almighty did not want me to empty my mind but rather fill it with Him. Yet I disregarded this awareness and persisted with my silent rebellion, for in this pagan practice my friendship grew stronger with Berengar. Daily, I averaged 500 pushups. Not at once, but in sets throughout the sun's shine. I was determined to reach 1,000 within twelve hours. After a few weeks of managing only 700-800, I finally hit the mark. Excitedly, with arms dangling like rubber and my entire body trembling, I orated the accomplishment. Berengar was indeed impressed and shared my excitement.

In many ways amid this season of alcohol sobriety, I thrived. One of the bar regulars commented, "Wing, maybe you should never drink again. I have never seen anyone grow and excel so quickly!" I laughed and responded in agreement. However, I knew I would return to drinking alcohol as soon as legally permitted. Although the sobriety was beneficial, I was only doing it because I must.

~~~

The day the court sentenced me and revoked my driver's license was the day Ol' Man Sam officially became my driver. He wasn't the finest driver, but he was my best option and companion. Apprehensively, I alerted him to each stop sign, curb and braking light from Rhino's passenger seat. I knew this annoyed him, but if I did not, he had already proved he would ignore them. To each of my instructions, Ol' Man Sam listened, then mumbled, "Thanks, mon. You got it, mon. Sure, mon."

During the summer, the University of Colorado in Boulder hosted the annual Colorado Shakespeare Festival. Both Ol' Man Sam and I, as lovers of all art and excellent writing, attended as many of the plays as we could. Sam had a friend who could secure us free tickets, so between my legal duties, when I could get my work shift covered, we observed the stage. On days I was required to drug test, I would tell my comrade we needed to get down the mountain immediately. He would shuffle his feet into the pattern of forward movement and then drive as mindfully as he could. After the drug test, we would peruse the festival's schedule, determine its exact location, park the truck and walk towards A Midsummer Night's Dream.

We always secured our post on the outskirts of the main seating grid, often in the shade or on a bleacher. From there we watched the actors attempt to portray Shakespeare's intentions, while munching on popcorn and sipping on something non-alcoholic and cold. After the show, we ambled around the university campus, pausing at his favorite benches, discussing what we thought of the program and how Shakespeare's works shaped the world of literary and performance arts. When the sun moved behind the mountains, allowing the town of Boulder to settle in evening's summer hues, we sauntered our way back to the gray, four-wheeled automobile and returned to mountain camp. "Two down, many more to go. Next up, The Merchant of Venice." Sam stated with a grin.

A week later, after my mandatory urine appointment, I hopped back into the truck's passenger seat. I struggled to maintain composure, holding anger within. Ol' Man Sam joked, "Dang Wing, that took a long time." But when he recognized my demeanor, his tone changed. "What's wrong, mon? You've got something stirrin' you up."

"Oh Sam," I replied, forcing a methodical tone, "I don't know what to do. An extremely messed-up thing has been going on for some time now. I haven't talked about it because I don't like thinking about it." I slumped defeated in my seat and lit a cigarette.

"Common, mon, you can tell me anything. Best you get it out instead of holding it in." Ol' Man Sam eased the truck onto the road towards the university campus.

"Okay, I will tell you, but please promise not to tell the others. Just leave it as it is once I spill it." I looked at my friend, imploring him to hold this secret.

"You got it, mon. I'm a vault mon." Sam patted my leg, causing me to flinch, a movement I never made with him.

Reluctantly, I spoke. "There is this guy, the drug-testing monster, who goes into the bathroom with me. Well, there are two guys. The other one is fine, but it's the bad one I had today, and most days, which is a problem."

"What is the problem, Hot Wing?" Sam drove the truck carefully while listening attentively.

"This guy, he is always harassing me. It started somewhat minor, but it has gotten much worse." I sighed as I realized I was about to say the words out loud.

"Harassing you how?" He downshifted into second gear, decelerating for slow Boulder traffic.

I relented and let it out, my tone escalating into an angry ramble as I spoke. "It is crude stuff, man, vulgar. He is vulgar. He always makes comments about my dick, and how long it takes for me to pee in front of him. I physically can't just suddenly pee with him right there next to me staring at me down there. So, we just stand there, in the bathroom alone, until I can get it flowing. The first time he said, as he crowded up to my body, 'Turn towards me so I can see you aren't using fake urine.' To which I snapped back at him, 'I'm not going to use fake urine, just give me space.' But he only gets closer. I have him turn on the sink faucet to prompt my flow, which still doesn't help because the reason I can't pee is that he traumatizes me, scares me, harasses me. It's not his looking at me down there that bothers me. It's what he has been saying. Multiple times he's said, 'Would it help you get something out if I held your dick for you?' Like, what the hell, man! And that's the G-rated version of it. It only gets worse. I can't physically urinate because of his constant comments, and therefore I get stuck in a tiny room with no camera with him for a long time. I just want to punch him, and yell in his face, but I can't do that, so I just stand there helpless, physically trembling and waiting, being harassed and waiting, trying to pee, trying to pee, getting harassed, continually getting harassed! Ahhh!!" I yelled angrily and then continued my rant. "But dammit, Sam, his comments just keep growing worse, crude, sexually explicit, harassing assaults at me and laughing at my powerless state and fear. With each drug test, his actions escalate. I don't know what I am going to do, or what he is going to do. It's like he wants to rape me, or he wants me to think that. He loves that I have no choice but to take it… I hate all of it. I don't know what to do."

I dragged hard on my cigarette and glanced over to see Ol' Man Sam's reaction. He appeared disgusted with what I had been experiencing. He then asked the question I expected next. "That ain't right at all, mon. Truly messed up. Have you reported him?"

"I have!" I shouted. "But they did nothing about it. I have reported it to the check-in desk person and to my case officer. The check-in person said that what I reported isn't happening, like she literally straight up denied it and brushed me off and told me it is best I just complete my urine test and get on with my day. My case officer told me I was lying, and 'This experience isn't designed for my comfort.' Like, no shit, it isn't designed for comfort. I don't need comfort; I just need not to be sexually harassed every time I go drug test and that guy is working, which he usually is. No one believes me. So, it just keeps getting worse. Screw this. I don't want to think or talk about it anymore right now. I'm sorry, brother, to spill this on you, also sorry because I can't focus on Shakespeare right now."

Emphatically Sam responded, "Can't trust anyone in the government. They just look out for each other and don't care about us."

"I know it. I just need to get everything done, get out of the system, and I will never drink and drive or break the law again, don't want to be in the system ever again." My toe tapped anxiously on the truck floor while I lit another cigarette.

"Don't worry about the play, mon, let's go get those sandwiches we like and then sit by the creek or something." Ol' Man Sam forced a smile while changing the subject to a foodie idea he knew I would approve of.

CINEREAL

"Yeah, let's do that. I am freaking hungry. Freakin' angry and hungry. Wish I could drink some whiskey or smoke some pot, but a cheesesteak sub will suffice."

"In time, brother, in time. Your anger is justified. I am proud of you for how well you have been doing. You've really put your all into attending to what needs to be done. In this sober season, your emotions have been more balanced out. Your mind is much clearer and more stable without the booze. Use that emotional stability to stay strong, mon. If we end up needing to kill the man, then we will figure that out." The fearless author winked at me and caused a single laugh to slice through my anger. I knew he was joking, but it did help that he shared my frustration. What he didn't know was how deeply my frustration was turning into shame. I felt lost, helpless, and accepted that I would just need to keep subjecting myself to the pervert's sexual harassment.

~~~

In September, Berengar and I succeeded in our mission. We secured a new home for our family. The abode was a marvelous upgrade from the goldminer's cabin, just one gulch over from Gamble on Lump Gulch. Not only was it a part of another Rollinsville borough, but it sat at the very end of a long dirt road. The lane ascends upon mountain flanks, providing spacious views to the east and south. No longer would we be squeezed into the folds of the land but now hoisted towards the sky. Our new cabin was an A-frame, with three bedrooms, plus a spacious loft. In the living room existed a proper woodstove, one that was legally installed. Large windows and a sliding glass door opened onto a wide deck that overlooked the surrounding fields, aspen groves and the magnificent Thorodin Mountain.

At dawn, we packed summer camp and eagerly moved into our new home. Ol' Man Sam was quite content with a downstairs room. Mike took the one next to his. I claimed the cozy bedroom on the main, woodstove floor next to the bathroom, and Berengar burrowed into the loft above the spiral staircase. Bee and Basil also bedded in the loft, and with a futon in the living room we had plenty of space for guests. Before long we were all settled in, with the woodstove harboring a crackling fire, a large pot of homemade soup simmering in the kitchen and the traditional waft of cannabis smoke lingering in the living room. Although I could not smoke the ganja, I would still sit in its sunbeam-illuminated cloud, enjoy the aroma, and hope our

CINEREAL

family's home lifestyle would not negatively affect my already sexually harassed drug tests.

Berengar purchased himself an old blue truck. Our driveway looked the part with two mechanical steeds ready for tree-harvesting season. We promptly went to work gathering wood. Brumal weather would arrive early at nearly 9,100 feet above sea-level. After burning fifteen cords of pine the previous winter, we wanted to ensure we had twenty cords available in October when snow would start falling and not stop accumulating until spring. Mike occasionally joined Berengar and me in the forest for our dead-tree collection, but since he was often preoccupied with other endeavors, most days it was just the two of us, returning to the hardy craft we had become proficient at. Up at the end of Lump Gulch, forest service roads connected the tails of Lump and Gamble gulches. Therefore, we did not need to climb the mountain on foot to harvest our dead trees. We utilized the unmaintained, tire-worn paths to reach and gather the trees we felled, and to commute to our thriving marijuana grow at the end of Gamble Gulch. When we weren't working in town, gathering supplies, or I wasn't fulfilling my legal duties in Boulder, there was no reason to leave our backwoods life in the mountains.

My favorite addition to our new home was a brown upright Jacob Brothers piano I acquired in Boulder. Transporting the piano from 5,400 feet above sea-level to our mountain lodge was a laborious task. It required all four of us men, with Ol' Man Sam as the driver. When we arrived in Nederland, I asked Sam to pull over so I could hop in the truck's bed with the bulky secured instrument. As he drove us through town onward towards home, I jammed upon the keys for everyone to hear. Having my piano provided joy in a time of tribulation. Once settled against the wall in our A-frame living room, I poured my emotions onto and into it each day. As a fan of naming inanimate objects, I dubbed my piano Chaco, in honor of the horse I befriended in New Hampshire at Kensington Farm.

Our life settled into its original and updated schedules. Serve the town it's party and drinks at Backcountry Pizza, frequently ride with Ol' Man Sam down to Boulder for legal duties, harvest and chop wood with Berengar, play piano, cook food, exercise, read, write, work the marijuana grow and sleep. Although the sexual harassment gnawed within me, I attempted to block it out of my mind and remain focused on our bountiful blessings. Colorado had become home, and all I must do was get through to the other side of my legal requirements to be free again. Content with the life I was a part of and helped create, I harbored no plans to move anywhere else for a long time. With this established mentality, I opened my heart to a committed romantic partner and planned to adopt a dog.

I partook in a few dates and mini adventures that Lump Gulch autumn. There was even one lovely lady who swelled my heart from down near Boulder. We had dated casually in the summer, but once my driver's license was revoked, our visits dwindled. However, on October 14, 2014, the day I turned twenty-nine, I met the one who would walk with me into the final year of my howling twenties. Despite being comfortable at home, with no desire for a large observance, I chose to spend the day differently for the anniversary of my birth. My friend Andi, who once was our Gamble Gulch neighbor, currently lived with her partner Ben in Nederland's village grid and was hosting a birthday party for her new neighbor's child. The child was turning three or maybe four; I wasn't sure, but it didn't matter, I simply yearned to be around people in a celebratory manner with zero attention directed towards me.

While the others drank and smoked marijuana, I sat on the porch smoking my tobacco, playing with the dogs who roamed the streets. There was one new canine, a large puppy, I had not met before. Upon inquiring as to who was the owner of the fluffy rascal, a pretty lady I had never met claimed ownership.

"That is Juniper," smiled a brunette, wavy-haired, freckled pretty woman, pointing to the red and white fluff ball wrestling with my arms.

"Juniper is going to be big! She has snowshoes for paws." I exclaimed.

"She really does, and yes, she will be. Half Bernese Mountain Dog, half St. Bernard, she has already been growing so fast."

I stood up and extended my hand to introduce myself. "My name is Wing. Juniper is going to love her mountain life."

She reached out her hand and grasped mine, shaking hello in return. "Wayne?" She asked. A common question I received.

"Wing. Like a bird. And you?"

"Oh sorry! I'm sure you get that often, 'like a bird.' I like that. My name is Elly." She smiled with a little laugh. Her positive glow and mellow demeanor immediately impressed me.

Elly and I launched into talking about dogs. In our first conversation, upon mentioning I was ready for and had been keeping my ears alert for a mountain puppy who needed a home, she divulged that her friend's German Shepherd recently birthed a litter. "I think the dog dad was a mixed breed, a mutt, so I don't exactly know what they will look like as they develop. They only recently opened their eyes as they are about four weeks old."

This intrigued me. For the rest of the evening as everyone milled in and out of the home and sang happy birthday to the child, unaware that it was my birthday as well, I cultivated the seed she planted in my mind. By the time I left the party, I had decided. I walked over to Elly and told her I would love to meet the puppy litter, intending to adopt one. And would she, Elly, like to have lunch with me tomorrow? We could eat and then go meet the pups.

Elly accepted. With both pairs of our smiling eyes gazing into the others, while agreeing to have lunch and a puppy adventure the next day, we knew it was more than just about dogs. It was a date.

~~~

Occasionally in life, when you meet "the one," you instantly recognize your destined connection. For myself, the day after my birthday, and after my lunch date with Elly, this occurred when a small black puppy bounded over as I sat down amid a raucous scene. Puppies were rolling, wrestling, and exploring every nook in the confined cabin-room space. The mother dog named Sequoia watched attentively. Her German Shepherd's eyes seemed to pierce my soul, judging if I was a suitable caretaker. While each puppy greeted me in its own newborn way, it was the black one who was drawn to me most. In return, I could not remove the eyes of my heart away from her. The human owner exclaimed that the little black female I held was the second born, and she clearly liked me. "She is a good choice, Wing. Three of the five puppies have been claimed, but she and the clumsy white and black male are still up for adoption." I agreed with him as I held, caressed, and peered into the dawned eyes of the tiny rascal. *She is perfect.* In that moment, I made a committed decision, one that would marvelously alter the rest of my life.

"I will give this little girl a loving home and life for as long as she lives." I smiled like a child on Christmas morning. There was no need to continue searching for any other dog. I found my match. The idea of separating her from her entire family slightly irked me, which caused me to speak the words that came out of my mouth next. "What's going to happen to that little roly-poly guy there?" I pointed to the black and white unclaimed male who was purposely running into the wall and falling backwards repeatedly like a ram who hates fences.

"Well, unless someone claims him, I suppose I will just have to keep him. But I have too much going on as it is. I'm going to California for a few months soon, and even then, I'll need someone to watch Sequoia while I'm away. I honestly don't know. No one has been very interested in that guy." The human owner shrugged.

"California, eh, so will the puppies be able to spend enough time with Sequoia until they are naturally weaned?" I questioned him, concerned for the puppies' crucial three months with their mother.

"It all depends. I am still trying to figure everything out." The long-haired hippie shrugged again.

This guy doesn't seem to have his plans set properly, I realized. I didn't like it one bit. It seemed up to me to be the puppy hero. "Well, tell you what. I will adopt this black one here, and I will adopt her brother as well. I am also willing to take care of Sequoia while you go to California. That way, at least these two pups will have the appropriate length of growth time with their mother, you won't have to worry about your dog, and when you return, you can come to my home and retrieve her. This will be beneficial for all parties, other than those already claimed pups, I suppose..." I pointed to the three he had now separated from the rest.

The mountain kid, a few years younger than I, agreed, and just like that, I became a dog dad, to not just one, but two puppies, and temporarily, to their mother Sequoia as well. In seven days, when the puppies were only five weeks of age, he would deliver all three dogs to our A-frame abode.

Elly and I returned to town, eager for the new life chapter that was now upon me, and us. I looked at her and spoke, "I suppose now that I am a dog-father, this makes you the mother."

"Yes, I suppose it does, other than Sequoia, of course." Elly blushed and smiled, and for our first time, we spanned the gap between her front car seats and held hands.

~~~

I appreciated the lofted deck of our A-frame home. As autumn dissipated and winter boldly pushed itself in, I basked in the solar warmth on the south-facing perch and observed the puppies romp about. In the morning, I sat with coffee, no matter the weather, and to my left watched the east slowly brighten, the sun ascending and claiming the Colorado sky. At sunset, rays

CINEREAL

would blast upon Thorodin Mountain's cliffs, setting them ablaze as stone on fire. Unlike on the Gamble Gulch porch, where I eventually spotted a mountain lion, harbored in narrow views accompanied by the creek's lullaby, here, my views reached as far as my eyes could see. I had always been a lover of horizons and not of containment, of freedom not limitations, thus on this deck my soul felt at ease. At night, stars swaddled our home, appearing as portals in an ebony wrap, glimpsing into heaven's luster.

The noble moose was a common visitor to our new yard. Many of the giant undulates lived nearby at a pond in the willows surrounding the water. Occasionally, they strode up the hill to feast on the aspen trees flanking our cabin. When I spotted a moose approaching, I swiftly wrangled the dogs and brought them inside. I did not want to interfere with the wild animals' natural movements, nor put my canine children at risk of being trampled.

Sequoia proved to be a superb dog and mother. Whenever she needed a break from parenting, I opened the door, and she disappeared into the forest. When I called her, she returned. What she did out there on her own, only she knew. I learned much about the puppies while examining Sequoia rearing her two offspring. She treated them differently. For the fluffy male, she was gentle and patient, and for my little wild female, she often needed to rule with a harsh, reprimanding demeanor. I waited a few days to name them, as I desired for their appellations to be appropriate to their personalities. After studying them diligently, the perfect titles became clear. My darling girl earned the name Wylie Wizzle, and her brother I dubbed Bacon. Wylie proved to be tenacious, mischievous, slightly rebellious, very intelligent and often scheming up a plan. While Bacon was mellow, obedient, goofy, and sometimes a tad clueless. He didn't have a mean bone in his body, unlike his sister, who was fearless and willing to fight, if need be, or even need-not be. When eagles and hawks circled overhead, hunting for their next meal, Sequoia barked up at them, defending the puppies from the predator's intentions. It was apparent Sequoia understood I would take over the role as parent soon, and in her own way she showed me how to teach them, in the unique ways each needed.

On my long deck sits thrust atop the landscape, as the dogs explored their new environment, I prioritized leaning into the blessings of life. I sensed that at any moment, if I slacked in my gratitude practices, I would slip into despair. The ongoing sexual harassment during the drug tests hung as an exhausting burden, chipping away at my confidence and humanity. It triggered deep personal fury I harbored, sins of the church I had learned of as a child. I was on the outside looking in at the sin, but even the window into it all had scarred me for any notion of trust in the church.

When I was a young boy, there had been a man, a horrible evil human, who for many years was touted as a trustworthy, godly, family man in our congregation. I shall call him Dung. In the youthful years before my family had fallen apart, we would frequently go to other church family's homes for fellowship. Picnics and games in the yard created fun, wholesome environments. However, one house we would visit was Dung's. His wife was hospitable and selfless. His kids were of similar ages to me and my siblings. Dung played music on stage during the Sunday worship services, often making others laugh with his humor and charisma. But Dung was not the man he pretended to be. He had most everyone fooled. My parents and church leaders were unaware of what horrible things he had been doing. The day came when Dung's despicable actions were revealed. He had been sexually abusing children. He was a pedophile. Finally, he was convicted and sentenced to prison, where he belonged. Dung created and left behind torrents of pain and damage. Although he never abused me, the fact we were near him in a trusting manner, the fact he had abused some of my friends, the fact he professed to be a man of God and yet was a man overcome with evil, was a horrifying reality which seeped into my soul. My heart mourned for those he hurt. In time, some of them told me about their experiences, while weeping tears of shame and confusion. As an adolescent, after the awful, sinful abuse was brought to light, I did not know what to think of the church anymore, or of men in positions of influence and power who claimed to be virtuous. I became extremely wary of anyone who claimed to be good, when in fact they could be a lying, dangerous hypocrite. Sexual abuse became the sin I hated most in the world. *Anyone who would assault others in such a loathsome way, especially children, deserves to die, to be publicly beaten and hung in the town square...* Thinking of this boiled my anger again, turning my knuckles pale with how hard I clenched my fists on the Lump Gulch sundeck. In my fury, I suddenly remembered the words Hunter Larry had spoken to me. *"Do not let the sins of others keep you from an eternity with God... ...sin is not from God, while grace, love, forgiveness, healing and judgement are."*

Bee graciously interrupted my thoughts by delivering a homemade sandwich. I accepted the sandwich with a whispered thank you and set it by my side on the wooden lofted floorboards. She smiled kindly and laughed at

CINEREAL

Wylie and Bacon, who quickly assembled attentively in front of me. Naively, I fell for Wylie's affection distracting me to my right, only to have Bacon grab the sandwich on my left. I emitted a surprised, admonishing sentence. Having observed the suavely accomplished theft, Bee guffawed robustly and promised to make me another. *Those darn kids are working together. I had better smarten up. It is time to give them proper training lessons.*

~~~

Despite the pleasant apricity on our deck, the winter raged with its annual highland fury. Snow rapidly piled up on the sides of our A-frame home. From afar, only the wooden facet and green metal pinnacle of our cabin protruded from a white world. The roofs of our blue and gray trucks levitated above the snowbanks in our driveway, while the pathways we shoveled resembled roofless tunnels from the back door to our vehicles.

After Christmas and New Year's passed, a few days of oddly warm weather descended upon the Rocky Mountains. Elly and I took advantage of this window to retreat on a one-night vacation while the roads were clear for travel. Our destination, Taos, New Mexico. It was only a six-hour drive south through the mountains, and since I did not have to drug test that day, and I had two days off work, all the ingredients for a refreshing getaway aligned. I would still call in from Taos to check if I must drug test in the morning, and if so then we would zip back up to Boulder before five in the afternoon, and if I mustn't, then we could take our time and enjoy the Great Sand Dunes National Park in the Sangre de Cristo Mountain range.

I brought Wylie and left Bacon at home with the family. A brief separation from each other would be healthy, and an adventure with just my girls appealed to us. I loved Bacon, but Wylie was my wild little pup, my chosen one, my favorite, thus I desired to show her more of the world without the distraction of her brother. Although riding in the passenger seat was never my preference, I was grateful to have a girlfriend who could drive. My side-seat lounge allowed me to observe Colorado in a new way.

We departed early, allowing time for a mini side-quest into Vail to eat lunch at the rowdy pub I worked at two winters prior. We arrived before noon, so the establishment was mellow, and though I recognized a few long-term employees, I kept my hat pulled low, not wanting to go through the motions of meaningless conversations with past acquaintances. After sharing laughs over the Vail anecdotes I shared during our meal, we rolled

CINEREAL

onward. Up and over the high elevation town of Leadville, a short snack break in Buena Vista, arriving in Taos well after the sun had set.

Our lodging for the night was the historic Taos Inn. Infamous for being haunted by ghosts, its construction was of the old adobe Spanish styled casa. I loved the art and architecture of the Southwest, and the next day, if I did not have to drug-test, we planned to explore some galleries and fulfill Elly's desire of investigating the local earth-ship homes.

We were both quite exhausted and famished following our long day in the car. Therefore, after I paid for our hotel room, we lounged in the restaurant within the inn. It was here that I first saw the strange man, who held eerie knowledge that would baffle me for many years.

"Do you see that guy? The tall, skinny, pale one serving food and drinks to the tables?" I asked Elly while nodding in his direction.

"I do, but what of him?" She glanced his way and then returned her attention to the menu.

"Well, right when we sat down, I noticed him, and he noticed me. Our eyes locked in such a peculiar way. He kept looking at me from over there yet still delivered food without regarding where he was going. Like I would do when hiking the trails, however, somehow oddly different." I tried not to stare in his direction and focused on meal options.

"That is strange, but he probably just knows this restaurant so well he doesn't need to watch his step, and maybe he was looking at you like that because he thinks you are handsome, like I do." Elly giggled, tossing me a flirtatious look.

"Sure, sure, and thanks, but no, I don't think that was it. I don't know. Perhaps I am just more tired than I thought and am overthinking. Okay, what're you going to order?"

Elly and I feasted on chips and salsa, guacamole, enchiladas, and carne asada fajitas. When our hunger had been satisfied, we spent time with Wylie outside in the back dirt-patch parking lot. Our vehicle was the only one parked on this side of the inn. Beneath the bare limbs of a few overhanging trees and within the confines of a tall slab fence, there was no light to see over ten feet in front of us. We sat with our backs to the boundary and discussed the strange man.

"I'm telling you. He kept staring at me the entire time we ate. It was truly the weirdest thing." I pulled smoke from my cigarette, the orange ember acting as the only light around us.

CINEREAL

"Maybe he has seen you somewhere else before. Did he look familiar to you at all?" Elly wrapped her arm through mine, sitting closer to share our warmth. Wylie chewed on a stick.

"No, definitely not. I have never seen him. I would remember. His appearance is so unique. I mean, almost like a lizard-human, tall, thin, pale, with long fingers and nose, those eyes though, they kept piercing me, I could sense it. There is no way I have seen him, or he has ever seen me, I'm sure of it."

Just as I explained to her what was also abnormal, the fact I never saw him speak a word to any other employees during our meal, the back door opened casting indoor light upon the pathway. Although the light was distant, I covered the ember of my cigarette to avoid detection while we were snuggled against the fence in the dark. It was the strange man. Elly gasped quietly, muted enough that her sound could not have traveled to the light. The strange man carried a bag of trash and walked toward the dumpsters.

As the door closed behind him, and the light from indoors became concealed, he took long strides and spoke unnervingly coherent words directed at us. "You come all this way, you spend all this money, and yet here you sit in the dark."

Elly gasped again. I tightened up. *Did he really say that? Should we respond?* I placed my hand on Elly's arm, indicating we should remain silent. Wylie sat in my lap and looked towards the man, but she too did not utter a sound. The strange man threw the bag of trash into the dumpsters, walked back towards the door, paused before he opened it, and though it was difficult to see him, we recognized him turn and glance back in our direction. Without another word, he then opened the door and returned inside.

"Okay, that was incredibly weird." Elly whispered with exhilaration now that we were alone again.

"What the... what did he mean by all that? I mean, how could he know we 'came all this way' other than we are staying at the inn, I suppose?" I felt unusually nervous, and yet also animated by the adventure of the scenario.

"'And yet here you sit in the dark.' What?!" Elly stood up, shaking off nerves. "Like he could see us! I couldn't see you when I was by the car and you and Wylie sat down here, so I don't know how he could have seen us even with the brief light when the door was opened. That was cast over there, not towards here."

CINEREAL

"Right!? Those eyes, they pierce. So weird, almost extraterrestrial-like... Okay, let's go for a walk away from this creepy lot." I stood up and motioned towards the sleepy town.

Elly, little Wylie and I strolled through the town of Taos. All the art galleries were closed, but we enjoyed peering in windows and observing the art that was displayed. We took our time. I twirled Elly once or twice on the vintage stone pathways. We kissed, walked hand in hand and pointed out details in old buildings we liked. Wylie was already a well-behaved young dog on the leash, and in our simple moments, it seemed like the beginning of a new kind of family. Although I loved my home and life in Colorado, a brief break away from the stresses of legal duties was a worthy rest. I needed to be refreshed and not to think about the sexual harassment. I needed some Southwest pueblo vibes to soothe my blustery soul.

The time was ten forty-five at night. The inn's restaurant, where we ate dinner, closed at ten. Down the street was a grocery market open until eleven. Only two cars sat in the large parking lot, but the lights of the market were still on. Everywhere in town was subdued, as it was only a weeknight in the middle of winter. After our amble, we decided to purchase snacks and basic supplies at the store. Upon reaching the front sliding doors, Elly said she would go in and purchase the goods while I remained outside with Wylie.

I stood in the lot and looked around while Wylie sniffed and did her puppy exploration. No other soul was in sight. The area was so empty that in all directions I would be able to spot anyone arriving, and yet, after reaching down to confiscate a piece of trash from Wylie's mouth and rising, abruptly, ten feet in front of me, standing still and tall was the strange pale man. His sudden presence startled me. I had not seen him approach nor heard any footsteps, and I had only knelt for a few seconds. But there he was, staring at me, piercing me with his laser vision. He did not look at Wylie, who bounded towards him, nor even glanced down when I pulled her back. Feeling quite uneasy about his precipitous appearance and demeanor, I spoke first.

"Oh, hi. I saw you at the restaurant." My words seemed thin and forced.

"What are you doing here?" His words were sharp, just like his eyes.

"We are getting some snacks. My girlfriend is inside while I let the dog explore all the unfamiliar smells, like puppies like to do." I was rambling unnecessarily, and yet still he did not glance at Wylie, nor had he blinked even once.

"No." He disagreed with my honest answer and then repeated. "What are you doing here?" His words now jabbed almost like a threat or a warning. I was unsure of their purpose, yet they held a combative implication.

"We are on vacation. We live in Colorado, just down checking out Taos for the night." I attempted to display a casual attitude and then looked around to see if anyone else could see us. There was no one. I peeked at the market door, hoping Elly would return quickly so we could leave.

"But that is not where you are from." The tall, thin man remained firm. He had not shifted his weight from one foot to the other. His heart did not even seem to have a beat. He looked un-alive, like a zombie with poise and erect posture. My uneasiness grew into fear. To his accusation that I was not from Colorado, I could not reply. Opening my mouth to force words, I closed it again, saying nothing. I stared back at him. After a brief, uncomfortable silence, he spoke his last words to me. "I know you are not from Colorado, for we are strong in New Hampshire."

With this powerful drop of disturbing knowledge, and with one last fierce stare to my soul, he turned around and walked inside the store, leaving me in shock, exposed, confused and afraid.

Finally, Elly returned. Frantically, I informed her of what had happened. "Did you see him in there? He walked in just a few minutes ago."

"I did not, and what?! Tell me all of that again. How would he know you were from New Hampshire.?"

"I don't know, Elly, I don't know. He clearly knew about New Hampshire somehow, without ever having met me before. And he stated 'we' with emphasis, and 'strong' with emphasis. I know for a fact that we've never met. I just don't know how he knew, and honestly, I don't think he was human. There is no way that non-blinking, non-glancing-at-Wylie being was a human..." Bewildered, I looked over my shoulder to make sure he wasn't following. "Come on, let's go back to the inn, to our room for the night. After all, we came all this way and spent all this money, and yet here we are in the dark! I don't want to be anywhere near this store when he comes out."

We hustled back to the inn, locked ourselves in the room, and repeatedly reviewed the events of the evening, including his exact words. In the end, all we could do was accept that it was an extremely odd, unnerving mystery. A mystery we may never know the answer to. The next day I thankfully did not have to drug test, so we focused our attention on the natural beauty of New Mexico, exploring the earth-ship abodes and romping through the sand dunes of southern Colorado. On the drive home, my ebony fluff ball slept soundly in the backseat, curled tightly in a circle. Her nose tucked beneath her hind paw and tail, while her little body gently undulated with the rhythm of breaths in repose. Sand from her adventure now lay strewn across the seat, but that was alright. We would clean everything up later.

~~~

The light on the ceiling flickered, causing all three people in the room to glance up. The lady at the desk commented the lightbulb must be near the end of its life. She spoke almost comically, as if there were nothing to worry about in her world. She brushed a strand of brown hair behind her right ear, yet as she turned her head to answer the telephone, the strand of hair fell forward again.

Another lady, younger, sat in the same strip of seats as a young man. There were three empty seats between them. This lady with blonde hair peered over at the fellow who sat with his head down. His heel tapped steadily on the faded blue carpeted floor, as if his toe was glued down but the back of his foot was caught in a windstorm. She opened her mouth as if to speak, but as she did so, a woman entered the room and called, "Cassandra!"

Cassandra stood up, disregarded whatever she was going to say, and followed the lady, leaving the room. The man knew she wanted to talk to him. He could feel her glances. In his peripherals he saw rips in her jeans at the knees. The gashes looked intentional, as if cut with scissors or purchased that way. He wondered why she would wear such a garment in February. It was snowing outside. *She must be cold.* But after considering it, considering turning his head towards her and smiling graciously, he decided not to. *What was the point? There was no point. Just keep your head down, wait for the drug test, do the drug test, and then leave.* He focused on getting in and getting out. He was more than anxious. He was frightened. His body felt locked up, and yet the tapping of his heel upon the faded blue carpet was not because of anxiety; it was because he had to urinate so damn badly. This was the only way he could muster a few droplets for the drug test. Load up on water, create the

CINEREAL

uncomfortable urge to pee, hold it in, and then try to push it out despite the barrier that would inevitably lock within.

The clock on the wall had three hands. One for the hour, one for the minute, and one for the seconds. The hand for the seconds seemed broken, clicking by far longer than any second than he'd ever experienced. Everything seemed slower in here, except for his pulse. That was beating faster than a horse's heart at a derby finish line. Click beat beat beat beat beat click beat beat beat beat beat click. Only two seconds had gone by. *How much longer must I endure this dreadful anticipation?* His name was next on the sign-in list, and there was no one else here, other than the damn lady with her damn loose strand of hair who kept looking up at that damn flickering lightbulb. He never wanted his name to be called, but he knew it must. He was next, *but in how long? Get in, get out,* beat beat beat click.

"David." *There it is.*

David looked up and saw the man he hated. The man who looked like any other Caucasian in government. Short hair, shaved face, except for his eyes, his eyes which held a haughty air declaring, "I own you."

"Nice to see you again David, follow me." The man smiled in a way that only David understood. Although it sounded kind to the lady at the front desk, it was not kind. It was controlling and manipulative. It was evil.

David did not answer but stood up, grabbed his jacket he had set on the seat to his right and brushed back his shoulder-length brown hair with his left arm, the arm that wore his first tattoo. The tattoo he paid to have permanently inked on that specific forearm because it was where his grandfather had his tattoo. David clenched his teeth and considered punching the man when he said, "Nice to see you again," for he mocked. He had his knife in David's body, and he was intentionally turning it. But David did nothing out of normal, he followed the man down the hallway, turned left into the bathroom where he had been many times before and stood in front of the toilet. Next to him, he heard the man lock the door and turn on the water faucet. In the bathroom, the two men stood together alone. No one else could get in.

"You know what to do." The man he would not look at spoke to him. "Show me that dick, David. Show me your dick."

In the waiting room, David had needed to urinate urgently, but now that he was standing in front of the toilet with the villain next to him, he no longer could. Well, he still direly needed to pee, but it would be impossible to do so. The barrier within had locked into place. He did not want the blockade. All he wanted was to push out the urine and leave as quickly as possible, but after months of harassment from this man, the task of eliminating the barrier and releasing the urine seemed impossible. David was broken.

"Are you going to be a problem again, David? Are you asking me to help you? Can you not urinate in front of me because you want to spend more time with me? Turn more this way. I want a better look. Ah yes, there it is." The man moved closer.

David tried to ignore every comment the man made, turning the words into static in his brain, yet the words still seeped through. The man continued moving closer to David, so close that his left shoulder brushed up against David's right shoulder. David could feel the man breathing on his neck as he continued to say things that David would not listen to. David closed his eyes and focused on forcing out a few drops of urine into the cup he held in his right hand, holding it beneath where the urine should come out of his body. But no matter how hard he tried, even while mentally traveling to another world without this man, nothing would come out.

The man lifted his left arm and put it around David's shoulders. David flinched, his body tightened as he felt the man wrapping himself closer around David's body. The man whispered into David's ear. "Do you want me to lick it? Will that loosen you up? Tell me what you like, David, what do you like, Davvvidddd." He slowly pronounced the young man's name, vibrating David's own name into his own ear. David felt like the man was trying to push himself closer until he was inside him, testing to see how far he could go until David would snap.

David sensed a tear coming out of his tightly closed eyes. All he wanted to do was push out a few dribbles of urine, enough to satisfy the government, enough for them to test it and move on with life. Enough for him to leave, but still nothing would come out. *How could he produce a tear but not any other droplets!?*

This is as far as the evil man had ever pushed himself onto David before. It had come this far many times but never further. David hoped it would be as far as he would go, but then abruptly, the man whose left arm was around David's shoulder, and whose breath stung on David's neck, now took his right hand and placed a firm hold on to David's genitals. In shock,

CINEREAL

David recognized the man had his hand securely wrapped around his member, clenching it, and David sensed the man smile as he squeezed.

David did not know what to do. For one excruciating second, longer than the seconds had been in the waiting room, he froze, and then, he snapped.

In a seizure of fury, forfeiting all self-control, David violently lifted his right elbow and thrust it into the man's ribs, but the man still held onto David's genitals. The young, trapped man then forcibly flung his elbows and arms in all directions, twisting and turning as an alligator might perform a death roll, or as a tornado destroys. The two men, who had been standing stationary a few seconds prior, now scuffled in the small bathroom with a torrent of imbalance.

The evil man finally flew backwards, his hand ripping off David's naked groin. He hit the bathroom wall with a loud thud. Wincing yet maintaining an entertained grin, he hung against the wall, tottering on vile feet. David glared at him, unlocked the bathroom door and ran out of the room while zipping up his pants. Frantically, he turned right, struggling to slow his speed as he passed through the waiting room. The lady at the desk emitted a startled, "Hey!" David heard her but kept moving to the door. He pushed it open, bursting out into the cold air. Tears poured down his face, blurring his sight. He looked behind him expecting the man to chase after him, but there was no one, only the door closing behind him. David brushed the tears from his eyes and moved into the parking lot, desperately scanning each vehicle until he recognized the gray truck. In the driver's seat sat Ol' Man Sam, his head backwards, eyes closed, taking a nap while he waited. David furiously jumped into the truck and hurriedly awakened his driver.

"Now!" David forced a shout, but only a stunned whisper escaped. "We must leave now."

~~~

In the days that followed, I turned into the worst version of myself. I ruined everything. Directly after the incident, in a haze of shocked ferocity, I told Ol' Man Sam what occurred. I kept blowing snot out of my nostril onto my passenger truck door, chain-smoking cigarettes and gritting my teeth between spilled curses and jumbled sentences. I then demanded that Sam take me to Backcountry Pizza, where I was set to work in two hours at four in the afternoon. Once we arrived, I stormed through the kitchen entrance, called the boss outside, and told him I quit.

CINEREAL

People I knew and cared about strolled nearby hollering, "Wing!" Perhaps they witnessed my emotions overflowing. Ignoring them, I explained to the boss that I didn't want this. I didn't want to quit, but I had no choice; I would be gone soon either way. I repeated to him how much I loved my job, how thankful I was for it, how much I loved everyone I worked with, how much I loved every single person in Nederland, but my time at Backcountry Pizza had come to an end. There was no other choice. Torment blinded my decision. I must disappear.

Next, I instructed Ol' Man Sam to drive us home to our A-frame cabin at the end of Lump Gulch. I packed a bag of necessities, my preferred clothing, books, wilderness survival gear, tools, the dogs' toys and food, toiletries, anything I might soon need. Quickly, I stashed the supplies in my truck.

Berengar and Bee had recently left for an overseas adventure, leaving only Mike and dear Ol' Man Sam to explain my next step to. "I will be back for everything else, but I need to disappear and formulate my plan. The cops might come here, but if they do, you can honestly tell them you don't know where I am. I will be in contact with you soon."

I secured Wylie and Bacon in their spots, jumped into the driver's seat, and drove the speed limit to a discreet motel. Upon securing a room for three nights with cash, I then drove into Boulder. Cautiously, I purchased four days' worth of food, whiskey, wine, water gallons, cigarettes, all again in cash, then returned to the secluded motel. What happened in the next few days I am not altogether sure of. It is difficult to remember. Not so much because of the alcohol, but rather by descending into dissociative amnesia.

I do not know if I broke up with Elly, or if I just pushed her away and constructed mental walls. I know I severed ties with most everyone and everything. Additionally, I know I did not curse God. Although I had been rebelling against Him for my entire adult life, I still believed in Him. I feared His omnipotence and righteous wrath of my rejection. He had shown Himself many times in ways I could never deny. He faithfully called me to Him. There was no atheist ever to walk the earth who could convince me otherwise. But it did not matter what I believed, for even though I did not curse God, I once again buried Him away. Instead of trusting in Him, I leaned into the bottle. I got drunk.

The Unsettling & The Decision

"That happened to David, not to Wing. That happened to David, not to Wing," I muttered to myself repeatedly between sips of red wine.

I sat on the porch of a white house in a wide, flat countryside. The porch faced north, for that is where you place such a feature on a home that bakes in southern heat and humidity. Beyond the two-acre lot lay a large tract of fenced pastureland. Brown cows roamed, dotting the dull-green grassy expanse. Past the fields, creating my horizon, rows of straight pines rose tall. I wasn't familiar with what kind of pine trees these southern Georgia conifers were, but I would examine, research and learn that later. In front of the barricade containing the grazers, pillared in Grandma's front yard, stood two magnificent pecan trees. Naked against a sky that had morphed from blue to orange, faded into pastels, until it became the color which swallows all colors. Bleak twigs at the end of stalwart branches quivered in a manure-scented breeze.

To the west, the sunset was completing its descent beneath the darkened prospect. The day was March third, and my Colorado mountains were now far away. I hadn't planned to come here, to the place my grandfather had spent his last days, but my dad had stated, "The family needs your help."

I knew he only said this because he didn't want me to drive away from Colorado without a license. Or hoist the backpack and lead two young puppies on cross-country skis into the snowy wilderness. Both of which I had considered as my two best options. But they were not. A tempest of angry confusion had blinded me. It was not just the incident. Not just the physical act of the sexual assault. It was everything that led up to it. I burned with resentment of myself. Never did I feel irate that I was finally caught drinking and driving. I regretted I had made such a habit of the foolish behavior, that I had become so careless with my existence. If I had not become that person, the sexual assault would never have occurred. Even the fact that the incident mentally devastated and dismantled me so completely compounded my self-hatred. *Other people go through far worse. Many are raped. I was not raped. Who am I to let such a minor incident destroy me? Why am I so affected by this? Why am I so pathetically weak?* From every angle, my thoughts drove me further into loathsome depths. My psychological health spiraled into a tumultuous, tangled mess. *If not for being the wretch that I am, perhaps I could have built the life I desired in Colorado. If not for the wretch that I am, perhaps my decade of adventures would have led me somewhere far stronger than being broken and alone. The year of twenty-nine should have been the crown of my twenties. Instead, it has become the year of my unsettling.*

After I hid away for a week following the event in Colorado, I was done. My ability to summon any courage, to face what happened, was nonexistent. To save me from myself, my dad flew to Colorado, and together we moved the piano and everything else into a storage unit in Boulder. My home at Lump Gulch and the community of Nederland had come to an end. If I would go to Georgia, and help the family, Dad promised to afterwards drive me wherever I wanted to go. For the time being, my freedom and self-sufficiency had vanished.

He was correct. The family did require my help. Someone needed to go through all of Granddad's things, organize his work shed, sift through his many tools and projects. Determine what was to be kept and what was to be sold or donated. Everyone else was busy with their growing families, with careers, with the traditional busyness I had never partaken in. And I, well, I needed this time to process all that had happened. I needed to serve others and not wallow in darkness. I needed tasks, focus, purpose and mental rest. It had been just over a year since my grandfather's death. My grandmother wasn't planning on staying in the house they had lived in together much longer. She wanted to move closer to her daughter in South Carolina, but for her to sell the house, this mission must be completed.

My first project was to build a fence that would create a secure enclosure for the puppies and add value to the property. The cow fences that stood on the north and westside of the property were ample for securing the bovines, but not my canines. Dad and I went to the lumberyard on day one and purchased enough wood for this project. That night we enjoyed a meal together with Grandma, watched a Steve McQueen movie, then early in the morning Dad left, leaving Grandma and me to ourselves. Grandma had always been one of my favorite people in the world, she being the epitome of genuine kindness, but we had never had the chance to spend one-on-one

CINEREAL

time together for an extended period. We were close, but there had always been other family around. Now it was just the two of us, her eldest grandson no longer a child, and my recently widowed grandmother.

In the morning, I started working on the fence. She delivered me a kitchen-crafted ham and cheese sandwich for lunch, just as she would for Granddad. We walked the property together, where I noticed the leaves from the previous autumn still lay on the ground. I made a list of all the work that needed to be done. Build the fence, clean the yard, organize Granddad's shed, plus additional chores I discovered along the way. My days were focused on this work. In the evening, we sat on the porch with Wylie and Bacon, listening to the birds and discussing life. I drank my wine, yet I'd hold back any heavy consumption and emotional discharge until she went to sleep. She had observed me in my whiskey lows after my sister's wedding, but I did not want to burden her with my compounding darkness.

To protect her from this, I set up my tent outside under one of the pecan trees. I could not sleep the first night inside. As I dealt with the burdens in my mind, I thought it best to be away from the house. Harboring in my tent felt safer than any indoor room. It summoned soothing memories from my time on the long trails. My tent upon a patch of earth was my favorite sanctuary, and there I could, in my own ways, appropriately address all that had transpired. I still could not understand how everything had fallen apart. I remained blind to the definitive destruction alcohol had been causing in my life. Nor did I yet understand that the substance, which soothed me, was in fact akin to pouring gasoline on a fire. But there in my nomadic abode on the wide flat land of southern Georgia, I latched onto anything accessible that could alleviate my wretched soul's pain.

I hammered my versatile ice axe into the ground and attached two long ropes to it. At the end of each rope, I tied a loop knot, attached a carabiner, and clipped this onto the dog's collars. Ensuring that when I slept, they would not run off chasing cows in the night. When Grandma retired to bed inside the house, I retired to the small camp I had assembled. I listened to the gunshots beyond the cotton fields to the east. The ones Granddad had warned me about the last night I'd spent with him. I recalled his anger and wondered what he would think of my pecan tree camp now. I wasn't on that side of the property, and I was doing this to protect Grandma from my pain, giving myself space to be as I must, so I concluded he would understand. Grandma didn't know exactly what I was going through or what had happened in Colorado. What she knew was that her grandson was hurting, and she could provide me a haven to take a timeout from the world.

At night I surveyed the fields as fog rolled in. The levitating haunts swaddled my chaotic despair. I observed the moon poised hazily in the sky. Coyotes yipped mischievously, scattering their wild chatter, dashing as apparitions in the gloom. I listened attentively and regarded my pups' four ears turning and two heads tilting in response. I imagined they understood what the coyotes were saying. In a way, I did too.

When I entered my grandfather's workshop, greeted by the aroma of sawdust and tobacco, memories of my childhood returned. Grandma told me it had remained untouched, his man cave where he would go to be alone, think and craft. All the large toolboxes and saws he taught me to handle when I was a young boy were still there. The same large red Craftsman cabinets with layers of drawers I used to explore intently. It was a different shed then, a different house, but many of the same tools and scents. I remembered his workshop being more organized, cleaner when I was younger. *This shop is now a cluttered mess. Perhaps in his older age he became less tidy, or maybe my memory just romanticized those days and now I am facing reality.*

It is a deeply intimate sensation entering the personal space of someone after they have passed away. Arriving as they left it. Opening the door, they had shut. I placed his well-worn straw hat on my head. *He had been in the middle of a few projects*, it appeared, *or perhaps multiple pieces of the same.* The house's living room hosted a magnificent model of a vintage car he had crafted. Made of many individual parts meticulously designed, cut, sanded, stained, and fit together creating one immaculate wooden roadster. Other smaller wooden creations decorated the workshop. Layers of paper, sawdust, drill bits and blades covered all the hoisted spaces. Heavy metal legs elevated overflowing surfaces. *To clean and organize everything, I must tackle one corner at a time. Using this plethora of scrap wood, I'll build a new table to fit in the first corner I clean. Then, on the table, I will place one item at a time, to inspect, dust, polish, and organize a home for. Separate piles will need to be amassed for items to keep, trash, or donate.* I lit one of his old dry half-smoked cigarettes, which still sat in an ashtray, and plotted my course.

Each day I spent my morning hours working on the fence, then a midday lunch hour with Grandma, and the afternoon hours in the shop. It provided a healthy sense of satisfaction to observe the progress of the fence coming together. The activity in Granddad's workshop helped me to mourn and heal from the pain of his death. I wrote many poems in his space. I cried alone. Ultimately, I cultivated a new bond with him, one of a matured understanding of who he was. I grew closer to him not as a grandson, but as a human, perceiving him in his drawn blueprints, in the way he set his items, in the private way his mind worked. In the evenings, Grandma and I trained the puppies, ate a hearty southern dinner, and sat on the porch viewing the sunset. As I drank my wine, we shared stories and memories. I mentioned to her that playing music was another healthy outlet for me, and that I missed my piano. After this, we went hunting for a guitar at the pawnshops in town. It was a fun, successful adventure, as I purchased a used Fender acoustic for a decent price. The following evenings, I added strumming my guitar to our porch sits, playing and singing songs for Grandma like "Hello Darlin'" and other favorites she had lovingly experienced with her husband, my grandfather.

"Grandma," I spoke, setting down my guitar.

"Yes, Wing?" She looked up from her book of puzzles with a gentle smile.

"Did I ever tell you that my very first memory in my entire life was from when I was less than one-year-old, and it was of Granddad?"

"I don't think you have ever told me that. But are you sure!? A memory from that age is quite rare." Grandma turned slightly in her seat. Her body language revealed she was open to listening to my possible tall tale.

I laughed at her slight disbelief. "Yes, well, we are all quite rare in our own ways. Are we not?" I paused while she nodded in agreement and then explained. "My very first word ever spoken was 'duck.' Mother said I spoke this word surprisingly early, and the reason my first word was duck is from my first memory. My first memory is of this. The family was all out to dinner at a restaurant. I remember there being quite a group of us. You, Granddad, my mom, dad and a few others. We must have been at a Cracker Barrel or some similar establishment, and I will not get into how I feel about that place now as an adult... oof." Grandma chuckled at my additional comment. I continued. "Anyway, the reason I believe it was there was because before we ate, we strolled through a gift shop. Granddad was holding me, and he let me pick out a stuffed animal as a present. I remember being in his arms, reaching out and choosing a colorful, plush duck. With my new duck in my little awkward paws, we then sat at the table. I remember exactly where I sat, at the end corner by the head in a highchair. Dad was at the head or foot of the table to my right. My mom was across from me, next to him. To my left, you sat, and further to my left across from Dad sat Granddad. Although the rest of my memory's details are hazy, these glimpses remain vivid. The plush toy that Granddad gave me became the reason for my first spoken word, duck." Complete with my explanation, I smiled with delight while observing Grandma's face receive my recollection as if corroborating it with her own.

"Oh my," she spoke in her natural southern drawl, "yes, I remember that dinner as well. You were very young, nearly just born! That is lovely to have Granddad be your first memory. Did you ever tell him about it?"

I sipped wine, set the Rioja back down on a glass end table and shook my head. "No, no, I don't think I ever told him about that. But that's alright. We talked about many worthy things."

"Yes, you did. You two had a special bond. He loved you very much." Grandma petted Bacon as he moved from the yard to lie by her feet. It warmed my heart to see him sitting beside her. They trusted each other. Grandma always had a dog when I was growing up, but now it was just her on her own.

"We did, and yes, I loved him dearly as well. Loved and still love, and I love you." I gave Grandma one of those sad yet content smiles, grateful for my grandfather, and grateful to be next to her now.

Once the fence was complete, I spent the morning hours cleaning up the yard. In the damp end of Georgia's winter, I ignited a massive pile of gathered leaves and brush. Grandma and I sat by the warmth, watching the orange and blue heat flicker towards the sky. A large pillar of smoke rose from the land. The bonfire seemed symbolic, as closure in Granddad's death. Peace for him replaced the sadness in my heart. Despite my life unraveling into disarray, in my heart I could finally let my grandfather rest.

After three weeks, I accomplished everything I came to do in Georgia. Granddad's workshop was cleaned and organized. The property was prepped for my grandmother to sell the house. I felt ready to move forward once again. To Grandma and Dad, I announced I had secured a two-week employment in western South Carolina as a chainsaw operator, working with Lefty, who was a good friend from my Appalachian Trail thru-hike. But first, I would lead Wylie and Bacon on a rigorous puppy bootcamp. Hiking and training them through the first eighty miles of the Appalachian Trail. I knew the rugged land well. Leading the two young rambunctious dogs through the wet, steep mountains would certainly prove stressful and difficult, but the setting, my patience, and firm commands would provide worthy discipline. My time in Georgia had been of tremendous value and so would be returning to the backcountry for a stint. Lefty planned to pick the dogs and me up at the Georgia/Carolina border. We would then work the job harvesting many trees, convert them into firewood, and then Dad would drive us across the country to retrieve my piano and belongings in Colorado. After Colorado, the time had come to drive to Oregon. Dad agreed it was a solid plan. I packed up my pecan-tree camp and prepared for departure. Not being able to legally drive anymore was truly inconvenient, but I was thankful my dad was willing to deliver me to the places I desired to be. It was an era of uncharted transition, currently tumbling through an abyss yet attempting to land on my feet.

I hugged my sweet, generous grandmother goodbye and thanked her for all her love and hospitality. Our three weeks alone together had been a marvelous gift. Then, in the same gray Rhino truck I had been arrested in, on the first day of spring, Dad and I drove down the dirt road, past the horizon of trees I'd learned were Longleaf pines and onward northwest to the southern terminus of the Appalachian Trail once again.

~~~

On April 10th, the same date I started hiking each of my long trails, Dad and I returned to Colorado. Anxiety roared within me. Neurotic angst of paranoia squeezed me. I did not want to be back in the state, especially in the same truck I was arrested in. The thought of someone spotting the license plates and arresting me again weighed on my mind. I did not know whether law enforcement was actively searching for me, or what the exact situation was. A friend from Backcountry Pizza informed me the police had come by inquiring about my whereabouts, but beyond that, I did not know if there was a warrant out for my arrest. I presumed its existence. It was a realistic risk I had placed myself in when I left. All I knew was I had been doing everything they required for my DUI, actively, humbly cooperating until the sexual assault. Once that occurred, everything turned upside down, inside out, twisted, perverted and ruined. It was time to collect my belongings from the storage unit and depart from Colorado forever.

The day after we arrived, Dad had a work trip. He would need to drop me off and then return in a few days, at which point we would rent a small trailer to transport the piano to Oregon. I had him leave me at Elly's house in Boulder, where I would be safe. It was important for me to spend time with her before my final departure. I regretted the way my emotional immaturity had caused me to act at the end of February. And just as I produced healthy closure with Granddad, I needed to attempt such closure with my relationships in Colorado.

Elly and I spent our few days talking and walking trails around the Flatirons. She remarked on Wylie and Bacon's seasoned behavior. I smiled and proudly stated, "Yes, they went into puppy bootcamp as two wild-things and came out as little soldiers. Bacon fears getting into water, though. I had to carry him across many of the streams. We'll get there."

Although it was mostly quelling sharing time with the woman who had introduced me to my puppies, and her giant dog Juniper, things had changed. I wasn't the same anymore. My body flinched when she made contact, and my soul tensely held its breath. I opposed returning up to Nederland, but I still needed to see Sam and share a proper goodbye. When my dad returned, we rented the trailer and loaded it with the piano, a few heavy boxes, some acquired mountain-furniture and then drove to the prearranged location. This would be my last Colorado stop. Pizza with my best friend, my author brethren, Ol' Man Sam.

"Hey mon!" Ol' Man Sam approached excitedly, shuffling his feet with arms wide open. He wore a new tie-dye t-shirt I had never seen.

"Sam man!" I embraced him heartily.

My dad and the jolly gonzo journalist shook hands. "Good to see you again," they both spoke in their own ways.

We entered the familiar eatery, ordered two large pizzas, for Ol' Man Sam deserved his own, then feasted and talked outside. Sam and I caught each other up on all things new, recapped our golden eighteen months together, and both agreed it was best to cherish it all and learn from our mistakes. "We had a hell of a run, brother," Sam spoke sincerely. "You are a legend, Hot Wing. Never in all my years did I meet anyone like you until I met you." He beamed, shaking his head with a chuckle, leaning on his knee with his fist. To a portion of this, I agreed, as we each are unique, and had one hell of a run.

I thanked him for his enduring, nonjudgmental friendship, emphasizing how much it meant to me that he listened and communed with my weight. He helped carry the load. A glimmer of emotional moisture welled in both sets of our eyes. Ol' Man Sam and I shared one last long hug, a mutually orated, "I love you brother, see you down the trail, mon," and then it was time.

Dad drove us north to Wyoming. By nightfall, we had crossed the state border. In Laramie, we booked a motel room on the edge of town, acquired two bottles of red wine, and focused on a night of rest.

"How are you feeling, son?" Dad glanced over at me, wearing a smile that held both empathy and success. A lot had happened in a short period, yet we had reached a giant milestone. No more Colorado. We each lay with our backs propped up with pillows on our respective motel beds. Inwardly, I chuckled at our current commonalities. The way we both crossed our feet at the ankles, the way we clasped our translucent plastic cups filled with Rioja. *He is my dad,* I proudly thought. At that moment, an already strong love for him surged. All past suppressed feelings about the way the family had disassembled when I was a teenager, I let go of. They had become like dust anyway. All anger toward him died when he drove me to the southern terminus for my Appalachian Trail thru-hike when I was twenty-four. The decomposed corpses of those emotions had lain forgotten in a locked room of my heart. It was time to sweep them away and make it official. *I cherish him and officially forgive him. We are not who we were then. He has changed; I have changed. His love for me is unconditional, a love he has repeatedly demonstrated. He saved me from Colorado and my frantic, potentially reckless escape into the wilderness. He has always supported my adventures. Time and time again he has shown up for me, even when I did not deserve it. It is time to release all past follies and move forward.* I didn't reveal my thoughts, for I was too tired. But my simple response was an honest one.

"I feel way too much, Dad, an ocean amount. But I love you, and I am deeply grateful for all you have done for me. It doesn't go unnoticed. Thank you. I'm about ready to turn my brain off for tonight. In a few minutes I'll step outside for one or two more smokes beneath the Wyoming sky and then surely sleep deeply. But I am ready to move forward." Dad's smile shifted into one of gracious understanding.

"Of course, that is what dads do. I love you, too."

~~~

There is no place in this country I love more than the grand, expansive West. Dad and I drove with grins as wide as the views. The distant line of horizons aligned with how life rolls, upward, downward, flat and stagnant, sharply ascending towards the sky until inevitably plummeting into canyons. But it never stays low just as it never stays high. I had driven these roads before, the interstate which follows the original Oregon Trail. As we progressed westward, I pointed out places I had camped, towns I once got drunk in, dirt roads I'd explored and mountains I'd climbed. I confessed side-quest adventures to him that very few would ever know, escapades I would never write about. He shared stories of his travels as a pilot, his way of thinking when he was younger, and how time teaches us many lessons through failures and experiences. I listened, resonated and agreed. We sang along with Johnny Cash, belting out the words to "I've Been Everywhere." Dad and I had much in common as adventurers. We explored differently, but our souls understood each other. He in the skies and I in the mountains. A distant prospect, pursuit commonality. Although he had visited me at many of my howling twenty's locations, each visit usually comprised a brief catch-up, filled with the meet and greet of my current peers. However, being on the road together, driving across the country, sharing our thoughts between songs and silence, this exclusive time, which would not have been if not for the messy darkness, allowed quality fellowship.

"Dad, did I ever tell you about the coin jar when you went away on your six-month aircraft carrier missions?" I looked over to my trusty pilot as I flicked my cigarette into Granddad's portable ashtray.

"I may know about it but remind me." He said, turning down the music's volume.

"When you left for those two long missions, Mom filled up a coin jar and placed it on the kitchen table. She said, 'There are as many pennies in here as the days Dad will be gone for.' Which was a lot, six months' worth of days in pennies. Each day I took one penny out of the jar, and over time I noticed the line of coins recede in the jar. And then, of course, when there were only ten pennies left, it meant you would be home in ten days! I'm sure Mom probably had to adjust the penny amount at times, but on the ultimate day my eager child-self pulled the last penny out of the jar, and you came home." I smiled while reminiscing about those distant days at our home in Orange County, Florida.

"I think I remember hearing something about that." Dad nodded, glancing at me affectionately and then returning his gaze to the highway.

"And then, it must have been at the return of your second deployment, you walked in carrying a brown grocery bag and up popped the head of Bond, our cat. Of course, he was just a little kitten then. We spent that night all thinking of names for him." I chuckled. Dad again nodded his head and smiled.

"Yes, the old Orange County home. Your grandmother and grandfather lived nearby at the time." Dad clicked the truck blinker left, zoomed around a long line of 18-wheelers and then returned to the right lane.

"Yup, the home with the strawberry patch, and the place Granddad saved me from the rattlesnake. Plus, the dirt pile, his huge Mayflower truck, making homemade ice cream, and all the baseball in the yard." I could have continued with the memories, as there were so many from that special epoch.

"It was good to have them close, so they could help your mother take care of you boys when I was gone." Dad remarked.

"It was. I spent a lot of time sleeping at their house, waking up before dawn every day, because I could smell Granddad's coffee brewing, and his cigarette. I would go sit on his lap, and we'd eat doughnuts together, his smoke filling the room, his arm with his tattoo cradling me. Then he would go to work, and I'd crawl into bed with Grandma. Good days..." My voice trailed off. I peered deeply into the land we drove through.

Dad looked at me and slapped his right hand on my left knee. He gave me a smile as if tacitly stating, *we are blessed to have memories of those we love.* "So, what is the plan when we get to Oregon?" Dad asked.

"The objective is making Bend, Oregon, my home. But first, I secured a job on a marijuana farm in southern Oregon. That won't start for a month or so. We will drive straight to Bend and determine the next steps from there. I figure I'll lie low somewhere for about a month, then make my way south to the farm." Red walls of an Idaho canyon damp from snowmelt suddenly surrounded the road.

"You've already secured a job! Man, you keep picking up jobs wherever you go before you even get there!" He slowed the truck down and shifted from fifth to fourth gear as we navigated the canyon's tight, curvy route.

"You know it! I have connections all over the place because I know so many people from all the adventures, hikes and traveling years. I'm thinking the outdoor marijuana grow will be another solid learning opportunity, plus robust, dirty work, which I enjoy. And if all goes as planned, it should compensate well."

"Is it legal?" Dad questioned, knowing that although states were legalizing marijuana, such as Colorado, there were still many gray areas in the industry.

"It is, yes. Oregon just passed the law to legalize recreational cannabis, but that won't come into effect yet, but medical marijuana is legal, and I will first obtain my medical license. I am a prime candidate for it, so it will be no problem. Don't worry, Dad, I never want to do anything illegal ever again. Walking the line from now on, no more infractions with the law for me. I am done with all of that." I hit the eject button on the CD player and replaced the James Taylor with a Led Zeppelin disc. Spotting my music selection, Dad raised his eyebrows excitedly. I turned up the volume and onward towards Oregon we rocked and rolled.

~~~

"Today is the day!" I exclaimed as we pulled out of the gas station in Burns, Oregon.

"Today is the day," Dad repeated with a less dramatic tone. "Bend, Oregon, here we come."

We were both still a little groggy after getting tipsy the night before in a Burns tavern. Our lively billiard shooting night had been cut short when the motel called informing us the dogs were making too much racket by wrestling, barking and ultimately disturbing people in adjacent rooms. We paid our tab and returned with wine to resume our first night in Oregon together. But now it was time for coffee and gas-station breakfast sandwiches while progressing west. My excitement amplified as we drew closer. I could sense the Pacific Crest Trail up ahead.

"I call them my lifelines. The PCT and the AT, much like blood veins in the body," I informed my driver. "I don't like being too far away from any long trail, and as soon as I am near them, I can sense their pull. As I get further away, I become depressed."

"Is that so?" Dad sipped on his coffee, giving me a face as if he didn't believe I could sense the long trails.

"It is so." I stated matter-of-factly. "Soon we will see the Cascade Mountain range, with Broken Top and the Three Sisters Mountains directly in front of us. Washington, Jefferson and Mount Hood to the north, and though we won't be able to see them, Mount Thielsen and Crater Lake to the south."

CINEREAL

"Alright then." Dad winked, enjoying my enthusiasm, listening to whatever I had to say. He was still waking up, but I knew his cup of coffee would help.

By the time we could see the mountains, Dad was as enthused as I was. The Cascade Range appeared as a wide, mighty crown of volcanoes on the horizon. I gazed with wonder at the land I had traversed, and the land I hoped to settle down in and call home. When we finally reached the town of Bend, Dad was ready to jump in and try some of the famous Bend, Oregon, beer he had heard so much about. We stopped at the first brewery on the east side of town, Worthy Brewing. I reveled in the brewery decor of Ken Kesey, one of Oregon's successful writers. Dad nodded to it and stated, "Someday that'll be Wing Williams the author on these walls." I laughed in hopeful agreement. We lifted our beer pints and cheered to a new life chapter in Oregon.

After Worthy Brewing, we drove into the heart of town and ate lunch at Bend Brewing Company along the Deschutes River. Dad had never been to Bend, and I had only spent a couple of hours in the small city three years prior. We discussed the next steps. I told him about Camp Sherman on the Metolius River and how G and I stayed there with the two sisters we'd met in Sisters. Since I could no longer legally drive, Dad must return to work, and I needed to fill some time until the cannabis job in Southern Oregon, we decided to drop me in Camp Sherman for ten days. A temporary haven in the forest. When Dad could return, we would purchase a modest RV camper for me to reside in for the summer.

The plan was set. The Oregon chapter could commence. After lunch we drove north and located a cheap room for rent in Camp Sherman. Nestled in a thick woodland of ponderosas beside the peaceful Metolius River, I spent ten days writing, hiking, purchasing sandwiches from the small general store, and continuing my internal contemplations. I even picked up a small side gig cleaning hordes of fallen pine needles off rooftops at the nearby Black Butte Ranch. Two retired police officers hired me for the task. I discreetly chuckled at the irony of the situation while leaping from roof slant to the next, blasting dry brown resinous tinder from gutters and crannies onto the ground. The old officers gathered them up, and together we transported multiple trailer loads to the local landfill. When the job was complete, they handed me a wad of cash and offered to drive me back to Camp Sherman. The cash I accepted, but the ride I declined. I wanted to walk the seven miles alone through the forest, happily basking in a land with no cell-phone service. *My favorite kind of land.*

When Dad returned, we purchased the camping trailer and parked it south of Bend in Sunriver. I lived there peacefully for another ten days. Next, we moved the camper down to the trail town of Ashland, Oregon, where I remained for another stint. During each period, I wrote, hiked, worked in any way I could find, and focused on untangling my discombobulated mental health. Elly flew from Colorado to visit me and the dogs in Ashland. We visited the Pacific Ocean, where the dogs ran on the beach and tasted salt water for their first time. We explored misty redwood tree forests and camped on riverbanks. Although it was mollifying sharing some time together, it was also apparent that our relationship had come to an end. She returned to Colorado, while I set my heart on the present and future. Dad reunited with me when he was able and helped transport my little camper onto the marijuana farm near Cave Junction, a region of renegades with no police force.

Dad and I embraced briefly and shook hands lovingly as we spoke our farewells. "Son, stay out of trouble. If this doesn't end up being the right place for you, we'll figure out something else." He glanced apprehensively around the grow site. "I feel like I'm leaving you stranded in a foreign, lawless land out here…"

"I'll be just fine, Dad. And of course I'll try to behave. Don't you worry about me. Again, thank you. You've done so much for me." I grinned optimistically. He nodded in response, as he liked to do. It was time to part ways. It seemed that the massive mission of moving me and the dogs from Colorado to Oregon was complete. I was finally somewhere I could start a new life, or so I believed.

~~~

I should never have accepted a job on the marijuana farm. I should have moved immediately into Bend, rented a place to live and secured employment in town, but my decade of howling twenties wasn't yet complete, and as I buried my mental anguish deep within, I relented to the familiar comfort of new adventure. Musing that *if my Colorado settlement must be uprooted, then I shall return to what I know, the routine of unconventional life.* At first, the grow farm seemed like an ideal plan, outdoor labor among sugar pines, myrtles and elder woods. Cultivating a mighty grove of cannabis trees delighted me. The problem was I continued leaning into my increasing alcoholism, and one of the farm operators was a drug addict. Not only that, but the atmosphere seemed evil. This was not like the supportive, loving environment of Colorado. This crew openly mocked God while treating me as an unwelcome possible Christian. Although I was not living for the Almighty, the blatant blasphemy infuriated me. At first, we worked together somewhat amicably, but quickly the relationship developed into hostility, descending into bitter disputes. An alcoholic and a drug addict fight in the forest, was the tune of the season.

Wylie and Bacon encountered their first bear. The event was titillating as well as terrifying. On a sweltering afternoon by a creek lined with berry bushes, we stumbled upon a sow and her three cubs. While the cubs scampered up a tree, the mother charged directly at us. I had been in this position before, so I knew how to handle it, but it was the dogs' first time. Thankfully, they obeyed my firm, calm commands and cautiously backed away by my side instead of rebutting the protective ursid. Another positive amidst the farm chaos was a reunion with my trail brother Safari. He came to my aid at a time of severe crisis. His visit provided light in a dark, outnumbered environment. The events of this, however, shall for now remain in the memory of him and me, perhaps a story for another time.

Meanwhile, Wylie became pregnant, an unplanned event I attempted to protect her from. The farm comprised many roaming canines, and she freed herself on the last day of her first estrous cycle. The message was obvious. It was time to leave. I needed to locate a safe place for Wylie to give birth to her litter. Safari, the dogs and I abandoned the farm and spent a few days hiking on the Pacific Crest Trail. We then camped outside Bend, waiting for my dad to return. I decided to gift Bacon, now a well-trained, nearly adult dog, to my grandmother. He would provide her, and she for him, loyal love and company. Dad drove across the country again, this time from Oregon to the east coast, with only the black and white goofy canine and delivered him to Grandma. I was sad to see him go, but I knew it was the best solution for everyone involved. While Dad embarked on the long delivery, I searched for a room to rent in Bend. Despite interviews with many seemingly potential options, no one would rent to me, for it was not just me they must consider. It was the entire litter of puppies soon to arrive. Reluctantly, I accepted an offer solely for the sake of Wylie. We would temporarily depart my beloved West and go to the only available location where she could have the space and time to birth and mother the imminent babes, Dad's house in

CINEREAL

Florida. With Wylie Wizzle's biological clock ticking, the pilot again drove from Oregon, this time with a swelling Wylie and discouraged Wing, transporting us to the sweltering, flat, southeastern refuge. On August 17th, in the thick heat of summer, we arrived. On August 19th, beginning at five-twenty in the evening, my darling companion gave birth to five beautiful, healthy puppies.

~~~

Florida is not where I desired to be. Wylie birthing a litter of puppies was never a consideration. My plan was to have her spayed when she turned eighteen months old. I wanted to allow her time to thoroughly physically develop before the operation, yet nature took its course before human manipulation could take place. Therefore, I must deal with the reality of all that had become, exhausted and overwhelmed by all that had occurred in my wild twenties. Yet there remained much to be grateful for. Wylie and her offspring were safe, and I had another unlikely sanctuary where I could rest and strategize my next steps. After Dad dropped us off, he returned to his pilot duties. He had donated much of his time, nearly 10,000 road miles, and even his home bed to provide for his wayward son. I couldn't help but feel at a loss. Life had fallen apart. My own actions had stripped away the control I once assumed over my world. I sat in the backyard wearing only shorts and sunglasses, drinking a glass of ice water beneath a large oak tree, reflecting upon where it had all gone wrong. Although introspection had already consumed me in Georgia, on the puppies' bootcamp hike, on our road trips across the country, and during my spring and summer in Oregon, it seemed as if I had not yet come to an acceptance for all that had transpired. Inwardly, I continued to war against my deserved circumstances.

Rolling it back in my mind, I knew the sexual assault had surely derailed my sanity, but the unraveling had started before then. The reason for the arrest had been my drinking and driving, and the reason for my habitual drinking and driving had been delusional confidence in my remote mountain life. I foolishly acted as if I couldn't or wouldn't ever hurt anyone up in those mountains, that I was free to live as I pleased, and yet that was a false sense of security I had mentally concocted. That mindset was incorrect and irresponsible. I had become filled with immoral pride. The mass consumption of alcohol had mired my thinking. My detached years in the wilderness, on the trails, away from modern society had blinded me to very real consequences. Resulting in circumstances I must now accept. No longer could I legally drive. No longer could I up and go as I pleased. I was trapped, placed, set aside on some sort of weird house arrest, in a modest home in a gated community in Florida. *All I have done has led to here.* I could either wallow in self-pity and anger, or I could use the present time-out to reflect upon what my actions had created, learn from it, mature, and move forward without repeating old actions. As my mother often quoted to me from the Bible, "Pride goes before the fall," indeed I was living proof of that now.

There would be ample time for more contemplation. I would be stuck on flat land until weaning the litter of puppies from Wylie. Then, I must deliver the newborns to proper homes. Yet even upon such completion, I would still be at the mercy of my dad's time and kindness. If he did not want to drive me back across the country again, the options for returning west would be limited and difficult. No longer was I in control. *Perhaps I never was.* My decade of adventure had been filled with colorful victories and didactic failures, and through it all, one of the many things I had learned, so mighty in its truth, simplicity and power, that no matter one's circumstances, you must keep moving forward.

I spent the last few months of my twenties hidden away in the Florida house. I tried to make a few friends at a local pub, playing billiards with strangers and striking up conversations while sitting on stools at the bar top. The girls found me fascinating, but most of the guys disliked me. When I answered questions and told stories of my adventures, the men mocked and tried to fight. Therefore, I ceased attempting to integrate into the community. Daily jogs around the odd neighborhoods became a healthy habit and mental outlet. Wylie joined eagerly, welcoming the exercise break from her mothering. I observed the residences, flora, and people who seemed foreign. Everyone acted obsessed with golf and nice vehicles, and not one of them, for I asked many, had ever hiked up a mountain before. I accepted I did not need to fit in. I continued reminding myself, *this is temporary.* The local homeowners' association required everything to appear a certain uniform way. Thus, Dad's house was just another house modeled much like the rest. A simple two-bedroom structure, which he rarely frequented, as he was usually in a different state, a different time zone, a different country, flying in the sky from one to another. Occasionally he would come stay for a night to check how I was faring. We would live as we did many years prior, drinking wine, watching old movies or ballgames and playing chess.

CINEREAL

On the other side of the ponds and lake, a mile away, the residences comprised enormous mansions. I jogged through these lavish neighborhoods and wondered what was happening behind the gates and ornate walls. In one large domicile, with ivy growing up its ramparts, I noticed a young woman peering out a large upper window. She looked down at me from her second floor with an emotionless gaze. A long pastel-green nightgown adorned her body. Her porcelain face appeared pale, as if no southern sun had touched her skin for a long time. I sensed she might be trapped, confined to a place she did not want to be, much like I felt. There were no vehicles in the wide circular driveway, unlike the other houses, which frequently bustled with activity. I decided to run the same route the next day. Again, she appeared in the window, this time rising from a seat I could not see. I waved, and she waved back. A gentle smile formed beneath her melancholic eyes. Day after day we shared a few seconds in this manner. She in her window wearing a nightgown, I always slowing my jog in front of her abode, an intimate moment exchanged in silence. One day I did a funny sort of dance in my stride. She brightened with laughter I could not hear. Usually, we just lifted and fluttered our hands, grinned, and wondered about the other. I witnessed nobody coming and going from that mansion. I hoped she wasn't alone. After a few weeks of this daily innocent interaction, as I jogged by at our customary time, the curtains were drawn closed. The young woman in the gown was not there. From that day forth, the window remained concealed. I never saw her again.

Dad had preserved my old computer. An archive full of writings and photos from the first half of my twenties. I placed it in his care when I hustled off to meet G for our winter adventure. We must have transported it south along with all his belongings when he moved away from New England in 2013. Excitedly, I read each old story and poem and admired the photographs I had taken. Each piece summoned nostalgia. It amazed me how much I had written and how many unique adventures I had accumulated in those years. Along with the notebooks I had filled in Colorado, my young, scattered work amassed to volumes. I had lived my decade of adventure, for better and for worse, and now I did not desire to continue living life in the same manner. With my thirtieth birthday approaching, the plans for my new decade were forming. It was clear what I needed to do next.

CINEREAL

Berengar, my dear brother from Colorado, whom I could not say goodbye to, had returned from his international trip and was visiting family in Florida. He drove to my location, where we spent an afternoon sitting beneath the oak tree. Wylie was happy to see him, as was I. The puppies sniffed and pawed at his shoes. I wrangled the rascals and placed them inside so we could commune without disturbance. He divulged anecdotes from his travels through Mongolia, then I confessed the details about my Colorado downfall. We sipped cold beers, watched Florida birds flutter from tree to tree, and reminded each other that we were in a period of transition.

Despite life's hardships, there remained a multitude of blessings. I practiced gratitude exercises daily and focused on the positives. My soul had always been optimistically driven, and though some of the recent events sporadically dragged my mental health into a state of hellish wallowing, I battled against this pull. I remained determined to focus on the present, create steps for the future, all while intentionally burying the dark anguishes into a vault deep within. *No longer will I let the end of my Colorado chapter infect my thinking. Who was I to allow such an event to discombobulate my life? So many others have experienced far worse assaults and torments than I. This has hung in the mind for far too long. Shame on me for letting the incident derail my mental sanity. You are stronger than this, Wing. Bury the weakness, move forward.* As I shifted my thinking in this unresolved method each day, life, for the time being, glowed brighter.

In the late afternoons, mighty thunderstorms and torrents of rain drenched the land. These southern tempests soothed my mind and body, alleviated the sweltering terra, provoked the pleasant earthy scent of petrichor, dazzled the sky with gluttonous bolts of electricity, while pronouncing power from the heavens with majestic booms. After the daily deluge and thunderstorms passed, dense mist rose from the ground, adding to the atmospheric moisture, hanging like floating ponds. It was at such times that I would run, down the paved trails, through lush flora and snake-slithering grasses, through the extravagant neighborhoods and onward by that mansion window. Never seeing my delicate silent friend again exacerbated my loneliness, *but it is okay,* I reminded myself. *This is only temporary.*

~~~

When autumn arrived, I barely recognized it, for the weather remained hot and balmy. On October 14, 2015, the calendar proclaimed the howling twenties were officially complete. My thirtieth birthday had arrived, and Dad returned home to celebrate the milestone with me. I was full of mixed emotions and tremendously thankful to have my stalwart predecessor to share it with. Over tequila, beers, laughter, steak, whiskey and wine, I announced to him the plan for my thirties.

"All right, Pops, I am ready to declare the plan for my new decade." I tipped back a shot of tequila on the patio of a restaurant where people wore sweaters in the eighty-degree weather. I lit a cigarette even though the server had admonished my previous one.

"Well, Wingstar, before you declare the new plan, why don't we reminisce about your twenties first?" Dad took a sip of his beer and smirked at my freshly lit cigarette. He didn't care that I was smoking on the patio after the server had just told me not to.

"Yes, good idea, Dad. Let's say one highlight, year by year, for each year was certainly an era of its own. Year twenty, bad decisions in Hollywood. I did get on three television shows though, Entourage, Monk and Bones." The server watched me smoke and drink. She rolled her eyes and decided against any further reprimands.

Dad nodded in response to my statement and then spoke. "Year twenty-one, I visited you in Hawaii, we watched the sunrise from the summit of Haleakalā, and later that day played tennis in its shadow."

"Indeed. And we all know how Hawaii ended." I lifted my tequila shot glass to the server, showing I was ready for another.

Dad laughed and added, "Yes, in handcuffs."

"It wasn't long after Hawaii that we also played tennis along the Panama Canal. That was one of our most exotic matches."

"Yup, that was a great one. You flew down on that trip with me, which made you the only family member who has flown in an airplane that I was currently flying." Dad swatted at an insect that had landed on the rim of his beer glass as he spoke.

"To which I am honored. You're the best pilot, Dad." I winked. "What was it Neil Armstrong said to you when you flew him that time?" I questioned, reminding Dad of the words from the moon-walking man.

"Nice landing, son." Dad beamed proudly. "He was a navy pilot too, you know."

"Oh, I know." I loved when he smiled like that. "Alright. Year twenty-two. A glorious season at the Grand Canyon. I hiked all over that magnificent, rugged land. You visited me there as well."

CINEREAL

"I did. Everyone spoke well of you. You were really growing into your own."

"Thanks, Dad, yes, I took that job, and every job I work seriously. Alright, your turn."

"Year twenty-three, let's see," Dad threw a cluster of french fries into his mouth and chewed while he thought. "Oh right, you had the job with the horses at Grand Tetons National Park. I couldn't visit you for that one."

"That's okay, but yes, that was one of my favorite jobs. Also, my first time observing grizzly bears and wolves in the wild. Climbed a lot of mountains. Man, that was a successful year."

"You climbed a lot of mountains that year? More like you climbed a lot of mountains the next year!" Dad was getting in the mood now, finishing his pint of amber ale and raising it up for another.

"Hah!" I exclaimed. "Yes, in the next year, year twenty-four, I climbed hundreds of mountains, hiked thousands of miles, trekking the entire Appalachian Trail. A monumental season of my twenties."

"A monumental achievement." Dad smiled and hoisted his fresh pint. We clinked and cheered, and then he continued. "Year twenty-five. That was your Portsmouth year, correct?"

"It was." I affirmed. "I committed some very questionable acts that year, and each day played out like a ridiculous reality television show, but it was also the year I started publicly sharing my writing. Which was a harsh reality check that many people would rather tear you down than build you up. It helped to thicken my skin and to scrutinize my craft. Ultimately, it motivated me further. Now, and in the future, I can handle such criticisms much better than if I had not gone through such before."

"Yes, one opens themselves up to a hateful world when they share what is in their heart, but the right people will resonate with it. Keep thickening that skin. I know you are a passionate person, but you need to mature in not allowing your emotions to control you." Dad acknowledged and encouraged.

"Yes, I know, Dad. I have much I need to mature in... I'm working on it. Not to let my emotions govern my decisions. Thank you." I sipped my beer and then added, "Also in year twenty-five, I met and came to adore Lynx, a worthy silver-lining amidst the debacles."

"Who? Did you ever tell me about this... Lynx?" He questioned.

CINEREAL

"She is a dear, loyal friend. One who has supported and rooted for me no matter my faults and circumstances. I am extremely grateful for her. Next up, year twenty-six, the Pacific Crest Trail! One of my greatest adventures and yet also one of my greatest failures."

"Son, I wouldn't call that a failure. You hiked even more than you did on the Appalachian Trail that year, created some friends for life, learned more lessons, and realized that life is more than the things you do. That was a year of depth for you. I know you went kind of dark at the end, but don't let that tarnish what a magnificent year it was."

"Thanks, Dad." I pursed my lips together and raised my head up and down, recollecting it all.

"Alright, my turn. Year twenty-seven," the pragmatic pilot adjusted his posture. "You moved to Nederland. But first, you helped me move from New Hampshire down here to Florida."

"Yup, sure did. One of our many adult road trips together."

"It was. You were a tremendous help to me. It would have been very expensive if I'd hired professional movers!" Dad smiled, "just a man and his first-born man cruising to some tunes on Interstate 95."

"You know it!" I beamed with both an alcohol tipsiness and familial pride. "Okay onward, twenty-eight, I must dub that year the year of Ol' Man Sam. He was a good friend during my turmoil. Other than leaving for Granddad's funeral and Carmen's wedding, it was my fully dedicated Colorado year, spent with my Colorado family. A tale of two Wings it was. Of course I got arrested for DUI. In every way, it was another wild year that provided many new lessons."

"You certainly carved yourself out a fine life up in those mountains. I was proud to see you take your wilderness skills and turn them into a daily lifestyle. But then, unfortunately, twenty-nine, the year it all came crashing down." Dad now pursed his lips somberly as his eyes wore a tender look. He knew what had happened. I'd told him everything. Yet it was something we didn't really talk about, nor did I want to. His glossy-eyed gaze reminded me of how much he saw and listened, even when we didn't speak of such things.

"Indeed," I spoke. "The year it all came crashing down. Also, the year I adopted my Wylie girl, so it was all worth it. And now here we are, with five puppies pooping all over the floor of your house." I laughed, and Dad joined in, for despite it all we were alive and happy to be together.

CINEREAL

"Yes, that's a good way to look at it. So, what are your plans for age thirty and this new decade? Are you still wanting to move to Bend, Oregon?"

I lit another cigarette and cleared my throat. "Well, let me tell you. Yes, Bend, Oregon, I think will be the best place for me to move to and settle down at. That's where my piano is after all. Part of my plan is to set roots and build strong community. I crave genuine, lasting connections. The twenties were such a whirlwind, and home was always a backpack, or an idea, until Colorado, but that clearly wasn't meant to be. Bend has called to me ever since my PCT hike. Oregon has called me. For some reason, I believe I am meant to be there. My plan is to live in Bend for at least ten years, at least my thirties, and during that time, for all that time, my primary goal is to establish a solid career as an author. That is all I want now, to elevate my hobby of writing and transform it into my life. As you know, I have always been a writer, and now it is time to level that up."

Dad leaned back in his chair, smiling, nodding, and though he could, and occasionally would have much to say on the topic, in that moment he simply stated the phrase he often spoke at the end of my announcements. "Well, alright then."

~~~

In November, Wylie naturally weaned her puppies. I invested extensive time and care in locating a loving family for each of the five dogs. Her first-born son and daughter, whom I affectionately called Sonny and Claire, as he was born while Moonlight Sonata played, and she during Clair de Lune, were going to the home of my dear friend Andrew. The same Andrew whom I had played high school soccer with, shared wild college years with, driven across the country to Los Angeles with, was bailed out of jail on the Appalachian Trail by, whom I served best man at his wedding for, and now, gifting Wylie's offspring to. Dad and I would deliver the dogs to him and his wife in Missouri on our way across the country to Oregon.

The day of departure was upon us. My Florida term had come to an end. I deep-cleaned the house, always abiding by the practice of leave no trace, and packed my few belongings into the vehicle. The youngest three puppies were transferred to their forever homes. I bid the backyard oak tree farewell, then Dad and I began our journey westward once again. We crossed the Mississippi River for my last time, my back to the east for good. We spent a night with Andrew and his wife, delivering to them the pups and recalling old times over a glass of scotch. Wylie was ready to be rid of her offspring, as was I. She had fulfilled her duty as a mother marvelously. In the morning, Dad and I progressed onward, navigating around Colorado. There was no need to enter that state ever again. We drove into the sunset and deep into the night, rested in Idaho, then resumed our push into the Pacific Northwest.

With only a few sunrises until 2015's Thanksgiving Day, my feet stood upon Central Oregon soil. The Cascade Mountains wore a fresh coating of snow. Resinous, sugary aromas of juniper and ponderosa trees lingered in the air. My dad and I looked at each other, both thinking the same thing. *Finally, the great unsettling has come to an end.*

"Son, this is it. This is where we part. I have done all I can do." Dad spoke with a tone I knew well, his *it is time to get serious* tone.

"Thank you, Dad. Truly, thank you for everything. You rescued me from Colorado, you drove me across the country multiple times, you even delivered Bacon to Grandma. You provided me with a place to stay, a sanctuary for the puppies' birth, and you were patient with me through my anguish. I will never forget what you have done for me. I will make you proud, Dad." Tears welled in my eyes.

"You do make me proud. But now it is up to you. You have done it before, and you will do it again, succeed in a new place. We have spent many wonderful days together this year, but now it is time to focus."

"I know, Dad, I know. Next time you see me, all will be different. I am ready. Ready to build my life in this new decade and land. I have placed the events of Colorado behind me, and I will not allow my emotions to control me anymore." I extended my hand. Dad grasped mine with his, and we shook vigorously.

"Sounds good, Wingstar. I'll come see you in a year or so." He enjoyed calling me by that affectionate name. "Do you have the keys to the storage unit?"

"Sure do," I confirmed, patting my pocket to prove the keys were there. "I love you, Dad. See you in a year or so."

"I love you too, Wing." And just like that, after our many miles together, it was time for him to drive away.

As I watched my dad leave, a familiar sensation washed over me, the sense of being alone in a land where I did not know another soul. I didn't have a home, only a little bit of money jangled in my pocket, and everything depended on what I would do next. I looked down at my dog. With love in our hearts, excitement in our eyes and determination in my soul, I spoke. "Wylie, we have arrived. The Oregon Trail is complete. We live in Bend now. It is time to get to work."

Part II
From Death to Life

CINEREAL

Fierce Brown Liquor

Alcohol is not the enemy, yet for me it offered a powerful conduit for the true enemy. Alcohol was not the problem. I was the problem. When consumed moderately, the libation can provide a positive communal effect in society, but with a little slip and a seemingly innocent extra, the dopamine-inducing drug rages forth as a trickster spirit. I could never consume just one drink. Even the idea of such temperance seemed utterly pointless. It was the crescendo I sought. The increase, the ride, the surging frenzy and the emboldened passion. Alcohol both elevated and numbed me just enough to maintain the belief that it was advantageous to my life. I defiantly adhered to the lie that it kept me calm, rational, creative, happy, enthusiastic and resilient through pain. However, from the very first sip, it began to destroy my body and mind. It dug its tenacious, haughty, apathetic claws deep into my soul, and once it conquered me, the devastation escalated into an all-consuming fervor.

In Bend, Oregon, during the autumn of 2018, I resisted this truth. I recognized it only to twist and reason every fact into a false-positive. In my second book, *As a Wolf Breathes*, released in December 2017, I closed out the poem "Whiskey on an Empty Stomach" with the lines "If the whiskey kills me, the flowers will still bloom." I was not naive, and yet I was every bit a fool. I comprehended its destruction, I suffered within its prison, I wrote about it, I bathed in it, I clung to the misery it created as if it was my despicable, desired fate. For me, alcohol continued to expand the evil portal. With the delusion of one with Stockholm syndrome, this malevolence had become my security. If not God, then the other, I supposed. Because of the wretched willing immersion, a violent upheaval would occur. Yet even the brink of death could not force me to attempt an escape from my addiction.

~~~

The word cinereal first entered my ears during a mandated alcohol class in Colorado. The term was not in the coursework handbook, yet the instructor introduced it as one of her favorites. "While the common definition of this

CINEREAL

rarely used word is 'of or like ashes,' or as a color 'ashen gray,' the Collins English Dictionary states cinereal also means 'relating to the grey matter of the brain and nervous system.' Now, the grey matter," she continued to explain while placing her hands together in the air so softly they barely touched, "is essential for our crucial functions, such as movement and thinking. Alcohol harms the grey matter. Long-term drinking destroys it."

I liked her. The instructor's unassuming appearance, with aging brown hair pulled back into a single braid lying informally upon her hunching back, was paired with a muted strength. She did not accept impudence from our group of delinquents, and her eyes brightened with each personal exploration into etymology.

"While 'cine' in Latin means movement, and 'real' in English is derived from the Latin word 'realis' meaning actual, which we use the common meaning 'real' for, 'realis' is derived from the word 'res' meaning 'matter.' Therefore, it is not difficult to make our way towards understanding why 'cinereal' can pertain to grey matter." She smiled at my attentive gaze, speaking as if she were a poet at heart and an alcohol class instructor by trade. She had, after all, explained to us her journey into sobriety. Not a sip of booze for decades. *Now that is something I can respect in this ridiculous culture*, I thought back then and even so now years later.

Memories of Colorado education transitioned to the current reality. My mug of coffee sat steaming in the autumn morning sun. I had only consumed a few ounces because my body could no longer handle the caffeine. Each new day amidst the routine hangover, my heart palpitated disturbingly. Every sip of the once-reviving dark beverage now pushed my racing heart closer to explosion. After one more taste, I shrugged and walked inside to my favorite cupboard in the kitchen. Wylie lifted her head, investigating my movements, then laid her noggin back down, understanding the steps. From the lofted wooden box I retrieved the remedy, whiskey. *Just an innocent hair of the dog, as they say, even if I am indeed destroying my grey matter.* Following two long glugs straight from the glass bottle, all internal pandemonium subsided. *Oh, how the brown liquid soothes.* From the sink's faucet, I guzzled some water. Satisfied, I returned to lounge in the garden, smoke a cigarette, admire the tawny drooping stalks and remind myself that everything was alright. Wylie and I heard a noise from the bedroom. *My partner must have awakened.*

Three years after moving into Bend, despite my addiction, life shimmered with fullness and possibility. I was in love with a young woman, whom for this book I shall call Pearl. We lived together in a small one-bedroom home we called "the art cottage." The cottage sat with its front door facing a stone-pebbled alley between grid streets of the old-town neighborhood. Three lofty cottonwood trees, a cherry tree, which blossomed pink flowers in the spring, and one towering ponderosa pine sheltered our roof from the high desert's blistering summer sun. We filled this cozy space with the fruits of our souls and love. Pearl worked at her family's downtown restaurant and created beautiful paintings. Ten months prior, I released my second book of poetry and short stories, which continued to sell very well. Between writings, I played music on Chaco, the old brown piano, occasionally reaching for a wine glass, which sat in its own stained circle atop the stringed, percussive instrument. After our work and hobbies, we cooked together in the kitchen. Lively, fresh aromas wafted out open windows and doors. Together we developed a thriving garden in our small backyard, designed with consideration for the sun's arch, which we adapted upon each seasonal lesson. Wylie Wizzle romped around inspecting each pinecone released from the Ponderosa pillared above while we soiled our hands in earthly chores and harvests. Between our busy comings and goings, we sat together, Pearl with her brushes and paints and I with my paper and pen. We birthed story after story on parchment in our own ways.

My first three years in Bend had started as an awkward adjustment to the small-city, pedestrian life. Wylie and I were accustomed to a slower, quieter, mountain speed. Sidewalks along loud, bustling streets with vehicles zooming by proved difficult for both of us. However, we kept our heads focused forward and adapted. I worked multiple jobs, trekking on foot each day, uphill both ways, through any weather, including snow. Walking agreed with me. I had turned the motion of my part-time trail seasons into a full-time practice. My life in Bend began by drinking less alcohol and living modestly in a small room I rented in the southeast corner of town. Sticking to the concentrated repetition of one step at a time helped me accomplish productive days. I made a few friends, saved as much money as I could, eventually moved closer into the town's heart, then dove into the taverns and social scene all while compiling the pieces for my first book.

Shortly after the first book, *The Bear Within*, was released, I met Pearl in a bookstore. She was sitting on the far side of the room, by the bookcases and stairs, wearing a burnt orange turtleneck sweater, and I was by the window and door, wearing the same thing as yesterday. It was one of those occasions where, no matter how hard I attempted to remain focused on my writing, I could not. People notice people all the time, every day, we are everywhere, but sometimes, for whatever invisible tendril reason, a certain someone will arrest the soul. When I first laid eyes on her, she captivated me. A lock of her umber coiled hair sprung up as she released it, setting her fingers back to the table. We exchanged glances and smiles, then returned attentions to our own computer screens, squinting our eyes into focus, continuing to work on our tasks. Or maybe she did, I could not think about whatever it was I was typing with her over there. After I sat with a blank mind and fluttered heart long enough, I knew if I was to accomplish any work I needed to leave. But first, I must make contact. *I must give her this silly little note I wrote.* Although I had never considered her before that hour, it now seemed impossible to move forward in life without at least saying hello and offering her my phone number.

While packing my tabletop items into my satchel, I sensed her gaze return. As I walked towards her instead of the door, she lifted her chocolate eyes and smiled. She did not appear surprised that I approached. In fact, she received my note with a kind "Thank you" before I could speak, as if she had seen me writing it, or as if she received such notes often. After whispering her gratitude, the bookstore held the silence of a library, and with my nerves I only managed to utter the tawdry phrase, "I had to." These words verbalized in such a quiet space bellowed from wall to wall, causing me to turn and leave as quickly as a confident saunter would allow. Peering back at her glow as I exited the door, we shared one more eye lock, brown eyes to brown eyes. Both of our faces displayed rosy blushes and charmed smiles.

She didn't call me, which was alright, for my days were filled with hoping that I might eventually see her again. Eventually proved to be only a week as I bumped into her on my way to a poetry reading. On our second encounter, a few beers and a whiskey rendered me properly tipsy. In my hands, I held my first book and a few loose papers filled with new poems I had been scratching together at a tavern. The combination of alcohol, pre-performance nerves, and the sudden sight of Pearl standing in an alley behind her family's restaurant culminated in a boisterously spilled "Hello!" She reciprocated my greeting with the same energy. "I need to practice my poem for the cafe's spoken word event," I chattered next. "Will you amuse me by listening to it?"

CINEREAL

"I would love to amuse you, Wing." She purred when she spoke, or so it seemed to me. She listened to my lines with genuine exclamations and even a gasp. After I finished one, I paused and, per her encouragement, launched into another. "Oh my, you really are pouring your soul into your poems! I love them. Thank you for reading them to me." Pearl looked towards the restaurant door as if she had stayed outside longer than she should have. I thanked her, suggested we meet again soon and before I overstayed my welcome, skipped along to the cafe.

Our brief run-ins around town continued. Each of our few minutes together developed into deeper conversations. Bantering escalated into heavier flirtations and perhaps, I considered, even a desire from her to see me again. I knew I carried such an aspiration, but it wasn't until she finally called me on the telephone that I knew she felt the same way. "Wing, hi, it's me, Pearl."

"Hi Pearl, you kept my number from the note." My heart twitterpated as I sensed her eyes shining. Her telephone voice sounded like honey.

"I kept the note, so yes." A gentle pause and smile hung in the air. "I was thinking, we keep running into each other, but do you want to meet up intentionally this time? Let's go have some fun."

She spoke the words I longed to hear. I responded as calmly as I could, despite my heart's elation. "Yes, I agree, intentionally. Let's go have some fun."

~~~

While Pearl worked at the restaurant in the evenings, I wrote and progressed in building an audience for my craft. The more I conversed with people I had never met, the more books I sold. My recipe for success was simple. After a long morning walk or run with Wylie along the Deschutes River, even on days I needed to first level out with a bit of whiskey, I would then sit on park benches, bar stools, in cafes, on downtown stoops, observe, listen and write everything down. Both little and long poems constructed upon the shuffling beats of life in Bend filled my notebooks. On each occasion where I had deliberately, visibly placed myself, strangers repeatedly posed the same questions to me.

"Hey, what are you writing?" To this familiar inquisition, I would glance up to a curious smile approaching me in the park, or over to my side at the bored drinker setting down their glass.

"Hi. Oh, I write poetry and short stories, and sometimes thoughts that I shall form into poems later."

"What do you write about?" They would then ask.

"I write about everything. From people I have met, adventures I have lived, lessons I have learned, muses about existence, observations, the way sunlight dances on the river, or how my heart responds to the moon, every speckle of life's beauty and pain, the way my demons tenaciously torment!" In this last phrase, I varied my voice by tossing in a tinge of humorous inflection. Without skipping a beat, I then continued, "and my bondage to this stuff," lifting my glass of whiskey. "But in this moment, since you inquired, I am writing about an unhoused man I conversed with last night on Bond Street, and his resilience despite all he has gone and is going through."

"I see." The stranger may rub their sneaker'd toe on the ground or brush back slouched forward hair. "Do you put these poems into books, or on a blog where others can read them?"

"I do. I have two books published so far, *The Bear Within* and *As a Wolf Breathes*. The first one I call my rookie card. I am currently working on my third. I used to write on a blog, but now it is books."

"Where can I find your books?"

"You can find them at Dudley's Bookshop Cafe downtown, or any bookstore in the country, really. If they don't carry them, they can order them for you. Also, it is easy to buy them on multiple platforms online. However, tonight you are in luck, for I have a copy of both here with me now." I would then reveal two crisp paperbacks, and if the person was interested, which they often were, they would flip through and read a poem, or I would read a poem out loud for them.

"Are you self-published?" Was a common question, and my answer always the same.

"Yes, I self-publish. It allows ultimate control and freedom in my work. I don't want my art to be perfected into some ideally marketable book from the opinions of people I don't agree with or live anything like. My books, like me, are imperfect, raw stories from my soul. They are, in fact, me. I desire to display my artistic and human development from beginning to end, from *The Bear Within* to whatever the last book I write will be, and to use this season of my career to establish an organic audience." Then I would smile and ask them what they did, for as much as I enjoyed talking about my writing, I sought to know who they were. Often, they would hurriedly answer and then follow up with the next question.

"Your name is Wing?" They asked as they searched for my books online from their phones, or from reading my name on the cover of the book they held. They always asked this question with some disbelief, as if Wing couldn't possibly be my first name.

"It is."

"Is that your real name?"

For this, I would gauge what my response should be, how much I should reveal, for as you know, the truth is sometimes more ridiculous than fiction. The explanation would depend on whether I was talking to a local or a tourist, whether they were sincere, or if they were nosy and judging, if I was drunk or in full control of my mind. When the conversation had run its course, I would return to my writing. The tourist might then purchase my books and bring them to their part of the world, as wind carries and spreads nature's seeds. The local might become a friend or just an acquaintance. No matter the human's circumstance, I would always invite them to my next poetry reading.

Bend has a reputation for its vibrant outdoor culture. With the Cascade Mountain range and Deschutes River as part of its magnificent backyard, the opportunities for mountain and water recreation, hobbies, athletic endeavors and simple wilderness absorption are endless. One thing Bend is less known for yet pulses just as proudly is its artistic culture. As appropriately sung by The Grateful Dead, "Don't tell me this town ain't got no heart, you just gotta poke around," so was the high desert's art scene. All outdoor activities and creative engagement I pursued. From day one, just as I would retreat into the backcountry to hike and refill, so too I discovered and utilized an array of opportunities to speak, listen, and eagerly share my written words.

I shared my poems at drum circles, open mics, in the library, bookstores, around firepits, on park benches, amidst events organized and unorganized. Wherever people listened, I poured my soul. No matter how many times I stood in front of an audience, no matter the number of people listening, nerves rattled my entire body until I opened my mouth and spoke. As my meticulously chosen vocabulary flowed, my nerves calmed, and I locked into the oration, transforming into the very emotion and moment I had produced it. Upon each occasion of standing in front of spectators and sharing my art, my soul would travel through my entire body, from my toes, from my gut, from the depths of my verbal painting. Into the furthest reaches of the well I would dive only to rise, oozing and pouring through trembling lips, metamorphosing into an air of arrows and swords. Pillars, I dropped onto pillows. With truths I shattered hardened lies. In reverse, I laid the tenderness of tones upon metallic weights, softening all gusts, until tempests would gnash at the former and turn it all over again, color and sound, the whisper of terrifying screams. The beat, the passion, the tears trickling down each cheek, the exhaustion, the crumble, the strength to stand forcibly again, wobbling from the adrenaline of existence. All was shared, all was received, and all was silent. For what is noise outside of one's body when you carry every noise in your soul?

After such recitals, I was often told that my poems were better understood when performed by me than when the reader had silently ingested them from the page in my books. This conflicted me. I recognized that when orated, the poem came alive and was delivered exactly as I intended the poem's life to be. Yet I still strove for the poems to hold the same amount of weight on the page. Each constructive criticism was of value, for I was and always shall be developing as a writer. Each time I returned to my craft, the goal was to improve. I could write a million imperfect poems, yet if they had been born from my authentic self, I was content. *I am and will always be imperfect.* Rambling down dark streets, I tipsily strode and thought. *Perhaps someday, maybe the day I die, I will finally compose the perfect poem.* At this I chuckled, shook my head and sauntered on.

~~~

Once my day of writing was complete, on evenings when Pearl was working and I didn't have a live reading, I would meet up with my three good friends Vin, Hest and Rad for camaraderie, drinks and a romp about town. Vin was the first friend I made in Bend, on the patio of a grimy downtown dive bar. Older than I, shorter, sometimes a bit of a curmudgeon, but he was always down for a few pints and conversation. Vin was tough both inside and out. He had that bulldog in him. Hest became my second Bend friend. A few years younger and taller than me, a lanky young man who'd spent his life in New Hampshire. He was from a different county; therefore, we had never crossed paths in the northeast, yet he also moved to Bend around the same time I did. When I rented my first room on the southeast side of town, Hest had just recently moved into the same house.

CINEREAL

Together, we shared the upstairs bathroom and, powered by our New England background, explored our new turf. Rad was older than I but younger than Vin. We shared physical similarities in our hair color, height, and passion for the wilderness. He was recently divorced and the dad of three delightful children. Between time with his offspring, Rad spent his days at CiderBar, an establishment he co-founded with his ex-wife. In this communal space, Hest, Vin and I met the board-sports and skydiving aficionado, a space we promptly dubbed our "living room."

Rad wasn't sure what to think of us when we first met. Our introduction occurred amid mischievous misbehavior. I always attempted to behave when taking part in the adult playground that was Bend. I harbored no ill will towards anyone and endeavored to treat everyone respectfully. However, my partying sometimes crossed the line. In this manner, Hest and I were stirring it up at the new-to-us CiderBar. With a prime location in town and only three blocks from Pearl and I's art cottage, the discovery was only a matter of time. Not only did they brew and serve their own cider, but they also supplied local craft beer and wine. CiderBar provided a billiards table, a basketball shooting game and pinball machines indoors. Additionally, a large outdoor patio with cornhole boards, a large metal bonfire pit shaped like an apple and enough room to imbibe raucously without bumping too many elbows. Thankfully, no one cared about tobacco or marijuana smoke, a necessity for any place I was to become a regular at.

During our first day at CiderBar, as Hest and I roamed from indoors to out and then back in to shoot basketball hoops, pints of beer from many prior pubs accumulated boldly in our rambunctious selves. We jumped inside the walled court of the lifted arcade basketball court. A strictly forbidden act. With this, our drunken antics crossed well over the line. Employees stared at us unhappily. The other adults enjoying a beverage responsibly shook their heads in disapproval. For a moment I forgot I was not a child on a playground, I was no longer a thru-hiker in my twenties pushing the limits of a trail town, instead I was fortunate to be a new member of a civilized community, and I should not misbehave. The actions Hest and I were rumbling into were not respectful. We were not acting like adults. Later I learned our already boisterous behavior had alerted all employees to possible action. The boss, Rad, observed us scrupulously. And with our immature act of climbing all the way into the basketball game, he had no choice but to confront and reprimand us.

CINEREAL

"Yo! Guys! What the hell are you doing?! Get out of there now!" The loud, sharp words snapped Hest and I's drunken laughter back to reality. I looked at the man who yelled at us. He appeared furious. He stood with his hands on hips, while occasionally waving one arm in the air to gesture his commands. "Get out of there now." He repeated. We obeyed. "Come have a talk with me outside." We sheepishly followed him out to the sidewalk. The upset man, whom I already liked, lectured about how inappropriate our behavior was.

After his admonishing speech, I responded in the way I truly felt, yet not in the way he expected. "With respect, man, I am sorry." I stated. "Sometimes I get carried away and honestly needed you to come down on me like this. I love this CiderBar place already. It's our first time checking it out, and in no way do I mean to be tromping all over it. That was wrong of me. I was being an idiot. I admit my actions went way too far. It won't happen again, I promise."

Hest responded similarly. Rad appeared almost stunned at our sincere replies.

"Guys, honestly, I wasn't thinking you would respond that way." Rad spoke as if he had never met apologetic young men before. "Most guys would curse at me and leave, but you both literally reacted in the opposite way I expected."

"Well, we aren't most guys, and I am still working on taming my woodland behaviors. I respect anyone who will call me out on my bullshit. My name is Wing." I extended my hand to shake and properly introduce myself.

Rad grasped my hand and shook it in return. "Right on Wing, my name is Rad."

Hest then introduced himself, and the tension from a few minutes prior soothed into laughter and understanding. I pulled out a cigarette, offered an American Spirit to both Hest and Rad. They shrugged and accepted. We stood on the sidewalk smoking, turning our bodies occasionally to the south, eyeing the three giant smokestacks in the Old Mill District, chatting and turning east, where the highway snaked by and Pilot Butte rose, then eventually north toward my abode. We dove into the first conversation of a new friendship. Rad explained to us the history of CiderBar and introduced us to some regulars who were playing cornhole. After a few more drinks, a few more behaved games and stories exchanged, Hest and I assured Rad we would be back soon.

"I live right over there," pointing towards the art cottage. "You can spot the giant Ponderosa, which stands in my backyard."

"Good locale. I live in the Old Bend hood as well." Rad nodded approvingly.

"Yeah, man, blessed to live where I am. With intention and hard work, one finds themselves where they desire to be. We will be back here often, and I promise no more crossing-of-the-line shenanigans! Great to meet you, Rad, until next time."

Although CiderBar became our living room, it did not serve one precious drink, whiskey. To provide for this need, I established myself at a business right around the corner, The Saloon.

I had been eyeing The Saloon for a while. It had been under construction across the street from my neighborhood marijuana dispensary. A small neon sign in the window humming its promise stirred my curiosity each time I walked by. When opening day arrived, straight to The Saloon I hustled. Eagerly, I sat alone at the long wooden bar top as one of its first customers.

"Whiskey please, well is fine. I dig the vibe in here." I observed a giant bison mounted above the bar, a plethora of old guns and a giant American flag. The interior exuded a cowboy country atmosphere with dark wood and even an upright-style piano hoisted high on the wall.

"Thanks, we just opened." The bartender, who turned out to be one of the owners, handed me my drink. It was a healthy pour, a good start.

"I know. I've been eyeing this place for a while. Welcome to the neighborhood. I'm Wing. You'll be seeing me. One problem though. Why is that piano not on the ground?" I poured back my whiskey in one full swig and then nodded, indicating a second.

The owner chuckled. "Well, I guess it is kind of weird we placed it up there. I don't know. We'll have to ask my cousin. I didn't make that decision."

I looked back at the mounted piano again, then to the man acting as day-one master of ceremonies. "I suppose I'll have to ride in on a horse sometime, stand on its back and play y'all a tune. Unless you can convince your cousin to lower the damn thing." I drank my second whiskey and pulled out my wallet. The man laughed at my comment and shook his head at my money.

"I'll see what I can do, Wing. Today's whiskey is on me. It is great to meet you. Bring your friends!"

"Thanks, boss, will do." I stepped outside onto the small front patio, lit a cigarette and breathed in the magical warm combination of smoke through a freshly liquor-coated throat. It paired well with the clean Oregon air. I always loved that blend, just as much as I reveled in the looks of disdain people would give about my cigarettes. For some reason, I always felt more comfortable being disapproved of than the opposite. After one more glance at the details of The Saloon's facade, onward I strode, home to the cottage to see my Wylie and play on my own upright piano. *On the ground, where a piano is supposed to be.*

Following the daily piano practice and tussle with my darling dog, I would resume my writing until Pearl texted informing me she was nearing the end of her work shift. Every night, no matter where I was or what I was doing, when her message summoned, I would go to her. Hand in hand, or arm in arm, we then traversed home through town. Once at our cottage together again, my heart was content. For what could be more important than ending each day with the ones you love?

~~~

Although my Bend life had become rich with love and activity, it could not erase the angst in my soul. Pearl recognized it. She learned about the darkness deep inside me. A darkness that occasionally tormented and always lingered. The events of my past had shaped me into a troubled being, who on the surface appeared to have life managed and controlled. I attempted to prohibit my demons from spilling out into the streets, into the stability of the community, but those reins I could not always hold fast. There raged a blustery wildness within, an erratic wind, a pacing anima. I had buried the trauma from Colorado's end, yet it manifested itself in eviscerating ways. No longer could I successfully go to the bathroom in a public stall. If there was any other human inside the restroom with me, I would clench my fists, grit my teeth, and the ability to relieve myself remained disabled until they were gone.

Extreme panic attacks often set in. Only Pearl understood, as she was the one who lived with me and witnessed them. Even on the way to visit her local family, all of whom I loved and felt comfortable around, I would spiral into a panic until I had a drink of alcohol. Then, only with the poison in my system, could I present myself to anyone other than Pearl. She was the only one with whom I felt safe. In my tears and melting mental demise, she would firmly place her hands on my salty wet face and breathe with me, listen to me, providing me the steadfast tenderness I so direly needed.

My claustrophobia had grown to be debilitating, a condition that started when I returned to society after my Appalachian Trail hike. It acted as another trigger for panic attacks. When I drank alcohol to hold the stitches of my sanity together, I began to realize how severely dependent on booze I had become. This awareness added to self-anger, to self-hatred, and yet I did not consider trying to eliminate the alcohol. The liquid poison was a blanket that covered me from the rest of the world.

It was during this time, living together with Pearl, that my mother strongly pulled away from me. I knew why. She told me. She disapproved of my relationship, considering it to be immoral. I was not following Jesus, I was not submitting to God, and yet "This is what she wants from me but not who I am! How can Mom hold me to a standard that I have not chosen to live!" I yelled these words and shook my fist. I knew I was in the wrong. God's presence lingered like a stern bystander, one who was no longer engaging and yet had not completely disappeared. A mixture of guilt, shame, stubborn pride, and hurt haunted within, so the only emotion I attempted to focus upon was my devoted love for Pearl. *If living with Pearl means my mother will have nothing to do with me anymore, so be it. This is the woman I want to marry.*

Often Pearl, Wylie and I departed from Bend for small vacations, mental health retreats. Although I missed the freedom of legally being able to drive, I was grateful that my partner could. Occasionally, I still took the wheel to provide her a break, but only when I was sober. The paranoia of being pulled over without a license always loomed. I was not hiding from the law. The authorities had run my government identification and background check multiple times since leaving Colorado. There was never an issue. They knew where I lived.

Our plethora of excursions amassed into a pile of adventures. We frequented the Oregon coast, exploring it all bit by bit, partook in outings to Portland and visited more of her family in Tucson, Arizona. During the solar eclipse on August 21, 2017, we immersed ourselves in the eclipse's totality atop Round Mountain in the Ochoco National Forest. Often, we went

CINEREAL

camping just for the night, always seeking cozy hidden nooks next to rivers beneath canopies of trees. We ran together, hiked together, existed on the planet together, united our lives together. She and I, with little Wylie by our side, built a framework for peace together. And yet the darkness I had buried deep within relentlessly emboldened, threatening to destroy all solace like a cancer breaking through a tomb. This living infection spread to every branch of my life. In the autumn of 2018, on one of our coastal adventures, I could sense all the peace she and I had assembled crumble.

For vital context, during our trip to Tucson in the summer of 2018, I suffered heatstroke. This miserable incident greatly discouraged me, as I had often exerted myself in such extreme heat before. During the Pacific Crest Trail hike, I regularly trekked in temperatures well above 100 degrees with no shade. Other than the heat's discomfort, it had never struck me down or caused debilitating illness. With the same confidence I carried traversing the Mojave Desert at noon, so too I boldly implemented during our week in Arizona. However, something in my body had changed. *Was it my age? Was it my perpetual drinking?* Whatever the factors were, it caused the scorching weather to torture my brain, strike down my strength, initiating the long sharp decline in health I was soon to face. Heatstroke acted as round one in a long, compounding descent into hell on earth. With each day of confused suffering, I persisted in consuming more alcohol. Whiskey shifted from what I considered to be a jovial friend and gripped me as an evil-spirited menace. No longer was I a fun drunk on the brown liquid. Rather, I turned into a mean, stubborn, fiercely defiant alcoholic. Two whiskey swigs balanced me out; three, four and more turned my soul and behavior from kind to harsh. Yet even with this knowledge I rarely ceased at one or two. Instead, I drank incessantly from the bottle. Unremittingly degrading my heart of love and kindness down into a projectile of filth.

Pearl acknowledged my change in behavior and remained patient towards me. During our intimate home parties of two, she would guide us towards tequila, my favorite red wines, the alcohols which did not cause the beast within to bray. We started to fight passionately, and yet our love would ultimately soothe all anger. After shaking the cottage with elevated arguments, we would sit and intentionally communicate. She treated me with grace and affection. Together we mended our disputes and moved forward. Never did my whiskey drunks encourage me to physically hurt her or anyone else. Violence had never existed in my core, but the mulishness, the chaotic

CINEREAL

fury which spilled into our lives exhausted all who knew me. It did not matter how much I loved and attempted to show it. My daily drinking outweighed everything. The alcoholism drained all light from our home. With each day, self-loathing continued to propagate. "This is not me," I whispered alone, drinking wine in the garden at night. "I adore others so deeply. Many of my favorite poems are about practicing a life of genuine kindness and love. And I mean it! It is not a front, nor a lie. Therefore, what have I become? I am a wretch. I have become what I plead with the world not to be."

That autumn of 2018, we drove to the southern Oregon coast with two of Pearl's friends, whom I had grown to love as well, Marissa and Stíofàn. With us I carried the whiskey bottle, and my sullen anger. As we hiked to the Natural Bridges in the rain, amidst the magnificent beauty where the Pacific Ocean meets the continent's rocky edge, I sensed the weight of my internal darkness escalating. Unable to stand beneath its weight any longer, I sat down on the edge of the cliff. The abyss audibly called to me, encouraging me to jump off, kill myself, finally die and rid every one of the incredible ugliness that was me. As I sat there bathing in the pull of ultimate decision, while Pearl, Marissa and Stíofàn skipped about admiring the environmental grandeur, I vividly observed a large wispy gray hand reach up from below the cliff's edge and crawl towards me. Instantly I recognized the wispy being. It was of the same living darkness I had communed with many times prior in my demonically tormented years. The hand summoned. All I needed to do was accept its grasp and be irrevocably pulled into the depths of the underworld where I belonged. Yet as I sat contemplating this end, Pearl sat down next to me. She could not see the hand, but she gave me hers. As she offered this tacit gesture, the wispy appendage retreated to the pit it had come from.

Once we returned home from our retreat, everything had changed. From the edge of the cliff onward, I remained outside deep into the night, longer than my evening routine had ever comprised. For as a villainous army, the incessant wispy, ethereal bodies of the living darkness had returned. Although their voices had beckoned at the cliff, at home they stayed muted for the time being. With this vile, vivid hoard, I obsessively communed.

~~~

Our daily routines remained the same, yet distance grew between us. I romped around the town, writing and selling books, drinking alone and drinking with friends, frequenting CiderBar and The Saloon. Pearl continued her busy involvement with the restaurant, painting, and spending more time away at her family's home. When there was a family event, they invited me, yet my attendance dwindled. At night, while I ruminated in our garden, drinking wine beneath the moon, she went to sleep without me. Our bodies lay but thirty feet apart, I in the dirt and she in the bed. All we had built was evaporating.

In the spring we agreed on one last grand Oregon road trip together. Perhaps we could repair all that had been unraveling. The day was April 10th, declared as an unofficial holiday dubbed Wing Day. April 10th was the day I started both my Appalachian and Pacific Crest Trail hikes. "Each and every April 10, I raise my head and begin again." I quoted from *As a Wolf Breathes*. Pearl laughed and placed her arm through mine while we strode from the parked car into Fort Clatsop. April 10th also served as an alternative day to celebrate me, for both Pearl and I were born on October 14th. Same day, different years. Our shared birthday was cute at first, but ultimately not ideal. On October 14th, my heart preferred for it to be her day, not mine. I did not want my birthday to detract a single moment from commemorating her. Additionally, April 10th seemed more to me like the beginning of my new year, and thus it became Wing Day.

History had always captivated me, therefore, I'd long desired to visit Fort Clatsop. It was a replica of the original fort, constructed and lived in by Lewis and Clark at the end of their mighty journey west. Close to the Columbia River, a few miles from the Pacific Ocean, nestled beneath fir and spruce trees, kicking pinecones with each step, we dove into an hour of historical education. We read each panel, studied each display in the museum, viewed the provided videos, strolled through the fort's rooms and imagined what life was like hundreds of years prior. We set aside our grievances and kissed in the rain. Away from life in Bend, while keeping me off the brown bottle, "Tequila today, Wing, not whiskey," as Pearl stated, all seemed possible again. Our relationship wasn't tarnished on the road, and yet, that is how one feels on a vacation. There is an atmosphere of impersonation. It is returning to routine life when one perceives the truth. Perhaps we both understood this, for we procrastinated going home.

Together we charged into ocean gusts and bellowed into thick salt air. On Cannon Beach, we sprinted like snails upwind and galloped like wild horses downwind. We expended ourselves until collapsing into sand dunes, ensconced with clouds drifting across the sky, sitting in silence, staring into the horizon, searching for the breach of whales and ourselves, until we rose, shook our messy hair clean and ambled back to the car to commence our drive southeast.

In Portland we rented a cottage, and she, knowing my anguish with that city, said I could drink whiskey that night. On our way to dinner, I jumped into the first liquor store I spotted and purchased a bottle. After our meal, I led her to the bar Dig a Pony. The very one where I had erupted into a volatile monster and was thrown out of during my first visit to Portland with G. The same piano I had madly played then still sat in the corner. So again, I played, and again they told me, "Not now." With my rebellious whiskey soul stirring, Pearl pulled me onward into our night away from that place of toxic memory. Eventually, having returned to our rented abode, the whiskey poured heavily into our throats, and torrid intoxication ignited the silent neighborhood night. Our voices thrashed, carrying piercing words across the nightscape.

In the morning, with the weight of poison in our blood, we drove on, but not yet to Bend. We knew what home would bring. At Cascade Locks, I proudly presented the Bridge of the Gods, where the Pacific Crest Trail traverses the Columbia River from Oregon into Washington. I touched the dirt, remembering when my footsteps had crossed this way nearly seven years prior. We drank beer and played a game of billiards in the same tavern I partied at on my long hike. Onward east to Hood River, our last stop before we must turn south back to Bend. We stayed in the brewery town to prolong our trip one more night. We understood this night to be the end drawing near, but we did not speak of it. Instead, we drank more beer and frisked atop hilly midnight streets.

"Tonight is not tomorrow, so let us not live as if it is." I whispered into Pearl's ear. She giggled and grasped my face, agreeing with puckered lips. But night only holds so many hours, and the road I once blindly boasted as forever, too, has an end.

Once home, we slid back into our separate lives, routinely crossing into summer. I worked on book three and tended our garden. She busied herself with projects and employment. It became apparent that my body and brain had sustained long-term symptoms from the previous summer's heatstroke. I could no longer tolerate hot weather. No sweat would excrete from my skin. My brain would blacken into a painful fritz as my internal temperature rose and be unable to cool itself. My body felt physically broken. I simply could not do the things I had previously done naturally. This added to the strain on our relationship, yet we persisted. Pearl drove me into the mountains on scorching days, to bathe in alpine lakes and rest in higher elevation shade, but it was only a temporary fix, a way to soothe pains and prolong our remaining time together.

As the cooler weather of autumn arrived, she had poured all the strength she could into our partnership. In early October 2019, a week before our birthday, on a bench beneath a tree, she announced she was done. The relationship must end. Although my heart and words fought against our complete separation, deep within I understood. I knew it had been coming, even though I never wanted to admit it. To repair our break, I would do anything except for the one thing that must change, my chronic consumption of alcohol.

She told me I could stay at the cottage as she wanted to move into her own space. The day quickly arrived. She cleared out all her belongings. We divided the things we had built and gathered among us. Two and a half years was the longest I had ever united my life with someone. Never had I loved anyone romantically more deeply than her. When Pearl was gone, when she was no longer my darling partner, I sank. Only Wylie and writing saved me from descending to the furthest depths. I believed I deserved it. I comprehended that my drinking had twisted me into someone I did not want to be. Bound within a prison of one's own creation, how does one change? As the taillights of her car disappeared into the tangle of streets, I laced up my boots, lit a cigarette and walked to The Saloon. It was time to drown in fierce brown liquor.

CINEREAL

The Beast with Many Heads

The Saloon became a sanctuary for me, or so it masqueraded for some time. Every employee knew my name, and I knew theirs. Rarely did they charge me for any more than half my drinks or reprimand me for my wild antics, and not once did they cut off my incessant alcohol consumption. When I pounced from a barstool onto the top of a large dining table, accidentally flipping it over, causing both my body and a dozen pint glasses to crash upon the ground, they helped up my dazed self, swept up my mess and handed me another drink. If I left my bar tab unpaid, they either waved it off or held it open until I returned. When I lit marijuana joints while lounging on the indoor loft's couch, they looked the other way. Only when I savagely kicked over the welcome sandwich board sign with a swift deliberate swing of my boot did they later state, "We know you were in a rough mood last night, but you can't be doing that Wing." I apologized sincerely and we carried on. I was a spectacle, a catalyst for a party, always bringing in more patrons and their money. "We put up with Wing's antics here because it's worth it. He may be wild, but his intentions are harmless, and he kindles a lucrative party nearly every day. Therefore, keep him happy," the owners must have instructed the employees. The wooden floor and beams, the tall ceiling with the out of reach piano, the cozy patio with a log burning furnace, even the bathroom stall where I could lock myself in with the drunken graffiti, every detail that comprised the sticky saloon became an escape from my abode. Memories haunted the art cottage. Pearl and I's faded love remained in every nook. Memories I wanted to paint over instead of dwell upon. Whiskey was a mighty soldier for this. Although blacking out on booze was a rarity because of my tolerance, it provided a hazy, numbing barrier allowing me to float about the world undisturbed.

When I sought a familial sort of camaraderie, CiderBar waited around the corner. Rad, Hest and occasionally Vin would rally together with me to partake in competitive games, rowdy conversations and to create new connections with townsfolk and tourists. Most everyone in Bend frequented

CINEREAL

CiderBar, and everyone who attended, met an enigmatic Wing. Away from the cottage, it was easy to shut off the painful compartments in my heart and focus on meeting new people, selling books and romancing new thrills. I had become adept at burying pain, unaware that its lack of resolution only strengthened its brewing force within. Approximately every day my friends and I met in our vortex, discussing elements of life, tangling with deep questions, sharing stories of adventures, and elevating ourselves into the highs of being alive.

"Rad, I wish this place had existed when I hiked the PCT. But then again, if we had met back then, it would have been difficult for me to continue hiking on! G would have loved this spot."

"You were one year early. In 2013 we opened our doors." Rad nodded, understanding my love for his business. He was proud of CiderBar, as he should be.

"2019 was a solid year for PCT hikers here. We received a plethora of signatures in the trail journal. In fact, I'm going to grab it so we can have a look back at the season. Do you need another drink?" I swiftly finished the last half of my beer, acknowledged Rad's nearly empty glass and hustled inside to grab the leather-bound journal and two fresh pints.

When I moved to Bend in 2015, it was no accident I landed in a trail town. Bend's proximity to my "lifeline" was one of its primary appeals. Operating as a trail angel to all hikers passing through was a personal priority. When I met Rad and CiderBar, it was clear the location would serve well to conduct my self-declared Pacific Crest Trail ambassadorship from. In the summer of 2019, while Pearl and I were still living together, I immersed myself in this duty. Within a leather-bound blank-paged book, I had drawn, written, styled and assembled an inviting ledger for all thru-hikers to sign and share whatever words they desired. This was a common practice across the trails, and now with CiderBar having its very own record, it facilitated in making CiderBar a go-to destination for all hikers. It served as my way of bringing in more business for the company and congregating the trail community at a compatible hangout in Bend.

Every time I spotted a hiker rambling through town, immediately I'd introduce myself, often by hollering, "What up, hiker trash! I'm Hot Wing, class of 2012. Have you been to CiderBar yet? Go get yourself a cold pint and sign the journal. If you need anything, a yard to camp in, a shower,

CINEREAL

laundry, questions about town, just ask for Hot Wing, they'll text me and I will swing by. Hope to see you there!"

Clasping the journal and refilled glasses, I returned to Rad on the patio. With a few tokes of marijuana, followed by cigarette drags and alcohol sips, we read each signature and entry in the log from the season.

"It was a good year." Rad agreed.

"Indeed," I said candidly. "And now on to a worthy winter. Let's see, we have the Halloween party to prepare for, two full moon parties and then the New Year's Eve party in just a few months."

I contributed my social skill sets and time to Rad, helping with his plethora of CiderBar parties in every way I could. I missed Pearl, but between my vivacious community, long walks and jogs with Wylie, writing, live poetry readings and selling books, life was full enough not to ruminate on the past and remain focused upon the present and future.

With Rad as conductor, all the passionate employees and an animated group of CiderBar regulars, including myself, we created and hosted a series of epic events. We seized the culmination of 2019 without knowing what 2020 would bring. Long strands of lights were hung, flashing party lights were mounted, a rotating disco ball reflecting multi-colored lasers lofted in CiderBar's heart, decor supplemented into every cranny, a DJ booth and large speakers filled a corner pulsating the air, we inserted smaller firepits across the patio adding blazes to the main apple shaped incinerator. The billiard table, infamous basketball game and pinball machines were ready to be gamed. CiderBar vibrated and glittered, inviting all to forget their troubles and come play. And come they did, skipping towards the colorful spotlights. Throughout each event, the taproom's indoor space became crowded, shoulder to shoulder, with elated humans cohering and dancing. Attendance required many to spill onto the patio, which also brimmed amidst the firepits and picnic tables, bright-eyed souls smoking, laughing, howling and exchanging alcohol-laced social joyous energies. Rad, Hest, Vin and I, together with many of our CiderBar peers, often gathered at our favorite outdoor perch to pause from crowd weaving, and proudly observe what we as a team had created, another successful zesty party.

"Thank you for CiderBar, Rad!" I hoisted my glass; the others mirrored my move. "If you hadn't founded this fantastic business, all this delight would not be." The crew chimed in agreement. We clinked and cheered to Rad, to CiderBar, with gratitude for our eclectic community.

CINEREAL

~~~

I do not know if my friends recognized the depth of my drinking problems yet, or my inner turmoil, the battles with darkness. It seemed like everyone else around me also drank frequently, though perhaps not as heavily, and I endeavored to leave my burdens at home. However, the friends I made and the environments I regularly attended were drinkers and drinking establishments. From my first alcoholic beverage until one too many, I appeared to have everything under control. At home following each event, after each poetry reading and after each bar had locked its doors, it was then that I would open my preferred comforting drink, a bottle of red wine. With this, I lounged outside in the garden. Wylie sat close and guarded the yard, invisible on moonless nights and a bold black figure in winter snow. With my wine, I melted into the withers of my mind. The living darkness was yet to speak ever since its wispy hand had reached up from the coastal cliff, and before that it had been many years since they verbally haunted my ears and brain. But once the hand summoned, the wispy gray bodies had returned and remained. In rows entering my peripherals until filling my frontal vision, they paraded. In the absence of light, their bodies shimmered, as ghosts may present themselves, or as fog shifts its shape in a dream. Beside the remnants of corn and tomatoes, bundled in blankets beneath the moon, defying hibernation, transfixed upon the ethereal, I drank one bottle of wine then persisted with bottle two. While others slept and the distant highway's hum pacified, I could finally let go of the internal grip I publicly held tight and allow my sanity to erode.

Pearl called me around the holidays. She wanted to show me her new apartment. Excitedly, I obliged, although my heart felt confused. Despite my feelings, missing an opportunity to spend time with her was not an option. I was happy she was moving forward as she desired, for love does not limit the other. My sadness stirred upon noticing the paintings, which once hung on our quirky yellow walls, now mounted upon fresh white panels. Yet I controlled all my emotions and forced a smile at each new setup she cheerfully presented. Peacefully, we tried to sit on her new couch together and attempted genuine laughter as we shared a bottle. We even let our knees brush against each other. I forced the rapid beating of my vital organ to temper when she rubbed my beard and stated she missed it. When she kissed me, I kissed her back, but I could not allow myself to assume we were reuniting. We were not. Everything had changed.

CINEREAL

After visiting her apartment, embracing goodnight and stealthily brushing a tear from my eye, I called a taxi and returned to the cottage. Wylie whimpered when she smelled my clothes. She knew I had spent time with Pearl but could not understand where she had gone. I did not know how to quell the emotions within either of us, so I implemented the only things that soothed. First, I held my dog and cried. Then I opened another bottle of wine and vented every broken piece of me upon the keys of my piano. Finally, I clipped Wylie onto her leash, and we walked down to the river. Next to the gentle currents curling around each stone and log illuminated by the moonlight, I wrote a poem.

~~~

When I awoke on January 17, 2020, I did not know that in less than twenty-four hours my life would change forever. I knew I'd rested well, for I'd only drunk one bottle of wine the previous night and fallen asleep before the lonely train screamed. With a calm brush of my hand, the eastern window's drapery slid open. Light poured into the room, highlighting the dust the fabric stirred with its movement. The world outside my window sparkled. Sunbeams danced upon snow. Winter hats atop my neighbor's heads bobbed down the alley, Sue and Jim were on their daily voyage to the market. It looked and sounded like ten o'clock. Sue's familiar voice and the crunch of boots as they trudged provoked a smile. My windowpane was thin and cold to the touch, allowing each subtle noise to leak through along with winter's chill.

I stepped into well-worn moccasins lying where I'd stepped out of them and wrapped myself in a tattered robe. Wylie stretched and yawned, alert to the fact that I was moving. After opening the backdoor allowing Wylie to charge into the yard with the force of a cannon, striking the neighborhood with barks she had saved all night long for each suspicious noise she catalogued in her mind, I drank a glass of water and ate a banana. Brumal gusts from the door ajar poured into the cottage. After a few loud minutes, Wylie trotted inside, pleased with herself for reminding every critter whose yard it was. I shut the barrier, poured a cup of grain-free organic food in her bowl and stood in front of the southern living room window munching on almonds. My heartbeat wasn't erratic. I wasn't hungover. I didn't need to drink a glass of wine or whiskey immediately to temper my pulse. "This is good. That means I can get a coffee," I spoke for Wylie to hear. "Today will

CINEREAL

be a great day." Ever since 2019 clicked into 2020, I'd been attempting to curb my alcohol consumption. In response, my mood had brightened.

After brushing teeth and adorning the usual January layers of clothing, Wylie and I ambled through the neighborhood. Our first stop would be the coffee shop. Walk past Poetry Corner, say good morning to whichever barista was working and order drip coffee with no cream nor sugar. Poetry Corner was known only to me and Pearl, plus everyone who read that specific poem in book one. Rambling past the auburn junction always sparked a grin on my face. Following our walk, which comprised shifting between the edges and center of streets depending on traffic and snowpack, I returned Wylie to our abode, grabbed my laptop and tromped down to an eatery for a proper meal and to work on book three.

By the middle of the afternoon, the sun's strength upon the volcano-pimpled land was diminishing. *Time for a beer and whiskey.* The new book was coming along well. It differed stylistically from the first two and was certainly the most comprehensive. Our breakup had birthed many poems portraying an array of emotions; however, the pieces were growing more positive again. As a mirror to my heart, this was a welcoming sign. I decided I would read a few of the new ones to my friends later that night. It always helped to orate my written words to them, along with everyone else who stopped to listen.

As I strolled through downtown on course to a preferred tavern, I spotted one of the unhoused men I had written a poem about. His head hung low, but he was wearing the insulated gloves I had given him. *I'm glad he is still alive,* I thought, while waving to an acquaintance on the far side of Minnesota Avenue. Once I reached my destination and sat on a barstool, the barkeep nodded in my direction, acknowledging my arrival.

While counting money from her till, she asked, "Hi Wing, the usual?"

"Hey Carrie, yes, please." I pulled out my iPhone to text the crew. It was a Friday night, and our usual end of week plans agreed upon, meet at CiderBar at five. As Carrie delivered the whiskey and India Pale Ale, I handed her the proper amount of cash, thanked her, then moved outside to sip and smoke. At all my spots, I had a preferred seat, and this one on a sidewalk on the edge of downtown always provided interesting activity to observe.

Once the drinks activated the cozy internal boozy layer, I proceeded home to let Wylie out again and chop wood as she frolicked in the snow. I always maintained a stack of firewood for the backyard firepit I frequently

CINEREAL

used, and chopping firewood was a favored lifelong pastime. At four-fifty it was time. After wrangling Wylie inside, tussling her fur and promising to "Be back later girl, love you," I locked the cottage and turned right down the alley, to first stop at the nearby market, the same one Sue and Jim utilized, for a quick slice of walking pizza and then on to CiderBar. There, the regulars and friends would gather for our usual Friday shenanigans.

I arrived chewing the last bite of my greasy snack, content a day of food coated my belly ensuring a controlled dive into an evening of revelry. The apple firepit crackled modestly, so I promptly added a few logs to revive its tenacity. Hest and Vin were already standing at the bar waiting for their pints to be poured. I nodded to Simone and Tania, expressing one for me as well. They knew what kind of beer I preferred. Everyone exchanged greetings, plus a hug for Brittany who sat observing the recent sports scores. Rad walked in the side door by the billiard table with an eager smile on his face. Soon we all cheered our togetherness. CiderBar vibrated with its standard weekend energy. Since there was no big party that night, the extras would be fewer, and the regulars would be more. The nights when most everyone knew each other were our favorites. We were one big quirky, unique, colorful family. After talking athletics with Brittany for a few minutes, the crew shuffled to our customary winter spot outside, standing around the apple firepit.

The work week was discussed, Vin and Hest highlighted a recent date they'd each been on, Rad mentioned a punk rock show he wanted to catch in Portland, I told of the folks from Switzerland I had chatted with and sold books to the night before. I provided cigarettes to whoever desired, our first pints turned into seconds and then thirds, more logs were added to the fire and mellow conversations escalated a few lively notches. It was time for a marijuana joint. Vin winked and grinned as I lit and hit the tasty bud and then handed it to him. He dragged a few tokes and then passed it along. Eventually, it would make its way around the circle. Any fleeting tones of skylight to the west had all but dissolved into night by now. With each breath, misty clouds protruded from our mouths. It was a frigid January night. The temperature settled in the teens. As the taproom grew busier, more people joined us around the fire. We squeezed closer together, shoulder to shoulder, rotating our fronts and backs to the warm blaze.

On this night, like many others, a few people we had never met wove themselves into our fireside conversations. We were a welcoming bunch,

CINEREAL

and with each chat and drink, strangers morphed into acquaintances. After a session of banter, Vin, Rad, Hest and I played billiards indoors, only to return to the fire after a few games for more smokes with hoods pulled over our heads. It was at this time that I shared some of my new poems, to the intrigue and applause from the others. A small crowd gathered around and listened intently to my verses. An older couple on their way out, who had paused as I performed, purchased my books from their phones on the spot. Eventually the evening surge dwindled, and when ten o'clock arrived, the CiderBar closed early for a Friday. However, we were not ready for our night to be over. Our beer buzzes draped lightly while my poetry adrenaline surged high, and many of us craved liquor. Vin, Rad, Hest, a few new companions and I agreed to turn the party up at The Saloon. As a gleeful pack, we migrated around the corner.

The Saloon boasts its own mighty firepit, shaped like a furnace with a chimney. Once everyone had their shots of choice liquor and fresh beers in hand, the gathering resumed outside again in its new location. As we grew from tipsy to raucously inebriated, our party danced about the patio tossing snowballs at street signs in the distance. We added firewood to the metal box while laughter, drinking and smoking accompanied us into the night. One man we met at CiderBar hung closely as if he was fully knit into our crew. We did not mind, nor did I question who he was or why he had intentionally become a part of our group so hastily. This was not uncommon, so I proceeded without caution. Hundreds of nights had been spent at this location, and each night I met new people. Socializing with strangers was a part of my book-selling routine, and I had always returned home safely. At The Saloon, I would confidently set my beverage down, wave my hands animatedly as I divulged a ridiculous story and turn my back without regard to the open pint glass. In other locations I practiced more caution, but CiderBar and The Saloon were an extension of home. Naively, I let my guard down. Never should I have trusted the dark-eyed man who had joined us that harrowing night.

~~~

The following is a summary of the harrowing incident. Details I did not fully comprehend when they occurred. A mixture of what I recognized and understood at the time, locations provided by my cellphone's data, terrifying flashbacks I would later frequently remember, video camera footage from

CINEREAL

The Saloon, and even footage from my phone's camera, for I documented much of our party with pictures and videos until the incident.

Shortly after midnight, as the calendar rolled from January 17 into 18, the dark-eyed stranger who had joined us drugged my drink. He stood by and watched my antics as the drug integrated with the alcohol in my bloodstream, waiting for the opportune moment. I began to feel strange, an odd inebriation I had never experienced before. My body and mind turned extra hazy and debilitatingly sloppy, not in tune with the usual cause of whiskey or lack of food. I had eaten enough. I balanced the number of drinks to ensure partying late into the night, aligned with my common routine. There was wine at home I still planned to drink beneath the moon. Hest, Vin and Rad were unaware of what was going on, for like everyone else at The Saloon, they were enjoying the casual events and conversations. It was nobody's job to take care of me, not even the employees. I was an adult who must look out for myself. As the drug took effect in my body, and my brain darkened, I stumbled outside alone to smoke a cigarette. My friends sat at the bar where I planned to return, as last call was not until one-forty-five in the morning, the time we each intended to stay until. When I ventured outside, I stumbled along the side of the extensive building in a state of confusion. Rapidly, I was losing proper function and mobility. My legs were giving out on me. The stranger and another face I did not recognize followed closely. Once I had staggered away from the front of The Saloon, leaning forward upon the red wall struggling to stand, both men grabbed my arms and dragged me into a vehicle. They threw me into the backseat and punched my head while wearing thick winter gloves. This brutal action forced my body into a state of dull mindlessness, too stupefied by the drugs to fight back. They drove me east, to the other side of the highway, into a pocket of town hidden by trees and yards of industry where train tracks pass through. They dragged me from the vehicle into the snow, over to the train tracks, and bludgeoned my head repeatedly with their gloves on. The temperature was around fifteen degrees. All was dark except for the white frozen ground. After beating me and ensuring I could not move on my own, they drenched me with a bottle of water. Quickly, the cold, dry air started turning the water into ice. They stole my phone, but not my wallet, planted drugs in my back pocket, drugs I never carried or ever used, but likely the same ones they had dosed my drink with. They then left me unconscious in the night to die alone, far away from where any other human would pass by or see. I do not know how long I lay there, or how many more minutes or seconds it would have been until I perished. I do know I should never have woken up. Death approached. Only one thing saved my life.

"MOVE! OR YOU WILL DIE." It was these exact loud, firm, audible words which awoke me. I did not know where they came from, yet in the pit of forced slumber they stirred my consciousness awake. Feebly, I opened my eyes, yet I could not lift my face from the snow. My entire body ached. My head throbbed with pain. I tried to move but could not. My clothing had become rigid and frozen. My body would not function. I let my head remain horizontal. Nose and eyes set into the cold ground. I shut off all effort and faded into nothingness. "MOVE! OR YOU WILL DIE!" Again, I heard these words. The voice shook me to my core, demanding my attention, and with the reiteration of this command my throbbing brain awoke again, grasping the urgency of the situation. *I cannot stay here. I cannot remain in the ease of obscurity. Urgently, I must force my body to move.*

Struggling to lift my head with strength I did not have, I shuddered. I attempted to stand, but this too seemed impossible. Slowly, with determination and obedience to the voice, I breathed in deeply and forced my torso up onto one bent arm. My head spun between light and dark. Once on my elbow, I forced one leg to shift upward. With this motion, I managed myself up onto the other arm and pushed forward with my leg. Gradually, I slithered forward. As I crawled, I strained my vision to comprehend where I was. It was difficult to see due to a harsh dizziness, so I continued inching along at a tedious pace until finally reaching a small tree and clutching my hands at the base of its trunk. Here I contorted into a sitting position. I recognized the train tracks and listened to the occasional rumble of a truck on the highway. The highway was now to the west, the opposite direction of where I was accustomed to hearing it. This provided an idea of which way to go. Eventually I stood hunched over, yet with each few steps forward my strength would fail, and my body collapsed again. For what seemed like hours, I continued this minuscule advancing motion. In time, I realized exactly where I was. Stumbling down a road passing large mounds of dirt, I recollected, *this is the landscaper's yard where I once purchased soil.* As I moved along, I prayed a vehicle, any vehicle, would come help me. In my pocket, I searched for my phone to check the time and call for help, but my phone was not there. Onward I swayed and stumbled until reaching the overpass of Highway 97. Beneath the highway there is a street which leads towards the Crux Fermentation Project. I knew where I must go. Past Crux, onto Colorado Street's edge, across and down into the east side of the Old Bend neighborhood. Once I arrived at Florida Avenue, the street my cottage was on, it was only a few blocks to the west. I persevered with a slow stagger. Never did another vehicle pass or see me all night.

When I finally arrived home, the front door caught my exhausted fall. Although my phone was gone, the cottage key remained tucked in my wallet. Wylie started barking, worried by my absence and the thud my body caused against the entrance. Once indoors, I collapsed on the wooden floor. Wylie investigated my body and licked my face. Her concerned affection provided immediate warmth and comfort. I reached up to the countertop to clutch a half-full bottle of water and rolled towards the carpet. Breathing deliberately, I struggled to fathom everything that had occurred. The magnitude of the incident was so profound it was difficult to accept. Attempting to piece each scene together with an injured brain was like trying to brush pinesap off skin. I remembered being pummeled in the head, riding painfully on my side in the vehicle, my feet dragging in the snow... But it was all too much to consider. I needed to fall asleep... Everything was fading... Through blurry vision, having staggered a few toilsome cold miles home, I squinted my eyes to read the oven clock. Almost five in the morning. Submitting to sleep could be dangerous; this much I discerned, so I forced myself upward onto the couch, sipped on water, and lay in pain and terror holding Wylie until the sun rose.

My head would not stop throbbing, but it was not the pain a hangover creates. It eclipsed, it pressed, it gripped, surpassing the worst headache I had ever experienced. When the sun rose, I knew I must summon help. If I could locate my cellphone, perhaps its location would provide more information. From my computer, I messaged Hest on social media, briefly explaining something awful had happened and my phone was gone. When he awoke and read my message, he promptly drove to my cottage. He joked I must have had a wild, fun adventure when I left them. He did not understand, nor did I entirely, but my thinking proved far too muddled to make any sense of it yet.

Using the "Find My iPhone" app on the computer, we learned my device was still on. Hest drove us to the area the application indicated. Further north up Highway 97, well beyond the route I shuffled home, they had thrown the phone off the highway into the snow. After an hour of searching, with my contributions extremely minimal as I could barely stand, see or think, Hest successfully recovered my device. Despite lying in the frozen snow all night, the phone case had protected it. Happy with our minor victory, Hest returned me to the cottage then went on his way, assuming I just needed to rest after a weird, confusing night. Grateful for his help, I collapsed in bed. He did not seem to understand, but I could not precisely describe what had occurred. I was barely holding on, optimistically smiling as I usually do, repeatedly promising him, "I'm fine, brother, thank you. I'll be alright."

After Hest left, I spun into a daylong sleep. When I awoke, the excruciating pain in my head continued to worsen. Recognizing two facts, I considered, the sun is setting, so it must be almost five, and I need help. Despite our breakup, Pearl was the only one. My fingers trembled as I dialed her number. My voice shook as I told her what had occurred. Promptly, she arrived and drove me to the emergency room at the hospital. The care at the ER was minimal. They were busy, so there was no room available for me, and my story confused them. Although I maintained a natural, cheery demeanor, I could not lift my head or communicate properly.

"You have suffered a traumatic brain injury. There might be bleeding in your head." The doctor stated and then asked, "Have you reported this to the police? Do you have health insurance? Wait here until we can get your head tested."

I did not have health insurance, nor had I reported the incident to the police. The very idea of talking to the police terrified me. Every year since Colorado, I had been doing everything I could to avoid law enforcement. The fear of this forced my mind to shut down even further. Talking to the cops was something I simply could not do. The sexual assault had erected strong internal walls against this. Perhaps if they had taken me seriously when I had reported it, I would feel differently, but they did not. Therefore, in my delirious mind, the cops were just as much to blame. I lay on a hospital bed in a busy hallway with ice on my head and Pearl tenderly by my side. After hours of waiting and realizing I could not afford the tests they were to run on me, amplifying my already maxed out stress, I told her we must immediately leave. A panic attack on top of everything else was rapidly overwhelming me. She promised to spend the night, not as my girlfriend, but as a chaperone to ensure I did not die. Grateful for her presence and support, I disconnected myself from the IV and escaped the hospital. An ocean of anxiety boiled in my soul. Far too much pain tormented my brain to lay and wait in a sharp world that seemed to only condemn and not care. Too many eyes cast suspicious glares as if I had done something wrong. The damage had been done. I could not change what had occurred. All I wanted was to be away from every piercing light and harsh noise, home in the dark silence with Wylie.

~~~

In the immediate days following the traumatic brain injury, the beast with many heads rose and viciously tormented. The living darkness had already returned in sight, but now it returned in sound as well. These voices, which plagued my childhood until my young twenties, harried again. It was as if in their years of silence, they were developing in strength, force and ferocity to unleash their fury at the opportune time. Each day and night, wherever I walked, wispy figures haunted my peripherals. Behind me, I would hear footsteps, yet when I turned around there was often no one there. In the evening as I drank my wine, the voices called to me, in taunting murmurs, in shrieking screams, stalking my mind wherever I strode. "Wing, David, Wing, David, we must finish the job. We must finish the job, Wing David! You should not be alive. We must finish the job!" At night, black figures circled my cottage. By day, an evil cloud pressed from every direction.

In my crippling anxiety, I decided against reporting the murder attempt on my life to the police. Instead, I conducted my own investigation. This I did without the help of my peers. Although I conveyed the incident to my friends, each of them seemed confused and brushed my story off as if I had simply experienced a wild Friday night. *Perhaps they are only my friends in the good times, and not when everything goes dark,* I considered. This thought I buried, for I needed to believe they genuinely cared. I knew Hest did at least. He had proven it by helping me retrieve my phone, and through many other selfless actions. Rad and Vin also displayed love beyond the pints in their own ways. My head throbbed, my vision sputtered, and constantly my brain spun into incapacitating spells of vertigo. Frequently my mind went black, impeding my vision, not allowing me to know where I was walking or sitting. I lay in the fetal position, digging my fingers into my head, forcing pressure into my agonizing skull until it eased. Alone in my torture, the only remedy that helped me live was drinking alcohol. To be numb to everything is what I sought. I considered the powerful words I had heard. The words that saved my life. "Move, or you will die. Move, or you will die." I understood where the voice had come from. It was impossible to deny. It wasn't my subconscious, far too distinct and omnipotent than anything I could produce. The voice was God's. His voice was irrefutable. Yet even though I comprehended He had saved my life, the haze of alcohol between me and God, between me and everything, created such a barrier it was as if I had buried myself in a poisonous cocoon.

As I moved around town daily, walking my errands and dog, not only did a supernatural enemy stalk me but also a human. A few days after the incident, as I strolled a public pathway along the Deschutes River, my head whipped over my shoulder when I heard the slowing wheels of a bicycle approach. A creepy man whom I did not recognize slowed his speed, matching my stride. He looked me in the eye and stated, "You should not be alive." He then sped up, biking away before I could retort. This event added to my dread and became the first of many times I would see him. For weeks afterward, no matter where I was in Bend, he appeared. Often, he moved deliberately, at a parallel distance, eyeing me down. Sometimes he would rush by on his bicycle from behind or speed up from my front as if threatening to run me over. At the last second, he would veer. One time I grabbed a stick as he approached, ready to jam it into the spokes of his wheel, but he saw me wield my makeshift weapon and remained at a distance. He knew something about the incident. He had made that clear. *Perhaps he is the second man who had thrown me into the vehicle.*

During these weeks of in-person agitation, the creep also found me on social media and messaged with the words, "I know who did it. But I will not tell you. There is a sadistic group of people who have been watching you and planning this for some time." When I messaged him back, he retreated into aloofness, choosing silence to compound my fears. I tried to pry and dig answers out of him, but he had already succeeded in intensifying my anxiety, just as I assumed he desired. Eventually, all I could do was save screenshots of his messages, in case I needed them as proof in the future, block him online and attempt to maintain a safe distance from him. Every day for the rest of the 2020 winter was fraught with fear and pain. Around my home, I built booby traps to alert me if anyone entered my yard. I drank wine and whiskey with all windows veiled. Rarely did I go to the taverns as I used to, and when I did, it was with a mutilated spirit of paranoia. Insanity loomed one step away from me each day. When running into friends, I maintained my usual positive grin, endeavoring to appear alright, for they just wanted to uphold their normal lives and not be burdened by my tribulations. Haunted by the living darkness and the fear of my abusers, swallowed up in pain and misery, I desired to rid myself of existence. Yet, my commitment and responsibility to Wylie prevented me from finishing the job and killing myself. Perhaps only God preserved my last tendril of safety from what would, could, and to some, should have been.

My dad came and visited me after I confessed the harrowing news. Rarely had I ever witnessed him cry, but there he stood in front of me with tears streaming from his eyes. When I asked him if he was alright, he voiced with a helpless surge, "People tried to kill my son. People wanted or want my son dead, so no, I'm not alright." I nodded my dizzy, damaged head, looked down to the dirt and then tilted the whiskey bottle to my lips. Still confused by all that had occurred, I was just grateful he was with me for a few days. He asked if I wanted to leave, that maybe Bend was not the town for me after all, but I said no. I didn't want to leave another place because of a traumatic incident again. I did not want to keep running. This didn't happen because of the place. It somehow had to do with me, wherever and whoever I was. I could blame only myself. The whoever I was, always seemed to attract an inescapable evil. Someday the wickedness would either finish the job, or I must somehow muster the courage to face it and fight it head-on.

~~~

There is a grime that exists beneath the rotting floorboards of our soul, where half-eaten worms decay and the feces of shriveled hopes shriek in despair. There, a murky, heavy, suffocating air tortures the grime, letting it neither live nor die, only suffer, suffer, suffer. "I am the grime." I whispered, my toes naked to the snow, my brain too hot, lungs burning with smoke, esophagus and belly aflame with whiskey. And though I did not want to be this grime, I wallowed in it for I did not know how to escape. "Something must change. I must change. Everything will remain the same, continue to rot into darkness, if I do not change."

It is an odd reality, which generates strange feelings, when someone tries to kill you. The fact that some people wanted me dead so resolutely that they acted upon their desires stirred nearly intimate sensations in my soul. Initially, I numbed myself so much I did not even know if I was angry. Nor was I sure if it directly added to my self-hatred, for I was already there. If anything, paired with a lingering fear, I almost agreed with them. It resonated as if someone else finally understood me. Suicidal ideation had recently been drowning me. The only difference is they had the courage to act on it, and I, well, I felt like a coward. Other than slowly drinking myself to death, I had not committed to its totality. I knew the reasons I had decided not to end my life. Wylie, I could not abandon her. She trusted me to love and care for her. My writing was another reason. Out of pain, I created art. At my core, I genuinely sought to help anyone in need. Utilize my suffering to inspire others to persevere no matter what they face. And to inspire such, I must do the same. The hiker in me was resilient, the child in me loved God, loved Jesus, loved my family, loved the concept of what was right in this world, abhorred what was evil, loathed when others committed violence, hated abuse, and yet, somehow, I had become caught in the middle. *What does it matter if a heart seeks purity and kindness if the body acts otherwise?* I knew my drinking had created a prison around me, a self-made suffering, the walls grown so thick I did not know how to break through, nor did I know if I even wanted to. Consuming alcohol seemed to be the only thing helping my recently acquired debilitating symptoms, the most incapacitating of them all, the persisting vertigo.

Ever since the traumatic brain injury, the dizziness arrived and would not cease. For the first few weeks, I assumed that my brain needed time to heal, and the symptoms might linger for a while. *But for how long?* I noticed the dizziness was much stronger when I was sober, but it would ease after two drinks. This brings me to the analogy I shared at the beginning of the book, of my season on the cruise ship when I was a strong young twenty-one. I was now on a boat again, an allegorical boat, lying on the earth in my backyard, with the constant rising and falling, spinning and quaking upheavals in my brain. My body was so accustomed to the alcohol that it would calm the symptoms, numb them, dull them, much like when my body had acclimated to the motion of the cruise ship that I no longer sensed the unstable rocking of the ocean. It was only when I stepped off the boat and stood on firm solid ground that the wavering returned. When I was drinking, I felt better. When I was sober, I was unsteady. Not only was I unsteady or merely dizzy, but the slightest visual disturbance would rocket my brain into extreme vertigo. Flashing lights tortured, neurologically slicing and triggering the mental spin. Movement in the car, turning my head too quickly off center, cacophony of noises drummed my brain into a hellish blackened oblivion. It was as if anything more than focused gentle existence would destroy my brain, that all became shaken up as a disturbed snow globe and could easily erupt and splatter across the planet. My brain was delicate now, broken, but alcohol provided the semblance of cohesion and strength. Therefore, even though I discerned my addiction to booze had become a prison, *perhaps leaning into this prison is the only medication I can access.* Aware of this folly, I desired to change what I had become and not hold on to my wretchedness as a life raft. *But what else can I do?*

Lying in my dizziness, I meditated upon the voice which saved my life. I thought about the plethora of instances He had revealed Himself. I returned to prayer and called out to God, begging Him to help me change. Again, I implored Him not to give up on me yet. His love was faithful although I did not deserve it. His presence steadfast despite my rebellion. He, the truest Truth that exists. These facts glared into the face of my soul with both Fatherly austerity and Fatherly tenderness. I needed to change my heart posture toward Him. Most of my friends and many of the people I met didn't believe He existed, let alone trust in Him. An adamant closed-heartedness towards Him existed all around me, and yet my belief in Him remained unshakable. Perhaps others had not witnessed the supernatural in both its glorious light and its decrepit darkness, but I had experienced such unveilings so many times I could not deny what was real. Despite this, since my youth, I persistently, irrationally rebelled against Him, seeking earthen pleasures and my strength, leaning into the decisions I wanted and not His, not Him. I understood why so many denied Him. Accepting Him would require refuting one's own self-godship. The world uplifts and worships pride. For this is secular instruction, our own strength, that we each are our own god. It sickened me each time I noticed a meme, picture or post on social media celebrating this fallen, misleading, dangerous mindset. Our culture's regard for autonomous self-love clings to ego and pushes away humility. And yet I was no different.

While suffering physical, mental and spiritual anguish, I opened my dusty Bible and attempted to unlock my stubborn, prideful heart. On the page I turned to, Jesus' words called to me. Matthew 11:27-30 (NKJV) "All things have been delivered to Me by My Father, and no one knows the Son except the Father. Nor does anyone know the Father except the Son, and the one to whom the Son wills to reveal Him. Come to Me, all you who labor and are heavy laden, and I will give you rest. Take My yoke upon you and learn from Me, for I am gentle and lowly in heart, and you will find rest for your souls. For My yoke is easy and My burden is light."

Another passage God led me to was James 2:19-20 (NKJV), which states, "You believe that there is one God. You do well. Even the demons believe - and tremble! But do you want to know, O foolish man, that faith without works is dead?" A few verses later in James 2:26 (NKJV) he says, "For as the body without the spirit is dead, so faith without works is dead also."

If change is to come, I must start by looking to Him. He is strength, not I. Only through Jesus Christ the Son, can I know the Father. But despite my earnest belief in Him, even the demons know He is the I Am. Is my belief solely an intellectual one and not one of a true trust in Him? For my fruit, my actions, my works are not godly. They are the opposite.

I knew that nothing of my merit could save my soul. Intellectually, I understood Jesus did it all. I believed He is the true and only Savior, that He is the only Way. Works do not save, but true faith, absolute trust in Him, creates works that reflect this. Our actions demonstrate where our faith exists. And I also knew that when I was an adolescent, my earnest, trusting faith in God was indeed whole, complete, and my works were once honorable to Him, but then I fell away and rebelled for so long, becoming lost in the fallen world which hates and denies Him. I replaced my trust in God with sinful pride. *If my natural actions are not reflecting Him, then am I even His anymore? He does not revoke the gift of salvation, but I can certainly reject it! Which is exactly what I have been doing for many years.*

~~~

In March 2020, COVID-19 arrived in the United States of America. March 17th, Saint Patrick's Day, was the first day in Bend, Oregon, when all taverns, bars, saloons and restaurants shut their doors due of the pandemic. I wrote a poem that Irish holiday night, sitting on my back stoop, drinking a soothing Malbec while listening to the silence St. Paddy's Day never wears. The world tumbled into a state of fear and confusion. Although I did not want people to be hurting, dying, or arguing, I welcomed the hush of society and the locks on tavern doors. I craved silence, embraced the social distancing, so direly desiring for the chaotic world to slow down. My previous romps around town turned into long walks with Wylie down dormant streets, strolling through empty parking lots, pausing introspectively by the river, and listening to the notes of a distant, lonely violin drift on the air, floating in an atmosphere of uncertainty.

I contracted my first round of coronavirus near the end of March. After suffering through heatstroke, years of alcohol abuse and the recent traumatic brain injury, the illness overwhelmed my body. Miserably, I continued to lie helplessly in bed, breathing deliberately with my tongue on the roof of my mouth, praying, peering out the window for seventeen days until it passed. Hest delivered groceries to me. From afar, my friends occasionally stopped by or waved. The virus ravaged my ailing brain, liver and heart, leaving me weaker than before. Somehow, I managed to diligently sip enough wine throughout the bedridden weeks to stave off any potential alcohol withdrawal symptoms.

When the illness passed and I could rise and return to daily life amidst the sprouts of spring, I planned to continue studying the Bible and seeking God, but this notion was only one of comfort to my feeble, battered self. Despite my prayers, numbing my body and mind remained my top priority. It was as if I had been fooling myself all along. I was not surrendering to Him nor wholly committing to Him, just partially enough as I lay nearly dying to convince myself I was doing what was right. On April 10th, the unofficial Wing Day, instead of repenting of my sinful lifestyle, placing my full trust in Him and obeying the Almighty, I rushed out of the cottage in a pridefully crazed dizzy bluster. And when my feet finally stopped, I stood inside a liquor store in front of a shelf of whiskey. One can deceive oneself, but one can never deceive God.

CINEREAL

The Dark Ages

When I was a young boy, before my parents divorced, I frequently dreamt a recurring nightmare. The dream would rattle me awake, fearfully distraught, terrified by its every sight, sensation and ominous implications. Any other nightmare I could shake off and return to sleep, but not this one. This vision of terror etched itself into my memory, haunting each day, pulsing within. On nights it replayed, I would wake and dash downstairs to my parents, who were often on the couch with popcorn and a movie, or in their room with the door shut. In tears I'd rush into their arms and sob uncontrollably from the perpetual vivid horrors or sit in the hallway by a thin stream of dim light slipping beneath their door, holding my knees to my chest, wrapping my arms around my young frame, attempting just to breathe.

Beneath a giant millstone, I was ground, my flesh destroyed and pounded into paste, continuously pressured into powder, never falling away but remaining in the lack of space between mighty circular boulders, generating a potent wrenching pain. My soul trapped with the flakes of my flesh, tortured ceaselessly with no ease, no pause, no release, no break, stifled, smashing, suffocated screaming, thrashing heat of grinding, expanding and pressing repeatedly, for forty years.

These forty years represented eternity in my young mind, for as each dream started again, so did the forty years. Never would I complete the torture. Forever, I must endure the pain. The reality of this hung on my soul every day. After the sun had risen and nightly sleep had concluded, it lingered. This representation of the worst feelings my juvenile brain could imagine fastened its grip. After the dream, after my scurry to seek comfort, once I had returned to bed and laid down to attempt sleep again, in the corner of my room, two, sometimes three vivid demons would sit by a little fire. They placed themselves with their backs towards me, but their faces turned over their shoulders, snickering as they whispered together, conspiring against me. Their fingers, noses, eyes and malevolent auras became imprinted on the inside of my eyelids when I closed them.

CINEREAL

~~~

I did not deserve to live another day. I do not deserve to live another day. Nor did I deserve Him saving my life each of the times He did. Never did I deserve His forgiveness and steadfast love. Why He stayed, why He did not break my hardened neck forever casting me away, I do not know, other than He is grace, He is patient, His love is immense. When sober from alcohol, my heart would seek Him, and when consuming alcohol my heart would return to stubborn blindness. For the thirty-three months following my first round of coronavirus, it was as if I only sought Him in my dreams, waking with desperate gasps, filled with remorse and shame from my pathetic weak ways, screaming the name, "Jesus!" As the fog of demonized rest wore off, I'd peel myself off the ground or force myself out of bed to face the day. Instantly the brain would spin into its awakened state of darkness, so I'd crawl to the alcohol closest to me and pour the numbing toxin down my throat until the vertigo eased. Trapped in a prison of poison, clamoring upon the walls to break out, I shrieked my voice into silence, drowned by the endless torrent of booze. Without it I could not stand, and with it my heart perpetually shut itself to God. For thirty-three months, from April 2020 to December 2022, I battled in this forlorn manner. My alcohol intake rapidly rose beyond an average of twenty drinks each day.

As spring matured and garden sprouts breached the soil, reaching as hungry babes to the nourishing sun, my friends and I retreated into the mountains to camp, ingest psychedelic mushrooms and romp beneath the vast starry sky. I was no stranger to psilocybin, the psychedelic compound in "magic" mushrooms, having consumed them often throughout my young adult life. Already that spring I had partaken in several such hallucinogenic "trips," one awful event and many beneficial ones. These mushroom trips held the ability to terrorize if handled rashly, but when utilized mindfully they could be helpful in clearing anxiety, humbling the ego, exploring the ethereal and ultimately resetting oneself back upon a proper mental path. Psilocybin trips were my preferred choice of the psychedelic realm, personally superior to the chemically manufactured LSD, which I'd enjoyed abundantly as a party drug, and calmer than DMT, which I had also intimately experienced on multiple occasions. However, mushrooms, like cannabis, were straight from the earth and as natural a drug as could be.

Camping in the mountains with friends was always a cherished activity. There upon the elevated earth I was home, and there in this home I communed with my Oregon family. We each were quite different — Rad, Hest, Vin and I, in our personalities, beliefs and experiences lived, but we shared a bond of adventure in the magnificent outdoors. Once the tents were pitched, the bonfire ablaze and mushrooms ingested, we sat upon the cool spring ground, still damp with winter's highland idle. Melting snow trickled downhill from large white mounds in the shade. We each sipped our choice drinks and observed as nature's hues shifted, morphed and developed. On mushrooms, every living object shows its value. One can see each tree and blade of grass breathe. The spectrum of light and sound usually diminished by what a human can perceive becomes amplified, the veil abolished, the molecules of existence pixelated and vibrant. The selfish ego of human importance melts away into an understanding of shared space and place on the planet. In many ways, the mushrooms open the portal to broader sight, for they help dissolve each cultural lie, eliminating the allusions a greedy capitalistic society constructs, leaving only the intricate raw portrayal of presence.

A mushroom trip with my crew in the Cascade Mountains served as a timeout from all I had been battling. Our conversations revolved around the beautiful intricacies of nature's balance, all while culminating in the simpleness of being. We basked in the intense hallucinogenic journey, and then in the clarity after we spoke about what it encouraged us to ponder. Often, on this camping trip and in future conversations together, we delved into the depths of philosophical questions, such as the purpose of life, our internal responsibilities or lack thereof, that being alive cultivated in each of us. Despite each conversational venture, I found it difficult to speak on what I understood, for despite my actual beliefs, in my alcoholism I was still wafting between continued rebellion against God or submitting and being transformed to live for Him. I believed one way and lived another. I felt like a fraud, filled with shame, conviction and self-anger each day. No longer was God buried away in my mind. He was at the forefront of my every morning, watching me pour the drink then carouse into each sinful day. In time, over wine, I did honestly state I believed Jesus is the Son of God as God incarnate, that I believed in His death on the cross and His victorious resurrection on the third day, and that His sacrifice, if we should truly believe and accept it, would produce in us repentance and earnest surrender to Him. However, upon stating this, it led to awkward silence, to confused head-shaking disagreement from my peers, and to other's fear of what ungodliness in the name of God has historically led to. Yet, in my mind, I had come to understand that all actions under the banner of God which led to any sins, to anything less than pure selfless love for another, were not from God at all. Too often the enemy has deceived by using the name of what is holy, only to stain what is holy and true. Once I stated this confession to the crew, hearing me say it strengthened my guilt of not living it. Each day God was convicting me, yet I remained on the fence, with one foot desiring to be with Him and the other unwilling to submit my torrid alcohol addiction and the sinful lifestyle I caroused. For me, alcohol had become an idol I served before Him.

On this magical night, at this camp, the timeout from all that occurred down the mountain was a holiday of refreshing camaraderie. I chose not to dwell upon the violent murder attempt for a day, and the looming physical health and spiritual battles. Instead, I silenced the internal turmoil. With an intentional dive into the psychedelic adventure, I chose simply to breathe, to lounge in gratefulness, to leave the anxiety of all symptoms down in town. My friends did not grasp my daily struggle with dizziness and vertigo, as whenever I was with them, I was drinking, and the alcohol held my vertigo under control. The boat did not rock as much when booze was in my bloodstream. Thus, with laughter and revelry after gallivanting around the forest and meadows, we gathered around the bonfire long into the night, proclaiming exclamations at the moon's voyage across our celestial ceiling. But, as all vacations, they must end, and back home we must return, they to their lives and I to the torments of mine.

In the cottage, an insatiable need to rage my soul deep into each night filled me. After waking at one in the afternoon and replenishing the alcohol in my bloodstream, I spent the rest of the post-noon daylight hours attending to the few positives in my life. Wylie and writing, sell my books, then proceed into another long night of drinking. Having progressed through part of the pandemic, the bars and restaurants that owned outdoor spaces opened to the public again. Each evening, I returned to my post at CiderBar and the ominous saloon to socialize with whomever was available. After the bar patios closed for the night, the party would often continue at my cottage until my overwhelmed and exhausted visitors took their leave and only Wylie, the wispy bodies of the living darkness and I remained. Here, communing with each demonic head of the beast, I would continue to consume my booze until the birds sang of the sun's imminent rise. Never during these thirty-three months was I awake and not drinking, and never was I not a breath away from death. Life had become the eternal grinding nightmare of my youth.

Near the end of May, Pearl returned for another dedicated chance at growing and sharing life together. I welcomed her return and, other than decreasing my alcohol intake, attempted to be as she wanted me to be. And yet, we were not the same people we had been during the first years of our romance. She had been maturing, and I had been disintegrating. When the weather grew hot, my damaged brain could not take part in the activities of old. She again endeavored to remain patient with me. I knew each day with her was one day closer to our definitive end. In September I published my third book *Owl of The Moon*. The lengthy collection of poetry sold well at first, speedily reaching six continents, but I no longer possessed the physical stamina to remain as focused on my writing career as I had during the first two books. Every layer of myself was crumbling. As a final push to help save both me and our relationship, Pearl proposed we eliminate alcohol from our lives for ten days.

To her, the ten days was an achievable, reasonable stint. To me, it sounded impossible, but for her, this time around, I was willing to try, at least that is what I verbalized. I had not abstained from alcohol for a single day since my departure from Colorado five and a half years prior. Therefore, I was not sure how my body would fare. During my first coronavirus spell, I drank a tad less, and here and there I would reduce my consumption, *but none?!* I realized this would decide our next, or last, step as a couple. It was in hour twelve of no alcohol that I comprehended how truly addicted I had become. Unsurprised by this, it glared as another proof of the truth. Withdrawal symptoms ravaged my body. Extreme heart palpitations, a raging angst, enveloping dizziness, descending into bouts of vertigo with each turn of my head. I knew our relationship was soon to be over. By the first afternoon, my heart rate escalated to dangerous speeds. I couldn't hold a pen without it thrashing back and forth, barely could lift a glass of water up to my trembling lips. Fearing a seizure, as soon as Pearl went to work, I chugged a bottle of wine. Before it was time to see her again, I brushed my teeth and thrashed my mouth with wash. It did not take long for her to realize what I was doing. In a fit of exhausted frustration, saddened by my failure, she announced she could do no more. We were truly finished. I knew this would happen, and though I may have fought against our breakup the first time, at this juncture it was easier to let it be. Alcohol addiction owned my body. I needed the poison to balance each symptom of my brain injury, especially the vertigo. In my heart, I wished Pearl the best. *She is better off without me. Broken Wing is already damned.*

That winter, as 2020 clicked forward into 2021, my decrepit mind, body and soul's condition exponentially worsened. The farther from God I fell, the further into the bottomless pit I descended. One afternoon when I awoke on the kitchen floorboards, I saw a demon I had painted on my wall during the night. Stretched out floor to ceiling, it loomed over me as one of the many beasts that governed my being. Surrounding my body on the wood were crude scribbles my hand had terrifyingly transcribed with a black marker. I hustled to grab a can of paint and coat the wall with multiple layers until the infernal being was no longer visible. The floor I mercilessly scrubbed with sandpaper. But it did not matter, for when night returned, so did each demon, each devil, each chain of hell led by their snickering leader. I knew that only one thing was keeping me undeservedly alive, but that could change at any moment. *If I had not given Him my heart and soul as a child, He surely would have given up on me long ago.*

~~~

When I was a young boy, my mother would read to me from the Bible, teaching me the depth of God's love. She explained that each one of us are sinners, and the only way to be redeemed and saved from an eternity separated from God is through His Son, the Lord Jesus Christ. Jesus died on the cross for each of our sins, serving as the Savior for our unrepayable debt. If we believed in Him, believed in His victory over death, rising from the tomb on the third day, accepted His incredible gift and repented of our sin, meaning to turn away from our sinful nature and turn towards and follow Jesus Christ, we would be saved. In this we would be born again through Him. This was necessary, for as God is a loving God, He is also just. The wages of sin are death, an eternal, torturous death of our soul beyond the passing of our fleshly body, a death which separates us from His love forever. But Jesus paid the penalty as the perfect, blameless sacrifice for all our sins, by taking upon Himself the weight of our wages. Justice was served, but we cannot receive this magnificently incredible gift of eternal life through our own actions, by living a "good" life. It is only through Jesus Christ, only through His grace. All our fleshly bodies will pass away, but our eternal spiritual life hinges upon the acceptance of His amazing sacrifice and dominion over sin and its consequential death. As my mother taught me all this, I did not accept and fall in love with Him blindly, for God worked in my heart helping me to truly understand what happened, what would happen, and what it meant for me. As a child, my soul burned with love for Him, and although I was just a boy who had not lived out in the world, nor yet understood the dire need of what Jesus' sacrifice meant to this world, I knew that no matter what, I desired to give Him my life as a servant because He gave His life for mine.

I remember the day I was baptized in New Hampshire, shortly after we moved as a family from Georgia. I recall another day when I sang "I Love You, Lord" in front of the church. My heart overflowed with adoration for Him and desired to share that love with all. I also remember crying after I told my neighbor Daniel about Jesus, for I had given him a Bible, but his mother confiscated it and threw it in the trash. Why the world hated Jesus so much shocked and angered me, yet I knew Jesus had made this very clear. In John 15:18-19 (NKJV), He said, "If the world hates you, you know that it hated Me before it hated you. If you were of the world, the world would love its own. Yet because you are not of the world, but I chose you out of the world, therefore the world hates you."

As I grew older and my family moved through its own disassembling tragedies, I held an anger I could not comprehensively place. Such pain justifiably hurt and surrounded me, yet I could not justly be angry at God or even stop believing in Him. He had presented undeniable evidence of His truth and love. *If I must place my anger anywhere, it should be at the sin, at the evil Satan always attempts to infiltrate lives with. In my misplaced anger, I became deceived and hardened.* Rebellion replaced my humility, so I left home as soon as I was able and pursued my own worldly ambitions. I knew this hurt God, but just as He is omnipotent, He loves each one of us endlessly. He wants us to choose Him. He does not force us to. If He forced us to love Him, then our love would not be genuine love. Most reject Him. Some of us become His as I had, and even though my actions and desires turned towards the world and away from Him, He would never let me go. He is the Shepard who knows where each of His sheep are, and when one falls astray, He leaves the fold to save His lost child. I had been lost for a long time, and yet He persistently called to me, standing by my side and never leaving me, despite my sustained rebellion.

CINEREAL

As a young growing adult living for myself and not for Him, everything the fallen, sinful realm offered fascinated me. The plethora of carnal pleasures my mother sheltered me from as a boy enticed me. I desired to experience each of these for myself. Immorality, drugs, worldly adventure, living my way, egotistic autonomy from serving Him and selfish pride in my own accomplishments. All of this drove me further away from His purity. However, my heart still retained Him, always sensing His Fatherly watchfulness. As I experienced cultures that hated Him, I educated myself, reading books about all religions, philosophies and mindsets. Questioning why is that Jesus is the Way, the Truth and the Life and not another way? Why does the world mock the fact He created the universe, and why is it believed by many that the Bible is just a fictional tale of stories? In searching for answers, I discovered all the commonly believed lies. But despite how much I could almost comprehend the world's godless point of views, and how much I also recognized the multitude of enduring proofs for God's Biblical truths (which the world effectively deceives many otherwise), He remained supreme in my soul although I was not living for Him. He had provided me sight to see vividly what many others could not, ensuring no matter how far away from Him I fled, no matter how much the fallen world's lies nearly made sense, an unshakable belief in Him would remain. How could I ever deny the supernatural things I witnessed? How could such things, which defy all laws of nature and science, exist if they were not from Him? I grasped why the world believes as it does, but I more so comprehended that His power is far above any of our earthly understandings. His wisdom is far greater than the world's wisdom. The wisest human on earth pales compared to God's wisdom. We are fallible. He is not. No matter how hard I strove to silence the Truth within me, it remained impossible. I could live in rebellion against Him, but in doing so, I was only living untrue to both myself and Him, and thus self-hatred propagated. As a boy, I surrendered my soul to Him, and as a man, I would either live and die in wretched misery and forever be separated from Him for rejecting Him, or I must finally submit and return to Him and no longer hide my love for Him. And to love Him means to obey Him. Not out of fear, but out of genuine seeking and Spirit-led growth in understanding the eternal depths of His love. The fear that does and should mightily exist is the consuming fear of living a life apart from Him. We are not meant to be our own; we are created to be His. And yet in the years 2021 and 2022, entrenched in an earthly controlling addiction, tormented by the enemy, despite my heart knowing the Truth, I continued in rebellion. For what, for why, I shamefully can make no excuse. I was full of a baseless, obstinate pride.

Occasionally I would meet a Christian, and when I did, I gravitated towards them. They shined the light I was dimming. My soul yearned for Christ-loving friendships. One such instance during the winter of darkness, a young woman with a wide-brimmed hat was sitting by the apple firepit at CiderBar. Her hat provoked my hello, but it was her heart for Jesus which enticed me to sit down and talk. We exchanged glowing chatter about the Son of God while my friends looked on with skeptical glances. At the end of our talk, we also exchanged phone numbers. She invited me to her church, but my active alcoholism hindered my ability to pursue growth in God. I wanted to seek Him, follow Him, obey Him. I knew I must, but one cannot serve two masters, and to me alcohol was the one I served. To the living darkness I repeatedly returned, grateful to know there were others in Bend who loved Him, yet remaining entrenched in my own sinful ways.

~~~

In the spring of 2021, my winter's outward rust polished a tad. Within me, I was corroding, but friendships produced enough light to keep me going. They lured me out of my cottage and forced my ailing body into life-sustaining movements. Rad and I occasionally ventured up to Portland. These trips away from our COVID bubbles stirred excitement amidst the doldrums. At CiderBar, on the patio by the apple firepit, I met a married couple of similar ages who recently moved to Bend from Asheville, North Carolina. Their smiles and earnest interactions enticed the small bits of remaining good in me to take part in optimistic thinking again. Max and Lena's enthusiasm, produced by the freshness of their new life chapter, reminded me of the elation I had experienced when I moved to Bend. They reveled in my poems and wild stories, and I leaned into listening to each word they shared. Although I knew many people and even more seemed to know of me, it was rare that such meetings developed beyond drinking buddies or town acquaintances to blossom into deep friendships. Max and Lena were two of these rare souls. I loved them immediately. Quickly, they became part of my inner circle. Hest, Rad, Vin and I wrangled them in, which they reciprocated, and by our second day lifting pint glasses and cheering together, we knew they would become chosen family for life.

CINEREAL

Again, I patted Rad on the back and thanked him for CiderBar, for without it we may never have met so many kindred hearts.

In May 2021, I started exclusively dating a woman I met in October 2020. We exchanged messages through the winter, and though she did not know the depths of my pain, or my battles with the living darkness, we dove into our new romance. I called her Flower, for she shined as such. Her kindness and genuine sweetness initially soothed my angst and self-anger. She pulled me into her embrace and whispered, "Do you want to go on an adventure with me?" I affirmed her offer with a kiss. Our new relationship, fueled by passion and promises, which I did not have the discipline or wherewithal to preserve, developed into a swinging pendulum of bliss and tempests. Truly, I loved her, but differently than I had loved Pearl. Flower was like an island respite amidst a gargantuan ocean I was miserably attempting to cross. Eventually in our partnership she discovered my darker side, as I too learned of hers. Beneath our charisma, we individually remained weary with baggage, as spiritual wounded travelers yet to heal. Together we struggled to build upon the rubble, but often the rubble must be sorted through on one's own. It must first be cleared and a new foundation restored before building upward again. These were lessons we would learn in painful ways.

~~~

In May 2021, my habitual correspondence with Ol' Man Sam ended abruptly. He and I had upheld our deep friendship for all the years since we parted in Boulder, Colorado. We maintained a frequent email exchange, sharing recent poems, philosophical writings and news of our latest happenings. After I survived the attempted murder, Ol' Man Sam encouraged my perseverance despite the compounding darkness. He had left Colorado and was living in the Dominican Republic for some time, where he too started experiencing vertigo. He also lost his balance. Because of this, he relocated to the northeast of the United States to live near loved ones. There he completed and published his second book, The Gonzo/Kukulkan Papers. On May 20th, Ol' Man Sam asked for my current address so he could send me a personalized copy, but after my response that same day, I heard nothing from him again. Two days later, D. Ro informed me of the tragic news. Ol' Man Sam had died.

His death trampled my already weary spirit. The tsunami of grief directly affected my relationship with Flower. I retreated inward, returning to dwell

CINEREAL

in an unnavigable labyrinth of chaotic darkness. She attempted to break through my densely established walls, but I would not let her in. Instead, my already extreme alcohol consumption continued to worsen. I bathed my organs with even more whiskey and wine every second I was awake, drunkenly floundering until dawn. Only when the robin's melody pierced the fading night, would I lay down in bed beside the woman whose pillow was damp with tears.

My thirty-sixth birthday arrived, yet I do not remember it. Flower informed me that before noon I lay in the dirt cradling a bottle of whiskey, drunk and blabbering after hurling hundreds of empty beer cans against the stone foundation of the art cottage one by one. Christmas arrived, and my river of rot persisted. On New Year's Eve, I might have been with Flower, or I might have not, I do not know. We might have already broken up, since I frequently pushed her away and only allowed her to return when I could not physically stand to go purchase my own basic supplies. Entering the year 2022, I teetered on the edge of death.

In the summer of 2022, D. Ro was on tour and set to open for The Lumineers at the Moda Center in Portland, home of the NBA Trail Blazers. He had moved on from Elephant Revival and begun writing and performing under his own name. Upon hearing that Ol' Man Sam and I's tall mutual friend would perform only a few hours away, I resolved to attend the show. Rad's company CiderBar served as an official sponsor for the large venue; thus, after a phone call, my friend revealed he had successfully secured two tickets in a luxury box suite for the musical event. Rad could not make the trip, but Flower could. Together, she and I drove north to the city. We stopped for my traditional respite at Government Camp on Mount Hood. There, I shared with her many of my Colorado stories involving D. Ro and Ol' Man Sam while drinking beer and whiskey. Flower listened intently, happy to see me donning an excited smile. After quenching my thirst, we rolled onward to the show. Once we had parked in the VIP lot and were seated in the VIP suite, when the lights shifted towards the stage, the curtain opened and the first notes of D. Ro's guitar and voice began, tears instantly started flowing down my face. Hearing his voice transported me to Colorado, to Ol' Man Sam. For the duration of his set, it felt as if my dear old friend was standing beside me. As D. Ro sang a familiar song that I first heard with Sam, I could smell the old man, perceive his braying voice, sense his portly mass shift from foot to foot. Throughout the performance I

CINEREAL

glanced over to where Ol' Man Sam might be, sighting only hazy air and the movements of a stadium full of strangers. After D. Ro completed his musical act, I informed Flower I needed to retreat outside immediately. I did not care to watch The Lumineers. My injured brain had absorbed all it could audibly and visually handle. I required the absence of percussion, lights and a tightly packed space. My lungs craved tobacco smoke, blood screamed for whiskey, and my heart must grieve. Flower followed me as I hurried through the upper hallway connecting the stadium suites until I located a bar, then onward with three portions of brown liquor in my hands and one fresh in my belly to a cement outdoor patio with multiple no smoking signs posted. The stadium's interior vibrated with the sounds of a rock band and its fans. For nearly the remainder of the event, I drank, smoked and mourned. It was as if a billion more tears were somehow still trapped in my body since Ol' Man Sam had passed away.

"He was sitting in his favorite chair out in the backyard." I leaned over to Flower and murmured. "I picture it one way, but I wonder what everything really looked like. The ground and trees, how he positioned his chair, his thoughts. He did it right, though. Took his last breath outside."

Flower placed her hand on my knee. I lit another cigarette and reached for the fourth whiskey.

When we heard The Lumineers play the first notes of their most popular track, signaling the show's culmination, and recognized D. Ro's voice join them on stage, we returned into the enclosed arena. As soon as the encores were complete, I grasped Flower by the hand and rushed her through a human maze against the tide of bodies retreating. We ventured to the stadium's lowest surface. Once near I hustled past a police officer on towards the back of the stage, jumped over a barrier fence and down onto the floor where the bandmates congregated. As the cop chased after me, I spotted my tall friend and yelled, "D. Ro!" Before law enforcement could reprimand my questionable movements, D. Ro spotted my wave and hustled over. With tears in our eyes, we embraced as two heartbroken poets.

"For Ol' Man Sam," I stated.

"For Ol' Man Sam," D. Ro agreed.

After all the commotion had ceased, and the Moda Center's lights were being turned off, Flower asked if I wanted to spend the night in Portland. "Perhaps a late dinner and a hotel," she suggested with a romantic flutter of tawny eyelashes.

CINEREAL

"No," I responded gently, "this city is no place for me. I accomplished what needed to be done. Thank you to Rad and CiderBar for providing the tickets, and thank you, Flower, for driving me to the show. It is time to go home."

~~~

From the day I met him, Max's friendship developed into a sanctuary amid a social wilderness of landmines. Hest, Vin and Rad were not landmines, but outside my crew, the CiderBar community and Flower, much of the world seemed to be. Paranoia, claustrophobia, vertigo, sharp internal organ pains, visual and audible battles with the living darkness, and the pervasive, debilitating alcoholism ruled my days. While mental health dragged despairingly low, Max and Lena recognized my struggles. Our conversations developed into deeper focuses, beyond the swapping of stories and the creating of lighthearted times. After receiving the seeds of closure for Ol' Man Sam's death at D. Ro's show, Max, perhaps without realizing, helped me begin to shift my mentality. As we discussed each facet of life, the history of ourselves, our patterns, our beliefs, I remembered significant parts of who I was, the me beyond the dizzy-brain injured-drunk. He aided in rekindling a dormant force within. The one who faced obstacles and hardships head-on, with the belief I could venture into the unknown and achieve anything I dedicated my mind to. Max helped me want to live and not die. We certainly enjoyed partying, elevating the volume to our rowdiness on multiple occasions, yet as our friendship progressed, we focused our thoughts and speech upon the ways we could and needed to mature.

By the summer of 2022, most of society had returned to its normal pre-pandemic ways. As I pushed forward, I endeavored into a new healing journey. I was reluctant, unable, and not ready to relinquish the alcohol, nor would I wholly admit I truly needed to. Within myself, I knew I should, but in my desires, I wished to skirt around that necessity somehow. *Perhaps someday, but not this day*, I considered with procrastination. *If I can fix myself without needing to quit drinking, that will be ideal.* Stubbornly, foolishly, I attempted to mend all escalating problems on my own instead of submitting everything to God. By continuing to include the omnipotent Creator partially in half-hearted prayers, tucking Jesus away in the mind's extra guest room, I convinced myself this was a satisfactory way to treat the One who saves. *After all, this is much more than I used to do!* Despite the internal pandemonium, paired with my self-deceiving approaches, everything was under control. I could handle it. At least, that is how I presented it. On the side, for entertainment, Max, Hest, Vin and I joined a bowling league. Together, the four of us formed our own team.

Joining a bowling league may sound like simple fun to those who like sports, and it certainly provided that, but it also supplemented constructive forms of thinking into my spiraling life. I had always been a competitive athlete before leaving college, and the bowling league allowed me to return to the mentality I applied in such competitions. Despite the vertigo, I bowled well with a balanced drinking routine. Two or three alcoholic drinks at breakfast, two or three alcoholic drinks at lunch, a shot of whiskey during bowling warmups, and then three pints of India Pale Ale and two more shots of whiskey throughout the event's three games. If I drank more by game time, I became slightly too inebriated to bowl well. If I drank less, my vertigo would ravage too severely, rendering me useless. Once the bowling night, filled with focused precision, weekly improvement and community connection was complete, I returned home to commence the real drinking. With only ten to twelve alcoholic drinks in my system by nine at night, I must drink ten more, usually involving red wine, before falling asleep. Consuming a minimum of twenty alcoholic beverages each day prevented withdrawal symptoms.

Max and I leaned into the mentality of developing our bowling craft, discussing each roll, spin, and adjustment beyond the bowling lanes. This concentration contributed to my consideration toward the rest of my disorderly life. *In what ways can I currently improve?* Since the beginning of the pandemic, the crew had been frequently utilizing psychedelic mushrooms. Now in the latter half of 2022, with the goal of healing my chaotically tormented, broken mental health, I intentionally dove into a solo journey of self-guided therapy involving months of daily mushroom consumption while completing my fourth book of poetry. Throughout the duration of summer's end and autumn, I ingested psilocybin 100 times.

While tripping on mushrooms can be an adventure worth sharing with friends, embarking on such trips was a vast psychological wilderness I preferred to explore alone. By myself, I could focus on specific thoughts and progressions. Once each "therapeutic session" ended, I would return into the next one where I'd left off. This continuation operated much like climbing a ladder. With each individual term, I progressed upwards another rung.

CINEREAL

My preferred setting was at night outside in my garden while Flower puttered around the art cottage wishing I would include her in my internal affairs. I knew I was ignoring her, but I did not have the capacity for any more than my demons. Although I loved her, many times I broke off our relationship in search of solitude. I wanted her to heal as well, but I knew I could not do that for her. Torn between companionship and alcoholic independence, regretfully I dragged her along the rollercoaster of my monstrously chaotic mind. Some days I sincerely behaved lovingly, and on others I could not stand the sight of another human. In such times, when feeling as if the world was constricting me so tightly that I could not mentally breathe, I pushed her and everyone far away. My callous behavior caused her to act out and harm herself, at which point I would promptly swoop in to save her. But then once more she would be at the cottage asking for what I could not give. My heart melted for her pain. She, like me, carried unresolved burdens from her past, and I placed additional burdens upon her. I did not want to emotionally harm her. Therefore, I would readjust my sights, hold the sweet withering Flower in my arms beneath a night sky until the claustrophobia returned, then frantically push her away again. The toxic cycle prolonged in its exasperating roll, yet in my darkness, I could not attend to it. All I could struggle to do was force myself to attempt cleaning up my own rubble.

During most of the mushroom trips and the writing of my new poetry collection *Grand Father Tree,* I lay on the earth beneath the colossal ponderosa pine in my backyard. With homage to my late grandfather, beneath the generational stature of a natural pillar, upon igneous soil, I meditated and travelled into spiritual depths. Each night I consumed a different weight of mushrooms depending on where I was in my expedition. Once a week I ate a macro-amount, upwards of three and a half grams. Biweekly, I ingested seven grams to experience a voluminous ego-death. Most often, between the higher spikes, I would consume only three-quarters to two grams, sensing in mind and body what would be the proper quantity for each night. These sessions usually started around ten and often lasted until sunrise.

The voyage of a heavy mushroom trip comprised three semesters. Prior to ingestion, I verbalized what my decided intention for the current session was. Such as, "Tonight I am going to focus on clean breathing and gratefulness. Tonight, I will not allow the living darkness to fester in my soul.

CINEREAL

I shall seek the purity beyond," then I would commence. The first trimester began about twenty minutes after consuming the organic hallucinogenic. I could sense it gradually approaching like a cat stalking a mouse, strengthening as a pounce, until enveloping my entire being. For a few minutes, I would then wrestle with anxiety, needing to pace, or yawn deeply. My skin crawled within compression, but I knew how to handle this sensation, having experienced it many times. As the mushrooms settled into me, it was as if I was passing through a giant womb, crossing from one dimension into the next.

The second trimester is the mighty one, returning to a world of shapeshifting beings, looming beasts, vivid pixilation and the ability to communicate with every living and un-living thing. I comprehended this world very well. In a way, it had become a comfortable home-scape. Here I could rapidly spin out of control if I slipped my grip upon intention, but I would not let myself slip, instead bathing in the intensity of the previously veiled dimension. The second trimester carried the ability to cleanse all distress. I would let go of my attachments to earth and venture far beyond where I lay. With practice, my capabilities to travel into other time periods and locations expanded. In a moment, my soul could transport to the furthest reaches of consciousness. When I needed to retreat, distinguishing myself entering a realm that I was not yet ready to tread, I would pull back and prepare myself to push even further in the next session. After weeks of this exercise, I became so proficient in my spirit's vast transportation that I comprehended if I wanted to, I did not need to return to my body. Rather, I could allow my physical body to die there on the dirt, while my soul remained beyond. I grasped the simplicity of the separate, defining the eternal nature of the soul and the temporal nature of the flesh.

The final trimester was one of settling back into the carnal casing, completely returning to self. As the hallucinogenic effect slipped away, mental clarity became revitalized where confusion previously dominated. Often this stage provided new inquiries I would ponder between sessions and explore deeper the next night. Like a grand staircase or ladder, constructed one step, one rung at a time, I climbed into uncharted mindscapes.

~~~

"Max, I have made an important decision," I announced to my friend the day after publishing *Grand Father Tree*. The September night prior I celebrated a successful book release. An exciting sensation of progress, cooler air and refreshing alcoholic beverages dressed our atmosphere.

"Alright, Wing, let's hear it." Max smiled between sips of his beer.

"Well, to others this may seem like a basic adult life staple. But to me, it will serve as an additional step towards healing." I gulped both my beer and whiskey and proceeded with animated hand gestures. "I am going to do all the steps necessary to obtain health insurance!"

Max laughed approvingly. "That is indeed a solid idea, brother. Health insurance will get you into those doctor appointments you so badly need."

"I know, man, oh, I know. I haven't been to a doctor for a long time. Last was when I had giardia on the Pacific Crest Trail, so, ten years! And that was expensive without health insurance. There was the emergency room visit following the murder attempt, but I left before any imaging, so it doesn't really count, even though that long lay in a hallway bed was still extremely costly."

"Yeah, that stuff adds up quickly," Max stated. "So, once you have active health insurance, are you going to get everything checked out?"

"Yes, I need to. I can't keep suffering this way, not without at least trying to fix this mess a little. A necessary step towards healing. In addition, no more cocaine. I only partied with it a handful of times here in Bend, not to the extent of my twenties, but from now on, no more. I proved this to myself when I declined it last week, which I honestly felt proud of. It does not serve my health, and each time I indulged in it since the incident, I felt like I could instantly die."

"Happy to hear it. I fully support that and agree. Let's keep moving forward, my friend." Max smiled and raised his pint glass for a cheer.

"Yes, to moving forward," I concurred.

After clinking and downing a mouthful of our tasty booze, Max added, "It sounds like this mushroom journey you are on is providing some needed clarity towards action."

"It certainly is yes, but there is a whole other side I am coming to realize, that perhaps in time I will open about. But I have been sensing that I have some major, life-altering decisions to make." My lips pursed while nodding seriously.

Max's eyes widened. "Well, I look forward to hearing about that when you are ready, Wing. Perhaps after your birthday, which is only about five weeks away!"

CINEREAL

"Yes, perhaps then I will be ready."

~~~

While indeed advancing in knowledge and clarity during my mushroom journey, I also perceived I was moving even further away from God. In a bizarre way, it was as if I was progressing at a dangerous distance, almost parallel to Him, but with an increasing chasm between us. My secular spirituality was maturing yet also emboldening in independence. Therefore, this form of spirituality was conclusively meaningless, completely misleading, outright dangerous, for I was doing something on my own that was not meant for me to do alone. Akin to what humans strove for at the Tower of Babel. My lengthy climbing journey towards enlightenment provided overwhelming conviction. When it comes to the reality of an afterlife, I already held zero doubts, but the hallucinogenic practice continued to prove its existence. The ability to separate the ethereal spirit from the tangible body is both remarkably fascinating and utterly terrifying. It demands the question, where does our soul ultimately go? The answer, regardless of our beliefs, is that our eternal destination is with God or cast far away from God. We either accept Him through His Son, Jesus Christ, or we reject Him. This freewill choice we each must make while still in our flesh, determining our soul's absolute eternal destiny, and no decision, or the attempt to operate within our own parameters, is in fact a decision opposing Him.

As the autumn of 2022 waned, my thirty-seventh birthday passed, and cold weather began crawling into the high desert of central Oregon, I contemplated the pressing persuasions surging within. A dominant sense of urgency to move beyond the depths of my dark ages compelled as now or never. I became consumed with the most important veracity. I needed to return to God, submit every layer and bit of myself to Him, genuinely trust in and follow Him with all my soul, or else be separated from Him forever. And yet, I did not completely know how. I knew how theologically, but I did not know how to rise beyond the barriers my alcohol addiction created, nor did not know how to tear down the walls I had constructed to maintain sanity. As I had been striving to heal, I had been doing so through my will, not surrendering to His. It was time for my season of psilocybin-therapy to end. But still, there remained the critical decision I must make.

While contemplating my necessary submission to God, the gusts of a thousand winds started to ravage. A multitude of the living darkness erupted

CINEREAL

audibly and visibly in every nook of my open and closed-eyed existence more ferociously than ever before. Violently, they waged their harshest battle. For so long they had succeeded, binding me in their chains, and finally I was fathoming the vital need to surrender to Him. *Not by my will or strength, but by God's.* Although Satan and his legions tremble at the Almighty's righteous power, they knew that they still clutched me as their prisoner. With all their demonic supernatural force, they would never let me go. In my solitary weakness, I collapsed to the ground, tormented by hellish claims on my soul. On elbows in November, just as I had that cold January 2020 night, I crawled towards the bottle, grasped it in my hand, then I crawled to my Bible, grasped it in my other hand, and devoured God's word while I drank.

What Matters Most

A solitary flame reached upward from the abating fire then disappeared. One last grasp, one final exhausted leap toward the sky before surrendering to slumber. End of November snowflakes fluttered down gently upon the dwindling coals. The base of my moccasins rested atop the firepit's metal rim. They would not get burned. The heat had lost its bite, and even if one more determined flicker followed the last, even if the worn leather soles were to be singed, it would not be the first time.

I reached instinctively to my left, locating my camp mug. It sat on a log, sawn into a flat round. My southpaw dominance preferred to set items on this side, upon this makeshift table, while my right-brained thinking favored this cup for red wine. For each flavor of drink I selected a distinct vessel, as for each moment I wrote a unique poem. A slow, exhausted sigh emanated from my lungs. I felt as the fire did, flickering low. No longer could I hold on to my rebellion. I did not want to fight against God anymore, not because I had no more strength, but because even in my obstinacy, He had continued to present who He is, and I had grown to love Him. For the last week, all I had been doing amid my drinking was devouring His scriptures and meditating upon every single way He had revealed Himself in my life. There were so many. He protected me from the forces of evil. He vividly pronounced His glory. He continually placed humans in my path who loved Him, encouraging me to set my sight on Him. And as I continued in my rebellion, He disciplined me as a Father will discipline His child. From every angle, through each day, He had been calling me to return to Him, to follow Him, to trust Him. *Why had I revolted against His love for so long? The truth is evident. It is time to surrender my life to the Almighty.*

Contemplation drifted to Psalm 46:10 (NKJV), "Be still and know that I am God." I took a sip of wine and looked away from the shimmering red cluster. My eyesight-to-brain could not handle the flickering of lights anymore. Although the modest coals mesmerized, glancing away and regaining my balance was necessary, even just sitting in my garden chair.

CINEREAL

Another sip of wine soothed my brain while allowing my vision to settle beyond the glow's reach. There in the dark I fixated upon the sturdy trunk of the mighty Ponderosa, the grandfather tree. While attempting to let my mind be still amidst the internal chaos of thrashing evil, I remembered Jesus' words in Revelation 2:4-5 (NKJV), and though He was speaking to the church of Ephesus, it still seemed applicable to me. "Nevertheless I have this against you, that you have left your first love. Remember therefore from where you have fallen; repent and do the first works, or else I will come to you quickly and remove your lampstand from its place - unless you repent."

In that moment, I moved from my chair and knelt on the ground. My knees imprinted into the dirt. My forehead pressed against the hardening soil. Tears escalated into weeping. I trembled beneath the weight my absence from Him had created. I called upon God with more sincerity and readiness than ever before. In His omniscient knowledge of my heart, He immediately spoke.

"Where is the boy who loved Me?" His voice was clear and calm. Perhaps Wylie, who sniffed concernedly at my bowed lamentation, could not hear, but in the silent night, to me His voice was undeniable.

Upon perceiving Him, my weeping intensified, for every truth and conviction encapsulated my soul. I spoke, "I am here, Father, I am here. I do still love You."

"If you love Me, then why do you not follow Me? Where is the boy who served Me so ardently?" His voice remained clear yet shifted to a tone of severity. Before I could answer, as I wept, He spoke more gently. "Do you remember your friend Trey?"

"Yes, Father."

"Do you remember before he died on Earth, you sat with him for hours, telling him about Me, answering his every question. You sat and prayed with him until he understood, until he gave his heart to Me. Do you remember the love you had for Me then?"

"Yes, Father, I remember. I so badly wanted him to love You too." My voice trembled as I responded.

"Yes, you did. And now, because of your love for Me, because you helped him understand and Trey gave his heart to Me, he is with Me for eternity. You helped save him. I desire that love from you again. I want you to love Me as you did then. Your love for Me shall grow each day. You have been lost. It is time to return. I will work in you."

CINEREAL

With these words, every molecule of my being vibrated intensely, with overwhelming remorse for my callous rebellion and gratefulness for His amazing grace and love. My adoration of Him swelled as tears spilled onto the earth. *How could I have been so selfish, so disdainfully irreverent, so wretchedly horrific to You for so long!? You are Truth, Father.* I begged God for His forgiveness. As a river of sincere repentance flowed from me, I trusted, knowing He forgave me. His Son had died and risen for this very purpose. I begged Him to create in me a clean heart, soul and mind, to aid me in following Him daily that I may never stray again. To guide me in my studying of His word, to strengthen my obedience to Him, to shed my sinful patterns, to fortify my strength and courage in Him no matter what the world may think. I asked Him to renew my soul. "I have believed in You, Father, since I was that little boy. I believe in Your Son, Jesus Christ, that He died on the cross and rose on the third day, defeating death, that He ascended to heaven and will return. I believe that through Your grace You have saved me, even though my sin has made me unworthy. You offer me what I do not deserve, and I accept Your incredible gift. I now fully place all my faith in You, holding nothing back. I trust You, Lord. I desire to live a life shining as a light for You, covered by the blood of Jesus, one that honors You, so that others will see Your glory and love. Thank You Jesus. Thank You Father. I commit my life to You, again and again and again each day, forever I am Yours."

Upon finally, humbly surrendering to Him, He spoke again before the silence of night returned. "Yes, my child, I have forgiven you. I shall give you the strength, but you know what you must do."

An incredible peace washed over me, into me, swaddling my soul within. He wrapped His love around me. There is nothing to fear when the Creator of the Universe, the One True God who is the entirety of goodness, is your Father. Yes, I knew what I must do, including the one thing I did not want to do, nor believed I could, but, with Him, anything can be conquered. I would face it, for following God, giving my life to Him as a bondservant for Jesus Christ, is what matters most.

~~~

The following days were full of deliberation, worship, prayer and humbled realization of my circumstances. My soul and commitment to Him were confidently renewed. His grace had saved me. Nothing I could do on my own would ever suffice. He must now and forevermore be my center, nothing else. Yet it was more than a matter of must; this was no chore; this was a leap of faith and growth, one that would continue to strengthen as the Holy Spirit worked within. He restored an infinite desire to please Him. My joy overflowed. Jesus' words in Matthew 5:29-30 (NKJV) ruminated in my soul, and though the context was Him speaking on adultery, I believed it could apply to my addiction as well. "If your right eye causes you to sin, pluck it out and cast it from you; for it is more profitable for you that one of your members perish, than for your whole body to be cast into hell. And if your right hand causes you to sin, cut it off and cast it from you; for it is more profitable for you that one of your members perish, than for your whole body to be cast into hell." I understood what He meant. As I now yearned to follow God completely, it became obvious that I had been placing alcohol between me and Him. I had been living for alcohol and not for my Savior; therefore, it must go.

I promptly noticed that the voices and presence of the living darkness had been eliminated. They had tormented since the traumatic brain injury in January 2020 and for much of my youth, but once I surrendered my life to God, He removed them. The chaos was ceasing, the beast with many heads was being defeated, and a mighty rest filled my mind. Actively, He was protecting me. I considered when I had observed the angels protecting the boy from the hoard of demons and imagined something like that was being done for me. This bolstered grateful awe of Him while praying and walking Wylie along the river, enhancing peace in my heart. One early December night I poured all the alcohol in my cottage into the toilet and flushed it away. Yet in my attempt to rescind from consuming booze, I suffered my first seizure the following morning. Battered by this event, I admitted I medically could not go from all to none. I needed to seek help to break out of the addiction prison. With this physical reality check, I focused on Him, trusting He would guide my path.

"In a few days," I said to Wylie, "Dad will be visiting. I will discuss this with him. Until I can secure help, I suppose I will need to keep drinking to survive."

As Wylie and I ambled on our walks, sipping on the stuff I did not want anymore, awaiting my dad's arrival, I sang the words of the song Amazing Grace in my mind. Every fiber of my being rejoiced in His steadfast love. "His amazing grace... ...that saved a wretch like me." I knew the journey ahead would be arduous, but it would be nothing less than worthy.

CINEREAL

On the day of Dad's visit, I arose with vertigo spinning out of control. To stand upright and receive my dear familial guest, I must begrudgingly continue drinking enough to survive. So, I drank my two drinks of whiskey, ate a meager breakfast of almonds and a banana, tidied up the cottage and prepared for his entrance. When Dad arrived and we embraced, I overflowed with emotion. Everything had been a battle since we had seen each other last. The morning sun bore warmly upon us despite snow also falling, as if the sky was split in two.

Dad stated, "You've now been living in Bend for seven years! Which also means you are now thirty-seven years old."

"I sure have, Dad, and yup, sure am. I'll always remember the road trip when you brought me here, both!"

"We had a lot of road trips together that year." Dad chuckled and jostled my shoulder.

Tears seeped out of my eyes as all sentiments within emboldened. Locating my whiskey mug, I poured a dram into it. While sipping, smoking and brushing wet salty cheeks, knowing the drink enhanced my emotions, I trembled uncontrollably. Dad peered at me with love. He understood I had been struggling. He observed all of me standing there, beneath the Ponderosa tree, drinking as a man who wished he could stop.

In that moment, Dad peered at the ground and kicked a pinecone Wylie had set at his feet. With his hands in jean pockets, he lifted his head, looked me in the eye and spoke candidly. "Well, Wingstar, what are you going to do about all this?"

I lifted my head, returned his gaze, and after a deep breath, I resolutely replied. "I am going to quit drinking alcohol."

Dad compressed his lips and nodded. He responded as he had when I'd announced I was going to hike the Appalachian Trail and many of my other colossal plans, with simple words but belief in his tone. "Alright then."

It was up to me, but I was not alone. What must be done must be done, or else it will not become.

A Worthy First Step

When one establishes a resolution, the stagnancy of indecision capitulates to the strength of momentum. I had rebelled against God for far too long, just as I had been indecisive on how I would handle my addiction. To express it perhaps most factually, only in the depths of my soul was I hesitant toward both my relationship with the Almighty and my relationship with alcohol, yet my actions had supported distance from Him and the prolonged enslavement. My foolish, supercilious obstinacy allowed the forces of evil and the poison of alcohol to wreak havoc on my life. While I adamantly lived for what was destroying me, the corrosion escalated as a gushing river erodes rock.

Upon my decision to hike the Appalachian Trail, which elevated the idea to a commitment, what followed was a plan full of manageable, doable, obtainable micro-goals, which led to the achievement of the macro-goal. *Now, I must do the same.* The primary objectives were to develop my relationship with God for the rest of my life and to secure freedom from the bondage of alcohol addiction. I must shed what prevented me from actively being a worthy vessel and servant for Him. By His grace He had saved me, yet through my own sinful nature, alcohol's reign controlled my life. But how can someone escape such a prison when the addiction is so deeply rooted? Essentially, I must simply stop consuming booze. However, since I could not cease drinking on my own as the level of alcohol withdrawals had reached life-threatening status, medical help was necessary.

During the month of December 2022, I suffered more seizures. Each seizure arrived when attempting to withdraw from alcohol too quickly. Medical guides suggested cutting back only ten percent of my average per week. A slow taper. One I impatiently and emotionally pushed too hard upon. The violent reactions from my body to even a tad less alcohol produced discouragement. Beneath the addiction existed the symptoms of my brain damage. I needed to locate an inpatient medical detox center to aid in surviving the withdrawals promptly. Until admittance, I must cautiously walk the line of not consuming too little and not consuming too much. While drinking alcohol was killing me, not drinking alcohol would also prove fatal. To me, this predicament held dark humor amidst the necessity to change.

I contacted every medical detox center in Oregon, yet every location was full. The facility must be one that would accept my health insurance, as I could not afford to pay out of pocket. For every facility that accepted my insurance, I placed myself on the waiting list and asked how to handle my current situation until being admitted. They all strictly directed, "Drink the amount of alcohol you have been, no more, no less, for with your level of addiction, your traumatic brain injury and now recent experience with seizures, one wrong move could quickly lead to death."

On December 17, I finally received the call I had been waiting for. A bed in a detox center only a thirty-minute drive away was ready for me. They provided instructions about what to bring and expect. Bring very little was the gist, for when I arrived, they would monitor or confiscate my belongings and provide hospital-style scrubs to wear. They recommended I bring a favorite sweatshirt, winter coat and slippers for my feet. They permitted cigarettes if I smoked, which I brought plenty of. Enough for myself and to share. While packing the carton of American Spirits in my bag, I smiled as it invoked memories of my grandfather. Often as a child, he would order me to enter his room and grab a fresh pack from the carton in his bedside dresser drawer. I relished this chore, for it seemed important. Every time I returned and handed him what he wanted, he would then smile and say, "Thank you, son," as he slapped the Winstons on his palm a few times, undid the plastic wrapping and pulled one out to smoke. He would often first smell the slim stick before lighting it, winking at me with the words, "Ah yes, nothing like a fresh pack." As I zipped up my detox bag, I admitted that someday I would need to quit smoking the nasty cancer-causers, *but not yet, one thing at a time, for now alcohol.*

The night before leaving for my detox, I became filled with apprehension, excitement, and relief. In the morning, my life would begin its drastic change. Falling asleep was impossible, so I drank wine and prayed until nearly dawn, confidently believing it would be my last alcohol consumption. As the sun rose and my eyes drooped low, as my stomach rumbled and esophagus burned with acid reflux, I forced myself forward towards the departure from my cottage. Flower would transport me and care

CINEREAL

for Wylie while I was gone. On the drive to the facility, to calm my soul while embarking into a new unknown, I recited Proverbs 3:5-6 (NKJV) repeatedly in my head. "Trust in the Lord with all your heart and lean not on your own understanding; in all your ways acknowledge Him, and He shall direct your paths." Many of the Bible verses I had learned as a child remained etched in my mind. For as two verses prior commands, "Let not mercy and truth forsake you; bind them around your neck, write them on the tablet of your heart..." My mother had always encouraged this action, to memorize scripture so that I would never be without truth. I was grateful she had instilled such in me, even when I rebelled against it.

I continued thinking about other things Mother taught me as a boy. Although I viewed her as strict, I was a child who required tough love. At dinner, she would frequently read to my siblings and me from George Washington's book *Rules of Civility and Decent Behavior*. If we broke one of these rules at the dining table, she would send us to the other room to complete math equations. Piano practice was rigorously enforced, as were daily chores and many other disciplines. Rarely was I allowed to drink soda pop, or consume sugar, or watch television. Video games remained out of the question. Dating and flirting with girls, I should not consider it. At the time it seemed like I was missing out on all the fun my peers took part in, but she was protecting me from turning my mind, body and spirit to mush. *Perhaps mush isn't the proper word*, I considered. *Perhaps it is more that my mother taught me the ability to hear deeply, not allowing my brain to be coated with murky noise.* Through her discipline, she provided me with the mental space for such. While other children ran to the television for shows and games, I ran to the woods to listen to the birds, sketch and write in my notebook. While they laughed at cartoons, I opened my heart to God. When others were busy filling their minds with nonsense, my mind was available for the whispers of the wind. I worried about kids now who were even more involved with smartphones, social media and the constant barrage of meaningless cacophony and wayward false importances. *Was anyone still cultivating the mental space to recognize when God called? I don't know...* Now, as an adult, my teeth remain cavity free, television and video games are a waste of my time. Reading, writing, playing musical instruments and exploring nature are far more valuable to me than mindless time spent. *No wonder my quiet sessions outside alone every night are so important. I always need to end my day by peering into the beyond, thinking, listening and finally again, praying. If only I had headed her guidance concerning alcohol… Instead, I have become a pathetic mess, but at least I can listen beyond society's vain commotion.* Slowly, my relationship with Mother was repairing. *But how much could it properly mend over my drunken sunrise phone calls to the East Coast? Or my sobbing, alcohol-saturated emotional ways? It could not. I need this sobriety not just for my relationship with God and for physical health, but also to build a worthy relationship with anyone in my life, including Mom. Learning to regulate my emotions and not be controlled by them will be an integral part of my development now.* I missed my mother dearly and decided to call her in detox once a few sober days had passed. *Hearing her voice without the weight of booze in my body will be a worthy delight.*

Once we arrived at the detox center, I hugged Flower goodbye, thanked her for her support, grabbed my bag and stepped out of the car into a frigid morning. My weak body trembled. I had not slept or eaten enough. It felt as if all the world's alcohol had passed through my veins. Although nervous, I was here. With one last wave to my darling dog and caring partner, I approached the somber building and knocked upon a locked door. A nurse with a medical mask covering her face greeted me and informed me she must test me for coronavirus before entering. She swabbed my nose and left me outside in the cold. While waiting for the test results, I filled out a hefty packet of forms and then crumpled into a sitting heap. I could no longer bear to stand beneath the weight of my addiction. My fingers had struggled even to hold the pen and fill out the many intake pages. Breaths of mist in the brumal air and smoke from my cigarette enveloped my shivering body. I waited and wondered, partially hoping the test would reveal I had COVID and then deny my admittance. *If that is the case, I could go home and continue to drink, but no. No, do not think like that, Wing!* I yelled at myself internally and then hastily turned to prayer. *Lord, give me the strength to make it through this.*

~~~

The nurse returned and welcomed me inside. I did not have coronavirus, so detox was set to begin. I entered a makeshift living room with a television and shelves full of DVDs, books and games. The walls were painted a fading gray hue. A large man lounged in one of the few bulky chairs. His head faced up to the ceiling while his mouth hung open, emitting gurgling snores. It was clear he had sunk into a deep yet potentially uncomfortable sleep. Beyond this initial area, there was a kitchenette. No wall divided the rooms, only the transition from a carpeted floor to tile. Here, a dining table, refrigerator and a few cabinets filled the space. Next to this area were separate doors leading to the men and women's chambers. Each room comprised three beds, end tables, bureaus and lamps, with hanging curtains available to slide between each bed. The bathroom door was located between the chamber doors in the kitchenette. Beyond this closed door, I could hear painful wrenching of someone vomiting between whimpers. As I observed my new temporary environment, the nurse instructed me to hand her my bag. Upon doing so, she immediately inspected each item I had brought. She confiscated my iPhone, handed me my Bible and writing journal, then stated that everything else would get locked up. When I needed them, I could request a writing pen and another pack of cigarettes. The nurse directed me into the bathroom once the vomiter exited looking pale and wearisome. The no-nonsense woman followed me in and shut the barrier behind us. She pointed to the shower, soap and towels, demonstrating that everything I needed other than my toothbrush was available. She then instructed me to remove all my clothes.

"All my clothes? Even my underwear?" I asked.

"Yes, even your underwear. I need to make sure you aren't trying to sneak in any contraband." She shot me a stern look, then softened as I blushed.

Obeying I tiredly joked, "Kind of like jail, huh? I promise you, no contraband; I am here of my own accord, for I want to get better." I stripped down naked and moved, bent and coughed in the ways she instructed.

With a sympathetic tone she replied, "We are much kinder than jail. This is just a necessary part of our intake. Okay, good, that is done. Put these scrubs on and wait in the living room. Next, we will need to take your bloodwork, go through more paperwork and prepare your medications. This will only take a few hours, then you can rest."

"Alright, whatever you say. Thank you." I pulled on the thin blue baggy pants and shirt she provided, then sat in a saggy chair next to the snoring heavyset man. As his chest heaved up and down with each rumble, I wondered if he and I would become friends. Other inpatients drooped around in slippers, grabbing a snack or filling their water cup then returning to bed. Everyone appeared to be in miserable condition. A few glanced my way with hollow eyes and then continued their shuffle. I counted five, making me the sixth. *Full house. This is clearly not a joyful place to be*, I mused silently. *I will also just keep my head down and do what I am told. It seems everyone is just trying to make it through.*

CINEREAL

Right when I was about to nod off into a desired nap, a different nurse approached and summoned me into the back room. This room resembled a doctor's office, complete with large windows facing a fenced backyard. With a cheery voice, she introduced herself and explained the procedures, rules and what I could expect. She tested my blood alcohol level, which showed a decent amount of alcohol was still in my body. I informed her I had experienced a few seizures when I didn't imbibe enough and explained my brain injury and allergy to ibuprofen. Everything I relayed, she typed into the computer. After our lengthy intake meeting was complete and an official doctor examined me, she acknowledged the shaking of my hands from alcohol withdrawals, vertigo rapidly setting in and my unsteady eyes. They promised I would have my first round of medication soon. "We just need the alcohol in your blood to clear up a bit more. But don't worry, we won't let you have a seizure. Once you take your first pills, you can go to sleep. We will then need to check your blood pressure every two hours."

"Okay, thank you." I stated sheepishly with a smile. My entire body hurt. Everything was spinning. It felt as if my brain would explode and I could have a seizure at any moment, but I held on tight and trusted everything they said. "Where can I smoke?" I asked, knowing I must tough out my symptoms until medication.

"Oh, Hunny, right through this door here, outside is a little covered patio and a yard for our patients. All the other doors remain locked for safety, but this one you can come and go as you please."

"Thank you," I stated again, my words now difficult to form. This nurse appealed to me more than the first, reminding me of my Aunt Jan. She spoke with a patient and empathetic demeanor. I walked feebly outside, unable to stand upright, gripping my throbbing brain with one hand and guiding my steps with the other. My vision scattered between hazy mental darkness and sharp bright lights. Finally, on a wooden bench beneath the outdoor roof, I slouched down into an exhausted sit. The cement foundation my feet rested upon also contained a canister for cigarette butts, yet it appeared many people nonchalantly tossed their trash towards it but not into it. Discouraged by this, I set down my cigarette and shuffled slowly back inside. The nurse looked up from her station and asked if everything was alright.

"Yes, I'm alright, considering. Do you have a broom and dustpan?" The nurse produced an inquisitive expression and pointed to a corner. I grabbed the tool, shuffled back out and swept up the mess, placing it all into the canister where it belonged, returned the broom, then lounged with my smoke in the frigid December air. Exhausted yet satisfied with the cleaner floor, I waited until my name was called again.

Finally, medication time arrived. Quickly, I swallowed the handful of pills and attempted to listen to the additional information provided, but my brain had expended all it could. I needed to lie down and sleep. Lunch was available, but I was not hungry. By now I could barely stand, so the kind nurse fastened her arm through mine and led me to bed. Before my head touched the pillow, darkness overtook my all.

~~~

I awoke to the scent of food and the sound of trundling footsteps beyond the slightly ajar bedroom door. Somewhere in the murky daze of rest I vaguely recalled having my blood pressure checked twice. *I must have slept for about five hours, and that aroma must be dinner.* My stomach rumbled, for I had not eaten in quite some time. While sitting up in bed and shifting my feet to the ground, I sensed a heavy lethargy. My body was not used to the medication. I had never ingested a heavy dose of benzodiazepines and gabapentin before. It was an odd sort of weight, as if it was keeping the erratic wires in my brain from rupturing into a thousand firecrackers. I forced myself into a slow walk, filled my water cup, relieved myself in the bathroom, then sat down at the dining table to inspect what was inside the plates with lids atop. The man who had been sleeping in the living room chair was no longer there, nor were the same nurses on duty.

I pulled one platter toward me and removed the lid. A homely fragrance of warm ham, cheesy macaroni and green beans rose into my nostrils. My stomach increased its rumble. A soft biscuit rounded out the entrée. I located a pad of butter in the refrigerator, squished it inside the bread and started forking at the rest of the food. The first bite satisfied my empty belly, and though the meal's quality impressed me, it was difficult to eat. Slowly, I forced another tasty bite down my hatch. An unfamiliar nurse approached and commented, "You must be Wing. Don't worry. Your appetite will return soon. Eat as much as you can and then come meet me at the nurse's station. We'll check your vitals and complete your second round of medication." I nodded and smiled while chewing on ham. My head bowed low to the food, for my whole body seemed to move at a quarter of its usual speed. To my left I heard a chair get pulled. I looked over to see the big man, who had

CINEREAL

been napping earlier, sit down. *He must have come from the bedroom, but I had not seen him behind the curtains pulled shut.*

I passively watched as he pawed at his meal much like I did. He looked around the table, his eyes lost, as if he were searching for something. Intuitively, I grabbed the salt and pepper and placed them by his plate. He gave me a tired look with a small nod, then pounded out way too much salt onto his food. *Oof,* I thought, *but who am I to judge?* We sat next to each other in silence, eating as much of our dinners as we could.

Abruptly, the crash of a lamp thrown at a wall followed by screams shrieked out of the women's bedroom. A fight erupted over what sounded like a possibly stolen item. Nurses rushed in, followed by a stout security guard I had not noticed prior. I looked at the big, salty man next to me. We said nothing, but our eyes tacitly agreed, *might as well keep eating. They can take care of that.* After completing half my meal, including the buttery biscuit, I spotted where to set my dishes and shuffled in my moccasins to the nurse's station for vitals check and medication. Another cigarette, another bathroom break, another full cup of water and back to bed to drift into another deep sleep.

Other than groggy awakenings for blood pressure and more medication, I slept through the night and awoke with a sense of excitement at five in the morning. *I have done it! Well, I am one-third of the way there. I have passed the twenty-four-hour mark of no alcohol.* To me, this was a successful achievement. Granted, I had been heavily medicated to ensure I did not die, and I still had two days of dangerous hours ahead, but this was positive progress. For an alcoholic, the first seventy-two hours are the most hazardous and vital. Withdrawal symptoms can be lethal. Seizures and heart attacks loom near, but after the seventy-two-hour mark, the window for such bodily responses diminishes drastically.

I rose from bed. The darkness outside my window held the calm of night. On to the nurse's station to complete what must be done. Next, I prepared myself a cup of decaf coffee. There is no caffeine allowed in detox as caffeine is also a drug and can easily interfere with medications. Then I swaddled myself in my thick alpaca sweatshirt, grabbed my Bible and went outside to smoke, sip and pray as the sky developed into its modest crepuscular shine. I read Proverbs 19, as it was the nineteenth day of December, and like many months have thirty-one days, so Proverbs has thirty-one chapters. Squinting my eyes in the darkness, holding the Bible close to my face yet tilted towards the indoor light modestly casting out the window, I slowly deciphered the words. Proverbs 19:16 (NKJV) stuck out to me. "He who keeps the commandment keeps his soul, but he who is careless of his ways will die." I understood what this meant. It resonated within. Of course, we all shall die, but it is the second death referred to here. This is the imperative death or life, an eternity with God, or an eternity cast away from Him. I considered that this Old Testament passage was written amid the old covenant with God, before Jesus came to earth as God incarnate, lived a blameless life, then served as the ransom for all who would believe in Him. Jesus established the new covenant. But this does not negate the fact that we should follow His commandments. We do so because we love Him. Our obedience results from our trust in Him and grows as a natural fruit of who we are in Him. However, it is not through our works that we are saved. "Thank you, Jesus," I whispered.

As I sipped my warm drink and blew smoke into the rafters of the patio roof, praying and watching the eastern sky grow slightly brighter, the door creaked open, and the big man shuffled out towards me. I had not heard him speak yet, but as he opened his mouth, I anticipated correctly what he would say. "Hey man, do you mind if I have one of your cigarettes? All I have are these crummy smokes." He held up a pack that looked like crushed Pall Malls.

I waved him over and answered. "Of course, man, come sit with me."

"Cool, thanks, I will." He turned back inside and returned donning a large worn winter coat. The weather was bitterly cold, like the temperature when I survived the attack on my life, some teen number of degrees. I handed him a cigarette and the one lighter the detox provided for us. They had confiscated the one I brought. At first, we sat and smoked in silence, each observing the eastern sky, which wore dark clouds. As the sun rose beyond their shield, the light revealed their woolen hues.

Halfway through our cigarette, I offered my salutations first. "My name is Wing. What's yours?" I pulled the alpaca sweatshirt hood down off my head, exposing my Carhartt beanie.

"George." He stated, looking from the distance to me, between an inhale of his smoke and a slow cherished exhale. "When did you get in? I didn't see you arrive."

"Yesterday morning. You were sleeping on the chair."

CINEREAL

George sighed. "I was drunk. They made me wait a while. My wife dropped me off drunk around dawn even though I didn't really want to come. But she said I can't come home until I am sober."

"I hear you. I didn't really want to come either, but I needed to. I need to stop drinking."

George nodded understandingly. "Me too. This is my third time in detox…" He paused as if he was about to speak more, then relented to the silence. After a few moments he nodded at my Bible. "That yours?"

"It is." I confirmed. "I didn't know if they'd have one here, but I saw another on the bookshelf. Where are you from, George?"

"The Warm Springs Reservation. Full blood native. They got mixed feelings about the Bible up there. Where are you from, Wing?"

I chuckled and stated, "Mixed feelings about the Bible everywhere, I'd say. I live in Bend, but kind of from all over. There's a bit of Choctaw in my blood, but I'm a mutt. Bend is home, though. Well, despite the mixed feelings of everyone else, what do you think about the Bible?"

George started to speak, but our chat was interrupted by the door opening again. This time, a woman I had yet to see came outside for a smoke. She muttered, "morning" reached out her hand looking for the lighter to be placed in it, sneered at my Bible, then sat between us. "Cathy," she offered as an introduction.

"Good morning, Cathy, I'm Wing." Once my name touched the air, the door opened yet again. A nurse poked her head out, announcing breakfast was on the table. That was all George and I needed to hear. Nodding to Cathy, the big man and I shuffled across the icy earth to eat.

The dining table had only five containers of food placed on it. I wondered if this meant one inpatient was now gone. I received the answer once Cathy walked in as George and I wolfed down our eggs and bacon. Eating was much easier than the day before.

"Sasha will complete her detox in jail." The blunt woman spoke liberally as she grabbed breakfast and carried it to the couch. Over her shoulder she added, "She assaulted the other girl yesterday, maybe you heard the racket."

Ah yes, that must have been what George and I perceived at dinner. Perhaps the interaction continued to intensify when I went to sleep early under the calming weight of medication. I had not met Sasha and had only seen the other girl exit her room briefly. I hoped they were both alright. George and I continued our breakfast without speaking. I liked him already. I could read his food thoughts. Again,

CINEREAL

his eyes searched the table, and without verbal communication I placed the packets of jam near him. He smiled, nodding his head as we chewed. My appetite had certainly returned. The food tasted marvelous, and within a few quick minutes we scraped both of our plates empty.

After breakfast, each inpatient went through the motions of completing their duties at the nurse's station. New employees arrived I had not met, and the surrounding day proceeded in full motion. George and I sat in dreary slumber. Our medications allowed little energy to course through our bodies. We shared another cigarette break. I gave him one of my full American Spirit packs so he wouldn't have to settle with the lesser smokes and promised another pack whenever he needed it. Inwardly I prayed, asking God that if George was open to discussing the Bible more, he would bring it up and I, in my immature experience, would be provided with the wisdom to know what to say. I didn't want to pester him in detox as our bodies and minds were already going through a tumultuous time. Beneath our medicated internal blankets, we each were fighting dangerous alcohol withdrawals. But despite the severity of our conditions, I felt safe in the care of trained medical professionals, and secure in the love of my heavenly Father. Following our post-breakfast chat and smoke, George chose a movie on the television's provided streaming services, and I returned to bed to read and sleep until lunch. The other guy in our room was packing up to leave. We never spoke, just accepted each other's presence. Once I awoke from my nap and dove into the sandwich and chips the kitchen had set out for our midday meal, both Cathy and the other guy had been released. George and I shared more time together, discussing our families and lives. He admitted he sensed his life was nearing its end if he could not stay sober. I agreed I recognized the same for myself then added, "But it brought me back to God, and for that I suppose it was all worth it." The detox center had grown somberly subdued. The one remaining girl rarely left her room. When she did, she sat shyly in her chosen chair, chewing slowly, glancing timidly, and then returned softly to her den. That night, dinner, a movie and sleep were all our medicated bodies could muster. With only a few days until Christmas, our full house of six inpatients had whittled down to a hushed sanctuary for three alcoholics attempting to break out of their addiction prisons.

~ ~ ~

On the morning of the third day, George joined me outside for decaf coffee at sunrise again. Our little repartee had been strengthening. *We are detox buddies,* I thought, smiling to myself as he grinned and waddled across the ice towards me.

"Mornin' Wing. Starting to feel better today. How're you?" George sat down. I tossed him the lighter. Gray clouds remained thick in the sky. We had seen little sun in the few days we had been here.

"Same bud, feeling better. Or I think so. The medication makes it difficult to tell, but I've been sleeping a lot, and food is building strength." I inhaled my cigarette and then exhaled away from him.

"Yup, a lot of sleep. The food here is pretty good, pleasantly surprised. Best I've had in all my detoxes. Hungry for breakfast." George prolonged his grin. This was the jolliest I had seen him.

"Grateful for that!" I chuckled in response to his food review. I looked to the east, sipping warm decaf coffee. My mind was still awakening.

George started to say something, paused, then released the words I had been praying to hear. "So, Wing, the other morning you asked my opinion of the Bible. I've thought about it, and I know we talked about family yesterday. Well, what I hadn't told you yet is that my mother became a Christian a few years before she died. I do believe in something of a God; I can recognize that in the intricacies of nature. Why many people adamantly choose to fight against that, I don't know. And when it comes to the message of Jesus and being a Christian in general, I guess I'm somewhat familiar with it. I just never really sought it out, took the time to grasp and accept it, or Him as my own. One thing I don't understand is, if Jesus was the Son of God, then why did He have to die? Why not just, I don't know, simply make everything good in the first place?"

"That's beautiful your mother accepted Him, George. She is now in so magnificent of a place that our minds cannot even fathom its perfection. And I hear you. I'm glad you've got some familiarity with that." I nodded my head and smiled, then dove in. "God did in fact make everything good in the first place, but He also gave us free will, allowing us the choice to sin or not. With the first sin came the fall. The world, which was pure, became a fallen world with sin. If He made everything only good without human's ability to sin, our love for Him wouldn't have been authentic, because our love wouldn't be a choice and therefore it would just be the way things were, which is not genuine love. He desires our submitting, repenting, full-hearted, by our own choice LOVE. He wants our faith in Him. 'For the wages of sin is death, but the gift of God is eternal life in Jesus Christ our Lord.' (Romans

6:23 NKJV). Therefore, because sin requires death and we each are sinful and there is no sinless human other than Jesus Himself, we were all doomed to an eternity cast away from Him. Jesus, the Son of God, needed to die to pay the debt for all our sins. Thus, God came down to earth as a human, His Son, to live the human life, experiencing all the pain and emotions we experience, yet since He, Jesus, was and is sinless, His death served as the pure sacrifice which would cover all our sins. His death was necessary for our salvation. But the best part is, that is not the end. He didn't stay dead. He defeated what sin causes, death, and He rose from the grave fulfilling the prophecies and promise for our opportunity of eternal life. Now, although He died as our sacrifice, we must accept this, believe this with our hearts, have faith in all of it, His resurrection, His forgiveness, that His death paid our debt in full. With this belief, we trust in Him and repent of our sins, which caused His death, turning to Him and away from our sinful nature, obeying His commandments, for true love is shown by our obedience to Him. We obey Him because of our trust in Him. While that may seem difficult, and can be, I certainly have a long way to grow in this, His love guides us in obedience. When we accept His gift of salvation, He sanctifies us, meaning He sets us apart from this fallen world for Him, purified from all unrighteousness. Nothing is of our own doing. Jesus did it all. We are spiritually bankrupt without Him. We shall always be sinners here on earth, but we shed our patterns of sin, recognizing what it is and what that means, for in our salvation and love for Him, like I said, we desire to serve and truly obey Him. Our works are not what saves us, but they become a fruit of our faith and salvation in Him. It's all incredibly beautiful, man! Praise God."

"Yeah, I suppose it is. Whew," George tittered as if his mind was overwhelmed taking it all in. "That is a lot to think about. Thanks for explaining it, though. When my mother gave her life to Jesus, many people on the reservation weren't too keen on it, some thinking it was a white man's religion and all, but then again, it isn't just a white man's religion, is it? I had never seen her experience more happiness and peace in all her life until those final few years. Must be something powerfully true there, I thought. I witnessed her change. But then, I just kept drinking and didn't think on it much more." George sat back as if he wanted to hear my thoughts.

"Well, I know in many ways the white man really messed things up. And even though some were spreading Christianity, many of them went about it in all the wrong ways. Murdering, taking control, lying, stealing land, breaking treaties, enslaving humans, none of that was Christ-like behavior. Unfortunately, evil sneaks its way into hearts and stains what is pure, like God's true message. Satan is tenacious, George, prowling around like a lion, devouring wherever and however he can. He perpetually deceives. Jesus wasn't even Caucasian. He was Middle Eastern. And Jesus is the only way for all people, no matter what race or creed. Greedy humans turned His image into what fit their power-hungry ventures. I'm pretty sure that pale-skinned, long-haired guy we see all over America and Europe isn't exactly accurate! There is much to be wary of in the sin of humanity. White supremacy is utterly nonbiblical and pure evil. Hatred and exclusion are not from God. Satan is the enemy. He pulls people away from following and representing a Christ-like life by misleading in every way he can. I am not proud of the sins my ancestors committed, nor of my own sins, but I am proud to be reborn in Jesus. Grateful that He did not give up on me and that I finally committed to following Him wholly. It certainly took me long enough… My identity is now in Him. A wise man once said to me, 'Do not let the sins of others keep you from the Truth that is Jesus Christ.'"

George nodded, "Alright, I get that. The reborn part. That is what my mother said she did. She placed all her trust in Him, and the peace she gained from that was incredible. I want her faith, and that peace. I want to go where she believed she would go after she died."

I sat up straight, lit another cigarette, prayed in my mind and then spoke. "Maybe you've heard the popular Bible verse John 3:16 (NKJV) 'For God so loved the world, that He gave His only begotten Son, that whoever believes in Him should not perish but have everlasting life.'" I opened my Bible and turned to this page and continued to read as George listened. "It goes on verse 17 to 21 with Jesus speaking, 'For God did not send His Son into the world to condemn the world, but that the world through Him might be saved. He who believes in Him is not condemned; but he who does not believe is condemned already, because he has not believed in the name of the only begotten Son of God. And this is the condemnation, that the light has come into the world, and men loved darkness rather than light, because their deeds were evil. For everyone practicing evil hates the light and does not come to the light, lest his deeds should be exposed. But he who does the truth comes to the light, that his deeds may be clearly seen, that they have been done in God.' Jesus is true love, man. His gospel is the truest form of love. And the Bible," I held up my worn leather copy, "is the infallible word of God. The world tries to twist and tear at that, but it does not change the truth."

"I want that light and that love. Why do so many people hate and reject His love?" George astutely asked.

I snickered understandingly. "Because it exposes our darkness. It challenges our sinful nature. It requires that we humble ourselves to Him, submit our every way to Him. Many think they can go to heaven on their own merits, by quote unquote being a good person, but that is prideful and utterly untrue. We each need to accept Jesus' incredible gift or else we will spend eternity away from Him, and there is zero goodness in that. Hell is not a party, like many will scoff at and haughtily try to believe. And then, of course, many people think they are free from this condemnation because they strongly do not believe in any afterlife. However, that doesn't excuse them from God's judgement. Like Jesus said, 'I am the Way, the Truth and the Life, no one comes to the Father but through Me.'" As I spoke to George I wondered if I was occasionally repeating myself, or what I should say to help him understand better, but I trusted God would do that work in George's heart. I felt rusty at this and just attempted to provide George with the scripture to let God handle the rest.

"Sure, sure, I see that. I have had so much darkness…" George's voice trailed off.

"So have I, my friend. There is a quote by A. W. Tozer, who was a missionary and author, that puts it simply: 'Jesus Christ knows the worst about you. Nonetheless, He is the one who loves you the most.'"

"Ah yes, that is good. I like that. A great way to sum it up. Love a good quote." George smiled.

"Indeed, man. It is a solid quote." I chuckled and added, "Alright, here is one more I love that hits home. R.C. Sproul stated, 'It is one thing to believe in God; it is quite another to believe God.'"

"There we go!" George enthusiastically nodded his head and then settled into a somber expression of deep thought. After a few seconds of silence, I returned to where we had momentarily diverted from.

"There is no darkness Jesus cannot save and forgive. None whatsoever. With Him, as a child of His, with us a part of His eternal family, He will grow us more like Him. When our soul is reborn in Christ, that is only the beginning. He gives us the Holy Spirit, which maybe you have heard of. The Holy Spirit dwells within us as the voice of God, as part of the Trinity which is God, 'However, when He, the Spirit of truth, has come, He will guide you into all truth; for He will not speak on His own authority, but whatever He hears He will speak; and He will tell you things to come. He will glorify Me, for He will take of what is Mine and declare it to you,' (John 16 13-14 NKJV)."

"Gotcha," George nodded slowly. "The Holy Spirit. That will be powerful, I imagine."

"Yes, extremely powerful, George. It acts as a counselor, teacher, guide, comforter, it convicts us and provides true wisdom. Those who do not become reborn do not receive the Holy Spirit, so the world does not know or understand how mighty it truly is. An incredible gift, you'll see." I winked at him and smiled, feeling my skin horripilate, not by the cold air but by the power of the Heavenly Father and the excitement of George's open seeking heart.

"So, what now?" George inquired curiously.

"Well, as Romans 10:9-10 (NKJV) states, 'that if you confess with your mouth Jesus as Lord and believe in your heart that God raised Him from the dead, you will be saved; for with the heart a person believes, resulting in righteousness, and with the mouth he confesses, resulting in salvation.'"

George looked towards the horizon, his mind working through all we had discussed. After a moment he asked, "Do you mind if I think on this some before, I don't know, before I take the next step?"

"Of course, George. I tell you what, I'll show you some places in the Bible to read today. I'll bookmark them in the copy from the bookshelf. Spend some time in prayer. Challenge yourself to truly seek Him in your heart, then truly listen. 'Seek and ye shall find.' Later this evening, we can talk more about it and even pray together. You can be saved today! But it is not the act of a prayer that saves you. It is not a matter of saying certain words, for remember our works do not save us. It is the genuine faith in your heart in Him, and we confess with our mouths what our heart believes. Oh, George, I am so excited for you!"

George stood up and grinned. I followed him upwards but not reaching as tall as he. "Sounds great to me, Wing." My big friend patted his belly. "Hungry, should be about that time."

"Should be," I agreed. Towards the door we shuffled together, slipping on ice and laughing as we strode. Three breakfast platters emanating scrumptious aromas were being delivered to the dining table right when we entered the door.

~~~

After breakfast, our medicated lethargy overtook us again. We both slept, but when I awoke, George was reading the ragged Bible the detox center had provided. I smiled at this while rubbing my eyes and returning to the nurse's station.

"Your body is doing well, Wing, no setbacks. How're you feeling?" The nurse I liked the best turned her chair to face me.

"Other than always being drowsy, I feel pretty good. Eating everything and stoked that come four in the morning, I will have passed the seventy-two-hour mark." Joy beamed from my face.

"Yes, tomorrow is a big day for you. If things remain on this positive trajectory, next we will have you meet with the doctor once more, then our alcohol counselor, and taper back on your medication. Of course, monitor how your brain and body respond to that."

"Of course. I dig it."

"You what?" The elder lady smirked.

"I mean, that sounds great to me, thank you." I laughed while her eyes expressed humor. She knew what I meant. "So, I should be able to get out of here by Christmas?"

"Oh yes, if all goes well, a couple of days lowering your medication and possibly we can release you on the twenty-third, Friday. Do you have a plan for after we release you?"

"A plan? I mean, not drinking is the plan. I am determined to stay sober from alcohol."

"I know, Hun, but it is more difficult than you may think now. Our counselor tomorrow will help you with all that. You just keep resting. Lunch should come out soon. I'll see you in two hours." She patted my knee kindly and sent me on my lethargic way.

George had fallen asleep with the Bible on his chest, leaving me to eat lunch alone. After cleaning every crumb off my plate, I returned to bed. When I awoke for dinner, George was sitting at the nurse's station looking ill. This worried me and left me to eat another meal alone. After dinner, I called my mom and dad on the detox center's landline telephone. It was uplifting to provide them both with positive updates. They encouraged me heartily, each in their own way from their different locations in the country.

CINEREAL

I hung up in time to see George ambling awkwardly next to the dining table. It appeared he was about to fall, for he quickly reached out his hand and placed it on the table while stumbling forward. Instinctively, I jumped up from the living room chair and rushed to his side. I pushed my body under his shoulder and chest as his large mass fell forward like a heavy tree.

"Nurse!" I shouted, holding up his body to keep him from hitting the ground. The nurse swiftly summoned the security guard and ordered me not to touch him. But what could I do? I was protecting his body from crashing down hard onto the floor. The security guard helped me lower him safely while the nurse called an ambulance. She pulled me aside and apologized for snapping at me, explaining it was about legal liability. Within a few minutes, the EMTs carted a discombobulated George out to the ambulance and on to the hospital. I didn't know what was going on. My mind filled with anxiety. All I could do was pray and wait, hoping he would return.

That night I went to bed as the only one in the room. The only other inpatient was the girl whose name I did not know. I had asked her once, but she only smiled and nodded. In fact, I did not hear her speak to anyone even once. Despite being heavily dosed with medication, I had a tough time falling asleep. Too many concerning thoughts for George rushed through my mind. *Trust in the Lord with all your heart and lean not on your own understanding*, I meditated upon persistently. Outside, I smoked alone, peering into the night sky. By myself, I snacked on popcorn and pudding cups until exhaustion won and drifted into a dreamless sleep.

~~~

On the morning of day four, I awoke from the depths of medicated slumber and noticed I'd slept in. Breakfast was already on the table. Upon spotting the two covered platters, I hoped the girl had already taken one to her room and that George would be outside waiting for me to join him for our daily sunrise smoke and talk session. I rushed to the backyard to check and congratulate him on our passing of the seventy-two-hour sobriety mark, but he was not there, and the platter of food was for the girl still to wake. My excitement descended into melancholy. I proceeded through the motions at the nurse's station with a forced cheer. "Day four! Have you heard anything about George?" I asked the nurse, who I deemed to be the only grumpy one of them all.

CINEREAL

"I cannot talk about the other patients, Wing. Here, take your meds. We are giving you slightly less today." She slapped the cuff around my arm to check my blood pressure.

"Yes, ma'am," is all I could mutter, following her orders, then sitting alone at the dining table again.

After breakfast, I met with the doctor and then an alcohol counselor while wondering how George was faring. Detox wasn't as fun anymore, and even if he couldn't return, I prayed he would at least be alright. *Perhaps he is thinking about what we discussed.*

"While everyone here has raved about your optimistic attitude and determination to remain sober, you need to understand that a healthy support system outside of detox is vital. Many people end up having to detox multiple times, and that is extremely difficult on the body." The alcohol counselor encouraged me, but she had a beer brewery sticker on her drinking canteen I could not take my eyes from. The sticker made it difficult for me to listen to everything she said. I could hear her, and the sticker did not make me want to drink, but it soured my belief in anything she spoke.

Finally, I could hold it in no longer. "Do you drink alcohol?" I asked her, nodding towards her canteen. This question caught her off guard.

"I do, yes, responsibly, but I don't see how that concerns our meeting now." She shifted in her chair as if my question was inappropriate.

"Ah, never mind. I hear you. Yes, I agree that a healthy support system is important. My girlfriend doesn't booze, nor does my dog, so I should be fine at home. Outside of that, I will seek therapy, I place my faith in God, and I'm meeting with my new primary care provider in early January, so she can help me research further steps. Also, I am unsure how my brain's chronic vertigo will affect my life once the medication wears off. Right now, my brain feels like it is being gripped in a warm sweater. Which is ideal, but out there I self-medicated my vertigo with alcohol, so that will be one of the first things I address with my new doctor." I looked towards the door, ready for our meeting to conclude, then pridefully added. "I won't need to go through detox again. Once was enough. I will make it stick." Within a few more questions, a few more pamphlets and the turning of her canteen backwards, she finally released me from her windowless office.

I sat outside in the cold. The day was still gray, and my cigarette smoke still rose toward the clouds, but my mind could not concentrate. I tried to pray, but even then, my silent words seemed jumbled. In time, I conceded to another nap. When I awoke, lunch had been served, and there were three containers of food on the table. Quickly I hustled out just as I had in the morning, now with a revitalized hope. "Is George coming back?" I asked, poking my head over the computer.

"Wing." Her eyes darted as my name stung its point.

I sat at the table eating my sandwich and chips when suddenly the front locked door beeped due to being unlocked by an electronic key from the outside. As it opened, dragging in cold air, first there was a detox employee and second, standing wider and taller than anyone else, was George. He advanced slowly on his feet, fitting himself tightly through the door frame. When the door closed and he turned forward, letting his eyes meet mine, his face brightened into a beaming grin.

"George!" I exclaimed with food still in my mouth. "Welcome back!"

"Wing! Guess what?!" He held up a Bible in his hand. "I did it! Or rather, Jesus did!"

Moisture filled his eyes as he triumphantly spoke. Instantly I knew what he meant. A brother recognizes a brother. *He had not gone to the hospital with a Bible, he must have asked for one when he was there and if he had done that, and he just said, "Jesus did it," well that could only mean one glorious thing, he believes.* George gestured, implying he would meet me in a few minutes. Eagerly, I finished lunch, accomplished the medical duties, and then waited outside for him to join me when he was ready. Within thirty minutes we sat together again.

"Tell me everything, or everything you want to share." I leaned forward in anticipation.

George couldn't remain seated. He stood up, lit his smoke and with a wide grin let his words spill out. "Alright, it was touch and go there at the hospital. I was kind of scared about it, but I kept thinking about everything we had been talking about. Plus, I had been reading the Bible passages you showed me before the ambulance. I wanted to read more, but I didn't have that Bible with me, so I asked the hospital nurse if they had one around, and she promised to go look. While she was gone, I laid there and prayed, genuinely prayed. I didn't have to force it as if it were some mantra or duty. My heart seeking Him in full trust of who He is. With complete faith that He was hearing my prayer, I realized I believe in Him and all He has done for me. Right there, lying with hospital things connected to me, I placed all my faith in Jesus. I gave Him my life. I asked Him for forgiveness and repented of my ways, turning away from my sin and to Him. I promised

CINEREAL

Him I truly desire change and to follow Him, asking Him to do His work in me, and to help me grow in understanding and to guide me. Wing, I believe in Jesus as God's Son and sacrifice for our sins and that He rose from the dead! While I was praying, something incredible came over me, much like the peace my mother had, knowing and even feeling Him as the truth. It was so incredible, Wing! After my hospital bed prayer, I was lying there with joyful tears in my eyes when the nurse returned with the Bible she found. She asked me if I was alright, and I looked up to her and couldn't help but tell her, while the happiest tears I've ever felt streaming down my cheeks, 'I just became a child of God.' I mean, incredible Wing, He is incredible."

"Incredible George, He is incredible indeed!" Tears filled both of our eyes as I listened, while he spoke his testimony with fervor. Excitement and joy radiated from the detox center's backyard smoking outpost. I stood up, extending my arms, and George wrapped his big-bear body around me with a fervent embrace.

"Thank you, Wing." George wiped tears away from his face after our arms returned to our sides.

"Not me, George, I did nothing. That was all from God. He wanted you, man. He called you, and you listened. I couldn't be more overjoyed." I wiped my cheeks as well, feeling the cold air highlighted in their dampness. We both stood lifting our smokes back up, nodding at the beauty of all, breathing deep breaths in, unable to remove grins from our faces. "Praise God, man, praise God! So, are you alright medically? What was that all about?" I didn't want to pry beyond what he wanted to share, yet I remained concerned after his emergency episode.

George just looked me in the eye with a glint of humor and said, "Eh, too much salt." At this, we both laughed enthusiastically. "No, really, it'll be alright. My organs, man, drinking and eating, I have a lot of work ahead, things I need to change."

"And you will, God will give you the strength. Same with me, man, we will, He will. He is and we are." I nodded, understanding the truth behind his humor and the seriousness beneath all that was. "Quite the detox we have had, huh, George?"

"It certainly has been, Wing. Never thought it could be this good. Eager to see my wife and kids. I should get out of here on Christmas Eve."

CINEREAL

"Perfect. I think I am heading home tomorrow, just a tad before you. But I held down the fort solo last night, so you'll have to hold it down without me tomorrow night. And yet, we are never truly alone with Him."

"Not a problem, buddy. Yup, He is right here with us. Okay, let's go inside. It is freaking cold today." George and I realized we were shivering, so we returned indoors to spend our last lethargic afternoon of detox together.

~~~

In the morning, George and I ate breakfast together for our last time. I traded him my pancakes for his fresh fruit cup, as we liked to do, and laughed with cheeks full of bites and bodies free from alcohol. Afterward, I met with the doctor for final clearance. All the medical staff agreed I was ready to be released. If I did not return to boozing, my liver should recover from the decades of alcohol abuse. The last round of medication was served, and instructions were provided on what to expect moving forward. My brain injury and impending vertigo would need to be thoroughly examined outside of the detox. Natural elation flourished within. I was finally on the other side of the addiction's prison walls. I could not thank everyone who had helped me enough, so I left a handwritten note on my bedside table emphasizing my ecstatic gratitude. The staff returned my belongings and iPhone. I gifted one last pack of cigarettes to George, called a taxi to deliver me home to the Bend art cottage, then sat talking with my friend until the transportation arrived. We discussed the next steps in our lives, prayed together, and agreed our time in detox had been of monumental value. I encouraged him to keep his heart focused on God, to grow in learning, to trust Him in all things and not to lean on his own understandings. The way God had used me, a messy alcoholic, one who only recently returned to Him, to help another alcoholic enter Christ's eternal love, humbled me immensely. *You are incredible, Father. I entered here with zero joy, and now I am overflowing with it.* When my taxi arrived, George and I shared a last embrace, bid our sincere farewells, and then parted ways.

As I finally stepped out the front door, the same one I had entered six days prior, all of life glowed with a fresh commencement. "I will never drink alcohol again." I naively stated into the central Oregon sky, to the magnificent Creator of all creation beyond the scope of our universe. Although I was freshly liberated on that frigid December 23, 2022, morning, little did I know the trials and tribulations to come. For what does one truly understand about their addiction when they are immersed in it? It is not until one detoxes the poison and then begins a new direction that they learn what and why addiction was and is. I would now need to face everything I had buried beneath the booze. A worthy first step had been accomplished, and it was time to learn how to walk a new path. There was much to be done, but first I would relish the enriching freedom, return to Wylie and Flower, clip my prancing dog to her leash, and beneath the protection of a medicated brain, in the tread of sturdy winter boots, set off on a snowy walk to purchase a proper, non-decaf coffee.

Turbulence

The sky was tumbling as I sat hunched over in the snow. My head hung low, eyes closed, left hand pressing firmly into my furrowed brow attempting to ease the escalation. I could not open my eyelids or lift my chin, for if I did, I would see the sky falling again. My whirling brain would roll right out of my skull and shoot across the earth into the river and flow so far and so fast I could never catch it again.

Wylie whimpered by my side. The speeding flakes crashing to the ground did not irk her, nor did the brisk temperature. She was merely concerned, worried my injury might inhibit me from standing again. I perceived the footsteps of a lone walker, another human enjoying the tranquil park on Christmas Day. Their shuffling strides sounded like boots on Styrofoam. They must have looked at me and assumed I was fervently praying, or crying, the way my body curved forward in disorder. I surely prayed a plea, but I did not cry a tear. The only wet on me was from the deluge of white when the sky plummeted and the calm horizon erupted, causing my vertigo to descend into debilitating spins. I sat this way, for there was no other choice. No more could I stand without collapsing. I must sit and wait.

After twenty mindful minutes filled with deep breaths and frustration, the torrent simmered. Slowly, I cracked my eyes ajar just enough to glimpse at the monochrome ground in a monochrome world. Even the silhouettes of evergreen trees had become lost in the whiteout. Wylie sensed my timid movement as I eased myself up to stand, holding the slit in my eyes as conservatively as I could. Open just enough to observe my steps yet not enough to bear witness to the mayhem of a real-life shaken snow globe. Although it had only been two days since the detox drugs wore off, I had been learning what my physical triggers were for the vertigo. Quick movements, turning my head to the side while walking forward, flashing lights, any visual disturbance would suddenly lurch my brain into a heightened attack. Even if I had my driver's license, driving would be

CINEREAL

impossible. The squall became a knockout punch I could not withstand. *But I must make it home to the cottage, to Flower and our holiday dinner. There is only one mile to go.* By focusing on each step while keeping my head low, perhaps I could progress without the need for another long, miserable stoop. Wylie pranced at the end of her leash. We were moving again, and even though both of our bodies brimmed with physical energy, mine in new sobriety and hers from her canine ways, the energy could not be utilized when my brain was under such duress. "One step at a time, Wing, one step at a time, just like on the long trails," I muttered. Forward we progressed, smirking as I remembered a quote by Albert Einstein. *"Life is like riding a bicycle. To keep your balance, you must keep moving."*

"How was your walk!?" Flower greeted us with an eager smile as our 2,000 steps were finally accomplished. The pleasing aromas of garlic, onions and roast filled the cottage.

"Not how I planned. When the snow started falling, the motion of the precipitation pulled my brain into an unbearable spin, like a string forcing a children's toy top into action. Suddenly I did not know what was up or down, left or right. Everything became violently discombobulated in here." I tapped my head and lifted weary eyes, forcing a grin. "However, it is wondrously beautiful out there. I have always loved a snowstorm, and always will, but there is something about its movement that makes my brain extra delicate. So, we sat by the river when it happened, which forced us not to complete the loop I'd originally planned. When I could stand again, we just came back. This vertigo is relentless." I lay down on the couch, shifting to my side, and closed my eyes. "I'll get up when I can. Crock-pot certainly smells good, makes it extra cozy in here. Glad I got that started when I did."

"It was so much fun having dinner with Max and Lena last night, but this meal will be even more delicious!" Flower's voice flourished with upbeat holiday cheer.

"Yes, that was a grand time. Fortunately, I didn't have a vertigo episode this debilitating with them, would have greatly hindered the mood." I emitted a guffaw.

Flower sat on the edge of the couch and rubbed my forehead. "I'm sorry this has been so hard on you. The alcohol really helped a lot, didn't it?"

"Yes, in the vertigo ways it did. But in all other ways, it didn't." I sighed.

"Well, it is only the beginning of your sobriety. Hopefully, it fades, or the doctors help you figure everything out."

"Yes, hopefully. But, eh, never mind, I don't want to think about it right now…" My words trailed off as I submitted to the medicine of rest and eventually drifted into a hazy nap.

~~~

After the holidays passed and the year 2023 began, the excitement of all things new dissolved into the reality of hardships. If I were to remain sober from alcohol, it was clear I must do so with the constant burden of vertigo. Between the violent episodes of brain spinning torture remained the constant instability, which mimicked the rise and fall of floating on a boat. I'd gained new tools to access, so I turned towards these for help. I went to my new doctor, and we initiated the medical journey with bloodwork, natural supplements and imaging of my brain and body, such as MRIs and CT scans. The results indicated what I already knew. My brain had been damaged, yet the affirmed knowledge provided nothing in the way of repair. The first neurologist I met with only wanted to medicate me. He acted like a grown-up smug frat-boy boasting he was a legal drug dealer. I did not like or trust him at all. The second neurologist would require waiting nearly a year for an appointment. My doctor helped my body even out mineral and vitamin imbalances, but all the other work would be a tedious process, waiting many months between each next step.

There was an outpatient rehab program the detox center's alcohol counselor had encouraged me to take part in. I walked there and attempted to have a meeting with the staff. Boxed inside a small room with no windows, with the insides of my head spinning while I sat, I explained to them my situation. In response, they instructed me about what to expect. Quickly I realized this program was much like the one I took part in, per court order, in Colorado. Only now would I be doing so voluntarily. As soon as the lady informed how often I would be required to provide urine samples as a drug test, I balked at any participation. No more urinalysis. I had already learned that lesson the harsh way. In fact, I did not want a single person telling me how I should live my day to day. Having someone monitor my activity was the last thing that could help me. Exasperated by it all, I tore myself out of the claustrophobic room to stumble dizzily, frustratedly, home.

CINEREAL

At the beginning of the new year, the old toxic tensions between Flower and me became reignited. There were many positive qualities between us, such as her shared, refocused desire to follow God, one that He utilized me to help her rekindle, and her willingness to aid me in my sobriety. But there also remained qualities detrimental to our partnership. I aspired to shed everything that had contributed to my old sinful lifestyle patterns. And in this, I craved solitude.

Daily, in the effort not to drink, I was no longer the silly, playful, fun Wing I had often been prior. To remain sober, each day became one of miserable grit. For so long I had only known myself with booze in my bloodstream. Alcohol had been a major part of my identity. As my friend Safari relayed over the telephone, "Other than being an adventurer, it was your identity, Wing." Now I barely knew who I was without it. I was a child of God, I knew that, but every day required dedicated focus in reminding myself to trust in Him solely. *I am His child, yes, but still an immature one.* My mind and body became vastly disconnected. Most everything triggered my desire to drink. Waking up, walking around town, eating, gardening, writing, playing piano, looking at Flower, talking to my friends, listening to music, entering every single Bend public space, simply existing surged the crave for alcohol. While I slept, my dreams became saturated with booze. In my dormant imaginings, I would get drunk, only to awaken terrified that I had truly wrecked my alcohol sobriety. The only two things in life that did not trigger this urge were Wylie and God. I needed time to face each monstrous moment without the responsibility of everything else, all while constantly struggling to stand up without vicious dizziness. When Flower tried to touch me, I flinched. Everyone and everything needed to leave me alone, for everything in the world aggravated me. Many times, my frustration leaked, displaying itself in sharp words. I knew my demeanor was not one of gentle Christlikeness, but taming my new exasperations presented as a vast, rugged wilderness I needed to learn how to navigate. Flower did not respond well to my changes in attitude, and I did not respond well to a single ounce of external pressure. Near the end of January, I broke off our relationship again.

During this month, I severely missed spending as much time with my friends as I had grown accustomed to. A few of them I saw on Thursdays at bowling league. We entered our second season, and even though it seemed like everyone else in the league was constantly drinking, Hest and Max lessened their alcohol intake. Vin's participation on the team was replaced by our friend Cooper. The league needed a new vice president, a position I decided to volunteer for, recognizing it to be an opportunity to serve. Upon announcing my candidacy, the members voted me in. Mostly, other than my perpetual dizziness, which caused me to miss some weeks, I continued to enjoy the competitive atmosphere and my new community-serving duties. Despite the league interactions, I dearly missed my long talks and wine nights with Rad. In the absence of our intimate conversations, I walked Wylie around CiderBar from a distance, listening to the jovial laughter I once participated in. With each despondent, sober day, it was difficult to find happiness in anything. Instead of consistently refocusing my heart on God and resting in His peace, I began to ruminate in the misery of what I no longer had.

Early in February, when Flower and I had only been broken up for about a week, her mother informed me an ambulance had rushed her from her apartment to the hospital. Once I talked to Flower on the phone and learned that she would make a full recovery, I, after only forty-eight paltry days without alcohol, caved into my weakness and walked straight to a bar. I chose a discreet establishment where no one would bother me. At four in the afternoon, I poured two whiskeys and two India Pale Ales into my body. I called Dad from the patio nook as shameful tears welled in my eyes. Exhausted from every ounce of life, I confessed to him my stumble. He warned me to be extremely vigilant not to fall into old patterns. In response, I emptily promised I would not, but to myself I could not ensure that guarantee anymore. The miserable, weak, malfunctioning, wretched creature within me was pugnaciously attempting to return. After the four drinks, I shuffled back to the cottage, half-heartedly praying to God, feeling like I needed to hide from Him even though I knew He saw all. Despite my slip, I resolved not to collapse completely into my alcoholism. Once home with Wylie, I invited Flower to come back when the hospital released her.

Two despondent sober days later, I learned my five and a half years of living in the art cottage was abruptly coming to an end. The owner of the property had sold, and the new landlord carried vastly different plans for the property. Although I originally believed I would have more time to locate a home, the construction was set to start, so the inability to let Wylie out into the yard rushed me into urgency. All of life seemed to be suddenly turned upside down. I did not want to drink alcohol, but I considered I might not have completely broken out of addiction's prison as I had naively believed. Despair silently crawled in.

Even though I genuinely cared for Flower, being in a romantic relationship was not what I desired, yet through my vacillating choices, I was back where I had been before. *I should never have invited her to return, for I know I will soon push her away again... It was a selfish decision, which will only lead to my emotionally hurting her more.* Trapped on all sides by all things I did not want, including feeling trapped by my own weak mind, I endeavored to lean into God, but my angry heart blocked out His voice and guidance. I imagined the Holy Spirit rolling ethereal eyes, muttering, "Here we go again." My faith and trust in Him remained strong, but my maturity lacked resolve. With the availability of alcohol around every corner, the ease of sinking into old patterns loomed. Every day my physical brain symptoms destroyed all basic movements. As friends happily proceeded with their lives in the distance, my sanity deteriorated.

~~~

At the beginning of March, I moved into the Prixon. The massive apartment building was titled the Hixon, but after only a few days of residing within the characterless cube, it seemed more like a Prixon to me. "Everyone who lives here loves this place, and they are all pricks," I bitterly mused. Moving into a small, contained box on the third floor had forced me to part ways with my favorite possession. My precious piano from the mountains of Colorado was no more. Without my keys, without the wooden and stringed creative outlet, I paced back and forth as angst intensified. I tried to deliberate positively, telling myself this is where God wanted me, *but why would He want me to live in a place with no yard, no trees, no porch, no balcony or any private outdoor space to stare unbothered into the stars and ponder amid each seasonal breeze?* It was as if everything my soul needed was taken away from me. "Probably because I drank. This is my punishment," I inconsolably muttered, while wavering between choosing sobriety or the bottle.

On such short moving notice, the Prixon was the only place I could afford that was available in a location I could walk and access my daily living needs. Contemptuously I became like a rat in a wall, hoarding anger, hiding from the urban, concrete, parking-lot-world outside and staring at the liquor store with its blaring red sign directly across the busy street in the western view of my only window. At first, I did not enter the enticing establishment. Despite my recent minor relapses, I still aspired to refrain. *All that hard work*

CINEREAL

of ridding the poison from my body cannot be wasted, and yet, that liquor store is calling to me, right there, only 300 feet away…

I had not allowed Flower to come to the Prixon with me, fancying the idea that the new location would be a fresh, peaceful chapter in life. She was not the problem, I was. Initially, my attitude about the apartment was optimistic. *This might not be where I want to live, but I will make the most of it.* I missed Flower's company and wanted her to thrive and be well, but if I was to remain sober from alcohol, I needed to face everything alone. I needed to pour out all my weaknesses and pain before God and break every sinful pattern. However, the liquor store continued to shout its silent taunts at me, diverting all worthy goals from my mind and turning them into a sottish mindset. In my fragility, my focus on God became overshadowed by my entrenched alcoholism. By the end of March, once again I failed. In sober anger I succumbed to addiction, walking directly across the street into the store with the obnoxious red sign, purchasing whiskey and wine then returning to my sealed room to smoke, drink, write and maybe for just a little harmless break, relieve myself of all the pent-up disgusting mentalities I spiraled in. Once back at my desk chair while looking upon the western edge of urbanized sprawl, I opened my whiskey first, drank two long swigs, then in the ease of immediate reprieve pulled out my favorite wine mug, relishing the simple pop the cork exclaims when pulled from its glass neck, filled the mug with a soothing Rioja, turned on three fans, lit a cigarette and sat again, to watch the line of cars incessantly creep the McDonald's drive-through and write late into the night until the sun rose again.

"The sky is losing its ebony," I scribbled furiously. "I hear the neighbors starting to shuffle. Flushing toilets, moving tables, slamming cupboards. I'm sure they hear me hacking phlegm and smell my rebellious indoor chain smoking. There is a car siren that hasn't stopped for eighteen shrieks. Screeching opioid construction workers already arrived, to fade into day as engine rumbles like hungry destruction grumbles, as I pace here for hours attempting to drown angsts, with 'This is why you should take that medication' thrown at me. I will not throw my bowling ball through the window, although I want to, although I desire to tear down the walls so that no wall will ever again contain me. I used to listen to birds. Now I listen to trash. Must get to the forest. Must break out of this Prixon, this Hixon filled with pricks who lazily delight in leaving their dog's shit in the stairwell. Must find one straight month of peace, far away from here, to write, to be left alone, to perhaps truly obtain sobriety, to listen to robins and sparrows and remember the joy of what He wants me to be. A plant in the wrong environment shall wither, and I am that wilt."

For days I spiraled in my filth. Many nights I did not sleep yet continued drinking beyond the sunrise. While setting patterned steps in circles around the 500 square foot box, pouring wine for breakfast, chain-smoking cigarettes and scoffing at each smiling resident from my lofted window, the Holy Spirit convicted me relentlessly. Paul's words from I Thessalonians 5:16-18 (NKJV) prodded my mind. "Rejoice always, pray without ceasing, in everything give thanks; for this is the will of God in Christ Jesus for you." I knew this was right, and I was wrong. He had placed me in this space even though I did not understand why. *I should be grateful, rejoicing for all I have been given, so many have so much less. I should be cultivating a heart of continual prayer and therefore act like I trust Him. For what does trust look like? Not like this. Not by grumbling and easily falling into old destructive patterns. But why must I be here in this place, which revolts the very essence of my being!? I would rather die. And why must He constantly prompt me with truth instead of letting me slip into my numbed stupor? Because He loves me, I know, I know. But...* Ignoring God's convictions holds consequences, which I also knew, but in my anger, like Jonah, I did not want to accept my circumstances. With each swig from the bottle, my prideful obstinance strengthened, the alcohol nourishing the sin I should flee from.

For the rest of March, I wrote, paced, read my ridiculous words aloud, drank from my well, the liquor store, until all my utterances and angers culminated in a massive panic attack. Miles away in the darkness, in the snow, in the woods, in a drunken mess of suicidal ideation, beneath a tree, crying as I held Wylie on my lap, I called Flower. I knew it was best to just leave her alone. I had stressed her heart enough by constantly pushing her away then calling her back, but in my drunkenness, I did not know what else to do. *She will let me drink. She will drive me away from this place.* Again, I considered Jonah from the Old Testament. Although I loved God, when He called me to be one way, His way, I turned and ran away from Him. When He called me to do one thing, I did the opposite. *I am supposed to be growing in Him and turning away from the alcohol and my worldly sinful ways, but no, I am nothing but a decrepit wretch crawling back to the bottle and a world of emptiness away from Him. I am nothing but ash, the cinereal grey of the no more which remains. Destroying my already broken brain, I disappear. Discard this leftover soot from the fire of my life, scatter me away into nothingness and forget I ever existed.*

CINEREAL

Was my thinking drastic and exceedingly dramatic? Absolutely. Could I comprehend this flailing while drenched in the poison of alcohol? Certainly not. Would I later regret every sip of alcohol I consumed after my first detox? Entirely. Should I have continued to pull Flower back into my darkness? Emphatically no. But that is what alcohol does, as a depressant, as a poison, as the enemy to my mind, soul and to all those who loved me.

Upon my drunken panic attack phone call to Flower from the forest, she rushed to my aid. I could not return to the Prixon yet. Therefore, in the middle of the night, she drove us to a motel on the edge of town. We stayed there for three days until I gathered my scattered senses. Although I did not want to return to the modern block of claustrophobic apartments, I must. I had signed a one-year lease, and perhaps God wanted me there for reasons I did not understand. Again, I attempted to stop the alcohol consumption, but already the intensely rooted addiction had regained its grip. Thus, the decision was to drink gradually less and lean into the silver linings that wine and Flower's company could provide. It was as if I were making a futile compromise with both God and myself. Reasoning that since I could not fight my circumstances, I would flow with them and perhaps illogically float out of the abyss. In foolish pride and exhaustion, I resubmitted to my addiction instead of continuing to surrender all to Him. Of what I had given to Him I seized the portions I wanted back. With this mindset, on a day I struggled not to drink any whiskey, I suffered another debilitating seizure.

~~~

"This place isn't all bad," I said as I cleaned up the mess I had created, and Flower lounged on my mail-ordered couch. "At least I have modern appliances and a decent air-conditioner for the summer. Although I cannot garden this season, at least I have a plethora of indoor plants. And even though I must stare at the liquor store, above it I can watch each sunset! And as far as smoking goes, even though there is no place I am allowed to smoke on this miserable, concrete, dog feces covered property, I have figured out my three fans plus towel under the hallway door system. Getting the hang of this place."

"That's the attitude to have, Wing!" Flower giggled, delighted to be back and happy to have tipsy wine-Wing dancing in his pajamas to jazz emanating from the speaker. "You do well with wine. It is whiskey that is the real problem."

CINEREAL

"Yes, wine is much better for me. I will write poetry daily and finally get to compiling my Louisiana Hurricane Katrina novel. If I reduce extremely slowly how much I drink each week, like five percent less per week, I should be able to avoid any more seizures and eventually crawl out of my addiction again. One step at a time. All will be well." I poured another glass of wine while deceiving myself, pulled out the chessboard and motioned to Flower. "Care to play a game?" Her eyes affirmed my request.

Besides pitifully attempting to balance my consumption, I excitedly returned to my friends. My reunion with the CiderBar community was a celebrated event. It felt like coming home. At first my peers were wary I was drinking again, but I tried to persuade them with stable words. "I am not an alcoholic; I am simply someone who created a bad relationship with alcohol. I fixed that, so everything is better now." Temporarily I convinced myself of this lie, but I am not sure anyone else believed it. Sometimes, for old times' sake, I ventured to The Saloon, ignoring the haunting aura of the living darkness. I forced myself to believe I was thriving amidst difficult circumstances, but I was not progressing at all. I was only fooling myself.

In June 2023, summer's brutal heat arrived in the central Oregon high desert. My body still could not handle temperatures above eighty-four degrees Fahrenheit. To evade this danger, Wylie and I walked early in the morning and after the sun had set. On brutal days when I could not bear to exist inside the Prixon any longer, Flower drove us to higher elevations in the mountains. There we swam in alpine lakes and lounged in the shadows of trees. We constructed a steady daylight routine, laced with booze and picnics, and though I was avoiding the way I should be existing, for a few months everything seemed to be alright.

Despite my distractions, deep in my soul I knew I was living in sin. Occasionally in the quiet I would hear God's whispers, causing tears to form in my eyes. In response, I would fall on my knees in earnest prayer. "Please, Lord, do not give up on me yet. Please just give me a little time to figure out how to truly move forward. Although it may not look like it, I have not given up. Call it a vacation, a cowardly vacation, but I know I must continue to focus upon ridding this poison from my life."

After prayer one night, I was prompted to open my Bible to the Gospel of John, chapter fifteen. Upon reading Jesus' words, I understood His message. John 15:1-6 (NKJV) "I am the true vine, and My Father is the vinedresser. Every branch in Me that does not bear fruit He takes away; and every branch that bears fruit He prunes, that it may bear more fruit. You are already clean because of the word which I have spoken to you. Abide in Me, and I in you. As the branch cannot bear fruit of itself, unless it abides in the vine, neither can you, unless you abide in Me. I am the vine, you are the branches. He who abides in Me, and I in him, bears much fruit; for without Me you can do nothing. If anyone does not abide in Me, he is cast out as a branch and is withered; and they gather them and throw them into the fire, and they are burned."

While each day played out as a battle to remain alive, to stand upright, to not have another seizure or explode from a brain aneurysm, as I drank to stay sane and breathe, all while loathing myself for drinking again, I tried my hardest to abide in Him. My soul craved the companionship of someone who was actively following Christ. My friends didn't understand or care about God. Flower seemed to only consider Him when I brought Him up. My mother was my only source of Christ-loving companionship, yet only as a long-distance relationship. I craved someone to sit with me and pray with me. Twice I called the pastor of a church I had never met nor been to, introduced myself to him and begged him for guidance. During the conversations we shared, I could not control myself from discharging torrential emotions as I testified to him about my deep love for Jesus, my desire to follow God purely and my wretched struggles in sin. He listened and instructed patiently, but as we talked, I shamefully concluded that I could not be seen in my despicable emotional state. Thus, even the pastor I kept at a phone call distance. His instructions were accurate. I knew he was right, for the godly answer is always the same.

Outside my window at the Prixon, lined along the street with the liquor store and McDonald's, were also bars and taverns. This is not unusual for the town of Bend, and much like my old cottage in the old town neighborhood, a plethora of drinking options existed within a short walk from my apartment's hallway door. One of these establishments, named CDubs, was a classic alcoholic drinking hole. At night the rustic environment erupted into a party of youthful revelry, billiard games and raucous socialization, but in the light of morning and the leisurely pace of midday, it is where the drunks would stagger to drink alone and slowly waste the precious minutes of life remaining. While drinking my lunchtime whiskey one day, sitting alone on the back patio with my cigarettes and an ashtray resembling the one Granddad had set for me on his kitchen table, I remembered the words of my Christian friend I met by the CiderBar firepit. When she learned I was moving into the Prixon she had stated, "I only fear Wing, that you will end up drinking at CDubs all the time, just like you did at The Saloon." Hearing her speak this in my memory caused my uncontrollable emotions to surge again, for she was correct. There I was, drinking in the most pitiful fashion, not for fun, not for socialization, but alone to ward off the shakes and maintain my breathing. I had returned to walking the line between drinking is killing me and not drinking will kill me. *Why am I like this!? Why have I fallen so far again?* I longed for her company. That she might sit and talk with me. Not as a date. I did not want to be currently dating anyone, but as a friend who also loves Jesus. Picking up my phone, I considered texting her, but I could not. *What would I say? "You were right, I can't keep myself from getting drunk at CDubs and it isn't even noon."* No, I must get out of here and never return. I must walk home through the rising heat, drink water and read my Bible. I must focus my heart on God. I must abide in Him.

~~~

For the reader and for one who has not battled active addiction, I am sure the reasons for my redundancy and insanity in the recurrent miseries are obvious. Now as I write, it certainly is. I regret who I was and wish I could have shaken that old foolish me in the Prixon out of my needless, ceaseless torment. Every time I took the eye of my heart off Him, I became lost. Every time I tried to control the situation, I failed. When I did not drink, my brain injury symptoms debilitated any ability to progress without vertigo. Yet when I drank, the alcohol destroyed my positive decision-making process, hindering my ability to remain focused on God. By drinking alcohol, I was pouring poison onto pain. Alcohol was not medicine but fuel for despair, yet somehow, when imbibing, I could not comprehend this fact. My addiction would tell me things that were not true. "You are not an alcoholic. You just need to monitor it better. You can follow both God and drink. You need the alcohol to walk, to live, to breathe." These lies and more my addiction viciously whispered, convincing me to be the truth. And yet, beyond these lies endured the one and only steadfast Almighty Father. He knew what I was going through, providing all the tools I needed to grow beyond the addiction. However, the work to implement them was up to me. I may have hated where I lived, and hated feeling trapped in every regard, but looking back, I needed it to learn how to focus beyond circumstances and recognize the root problems. Like my mother had told me as a boy,

CINEREAL

"You do not learn things the easy way." Myself, and many others like me, needed to fight our way through a hell of our own creation to grasp surrendering everything to the one who purely loves, Adonai.

As summer turned into autumn and I unrelentingly raged against life in the Prixon, some bittersweet news was presented to the community. CiderBar had sold, and its taproom location we all loved would soon be closing. Bittersweet, for though our beloved hangout spot would soon be no more, for me this meant I could finally let go of that world. I needed this forceful end to inhibit slipping back into the perpetual temptation to return day after day. CiderBar had provided many friends and fun times, and the closing of its doors determined the elimination of part of my old Bend life. I did not confess to Rad my underlying relief, simply, "We must go big and end this chapter with revelry, celebrating what it has meant to us all! Thank you, Rad, for CiderBar. We are going to party!" And so, we did. At the end of October, as a recently turned 38-year-old alcoholic, I and many friends partied late into the night. When everyone left CiderBar for the last time, Rad and I remained by the firepit, burning logs until nearly sunrise. We gave it the goodbye it deserved.

"What is next for you, Rad?" I asked as the last log crackled sentimental flames.

"Well, the kids are growing older, almost teenagers now, so I will lean into all that brings. I need and want to devote more time to them. CiderBar closing will certainly help." Rad pursed his lips, staring into the final blaze. "How about you, Wing?"

"Sounds good, Rad. You are a great dad with wonderful kids. There will be many worthy, life-shaping years you share with them ahead. Me? Well, I need to refocus my efforts on breaking this alcohol addiction. I am right back where I was last year, deeply saturated in booze. Therefore, although I hate to do it and am ashamed of my failures, I need to be admitted into a medical detox again. I see no other way forward."

Rad looked at me with understanding eyes. He had observed many of my struggles over the Bend years, and though we valued our camaraderie over drinks and late-night talks, some things in life are far more important than holding on to the ways of old. "Yes, if you feel it is time, then it must mean it is. I wish you the best, Wing." We lifted our cups and cheered, for in many ways, it was the end.

~~~

CINEREAL

Ten and a half months after being released from my first medical alcohol detox, I was released from my second. Autumn sauntered past its peak as trees began to bare skeletal limbs. Round two was far different from round one. There was no "George" to befriend. There was little light and much darkness. Most of the other inpatients were detoxing from opiates. Therefore, their battles differed from mine. I sat and talked with the other lone alcoholic, but our conversations fell short of understanding, so we spent more time staring off into the distance under the weight of our medications than anything else. Unlike the considerable quietness of detox one, detox two was a smaller center adjacent to a large rehab facility. The participants of the rehab were loud, crude, and a few involved with smuggling in drugs and contraband. I tried to avoid everyone except the nurses and doctors altogether, but I was where I was, so I must endeavor to exhibit grace, kindness and patience. In a journal entry on the afternoon following my release, I wrote these words, among others, describing my time.

"…Obnoxious television in bedroom blaring How to Catch a Killer, accounting murders of children. Earplugs and pillows mashed over my head trying to ignore it all. Drugged-up nightmares, profuse sweating paired with constant trembling. Outside, sitting in the sun, attempting to soak positive energy, attempting to talk to God without disturbance, smoking cigarettes, drinking decaf coffee, meditating, until the daily pound of basketballs upon cement taunts every fiber of sanity. Nowhere to scream, so I scream within. They drug me more. I sleep and weep, falling into tormenting depths. The kind tenderness of nurses is overshadowed by racial slurs and hate speech screamed at us by locals on the other side of the fence. Skinheads and swastikas, denying space for anyone unlike them. I focus, I pray, I grit, I block it all out, but it digs and seeps into tranquility. Lying in a room where there is no peace, I close my eyes and breathe one second at a time. Upon returning to the Prixon, the liquor store sign stares me down. This, my window's only view. But I will not drink, I will not fold, not this time…"

Having returned to my residence, I sincerely desired never to drink alcohol anymore, and yet I did not believe I could hold to that determination. Staring at the liquor store sign, unable to perceive any of Flower's words, I slumped into exhaustion, worn out by all that was.

I trudged through the motions of life, gritting through each day to maintain sobriety. Bowling on Thursdays, ignore all the drinks, study the

CINEREAL

Bible, look away from the liquor store, dream about alcohol when I sleep, long walks with the dog, write each day, sell the old drunken books... I prayed I might locate some Christ-loving friends and prayed that Flower would grow in her own faith, but I could be no one's rock yet, I needed to be alone with God to grow. Inwardly, I started peeling back the layers of past traumas, writing everything out into poems and prose. The deeper I dove beyond the calloused scars from the sexual assault, the murder attempt on my life, the dissolution of my sturdy family long ago and the decades of self-loathing, I drowned in sober emotions. With alcohol my emotions were heightened and uncontrolled, but in sobriety, I was discovering, my emotions were even more intense, yet they were different. They felt cleaner and more authentic than when savagely dressed in booze. Alone without the guidance of wiser souls who could maturely help me navigate these new sober focuses, I remained lost and melancholic. "What an oxymoron I am," I muttered, "desiring to be alone and simultaneously not to be alone. I think it is just the kind of alone that matters. I want nothing that holds me back, and I want everything that helps me grow towards purity, truth and godliness." Reaching out my soul's hand to Him, He held it. He spoke to me and guided me, yet I still craved the friendship of a Christian human mentor.

Despite the trudge and difficulties of alcohol abstinence round two, I both applauded myself and thanked God for successfully making it through each day. When I craved alcohol, I reminded myself that when I was imprisoned in my addiction, I had craved sobriety more. During the moments when my grip almost unfastened, I called out to Him, and He lifted me above death. My daily dizziness and vertigo slowed me down, but in this despair, I continued to nourish my soul with His word. I realized this suffering was for a very specific reason. *Why would He grant me the physical healing and stable health I desired if that led me away from the amount of time I was now dedicating to Him?* Confusions slowly morphed into acceptance and understanding.

Flower and I shared a few positive days and many strenuous ones. She wanted things I could not currently provide. Her contentment was important to me, but I could not be the sole reason for her happiness. Ultimately, we each needed to heal and grow on our own. Feeling torn between continuing to fight through our discrepancies or a final breakup, I did not know what to do about our relationship. It was more than I could focus on if I was to remain sober. As I prayed about what to do, a Bible passage promptly dominated my mind. Jesus speaks in Matthew 18:6-7 (NKJV) saying, "But whoever causes one of these little ones who believe in Me to sin, it would be better for him if a millstone were hung around his neck, and he were drowned in the depth of the sea. Woe to the world because of offenses! For offenses must come, but woe to that man by whom the offense comes!"

I understood what this meant. She was a little one in her faith, and if any of my actions caused her to sin, well, the verse makes it very clear. I did not want our conflicts, or our intimacies and expulsions of such, nor any of my battles to cause her to sin. Every time I drank alcohol, it was easy to slide backwards into the old, sinful, immoral patterns. When I did not drink, I became shut off and reclusive. *Soon I must let her go, especially if I cause her to stumble in Christ. For now, all I can manage is to focus on sobriety, healing and growth in God.*

Would You?

On the top floor of the Prixon building, with views to the west and south, there is a communal deck. The space is modest, but it provides a few barbecue grills and a gas firepit for the residents to use and enjoy. During my drinking days, I would often come up to this sixth-floor airy loft in the evening with a mug full of wine and a book, and sometimes my chessboard in case some lone stranger had the will to play me. If the space was full, with either chatty residents or a raucous party, I would turn and leave, for despite my wine, I no longer desired to be around cacophony.

At the end of 2023, amid the season of alcohol sobriety round two, I preferred to only sit up top by the fire if no one else was there. Midweek evenings during the early winter sunsets were usually prime opportunities. On one such day, I sat bundled in layers, feet close to the edge of the cozy flames, body facing west, while observing deep rich orange hues fade into royal purples above the Cascade Mountains. Instead of wine, I had a steaming cup of turmeric-ginger tea, and instead of a chessboard, I carried my Bible. I smoked a cigarette alone, shifting my eyes from the sky to the passage I was reading. In these peaceful moments, once the sun had slipped beneath the volcanic mountain's silhouettes, the door behind me creaked open and the footsteps of one human approached. Disheartened at losing my solitude, I turned to see a man perhaps five years older than I carrying a six-pack of beer and donning a warm coat. He smiled and asked if it was alright to join me by the fire. "Of course," I smiled in return. "It was a beautiful sunset, but I doubt I will be up here much longer."

He nodded and agreed it had been a lovely one, as he had viewed it driving home from work. "But now I am ready to relax." He sat in the chair two over from me, cracked a variety of ale I used to enjoy, and emitted a long, satisfied sigh after his first gulp.

"I hope my cigarette isn't a bother to you." I stated, recognizing society's growing distaste for my calming habit. Although they gratifyingly acted as a social distancer, an effect I employed, here on this communal loft, smoking was not permitted.

"Not at all, smells good. Reminds me of my childhood. My old man always smoked. Do you want a beer?" The man generously offered, which I thanked and refused.

Returning the politeness of his bid, I lifted the tobacco held in my fingers. "Do you want one of these?"

The man leaned forward as if almost to say yes, then paused, sat back and waved it off. "Thanks, but I'm alright for now." He took another long drink of his beer, which caused the addiction in my body to somersault. I certainly wanted one of the locally brewed IPAs, but I must become comfortable being around alcohol while still holding strong in my abstinence. I nodded understandingly, smoked the last few drags and then discarded the butt into the firepit. As I did so, the man stated, "Are you enjoying your book of fairy tales there?" He snickered at my Bible.

I did not mind the question, nor was it rare, so I chuckled and responded, "I am enjoying it, but it is not fairy tales. It is the infallible Holy Word of God."

"Yes, I imagine you believe that." He shifted in his seat, settling in.

"Have you read it?" I leveled my voice with a direct tone.

He laughed abruptly. "No. But I know the gist, the classic Christian story." He applied air quotes as he articulated Christian story.

"Then how can you call it fairy tales if you haven't read it?" I spoke with an attitude of both defense and offense. "Is your opinion solely based on the opinions of others?" His eyes squinted into a slight glare, I continued. "It baffles me, well that isn't the right word, it truly irks me that so many are adamantly opposed and disdainful towards something they have never read nor sought to understand." Upon saying this, within myself I sensed a voice encouraging me to calm my tone, so I tried to soothe the energy with a kind smile.

"So, are you like, really religious then?" His tone changed from an attitude of condescension to one with a hint of impartiality.

I proceeded gently. "Not so much religious but more in an active relationship with God. I prefer the term faith rather than religion, for the latter connotes the idea of practices to achieve a spiritual goal, rules and traditions that if done will bring someone to heaven. We are saved through His grace, redeemed by His death and resurrection. He paid our debt. There is nothing we can do on our own to earn our way. One must believe, trust, repent and love Him. Jesus said, 'I am the way, the truth, and the life. No one comes to the Father except through Me.' (John 14:6 NKJV). And when we love Him, we desire and strive to obey Him."

"So, you really believe Jesus was raised from the dead, then, huh?" He eyed me with a bit of a comical look, as if he thought all I said was wacky.

"I do." I looked to the west and the fading light lingering as a hovering ribbon between the darkness above and darkness below. Within, I mulled whether I should stay and entertain his questions for a bit, or if I should go ahead and return to Wylie three floors below. The man didn't speak after my affirmation, *perhaps on his approach he was hoping he'd have the patio to himself as well.*

After a brief silence, with both of us settled into our chairs, he spoke again. "What is one reason you believe Jesus rose from the dead? That is, if He even existed or was even crucified."

I looked over to see that his demeanor was curious, so I decided to stay for at least this question. "There are a multitude of reasons I believe. First, many sources outside of scripture have corroborated Jesus' existence, even attesting to his miracles by the first century Jewish historian Flavius Josephus. But for myself, one of the most powerful testimonies is the incredible fervor, lived out for the rest of their lives, by the eyewitnesses of Jesus' death and resurrection. After His resurrection, He appeared to at least 500 people in His glorified body. And after Jesus' ascension to heaven, forty days after He rose from the dead, which was also widely observed, all the witnesses lived forth adamantly unwilling to deny what they had seen, even under the cost of persecution and death. Out of Jesus' twelve disciples, excluding Judas who died from suicide and John who survived unscathed from being thrown into a vat of boiling oil then lived into old age, but the rest of Jesus' disciples died brutally for their steadfast belief that He was indeed the risen Son of God." I paused to sip some tea which was getting cold, noticed my fire-mate was still listening and proceeded with slow, annunciated words. "To be tortured, persecuted and put to death, one must thoroughly trust in what they believe. There is zero room for doubt. From them, the church was born. By the thousands, people who listened to Jesus' disciples and the witnesses of Jesus' resurrection but had not seen the Son of God themselves, believed. The Holy Spirit, who is the divine and living presence of God, for God is three persons in one, known as the Holy Trinity comprising God the Father, God the Son and God the Holy Spirit, then indwells all believers." I tapped my Bible. "Just as Jesus had promised before His ascension in the Gospel of John and is described thoroughly in the book of Acts. This living Spirit of God cannot be known unless one has accepted His salvation. Therefore, a nonbeliever cannot understand just how mighty the Holy Spirit truly is. I believe in Him with all my heart, soul, mind and strength, but it took me far too long to surrender my life to Him. Wish I had sooner." I nodded and pursed my lips, signifying I was done for now.

The beer drinker sighed with less relief than when he first sat down, then sputtered apathetically, "Yes, one would have to believe something fully to die for it or just be a crazed lunatic. They all could have been loonies, you know."

I forced a chuckle and responded. "Well, you read the Sermon on the Mount, one of Jesus' most comprehensive public addresses, and tell me any of that was from a lunatic or told to lunatics. Interestingly, Robert Cole, a Harvard psychology professor, stated, 'All the writings on ethics over the past 2,000 years are simply footnotes to the Sermon on the Mount.' Therefore, Christianity most certainly did not originate nor was carried forth by any lunatics."

"Huh, okay then, say they weren't lunatics. I just don't see what is has to do with me. My whole life I have been happily not believing in God, and I still strive to live a moral life. I really don't care that you are reading your Bible. If that works for you, then good. I just don't like when Christians are out there being loud about it. I'm not saying you were. You were just here reading quietly, but many people."

I moved uneasily in my seat, ready to move on with my evening away from the smell, sound and sight of alcohol. However, I felt urged to say more. I could not just leave this man in his lost mental shrug without explaining our vital need for the Lord God Almighty. "It has to do with you, and each of us, because we all are sinners who deserve eternal death, separated from the glory of God. There is not a thing we can do to change that. Yet God is just. He is not unreasonable or sinister. However, His wrath towards all who reject Him is to be greatly feared. And in being just, the price for our sin must be paid. But not only is God just, He deeply loves us. Out of His immense love, Jesus paid our debt through the shedding of His blood, through His death and resurrection. He paid our debt for us, but we need to believe and accept it. Jesus did it all, man. Consider what He went through, a brutal public execution, flogged, tortured, killed slowly on a cross. A death that, as God, He did not have to do. He was and is blameless, pure, and yet He did it so that you and I might receive the eternal blessings of His love. He loves you so much that He died for you. But of course, He did not stay dead, and He will return." I paused with a grin and drank the last swig of my tea. The man remained silent, so I proceeded to answer the latter of his prior verbal disgruntlements. "As for why Christians are loud about it, is also purely out of love. Because they do not want you to suffer an eternity in hell. Whether or not you believe in hell, does not change the fact that it is real. Even more so, they must make it known to those who do not believe! Think about it this way. Say there is a road that winds through a rugged mountain landscape, carving in and out of gorges with steep rocky walls on either side. Every subsequent view is obscured. Around the next turn, there is a bridge across a deep chasm that has broken apart, destroyed, is no longer intact. Anyone who continues along this road will plunge to their deaths. Everyone who knows of this impending doom would then be compelled to tell everyone who does not know or believe about the bridge being broken to save them. It would be extremely cruel, the very opposite of decency and love, not to warn them adamantly. And yet they not only warn, but they also proclaim the lifesaving solution. It is then the driver's choice to either trust and humbly accept the solution, or pridefully ignore it and plummet to their demise. You can see that, right? And yet hell is far worse than simply plunging to an earthly death. It is eternal, horrible, inescapable suffering. Thus, they are out there, and now me right here, sharing the good news of Christ, our one true hope, entirely out of love. I must add, urge, and ultimately pronounce how vast eternity is. To our human minds, which understand things within constructs, beginning and ends, it is impossible to fathom. We throw around the simple eight-letter word, eternity, so often, but really think upon its depth. Forever, man. There is no end. Not one-thousand years, not millions, nor trillions, it never ends. The life we live here on earth is less than even a scratch compared to eternity, and yet this is our only chance. We must not waste it."

The man set his empty can onto the ground and reached for another beer. The crisp snap of it opening caused shudders to ripple through my body. I had to get off the patio, but I must first listen to what the man had to say in response. He drank and then spoke, "Alright, I suppose that makes sense. But I don't know. There are a lot of beliefs in this world. Plenty that have nothing to do with some eternity beyond here. Mine is just to stay in my lane, work hard, and things like that."

My addiction anxiety intensified. *I must get far away from the alcohol, and this guy doesn't seem to want to even consider the truth,* but the need to at least leave him with a new sense of considered perspective held me a moment longer. After a deep breath, a quick silent prayer and a glance back to the sky, I stated, "No one wants their lives to be disturbed. But it is of utmost worth to seek for the more, for the truth, rather than shutting it out. Seek and ye shall find, man. You owe it to yourself. Everyone does. It would be more than an awful shame not to give oneself a real chance. For what otherwise, stubborn pride?" I grabbed my empty mug, placed my cigarette pack and lighter in my jacket pocket, tucked the Bible under my arm and rose to make my way to the door. The man forced a smile and remained silent, perhaps thinking about my words or maybe just looking forward to my departure. "A rhetorical question before I go." He looked towards me again after he rolled his eyes. "And I challenge you to contemplate the why of your answer. If you were to seek, and you were to truly, humbly, listen for Him, and you were to understand that God has in fact already revealed Himself to each one of us within all His creation, would you allow yourself the chance to believe in Him then? If you gave yourself a genuine opportunity and read His Word, read the Gospel story of Jesus and you felt convicted in the Truth, would you strive to follow Him then? If you were to come to an understanding of what our separation from Him means, would you repent and follow Him?" I stood for a moment, a few steps from the door, letting my questions linger in the air. I tried my best to speak tenderly, but so much urgency filled my heart, yearning for him to care. He heard me. The look on his face made it apparent, yet it was also clear he was choosing to shut it all out. "Alright, man," I concluded encouragingly. "In the New Testament, read the books of John and Romans, but it's up to you. I will be praying for you, and I hope you have a restful evening."

The man jabbed with a harsh tone as I turned my back to leave. "Damn, dude, don't pray for me. I really don't care. If all my friends are going to hell, then I might as well go too. I see what you are saying and challenging me to consider, but humble myself?" The man scoffed, swigged his beer and then leaned back in his chair.

His tone affected me to leave him with a final thought. "There is a wonderful quote by C.S. Lewis which puts it into perspective. He said,

'Christianity, if false, is of no importance, and if true, of infinite importance. The only thing it cannot be is moderately important.'" I let the words hang in the silent air. "I will pray you dwell on it deeply. Read God's Word, seek Him. You do not know what you scoff at, and that is dangerous. Truth does not change just because you choose to shut it out." The door closed behind me as I departed. Sometimes when I aspired to be alone, God held other plans for His own reasons.

In my heart, I prayed for the man, that our brief conversation would remain within him and his heart would soften towards God. That he would recognize God all around him and perhaps, maybe, someday, humble himself enough to come to know Him. *Wouldn't that be amazing*, I considered as I scurried down the stairwell steps avoiding the vertigo triggering elevator, rushing to Wylie to take her for a walk to the east away from the liquor store, *if the whole reason I ended up living here was to have a simple conversation with that guy. I may never know the outcome, but if he does come to know the heavenly Father through Christ, it would make this entire Prixon year worth it.* In prayer I added, *Lord, please open that man's heart to You. Wherever I am, I shall keep sowing seeds. May there be ears that hear. Please keep working in me and through me. Help me learn how to share Your Word precisely and effectively. Help me grow, Lord. I am nothing without You, Father. Thank You for placing me where You want me, even when I don't understand it. All of me trusts all of You. In Jesus' name, Amen.*

CINEREAL

If He, then I

On January 5, 2024, I retreated from my urban apartment to a small log cabin in the forest. Alone with Wylie on the western flanks of the Pacific Crest, nestled in Grand Fir trees by a lake safe from the mayhem of the masses, I bathed in a silence I so direly craved. The cabin was one of maybe fifteen others on an incline above the water, a part of a small resort which bustled in the summer yet hibernated in the winter. When I arrived, I saw no other humans. Only two long-bed pickup trucks dormant in front of the caretakers' quarters signaled any sign of activity. I had already received my cabin door code from the forest service website, so there was no need to seek anyone out. The sun would set soon. Once I unloaded my supplies for the three nights I paid to hide away in the one-room modest structure, and the rumble of my ride withdrew to whence it had come, Wylie and I walked down to the lake to sit upon the shoreline. From above where the eagles fly, the lake must appear lost beneath the evening mist, but under this somber blanket, the water stood as still and clear as glass.

I exhaled a long, silent breath, releasing all the angst incurred in town. Here I could finally relax, listen, and fully be without holding on to an edge of gritting, flexing self-protection. Free from the tumultuous racket of truck engines peeling out of parking lots, from the arguments of disgruntled couples, the vulgar yells of teenagers loitering outside the store below my Prixon window, and the banal banter from tech guys partying on the sixth-floor patio between their bumps of cocaine and vodka swigs. Free from the obnoxious whine of leaf blowers, shrill car alarms, the perpetual questioning if I was alright, and the incessant hum of electricity in the air. Here I was temporarily emancipated from all the grime, Wi-Fi and unabating noise that society produces.

Wylie sat beside me calmly, understanding we were home. Home in the forest, in a land much like her birth and location of my true happiness. Although it was winter, not a single patch of snow dotted the landscape. *The precipitation is late this year, but perhaps it is there in the clouds waiting for our arrival.*

CINEREAL

I could smell the humidity mounting, sense the possibility of a pending storm in the condensing grays above us. A chilly breeze navigated its way across the placid lake, revealing its direction by the tender undulations it created in the water and in the gentle waver of evergreen boughs. One ripple after another neared where we sat until reaching us, applying all the woodland scents it carried upon our faces. Wylie smiled, as did I. We glanced at each other with agreeing eyes, but we needn't speak anything, for in this paradise our communication was like every living plant around us.

There would be no visible sunset on our first evening, so after exploring a portion of the lakeside trail, we returned to the cabin to organize our lodging for the next few days. *Organize*, I thought. *When I first moved to Bend, I called it "Oregonize."* I chuckled at this memory while unpacking supplies. The cabin itself was a four-walled square space smaller than a single-car garage. It provided a two-burner gas cooking stove and an ordinary gas fireplace with flames that mimicked a wood-fire. The walls were not thick enough to hold industrial insulation, so I joyfully put on a sweater and arranged my food. I only brought the necessities of camp chow, a diet much like I would carry on my long hikes. *Tonight, will be a simple meal of baked beans, beef jerky, bread and an apple for dessert.*

After eating, I inspected the bed. It was old and saggy. I dragged the worn mattress onto the floor and spread out my sleeping bag upon it, the same tattered bag from my Pacific Crest Trail hike. My backpack and jacket I would use for a pillow. The gallon jugs of water I set beneath the one small table after making a hot cup of tea. While my beverage steeped, I ventured out to locate the bathhouse and then returned to settle on the small porch to read, smoke and write until succumbing to slumber. Just as my eyes started to ache from staring intently at words I could barely see, I looked up to spot a few snowflakes beginning to fall from the dark sky. Wylie and I exchanged delighted expressions. The winter weather had finally arrived.

~~~

We awoke to a world transformed. The dry brown day of yester was now a landscape covered in fresh snow. At least twelve inches had fallen in the night, and the flakes still descended heavily. With little breeze in the air, all was calm. Only the gentle patter of flakes meeting trees and cabins stirred a nearly muted hum. Staring across the lake into a world of monochrome haze exasperated my delicate brain. I knew not to gaze directly at the falling motion, or far off into a visually consuming distance, for I had been learning how to avoid vertigo triggers. Instead, my observation fixed upon nearby steadfast tree trunks as we galloped into the powder. I ate breakfast by a stream in the forest far from the cabins. The stark difference between the dark water flowing towards the lake and the billowing colorless mounds teetering on the edge emphasized the amount of accumulation. I chewed slowly, absorbing each second of peace as if in heaven itself. Peering beyond our exploration, the snowy swaddle remained undisturbed, yet looking from where we had come, our tracks showed our venture of solitude was a success. Wylie's and I's were the only ones. Large plops fell from the boughs above, creating sudden craters in the thick white floor. I laughed with the glee of a child and in return Wylie romped in circles around me while we progressed deeper into the Narnia-like land. When the chill reached our bones, we turned around and returned to the cabin for coffee, only to set out into our forest adventure after the hot drink had warmed my body from within.

Waking up in a place where the soul feels most content allows the mind to rummage through the mental lists it amassed in the pandemonium of "back there" and ponder clearly upon each item with no distractions. My friend Max and I had recently been discussing the idea of "building our new roads." For me, this new road, path, trail, whatever I wanted to call it, was the way of sobriety from alcohol. For so long, my road had been that of constant alcohol consumption. It is what I was used to, the way my brain was comfortable with. Now I was challenging my brain to operate in new ways. I was rewiring my mind. With each additional sober day and each decision not to drink at a time I previously would, my road and mentality towards sobriety matured. Max was a supportive friend in this venture, as he too, along with Hest, had been reducing their alcohol intake and even deciding to go long stints without a drink. They did not battle the same addiction as I, but they also recognized the harm of ingesting poison and the value of its opposite. Their shared focus helped me not to feel as alone in my alcohol sobriety battles.

"Yes, Wylie Wizzle!" My black dog smiled with her snout covered in powder as I chimed her name. "I am creating a new road girl, a cleaner, stronger, far more beneficial road than the one I traveled for so long. It benefits both of us. You like this new road, don't you?" She tilted her head playfully, then turned and zoomed up a slope, stopping once she could not see me, and then she zoomed right back to my feet again. Her black body darted through white accumulation as thick as she was tall. I hooted and proceeded further into the idyllic landscape, enjoying the fact that she could roam the forest as she pleased.

Another new road I had been building and traveling upon was my relationship with God. Much like my alcohol path, too much of my life had been off this godly way. Now that I was back on it, intentionally focused and trusting Him, no hardship, suffering or difficulty in life held any negative weight. I was with Him and He with me. As Isaiah 41:13 (NKJV) states, "For I, the Lord your God, will hold your right hand, saying to you, 'Fear not, I will help you.'" The confidence one can have in the Lord when they walk with Him is unlimited. The strength one has in the Lord is a well that shall never go dry as His strength is omnipotent and eternal. Such incredible secure joy this provides. Onward through the snow, Wylie and I explored until we both collapsed in euphoria, staring up into laden tree boughs. *They are the decor of our beautiful ceiling, and He is my stalwart fortress.* I pulled a ham and cheese sandwich out of my pocket that I had prepared at the cabin for a moment like this. I ate all but the last bite, which I gave to my darling, drooling companion.

When we returned to the small resort, concealed by the sky's generous emission, the rumble of one truck hummed acceptably in the air. The noise of a plow scraping dirt beneath the white indicated work was being done. Wylie and I warmed ourselves by the cabin's small pseudo-woodstove. I hung my wet clothes to dry and pulled my alpaca sweater around my body. We sat on the porch and watched as the plow occasionally grumbled by. I nodded to the man driving the old truck, and he nodded in return, perhaps appreciating that I was here renting a cabin when all the others sat empty. *He is probably wondering where my vehicle is, but it is as I prefer, unattached to things of the world with nothing but a backpack, shelter and two legs on which I could walk into the wilderness and forever disappear.* I laughed again at this delightful idea. In fact, all day I had never ceased laughing. My transportation would return for me once the short vacation ended, and then I would jump into that vehicle gratefully, thanking Flower for her willingness to help me retreat to my off-grid woodland getaway, but as always, I enjoyed reminiscing the seasons of long trail freedom, when no car was needed, only appreciated.

~~~

As evening set in and the sun hidden behind the storm clouds dimmed its passive shine, the wind returned. The snow continued to fall, but no longer did it descend gently. It ravaged through the air as a multitude of innocuous bullets on a determined sideways slice. I focused my mind on the intention I had saved for this getaway, forgiveness. God had stirred this need in my heart recently, but back at the Prixon it was difficult to focus upon completely amid the turmoil of circumstances and commotion. I had written a long list of things in my life I was grateful for, and when my thoughts drifted into angst, to this list I returned, rereading, re-centering and continuing to add to it. I knew my struggles paled compared to the blessings I had, yet no matter how much I prayed and meditated upon the good, an unrelenting anger I carried for many years persistently festered. *Where was this anger coming from? Why must I continue to sway between the light and dark?* Like a pendulum, one day I was filled with joy and the next I was filled with bitterness. For so long it acted like a cancer, pillaging my body. This anger, this tormenting, terrible root shooting tendrils into each nerve. Finally, through prayer, I fathomed exactly the source of the rage. And yet, it scared me to face it, to forgive it, to let it go, as if holding on to the animosity was giving me some reason, some excuse, some… "Ah, it is time. If He will, then I must. I must, I must!" Wylie glanced up from her fox-pose cozy curled position on my sleeping bag as I audibly murmured and paced inside the cabin.

Releasing an exhale of decision, I sat down on the floorboards and turned to Colossians 3:12-14 (NKJV) to read the passage I had known since I was an adolescent. "Therefore, as the elect of God, holy and beloved, put on tender mercies, kindness, humility, meekness, long-suffering; bearing with one another, and forgiving one another, if anyone has a complaint against another; even as Christ forgave you, so you also must do. But above all these things put on love, which is the bond of perfection."

I paused, praying to the Lord to provide me the strength to forgive whom I must. Then, turning to another verse, I read.

Ephesians 4:31-32 (NKJV) "Let all bitterness, wrath, anger, clamor, and evil speaking be put away from you, with all malice. And be kind to one another, tenderhearted, forgiving one another, even as God in Christ forgave you."

Another one, as I needed His Word to fill and nourish my soul. My body trembled knowing what I was about to sincerely do. Like standing on the edge of a cliff before heaving a trusting leap into cold alpine water below.

CINEREAL

Here, I chose a passage from the Sermon on the Mount, a time when Jesus spoke to thousands.

Matthew 5:43-45 (NKJV) "You have heard that it was said, 'You shall love your neighbor and hate your enemy.' But I say to you, love your enemies, bless those who curse you, do good to those who hate you, and pray for those who spitefully use you and persecute you, that you may be sons of your Father in heaven; for He makes His sun rise on the evil and on the good, and sends rain on the just and on the unjust."

Yes, just as my Father in heaven forgave me, wretched terrible me, then I too must forgive. It is time. And so, I bowed my head and prayed these words. "Oh Father, holy perfect Lord, I thank You for Your love and guidance. For so long I have held a vehement anger in my heart towards the man who sexually assaulted me in Colorado, and the man, or men, who tried to kill me in January 2020. For so long I have blocked their faces from my mind, swept all memory of it under my mental rug, ignored it, run from it, hated them, hated them so deeply and yet, I cannot hate them anymore. I need to love them too. I need to forgive them. Father, please give me this strength and hear me as I say with all my heart and soul that I will no longer hold on to this anger. Just as You have forgiven me and just as You love every soul on this earth and desire for them to love You, so I will also love them. I forgive them. Wherever they are, and whomever they are, please send Your love down into their hearts. Please soften them and turn their minds and souls to You. Since they too are loved by You than they too shall be loved by me. No longer will I think hatefully of them, but only lovingly. I let it go, Lord, I let all my strife go. With Christ-like love, I forgive them, and with love, I pray for them to find You and to accept Your gift of salvation. Please, Lord, save them. Your love is whole and true, and that is the love I strive to love with. I am Yours, Father, and I pray that someday they will be Yours as well. In Jesus' name, Amen."

As I slowly lifted my head from prayer, tears poured out of my eyes, down my face, dripping onto the cabin floor. An immense weight lifted from my entire being. I let it go. I forgave them. I chose and will continue to choose to love every single person, no matter the harm and hatred anyone produces. Forever forward with love, never backwards with animosity. Trembling, I stood and smiled at Wylie, who was peering compassionately at my emotions. "It's alright girl, everything is going to be alright." I rubbed her head, drank some water, wiped my face clean and smiled. "Wow, Lord, truly wow, thank You, Father." I couldn't help but feel a powerful sense of awe through my entire body for Him. I but His quivering child, trying my hardest, leaning into Him. *He is with me, guiding me, and this forgiveness was long overdue.* I could not know what these men thought, where they were, or even exactly who they were, but no longer did I wish them anything but the greatest gift of Christ's salvation. And with that, I made myself a cup of tea, sat on the porch and watched the central Oregon snow continue to fall upon our magnificently beautiful planet.

~~~

As the days of January clicked by at the Prixon, I read books on sobriety, prayed and studied the Bible daily, filled time with exercise, writing, and practicing vertigo patience. On Wylie and I's frequent long walks, I kept my head turned away from all moving vehicles and flashing lights so as not to disturb the brain. Each meal tasted far more delicious than when paired with alcohol. Flavors popped, emotions stabilized, and my internal anger had been eliminated. In many ways, it seemed like I was doing alright. There is a phrase I heard everywhere, on televised shows, in movies, from my friends, a phrase I had often used, which now maddened me every time I heard it. The phrase "I need a drink." Although stated casually, seemingly innocently woven into the fabric of our society, it acted so powerfully in holding people to the assumption that they did indeed need a drink to feel better, to handle stressful situations, or to celebrate an event or achievement. This weak-minded wording tormented the core of my being. I despised that it was everywhere. The more I focused on its opposite, the more I heard it. I stopped watching any shows or movies altogether, refrained from entering any establishment that served alcohol, and hid away from the world in my awful box of an apartment.

However, my frustration and shedding of all things went too far. I took this out on Flower, pushing her away with no warning or closure. Obsessed with the compulsion of riddance, it appeared as if I was winning, winning the battle against alcohol addiction. In retrospect, I recognize that the deceiver was utilizing even this against me. God in His convictions through the Holy Spirit warned me of my behavior. I was not winning, but rather proudly veering into the mindset of my self-control. I aspired to cast all my cares upon God, and thought I was, yet when it came to anything with alcohol, I gripped the situation in my hand and ran away from it. The danger of this mindset remained obscured by my sober arrogance. So much so that the very temper I held against alcohol ironically brought me back to it. While hiding away from the world, forcing myself to grit through, depriving myself of community, friendship, support, things I direly needed, I eventually snapped.

It started with the confidence that I had indeed conquered my addiction. The circumstances I built for myself bolstered it. So many erected walls surrounded me that no one could know if I drank. "If I indeed do not need alcohol, then why would a little bit of wine hurt? I will not get drunk; I will simply reward myself for how well I have been doing." Speaking these words like a blind madman, inadvertently ignoring God and all previous goals and priorities, in this haughtiness, I formed a plan. Alone in my apartment, no one could frown upon its foolishness. The plan would aid my writing, or so I alleged. I had been working on my Louisiana novel, a true story dear to my heart, and by rewarding myself with one bottle of wine for every 10,000 words written, there would be no way I could abuse drinking. That would mean, in my imprudent assumption, I would only consume a bottle of wine, a paltry four drinks, every three to four days, which would encourage me to write many words each day. To my deceived alcoholic mind, it seemed like a foolproof plan, a win-win.

As soon as deciding this arrangement, while looking out the window at the liquor store, knowing I was about to walk across the street instead of determining, "I will not drink today," a flurry of disagreement surged in my soul. But this warning I ignored, convincing myself everything would be alright. After all, "I do not NEED a drink. This is a well-earned treat."

The first bottle of wine tasted like victory. *I have succeeded!* Stupidly, I announced within. *I have conquered the grip alcohol had over me.* The voice of addiction spoke differently than it had to lure me into my first relapse. Casually sipping the four glasses over four hours, I did not get drunk, nor drink whiskey, and when the bottle was empty, I carried on with no need to buy more. Having been fully sober from alcohol for longer than the first round, I had solved the intricate puzzle. *I can now carry on with my life as a mature drinker in moderation.* In this deception, I wrote for the next few days until reaching another 10,000 words. At which exciting point, I hustled across the street and purchased another bottle of wine. "Oh, how marvelous this is, Wylie! The Prixon ain't so bad when I do it like this!" While tipsily skipping around my apartment, dancing and singing to my dog, I ignored every text and call, continuing to hide away in my addiction. Even Wylie knew I was a fool.

The pattern of my stupid plan only lasted a few rounds. After one week of writing and sporadic bottles, in the early days of February after arguing again against the woman who loved me, I spiraled into wretched alcoholic Wing. On a gray day while snow spit sporadic flurries from the sky, in my exhaustion of attempting to walk the line of moderation, I looked at my Bible then turned away and stated, "Screw it." Straight to CDubs I ran, the bar my Christian friend had worried I might turn into a second home. With a returned contempt towards my weakness, I ordered a shot of whiskey, then another and another, until weeping in my returned boozy emotions on the back patio over a pint of beer next to an ashtray full of my cigarette butts.

While wallowing in my whiskey drunk, I texted Rad asking him to come have a drink with me. I missed him dearly and figured if I was already drinking, we might as well spend time together as we used to. He said no to alcohol but agreed to pick me up for a calming tea away from the bar. In the moment this exasperated me, but eventually I would look back and understand he was being a supportive friend. We sipped our wholesome beverages by the river on my favorite bench. The Cascade Mountains bearing the Pacific Crest Trail dressed our horizon as I poured out my discouraged soul. Rad listened and spoke mildly without judgement. After the sun had set, he drove me home.

I knew I'd fallen hard. The relapse discouraged me. But I also knew I must not let it imprison me into another long season of alcohol as I had before. I called and apologized to Flower, and she promptly came to my aid. That night I decided to stop before my addiction trapped me again. And yet the next day I suffered another seizure. It was too late. Although it had been such a short time of drinking, my body already remembered that it could not live without the booze. The tenacity of my addiction was frightening. Flower knew what to do. She ran across the street to the liquor store, purchased the items I requested with the cash I handed her, then returned to my side. My body and brain teetered on the fringe of death once again, exhausted by the seizure, worn down by decades of poison. I decided not to tell my doctor, desiring as few people to know as possible. And again, I would try to step the consumption down on my own, avoiding another dangerous health episode and ultimately returning to my sober road. "How fast I have fallen! How deep my addiction is rooted! Why did I throw it all away? Why did I trade my sobriety for the prison I thought I had escaped? I am a weak wretch…" I exclaimed these statements with self-ridicule to Flower as she held Wylie on the couch. And yet God reminded me that on my own I would continue to fall, but with Him all things were possible.

Each day I tried to drink less, but every other day I slipped up and drank more. The old destructive pattern devoured me. On Thursdays, I went bowling and did not drink, hiding the relapse from my teammates. They knew, they could tell, for my body shook with each roll, my eyes appeared as if I was mourning, my usual confidence fluttered as a dying moth. Max asked me if I was alright. To his question, I honestly confessed my second relapse.

"Don't be so hard on yourself, Wing, remember that new road you've been building. Return to that road." He placed his hand on my shoulder and offered an encouraging smile.

"Don't be so hard on myself!?" I retorted. "I am always hard on myself; I must be. When I was a kid, if I made an error on the baseball field, if I didn't place the baseball exactly on the edge of the strike zone like I intended, I would practice that play and pitch hundreds of times until I eliminated all errors. If I do anything wrong, I must practice it until I do it right. I messed up, and I will be furiously hard on myself with this. But I will get it right."

Max listened with understanding, while maintaining his kind smile. With patience he spoke, "I have always admired your drive, Wing. You are tenacious. But there is a difference between striving to grow and beating yourself up for mistakes. You know this. Remember what you tell me when we bowl a bad frame? You say, 'We cannot change what has happened, let it go. Don't let the past bad shot affect your next one.' You are mentally strong in your competitions. I admire that about you, but you need to utilize that mental strength in your battles toward alcohol sobriety as well. Use that asset here. You need to let it go and move forward. You cannot change that you drank, but you can be kinder to yourself. Encourage yourself. Don't mentally beat yourself up. Forgive yourself and get back on that new road."

~~~

As the end of February and the end of my Prixon lease approached, I frantically searched for a new place to move. I had been scouring all available housing listings for months, but the lack of availability in my price range and location needs remained extremely slim. I could not stay at the Prixon any longer and prayed daily that it would be God's will for me to move on from the apartment complex. My ideal spot would be a one-bedroom or studio, no shared space, plus contain a small yard for gardening and Wylie. I needed to sit under the stars at night and remain sober, but first I must detox, again.

"Ahh, there are so many agains!" I paced back and forth in front of Flower. "But I will not hold on to my failures. They happened. I accept them. I must only move forward, and I can only do so with my heavenly Father as my strength." We discussed my relationship with alcohol, God and ourselves. We agreed I would face this detox with Him in Spirit, with Wylie curled by, but me on my own. "If I cannot get sober, I do not deserve to leave the Prixon. I must get through this without any medical care. I have anti-seizure pills. The same ones I took at detox, which the doctor prescribed me for emergencies, and this is an emergency. Plus, I can get my hands on more benzos if I need to. I know it is a risk, but I must physically do this alone with only God and Wylie by my side. I trust Him. He knows my heart. He knows how deeply I yearn to live without alcohol despite my failings."

Flower listened to my rant with tears in her eyes. She did not want to go. Even though in my frenzy I decided that we mutually agreed I would detox alone, in this she was not of the same attitude. She loved me and wanted to remain by my side. Yet every time I drank, I faded into my alcoholism, and every time I didn't drink, I pushed her away. She did not deserve the back and forth pull on her heart. In my drenched mental furry I could not perceive anything clearly. I could not see her, only a tunnel, and that tunnel seemed like one I was furiously digging, trying to get back out of the torrid, boozy underworld I perpetually descended into.

Six days before the end of February, I drank my last drink of alcohol, again. In the morning, Flower left with her packed bag as I ingested my first round of pills. For three days I lay in the fetal position and gripped my fingers into my brain. I ingested the anti-seizure drugs at intervals based on what I had learned in my previous two medical detoxes and a Harvard Medical report I studied online. Three times a day I stumbled outside with Wylie into the harsh parking lot so she could go to the bathroom across the asphalt in the grass. Minute by minute I breathed intentionally, repeating, "Trust in the Lord with all your heart and lean not on your own understanding."

At times as I lay in bed, I wept, saddened by the pain I had been causing Flower. Once I began detoxing, my actions glared harshly. I did not want to hurt her, but I was yet to know how to balance everything in my life. "Please,

CINEREAL

Lord, forgive me for the pain I've caused Flower. Forgive me for my continual sin. Please help me to truly grow. Renew a spirit that honors You within me. Please help Flower heal. Guide and protect her in all ways. I am Yours, Father. Thank You, Jesus, for all You have done, for paying the debt I owed that I could not pay." I knew He forgave me and trusted He would protect her. He gave His one and only Son, who died and rose from the dead. He forgave all my sins, past, present and future, when He atoned for our sins on the cross, when I placed my faith in Him. *He is good, He is love, He is merciful and full of grace. His incredible gift, I have received. In this faith, no matter where we are in life, I and Flower and all who believe in Him are eternally His. There is no greater safety than this.* Ephesians 1:7 (NKJV) "In Him we have redemption through His blood, the forgiveness of sins, according to the riches of His grace."

During the detox, I received a text from a friend. She asked whether I was still searching for a new place to live. Aware of my limitations and needs, she announced she knew of the perfect spot. I contacted the landlord and within hours, pending approval, the place could be mine. I laid back with tired relief, humbled by God's greatness, thanking Him. It was obvious, despite all my worries, God provided exactly what I needed at exactly the right time.

Finally, I reached the seventy-two-hour mark of no alcohol. The body successfully detoxified without experiencing any seizures or heart attacks. I was back on the sober road and had even potentially secured a new place to live. Over the telephone, I excitedly relayed the news to my mother. Together we praised God's enduring goodness.

The next day I visited the new prospective home and signed the lease. It was little more than a glorified shed, with a tile floor and plumbing. But it was a small stand-alone studio on the ground, an additional dwelling unit behind a larger home and perfect for me. A small private fenced yard was included, and just enough indoor space to fit my simple belongings. Additionally, the abode sat in a peaceful neighborhood close to the Deschutes River and an organic grocery market, tucked away from all taverns, liquor stores and late-night boisterous activity. *The writing shed. That is what I shall call it. And soon I shall finally be able to get another piano! He is looking out for me,* I joyfully acknowledged, beaming enthusiastically and hustling back to Wylie.

CINEREAL

There was a lot to do in a short time. *First, inform the Prixon I am leaving. Next, pack everything, scrub the entire apartment with white vinegar and hot water, and hire someone to help me move. Max has a truck and a trailer. If I pay him a proper day's wage, and he agrees, we could complete the transition in one day.* Logistical thoughts eagerly rushed through my head as footsteps scurried me to the claustrophobic cube hoisted three floors above a parking lot. Refreshed, sober energy filled my body. Occasionally, suddenly, the vertigo would mercilessly strike, forcing me to stop until it abated, but then at the pace I could handle, I resumed the required busyness of my last Prixon days.

On the last night of February, I stared out the window at the liquor store sign for the last time, allowing my mind to slow down. "Be still and know that He is God," I murmured. Earnest prayer to the Almighty consumed my mind. It was then, just as Max had said, that I finally, thoroughly forgave myself. I had forgiven the ones who hurt me, but I too was one who had been hurting me. *Since God forgave me, then shouldn't I too? Yes, if He will and did, then I must.* As soon as I genuinely forgave myself, all the self-loathing that had developed from my relapse disappeared. For that is where anger thrives, in a heart of unforgiveness. When I forgave those who hurt me, the anger I once held was abolished. And when I forgave myself, my inward resentment dissolved. Pride upholds anger. The enemy deceives us into thinking we must control all things. But no, we must simply, sincerely, humbly, give every single emotion and control to Him. Let Him guide us, trust Him with all, for His love is pure.

On March 1, 2024, Max helped me move out of the Prixon and into my new home, the writing shed. The turmoil of the past year faded into awe and gratitude. Humbled and revived, I finally sat outside again. My chair faced west, just as it had at the Prixon, but now there was no liquor store. Instead, only the neighborhood fences, treetops and colors of a magnificent sunset displayed before me. Psalm 19:1 (NKJV) entered my mind, just as it had atop Mount Thielsen. Yet unlike then, I did not tremble fearfully for rejecting of the Almighty, rather, I sat swaddled in an incredible peace, my soul safe in the assurance of His love and promises. I whispered the words of the verse as bold hues faded, and stars appeared in the celestial canopy. "The heavens declare the glory of God; and the firmament shows His handiwork." After some time in prayerful silence with Him, I observed my new small yard. Although it was nothing more than a rectangle patch of dirt, in the night's cool air I started planning my new glorious garden. *Take what*

CINEREAL

you are given and make the most of it. To start, I will gather supplies and build soil beds, but tonight I shall rest.

CINEREAL

Angels, Demons & The Lion

Two months and a few days after moving out of the Prixon and into the writing shed, amid a rejuvenating breeze in early May, I sat outside a coffee shop in the morning hours anticipating the confirmed arrival of a new Christ-loving friend. She and others I had met at a church God directed me to, in His creative signaling ways. My participation was limited, as indoor cacophony mangled my injured brain, twisting stability into a hazy void of erratic static and vertigo. Despite this chronic struggle, I eagerly attended as frequently as I could manage. My awe and appreciation of how He works continued to increase, as He provides exactly what one requires. He knew I needed a Biblically focused community, and even on the days I could not partake, He nourished my soul with His word, delivering peace and mental rest through His promises, understanding through His guidance and companionship through His steadfast fellowship. At this specific cafe meeting, I had a very important story to impart. In preparation, I breathed calmly and prayed silently. Not a single drop of alcohol had been consumed since moving into the new abode. Each dawn presented as a precious gift. With over sixty days sober from alcohol consecutively behind me, every moment acted as a lustrous new horizon. *Much like climbing to the top of another mountain and viewing land ahead I was about to dive into for the first time,* I considered, ready to share the story which served as an unbreakable root within. Life was not easy. My brain still incessantly rose and fell like a boat at sea. My body remained confused. Learning how to interact soberly without social anxiety was in process. Maturely handling triggers and emotions without alcohol endured as a duty, a duty I focused upon patiently and intently. But amidst this work, my mind was sharp and clear, and my soul confidently serene.

"So, Wing," once settled at the table I chose for us, Reina sat holding a decadent latte. Following our salutations and a sip from her artistically poured beverage, she curiously entered the topic we had met to discuss.

CINEREAL

"What is this wild story from your youth about angels and demons you have only alluded to?"

"Ah yes, it is time to reveal in detail what I experienced. Many do not comprehend these events. Therefore, I tell it sparingly, but I know you will understand, as you also trust the Lord and believe in His omnipotence."

She nodded and smiled, folding both hands snugly around her café branded cup. I gazed up at the heavens and began.

"Foremost, as I like to preface all my important stories, I must explain to you the context. After the context, a visual map of the land where the events took place. And then, exactly what happened upon the land."

"A layered approach to convey it properly, got it." Reina accepted the outline for my narrative.

"Yes, exactly." I picked up my dark drip coffee, sipped, set it back down and proceeded. "When I was twelve years of age, I went to camp at a place called New England Frontier Camp in the forests of Lovell, Maine. Nestled next to Kezar Lake, I spent a few of my young summers, learning to sail, water ski, practicing archery, strengthening woodland survival skills and competing in sports. Along with all the recreational activities, NEFC was Biblically focused, geared towards providing the tools to develop boys into someday, godly men. The region was beautiful. Dense woodland with many trails by the lake. A rustic place I loved and still reminisce fondly about. Everything about the camp, produced joyous summers."

Reina acknowledged, "Sounds like your parents discovered the ideal spot."

I nodded in agreement. "Oh yes, they certainly did. It was a wonderland to me. This specific summer there was a bully, much larger than I, as I was a medium child. The bully kept picking on one of my smaller, younger friends from our church back home. For the sake of the story, I will call the bully, Billy. One day I saw Billy really hassling my friend, so without hesitation I confronted him, demanding that Billy cease his harassment, but he did not, so I punched him in the stomach. Billy then turned his strength from my friend to me. We fought a scrappy skirmish until the camp counselor broke it up. Furious at us, the camp counselor, who was a young man himself, no older than probably twenty-two, tried to determine our punishment after listening to both of our reasons for the fight. It was clear to the counselor that something must be done, so he drew a large circle in the dirt and told us that if we wanted to fight, we must do so with rules. Into the circle, Billy and I went. The rules, no punches, but whoever wrestled the other out of the circle first would win and the loser would have to clean all the dishes after dinner. A chore none of us desired. We agreed, and when the counselor counted down, along with the boys gathered around, and everyone shouted 'go,' the match was on. It did not last long, for though Billy was stronger, I was faster. When he came barreling towards me, I faked one way, forcing his momentum in the direction I wanted, then I jumped aside and pushed his bulky body out of the sphere. Everyone cheered, except for bitter Billy in the dirt. The contest was over. As a respectable competitor, I reached my hand out to Billy to help him off the ground, but he madly refused my offer. I felt sympathetic towards him, as all week he had carried a mean attitude, and I knew he must have some internal issues we did not understand. I may have been standing up for my friend, but I wanted to befriend Billy as well. Billy is the main character in my upcoming event, so now that you know who he is, I will explain to you the lay of the land."

"Alright then. Step one achieved." Reina's eyes and words relayed invested interest.

"Aye," I confirmed. "Step two. New England Frontier Camp sprawled across many acres. To the west sat the main lodge, dining hall, marina and lake, but that doesn't concern this story. To the south was a large woodland firepit, called the amphitheater, one of many firepits at the camp but the one you need to know. Nearly half-a-mile north, up a small hill, were the campers' cabins. Between the cabins and the amphitheater, lay large soccer fields and a full-size basketball court. A forested trail connected this firepit to the fields, then on to the basketball court, which sat below a little hill leading to the campers' lodging cabins. The court had a tall, lofted ceiling above its cement floor, but it had no walls. This is important. Thick metal beams held up the roof. Between these beams, there was nothing but open air where walls could have been, allowing anyone to walk onto or view the court from any side. The route everyone trekked when going from the soccer field to their cabin would be to cut straight across the court, under the roof and out the northern side, up the small hill. Atop this slope on the left lay a large bathhouse with showers, toilets and such, and further beyond were the cabins with our bunks. All of this is crucial to comprehending the story."

I pretended to draw the described map with my finger on our outdoor coffee table. Amphitheater firepit, trail, sports fields, basketball court, hill, bathhouse, cabins. Reina conveyed that she understood the layout.

CINEREAL

"Alright, now that the context and map are laid out, here is what happened." I raised my eyebrows, expressing the supernatural occurrences to come. "One summer night, about twenty of us boys, including Billy and me, and a few camp counselors were enjoying a post-sunset bonfire at the amphitheater. We were roasting marshmallows, building s'mores, singing camp songs, telling stories, everyone gathered around happily except for Billy, who paced nervously on the perimeter. I was keeping my eye on him, more so than the camp counselors, it seemed, because I recognized that something was deeply bothering him. Suddenly I felt a gust of wind, but not a normal gust. It was a violent, ominous blast, and as this wind poured in, Billy erupted into terrified screams and immediately took off running up the trail, frightened out of his mind. As he ran, he continued screaming. Instantly, I looked at the counselors, who appeared stunned. The other boys were visibly alarmed, so without hesitation I sprinted after Billy. Since it was a summer night, light lingered in the sky until at least ten o'clock. Therefore, I could see my surroundings adequately. When I exited the forest and entered the soccer fields, I spotted Billy about fifty feet in front of me. I continued to close the distance as he dashed towards the basketball court as if making a direct line straight to his cabin. But this is when it happened. Abruptly, with me close behind him, I was stopped in my tracks by a vision so powerful, vivid and heavenly. Surrounding the court from ground to ceiling, on the perimeter where the walls would be, was a multitude of massive, tremendously glorious, illuminated angels. Yes, actual angels. At first, I couldn't believe what I was seeing. As I attempted to stare at them closer, their brightness nearly burned my eyes. It was obvious that Billy could not see them, for he ran straight at them, preparing to run onto and through the court. I stood in awe and watched as Billy ran into one angel and fell backwards onto the ground. He appeared extremely confused, and rightfully so, because to him there was no wall. To him the angels were invisible, and he should be able to progress onward, but to me, I could see exactly what was happening. Billy stood up and tried to proceed again into the court, but again he ran into an angel. After a few tries in different locations, each time running into another angel and falling backwards, with his confusion increasing, he eventually ran around the court by way of the perimeter trail, then up the hill still screaming out of terror all the way to his cabin. But it was not the angels he was so fearful of. It was what the angels were protecting him from. What I would see and experience next."

"Whoa," Reina spoke aghast. An appropriate response. I bobbed my head in agreement.

"Now, at this moment, once Billy had made his way safely around the court, the angels vanished. Their sudden absence left a vision-swallowing darkness. Once my eyes readjusted to the night, with a faint ribbon of light still far on the horizon, I looked behind me, but no one was coming, so I slowly approached the basketball court. As I neared and stepped my foot onto the cement floor, through the air where the angels obstructed, I heard a vicious, despicable hum of activity inside the court. Much like a beehive if the bees were all the size of buses. I felt a wrenching, overbearing heat. I smelled burning flesh. Fearfully, timidly, I walked forward. Instantly, as soon as I entered beneath the roof, my eyes were opened to the sheer horror of flying demons. There were hundreds of them. The space was filled with them. From every angle they darted at me, seething, shrieking, bellowing first Billy's name and then mine, calling for his soul as if they were predatory, life-sucking beasts. Their horrendous faces burned in front of mine. I could not swat them away, only be wrapped and consumed by them. It was sadistically, nightmarishly horrific. I didn't know what I would walk into when I stepped into the court, but there I was, enveloped in an ocean of evil. I attempted to sort of swim through the thick mass of demons, moving through them the way molasses moves, barely progressing. Down into my face they incessantly flew, sneering at me, maniacally jeering with harsh, haughty cackles. Determined to reach the other side, I struggled, physically pushing them aside, shouldering, combatting, fighting to gain a foot of progress amid a crowded hell. Once I finally reached the other side and stepped out of the court, I breathed fresh air again, relieved to be out of the demon's den. At this point, I looked back from where I had trudged, hearing and slightly seeing the camp counselors and other boys trotting across the soccer field. They stepped onto and traversed the basketball court as if it was just another night. The demons did not bother them. They did not know what Billy and I had just experienced. Gasping to articulate, I voiced Billy was in his cabin. The counselors thanked me and then rushed to his aid."

"Oh, my incredible God. As in, I am not taking His name in vain, but I say that with true reverence to Him. His angels, and the vile enemy, wow." In her reaction, I pursed my lips perceptibly. Reina spoke again. "What happened next!? What did you do?" She gripped her empty cup of coffee crushingly in her hand.

CINEREAL

"Yes, so, I tried to talk to the counselors, but they told me, 'Not now,' so all I could do was go to my cabin and wait. But you think that was powerful, what happens next is possibly even more so."

"There is more!?" Reina set her compressed cup down on the table.

"About two hours later, probably around midnight, when all the mayhem of the night had passed and most everyone had fallen asleep, I walked outside in my bedclothes to go to the bathhouse. The events of the evening would not rest in my mind. But before the bathhouse, I veered over to the hilltop to peer down towards the court, to look upon the location of the wild scene. Yet walking the tiny detour wasn't all my decision. I felt pulled to go look, as with a beckoned curiosity, as if there was one more thing for me to see, and there was."

"What was it??" My audience of one tilted forward on the edge of her seat.

"It was something I did not expect, nor can explain in any way other than exactly how I vividly saw it. Down the hill, in the dim glow of trail lights, strolling around the perimeter of the court, was a lion. A fully maned, large male, wild lion."

"A what!?"

"Yes, a lion. Exactly what you are picturing in your mind. Just like one you would see in Africa, or what once roamed the Middle East, or at a zoo. An actual, huge, imposing lion. This lion walked around the demonic infested structure. I again stood nearly frozen in awe, much like I halted when witnessing the angels, but now I watched the lion for a few minutes. The lion walked with confident intention, as if not allowing anything from going in or coming out of the court, but I do not think it was people he was managing. It was the evil legion he was containing. When the lion reached the closest point to me on the perimeter trail, a mere thirty feet away, it stopped. The lion gazed up to me standing on the hill and settled his eyes into mine. Of course, I could not take my eyes off him, but I felt no fear. No part of me questioned the radical improbability of it. My mind did not freak out like, 'Oh no, there is a wild lion!' For, somehow, it was far more than an animal. It exuded a magnificent, indescribable amount of peace. As it gazed at me, into me, it produced immense calmness in my soul. He looked at me as if he knew me, emanating a strength I did not know existed. After a moment, it strode confidently onward. It was the single most dynamic sight I have ever witnessed." Sitting back in my chair, exhausted from the heightened emotions that stirred as I relayed the events, I sipped my neglected cooled coffee and laughed mildly. We both laughed, not in humor but in astonishment at the immensity of God.

Reina spoke after our inspired reactions. "So, I mean, I can't even begin to wrap my mind around all this. You witnessed the angels guarding Billy, and then you were immersed in the demons, and then you witnessed the lion, who was probably, not probably, it must have been - God. Did anything come of it all? The next day?" She asked the question I needed to complete the account.

"Yes, yes, and yes." I affirmed. "The lion was definitely God, at least in the form He chose to present Himself to me," I agreed. "I don't think anyone else would have been able to see Him. Unless He unveiled Himself to them too, of course. But that I was permitted to witness the angels, demons and the lion was undoubtedly for a greater reason. To answer your follow-up question, the next day I learned more details that now complete all I know about the event. That night, after much confusion and fervent prayer over Billy by the counselors, the bully surrendered his heart to God. The gust of wind and his terrified screams had been demons coming after him and leading him to the hoard. Who knows what would have happened if they had succeeded, but God did not allow it. After prayer over Billy in Jesus' name, the demons left his body, and Billy then understood the spiritual attack and committed his life to Christ. It was miraculous. When I saw him the next day, his demeanor had completely changed.

"Praise God. That is so amazing!" She beamed enthusiastically.

"Indeed, praise God. Also, the following day, I needed to tell some adults what I had witnessed. I couldn't keep it all to myself. Therefore, I relayed my experience to a camp counselor, and he brought me to one of the camp leaders. In a rustic Maine office, I divulged my full account. The man listened calmly, without displaying surprise or disbelief. After I finished, he wanted me to communicate all I had told him to another man on the board of directors. Right there, he picked up the telephone, dialed the numbers, explained the reason for his call, handed me the phone, and I repeated the events. Upon finishing, the man told me this. 'You have witnessed God's work. Why He wanted you to observe it, I do not know, but I will tell you what I do know. Yesterday, God firmly placed a message in my heart conveying that something monumental was going to happen at camp last night. I informed the other leaders, and we spent all night praying, not knowing exactly what we were praying for. We believed there would be an event of spiritual warfare, and young man, you witnessed it.'" My eyes looked to the sky, then down to my coffee comrade.

Reina mirrored my movements, peering towards the heavens and back at me. "So incredible, Wing. God displayed to you a glimpse of His work. He wanted you to observe the spiritual warfare in action."

"Exactly," I nodded with sincerity. "He wanted me to see it. Perhaps so that for the rest of my life I could never dismiss His power and the certainty of the greater world beyond the limited tangible one we see and live in. He showed me a sliver, a sliver that shall never leave my memory. No matter how much I resisted and strayed from Him in my life, I always knew the truth, and for my years of rebellion I am ashamed. Living against Him while knowing His undeniable omnipotence bred an atrocious darkness. Yet in His mercy and grace He forgave me and does not want me to live in shame, only to look upon Him. He is the Lion, He is the Commander of Angels, He is the Creator of the Universe, He is the King of Kings. And though Satan and his army fight against the Almighty, they have no power over Him. In His time, God will destroy all evil, for He is the Victor. I trust and believe in Him with all my heart, mind, soul and strength. I thank God each day that He is who He is and that He never gave up on me. Now I just need, am, and will, forever live for Him. I owe Him my all. He is working in me just as He is working in you. There is still a lot of work to be done, of course! But no longer will I be silent about who He is and how much each person needs Him, whether they know or agree. As His children and servants, we have a duty to His kingdom. For all He is, I worship Him with immense awe and gratitude."

"Amen!" Reina emphatically spoke. She gathered her tabletop items as if it was time to leave, but with one more question she paused her movements. "Did you ever experience any more angels or demons like that again?"

"Oof," I guffawed. "So many times. But never again did I witness angels in their celestial radiant splendor like I did that night at camp. I have come across angels disguised as humans, and even the odd man who led me to this church I think was an angel. I told you about how all that occurred."

"Yes, that is another amazing story. Have you told that one to Sherry and Val?" Reina smiled inquisitively.

CINEREAL

"Not yet, but I will tell them. They deserve to know. Oh, how I love Sherry and Val. God bless them both." Reina agreed with a tender acknowledgment by holding her hand to her heart. I then continued, "As for demons, they became a torturous infestation in my life for many years. A few years after the camp event, I heard and felt that demonic gust of wind enter my family's home in New Hampshire. And during my childhood and then later in my era of running from God, I was often plagued with demonic activity. Seemingly forcefully bathed in them. That vile beehive-like hum inside the basketball court became a sound that tormented me. Every time I'd hear it, I'd know exactly what it was, having grown very attuned, or rather, sensitively aware when evil is present. But now, as I am covered by the blood of Jesus, they can do no harm. They still try sometimes, but in prayer and commanding them to stop in Jesus' name they are silenced. When I recognize others suffering in the same way, I immediately pray for them and speak to them about Jesus. And that is just it, isn't it? He delivered us, and so we continue this work for Him. We love others as He loves, even our human enemies. In all things, to God be the glory."

My friend sat up straight. "To God be the glory." She affirmed. After a long sigh demonstrating our mental saturation, we both tacitly shook off our brains. We grinned and stood up. The sun had risen high into the spring sky. Adolescent green leaves fluttered softly on the trees. It was time to go our own ways and proceed with our day. It was time to live for Him, now and forevermore.

CINEREAL

The Writing Shed

Drinking alcohol is not sinful. Jesus drank wine with His disciples and friends. However, drunkenness is, the Bible states this clearly. Unfortunately, I had proven many times I could not imbibe responsibly. Therefore, sobriety from the drink became my only option. While my reasons for abolition of booze were to serve God honorably and sustain my organs, I foolishly continued to clutch a tucked away hope that perhaps someday I could enjoy the beverage in controlled moderation. This persistent, seemingly innocent mindset had slowed my progress, contributing to the previous relapses. Overall, the idea of never drinking alcohol again, especially wine, seemed impossible. *The whiskey, alright, not that one, but wine!?* Like Jesus did, I wanted to sip the soothing fruit of the vine in small amounts without it leading to sin. Compared to the years prior, I had improved significantly, with the most significant transformation being Christ's ongoing work in me. Now, I only aspired to emulate Him.

Since the idea of never drinking alcohol again was still too daunting for me to handle, I shifted from that focus and reapplied the mentality I utilized when hiking the Appalachian Trail. Consistently accomplish the micro-goals to achieve the macro. Don't obsess over the massive objective. Instead, assemble consistent daily practices that support alcohol sobriety all the way from awakening until sleep. Early to bed, early to rise, and repeat.

In my new home, the writing shed, I arrived much like a withered plant. A metaphorical plant that had been struggling to survive in its unnatural ecosystem. I now found myself in a suitable environment. A genuine revival was upon me. Life became much quieter than I had ever lived. My structured routines were filled with valued life staples and nothing more, consistently nourishing my soul, body and mind with His word, church community, prayer, exercise, healthy meals, walks with Wylie, writing, reading, gardening, long sits beneath the sky and the occasional coffee, chess match or lunch with a wholesome friend. In this fresh life chapter, I distanced myself from many people, not for lack of love but out of necessity to concentrate on healing and alcohol sobriety. If something did not assist my goals, I attempted not to partake in it. The season of silence and solitude I had craved was now upon me.

Occasionally, old rebellions attempted to raise a defiant head, prompted by loneliness and a slip into self-ambitious pride. When this occurred, I sensed all stability waver off track. But God in His gracious love steadily guided me back. Placing Him at the center of my life, every obstacle was manageable, yet when I veered off course, I would start to drown. Amid such falls, my hand reached out to Him. On every occasion, He pulled me out of the chaotic darkness. The daily dizziness and bouts of vertigo persisted, creating a discouragement God was teaching me how to manage. Sometimes, my brain blacked out, causing me to collapse inside markets or nearly tumble into traffic. Trying to stand still in one spot, beneath claustrophobic ceilings pressing down, proved to be the most difficult. My brain episodes usually occurred while waiting in lines or wavering in place in front of a market cashier. However, as Einstein noted, I just needed to keep moving.

One spring day, two friends from church rushed me to the hospital emergency room straight from my writing shed. The week following included heightened difficulty to cope on my own, yet I persisted with God's strength. While no healing medical remedies had been determined, I adapted to the physical impediments with patience, gratitude, resolve and controlled routines. With the aid of doctors, frequent imaging, multiple therapies including ocular, vestibular, cranial sacral and mental health therapy, the mystery of my condition faded and understanding grew. The traumatic brain injury had incurred permanent damage to the sensory control function in my nervous system. Visual disturbances dominated as the most debilitating trigger. And even though I had hoped to correct my judicial issues in Colorado, restore my driver's license and someday legally drive again, unless God chose to repair my brain, driving would remain impossible for the rest of my life. However, this reality did not discourage me, for I had driven enough in my life and grown adept at walking anywhere I needed to go. *The thousands of miles hiked on the long trails were preparing me for this,* I cheerfully thought. *God knew what He was doing. He always does.* Aside from the symptoms the brain injury had solely created, the heatstroke, excessive alcohol abuse and even multiple coronavirus infections, compounding with the TBI, resulted in my body producing an auto-immune condition. This explained why, for the past few years, I could no longer handle excessive heat. While such complications and sufferings hindered daily movements, they no longer produced even a hint of anxiety; rather, my joy flourished in the secure promises of my heavenly Father. Because of Him, any fear of death I had ever held was eradicated forever. For what can cause true harm when we are His? Surely flesh can be maimed, mangled and killed, but our flesh is not coming with us, to eternity with Jesus, to our true home.

During my third refocused alcohol sobriety, many people asked if I attended Alcoholics Anonymous. My simple response, not desiring any conversation on the subject, was always the same. "No, I do not. It is not for me." Usually, they would then let it be. Occasionally, someone would admonish my choice, judgmentally expressing that I would fail in alcohol sobriety without it. But their comments never bothered me, for they did not understand. Thus, I would smile and quietly proceed with my day. The main reason for not partaking in A.A. was never one of pride; rather, the environment of many bodies squeezed into a room was the exact opposite of a conducive environment for my brain. I already had some experience with Alcoholics Anonymous. Following my first arrest at age nineteen, mandatory A.A. meetings were part of my disciplinary package. To me, A.A. felt like a punishment, and the very notion of claustrophobically listening to others dwell upon their alcohol experiences, be they stories of failure or success, was not the way I preferred to apply my attention. Through the previous New England A.A. meetings, I had become familiar with the twelve-step program. I did not need to be convinced of a higher power, as I was daily focused upon my relationship with Him. And the root of each step I actively implemented outside of controlled meetings. Honesty, hope, faith, courage, integrity, willingness, humility, love, responsibility, discipline, spiritual awareness and service were utmost practiced personal priorities. For community, I sought like-minded Christ followers instead of other alcoholics. I believe that A.A. is an advantageous program for those who choose to utilize it, but for myself, as stated, "It is not for me." I pledged to myself that if I plunged into one more dangerous relapse with alcohol, then, and only then, out of self-punishment I would attend an A.A. meeting and continue attending if it proved beneficial.

Upon completing 100 consecutive days of alcohol sobriety, the newly achieved milestone was encouraging. *But what are 100 days in the scope of a life, or eternity? It is but a speck, a grain, a flicker within the universe.* I allowed myself to revel quietly while perched on a large rock in the river. The current curled around my body, gurgling pleasantly the way moving water does. My eyes focused on the sparkling sun-glitter atop each undulation. In prayer, I thanked Him for my progress and each blessing He bestowed, bathed in the peace He provides, and then rose and persevered forth, for that is what one must do.

As the heat of summer heightened and the volume of humanity clinking their drinks in cheers rose around me, I retreated into my den for hibernation. I knew myself well enough to understand this would be my toughest summer yet. Between my brain's symptoms and my first hot season of alcohol sobriety, hunkering down to preserve the focus was a necessity. Every day wore a different emotion. Some days were filled with effervescent joy, knowing I was living exactly as He wanted me to. Other days, I could not escape the weight of melancholy and other heavy internal perceptions. Yet on each occasion, I sat in them, focusing upon how and why I felt the ways I did, considering the roots while not allowing them to control me. With alcohol, my emotions had often tossed me around as a boat without a rudder, but in my sobriety, emotions were simply a window into internal depths, no longer governing my decisions.

As the season progressed, as I examined how all my life had unfolded, every memory, each action and reaction, all what, how and whys became clear. Understanding replaced murky confusion. God's faithfulness had been steadfast, even when I'd rebelled for so long. His love endured despite my selfish desires. Although I had thought I was existing with a loving heart, my heart had become tarnished and twisted by the sinful patterns I persisted in living in. My alcohol abuse created a wake of destruction, hurting many in my life. The pain I had caused others hung heavily around my heart. I mourned the lost days I had lived apart from God. Yet He forgave me for every single one of them and was providing new days that I might use them to serve Him, that I might witness His love to everyone around me. With His immense love, my Savoir removed the weight and eliminated all shame. Just as it is declared in Psalm 34:5 (NKJV), "They looked to Him and were radiant, and their faces were not ashamed." And yet, it remained paramount that I always look to Him, for if my eyes shifted, my weakness would return.

In late July 2024, I reached five months of sobriety from alcohol. In this month, the persistent fog of mental detachment lifted. My mind and body reunited. For the first time since eliminating the poisonous consumption, no longer did I feel awkward speaking with other humans or the need to daily state, "I will remain sober today." A new enhanced normal replaced the remnants of old battles. Yet in this relief, addiction's voice disguised as gentle encouragement insinuated that the goal was nearly accomplished. *Perhaps when I reach six months, the war will be won, and alcohol will relinquish its rooted grip.*

Flower and I ran into each other, resulting in a pleasant conversation. We reminisced about old times and shared events from our modern chapters. A month after I moved out of the Prixon, our back-and-forth intimate relationship had come to its necessary end. Now, following months of absence from each other's lives, we decided it would be worth attempting to remain friends. After all, we both knew each other very well. "If you ever need an escape from the summer heat, because I know how difficult that is for you," she kindly offered, "just let me know and I will drive you somewhere cooler. As friends, of course." I thanked her, promising to consider it, and then moved on with my dizzy day.

In late August, I accomplished six months without drinking a single drop of alcohol. Reaching this half-year checkpoint stirred successful excitement within, an achievement I decided was worthy of celebration. The summer had been exhausting. One I longed for a brief break from. I contacted Flower, suggesting we leave Bend for a few days and go somewhere refreshing to relax. "Mount Hood is the spot, our old spot. We can lounge in mountain shade and swim in the lakes, but only as friends."

She agreed. Within a few hours, Flower, Wylie and I cruised north through the smoky arid air of a central Oregon late summer. Yet despite our familiar cheerful conversation and the potential for a revitalizing respite, a voice within warned of the hazards of my folly.

~~~

As we approached the edge of the high desert, passing through forlorn hues of the Warm Springs Reservation, I thought of George. Thinking of him did not conjure happiness but guilt, for I knew what I was about to do. Once we entered the Mount Hood National Forest, the voice advising of the risks in our getaway emboldened. I pushed it away, desiring to romp on as I pleased. Holding my arm out the window, piney aromas refreshed my senses. The internal warning persisted. *Turn back now? No, not now,* I silently defied. Retreating from Bend's daily toils felt far too good to observe the warning. *A break from my routines is necessary,* I adamantly refuted without admitting the true objective. As the road and those upon it ascended the flanks of Mount Hood, the temperature dropped one delightful degree at a time. A reinvigorating sense of adventure replaced the tedium of home hibernation. In honest depths, I knew I shouldn't be retreating from my focused, effective practices. *I am not yet solidified enough in alcohol sobriety for this.* A weakness I was allowing to take control. *Nor should I be spending time with Flower in this manner, risking negatively affecting her heart, undoing stitches that have probably not yet completely healed.* Foolishly, for the fleeting fancies of immediate satisfactions I continued to ignore all possible consequences under the banner of a supposedly needed vacation.

When we pulled into our pastime haven of Government Camp, I accepted my doom. While exiting the car, I reminded Flower that we were not getting back together. "If anything, this is a test to determine if we can actually be friends." But I already knew the real reason for this trip. The three drinking establishments I frequented on past stopovers and escapes lay before me. A pub, a tavern and a bar. Eyeing them each, remembering my old steps, addiction's silent decision emerged. *I will not get drunk.* Half-heartedly, I told myself. *But I accomplished six months without a drop, and this is a "vacation."* The word I kept exploiting as if it allowed my wrongdoings. *Therefore, a few controlled drinks will be good for me…* Flower's eyes pleaded for my affection. I did not want to dwell upon her notions, but here we were. I had volunteered the situation, succumbing to the internal deception that a drink away from Bend would not count against my goals, forcibly ignoring every internal warning on the drive. With a forced smile, I glanced at her and suggested we get food. "I'll meet you and Wylie at that spot in the back corner of the yard we like." Upon her affirmation, I walked straight into the bar.

While Flower and Wylie waited outside at the same table that we had lounged at on our way to D. Ro's performance in Portland, I eyed the beers on tap. They had one of my favorites. When the barkeep asked if I was ready to order, spotting the two menus in my hand, I told him we had just arrived, but I would take one of the Double Mountain Hop Lion IPAs. As he poured the golden goodness, I remembered the time Pearl and I visited its brewery in Hood River. Simultaneously, anxiety formed in every cell of my body. When the barkeep set the full pint in front of me, the words "I'll also take a shot of Jim Beam and start a tab," fell out of my lips. "Be back soon with a food order." He nodded and poured the bourbon, which I always improperly, without caring for accuracy, referred to as whiskey. In my alcohol-saturated lifestyle, whiskey had served as a blanket term for all fierce brown liquor. I offered him my bank card to hold for the tab. He waved it off with a shrug and a waggle of his head.

"No worries, man," he stated casually, "I remember your face. You aren't running out on us, I trust you."

"Thanks, man," I muttered, matching his casual tone, having remembered his face as well. *He trusts me, but suddenly I don't trust myself,* I acknowledged. *All of this feels so… wrong.* Brushing my thoughts away, I instinctively grabbed the liquor, poured it smoothly down my throat, relished the warm, memorable burn, then grabbed the frothy-topped beer and sauntered outside. Flower and Wylie both sat waiting with smiles on their faces, and with one drink in my body, to drown out the escalating anxiety, I allowed myself many more.

Two days later we returned to Bend. On the ride home, Flower cried. My heart overflowed with guilt and shame. I should not have consumed alcohol. I should never have allowed us to spend the time together. We shared a few deep conversations, and Flower even attested I did not let my drinking spiral out of control, but none of that mattered. It all teetered toward the old life, the one I had been battling so hard to leave behind. Despite not allowing physical intimacy to ensue as it once did, my soul ached knowing our shared days confused her. In my exhausted summer loneliness, I betrayed what was right for what felt good, a false good which only did the opposite of nourish. *I should not have called her. The second I considered our getaway I should have fallen on my knees and poured out my considerations to God. Why did I slip backward again?* The answer was obvious. Instead of obeying Him and holding my eye upon Him, I let it slip away and obeyed my addiction.

When Flower dropped Wylie and me off at the writing shed, the sighs were not of satisfaction. They were of heightened realization that what we once shared was no more. She held on to a hope I wished she would let go of. But with my thoughtless actions allowing us to commune emotionally after months apart, it was no wonder. *Of course, she would proclaim she had healed, that we could be friends. It was up to me to protect her heart. It was up to me not to let my addiction take control. It was my fault I did not keep Christ at the center. In all those ways, I failed. Damn my selfish carelessness. It only causes pain;* I regrettably considered as the sound of her departing car faded into silence. Once inside the writing shed, my body trembled beneath the weight of my sin. Waves of filthy sorrow drenched me. As a despicable sinner, I crumpled to the ground and prayed two days too late. Tears poured onto the carpet, embarrassed in front of the Almighty by how callously I had acted. My sin not only hurt Flower and myself, but Him, He who died on the cross for me, and here I had acted as if that didn't even matter.

Beginning the moment I drank, remorse clung within. As soon as we decided to retreat from Bend, the Holy Spirit warned me, and yet I buried it all until we left Mount Hood. It was clear that despite six months without alcohol, my body had not forgotten its addiction. Even the old tolerance had not diminished. The beast was waiting for one drop. *Perhaps it will never go away…*

September had begun. Sounds of Labor Day weekend reverberated across the land. Closing my curtains and turning off the lights, I hid from the world, wallowing in regret. For six months I had been doing so well, but the reality of how rapidly everything deteriorated terrified me. The brutality of my alcoholism and the decisions I made continued hurting everyone around me, especially the ones I loved.

~~~

My dear friends Hest, Max and Lena were moving out of Oregon in the fourth week of September. Hest was returning to New Hampshire, while Max and Lena had purchased a home near Ashville, North Carolina. Hest announced a going-away party at The Saloon, the very place where the murder attempt on my life originated. I did not want to go, but I also did not want to miss out on one last soiree. The idea seemed harmless, and though I had not decided to fully partake in the carousing by drinking alcohol, I also did not firmly determine that I would not. Having returned to alcohol sobriety following the Mount Hood getaway, the disposition for the month had been one of internal squalor. While my heart remained on my Savior, my mind struggled to let go of my recent sin. Other than a few brief coffee meetups and one last mellow bowling outing with the crew, Hest's party would be my first full public appearance in September. While striding toward the infamous location to bid my Bend chosen family farewell, anxiety escalated. I knew I was in trouble. My indecision not to drink was a decision.

When I walked into The Saloon, my former persona returned. Swiftly I morphed from hesitancy into a bravado attitude of "let's burn this place down." As if nothing had changed, we stood at the bar ordering naturally.

CINEREAL

With my arms around Max and Lena's shoulders, my face blazed with a mischievous grin. Ignoring the ghostly memories of the living darkness, I snatched a shot of mixed liquors as the colorful row was placed on the wooden slab in front of us. To my comrades, I stated, "This is a vacation. I will be fine. Do not worry about me. I will immediately go back to sobriety after tonight." They all shrugged, for our long Bend life chapter together was ending. We clinked our little shot glasses and cheered. It was not their responsibility to take care of me or determine my actions; that was on me, and for what I chose, I could only blame myself. The first shot led to the usual beer, then to a second and eventually, whiskey. The patio filled with cheerful faces we had partied with for many raucous years.

As I leaned into the frivolity, laughing and slowly becoming inebriated, initially I appeared to be a man in control. I enthusiastically answered and asked questions about how life had been going. Yet despite my outward tipsy radiance, privately I felt like a fraud. The drink in my hand and the drinks in my bloodstream was no longer the me I desired to be. Until the Mount Hood getaway and even since, I was not that drunk person anymore. But there I was, imbibing again at The Saloon. In the past, I felt like a hypocrite by not living for God and now for casually abandoning my sobriety. "As long as I do not get drunk, I will not be in sin, nor will it trigger my addiction into a full relapse," I whispered into the bathroom mirror, knowing I was lying to myself. Already I was committing sin, as sin is not only the letter of the law but also the spirit of it. However, that is the trick of addiction's voice. An alcoholic can promise themselves they will not get drunk, but as soon as they consume one drink, such determination is lost.

While night set in, we swayed on the brick veranda like a gluttonous band of jesters. I was delighted to be with my friends but also, having returned to a pit of shame, relieved they were moving away. Just like when CiderBar had closed its doors for the final time. Not because I did not love them, but it was evident my sobriety strength was still very fragile. I still needed to persist in the season of solitude, away from the temptations of the world. God had provided this term for a reason, and until I matured in the ways He desired, the season may never end. If I could have said no to imbibing at my friends' going away party or even stopped by but chosen a non-alcoholic drink instead, only then would I have proven to myself I was solidified. Rad slyly presented me with a skeptical eye as we reeled into the night, the look of a disappointed brother. He knew I was not staying true to who I was striving to become. As I hopped from one frivolous conversation to the next, I wished that once the alcohol had left my bloodstream, I could immediately return to my new road without a major setback. Drunkenly, I asked God not to allow my seizures and severe withdrawal symptoms to become activated. But in my heart, I knew this would not be the case. There would be consequences for my callous actions.

Two days after the night of the party, my old friend Berengar from Colorado was set to visit. His arrival had been rescheduled many times because of my inability to handle summer temperatures. Consequently, regardless of my alcohol failures, I could not reschedule it again. We had not seen each other for nearly ten years when we shared an afternoon together surrounded by Wylie's puppies in Florida. Since then, we remained in frequent contact throughout the decade. Berengar was arriving with a woman he had married in Japan. Originally, I was eager to greet them as the stronger, sober new me, and yet I must greet them as the mess I once and still was. Knowing their visit was swiftly approaching, I had to make an important decision out of three choices. One choice was to cancel and immediately ingest detox drugs to avoid potentially lethal withdrawals. The second, not cancel nor take medical drugs and pray I didn't have a seizure, and the third option, drink alcohol through their visit and self-detox once they left.

By ten in the morning, my entire body convulsed. The withdrawals were already wreaking havoc on my delicate brain and nervous system. Recognizing the sequence of this, I knew it would only be a matter of hours until my body succumbed to the danger. Upon deciding not to cancel our plans, but to remain capable of hosting Berengar and his wife's visit, I struggled to a store where I purchased and urgently drank more whiskey. The rush of poison into my blood stabilized my shakes and firecracker brain, while also causing extreme sadness to return. Not the lonesome wholesome melancholy, but a mighty grief acknowledging that due to my relapse I was back in addiction's prison, having fallen and spiraled into the wretch I strove to never be again.

"I just need to drink to get through Berengar's visit, then I will stop forever," I muttered to God, while pacing back and forth sipping from the bottle. Wylie observed with concerned eyes. She understood what was going on. She had witnessed my debauchery for most of her precious life. Tears streamed down my cheeks as the poison coursed through my body. For over

CINEREAL

six months I had not brought a single alcoholic beverage into the writing shed, and now the purity of the abode had been tainted.

When Berengar arrived with his wife, our time shared was contaminated by my active addiction. I could offer very little other than provide a place to sleep and a garden to sit in. We played chess and ate sloppy meals. We drank wine and talked about life, about the memorable times we'd had and the struggles we'd faced. Amidst one conversation, Berengar and I sat on the dirt as both of us released emotions we had confined within. Liberating our burdens with each other reminded us of the bond we had forged in the mountains. After two hazy nights, they were gone. I regretted not being able to show my Colorado brother a cleaner version of myself, but it was raw and honest. Our time together still held value.

The moment their truck drove away on the morning of September 27, 2024, the same day I completed the Appalachian Trail only fourteen years later, I collapsed. I expended all remaining strength to make it through the visit. Breakfast wine stained my teeth. The tiled bathroom floor held my quivering body. I called my doctor and confessed. Understanding the severity of how deeply my addiction was rooted, knowing how quickly the potentially fatal withdrawal symptoms would return, she prescribed the exact medications I would need to detox on my own. She warned me of the hazards, which I assured her I understood, but I had created this problem and so, if it be God's will, with His grace and strength, I would survive. Using the stabilizing false strength of alcohol, I collected my medications at the pharmacy and returned home to finish the day. Come morning, I would begin what unquestionably must be the final detox.

In the evening while lying on the dirt of my writing shed's garden drinking the last bottle of wine, I intently focused upon the misery I placed myself in. With tears, I prayed to God, knowing how disappointed He was in me. I drank as moderately as I could, just enough to evade tremors, yet enough to fall asleep. In the morning, once the alarm clock announced it had been twelve hours since my last sip, I swallowed my first round of pills. The arduous process commenced for my fourth time. I thanked God for providing me one more chance. Wylie curled at my feet as I lay in the fetal position. It was time to return to the season of solitude. The season I should never have left. My consecutive days without alcohol had dropped back to zero. *The six months were not a waste. They were worthy days on my new road, and perhaps I can continue where I left off, but my failures have proven I still have much to learn.*

As I waded through the blurry seventy-two-hour drudge, I prayed and read the Bible every moment I was awake. He forgave me, so I forgave myself. I would not hold on to this one. With the deserved weight of remorse and understanding, I fully let it go. *But I can no longer live the way I used to. I cannot keep falling into old destructive patterns. I am not that person anymore. Just because He has forgiven me with His amazing mercy and grace never excuses my behavior.* Paul the Apostle's words in Romans 6:1-2 (NKJV) stresses this point. "Shall we continue in sin that grace may abound? Certainly not! How shall we who died to sin live any longer in it?"

After three days, I weaned off the heavy medications. Gradually, my body readjusted back to pre-relapse form. For two years I had been placing increased strain upon my whole with the perpetual cycle of alcohol, medications and sobriety. My brain and organs did not have the strength for another series. *That must be the last time,* I silently reiterated. I wrote out a list of dates encapsulating my two-year journey. After my first detox, I remained sober for forty-eight days and then relapsed for almost nine months. Following my second detox, I lasted nearly three months without alcohol and then relapsed for one month. Upon completing my third detox, I proceeded not to drink a sip of alcohol for six months and a few days. In my final relapse, I fell for a weekend, returned to sobriety and shame and then a few weeks later saturated myself with alcohol for five dishonorable days. Examining this list on paper encouraged me. Despite all my failures, I was making genuine progress. With each relapse and stint of alcohol sobriety, my time drinking lessened and my abstinence lengthened. In a moment of seemingly innocent pride, God's conviction overwhelmed me again. Immediately, I bowed on my knees in prayer.

I cried out to the Lord, "Father, it is You who created this universe. It is You who gives life. You who sustains and allows each breath. I am but a servant to You, a woeful servant who falls away repeatedly. My God, my Father, my King, my Every Reason, please draw me closer to You each day. Embolden Your Holy Spirit within me. Shine Your love and face upon me. Thirst me for only You, the Living Water. Hunger me for only You, the Living Bread. I nourish on Your Word, Lord. Create in me a heart that grows purer each moment of each day. All I want is to honor You, to serve You, to listen for and seek You. On my own, I am nothing, but with You I will

CINEREAL

fulfill Your desires for me. Raise me up from my shame and give me the strength to follow You entirely. Guide me, Lord, where You want me to be. Give me the courage to always follow where You lead, standing and shining as a light for You. Search my heart and see my love for You. It flows from depths eternal, from a spring which You seeded in me. Convict me in my transgressions, the ones I know and the ones I am blind to, that I may abandon every sin and grow more like You. Please instill in me Your wisdom, help me to always discern what is from You, what is Your will and what is not. Please help my heart to grow in kindness, patience and humility. I do not want my sinful pride anymore. Blot it from me. Deepen my ocean of faith in all that You are. Oh Lord, You are my rock and shield, my fortress, my steadfast tower I run to and am safe. You move the waters and with Your fingertips shape the mountains. With a sweep of Your arm, all galaxies tremble. The universe is Your invention. You are the Artist of Greatest Design. Your power and love are more than my mind can ever fathom, and to You I shall forever surrender my all. I hold on to nothing of myself, and I seek all of You. I love You, I love You, I love You. Thank You Jesus, for Your sacrifice, for paying the wages of my sin, paying my debt I could not pay. Thank You for defeating death and rising from the grave. Thank You for sanctifying me, for setting me apart, for calling me, choosing me, and adopting me into Your righteous family. Please help me share the truth of Your gift and the mighty truth of You to all those who do not know You. Lift me up so that I may be a witness of truth and love for You. All the glory in the world is Yours, is You, for there is no true glory other than You. You are the Alpha and the Omega, the Beginning and the End. You are God, the one true God, my Father. Protect me from evil, wrap Your arms around me, Lord, and hold on to me forever. I rest in the truth that I am covered by the blood of Jesus. I love You with all my heart, with all my soul, with all my mind and with all my strength. In Your Son, my Savior, Jesus' name, Amen."

~~~

Although I had not stayed true to my objective when I relapsed, I stayed true to my pledge to attend Alcoholics Anonymous if such a relapse occurred again. On October 7, I begrudgingly walked into a tightly packed room inside a small church close to the one I occasionally attended. The room's cacophony resonated harshly in my brain. The constant baseline dizziness already threatened to spin into vertigo. *But,* I thought, *I must do this, for I failed again, and this is a resource available. Please keep me stable, Lord. Remain open-minded, Wing.* As my body breached the doorway, numerous eyes observed my presence. Promptly, many hustled to greet me. As I politely extended my hand toward each overwhelming welcome, one pulled me in for a hug. I did not like that. Other than a handshake, I did not want anyone to touch me. Squeamishly, I sat where the crowded bodies directed me. The guy grazing my shoulder on the left and the woman grazing my shoulder on the right both asked how many days, if any, I had abstained from alcohol. "Today marks ten," I replied. Their excitement at my answer bothered me. I could not process the words of one as another waited eagerly to ask the same questions. *This is all too much.* Finally, the meeting started, and only one person spoke at a time.

When it was my turn to introduce myself, I spoke honestly. Talking to the masses was never a problem for me. I confidently enjoyed public speaking, but in the A.A. meeting, as I sensed the man by my side place his hand upon my shoulder, I wanted to snap. Shrugging off his infringing paw, I closed my eyes while continuing to introduce myself and my journey. *Gentleness, kindness, self-control,* prodded my mind, causing me to turn mid-sentence to the man who was only being sympathetic, offering him a smile in place of my cringy shrug. The room spun. Sitting up was a struggle. Fifty close breaths wafted towards mine. I admitted my deep faith in Christ and that I did not desire to be here. That it seemed like a punishment, but I had pledged to myself I would come if I relapsed again. Upon completing my few orated minutes, everyone offered too much encouragement and then excitedly presented me with my first A.A. sobriety coin. I did not want the coin, *patience, goodness, love,* but I smiled and thanked everyone for their support, promising I would include everyone in the room in my prayers. A few smirked at my comment. The room continued to spin.

Throughout the hour, many people shared valuable, vulnerable insights about their own struggles and successes with sobriety. I appreciated the raw humanity. As each one spoke, I prayed for them within. To manage the claustrophobic swells, my eyes remained mostly closed, allowing a slit of openness for visual perception. When the last words were shared, I stood to push hastily beyond the many more assuming hugs, hands and words of advice thrown in a mass of jumbles. Once outside, beneath the refreshing sky again, my angst subsided. Here I was willing and more able to talk, with

CINEREAL

a step back from the steps they each took closer, but not in there, no, in there was far too much.

I wobbled home, satisfied I had attended but doubtful I would return. *Only if another relapse befalls, then yes, but another drop of alcohol is not an option.* Imagining that every person in the world is allotted X number of such drinks in their lifetime, my allotted number had already been consumed. *I am retired from that life. But it is You, Father, who will help me with my sobriety. It is You who works within me. Please stir the hearts, minds and souls of each person at A.A. that they may seek You. Let them find You and place their faith in You. More than just the recognition of a higher power, but the truth of You, for every single person needs Jesus.*

That night, one week before my birthday, God presented a gift I direly needed. While studying the Gospel of Matthew, the first book in the New Testament, I read a verse of Jesus' words and promise which provided more peace and strength in my battles with alcohol than I had yet to experience. I'd been consuming all of Jesus' teachings, nourishing my soul as much as possible, so that I might finally succeed and not fall into my addiction again. Matthew, Mark, Luke and John I had read at least a dozen times in my life, yet upon each study He revealed more understanding to me than the time before. He was actively cultivating my knowledge of Him. Matthew, Mark and Luke are considered the synoptic gospels, carrying similar viewpoints, offering biographical accounts and containing many of the same stories and teachings of Jesus. The Gospel of John, my favorite, holds a distinct style, focusing more upon the heart of Christ and His divinity.

Before my reading, I asked God to provide me with wisdom of understanding to hear His words through the clarity of the Holy Spirit and not through my faulty earthly perceptions. An earnest, frequent prayer as I never desire to absorb the scriptures to fit my preconceived mindset, but only in the way He intends.

When I reached the passage of the Lord's Supper, the institution of the Eucharist in Matthew, which is accounted for similarly in Mark and Luke, a common verse I'd read and heard a multitude of times stopped me, bore into me, transformed and emancipated all my previous wonderings and subtle desires about someday being able to drink moderately again. His words swaddled me in a blanket of peace, helping me to abandon forever every remaining drop of angst within, for the man speaking is the Son of God. He is God. He is the very One who has done it all. He, my Savior, the One I seek and strive to become like, declares the words I didn't know I needed to hear. Matthew 26:27-29 (NKJV), "Then He took the cup, and gave thanks, and gave it to them, saying, 'Drink from it, all of you. For this is My blood of the new covenant, which is shed for many for the remission of sins. But I say to you, I will not drink of this fruit of the vine from now on until that day when I drink it new with you in My Father's kingdom.'"

There it was. Boom, it struck my addiction with a knockout punch. Jesus, who drank wine with His disciples and friends, promising that He would no longer drink wine until He drinks it new with them in heaven. Yes, Jesus knew He was soon to be crucified, that He would defeat death and rise from the grave. He knew that after His resurrection, He would spend forty days on earth in His glorified body for hundreds to see, touch and spend time with before His ascension to heaven, but no longer would He drink wine. "No longer would He drink wine," I spoke out loud. "If Jesus set down the cup, then so must I." I imagined that this Bible verse was not necessarily written for my circumstances, or for other's who struggle with addiction, and Jesus undoubtedly did not have a sinful problem with alcohol that would require Him to stop consuming it, He was blameless! But the mere mention of this truth encouraged me, lifted my soul, it affected all my internal battles to cease permanently. Jesus provided extraordinary peace. *Not only did He set the wine down, but He also promised there will be wine in heaven. Therefore, I do not need to worry about never being able to drink a glass of wine ever again, for I will, with Him.* The Bible talks of feasts in God's kingdom many times in other passages. Ones I mentally devour and envision with immense belief and excitement. Just as He urges us to do through Paul's words in Colossians 3:2-4 (NKJV), "Set your mind on things above, not on things on the earth. For you died, and your life is hidden with Christ in God. When Christ who is our life appears, then you also will appear with Him in glory."

As I closed my Bible for the evening, joyful tears of relief trickled down my cheek. *If He will, then I must. No more anguish, no more worry, no more anxiety as if I am somehow missing out. I am not missing out on anything. I have everything, for I am His.*

~~~

Amid the interior of October, I celebrated my first adult birthday without a single sip of alcohol. At age thirty-nine, I was finally free from the prison that had held me captive for so long. I spent the day alone with only my darling Wylie and my Father in Heaven. We walked down to the river to pray, and though my feet tread upon steady land, my brain sensed the constant rolling of the sea, a rising and falling as if the ground was breathing. *Perhaps I will always feel this way. Perhaps the constant dizziness and abrupt episodes of vertigo will never be healed. But if that is so, then it is His will. I do not mind anymore. I know He can heal me in a blink if He chooses, and yet He always has a greater reason. In so many ways, in the ways that matter, He has already healed me.*

"He has me where He wants me. Even when I do not understand, I trust and love Him. And I love you, girl." I said this to Wylie Wizzle as we bopped along. She peered up at my face with a smile. "We make quite the pair, us two, a W.W. and a W.W. - two creatures just doing our best amid a beautiful volcanic landscape."

With autumn's recent arrival, cool, clean air pleasantly caressed my skin. It was time to get back to work. I had compiled hundreds of new poems I could shape into a new collection. Also, there was my Louisiana novel set amidst the aftermath of Hurricane Katrina I had been progressing on. *Yes, but first I must pray about that.* Wylie pranced as we approached the river. We sat in a favorite spot, one by wide, calm waters where otters often swam. Golden leaves in the shape of teardrops shimmered on aspen trees. Red-winged blackbirds sang melodic trills. I poured out my heart to God, asking Him to lead me into my new year. Between silent prayers, I pondered all I had been working on. This mighty transformation in my life was one I earnestly desired. Despite failing and falling many times, because of Him I always rose again. *I will keep persevering onward, one step, one day at a time. I have a long way to go, but He shall always be with me, and with Him all things are possible.*

After our silence, sitting as but a child in His creation, I sensed a powerful directive from Him pressed upon my heart. Until that second, it was a notion I had never considered. *A fifth book of poetry would be lovely, and the Louisiana novel might have its time, but both projects must wait. There is a new book He wants me to write, starting immediately.* Filled with tingling inspiration, I obediently rose from the riverside's matted, tawny grass and hustled home with Wylie. As soon as we returned to our abode, I opened a blank page, and with His guidance, words promptly flowed. On October 14, 2024, the first day of my final year in my thirties, I started writing this book.

The Purpose of Life

Today is September 28, 2025. Last night, following prayers of gratitude and praise to the Creator from my garden beneath the stars, as I slept serenely with Wylie curled snugly by my feet, I officially reached my one-year anniversary for sobriety from alcohol. When I awoke to the chatter of finches and sparrows, the ascending sun shining tender autumn light upon the little birds feasting on sunflower seeds, a wave of both exhilaration and profound awe for our Creator washed over me. For by His grace, I am here, living the life He intended for me. Not the one I had rebelliously drowned myself in for decades, but the enriched existence that He benevolently desired I embrace.

This entire year of age thirty-nine has been a gift filled with colossal quantities of unrivaled peace and joy. A treasure He held in His hands since before the beginning of time, eager to bestow on His child's surrendering, obedient heart. As I arose to stretch my limbs and prepare some coffee, my mind recollected His words in Jeremiah 29:11 (NIV). "'For I know the plans I have for you,' declares the Lord, 'plans to prosper you and not to harm you, plans to give you hope and a future.'" *Thank you, Father. Yes, you have given me exactly that.*

The year of alcohol sobriety has not been difficult in the ways my previous sobriety stints and battles were. Ever since recognizing that Jesus Himself had set down the cup, so too was I wholly able to do so. Once I relinquished the foolish hope of someday moderating my consumption, my desire for it has not returned. Every trigger, such as noticing others enjoying the drink, was abolished. No part of me craved or considered imbibing again. Acquaintances who only observed my failures but not the intimate increasing depths of my relationship with God did not understand. They still considered the need to relay comments such as, "Without A.A. you'll never make it." Or, "We know who you were, and people never really change." Yet their proclamations bounce off my God-instilled armor like raindrops upon steel. One person noted, "Something in you truly has changed. How did you do it?" And to that I enthusiastically responded.

"It is not me; it is Him. It is Jesus. He has done it all." My face aglow with the bliss of my Savior's love.

Despite this year's joyous emancipation, challenges still occupied the worthy term. Writing this book has not been easy. But in His greater plans for my healing and growth, the process of my memoir's creation has also provided abundant blessings. I think back to a year and a half ago, when my friend Reina from church offered supportive words in front of a small gathering of people. She stated, "Wing, I am so eager to see what God's plans are for your writing." At the time, although living for Christ, hearing her speak this landed sharply on my soul. For even though I had surrendered my life to Him, somehow, I had not considered that maybe He wanted me to write differently than the way I had been.

To her statement and the harmonizing nods from her honorable partner and others, I genuinely responded, "Yes, we shall see where He leads." But within, I defensively considered, *well, I am writing my fifth poetry collection, and the Louisiana novel. Neither is explicitly for Him and His kingdom, but they won't be against Him either.* Even though her exclamation was virtuous, my reception of it felt sharp because the Holy Spirit instantly prodded me. Helping to realize that maybe I hadn't surrendered everything. Perhaps a part of me assumed I would still construct my career and express my art in the way I had previously envisioned. Yet, because I sincerely did not want to hold anything back from Him, I promptly communicated my thoughts. *Lord, you know I desire to surrender all of me, so I give you my writing as well. Lead me in the paths of your righteousness and I shall follow, even when it is challenging.*

And then, my thirty-ninth birthday occurred. There in my supplications next to the river, He steered me onto this fresh course. As I recognized His voice and launched into the new direction, each day I started and ended my writing sessions with prayer to Him. When mental blocks arose, my mind unsure of exactly what to share or not to share, when I became fearful of exposing the most vulnerable parts of my life, and my mettle to stand boldly for Christ seemed feeble, I called out to Him. "Give me the strength Father. Provide me with the courage. Impart to me your wisdom and direction, for I only want this book to glorify You." While I paced between pages, as I sought His governance, during my long meditative sits listening for Him, He steadfastly led. And to His daily guidance I obeyed and followed. Leading me to right here, right now, one year sober from alcohol, completing this book, brimming with the peace and joy that is only attained in Him.

Upon commencing the creation of *Cinereal*, I wrote the first brief chapter on my birthday. I then constructed a crude outline of the manuscript's entirety. The further I advanced into the first draft, the more details and accounts necessary were presented. As the structure developed, the substance became defined. I compiled multiple lists of notes to supplement the second draft, an inventory I added to whenever an applicable idea occurred. At night, nearly asleep, I often reached for the list and scribbled upon it. On walks with Wylie, when the Holy Spirit gently nudged, I wrote it down. For the first draft, I established and committed to an effective schedule, determined to write at least one-thousand quality words a day. Some days the writing poured, easily reaching three thousand. On other days, accomplishing the bare minimum was arduous, needing to erase, rewrite, delete again, ponder and pray, write anew, frequently multiple times until I became satisfied. Before the end of each lengthy session, I asked myself two questions. Have I given it my all? Is the project better than when I awoke? If the answer was yes, I would set it aside, attempt to let my mind rest, and then do it all again the following day. Step by step, just like on the long trails, one micro-goal at a time. Once the hundreds of micro-goals had been accomplished, so too would be the ultimate.

Upon completing the first draft at the end of March, I promptly proceeded into the second, implementing all the transcripts I had amassed. After the second draft's completion in August, I scrutinized it with a third draft, applying all necessary revisions, shaping it towards its definitive form. The fourth and final draft I rigorously polished, fine-tuning every detail. The first two drafts compiled the book, while the last two drafts molded it. Each draft proved to be distinctively valuable and necessary. Now, as I write the last chapter, which I purposely saved for this anniversary day, I fondly reminisce upon my diligent year. Autumn, I executed my new schedule until my mind knew it as a habit. Winter, I labored starting in the morning's dark hours into evening's dark hours. Through the spring I persevered, allowing a break to build my garden, then resuming my craft while flora seeds leisurely grew. Into the heat of summer, I remained self-disciplined and persisted, ignoring the surrounding commotion of the rowdy season. Upon autumn's return with the finish line approaching, I vigorously pressed onward, much

CINEREAL

like I had on the Appalachian Trail, yet this time humbly listening for the guidance of the Almighty.

The process was often a lonely one. My old life had been shed. In its place existed a modest subsistence and a matured ability to be still and know that He is God. But even in this sacred season of solitude, despite the flourishing blossoms of my active relationship with Him, my humanism still craved companionship. I would not revert to old patterns, but my heart yearned for romance, for a partnership with a Christ-loving woman befitting me. Someone to share life with, to continue growing closer to God with, a wife to adore, pray and abide in His peace with. In reflection, I grasped that although I had loved in the past, it was not led by Him, it was not pure, righteous love. And despite my then worldly entanglement, He had protected me, even from myself. On one particularly melancholic winter evening, my mind having slipped into focusing upon what I did not have rather than the abundance of blessings He lavished, I asked God what I should do about my wholesome amorous longings. After a few moments of silence, He presented these exact words. "This too is a gift."

His statement struck me powerfully, comprehending exactly what He meant. *Yes, this loneliness, this absence of distraction, this spell of seclusion, this too is a gift. For I cannot fulfill Your plan for this book and my Christ-centered growth without being set apart, tucked away, allowing total focus upon You. You are preparing me for all that is to come. If it is ever Your will that I might share this life with a romantic partner, I eagerly welcome it when You know I am ready. And if it is not Your will for my life, I am content, for You provide everything I need in Your perfect timing. I trust You. Thank You, Father.* Per His reminder, renewed peace replaced my melancholy. *All is well. Continue writing the book. Complete this task He has designated for me. Persevere to the finish line.*

Each day of this book's compilation has helped to tremendously strengthen my faith in Him. His steadfast love in my life is transparent. Every aspect of existence proclaims His omniscience and omnipotence. My faith, that once was strong, now bursts as a mountain range expanding ever vaster, stalwartly exuding, reaching every person I meet. This year-long mission has allowed me to examine my life, untangle each internal perplexity, and ultimately understand God's enduring faithfulness. He utilized this method to heal all the broken places in my soul. My brain still rises and falls like a boat at sea, or as a man standing on solid ground following a period aboard a ship, but the weighty depression, the living darkness, the debilitating

CINEREAL

PTSD, the consuming anxiety, unresolved grief, the chaotic torments that once wreaked havoc upon my being, He healed them all. I now cherish the difficulties my traumatic brain injury created, as it forced me to slow down to the speed at which I can completely commune with Him. In this, in Him, I am whole.

In a few days, it shall be October. Autumn hues are emboldening across the vast expanses of Oregon and beyond. I imagine my sister guiding her little children through New England forests, imparting to them ecological essentials. Perhaps she holds a red maple leaf in her hand, and perhaps my adoring mother smiles on. I visualize my brother on his sailboat in the fog. Squinting eyes upon thin landscape lines, navigating around the islands of Maine. His family wiping wet brows, beaming with adventurous glee as the boom is swung to the starboard side. The venerable pilot, my dad, retired from his career this year. In July, we retreated to the ocean. In the past, he and I had shared little time without wine bottles between us. With alcohol's absence, our companionship seemed cleaner, more genuine and present. I could clearly see and hear his soul without the murk of poison layered between. *And*, I considered, *perhaps he can finally see the me he had hoped I would become when I was born.* My friends and I, although now dispersed across the globe, communicate frequently. Daily, I pray for each of them by name. Recently my dear chosen-brother Max accepted Jesus as his Savoir. His decision fills me with boundless euphoria. My mother and I's relationship, regardless of our eleven-year physical separation, is the strongest we have ever known. She has always loved me with a Christ-like devotion, one I could not recognize and thoroughly value until I also grew to love Him. My heart yearns to see her again in this life and wrap my arms around her with the sincerest embrace of gratitude I have ever given, but I know that whatever be His will for our brief earthen existence, she and I shall share the infinite blessings of an eternity in heaven together worshipping our Father, and that is what I eagerly await the most.

Now, as my mind and fingers lay this book's last words, while my eyes occasionally peer upward fervently awaiting Christ's return, afternoon drizzle has dressed the autumnal air with the pleasant aroma of petrichor. In a few weeks, I will graduate from my thirties and turn forty. The culmination of a decade and the inauguration of new. Come Thanksgiving Day, I will have lived in Bend for ten years. The plans I once carried for this town have been accomplished and, I believe, God's lessons for me in this land have been learned. Whatever the Lord has planned for me next, I am ready. Wherever He leads, I will faithfully follow. In every way that He calls me to lead others, I will do so with a humble servant's heart and the loving strength of the Almighty.

What is the purpose of life? The answer is simple. To seek, surrender to, grow to know, live for, serve and worship the one true God, through Jesus Christ our Lord. The internal empty void every human has sensed in their lifetime, the insatiable pit that so many try to fill with money, fame, lust, pride, with the temporary things of this fleeting world, none of it shall ever satisfy, for He created us to be His children. Without fulfilling this, without repenting of our sinful nature and accepting His incredible gift of grace, without saying yes to His love and trusting in Him, we shall always be incomplete.

Out of deep, sincere love for you, if you have not already done so, I urge you to submit your life to Him. I challenge you to surrender to Him your ego, your doubts, anger, hatred, discomfort, confusion, reluctance, everything that holds you back from seeking Him. If you are unsure of how to even begin, start with that, admit your uncertainty to Him, and then pick up His Word and read the Gospel of John. As the Savior told us in Mark 8:36 (NKJV), "For what will it profit a man if he gains the whole world, and loses his own soul?"

It is He who lifts us from death to life, just as it is He who paid for our sins and rose from the dead. And it is He who will come again to deliver His children home. Jesus has done it all. With a heart full of gratitude, and a healed mind that now rests in His love, I thank you for reading this book. Although in the past I was like that of ashes, because of Him I am cinereal no more. Onward.

Romans 8:38-39 (NKJV)
"For I am persuaded that neither death nor life,
nor angels nor principalities nor powers,
nor things present nor things to come,
not height nor depth,
nor any other created thing,
shall be able to separate us from the love of God
which is in Christ Jesus our Lord."

Acknowledgments

Accomplishing *CINEREAL* feels surreal. I poured all of me into its creation, holding nothing that was essential or valuable for this book back. As Rad would say, it was a "full send." The reality of completing this project hasn't entirely sunk in yet. However, what has sunk in is the vast amount of love and support I have been blessed to receive throughout the first forty years of my existence. My life would have been only pebbles and leaves, perhaps not even that, without you.

If your name or pseudonym was in *CINEREAL*, even if just a brief mention in one line, know that I am profoundly grateful for you. Including you in my book is my way of expressing my love to you for as long as publications endure. You impacted me in the way I needed to process, grow, be myself, and live to the fullest. Your companionship through little and grand moments of fun and joy, seriousness and pain are worth more than gold can ever afford. Life is richer because of you. Thank you, for you. For my friends and acquaintances along the way whom I did not mention, my gratitude for you is no less, yet I could not tell every meaningful story within this saga. Perhaps in other books.

Thank you to every tree for providing the paper for this book and oxygen for us to breathe. May your seeds flourish. Thank you to all my athletic coaches throughout my young amateur "career." Thank you, Mrs. Philbrick, who spent many (probably at times stressful) hours instilling piano discipline and knowledge into my adolescent mind. Thank you, Mr. Beal, the very one who listened while I read the poem about my dead cat in front of the class. You were my favorite writing teacher because you challenged me. Thank you to the English professor at UNH, whose name I cannot remember, for encouraging me to go out and seize my life. Thank you to the police officers, lawyers and judges who treated me decently. And to those who did not, I will always hold a Christ-like love for you as well. Thank you, Pastor Clinch, who filled my young mind with godly wisdom as a child. Despite my years of rebellion, the sermons you instilled never perished. Thank you, Alyssa Hoch, for proofreading the third draft of this massive manuscript. Your Christ-loving heart and joyous service provided me with the valuable literary "second set of eyes" I so direly needed. Thank you, Sarah, for helping me with the technical difficulties. Sometimes it is the "simple" things I just cannot figure out how to do on my own.

To all the trail-angels who provided any form of trail-magic to me or any other hiker on the wonderful system of long trails our country preserves, thank you! Your selfless actions create positive impacts that ripples onward for lifetimes. To all those who maintain and protect the long trails, thank you. Vast wilderness spaces and corridors we must preserve.

Thank you, Tom Beans of Dudley's Bookshop Café, and Justin Schlosberg and Bernadette Foley of the Underground Book Gallery, for owning my two favorite bookstores and helping to advance my Bend, Oregon, poetry audience. Many worthy events in my life have either begun or been nourished at your treasured establishments. Thank you to my decade-long trustworthy friend Linda for the occasional care of Wylie Wizzle, and for aiding me in acquiring my new piano for the writing shed. Dan and Pam of the bowling league, thank you for being strong peers and friends during a time I was hiding many struggles. You have a friend in me for life. Lyle, thank you for always believing in me and not just saying it, but demonstrating it through your kind actions. Thank you to all the doctors, nurses, therapists and technicians who have aided, guided and informed me through a confusing medical journey. Thank you to each barista and cashier who has interacted with me amid my writing routine. The kindness you always provide has sustained my spirit throughout this yearlong process. Thank you to everyone who has ever prayed for me, reprimanded my wayward ways, encouraged me to seek God, even when I did not listen. Your prayers for my life have not gone unanswered. He is always listening and working by His wondrous timing. Praise the Lord!

To my family. I must first address the Most High, my heavenly Father. Thank You for Your faithful love, for Your Son, Jesus' sacrifice, for defeating death, healing my internal chaos and transforming my life into one of peace. Thank You for every detail of Your immaculate, magnificent creation. You are my entire reason for everything. I pray that this book and the rest of my life honor You. To my devoted Dad. From the day I was born until now and surely beyond, you have always supported my unique adventures. Even when I was a troublesome son, you were always there for me. Thank you for always transporting me from A to B, visiting me in my wild places, and reminding me to take everything "one step at a time." From my innermost depths, I am grateful for and love you. To Grandma, the kindest woman I've ever known, thank you for harboring me, rooting for me, and always living as an example of godly, patient, unconditional love. To your late husband and my grandfather, a man we both cherished, we shall see and rejoice with him in heaven someday. Thank you to all my aunts, uncles, cousins, and extended family members spread across the globe, even in unfamiliarity, I appreciate you. Love you Aunt Brenda! My dear brother Michael and darling sister Carmen. Despite our earthen distances, nothing could ever diminish the fervent love I carry every mile and across every mountain for you in my heart. May God always bless and protect you, your spouses and children, my beloved nieces and nephews. And finally, the woman of my entire life's hour, Mother dearest. Thank you for bringing me into this world, for living as an example of righteousness on earth, and sowing in me the love of my first love, Jesus Christ. Without you, none of me would ever have been.

To all I have ever met, quietly ambled by, or never even known to exist, this book is for you. My greatest desire in this world and dedicated prayer is for you to come to know the amazing love of God through Jesus Christ. Gratefully, sincerely, and with a sparkling smile in my eyes, may His peace be with you. ~ Wing Williams

www.ingramcontent.com/pod-product-compliance
Lightning Source LLC
Chambersburg PA
CBHW020339010526
44119CB00048B/527